ENGLISH

A Powerful Language Arts Program

Contents of the Teacher's Edition

McDougal, Littell
ENGLISH
A Powerful Language Arts Program

McDougal, Littell English is the perfect companion to your reading series. It has more of what you buy an English book for: solid, in-depth instruction in a manageable, easy-to-use format. *McDougal, Littell English* offers the right balance between writing and the related language skills students really need. Focused, single-topic instruction is integrated with writing, listening, and speaking applications that help your students become more effective communicators.

Literature—Exemplary models from whole works of literature are found at the beginning of units and throughout the lessons to motivate students and to illustrate effective writing. This poem precedes the chapter on narrative writing.

Thinking—Students are guided through a variety of thinking processes. They read and think about each type of writing *before* they write.

Writing—Thorough instruction in the writing process teaches all students to write effectively.

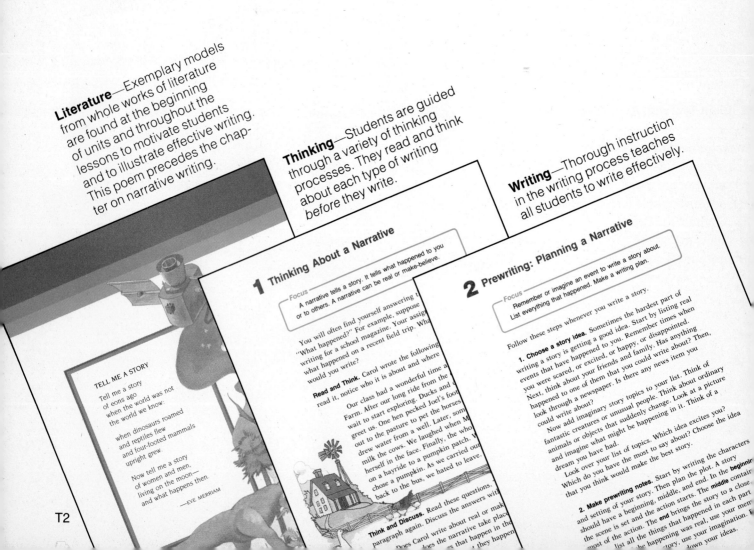

TELL ME A STORY

Tell me a story
of eons ago
when the world was not
the world we know:

when dinosaurs roamed
and reptiles flew
and four-footed mammals
upright grew.

Now tell me a story
of women and men,
living on the moon—
and what happens then.

—EVE MERRIAM

1 Thinking About a Narrative

Focus
  A narrative tells a story. It tells what happened to you or to others. A narrative can be real or make-believe.

You will often find yourself answering t... "What happened?" For example, suppose... writing for a school magazine. Your assig... what happened on a recent field trip. Wha... would you write?

Read and Think. Carol wrote the following... read it, notice who it is about and where...

Our class had a wonderful time a... Farm. After our long ride from the... wait to start exploring. Ducks and g... greet us. One hen pecked Joel's foot... out to the pasture to pet the horses... drew water from a well. Later, som... milk the cows. We laughed when M... herself in the face. Finally, the who... on a hayride to a pumpkin patch. V... chose a pumpkin. As we carried ou... back to the bus, we hated to leave.

Think and Discuss. Read these questions. ... paragraph again. Discuss the answers wit... Does Carol write about real or mak... ... does the narrative take place... ... s that happen in th... ... they happen...

2 Prewriting: Planning a Narrative

Focus
  Remember or imagine an event to write a story about. List everything that happened. Make a writing plan.

Follow these steps whenever you write a story.

1. Choose a story idea. Sometimes the hardest part of writing a story is getting a good idea. Start by listing real events that have happened to you. Remember times when you were scared, or excited, or happy, or disappointed. Next, think about your friends and family. Has anything happened to one of them that you could write about? Then, look through a newspaper. Is there any news item you could write about?

Now add imaginary story topics to your list. Think of fantastic creatures or unusual people. Think about ordinary animals or objects that suddenly change. Look at a picture and imagine what might be happening in it. Think of a dream you have had.

Look over your list of topics. Which idea excites you? Which do you have the most to say about? Choose the idea that you think would make the best story.

2. Make prewriting notes. Start by writing the characters and setting of your story. Then plan the plot. A story should have a beginning, middle, and end. In the **beginnin...** the scene is set and the action starts. The **middle** contai... most of the action. The **end** brings the story to a close... list all the things that happened in each par... ... be happening was real, use your men... ... story, use your imagination... ... down your ideas...

I never knew I was so good at writing a story!

From *McDougal, Littell English*, Brown Level, page 32

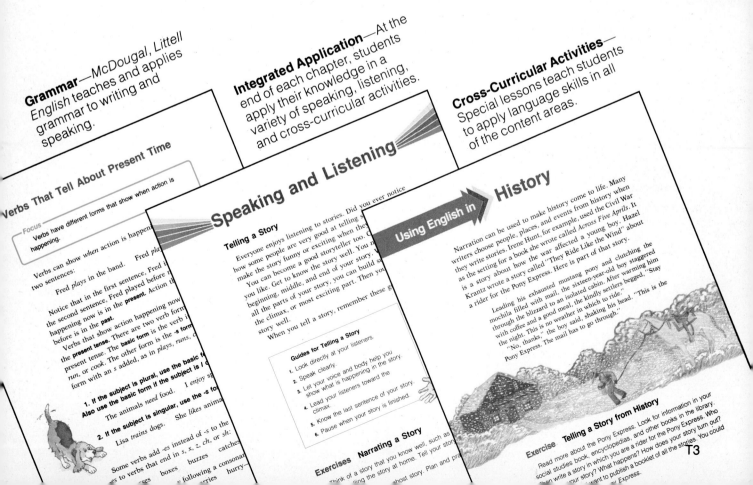

Grammar—*McDougal, Littell English* teaches and applies grammar to writing and speaking.

Integrated Application—At the end of each chapter, students apply their knowledge in a variety of speaking, listening, and cross-curricular activities.

Cross-Curricular Activities—Special lessons teach students to apply language skills in all of the content areas.

Verbs That Tell About Present Time

Focus

Verbs have different forms that show when action is happening.

Verbs can show *when* action is happening.

Fred *plays* in the band.   Fred *pla*

Notice that in the first sentence, Fred the second sentence, Fred played before before is in the **past**. Action th

Verbs that show action happening now the **present tense**. There are two verb form present tense. The **basic form** is the **-s** form *run,* or *cook.* The other form is the **-s** form with an *s* added, as in *plays, runs,*

1. If the subject is plural, use the basic f
Also use the basic form if the subject is *I* o

The animals *need* food.   I *enjoy* s

2. If the subject is singular, use the -s fo

Lisa *trains* dogs.   She *likes* anim

Some verbs add *-es* instead of *-s* to the *es* to verbs that end in *s, x, z, ch,* or *sh:*
boxes   catches
sses   buzzes
following a consonan-
ries   hurry-

Speaking and Listening

Telling a Story

Everyone enjoys listening to stories. Did you ever notice how some people are very good at telling s make the story funny or exciting when the
You can become a good storyteller too. O you like. Get to know the story well. You n beginning, middle, and end of your story. all the parts of your story, you can build s the climax, or most exciting part. Then yo story well.

When you tell a story, remember these g

Guides for Telling a Story
1. Look directly at your listeners.
2. Speak clearly.
3. Let your voice and body help you show what is happening in the story.
4. Lead your listeners toward the climax.
5. Know the last sentence of your story is finished.
6. Pause when your story is finished.

Exercises Narrating a Story
Think of a story that you know well, such as _ing the story at home. Tell your stor ____ host story. Plan and pr

Using English in ▶ History

Narration can be used to make history come to life. Many writers choose people, places, and events from history when they write stories. Irene Hunt, for example, used the Civil War as the setting for a book she wrote called *Across Five Aprils.* It is a story about how the war affected a young boy. Hazel Krantz wrote a story called "They Ride Like the Wind" about a rider for the Pony Express. Here is part of that story.

Leading his exhausted mustang pony and clutching the mochila filled with mail, the sixteen-year-old boy staggered through the blizzard to an isolated cabin. After warming him with coffee and a good meal, the kindly settlers begged, "Stay the night. This is no weather in which to ride."
"No, thanks," the boy said, shaking his head. "This is the Pony Express. The mail has to go through."

Exercise Telling a Story from History
Read more about the Pony Express. Look for information in your social studies book, encyclopedias, and other books in the library. Who ___en write a story in which you are a rider for the Pony Express. Who _your story? What happens? How does your story turn out? You could ____want to publish a booklet of all the stories. You could ___ Express.

T3

Setting the Stage for Clear Communication

The following pages illustrate how the complete Language Arts Program works, using writing a description as an example. Here, as in every writing chapter, the lesson begins with literature models and thinking activities.

Focused Instruction

Thinking—Appropriate examples and a full range of questioning strategies equip students with the thinking power they need to write confidently for various audiences and purposes.

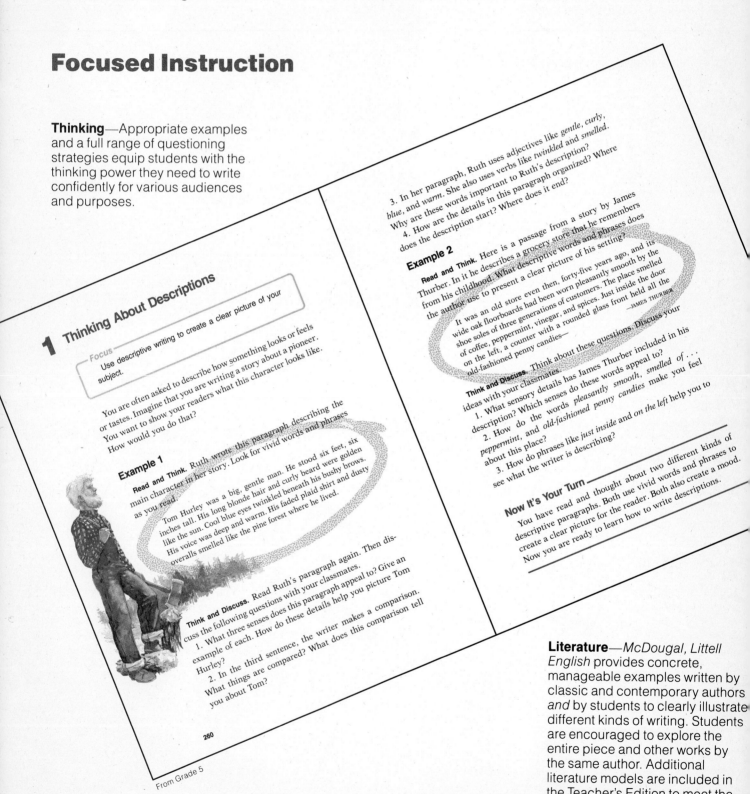

1 Thinking About Descriptions

Focus Use descriptive writing to create a clear picture of your subject.

You are often asked to describe how something looks or feels or tastes. Imagine that you are writing a story about a pioneer. You want to show your readers what this character looks like. How would you do that?

Example 1

Read and Think. Ruth wrote this paragraph describing the main character in her story. Look for vivid words and phrases as you read.

Tom Hurley was a big, gentle man. He stood six feet, six inches tall. His long blonde hair and curly beard were golden like the sun. Cool blue eyes twinkled beneath his bushy brows. His voice was deep and warm. His faded plaid shirt and dusty overalls smelled like the pine forest where he lived.

Think and Discuss. Read Ruth's paragraph again. Then discuss the following questions with your classmates.
1. What three senses does this paragraph appeal to? Give an example of each. How do these details help you picture Tom Hurley?
2. In the third sentence, the writer makes a comparison. What things are compared? What does this comparison tell you about Tom?

260

From Grade 5

3. In her paragraph, Ruth uses adjectives like *gentle, curly, blue,* and *warm.* She also uses verbs like *twinkled* and *smelled.* Why are these words important to Ruth's description?
4. How are the details in this paragraph organized? Where does the description start? Where does it end?

Example 2

Read and Think. Here is a passage from a story by James Thurber. In it he describes a grocery store that he remembers from his childhood. What descriptive words and phrases does the author use to present a clear picture of his setting?

It was an old store even then, forty-five years ago, and its wide oak floorboards had been worn pleasantly smooth by the shoe soles of three generations of customers. The place smelled of coffee, peppermint, vinegar, and spices. Just inside the door on the left, a counter with a rounded glass front held all the old-fashioned penny candies—

—JAMES THURBER

Think and Discuss. Think about these questions. Discuss your ideas with your classmates.
1. What sensory details has James Thurber included in his description? Which senses do these words appeal to?
2. How do the words *pleasantly smooth, smelled of . . . peppermint,* and *old-fashioned penny candies* make you feel about this place?
3. How do phrases like *just inside* and *on the left* help you to see what the writer is describing?

Now It's Your Turn

You have read and thought about two different kinds of descriptive paragraphs. Both use vivid words and phrases to create a clear picture for the reader. Both also create a mood. Now you are ready to learn how to write descriptions.

Literature—*McDougal, Littell English* provides concrete, manageable examples written by classic and contemporary authors *and* by students to clearly illustrate different kinds of writing. Students are encouraged to explore the entire piece and other works by the same author. Additional literature models are included in the Teacher's Edition to meet the needs of all your students.

From *McDougal, Littell English*, Gold Level, page 396

Literature woven throughout the text sparks a love of learning outside the classroom.

Integrated Application

Oral Language—Students apply the thinking strategies learned in each lesson through writing, speaking, and listening activities that develop strong, well-rounded communicators.

Speaking and Listening

Making Introductions

Introductions help people get acquainted with one another. A good introduction should include some description.

For example, imagine that your cousin Tony has come from California to visit you. He will be going to school with you and meeting your friends. You know it will be difficult for Tony to remember everyone, so you have thought of a way to help him. You will include a short, descriptive phrase with every introduction. The description can tell what someone does or is, not just what someone looks like. For example, you might say, "Tony, this is Angela. She is the fastest runner in our class."

When you introduce people, remember these guidelines.

Guidelines for Introductions
1. Say both names clearly.
2. Tell something about each person you introduce.
3. Introduce an older person or a person in authority first.
4. Smile and show interest in both people.

Exercises   Using Description in Introductions

A. Imagine that you are introducing three friends to your parents. Write a descriptive phrase you might include in the introduction. Make sure it is something that makes that person special.

B. Write a short introduction for someone you and your classmates know. Do not use the person's name. See if others can guess whom you are introducing by the descriptive phrases you use.

268

From Grade 5

Thought Bubbles—This unique feature helps students visualize the thinking process used in each stage of writing.

You can make a model volcano in your own kitchen! First, you'll need to get some newspapers, a 6-ounce paper cup, some modeling clay, 4 tablespoons baking soda, and ½ cup vinegar. Cover the table with newspaper. Put the cup, right side up, on the table. Form the clay around the cup. Next, put the baking soda in the cup. Add ¼ cup vinegar.

I should be more specific.

4 layers of

sides of the

The clay must touch the sides of the cup.

You can add another ¼ cup vinegar if you want to.

I'd better tell them how to keep the volcano going.

The Complete Writing Program

After reading and thinking about each type of writing, students begin a series of lessons in the process of writing—prewriting, drafting, revising, and sharing.

Focused Instruction

Writing—*McDougal, Littell English* provides students with a variety of strategies for each mode of writing. Carefully sequenced lessons guide students through the writing process.

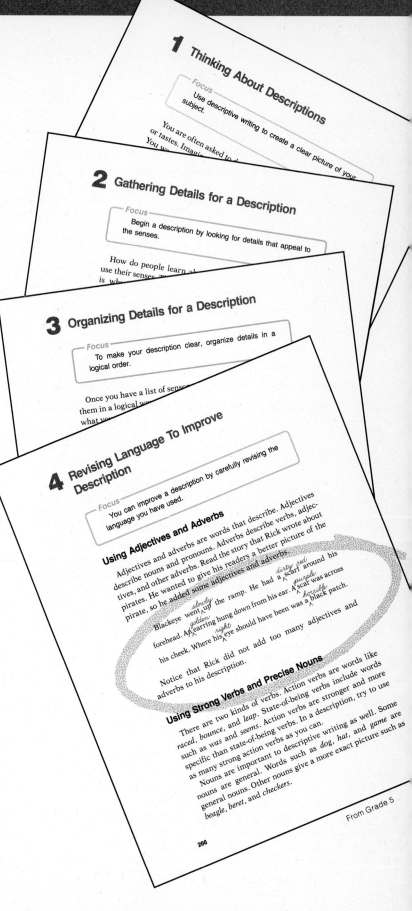

1 Thinking About Descriptions

Focus
Use descriptive writing to create a clear picture of your subject.

You are often asked to ... or tastes. Imag ...
You w ...

2 Gathering Details for a Description

Focus
Begin a description by looking for details that appeal to the senses.

How do people learn ...
use their senses ...
is wh ...

3 Organizing Details for a Description

Focus
To make your description clear, organize details in a logical order.

Once you have a list of sens ...
them in a logical wa ...
what yo ...

4 Revising Language To Improve Description

Focus
You can improve a description by carefully revising the language you have used.

Using Adjectives and Adverbs

Adjectives and adverbs are words that describe. Adjectives describe nouns and pronouns. Adverbs describe verbs, adjectives, and other adverbs. Read the story that Rick wrote about pirates. He wanted to give his readers a better picture of the pirate, so he added some adjectives and adverbs.

Blackeye went up the ramp. He had a scarf around his forehead. An earring hung down from his ear. A scar was across his cheek. Where his eye should have been was a black patch.

Notice that Rick did not add too many adjectives and adverbs to his description.

Using Strong Verbs and Precise Nouns

There are two kinds of verbs. Action verbs are words like *raced, bounce,* and *leap.* State-of-being verbs include words such as *was* and *seems.* Action verbs are stronger and more specific than state-of-being verbs. In a description, try to use as many strong action verbs as you can.

Nouns are important to descriptive writing as well. Some nouns are general. Words such as *dog, hat,* and *game* are general nouns. Other nouns give a more exact picture such as *beagle, beret,* and *checkers.*

From Grade 5

266

Writing options help each student develop an individual writing style.

Integrated Application

Composition—Students integrate thinking and language skills to make their writing more precise.

Creative Writing—Diverse creative writing activities help students develop fluency and style as they unleash their creativity.

Cross-Curricular Activities—Students apply writing lessons across the curriculum to learn the importance of writing in the real world.

The Power Handbook—This handy writing resource serves as a reference and promotes independent learning.

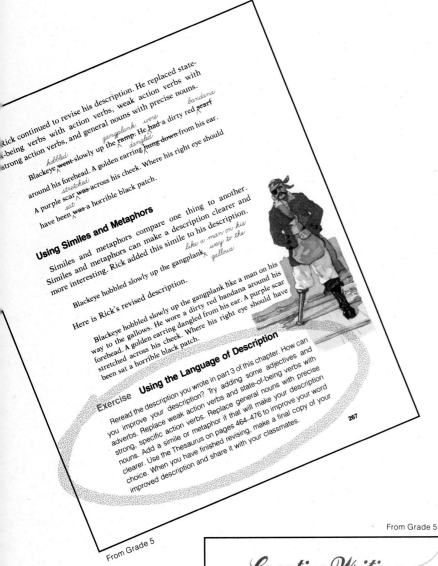

Rick continued to revise his description. He replaced state-being verbs with action verbs, weak action verbs with strong action verbs, and general nouns with precise nouns.

hobbled
Blackeye ~~went~~ slowly up the ~~ramp.~~ *gangplank* He ~~had~~ *wore* a dirty red *bandana* ~~scarf~~
dangled
around his forehead. A golden earring ~~hung down~~ from his ear.
stretched
A purple scar ~~was~~ across his cheek. Where his right eye should
sat
have been ~~was~~ a horrible black patch.

Using Similes and Metaphors

Similes and metaphors compare one thing to another. Similes and metaphors can make a description clearer and more interesting. Rick added this simile to his description.

like a man on his way to the gallows

Blackeye hobbled slowly up the gangplank

Here is Rick's revised description.

Blackeye hobbled slowly up the gangplank like a man on his way to the gallows. He wore a dirty red bandana around his forehead. A golden earring dangled from his ear. A purple scar stretched across his cheek. Where his right eye should have been sat a horrible black patch.

Exercise   Using the Language of Description

Reread the description you wrote in part 3 of this chapter. How can you improve your description? Try adding some adjectives and adverbs. Replace weak action verbs and state-of-being verbs with strong, specific action verbs. Replace general nouns with precise nouns. Add a simile or metaphor if that will make your description clearer. Use the Thesaurus on pages 464–476 to improve your word choice. When you have finished revising, make a final copy of your improved description and share it with your classmates.

267

From Grade 5

From Grade 5

From Grade 5

From Grade 5

POWER HANDBOOK

Guidelines for the Process of Writing   410–

Topics for Writing   412–414

Guide to Capitalization   416–431

Creative Writing

A. Find an unusual picture in a newspaper or magazine. You might choose a photograph from a news article or a glossy magazine advertisement. List all the details about the unusual person, place, or thing in the photograph. Use your list to write a descriptive paragraph about this person, place, or thing.

B. Imagine that you have a room in your house all to yourself. What would this room look like? What would be in it? Write a description of your room. Be sure your description is well thought out. Try to help your readers see this room as clearly as you do.

C. Use sensory details and descriptive language to write about each of the numbered items below. Write your descriptions in riddle form. See how many your classmates can guess.

Example: I crunch when you munch me. I'm green as a lettuce leaf. My top is quite leafy, my body quite stringy. I'm a dieter's best friend. What am I?

1. spider   3. sand   5. lemon
2. peanut butter 4. raisins   6. clock

Using English in ➤ Science

In this chapter, you have learned how important observing is to describing. Scientists know the importance of observing, too. Some scientists observe through microscopes. Other scientists observe through telescopes. Scientists can even "observe" by carefully studying the information on computers. In all cases, scientists write descriptions of what they see.

In your science class, good describing skills can help you to describe what all or part of a plant or animal looks like. You can use your skills to describe the materials for an experiment. When you write descriptions for science class, remember what you have learned in this chapter. Use good adjectives and adverbs, strong action verbs, and precise nouns. Give your readers a clear picture of what you are describing.

Exercise   Observing and Describing

Below are two photographs. These pictures were taken through an electron microscope. An electron microscope enlarges objects to thousands of times their normal size. Choose one picture and use your describing skills to write what you see. When you have finished your description, look on page 488 to find out what each object is.

Grammar to Support Good Writing

Students learn how grammar, usage, and mechanics can improve their spoken and written communication.

Focused Instruction

Grammar—Single-topic lessons begin by stating the focus of the lesson, then move to concise explanations and meaningful examples.

Writing and Speaking—Students learn how applying new concepts to writing and speaking can help them communicate more effectively.

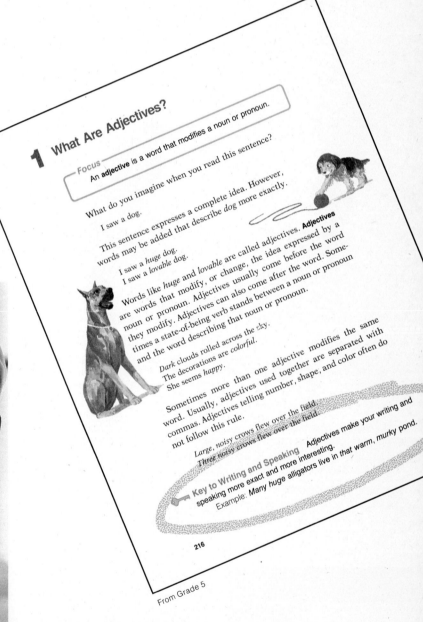

1 What Are Adjectives?

Focus
An **adjective** is a word that modifies a noun or pronoun.

What do you imagine when you read this sentence?

I saw a dog.

This sentence expresses a complete idea. However, words may be added that describe *dog* more exactly.

I saw a *huge* dog.
I saw a *lovable* dog.

Words like *huge* and *lovable* are called adjectives. **Adjectives** are words that modify, or change, the idea expressed by a noun or pronoun. Adjectives usually come before the word they modify. Adjectives can also come after the word. Sometimes a state-of-being verb stands between a noun or pronoun and the word describing that noun or pronoun.

Dark clouds rolled across the sky.
The decorations are *colorful*.
She seems *happy*.

Sometimes more than one adjective modifies the same word. Usually, adjectives used together are separated with commas. Adjectives telling number, shape, and color often do not follow this rule.

Large, noisy crows flew over the field.
Three noisy crows flew over the field.

Key to Writing and Speaking Adjectives make your writing and speaking more exact and more interesting.
Example: Many huge alligators live in that warm, murky pond.

216

From Grade 5

Lessons use the inductive method to actively involve students in the learning process.

From *McDougal, Littell English*, Gold Level, page 126

Integrated Application

Three Levels of Exercises—
Three levels of practice, including
a writing application, promote
long-term retention.

Writing in Every Lesson—In
McDougal, Littell English, students
move beyond sentence writing to
practical and creative application
of the concept just learned.

Extra Reinforcement—Each
chapter ends with an interesting variety of activities that
encourage students to apply
grammar in written and oral
language.

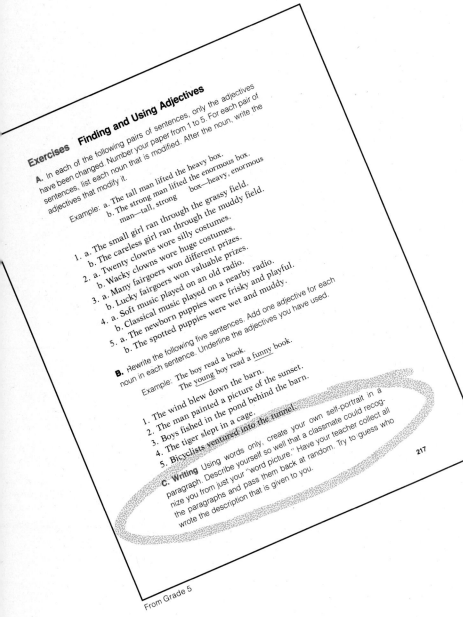

Exercises   Finding and Using Adjectives

A. In each of the following pairs of sentences, only the adjectives
have been changed. Number your paper from 1 to 5. For each pair of
sentences, list each noun that is modified. After the noun, write the
adjectives that modify it.

Example: a. The tall man lifted the heavy box.
b. The strong man lifted the enormous box.
man—tall, strong   box—heavy, enormous

1. a. The small girl ran through the grassy field.
   b. The careless girl ran through the muddy field.
2. a. Twenty clowns wore silly costumes.
   b. Wacky clowns wore huge costumes.
3. a. Many fairgoers won different prizes.
   b. Lucky fairgoers won valuable prizes.
4. a. Soft music played on an old radio.
   b. Classical music played on a nearby radio.
5. a. The newborn puppies were frisky and playful.
   b. The spotted puppies were wet and muddy.

B. Rewrite the following five sentences. Add one adjective for each
noun in each sentence. Underline the adjectives you have used.

Example: The boy read a book.
The <u>young</u> boy read a <u>funny</u> book.

1. The wind blew down the barn.
2. The man painted a picture of the sunset.
3. Boys fished in the pond behind the barn.
4. The tiger slept in a cage.
5. Bicyclists ventured into the tunnel.

C. Writing Using words only, create your own self-portrait in a
paragraph. Describe yourself so well that a classmate could recognize you from just your "word picture." Have your teacher collect all
the paragraphs and pass them back at random. Try to guess who
wrote the description that is given to you.

217

From Grade 5

From Grade 5

From Grade 5

Using Grammar in Writing

A. Unicorns and dragons are creatures that we learn about
from folk tales. Imagine that you are a knight on an adventure.
You come across a very strange, never-before-seen creature. As
you ride back to the castle, you think about how you will
describe what you have seen. Write a brief paragraph giving
all the details of this unusual beast.

B. Use some of the following twelve adjectives to write a
paragraph about a day in the life of one of the seven dwarfs.
Underline each adjective as you use it.

beautiful	more hopeful	wrinkled	poor
seven	sillier	most wonderful	sad
smartest	worse	curious	best

C. Using Adjectives To Write About Art Visit a museum or use
an art book to look at several paintings. Choose your favorite
painting. Write a brief paragraph that describes it.

230

Exercises for Mastery   Chapter 12

Adjectives for Strong Description

A. Finding Adjectives In each of the pairs of sentences below,
only the adjectives have been changed. Number your paper from
1 to 5. For each pair of sentences, list each noun that is modified.
After the noun, write the adjectives that modify it. Do not include
articles.

1. a. We swam in a large, clear lake.
   b. We swam in a warm, shallow lake.
2. a. Tiny birds perched on the bare branches.
   b. White birds perched on the dark branches.
3. a. The powerful speaker talked to a joyous crowd.
   b. The fearful speaker talked to a rowdy crowd.
4. a. A hot, gusty wind swept the area.
   b. A fierce, cold wind swept the area.
5. a. Six old horses lived in the dirty stall.
   b. Young, spotted horses lived in the other stall.

Powerful Components

All components in *McDougal, Littell English* are aligned to work together to deliver powerful language arts instruction.

Pupil's Edition
The Pupil's Edition is available in a softcover, consumable format for grades 1–2 and in a hardcover format for grades 2–8.

Teacher's Edition
The annotated Teacher's Edition provides comprehensive teaching support with objectives, teaching suggestions, and strategies for individualizing each lesson. Suggestions for *Motivating Through Literature* and *Teaching Special Populations, Unit Projects,* and specific *Guidelines for Evaluating Writing* provide added support.

Teacher's Resource Binder
Time-saving materials to reinforce, extend, and evaluate include: *Process of Writing Transparencies; Skills Practice Book (Blackline Masters); Enrichment* and *Reinforcement; Tests; Ideas for Creative Teaching; Teaching and Evaluating Student Writing; Lesson Plans for Integrating the Language Arts;* and colorful posters.

Skills Practice Book
Hundreds of exercises reteach and reinforce concepts in writing, grammar, usage, and mechanics. (Also available in Spirit Master form)

Skills Practice Book Teacher's Edition

Tests
Pretests and *Mastery Tests* for each chapter, *Mid-Year Test,* and *End-of-Year Test* help you identify problem areas and evaluate progress. (Available in Blackline or Spirit Master form)

McDougal, Littell Instructional Software
Tutorial writing programs for grades 3–8 (Apple IIc, II+, IIe)

- *Writing Better Sentences*
- *Writing Better Paragraphs*

A Complete Kindergarten Program

McDougal, Littell English, Cherry Level, meets the needs of children entering kindergarten with a diverse range of experiences and abilities. It offers a flexible readiness program with the features you want.

- *Manageable organization* of units, chapters, and lessons helps you tailor instruction to meet individual needs and provide a strong foundation of language arts and social skills.

- *Flexible time-management plans* accommodate full-day or half-day schedules—saving you valuable planning and preparation time.

- *Lively, enjoyable activities* offer countless ways to involve youngsters. Multisensory activities keep children of all abilities thinking and doing.

Components
The kindergarten program includes a comprehensive *Teacher's Guide,* a complete book of *Activity Masters,* a *Big Book* of captivating, full-color illustrations, and an optional, full-color *Student Workbook.*

Designed for Flexible Teaching

The *McDougal, Littell English Teacher's Edition* was designed to help you meet students' individual needs and enhance your teaching style.

Flexible Organization
Single-concept chapters can be used in sequence or at the critical time when your students need them.

Individualized Learning
McDougal, Littell English provides effective strategies for meeting the needs of students of all ability levels, students with limited English proficiency, and students with special needs.

Independence and Cooperative Learning
Individual thinking enriches cooperative learning experiences in speaking and listening activities and unit-long group projects.

Professional Growth
Creative ideas for teaching and up-to-date research give you insights into new teaching strategies.

A wealth of teacher-tested ideas help you establish a positive learning environment.

*With **McDougal, Littell English,** you can facilitate a variety of learning styles.*

A comprehensive, conveniently organized teaching resource

McDougal, Littell English is organized for ease in teaching. Four manageable units in each text present a series of composition, grammar, and related skills chapters that reinforce an integrated approach to teaching language arts.

Beginning the Unit

UNIT 1

Introducing the Unit

1. Introduce the students to their new English books. Have them examine the cover and find the table of contents. Ask them to look through the table of contents and name some things they are going to learn about this year. Then have them turn to the **Power Handbook** beginning on page 329. Have them look through each part of the handbook.

Now have students turn to page 2. Ask a student to read the titles of the five chapters in Unit 1. Show how the chapters progress from the study of words to sentences, and finally to paragraphs.

Read and discuss the unit introduction. Ask students for more examples of how they can use these skills in school and outside of school.

2. Use the **Unit Management Guidelines** below to help you develop your weekly lesson plan. An optional week 9 has been provided to allow for variations in the length of grading periods. You may wish to use this week for review, additional practice, and the presentation of selected special feature pages. The chart can be adapted as needed for four- or six-week grading periods.

Motivating Through Literature

Have students read the poem "There Isn't Time" silently. Then have one student read it aloud. Ask these questions:

1. What are the things the poet says there isn't time to do? *(lines 1 to 8)*
2. What does the poet say there is time for? *(lines 9 to 12)*
3. This poem is about things the poet wants to do. What are some things other people may want to do? *(Answers will vary)*

Pass out strips of paper. Ask students to write one exciting thing they would like to do some day. Have students read their ideas to the class and attach to the bulletin board. Choose a few of the ideas and ask students what skills they would need to achieve those goals. Lead students to see how better speaking, writing, and sharing can help them to fulfill many dreams.

2   Unit 1

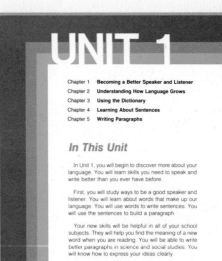

UNIT 1

Chapter 1   **Becoming a Better Speaker and Listener**
Chapter 2   **Understanding How Language Grows**
Chapter 3   **Using the Dictionary**
Chapter 4   **Learning About Sentences**
Chapter 5   **Writing Paragraphs**

In This Unit

In Unit 1, you will begin to discover more about your language. You will learn skills you need to speak and write better than you ever have before.

First, you will study ways to be a good speaker and listener. You will learn about words that make up our language. You will use words to write sentences. You will use the sentences to build a paragraph.

Your new skills will be helpful in all of your school subjects. They will help you find the meaning of a new word when you are reading. You will be able to write better paragraphs in science and social studies. You will know how to express your ideas clearly.

This is just the beginning of your journey through language. There are always new words to learn. There are always new ideas to share. It is a journey that never ends.

THERE ISN'T TIME

There isn't time, there isn't time
To do the things I want to do
With all the mountain-tops to climb,
And all the woods to wander through,
And all the seas to sail upon,
And everywhere there is to go,
And all the people, every one
Who lives upon the earth, to know.
There's only time, there's only time
To know a few, and do a few,
And then sit down and make a rhyme
About the rest I want to do.

—ELEANOR FARJEON

3

Unit Management Guidelines

Week 1	Week 2	Week 3	Week 4	Week 5
Unit 1 opener, pp. 2–3. Chapter 1, Parts 1–5, pp. 5–17.	Chapter 2, Parts 1–6, pp. 19–31.	Chapter 3, Parts 1–3, pp. 33–39.	Chapter 3, Parts 4–6, pp. 40–47.	Chapter 4, Parts 1–3, pp. 49–55.

Week 6	Week 7	Week 8	Week 9
Chapter 4, Parts 3–4, pp. 54–61.	Chapter 5, Parts 1–4, pp. 63–71.	Chapter 5, Parts 4–6, pp. 70–79. Cumulative Review, pp. 80–81.	Additional review, reinforcement, and enrichment. See number 2 under **Introducing the Unit.**

Unit Projects

Independent Activity

Students can use rebus writing to express graphically what they have learned about word parts, prefixes, and suffixes. Ask students to create rebus stories on poster boards using pictures in place of words or parts of words. Have them each retell one familiar story or fairy tale in their own words or write an original story. As they write, they should find appropriate places to substitute pictures for words. Compound words such as *pancake*, for example, may consist of two pictures. Prefixes and suffixes can stand alone next to a picture, as in *relock* or *spotless.*

For Gifted and Talented Students—Have students write an original mystery story using rebus clues. The picture words should be the clues to solving the mystery. For example, if the missing jewels are in the garden, a picture of a guard followed by the letter *n* could be the rebus clue for *garden.* Students can begin by making up rebus words for clues and then writing a story using that vocabulary.

Group Activity

Verbally talented students can work together to create a language skills game. For example, they might create a board game with squares labeled *antonym, synonym,* and so on. If a player lands on the *antonym* square, the player picks a card from a word pack and must name an antonym for the word on the card.

Provide students with materials such as tagboard, markers, and dice. Challenge them to create a game about word meanings, word parts, and sentence parts. They must create the game so that players make use of a dictionary.

Computer Activity

Students are introduced to the process of writing in this unit. Computer programs are available which allow students to write, edit, and revise their paragraphs on the computer. Two such

(Unit Projects are continued on page 81 of this Teacher's Edition.)

Unit 1   **3**

● **Introducing the Unit**
The purpose of the unit and the relationship of the chapters are clearly explained.

● **Motivating Through Literature**
Each new unit is introduced with a two-page literature lesson. Colorful art and a thought-provoking poem help you motivate students, encourage creative expression, and nurture literary appreciation.

● **Unit Management Guidelines**
An easy-to-use management chart helps you prepare lesson plans for up to two months.

● **Unit Projects**
Each unit overview offers Independent, Group, and Computer Activities designed for students who enjoy additional challenge. Unit Projects applying several concepts taught in the unit can be used as long-term activities covering several weeks. Sections of some projects are designed for gifted and talented students.

T14

Beginning the Chapter

Chapter 21

Chapter Objectives

1. To understand how books in the library are classified
2. To categorize books according to the Dewey Decimal System
3. To use the card catalog to locate books
4. To differentiate among the three kinds of catalog cards
5. To understand and use the reference section of a library
6. To develop skills in note-taking
7. To recognize techniques for gathering information by interviewing
8. To identify and use graphic aids when appropriate

Motivating the Students

1. Read the following poem to the class.

The Library

It looks like any building
When you pass it on the street,
Made of stone and glass and marble,
Made of iron and concrete.

But once inside you can ride
A camel or a train,
Visit Rome, Siam, or Nome,
Feel a hurricane,
Meet a king, learn to sing,
How to bake a pie,
Go to sea, plant a tree
Find how airplanes fly,
Train a horse, and of course
Have all the dogs you'd like,
See the moon, a sandy dune,
Or catch a whopping pike.
Everything that books can bring
You'll find inside those walls
A world is there for you to share
When adventure calls.
You cannot tell its magic
By the way the building looks,
But there's wonderment within it,
The wonderment of books.
—Barbara A. Huff

2. Emphasize that to make the best use of a library, a person should know what services a library offers and exactly where everything is located. This chapter explains ways to find books and information quickly and easily.
3. Read and discuss the chapter introduction on page 349.

348 Chapter 21

Week 31
Chapter Management Guidelines This chart may be used to help structure daily lesson plans.

Day 1	Day 2	Day 3	Day 4	Day 5
Chapter 21 Opener, p. 349; Part 1, "The Classification of Books," pp. 350–351	Part 2, "The Dewey Decimal System," pp. 352–353	Part 3, "Finding a Book," pp. 354–355	Part 4, "Types of Catalog Cards," pp. 356–358	Part 5, "Using Other Resources," pp. 359–361

Chapter 21

Sharpening Library and Research Skills

Did you ever wonder why the grass is green or what makes the sky look blue? As a child you asked questions to find out about the world around you. Now, as a student, you not only ask questions but you have to answer them as well.

People never stop looking for information. That is why knowing how and where to find information is such an important skill.

This chapter will help you to learn how and where to locate facts about a topic. You will learn how to use the library and how to do research. You can use these skills to gather information, answer questions, and satisfy your curiosity.

349

Week 32
Chapter Management Guidelines This chart may be used to help structure daily lesson plans.

Day 1	Day 2	Day 3	Day 4	Day 5
Chapter 21, Part 6, "Taking Notes," pp. 362–363	Part 6, "Taking Notes," pp. 362–363	Part 7, "The Interview," pp. 364–365	Part 8, "Getting Information from Graphic Aids," pp. 366–367	Chapter Review and selected end-of-chapter activities

Special Populations

LD Use actual library materials as you discuss this chapter, or take the class to the library. Do the exercises in class with the students. Encourage students to use the library for work and pleasure.

ESL If possible, teach this section in the library. Give students as much extra library practice as possible. Have students find books relating to their native cultures in the library, and encourage them to borrow books on topics of interest to them.

Related Chapters

You may wish to refer to related material in other chapters as you teach the following concepts:
1. Techniques for scanning and skimming, Chapter 7, "Study and Test-Taking Skills," page 125
2. Using the dictionary, Chapter 8, "Exploring the Dictionary and Thesaurus," page 141
3. Gathering facts for report writing, Chapter 22, "The Process of Writing a Report," page 371

Additional Resources

Skills Practice Book—pages 132–139
Test Booklet—pages 121–128
Pretest—pages 121–122
Mastery Test—pages 123–128
Teacher's Resource Binder
Reinforcement Activities—
pages 83–88
Enrichment Activities—
pages 35–36, 41–54, 79–80
Ideas for Creative Teaching

Chapter 21 **349**

● Chapter Objectives
Clearly stated learning objectives are presented for each lesson in the chapter.

● Motivating the Students
An activity or discussion topic, often highlighted by a thought-provoking literary selection, draws students into the chapter, promotes literary appreciation, and encourages creative expression.

● Chapter Management Guidelines
A convenient management chart helps you create detailed, day-by-day lesson plans.

● Special Populations
Guidelines help teachers meet the special needs of certain students.

● Related Chapters
A handy cross-reference to other chapters containing related material is provided for your convenience.

● Additional Resources
A listing of additional resources refers you to the appropriate pages in the Skills Practice Book, Test Booklet, and Teacher's Resource Binder.

● To help you evaluate student writing
Criteria for the holistic evaluation of student writing are provided in composition chapters and in the Teacher's Editions. These criteria closely correspond to the guidelines developed by state writing projects.

Everything you need to introduce, develop, and individualize lessons

Teaching the Lesson

● **Lesson Objectives**
A focused statement previews the goal of the lesson.

● **Presenting the Lesson**
Step-by-step suggestions help you adapt the lesson for All Students, for Basic Students, and for Advanced Students. Potential problem areas are identified and additional examples are included.

● **To help you teach important thinking skills**
The critical thinking skills taught and applied in each lesson are clearly identified in the Teacher's Edition.

Part 1

Objective
To find and use definition, restatement, and examples in context to discover word meanings

Presenting the Lesson

■ **All Students**

1. Read and discuss page 6. Have students tell which words in the example sentences help to define the unfamiliar word. Be sure students understand the idea of *context*.

2. Stress that using examples to find meaning requires both imagination and logical thinking. The reader must understand the category the given example or examples belong to. Then, he or she can see if the new word fits in that category. For example, one simple sentence tells about "implements like screwdrivers and pliers." This is helpful only if the reader knows what screwdrivers and pliers are. Then the reader must correctly put them in the category "small tools used in repair work." Only then can the reader define *implements* as "small tools."

3. Emphasize the role of the key words listed on page 7, as signals to definitions or restatements. Also emphasize key words that signal examples.

4. Assign and discuss Exercises A and B on page 7.

5. Use Exercise A on page 14 for additional practice if needed.

▶ **Basic Students**

Before the students complete Exercises A and B, give them additional practice in determining word meaning from context. Work through the following examples. Then, have the students complete the exercises in the lesson.

1. Before he went on his vacation to France, Jason *accumulated*, or collected, as much information on France as he could. collected
2. Cleo always comes up with *unique* ideas. That is, her ideas are like no one else's. like nothing else
3. The catalog showed a wide variety of *cutlery*, such as knives and scissors. tools for cutting
4. Leaves on many trees turn *russet*, or reddish brown, in fall. reddish

6 Chapter 1

From Grade 5, Teacher's Edition

1 Using Context Clues: Definition, Restatement, and Example

┌─ Focus ─
Context clues can help you learn the meaning of an unfamiliar word in a sentence. A context clue may define, restate, or give an example of an unfamiliar word.
└

▶ Comprehension

When a writer knows that a certain word will be new to many readers, he or she may use a **context clue**. *Context* means the words or sentences around a particular word.

Definition or Restatement

The writer may give a **definition** of the word or **restate** the unfamiliar word in a different way. Read these sentences.

> She saw a colony of *gannets*—large, white sea birds—perched on the rocks. (definition)
> The balloonists *ascended*, or went up, more slowly than they came down. (restatement)

Example

Sometimes the writer helps the reader understand a new word by giving an example. When you read, check to see if an unfamiliar word is explained by one or more examples somewhere else in the sentence. Read this sentence.

> *Implements*, such as screwdrivers and pliers, are handy to have around the house. (example)

The context tells you that screwdrivers and pliers are examples of *implements*. This helps you understand the meaning of *implements*.

Advanced Students

Have the students choose four words from the following list, look up the meaning of each in a dictionary, and use each word in a sentence that reveals the meaning of that word. Remind them to use various types of context clues.

anchovies	ancestor
speleologist	cursory
graphic	tact
sphere	arroyo

Special Populations

ESL Help students break complex sentences into simple sentences before they work the exercises. For example, "She saw a colony of gannets—large, white sea birds—perched on the rocks" can be broken down into "She saw a colony of gannets. Gannets are large, white sea birds. The gannets were perched on the rocks."

Certain key words and punctuation marks signal that a writer is giving a context clue.

Key Words Signaling Definition or Restatement		
which is	or	also known as
that is	in other words	also called

Punctuation Marks Signaling Definition or Restatement
dashes, commas, and parentheses

Key Words Signaling an Example		
and other	for example	for instance
like	especially	such as

Exercises   Mastering Context Clues

Analyzing

A. Use the context clues in these sentences to write definitions for the words in italics. Check your definitions in a dictionary.

1. I enjoy Japanese food—*sukiyaki*, for example. a type of Japanese food
2. Samantha is a *philatelist*. In other words, she is a person who collects stamps. a stamp collector
3. Old pottery, like *majolica*, is hard to find. a type of pottery
4. Stay away from *toxic* plants such as poison ivy. poisonous
5. Diana can do a *half gainer* and other difficult dives. a type of dive

Analyzing

B. Write what each word in italics means. Then write what key words or punctuation marks helped you tell the word's meaning.

1. Dexter worked with a *farrier*, a blacksmith, to shoe the horses. a blacksmith, commas
2. A *vista*—a distant view—of pine forests and lakes opened before us. a distant view, dashes
3. Julio asked the grocer for *plátanos* (bananas). bananas, parentheses
4. Stock up on *gherkins* and other kinds of pickles. a kind of pickle, and other kinds
5. I used an *adz*, which is a flat-bladed ax. a flat-bladed ax, which is

7

Reinforcement

Have students follow the directions for Exercise A on page 14 using the sentences below:

1. The wide *plateau*, a high flat plain, was spread out before us. a high flat plain
2. Pedro can play a *marimba*, a guitar, and several other musical instruments. a musical instrument
3. Joe *feigned*, or pretended, surprise to see us at the station. pretended
4. Use a large dipping spoon, such as a *ladle*, for the soup. a large dipping spoon
5. The cheerleaders shouted through *megaphones* (large funnel-shaped horns). large funnel-shaped horns
6. Several wildcats roam the northern hemisphere—the *lynx*, for example. a kind of wildcat
7. We felt *torpid*—lazy and sluggish—in the hot weather. lazy and sluggish
8. Mother baked a *soufflé*, which is a puffy egg dish. a puffy egg dish
9. Lisa's *patella*—kneecap—was injured when she fell. kneecap
10. Mr. Jeffreys and I are *colleagues*. That is, we work together. people who work together

Enrichment

1. Divide the class into four groups. Each group should make up five non-sense words and a definition for each word. Groups should exchange word lists and write sentences that give context clues to the meaning of nonsense words. Exchange should continue until all groups have worked with all the words. The sentences should be shared with the class.

2. For additional enrichment activities see the Unit Projects in the Teacher Notes on page 3. One or more of these projects have special activities for gifted and talented students.

Chapter 1   **7**

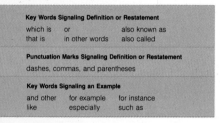

Additional Resources

Skills Practice Book—
   pages 1–2
Teacher's Resource Binder
   Reinforcement Activities—
      page 1
   Enrichment Activities—
      page 11

Special Populations

Suggestions are provided for modifying the lesson to meet the needs of students for whom English is a second language (Limited English Proficiency), students who use a nonstandard dialect, and learning-disabled students.

Reinforcement

Additional exercises and activities are provided to give students more practice with new concepts.

Enrichment

Additional activities and exercises give students an opportunity to apply what they have learned.

Additional Resources

A listing of additional resources available for the lesson refers you to the appropriate pages in the Skills Practice Book, Test Booklet, and Teacher's Resource Binder.

Additional Features in the Teacher's Edition

- Guidelines for Evaluating Composition
- Guidelines for Speaking and Listening
- Management Guidelines
- Class Record Sheet
- Individual Record Sheet
- Parent Letters in English and Spanish

Management Guidelines

The following guidelines are designed to help a teacher adapt the materials in *McDougal, Littell English* to suit his or her particular needs and schedule.

Determining the Topics To Be Covered
Before initiating the program, teachers should review the topics to be covered in light of these questions:
1. What are the curriculum requirements of the district?
2. How much time is available for the teaching of English?
3. What topics, if any, are taught elsewhere or as a separate course (for instance, library skills or spelling)?

These questions should help the teacher narrow down the topics to be covered in the time allotted.

Diagnosing Student Strengths
The Test Booklet for *McDougal, Littell English* contains a pretest for each chapter in the text. Teachers may administer these tests in several sessions at the beginning of the year, or prior to teaching each chapter. The results will indicate how much emphasis should be given to any specific chapter, and will also identify those students who need extra help with a particular concept.

Creating Lesson Plans
Time management charts are provided throughout the Teacher's Edition to help the teacher plan out weekly and monthly lesson plans. On every unit opener page are Unit Management Guidelines that show how the chapters for that unit may be scheduled over an eight-or nine-week grading period. Teachers who work on four- and six-week grading periods may adapt the charts accordingly.

Help for more specific lesson planning may be found on the chapter opener pages. There, Chapter Management Guidelines are provided that display how a chapter may be presented over several days.

A Unique Service for Teachers: Custom-Designed Management Plan
For school districts adopting *McDougal, Littell English*, McDougal, Littell & Company will, upon request, provide a customized time management plan geared to the curriculum requirements and time allotments in your district. Please write for details.

Individualizing
Initially, each lesson should be taught to the class as a whole. It may then be necessary for the teacher to provide additional help for some students while continuing to challenge the others. Suggestions for such individualization are provided in the teaching suggestions under these headings:

Basic Students	Reinforcement
Advanced Students	Enrichment
Special Populations	Exercises for Mastery

Teachers should become familiar with the suggestions for these pages before beginning to teach the lesson and plan sufficient time to incorporate them as necessary.

Using the Power Handbook
For more effective use of the Power Handbook, the teacher is strongly encouraged to introduce it to the class briefly at the beginning of the year and to remind students about it during the year. Teachers may want to develop the sections in the Handbook in the usual teacher-guided approach, in the order that the sections appear. For that purpose, teaching suggestions are provided. However, some teachers prefer to teach the various concepts as the need arises.

Week 28

Chapter Management Guidelines   This chart may be used to help structure daily lesson plans.

Day 1	Day 2	Day 3	Day 4	Day 5
Chapter 19 Opener, p. 319; Part 1, "Fact and Opinion," pp. 320-321	Part 2, "Errors in Thinking," pp. 322-323	Part 3, "Drawing Conclusions," pp. 324-325	Part 4, "Solving Problems," pp. 326-327	Chapter Review and selected end-of-chapter activities

Management of Program Resources

In the *McDougal, Littell English* series, all materials essential to the student for achieving the stated objectives are provided in the student text. All the materials essential to the teacher for presenting the student text are provided in the Teacher's Edition. Supplementary materials for reinforcing, evaluating, and recording student progress are provided in booklets or in copy master form.

The following chart shows how these materials may be used to develop every step in the teaching process.

Resource (* indicates more than one possible use)

Teaching Step	Student Text	Teacher's Edition	Skills Practice Book, Test Booklet, Duplicating Masters, Teacher's Resource Binder
Preparing the Students 1. Pretest/Diagnosis			Test Booklet, DM's
2. Motivation	Unit Opener Chapter Opener	Chapter Notes: Motivating the Students	
Teaching the Lesson 1. Basic Lesson	Part Lesson	Presenting the Lesson: All Students	

2. Individualizing		Presenting the Lesson:
		  Basic Students
		  Advanced Students
		  Special Populations	

Reinforcing the Lesson 1. Written exercises	Part Exercises*	Reinforcement*	SPB, DM's, TRB
2. Review of lesson, with practice exercises	Exercises for Mastery*		SPB, DM's
3. Group activities		Unit projects*	TRB
Extending the Lesson	Speaking and Listening, Creative Writing, Using English in Other Subjects*	Enrichment Unit projects	TRB
Applying Grammar and Other Skills to Writing	Using Grammar in Writing		SPB, DM's
Applying Writing to Other Subject Areas	Using Grammar in Writing* Using English in Other Subjects*		TRB
Testing the Lesson 1. Individual part check-up	Exercises for Mastery*		
2. Mixed review check-up	Chapter Review		SPB, DM's
3. Chapter test			Test Booklet, DM's
Reteaching	Part Exercises* Exercises for Mastery*	Reinforcement*	Any unused worksheets in SPB, DM's, or TRB
Maintaining Skills	References to previous lessons, Cumulative Reviews		Test Booklet, SPB, DM's or TRB

Teaching Critical Thinking Skills in the Classroom

During the last several years the term "critical thinking" has become the focus of educators throughout the country. Whether a student is being introduced to computer studies or to prewriting techniques, the ultimate purpose in all areas of education is the same—to teach students how to think critically and independently.

Yet, how much of a teacher's time is spent *specifically* developing thinking skills? And how many students even realize that thinking skills exist, or that by understanding and practicing them, they can more successfully approach situations and problems in every area of life? The most widely known general critical thinking tests—Cornell Critical Thinking Tests (Ennis and Millman, 1985) and the Watson-Glaser Critical Thinking Appraisal (Watson and Glaser, 1980)—indicate that neither teacher instruction nor student understanding is nearly as complete as one might hope.

It is this gap in education that teachers and other educators have recently begun to address. Probably the most influential work on this subject in recent years is *Taxonomy of Educational Objectives*, by Benjamin S. Bloom and others (1956). One of the goals of the *Taxonomy* was to outline the general categories of thinking skills.

A whole generation of teachers is now familiar with the *Taxonomy*. Its impact on education has been profound. However, since the work was published, other researchers have published variations on these categories of thinking skills. Many, for example, disagree with the sequential nature of the *Taxonomy* and argue that, depending on the context, different levels of the *Taxonomy* may be considered the "higher order" skills (Paul, 1985). Other researchers have published their own interpretation of what "thinking" is (Sternberg, 1985; Ennis, 1986; Feuerstein, 1980; Oscanyan, 1977). Yet all of these studies have had the effect of making teachers reexamine what and how they are teaching.

Impact on Teaching

One of the most direct benefits that these studies have had is to make teachers themselves aware of the thinking processes that go on in themselves as well as in their students. A second, more long-range benefit that research has had is to encourage educators to incorporate critical thinking instruction in the classroom actively. Such instruction can be accomplished using several different methods: (Quellmalz, 1985; Paul, 1985; Joyce, 1985):

1. By varying the types of questions asked in class to insure practice of different levels of thinking skills
2. By recognizing that there are different styles of learning; that some students learn best through memorization, some through analysis, and some through application
3. By teaching with and presenting models of different thinking strategies
4. By providing methods for finding answers rather than simply presenting the answers themselves
5. By designing tasks and assignments that permit multiple interpretations and solutions
6. By providing opportunities for the use of higher level thinking skills
7. By encouraging open formats in which students must explain their reasoning.

Application in *McDougal, Littell English*

McDougal, Littell English incorporates critical thinking instruction in the following ways:

1. **Thinking strategies.** Specific methods and strategies are given for such skills as these:

problem solving	determining relationships
making inferences and drawing conclusions	evaluation
analysis of information	recognizing errors in thinking

Bloom's Taxonomy

Taxonomy of Educational Objectives: Cognitive Domain

1.00 Knowledge
1.10 Knowledge of Specifics
1.11 Knowledge of Terminology
1.12 Knowledge of Specific Facts
1.20 Knowledge of Ways and Means of Dealing with Specifics
1.21 Knowledge of Conventions
1.22 Knowledge of Trends and Sequences
1.23 Knowledge of Classifications and Categories
1.24 Knowledge of Criteria
1.25 Knowledge of Methodology
1.30 Knowledge of the Universals and Abstractions in a Field
1.31 Knowledge of Principles and Generalizations
1.32 Knowledge of Theories and Structures

2.00 Comprehension
2.10 Translation
2.20 Interpretation
2.30 Extrapolation

3.00 Application
The use of abstractions in particular and concrete situations. The abstractions may be in the form of general ideas, rules of procedures, or generalized methods. The abstractions may also be technical principles, ideas, and theories which must be remembered and applied.

4.00 Analysis
4.10 Analysis of Elements
4.20 Analysis of Relationships
4.30 Analysis of Organizational Principles

5.00 Synthesis
5.10 Production of a Unique Communication
5.20 Production of a Plan, or Proposed Set of Operations
5.30 Derivation of a Set of Abstract Relations

6.00 Evaluation
6.10 Judgments in Terms of Internal Evidence
6.20 Judgments in Terms of External Criteria

From *The Taxonomy of Educational Objectives Handbook 1: Cognitive Domain* (Bloom and others, 1956, p. 201)

2. **Inductive Teaching.** Textbooks have traditionally presented rules and concepts with very little introduction and almost no elaboration. Students are not given opportunities to think through new concepts on their own, or to reach generalizations independently.

   McDougal, Littell English, in contrast, sharpens the thinking process by presenting most lessons in a simple inductive format. Students are presented with various facts and examples which they analyze carefully. From this point, students are led through steps of evaluation, generalization, or drawing conclusions and ultimately arrive at the key concept.

3. **Emphasis on Analysis.** Students are given abundant opportunities to explore models and samples in order to determine why these examples work well, or why they are weak.

4. **Variety of Methods and Activities.** Different types of learners require different kinds of teaching. Similarly, different types of thinking skills necessitate a variety of exercises to develop them. *McDougal, Littell English* recognizes these two facts by providing an exciting variety of exercises that address different requirements and needs. Some exercises are written and some are oral; some are highly structured while many others encourage creative thinking and application; some require only one answer and some stimulate divergent thinking and many acceptable responses.

5. **Levels of Exercises.** In grades 3 through 6, the thinking process is additionally developed through different levels of exercises. Each lesson contains two or three exercises. The first usually requires simple recall or identification. The second requires more complex analysis, application, or evaluation. Additional exercises allow independent application of the concept in new and creative contexts.

6. **Labeling.** The lessons and exercises in the Teacher's Editions of *McDougal, Littell English* are given labels that indicate the type of thinking skill being taught or utilized. These labels can help the teacher pinpoint skill areas where a student is weak. They can also be used to help students become aware of the types of thinking skills they are using and developing. The labels are based on general categories of thinking that appear in numerous bodies of research (Bloom, Ennis, Sternberg, and others). Both major heads and subheads shown below are used within the text.

Level 1. Literal Understanding (responds to what is explicitly stated)
   Comprehension
   Recalling
   Recognition
Level 2. Interpretation (responds with and to ideas and opinions not explicitly stated)
   Classifying
   Recognizing Relationships
   Generalizing
   Making Inferences
   Drawing Conclusions
Level 3. Critical Reasoning (investigates, evaluates, and integrates information)
   Judging
   Analyzing
   Evaluating
Level 4. Application (extends learning to new contexts or situations)
   Structured Application
   Synthesis
   Creative Application

Conclusion

All students have the right to be taught critical thinking skills. Their eventual success, both in school and beyond the classroom, will depend on how well they develop these skills. Through greater awareness of the thinking process, we, as their teachers, can help them achieve this goal. We can also share in the benefits that a generation of independent and creative thinkers can bring to us.

Sources

Bereiter, Carl. "How to Keep Thinking Skills From Going the Way of All Frills." *Educational Leadership* 42 (September 1984): 75-77.

Ennis, R.H. "A Taxonomy of Critical Thinking Skills." In *Teaching Thinking Skills,* edited by J.B. Baron and R.J. Sternberg. New York: W.H. Freeman, 1986.

Ennis, R.H., and J. Millman. "Cornell Critical Thinking Test, Levels X and Z." Pacific Grove, California: Midwest Publications, 1985.

Feuerstein, R. *Instrumental Enrichment: An Intervention Program for Cognitive Modificability.* Baltimore: University Park Press, 1980.

Joyce, Bruce. "Models for Teaching Thinking." *Educational Leadership,* May 1985.

Joyce, Bruce and Marsha Weil. *Models of Teaching.* Englewood Cliffs. N.J.: Prentice-Hall, Inc., 1980.

Oscanyan, Frederick S. "How Can I Teach My Students To Learn on Their Own." *Educational Theory* 27 (winter 1977): 76-79.

Paul, Richard W. "Bloom's Taxonomy and Critical Thinking Instruction." *Educational Leadership,* May 1985.

Quellmalz, Edys S. "Needed. Better Methods for Testing Higher-Order Thinking Skills." *Educational Leadership,* October 1985.

Sternberg, R.J. "Criteria for Intellectual Skills Training." *Educational Researcher* 12,2 (1983): 6-12,26.

Sternberg, R.J. "Critical Thinking: Its Nature, Measurement, and Improvement." In *Essays on the Intellect,* edited by F. Link. Alexandria, Va.: Association for Supervision and Curriculum Development, 1985.

Watson, G., and E.M. Glaser. "Watson-Glaser Critical Thinking Appraisal, Forms A and B." Cleveland, Ohio: The Psychological Corporation, 1980.

A New Approach to the Teaching of Writing

The inclusion of a strong writing program has always been deemed essential to any effective language arts curriculum. The means by which writing is taught, however, seems to change every several years as educators seek increasingly better ways to teach writing skills to students.

A Critical Look at the Process of Writing

During the past ten years or so, teachers have been excited by a concept of composing commonly referred to as the Process of Writing. This concept was a welcome innovation because, prior to its introduction, most student writers, their teachers, and their texts ignored the fact that there was a process to writing—a method of thinking and revising that is necessary to any successful composing experience (Graves, 1977). As it is usually described, this process consists of four main stages, which were to be completed more or less in sequence.

1. Prewriting, or planning
2. Drafting
3. Revising and proofreading
4. Making the final copy and sharing

As a way of clarifying for teachers the various stages of writing, this rather linear model seemed acceptable. However, most teachers began finding, to their dismay, that the process of writing wasn't working well. The reasons?

Problems with the Process

First, researchers discovered that this process did not accurately reflect the way people write. Most writers do not go through the steps of the process in quite the prescribed order (Rodrigues, 1985). Some spend a great deal of time prewriting; some begin, in effect, at the drafting stage, and some blur the stages. The correct model of writing, according to these researchers, is recursive—it circles back on itself, and takes different forms for different writers. (Graves, 1983; Murray, 1968; Haily, 1978; Gaskins, 1982; Haley-James, 1981, 1982)

A second reason for the failure of the process was a tendency of many of its proponents to utilize it in a very unsystematic, open-minded way (Rodrigues). Student choice and free writing abounded, while structured models, skills instruction, and attention to grammar, usage, and mechanics were given low priority.

Third, little attention was given to different learning and writing styles. It has long been recognized that there are different types of learners, and different types of writers. Each individual attacks a task or problem in a unique way, using different methods and proceeding along different logical paths. As composition has too often been taught, texts assume that all students can follow one rigid process.

Finally, inadequate attention was given to different types of writing. A report on computers and a fantasy story about small beings that live in a sewer system are two very different types of writing. The same writer would complete the prewriting for these two pieces in extremely different ways. Yet, in most texts, students are taught one writing process that is supposed to suffice for dramatically different genres.

The teaching of composition has been further hindered by the following deficiencies:

1. No development of the relationship between writing and thinking. Good writing is actually a series of thinking activities. Writing involves generating ideas (What can I write about? What details will I use?), seeking relationships (Which ideas belong together? How can I form a bridge between these two concepts?), problem-solving (How can I make this argument more effective for my audience?), and judging and evaluating (Why isn't this paragraph working? How can I improve it?). Yet the *thinking* aspects of writing are often taken for granted or treated incidentally.

2. No application outside of English class. One of the main purposes of writing is to communicate ideas. When this purpose does not exist, writing becomes meaningless. Unfortunately many composition texts try to attract students with "motivational" writing situations such as newspaper stories, while neglecting to show how the skills involved can be used in the students' real lives.

3. No recognition of the interdependence of writing genres. No type of writing exists in isolation. Narratives involve description. Expository writing often includes elements of narrative. Yet most texts treat writing genres as though they exist for and by themselves.

Composition Instruction in *McDougal, Littell English*

McDougal, Littell English has addressed the problems that teachers have faced because of incomplete or faulty treatments of the process of writing. This new program incorporates the following approaches to the teaching of writing:

1. A Multi-process Approach

No single process of writing is presented to the students. Instead, writing is introduced as a series of choices and decisions. Beginning with grade 3, students are led through a general writing chapter that presents an overview of the stages of writing and the choices that are involved in each stage. In subsequent chapters, students are led through different types of writing—description, narration, exposition—and are also shown several different processes of writing, one to suit each writing mode.

2. The Use of Models and Structured Presentations
To balance the more open format of the multiple-process approach, students are introduced to each type of writing through several carefully structured lessons. Frameworks and guidelines provide temporary supports for the students until they gain the confidence to make writing decisions on their own.

3. Recognition of Different Types of Writers
McDougal, Littell English is careful to recognize the variety of writing styles that exist among even the youngest writers. No two writers approach a writing task in the same way. Therefore, a variety of prewriting, drafting, and revising techniques is presented so that each student can find the methods with which he or she is most comfortable.

4. Emphasis on Thinking Skills
Since, as stated earlier, clear writing is dependent on clear thinking, these texts work to nurture the development of thinking skills through every chapter. (See Teaching Critical Thinking Skills in the Classroom, pages T20-T21.) In the writing chapters, this emphasis is especially apparent. Every chapter begins with a lesson in which students read, analyze, and evaluate two samples of the type of writing that is the focus of the chapter. Throughout the rest of the lessons, students learn to explore, implement, and evaluate writing choices.

5. Emphasis on the Recursive Nature of Writing
Stages of the writing process are not treated in isolation. The boundaries are purposely blurred. Revision (and the thinking behind it) is shown as early as the prewriting stage and continues into drafting. Idea generation and organization decisions are still evident during revision.

6. Application in Other Areas
McDougal, Littell English presents most writing situations in a context of some other subject area so that students can see the purpose for learning to write well. For example, one writing sample may be an explanation of the experiment for science class, another might be a narrative being written for social studies.

7. Recognition of Interdependence of Writing Types
A point is made of showing students that the different "types" of writing are used to strengthen and develop each other. The use of description, for example, is encouraged in both narratives and explanations. Narrative, in turn, may be used to highlight a point in an explanation.

8. An Integrated Language Approach
Good communication depends on more than good composing strategies. It also depends on sound thinking skills, vocabulary development , study and research skills, literary appreciation, and an understanding of basic grammar and mechanics. *McDougal, Littell English* develops students' abilities in all these areas.

9. In-depth Teaching
McDougal, Littell English covers each type of writing in detail, spending usually no fewer than six pages per type in the primary grades, and expanding to ten to twelve pages per type in the upper grades. Organized in easily manageable two- or three-page lessons, these chapters provide students with the in-depth teaching they need.

Goals of the Program
Writing is more than just a humming word processor or a pen scratching across paper. It is also a method of sharing information, a means of self expression, a way of discovering ideas, and a way of exploring oneself. Yet if students are not given the proper instruction, writing can become something else—a chore.

McDougal, Littell English strives to introduce students not only to the techniques of writing, but also to the excitement. By doing so, we are helping to make the teaching of composition a particularly rewarding experience for the teacher.

Sources

Boiarsky, Carolyn. "Prewriting Is the Essence of Writing." *English Journal* 71, no. 4 (April 1982): 44-47.

Cooper, Charles, and Lee Odell, eds. *Research on Composing.* Urbana, Illinois: National Council of Teachers of English, 1978.

Daigon, Arthur. "Toward Righting Writing." *Phi Delta Kappan* 64 (December, 1982): 242-246.

Gaskins, Irene. "A Writing Program for Poor Readers and Writers and the Rest of the Class, Too." *Language Arts* 59, no. 8 (Nov./Dec., 1982): 854-863.

Graves, Donald. "Language Arts Textbooks: A Writing Process Evaluation." *Language Arts* 54, no. 7 (October, 1977): 817-823.

Graves, Donald. *Writing: Teachers and Children at Work.* Exeter, New Hampshire: Heinemann Educational Books, 1983.

Hailey, Jack. *Teaching Writing K Through 8.* Berkeley, California: Instructional Laboratory, University of California at Berkeley, 1978.

Haley-James, Shirley, ed. *Perspectives on Writing in Grades 1-8.* Urbana, Illinois: National Council of Teachers of English, 1981.

Haley-James, Shirley. "Helping Students Learn Through Writing." *Language Arts* 59, no. 7 (October, 1982): 726-731.

Kantor, Kenneth J. "Research in Composition: What It Means for Teachers." *English Journal* 70, no. 2 (February, 1981): 64-67.

Murray, Donald. *A Writer Teaches Writing.* Boston: Houghton-Mifflin Co., 1968.

Rodrigues, Raymond J. "Moving Away from Writing Process Worship." *English Journal,* September 1985, 24-27.

Sudol, Ronald A., ed. *Revising: New Essays for Teachers of Writing.* Urbana, Illinois: National Council of Teachers of English, 1982.

Writing Instruction in the Classroom

In order to have a successful writing program, teachers must have more than a good text. They must also be given information on how to structure the writing class as a whole. Some guidelines for this are presented below.

Guidelines for Effective Writing Instruction

1. Create a positive atmosphere.
Writing is best learned in a structured yet encouraging and supportive workshop atmosphere (Graves 1978, Koch and Brazil, 1978, Beaven 1977, Gaskins 1982). The teacher must have a positive attitude toward writing in general and students' writing efforts in particular.

2. Establish a physical environment conducive to writing.
Arrange desks to permit sharing when helpful, and then rearrange them when independent work is necessary. Create "idea corners" or "conference corners."

3. Let the students write, and write often.
The only way students will learn to write is "through a private discovery of writing problems and their solution" (Murray, 1968). Therefore, allow frequent opportunities for writing on a daily basis, if possible.

4. Provide constant feedback.
Thoughtful evaluation is necessary for continued growth in writing (Hailey 1978). This evaluation may take the form of teacher, peer, or self-evaluation. (See "Guidelines for Evaluating Writing," pages T26 to T29).

Techniques for Writing
To enable students to find a writing process that suits both the writing they are doing and themselves as writers, *McDougal, Littell English* presents a variety of techniques and methods within the chapters. These are summarized below. The teacher should become familiar with these methods and may wish to reproduce a similar list for the students so that young writers may have an easy reference as they seek out the process of writing that is best for them.

Prewriting

Brainstorming
Independently or in groups, students generate as many ideas as possible from a given starting point. The ideas need not be related in any way and may indeed stray over into areas completely unrelated to the original idea. The purpose is simply to discover a number of ideas for possible exploration.

Charts, Clusters, Maps, Idea Trees
These are different methods of visually presenting the results of a brainstorming session. Students record generated ideas, using lines or shapes to show the relationship of one idea to another.

Cluster

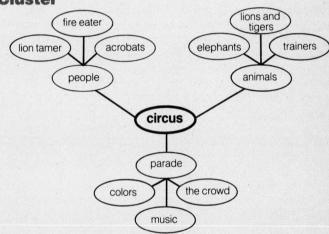

Creative Thinking
Students try to look at usual subjects in unusual ways: What if dogs could fly? What if there were no wheels? What would I get by combining a pizza and a hamburger? Where might this rock once have been?

Discussion
Often, the best source of ideas is other people. Discussion of a topic provided by the teacher, or of the students' own choosing, often leads to a wealth of ideas for writing.

Experiences
Field trips, lectures, and any new person or situation may stimulate writing ideas and break class routine. The teacher may wish to schedule activities regularly throughout the year.

Free Writing
Students write intensely for several minutes, freeing the flow of ideas.

Interviews
An expert on some topic can provide a writer with a number of interesting writing topics or supporting information.

Journals
Students keep a diary-like record of thoughts, ideas, and experiences.

Observing
Students try to remain sensitive to all that happens around them, looking for writing ideas in people, places, and events.

Questioning
All reporters know about the six basic questions of acquiring information: *who, what, where, when, why,* and *how.* Students can be taught to use these questions, too.

Reading
Books, magazines, encyclopedias, and newspapers are endless sources of writing ideas. Try to allow time in class each day for reading, and encourage students to be continually on the lookout for interesting topics.

Drafting
Drafting, like other aspects of writing, is highly personal. The following methods, and variations of them, seem to be among the most common. Help students to find the methods they are most comfortable with.

Highly Structured
The writer works from very complete prewriting notes, changing little of the content or organization.

Loosely Structured
The writer works from rough notes, experimenting with ideas and organization during writing.

Bridges
The writer begins with two or three main points or situations to be covered, and concentrates on building logical bridges between the points during drafting.

Quick Draft
The writer composes quickly, not stopping to refine ideas or rework copy until the "revising stage".

Slow Draft
The writer works meticulously, carefully drafting one sentence or paragraph at a time, revising continuously, and reworking the piece in its entirety when the draft is complete.

Revising
Whether revising is done during drafting or after the first draft is complete, students must find a technique of revising that best suits them and the type of writing they are doing. (See Guidelines for Evaluating Writing on pages T26 to T29 of this Teacher's Edition.)

Conference
Oral evaluations by the teacher concentrate on both strengths and problems, while the student asks questions.

Peer Editing
In pairs or small groups, students critique each other's writing.

Group Questioning
After one student in a group reads a piece of writing aloud, the other students ask questions to highlight any incomplete information.

Editorial Groups
Students assigned the roles of author, editor, and proofreader work together on an assignment and later may change roles.

Oral Reading
Students read their work aloud, or into a tape recorder. The ear often catches what the eye misses.

Performance
For explanatory pieces, another student follows the directions and points out unclear or confusing passages.

Sharing
Writing is communication. As such, its purpose is lost if the final product is not shared with others. Sharing also gives the students themselves more of a reason to be careful with their writing. The following methods may be used to encourage students to share their writing:

Booklets
Writing on similar topics is collected and "published" as a booklet.

Bulletin Boards
Writing on a specific subject is posted and illustrated with appropriate drawings and photographs.

Drama
Stories may be adapted to the form of a play and acted out.

Exchanges
Letters and other writing may be exchanged with other classes.

Letters
Writing may be done in the form of letters and then mailed.

Newspapers and Magazines
Students may submit their writing to children's magazines and local papers. Students may also create a newspaper or magazine of their own that involves different subjects and genres.

Readings
Students may read their materials to the rest of the class or in small groups, accompanying it, if they like, with music.

Guidelines for Evaluating Writing

Adapted from *Teaching and Evaluating Student Writing,* copyright ©
by McDougal, Littell & Company

Most educators would agree that constant, helpful evaluation of student writing is the only way to help young writers develop their skills. For many teachers, however, this "helpful" feedback has come to mean endless amounts of time spent with a stack of papers and a red pencil, marking every incorrect spelling or misplaced comma. Such an evaluation is suffered through for the good of the students. Yet how much does this evaluation system aid the developing writer?

When a child is learning to talk, a parent will accept and respond to single words or incomplete phrases, recognizing that the child has a message to communicate even if the form of the message is undeveloped. Similarly, when a student is learning to write, he or she needs the encouragement of a response to a written message, no matter how undeveloped the form of that message is. A teacher cannot afford to require correct sentence structure, grammar, capitalization, punctuation, and spelling before looking at the ideas in a piece of writing.

The practical classroom application of these ideas, advanced by recent research into the writing process, is that students should be given opportunities to write as frequently as possible and that they be given some evaluation of the sense and style of their writing as frequently as possible. This emphasis on quantity means that some teachers may need to rethink their evaluation procedures.

Types of Evaluation

In order to give student writers the constant practice and feedback they need, teachers must have a practical method of evaluation. If students are writing constantly, a teacher cannot be expected to evaluate each piece in a word-by-word manner. Nor would such an evaluation necessarily be useful to the developing writer. It is therefore suggested that a teacher use two different evaluation methods—the holistic method and the more detailed analytic method.

Holistic evaluation of writing is a quick, guided method of rating pieces of writing. It can best be used to evaluate daily writing samples or first drafts of more complex pieces. With holistic evaluation, an evaluator reads the written piece as a whole, considers certain features, and immediately assigns a grade. The grade may be a single rating for the entire piece of writing or a set of ratings for the different features being considered.

The evaluation form provided on page T29 of this Teacher's Edition is of this second type of holistic evaluation, but will also guide teachers who wish to use the single rating evaluation. It lists the major characteristics of content and form that can be identified in most types of writing. When the teacher desires to evaluate a certain type of writing, such as narrative composition, he or she might supplement the general questions about content with the more specific guidelines found in the last part of the writing chapters in grades 3 through 6.

Analytic evaluation should occur only when the student has turned in the clean, final copy of a piece of writing. In this detailed type of evaluation, the teacher analyzes each aspect of a piece of writing, including both content and mechanics. By this point, many of the student's errors will have been spotted and corrected during the revision process. Problems that remain in the final copy are likely to be indicative of where the student's real weaknesses lie, and both student and teacher can concentrate on identifying and correcting them.

Evaluators

The evaluation process can be utilized by three types of evaluators: the writer of the piece, other students, and the teacher. Each type of evaluation offers unique benefits to the developing writer.

1. Self-Evaluation

In this type of evaluation, a writer comments on his or her own work, noting which parts were successful and which were unsuccessful. During self-evaluation, a student may be guided by a chart such as the one on page T29, as well as by what "feels" right.

It will not always be possible for a student to pinpoint exactly what is wrong in a piece of writing. When this occurs, the writer should be encouraged to underline any sentence or section that doesn't "feel" right, verbalize the problem as he or she perceives it, and then seek further clarification and help from the teacher. This estimation of errors will eventually become more precise as the student learns to recognize similar problems in later writing.

It is very helpful for students to be guided through the evaluation process before they attempt self-evaluation. The teacher might, for example, project a sample composition using an overhead projector and then guide the class to an understanding of the types of questions they should ask during the revision process. Such guided evaluation helps the young writer develop a sense of when information is incomplete or ideas unclear. This knowledge can then be applied during self-evaluation.

2. Peer Evaluation

Evaluating the writing of others is often a strong learning experience. In peer evaluation, students work together in small groups to improve a piece of writing. Student evaluators should always be given a list of specific criteria that the writing is expected to meet and should then comment on how well each paper succeeds. Peer evaluation is most effective when the writer is given time to make revisions after the group suggests ways to improve the work.

3. Teacher Evaluation

The teacher's comments and suggestions may be incorporated at any point in the writing process. Studies indicate that evaluation by the teacher is most successful when it is done in combination with self- and peer-evaluation. The evaluation form on page T29, therefore, provides for such a combination.

Teacher evaluation should also involve direct communication with every student. Such help can be provided in student-teacher conferences. These conferences provide an opportunity for students to ask the questions they develop during self-evaluation. They also give teachers a chance to comment on the strong points of the paper, offer additional suggestions, and provide individualized instruction when it is needed.

Teacher evaluation of a final copy should be the last step in the evaluation process. When a student turns in a clean, final copy of a paper, the teacher should require that previous drafts be turned in with it. The teacher should then provide an in-depth analysis of the final copy, judging it not only on its final content but also on how well the student incorporated earlier suggestions.

Keeping a Record of Improvement

Both the teacher and students benefit when writing folders are maintained throughout the school year. A piece of writing from early in the year, along with its evaluations, can be compared with later pieces. Progress from one piece to the next will be erratic, as the writer takes risks using new techniques and appears to move backwards until gaining mastery of each new technique. However, over the course of the year, progress should be evident.

Sources

Beaven, Mary. "Goal Setting and Evaluation." In *Evaluating Writing* edited by Cooper and Odell. Urbana, Illinois: National Council of Teachers of English, 1977.

Cooper, Charles R. and Lee Odell, eds. *Evaluating Writing: Describing, Measuring, Judging.* Urbana, Illinois: National Council of Teachers of English, 1977.

Evertts, Eldonna L., ed. *Explorations in Children's Writing.* Urbana, Illinois: National Council of Teachers of English, 1970.

Gaskins, Irene. "A Writing Program for Poor Readers and Writers and the Rest of the Class, Too." *Language Arts* 59, no. 8 (Nov./Dec., 1982): 854-863.

Graves, Donald H. *Balance the Basics: Let Them Write.* New York: The Ford Foundation, 1978.

Koch, Carl and James Brazil. *Strategies for Teaching the Composition Process.* Urbana, Illinois: National Council of Teachers of English, 1978.

Murray, Donald M. *A Writer Teaches Writing: A Practical Method of Teaching Composition.* Boston: Houghton Mifflin, 1968.

Sager, Carol. "Improving the Quality of Written Composition in the Middle Grades." *Language Arts* 54 (1977): 760-762.

Using the Evaluation Form

The form for composition evaluation on the next page may be used at any stage of the writing process. The form may be re-used with a single piece of writing after each revision.

The form should be filled out by the student and turned in with the writing. There is also space on the form for peer evaluation, if desired. The teacher may ask students to turn in only final copies, or may ask to see work in progress. The student states whether the submitted writing is the final copy.

On the evaluation form, content may be rated at any point; mechanics should be graded only on a final copy.

Self-Evaluation: Besides the questions on the form, the student can ask himself or herself the questions concerning revising listed in the relevant composition chapter. These guidelines will help in distancing the writer from the work. The student may use 1, 3, and 5 subjectively.

Peer Evaluation: Members of the peer group should rate each feature as objectively as possible. So that attention will be focused on ideas and organization, the group is asked to evaluate content only.

Teacher Evaluation: The following standards for evaluating composition are provided to assist the teacher in rating papers with objectivity and consistency. In a conference, the teacher might discuss one or two of these areas in detail.

Ideas

	1—Low	3—Middle	5—High
1	Unclear, unimaginative writing. Boring or poorly defined topic.	Understandable but unimaginative writing. Topic adequately defined.	Imaginative, interesting writing. Well-developed topic.
2	Lack of organization or development. Unclear or missing main idea.	Identifiable main idea, but weak organization. Some ideas missing or out of order.	Strongly defined main idea. Clear, logical organization. Sentences related to each other.
3	Many irrelevant sentences or details.	Few irrelevant sentences or details.	Well chosen, relevant sentences or details.
4	Writing so lacking in development and detail that topic is not identifiable.	Boring description. Incomplete development of narrative or exposition.	Description rich in detail. Clear, easily-followed narrative or exposition.
5	Many fragments and run-on sentences.	Some fragments and/or run-on sentences.	Few, if any, fragments or run-on sentences.
6	Dull, general words, poorly chosen.	Suitable but unimaginative language.	Specific, figurative language.

Mechanics

1	Paragraph(s) not indented. Title missing.	On writing longer than one paragraph, not all paragraphs indented.	Paragraphs indented. Title in correct position.
2	Frequent mistakes in the use of nouns, verbs, pronouns, and subject-verb agreement.	Occasional mistakes in the use of nouns, verbs, pronouns, and subject-verb agreement.	Infrequent mistakes in the use of nouns, verbs, pronouns, and subject-verb agreement.
3	Frequent mistakes in capitalization of sentence beginnings, proper nouns, I, and titles.	Occasional mistakes in capitalization.	Infrequent mistakes in capitalization.
4	Punctuation marks frequently missing or misused.	Punctuation marks usually used correctly.	Infrequent mistakes in punctuation.
5	Frequent mistakes in spelling, without any pattern or indication of awareness of spelling patterns.	Occasional misspellings, usually indicating an awareness of spelling patterns.	Infrequent spelling mistakes, usually indicating an awareness of spelling patterns.
6	Badly formed letters of uneven size and slant, frequently illegible.	Some carelessly or inconsistently formed letters, sometimes hard to read.	Correctly formed letters with consistent size, slant, and spacing.

Composition Evaluation Form

McDougal, Littell English

Writer _____   Date _____

Title _____   Circle one: Unfinished   Final Copy

The Writer's Opinion
1 I want to work more on this.
3 This is all right.
5 I'm very happy with this.

Peer Group or Teacher's Evaluation
1 Please show this to me again after you've worked on it.
3 This is all right.
5 You should be very happy with this.

Ideas	The Writer's Opinion 1, 3, or 5	Peer Group Opinion 1, 3, or 5	The Teacher's Evaluation 1, 3, or 5	Teacher's Comments
1. Is the writing interesting? Is the topic a good one?				
2. Does the writing make sense? Are the ideas in good order?				
3. Do all the sentences and details stick to the topic? Should some be left out?				
4. Should more sentences or details be added?				
5. Is every word group a sentence?				
6. Is every word the best word for that sentence?				

Mechanics (Teacher grades final copy only.)		
1. Is the form correct?		
2. Is the grammar correct? (Note especially nouns, verbs, and pronouns.)		
3. Are capital letters used correctly?		
4. Are all punctuation marks used correctly?		
5. Are all words spelled correctly?		
6. Is the handwriting clear and readable?		

Developing Oral Communication Skills

Good communication depends on more than strong writing skills. It also depends on the ability to speak and listen effectively. Throughout both the teacher's and pupil's editions of *McDougal, Littell English,* suggestions are provided for strengthening students' oral communication skills. You may wish to duplicate the charts below in order to evaluate your students' development in these areas.

Use the Listening Evaluation Form when you have the opportunity to observe a student for at least five minutes in a situation that requires focused listening. Use the Checklist for Evaluating Speeches to provide prompt and effective evaluation of student presentations. The chart may also be used by students for peer evaluation. It is recommended that at least one of the evaluations be completed for each chapter.

Student's Name _____ Date _____

Listening Evaluation Form

For each item, circle the most accurate response. In the space below the choices, note any relevant behaviors.

1. The listener shows a conscious intention to hear by making an observable effort to eliminate or overcome difficulties.	Never	Sometimes	Usually	Often
2. The listener shows attention to what is being said by reacting appropriately, as by laughing at humorous statements and showing concern at more serious moments.	Never	Sometimes	Usually	Often
3. The listener shows understanding of what has been said by asking appropriate questions of the speaker, answering questions on the content, or using information from the presentation in a succeeding discussion or in later oral or written work.	Never	Sometimes	Usually	Often
4. The listener shows appreciation of what is said by a mannerly behavior during the presentation and by constructive comments concerning its delivery, content, or the like afterwards.	Never	Sometimes	Usually	Often

Checklist for Evaluating Speeches

Rating
5-Strong
3-Average
1-Weak

		Rating	Comments
Contents			
Introduction	—gets audience's attention —states the topic clearly		
Body	—supports the main idea —contains no unrelated material —states supporting ideas clearly —develops supporting ideas clearly —develops supporting ideas completely —is well organized —suits the purpose and audience		
Conclusion	—is brief —provides a summary of major points or draws attention back to main idea		
Presentation			
Nonverbal	—speaker has good posture —speaker is relaxed and confident —speaker has good eye contact —gestures and facial expressions are natural and appropriate		
Verbal	—volume is not too quiet or too loud —articulation is clear —pace is not too slow or too rapid —volume, pace, and pitch vary as appropriate —pauses are used effectively		

Integrating the Language Arts in the Classroom

Since the 1950's, educational psychologists and researchers have examined and reexamined the theories and techniques involved in teaching basic communication skills. Philosophically, most experts agree with Stephen Judy's contention that "The fully literate person uses language in every part of his or her life, not just as a tool for communication, but as a process for knowing." Consequently, there has been a concentrated effort in our schools to cultivate the crucial language skills of reading, writing, thinking, speaking, and listening.

What the Research Says

Although the methods varied, one basic tenet emerged from the myriad of research and methodological practices, one that forms the cornerstone of *McDougal, Littell English.* This tenet holds that reading, writing, thinking, speaking, and listening are interrelated and inseparable communication skills. They work together within a complex language system to help us "...categorize, abstract, define, and store experiences," notes Anne Auten in a recent article of *The Reading Teacher.* As students sharpen their facility in one or more language skill areas, they enhance the development of the others. For example, Walter Loban, in a thirteen-year National Council of Teachers of English longitudinal study, reported that young children who displayed superior oral language in their early school years were more likely to excel in reading and writing skills as they progressed through the upper elementary grades.

Applications of Research in *McDougal, Littell English*

The *McDougal, Littell English* Program reflects the conclusions of all of these researchers. Within each textbook, the interdependence of language skills is highlighted through the tightly-woven unit organization. Every unit contains not only chapters on grammar and composition, but one or more chapters on related language skills. Included are lessons on speaking and listening, critical thinking, study and research, and literary appreciation. Each of these skills is woven through the rest of the book as well, appearing in exercises, on special feature pages, and as reinforcing techniques for other concepts.

This careful integration of language skills helps students develop their abilities in a far more complete and sophisticated manner than when they are limited to books that present only grammar and composition topics.

The emphasis on integrated language skills is additionally reinforced through the method of presentation. As eminent educational psychologists Jerome Bruner, Madeline Hunter, and Benjamin Bloom have demonstrated in their research and application, students learn best when material is presented in small, meaningful, sequentially-ordered units. Both Hunter's learning model and Bloom's mastery learning plan utilize diagnostic testing, thorough treatment of a topic, and regular, specific feedback to ensure the student's smooth progress toward the desired goal. Segments of the learning process must be seen as meaningful not only by themselves, but also in relationship to the whole.

In *McDougal, Littell English,* all of these principles are carefully followed. Concepts are presented in one-focus chapters that are made up of manageable, two-page lessons. (One-page lessons in grades 1 and 2) Students are never asked to assimilate more than one new skill or concept at a time; however, chapters are carefully arranged so that each skill builds on what has preceded it. The relationships among concepts are repeatedly stressed and reinforced, and numerous opportunities are provided for students to combine and apply all of the skills they have acquired. Pretests, mastery tests, chapter reviews, and cumulative reviews allow both students and teachers to monitor progress.

We hope that you find *McDougal, Littell English* a reflection of the most respected educational research, an invaluable aid in helping you and your students to develop their greatest learning resource—language skills.

Sources

Auten, Anne. "The Ultimate Connection: Reading, listening, writing, speaking-thinking." *The Reading Teacher* 36, no. 6 (February 1983).

Brandt, Ron. "An Interview with Madeline Hunter." *Educational Leadership* 42 (February 1985).

Bruner, Jerome S. *The Process of Education.* Cambridge, Massachusetts: Harvard University Press, 1960.

Greenberg, Joel, and Christine Rath. "Empowering Students Through Writing." *Educational Leadership* 42 (February 1985).

Guskey, Thomas R. "Bloom's Mastery Learning: A Legacy for Effectiveness." *Educational Horizons* 62, no. 2 (Winter 1985).

Seaver, JoAnn Tuttle, and Morton Botel. "A first grade teacher teaches reading, writing, and oral communication across the curriculum." *The Reading Teacher* 36, no. 7 (March 1983).

Teaching Special Populations

Most classrooms in our society are likely to contain some students with special language problems or needs. Three of the most common groups of students with special needs are students with learning disabilities (LD), students for whom English is a second language (ESL), and students who speak a nonstandard dialect of English (NSD). This section is provided to make the classroom teacher aware of these special students and their learning problems. A teacher who is prepared in this way can make certain that these students are not penalized for problems that are beyond their control. He or she will also be better equipped to help them fulfill their potential.

Learning Disabled Students (LD)

These students typically have average or above average potential; however, specific areas of deficiency, which vary from student to student, make the processing of information and the acquisition of skills more difficult. Specific areas of dysfunction include the following:

auditory discrimination—ability to recognize the differences between sounds and words

auditory memory—ability to store and recall what has been heard

visual discrimination—ability to differentiate one object, letter, or word from another

visual memory—ability to recall printed letters, words, or numerals

spatial relationships—ability to perceive objects correctly in space

gross motor coordination—ability to make large muscle movements

fine motor coordination—ability to make small muscle movements required for handwriting

receptive language—ability to understand/comprehend what is spoken or written

expressive language—ability to express oneself through speaking and writing.

It is essential for the teacher to remember, in dealing with any of these problems, that they are beyond the student's control. Therefore, what may appear to be inattentiveness or an uncooperative attitude on the part of a student may, in fact, reflect his or her inability to learn through conventional channels. However, many learning disabled students can compensate for their handicaps and overcome their problems.

Whenever possible, the teacher should work with counselors and special education teachers to determine the specific nature of students' disabilities. Doing so will allow the teacher to devise strategies for circumventing them. Some general strategies follow.

General Areas of Difficulty

Whatever the specific nature of an individual student's disability, there are certain predictable problems that will impede his or her efforts to learn:

1. Low reading level
2. Inability to organize work or ideas
3. Laborious and illegible handwriting
4. Short attention span
5. Poor memory
6. Difficulty in processing information
7. Difficulty following directions and completing assignments
8. Difficulty in thinking, reasoning, and generalizing
9. Hyperactivity
10. Distractability
11. Low motivation
12. Poor fine motor coordination

General Strategies

Use these strategies to counter the disabilities themselves:

1. Seat the students in front of the classroom where there are no obstructions to seeing or hearing.
2. Present essential pieces of information both orally and in writing. Reinforce written material in the text with oral explanation. Conversely, write oral instructions and assignments on the board, and provide a written study guide highlighting key points.
3. Supply visual aids whenever possible to reinforce material from the text. Simple charts, models, diagrams, and illustrations may help clarify relationships among ideas. Color-key or asterisk important information.
4. To help students compensate for poor short- and long-term memory repeat important ideas frequently and begin each lesson with a summary of material covered the previous day.
5. When making an assignment, work one or several problems on the board, demonstrating how students should go about answering them. Break the process down into steps, and be sure that the order of the steps is clear.
6. LD students will need much more practice on each concept than regular students will. Most of this practice should involve the teacher, to avoid students making the same mistake over and over.
7. When grading written work, give one grade for content and another for mechanics, so that the student will receive credit for good ideas in spite of mechanical shortcomings.

8. Allow students to answer test questions orally, either to the teacher or with a tape recorder. This practice may eliminate the anxiety caused by the prospect of writing under time pressure.
9. When complete words or sentences are unnecessary, help the students find shortcuts to avoid writing long or difficult words repeatedly. Devise abbreviations for the complicated terms in each chapter. Also permit LD students to print or use a typewriter or word processor.

Adaptation of Material

In addition to using the strategies mentioned in the previous section, the teacher may find that some modification of the course material in *McDougal, Littell English* will be necessary.

1. Break long-term assignments into shorter, individual tasks that can be assigned on a step-by-step basis.
2. Shorten and simplify all regular-assignment work; students must put extra time and effort into completing their work.
3. Simplify the assignments for written work, and allow students to work with partners or to put first drafts on tape.
4. If the reading level of a chapter or section is too advanced, explain important vocabulary and concepts before students read.
5. Either supplement or replace difficult terms from the text with simpler ones. For example, use the phrase "time order" instead of "chronological order."

English as a Second Language (ESL)

Students whose first language is not English face a number of challenges. These vary in difficulty, depending on students' native language and culture and their familiarity with U.S. language, culture, and educational systems. However, most ESL students will share a multitude of problems that fall into two general categories: difficulty with the complexity of language and unfamiliarity with cultural references.

The chapters and sections of *McDougal, Littell English* are written at a level that may be difficult for many ESL students. Moreover, the exercises and assignments require students to analyze and manipulate a language that many ESL students will not yet have acquired fully. Once a teacher is aware of these problems, he or she can implement certain techniques for reducing the difficulties ESL students face.

General Strategies for Countering Language Barriers

To help students overcome the difficulties posed by an unfamiliar language, the teacher may employ the following strategies.

1. Preview the lesson to spot areas of difficulty (complex sentences and advanced vocabulary). Introduce new topics at a slower pace and provide guided practice with increased feedback and monitoring.
2. Read aloud the essential parts of each chapter, allowing time for explanations, examples, and the answering of questions.
3. Shorten assignments and allow extra time for the acquisition of concepts. Eliminate material that is too complex.
4. Simplify all activities and exercises linguistically whenever possible. Explain such terms as *italics* and *underline*.
5. Build into the activities as many visuals, manipulatives, and concrete experiences as possible. The teacher may have to illustrate and demonstrate meanings as if with small children. However, these aids should not be presented in a condescending manner—the age and intelligence of the students must be respected.
6. Suggest that students work as a group whenever possible. Encouraging each student to go through activities with the group gives him or her enough concrete practice and confidence to try it alone.
7. Correct written exercises and compositions carefully so that students will not continue to practice mistakes.
8. Precede every writing activity for ESL students with a similar oral activity. This procedure provides students with an opportunity to separate the tasks of clarifying ideas and translating them into correct written form.
9. Encourage ESL students to keep journals in English, recording thoughts and impressions without concern for grammar, spelling, and punctuation. It will help them to develop fluency and build confidence and enjoyment in their writing.
10. To reduce the demands on the teacher's time, recruit advanced students to help the ESL students understand written materials and to monitor their practice.

General Strategies for Countering Cultural Differences

The other major problem area for ESL students will be the many cultural references that appear in the text. Some ESL students will have trouble determining gender from proper names alone. They may also have difficulty understanding references to national holidays, sports, individual teams, famous people, geography, foods, and popular culture. Slang, jargon, and idiomatic expressions are tied directly to a specific culture and are often impossible to translate. The following approaches could alleviate these problems:

1. Encourage class discussion to clarify cultural references and provide general information to the whole class. This and other oral work will greatly facilitate the ESL student's acquisition of English.
2. Encourage discussion of differences and similarities between the ESL student's language and English. In covering verb tenses, for example, ask the ESL student to explain how his or her language expresses ideas of time.
3. Encourage ESL students to write about their native customs, holidays, geography, celebrities, and foods.
4. Encourage ESL students to read material, at an appropriate level, about specifically American people, places, and events. You might even provide these students with newspapers and popular magazines to read and discuss. This will help them acquire the common stock of information familiar to most Americans.

General Strategies for Countering Difficulties with our Educational System

ESL students entering in the upper elementary grades (3-6) may be unfamiliar with certain aspects of our educational system.

More traditional systems in other countries may depend more heavily on rote learning; therefore, foreign students might be stymied when asked for a creative response, or an "opinion." The teacher can encourage these students by giving examples of opinions, and helping the students evolve their own responses.

Students from traditional backgrounds may have difficulty participating in an American-style discussion. Form a small group where these students can feel at ease. Role-play examples of appropriate participation. Then encourage students to continue on their own.

Explain any procedures (following exercise directions, underlining, listing) by working out examples on the board with ESL students. They may have difficulty interpreting certain kinds of maps and graphs. Use techniques from earlier grade levels to explain these to them.

ESL students entering at an advanced level may not know how to use a dictionary, reference materials, or library. If so, use procedures from earlier grade levels to present this information.

Speakers of Nonstandard Dialects (NSD)

Everyone speaks some sort of dialect. The speech of Americans in one section of the country differs in at least some aspects of pronunciation, vocabulary, and grammar from the speech of people in other sections. In addition, certain social, ethnic, and racial groups share a distinct way of speaking. Sometimes, however, the dialect common to a particular group departs so much from the more widely used and accepted dialects that it is termed "nonstandard." It is with students who speak such a dialect that this section is concerned.

Teachers must be aware that nonstandard dialects are considered by many linguists to be legitimate language variations. Speakers of "nonstandard" dialects are not necessarily careless speakers of English, nor should the variant features of these dialects be considered "errors." On the other hand, speakers of these dialects should be led to recognize that they cannot participate fully in mainstream American culture and society without understanding and effectively employing its language, standard English.

General Strategies

The teacher of NSD students should bear in mind that one need not, and indeed should not, eradicate one dialect in order to teach another. Instead, the teacher should implement the following strategies:

1. Encourage students to learn the patterns and usages of standard English for use in contexts where it is considered more appropriate (for academic writing and speech; in job applications and interviews; at work).
2. Encourage students also to use the dialect that sounds natural to both speaker and listener in informal, casual, and family settings.
3. Tape-record samples of speech from various settings: playing fields, family gatherings, classrooms, committee meetings. Guide students in analyzing

the vocabulary, sentence patterns, and grammar used in these different contexts. This practice will make them see that various forms exist within a single language, each form being appropriate in a certain setting.

4. When covering the composition chapters in *McDougal, Littell English,* have the NSD students keep journals, in whatever dialect is natural and comfortable, of thoughts, feelings, impressions, and experiences. Read the journals periodically and comment in writing about potential uses for the material in later compositions. Do not "correct" variations from standard usage or point out misspellings. Such nonjudgmental reading will reinforce the lesson that writing in standard English is not abandoning one's identity but communicating to a wider audience.

5. Take note of the areas of grammatical variations that appear in the NSD students' written work, and be prepared to provide extra coaching, more detailed explanations, and additional practice, until the students have mastered the unfamiliar parts of standard dialect. Speakers of so-called Black English, for example, may have trouble with verb usage, for some of the principles of standard grammar and usage do not match their speech patterns. For similar reasons, speakers of Hawaiian dialect may encounter difficulties with articles and pronouns. Other groups may have trouble with word order in sentences.

Special Populations Consultants

Karyn Bailey, Teacher of the Learning Disabled, formerly with the Oregon Middle School, Oregon, Wisconsin

Alan Balter, Ph.D., Professor of Special Education, Chicago State University, Chicago, Illinois

Rebecca Benjamin, Educational Consultant, Albuquerque, New Mexico

Sharri Bressler, Learning Disabilities Resource Teacher, Reilly Elementary School, Chicago, Illinois

Margaret McNamara, Special Education Consultant, Tinley Park, Illinois

Deborah Perry, Special Education Consultant, Lake Bluff, Illinois

Sharen R. Stubbings, Teacher, Cove School, Northbrook, Illinois

Dr. Eleanor Wall Thonis, District Psychologist, Wheatland School District, Wheatland, California

Judy Veramendi, ESL, Spanish, Bilingual Consultant, Dixon, Illinois

Karen Bustelo Wehle, S.L.D. Teacher, Leon County School District, Tallahassee, Florida

Other Elementary Programs from McDougal, Littell & Company

McDougal, Littell Spelling Grades 1—8

McDougal, Littell Spelling is a research-based program that helps students learn spelling strategies for the list words—and for writing across the curriculum. The developmental approach moves from sound/letter relationships in the early grades to word structure and multiple word forms in the upper grades.

Reading Literature Grades 6—8

Reading Literature teaches essential reading skills through contemporary and classic works of fine literature. Thorough instruction in reading, writing, thinking, and language development helps students make the crucial transition from learning to read to *reading to learn*.

McDougal, Littell Handwriting Grades K—8

McDougal, Littell Handwriting provides a step-by-step approach to good handwriting. Lessons teach one letter and one stroke at a time, building skills that transfer to daily writing. Frequent checkpoints focus attention on handwriting improvement. Enjoyable application gives students creative ways to use and maintain their skills.

McDougal, Littell
ENGLISH

Dear Student,

When you open *McDougal, Littell English,* you are beginning a journey. You will be traveling through the world of words. You will discover your own talent for shaping ideas into words.

McDougal, Littell English uses literature as your guide. Below is a list of some of the titles and authors of the literature you will read as models of good writing. Let those models lead you to the books themselves so that you can discover and enjoy the power of words in the world of literature.

The Editors

Literary Selections in *McDougal, Littell English, Gold Level*

Annixter, Jane and Paul, from *The Great White.* ▶*The Last Monster*
Baggett, James A., "The Science of Fighting Fires," *Science World.*
Baldwin, James, from *Go Tell It On the Mountain.*
Belting, Natalia M., "The Dark Gray Clouds," *The Sun Is a Golden Earring.*
Bennett, Rodney, "Windy Nights."
Bold, Alan, "Lullaby," *A Very First Book of Poetry.*
Brooks, Gwendolyn, "Cynthia in the Snow," *Bronzeville Boys and Girls.*
Buck, Pearl S., from *The Big Wave.* ▶*The Good Earth*
Cane, Melville, "Snow Toward Evening," *So That It Flower; A Gathering of Poems.*
Capote, Truman, from "A Christmas Memory," *Selected Writings of Truman Capote.*
Chesterton, G. K., from *The Man Who Was Thursday.* ▶*The Spirit of Christmas*
Clark, G. Orr, "The Night Is a Big Black Cat," *The Random House Book of Poetry for Children.*

Continued on page 540.

McDougal, Littell
ENGLISH

Green Level
Red Level
GOLD LEVEL
Silver Level
Aqua Level
Brown Level
Plum Level
Pink Level
Cherry Level (K)

ML

McDougal, Littell & Company

Evanston, Illinois
New York   Dallas   Sacramento   Raleigh

Authors

Kathleen L. Bell, Assistant Director of Composition, Department of English, University of Miami, Coral Gables, Florida

Kraft and Kraft, Developers of Educational Materials, Stow, Massachusetts

Susan Duffy Schaffrath, Consultant in Educational Materials for the Elementary and Middle Grades, Chicago, Illinois

Mary Ann Trost, Former Elementary Teacher, East Cleveland City School District, East Cleveland, Ohio

The Editorial Staff of McDougal, Littell & Company

Consultants

Deborah Kay Bossmeyer, Middle School Team Leader and Language Arts Teacher, DuValle Middle School, Louisville, Kentucky

Patricia Brackenrich, Principal, White Sulphur Elementary School, White Sulphur Springs, West Virginia

Ann E. Davis, Assistant Superintendent, Washington County Education Service District, Portland, Oregon

Karla J. Dellner, Coordinator of Staff Development, San Juan Unified School District, Carmichael, California

Joy C. Fowles, Ph.D., Coordinator for Secondary Education, Clear Creek Independent School District, League City, Texas

Susan Vignes Hahn, Assistant Superintendent for Instruction, Archdiocese of San Francisco, San Francisco, California

Nana E. Hilsenbeck, Language Arts Supervisor, Volusia County School District, Daytona Beach, Florida

Bobbi Mulholland-Mahler, Coordinator of Curriculum, Irvine Unified School District, Irvine, California

James W. Reith, Program Coordinator for Language Arts, Foreign Languages, and Libraries, Scottsdale School District, Phoenix, Arizona

Cover Art: *Neighborhood Garage* **by an elementary school student, courtesy of The International Collection of Children's Art, University Museums, Illinois State University.**

Acknowledgments: See page 539.

ISBN: 0-8123-5108-8   TE ISBN: 0-8123-5109-6

Copyright © 1989, 1987, 1984, 1980 by McDougal, Littell & Company
Box 1667, Evanston, Illinois 60204
All rights reserved. Printed in the United States of America

Contents

Organization of the Book

McDougal, Littell English teaches chapter by chapter the three strands of grammar, composition, and related resources and skills. Each unit of the book integrates the three strands in a meaningful progression. The strand to which each chapter belongs is labeled and color-coded in the Table of Contents. The meanings of the colors are as follows:

Yellow   Grammar, Usage, and Mechanics

Blue   Composition

Green   Resources and Skills —Vocabulary Skills, Speaking and Listening, Research Skills, Study Skills, Literature Skills, Thinking Skills

Unit 1 The Magic of Language

Unit Organization

Unit 1 lays a firm foundation for the development of language skills in all three strands: vocabulary, grammar, and composition.

Chapter 1 introduces several resources available to the students for unlocking new vocabulary, such as by recognizing word borrowing or combining of words.

Chapter 2 provides the basis for grammar study as it analyzes the simple sentence and its parts, including compound parts. Chapter 3, on nouns, and Chapter 4, on verbs, enrich student understanding of these parts of speech and rules governing their use.

The last two chapters of the unit integrate and apply these grammar skills to composition. Chapter 5 shows how the sentences of a paragraph relate to each other and the whole. Chapter 6 introduces the process of writing and indicates how excellent sentence-writing skills are basic to longer compositions.

End-of-Chapter Features

Special feature pages, which provide practice and application of the students' learning experiences, appear at the end of each chapter in each unit. The choice of features in a particular chapter depends, typically, on the strand to which the chapter belongs.

Grammar Chapters

Grammar chapters include two feature pages.

1. Exercises for Mastery More practice, correlated to the chapter parts, for reinforcement and re-teaching of grammar skills.

2. Using Grammar in Writing A writing application of the grammar skill taught in the chapter.

Composition Chapters

Composition chapters include three feature pages.

1. Speaking and Listening An activity that applies major concepts of the chapter to a speaking/listening situation, providing opportunities for developing oral skills.

2. Creative Writing One to four thought-provoking topics to stimulate original writing.

3. Using English in . . . (Cross-Curricular Applications) Activities that relate the chapter concepts to other fields of study, illustrating the usefulness of language skills in all areas of the curriculum.

Resources and Skills Chapters

These chapters include the following feature pages.

Using English in . . . (Cross-Curricular Applications) Activities that relate the chapter concepts to other fields of study, illustrating the usefulness of language skills in all areas of the curriculum.

Unit 2
Building Memories

Unit Organization

Unit 2 gives strong attention to study and vocabulary skills, continues the grammar study of parts of speech, and integrates these developments with composition as it presents two types of writing.

As part of the resources and skills strand, Chapter 7 provides guidelines for efficient studying and test-taking. The next two chapters develop additional techniques for discovering word meaning and choosing words effectively: Chapter 8 builds vocabulary skills through the study of context clues, and Chapter 9 strengthens both vocabulary and research skills through the use of the dictionary and thesaurus.

Chapter 10 guides the students through the process of writing an explanation that tells *how*. Reminders to choose words carefully encourage students to apply skills learned in preceding chapters.

Chapter 11, on subject-verb agreement, and Chapter 12, dealing with pronouns, give the students better understanding of grammar and enable them to write more correct sentences.

Building on this improvement, Chapter 13 directs students in planning, writing, and sharing original narratives.

Unit 3
Painting
with Words

Unit Organization

With emphasis on descriptive language in speech and writing, Unit 3 shows how skills in all strands reinforce one another.

Chapter 14, in the resources and skills strand, concentrates on speaking and listening skills useful in school.

The next three chapters, part of the grammar strand, present concepts and techniques equally important to composition. Chapter 15 shows ways to improve sentence writing. Chapters 16 and 17 introduce adjectives and adverbs, both essential to description. Chapter 18, which points out the importance of description in literature, provides guidelines for poetry appreciation.

Chapter 19 logically applies to the writing of descriptions what was taught in the four preceding chapters.

Unit 3 Painting with Words   248

Unit 4
Going Forth

Unit Organization

Unit 4 completes the introduction of parts of speech and emphasizes the importance of original, critical thinking both in everyday situations and in written expression.

Chapter 20, the final grammar chapter, introduces prepositions and conjunctions.

Chapter 21, in the resources and skills strand, teaches thinking skills that help students discriminate between reasonable and unsound opinions and conclusions.

Chapter 22 challenges students to apply these thinking skills to state and support their own opinions in writing.

Chapter 23 discusses the resources of the library and the skills needed for effective research.

Immediately putting theory into practice, Chapter 24 takes the students step-by-step through the process of developing, researching, and writing a report. In gathering information for the report, students have an opportunity to use their library and research skills. Integrating both grammar and composition skills, Chapter 25 teaches guidelines concerning the form and content of both friendly and business letters and business forms.

Power Handbook   461

McDougal, Littell

ENGLISH

Gold Level

UNIT 1

Introducing the Unit

1. Help the students become familiar with their new text. Have the students locate the table of contents, index, and **Power Handbook.** Explain and discuss the purposes for each of these parts.

2. Organization of the Unit Have students read the titles of the chapters in this unit. Be sure students see how all the chapters in the unit deal with the basic elements of English and how these elements fit together to form our language.

Read and discuss the unit title and introduction on page 2. Emphasize that the students use language as an integral part of their lives both in and out of school. Introduce the idea that language is used not just for communication but can also be used creatively for artistic purposes. Then continue the lesson with **Motivating Through Literature,** below.

3. Use the **Unit Management Guidelines** below to help you develop your weekly lesson plan. An optional week 9 has been provided to allow for variations in the length of grading periods. The teacher may wish to use this week for review, additional practice, and the presentation of selected special feature pages. Teachers who work on four- or six-week grading periods may adapt the chart accordingly.

Motivating Through Literature

Have a student read the poem "Cast a Spell" on page 3. You might mention that William Shakespeare's *Macbeth* begins in a similar way. Witches chant words that create a magical spell. Point out that words have the power to make things happen. Use the following questions to stimulate discussion about the poem. Suggested answers are given, but discussion may lead to different responses.

1. What are some kinds of artistic creations mentioned in the poem? sculpture, painting, music, dance, poetry, weaving
2. Could "Cast a Spell" have more than one meaning? Yes, to create something magical, like a spell, and/or to create a work of art

UNIT 1

Chapter 1   **How Language Grows**

Chapter 2   **Writing and Understanding Sentences**

Chapter 3   **Nouns for Precise Meaning**

Chapter 4   **Verbs for Writing Power**

Chapter 5   **Learning About Paragraphs**

Chapter 6   **Choosing a Process for Writing**

The Magic of Language

In Unit 1 you will study some of the basic elements of English. You will see how you can make these elements work together to express your thoughts.

You will learn about how English has grown and continues to change. You will discover how to build a sentence by combining precise nouns and powerful verbs. You will explore the process that writers use to put their thoughts into writing.

The skills you will learn in this unit will help you understand more about the words you read and hear in other classes. Also, you will see how the process of writing can be used to complete any assignment.

Language can be magic. You can use it to weave a tale, paint a picture with words, or sing of your accomplishments. With words you can cast a timeless spell.

Unit Management Guidelines

Week 1	Week 2	Week 3	Week 4	Week 5
Unit 1 Opener pp. 2–3; Chapter 1, Parts 1–4, pp. 4–15	Chapter 2, Parts 1–5, pp. 16–29	Chapter 2, Parts 6–9, pp. 30–37, 38–43	Chapter 3, Parts 1–4, pp. 44–55, 56–59	Chapter 4, Parts 1–5, pp. 60–74

CAST A SPELL

Double, double,
Toil and trouble,
Coil of clay or rainbow bubble,
Woven, painted, danced or sung—
Sing the thing that you have done.

Cast a spell with eye and hand.
Bring it forth at your command.
Made of clay—or paint—or rhyme,
It will live. And truly time
Cannot touch what you have won,
By the thing that you have done.

—ZILPHA KEATLEY SNYDER

3

3. What does the poem say about time? A work of art may be remembered long after its creator.

Once students understand the poem, explain that this unit will help the students to use language to "weave spells" of their own.

Unit Projects

Independent Activity: Words from Names

To learn more about word origins, students will research and illustrate the origin of each word chosen from the list below. Students should select seven words: denim, lisle, champagne, cologne, hamburger, frankfurter, bologna, cheddar, argyle, damask, Edam, tweed, copper, and delftware. First, have the students look up each word to find its origin and meaning. Then direct them to draw a simple outline map of Europe on a poster. After consulting a map of Europe to find the location of the origin of each word, students should mark these places on their outline map. At each place marked on the map, they will write the name of the town, the word being researched and give some representation for the word. The representation could be a swatch of denim or a picture of a cologne bottle for example. Display the completed posters. Similar projects could be done using other words that have come from proper nouns, people's names, for example.

Group Activity: Word Game Magazines

So that students can see language activities as pleasurable, have the class prepare a magazine devoted to publishing student-created word games. Any student may submit a game for publication. Games might include crosswords, word searches, and brain teasers, for example.

For Gifted and Talented Students Allow these students to oversee the editing and selection of games to be included in the magazine. They should establish (Unit Projects are continued on T. E. page 123.)

Week 6	Week 7	Week 8	Week 9 (optional)
Chapter 4, Parts 6–9, pp. 75–83, 84–89	Chapter 5, Parts 1–2, pp. 90–97, 98–99; Chapter 6, Parts 1–3, pp. 100–107	Chapter 6, Parts 4–7, pp. 108–117, 118–121; Cumulative Review, pp. 122–123	Additional Review, Reinforcement, and Enrichment. See number 2 under **Introducing the Unit.**

Chapter 1

Chapter Objectives

1. To become aware of words borrowed from other languages

2. To understand that new words can be made by changing the form of existing words

3. To be aware that words can come from the names of specific people and places

4. To understand how discoveries in science add words to English

Motivating the Students

1. Read and discuss the introduction on page 5. Ask the students for other examples of echoic words *(boom, sizzle, chirp,* etc.).

2. Talk about language being alive, growing and changing—words dying out and being added. Ask students for examples of words that have become outdated *(horseless carriage* instead of *automobile).* Mention that some words almost completely disappear. For example *wer* once meant "man" and now exists only in the word *werewolf* (man-wolf). Tell the students that this chapter will help them to understand where many of the words in English come from and how our language grows and changes.

Special Populations

LD Students may require extensive practice. Utilize the exercises under **Reinforcement.**

ESL Students may need extra time to master linguistic concepts. Pair these students with native English speakers during drill and practice.

NSD Vocabulary study will help these students to learn standard words that are similar to the nonstandard words with which they are familiar. Help NSD students with the pronunciation of all new words.

Week 1

Chapter Management Guidelines   This chart may be used to help structure daily lesson plans

Day 1	Day 2	Day 3	Day 4	Day 5
Unit and Chapter Openers pp. 3–5; Part 1, "Borrowed Words," pp. 6–7	Part 2, "Clipped Words, Compounds, and Blends," pp. 8–9	Part 3, "Words Made from Names and Initials," pp. 10–11	Part 4, "Words for Your Future," pp. 12–13	Chapter Review and selected end-of-chapter activities

Chapter 1

How Language Grows

Have you ever wondered how language began? Perhaps people first started speaking by imitating sounds around them. Words like *crackle, splash,* and *roar* may have been the beginning of language. These words are called echoic words, and we still have them today.

Since that time, thousands of words have come into being. Other words have disappeared from use. This is because language is a living thing. Like all living things, it never stops growing and changing.

In this chapter, you will learn many of the ways that language grows. You will learn how new words can be made by clipping, combining, and blending existing words. You will see that many words we use today come from other languages, the names of people and places, and from science and technology. Most importantly, you will come to understand that the language never stops changing.

5

Related Chapters

You may wish to refer to related material in other chapters as you teach the following concepts:

1. Using base words, prefixes, and suffixes, Chapter 8, "Building Your Vocabulary," page 147

2. Using the dictionary, Chapter 9, "Discovering the Dictionary and Thesaurus," page 161

Additional Resources

Skills Practice Book—pages 1–7

Test Booklet—pages 1–6
  Pretest—pages 1–2
  Mastery Test—pages 3–6

Teacher's Resource Binder
  Reinforcement Activities—pages 1–4
  Enrichment Activities—
    pages 9–10, 39–52, 53–55
  Ideas for Creative Teaching

Part 1

Objective

To become aware of words borrowed from other languages

Presenting the Lesson

All Students

1. Read and discuss page 6. Ask the students for additional examples of words borrowed from another language (*taco* (Sp.), *pasta* (Ital.), *bouffant* (Fr.), etc.). Discuss what language the words have come from. If students do not know the origin, use this opportunity to review how to find the etymology, or word history, of a word in the dictionary. Be sure to review this procedure before assigning the exercises.

2. Choose one of the words on the list on page 6. Have the students look it up. Explain that the etymology is enclosed in brackets and that the symbol < means *derived from*. Then show the students the list of abbreviations used in the dictionary so that they will know how to interpret the names of the countries.

3. Assign and discuss Exercises A and B on page 7.

Basic Students

Either do the exercises as a class or allow the students to work in pairs to complete them.

Advanced Students

Add these words to Exercise A.

bamboo	juvenile	canoe
Malay	L.	Sp.
skate	banana	rodeo
Du.	Sp. & Port.	Sp.
callous	opera	raccoon
L.	It.	Algonquian
noodle	cheetah	babushka
G.	Hindi	Russian

Special Populations

ESL Encourage students to discuss their native languages. Encourage them to suggest other words English has borrowed that were not mentioned in the lesson. Have them tell about English words their language may have borrowed.

NSD Some dialects contain interesting words, such as *spider* for *skillet*. Encourage students to suggest some of these.

---

1 Borrowed Words

> **Focus**
>
> Many words in English have been borrowed from other languages.

▶ Comprehension

Throughout its history, the English language has taken many words from other languages. Even today, English is still borrowing words. The chart below shows some words English has borrowed. You will see that the spelling and meaning of a word may change slightly when it comes into English. However, the original meaning and the English definition are usually very close.

English Word	Original Language	Original Word	Original Meaning
bonanza	Spanish	bonanza	fair weather, prosperity
pecan	American Indian	pakan	hard-shelled nut
bouquet	French	bouquet	bunch of flowers
barbecue	Caribbean Indian	barbacoa	frame of sticks
bureau	French	bureau	writing desk
okra	African	okra	okra plant
chop suey	Chinese	tsapsui	mixed bits
cookie	Dutch	koekje	cake
drama	Greek	drama	a play
chipmunk	American Indian	chipmunk	type of squirrel
ranch	Spanish	rancho	large farm
robot	Czechoslovakian	robotnik	slave
pretzel	German	brezel	biscuit baked in the form of crossed arms

6

Exercises   Identifying the Origin of Words

▸ Recalling

A. Use the dictionary to find out from what language each of the words below is borrowed. Write the correct abbreviation.

Algon. = Algonquian (American Indian)
Fr.   = French
Sp.   = Spanish
Du.   = Dutch
G.   = German

1. kindergarten G.
2. chaise lounge Fr.
3. wigwam Algon.
4. sombrero Sp.
5. margarine Fr.
6. moccasin Algon.
7. ersatz G.
8. snoop Du.
9. patio Sp.
10. snorkel G.

▸ Structured Application

B. Sometimes a borrowed word does not come directly into English from another language. Use a dictionary to find out about the words *chowder* and *alligator*. In your own words, tell how they came to English and how they got their meanings. See answers in margin.

7

Additional Resources

Skills Practice Book—page 1
Teacher's Resource Binder
 Reinforcement Activities—
  page 1

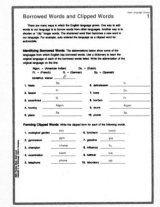

Reinforcement

1. Have the students find the language of origin of these words and phrases:

1. student   Latin
2. ambulance   French
3. ketchup   Malay
4. lacrosse   French
5. chocolate   Spanish/Mexican
6. salami   Italian/Latin
7. a la mode   French
8. bon voyage   French
9. per capita   Latin
10. vice versa   Latin

2. Follow the instructions for Exercise B on page 7.   curfew, berserk

curfew—From the French word *covrefeu*, which comes from the two words *covrir*, to cover, and *feu*, fire. In the Middle Ages a bell was rung every night to signal everyone to cover their fires, put out the lights, and go to bed. Now it means a deadline beyond which people, usually children, may not appear on the streets.

berserk (see *berserker*) From the Old Norse; a warrior in bearskin (*ber*, bear, *senki*, skin). In Norse legend, a warrior wore a bearskin and behaved like a bear and worked himself into a frenzy before battle. Today the "bear shirt" part of the meaning is gone and it means a violent rage or frenzy.

Enrichment

1. Explain that the English language is spoken differently in England and in America. The pronunciation of many words is different, and certain words are different. Ask the students to find out what each of these words means in England.

lift elevator
torch flashlight
petrol gasoline
boot trunk of an automobile
ring to telephone

flat apartment
underground subway
nappy diaper
pram baby carriage
dustbin garbage can

2. For additional enrichment activities, see the Unit Projects in the Teacher Notes on page 3. One or more of these projects have special activities for gifted and talented students.

Exercise B

chowder—From the French word *chaudière*, meaning "pot." Early American settlers used large French pots to cook a thick fish and vegetable soup. The soup was called *chowder*.

alligator—From the Spanish words *el lagarto* meaning "the lizard." When the first Spanish explorers came to the Western Hemisphere and saw alligators, they thought the alligators were lizards.

Part 2

Objective

To understand that new words can be made by changing the form of existing words

Presenting the Lesson

 All Students

1. Read and discuss page 8. Explain the three different ways to make new words and discuss the examples in the lesson. Make three columns on the chalkboard. Label them *clipped words*, *compound words*, and *blended words*. Ask the students for additional examples of each. Mention that some compound words are hyphenated. Point out that when in doubt about the spelling of a compound word, it is always wise to check a dictionary.

2. Assign and discuss Exercises A and B on page 9.

 Basic Students

Do the first column of each exercise as a class. Allow the students to work in pairs to complete the exercises.

 Advanced Students

Have the students give the long form for each of these clipped words or phrases.

photo   photograph
high tech   high technology
sci fi   science fiction
typo   typographical error
sitcom   situation comedy

Have the students tell from what two words each of these blends was made.

slumlord   slum + landlord
carhop   car + bellhop
gasohol   gasoline + alcohol
workahololic   work + alcoholic

Reinforcement

1. Follow the directions for Exercise A on page 9.

limousine   elevated train
saxophone   representative
metropolis   exposition
demonstration   information
examination   tuxedo

2 Clipped Words, Compounds, and Blends

┌─ *Focus* ───────────────────────────────┐
│   Some new words can be made by changing the forms of │
│   words that already exist. │
└──┘

▶ Comprehension/Analyzing

Words that are already a part of our language are often changed to make new words. Sometimes words are shortened. The shortened word then becomes a new word in the language. New words can also be made by putting two or more words together.

Words Made by Clipping

When a long word is used a great deal, it is often given a shortened form. For example, people say *fan* for *fanatic* or *vet* for *veterinarian*. Shortening a long word is called **clipping**. Look at the examples of clipped words below. Do you know the long form of each?

burger hamburger   gas gasoline   champ champion
lunch luncheon   bike bicycle   drape drapery

8

2. Follow the directions for Exercise B on page 9.

roommate
Medicare   Medical + care
telephoto   telescope + photograph
guesswork
output
laundromat   laundry + automat
seaworthy
cloakroom
breathalyzer   breath + analyzer
fairground
guesstimate   guess + estimate
seafood

Putting Words Together

Compound Words Sometimes two or more words are put together to make a new word. The new word is called a **compound word**. English has many compound words. New ones are being made all the time. Some compound words you may be familiar with are *bookkeeper, football, teen-age, downtown,* and *input.*

Blended Words Sometimes when two words are put together to make a new word, some of the letters are dropped. The new word is then called a **blend.** You may know some blends. The word *smog* is a blend of *smoke* and *fog. Paratroops* is a blend of *parachute* and *troops.*

Exercises Finding Clipped Words, Compounds, and Blends

▶ **Analyzing**

A. Study the following words. Write the clipped form for each.

omnibus	telephone
laboratory	periwig
taximeter cabriolet	mathematics
advertisement	promenade
gymnasium	submarine
influenza	dormitory

▶ **Classifying/Structured Application**

B. Write whether each word below is a compound or a blend. Write the two words each blend is made from. If you need help, look up the words in a dictionary. C = compound B = blend

carryout c	chortle B chuckle, snort
motel B motor, hotel	bellhop c
cloudburst c	bedspread c
drugstore c	telethon B television, marathon
turtleneck c	motorcade B motor, cavalcade
skyscraper c	brunch B breakfast, lunch

9

Enrichment

There are many books written about word histories. Books about language and words will be found in the 400 section of a library. Check some out of the library and read some of the more interesting entries to the class.

The Merriam Webster Book of Word Histories, G. & C. Merriam Co., 1976.

People Words by Bill Severn, Ives Washburn, Inc., 1966.

Place Words by Bill Severn, Ives Washburn, Inc., 1969.

What's Behind the Word by Harold Longman, Coward-McCann, Inc., 1968.

Words by Jane Sarnoff and Reynold Ruffins, Charles Scribner's Sons, 1981.

Additional Resources

Skills Practice Book—
pages 1–2

Teacher's Resource Binder
Reinforcement Activities—
page 2

Part 3

Objective

To be aware that words can come from the names of specific people and places

Presenting the Lesson

 All Students

1. Read and discuss page 10 up to **Words from Initials.** Ask the students for additional examples of words named after people: *Bowie knife* (James Bowie), *Geiger counter* (Hans Geiger), *Petri dish* (J. Petri), etc., and words named after places: *limerick* (Limerick, Ireland), *Clydesdale horse* (Clyde, Scotland), *bantam* (Bantam, Java). If they cannot suggest any, give some of the words above and have them look them up.

2. Next read **Words from Initials** on page 11. Write the word *acronym* on the board. Ask the students for additional examples of acronyms. Be sure the acronyms are pronounceable words.

3. Assign and discuss Exercises A and B on page 11.

 Basic Students

Have students work in groups to reduce the number of items for each student in Exercise A. For example, one group could look up the words in the first column, and so on. Groups should then confer so that each student has a complete list of words with the origins.

Have the students make a list of acronyms that they find in newspapers and magazines and write what each acronym stands for.

 Advanced Students

Have the students explain each of these acronyms.

sonar   sound navigation and ranging
WAVES   Women Appointed for Voluntary Service
CORE   Congress of Racial Equality
SEATO   Southeast Asia Treaty Organization
UNESCO   United Nations Educational Scientific, and Cultural Organization
Quantas   Queensland and Northern Territories Aerial Services

Cobol   Common Business-oriented Language
WAC   Women's Army Corps
CAT scan   Computerized axial tomography

Have students research the origin of the names of the days of the week.

---

3 Words Made from Names and Initials

> **Focus**
>
> New words come into our language from the names of people and places. Initials can also be put together to make a new word.

▶ **Comprehension**

Some words are taken from the names of people and places. Other words are made from the first letters, or the first few letters, of a group of words.

Words from Names of People

Read how one person's name became part of our language.

> The Earl of Sandwich lived about 200 years ago. He loved to gamble. He did not even want to leave the gambling room for meals. Therefore, he asked for a more portable kind of meal, something he could eat as he played. Eventually, his snack became known as a *sandwich*.

Here are some other examples of common words that came from the names of people.

> boycott (Charles Boycott)
> pasteurize (Louis Pasteur)
> teddy bear (President Teddy Roosevelt)

Words from Names of Places

Words can also come from names of places.

> In 490 B.C., the Greeks won a war against the Persians at the battle of Marathon. One of the Greeks ran twenty-six miles to bring the news of victory from Marathon to Athens. Today the word *marathon* usually means a twenty-six-mile race.

10

Here are other words that came from the names of places.

hamburger (Hamburg, Germany)
Tabasco sauce (Tabasco, Mexico)
cashmere (Kashmir, India)

Words from Initials

Sometimes the initials of a group of words are put together to make a new word. These words are called **acronyms**. An acronym is often a simpler way to say something. For example, it is easier to say NASA than to say National Aeronautics and Space Administration. Acronyms are always pronounced as words, not said as initials. Here are some common acronyms.

AWOL (absent without leave)
NOW (National Organization for Women)
ZIP (Zoning Improvement Plan)

Exercises   Discovering Where Words Come From
▶ Structured Application

A. Look up each of the following words in the dictionary. Find out what name or place each came from. Write the name on your paper.

Braille
Louis Braille
macadam
John L. McAdam
calico
Calicut, India
guillotine
Joseph Guillotin

cardigan
Earl of Cardigan
tuxedo
Tuxedo Park, NY
chesterfield
Earl of Chesterfield
pompadour
Marquise de Pompadour

tangerine
Tangier, Morocco
magnolia
Pierre Magnol
sousaphone
John Philip Sousa
macadamia nut
John Macadam

▶ Analyzing

B. Look at the following list of names. Write down the well-known acronym for each.

1. Wide Area Telecommunications Service   WATS
2. Cooperative for American Relief Everywhere   CARE
3. North Atlantic Treaty Organization   NATO
4. Radio Detecting and Ranging   RADAR
5. People United To Save Humanity   PUSH

11

Special Populations

ESL Encourage students to share acronyms, place, or name words from their native language.

Reinforcement

Have the students trace the source of these words.

frisbee   "Mother Frisbie's" cookie jar lids
zinnia   Johann Zinn
derrick   T. Derrick
diesel   Rudolf Diesel
lynch   James Lynch or Captain Wm. Lynch
maverick   Samuel A. Maverick
boysenberry   Rudolf Boysen
sideburns   Ambrose E. Burnside
watt   James Watt
doily   a merchant named Doiley
madras   Madras, India
mackinac   Mackinac, Michigan
blarney   Blarney Castle in Ireland
bedlam   St. Mary of Bethlehem Hospital in London
hallmark   Goldsmith's Hall, London
magnet   Magnesia, Thessaly
damask   Damascus, Syria
frankfurter   Frankfort, Germany
cologne   Cologne, W. Germany
badminton   Badminton, England

Enrichment

Many of our words are named after Greek and Roman gods and goddesses. Have the students do some research and find as many words as they can that stem from Greek or Roman myths. Some dictionaries contain a supplemental dictionary of classical mythology.

Example: *Cereal* is named after the Greek goddess Ceres, the goddess of the harvest.

Additional Resources

Skills Practice Book—page 3
Teacher's Resource Binder
Reinforcement Activities—
page 3

Part 4

Objective

To understand how discoveries in science add words to English

Presenting the Lesson

 All Students

1. Read and discuss page 12. Mention that many new words are added to English from science and technology. Since science and technology are making discoveries so rapidly, many new words are becoming part of our everyday language. Stress that this is why a person's vocabulary must grow. We cannot read, learn, or talk about these discoveries without the necessary vocabulary. Ask the students for additional examples of words that are the result of discoveries in science and technology.

2. Assign and discuss Exercises A and B on page 13.

 Basic Students

Have students work in pairs to complete Exercise A on page 13.

 Advanced Students

In addition to looking up the scientific definition of each word in Exercise A on page 13, have the students also look up the older meanings of the words for items 3–7.

Have students determine the language of origin and original meaning of the word parts for:

bio/engineering   ultra/sonic
video/phone   astro/naut

Special Populations

ESL, NSD Be sure students have help and practice pronouncing words that are new to them.

Reinforcement

Follow the instructions for Exercise A on page 13.

bit   a single character in a binary number
compact disk   an audio recording made with a laser
robotics   the art of using robots
Teflon   a polymer used in nonstick coatings

---

4 Words for Your Future

> **Focus**
>
> Discoveries in science and technology add new words to English.

▶ Comprehension

In this chapter, you have learned many ways that new words come into your language. Language also changes and grows because of discoveries in science and technology. As new inventions and discoveries are made, new words are needed to name them.

The space and computer industries, for instance, have added a whole new vocabulary of words to English. Here are some new words that have come from these areas

reentry   software
astronaut   magnetic recording
zero gravity   byte

Scientific improvements and inventions have produced the following words.

bioengineering   videophone
synthesizer   bionics

Some new words are really older, familiar words that have taken on new meanings. Do you know the familiar and the new meaning of each of these words?

memory   bug   a flaw in computer program
   computer memory
mouse   shuttle   vehicle that carries astronauts into space
   computer indicator

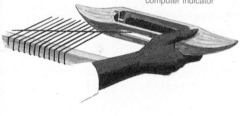

12

Exercises   Using Technical Words

Structured Application

A. Number your paper from 1 to 10. Look up each of the following words in a dictionary. On your paper, write the meaning that relates to science or technology. Then, write a sentence that uses the word correctly. See answers in margin.

1. ultrasonic
2. Skylab
3. booster
4. monitor
5. chip
6. burn
7. hardware
8. word processing
9. launch pad
10. countdown

Creative Application

B. Choose five words from this lesson or other technical terms. Write five "What Am I?" riddles. Write the answers to the riddles on another sheet of paper. Exchange riddles with your classmates. How many can you answer?

> Example: I am a kind of watch that does not use hands to tell time. What am I? Answer: a *digital* watch.

13

flowchart   a diagram showing the progress of work through a sequence of operations
microfiche   a small sheet of microfilm
laser   a device that amplifies focused light waves and concentrates them in a narrow, very intense beam
dialysis   a mechanical process to clear the blood of impurities during kidney failure

Enrichment

Suggest that students keep a log of scientific and technical terms that have been added to English. Have students read the newspaper for one week and record any words they discover pertaining to biology, medicine, astronomy, computer science, or other scientific fields. They should write the word and its definition in their log. Allow time at the end of the week for students to share their findings.

Exercise A
1. beyond the range of human hearing
2. an orbiting space laboratory
3. a rocket that launches a spacecraft
4. a computer viewing screen; a device that continuously checks or records information
5. a tiny integrated circuit for use in electronic equipment
6. one firing of a rocket
7. basic parts of a computer system
8. computer system for typing, editing, storing, and reproducing written material
9. the platform from which a spacecraft is sent into space
10. counting time backwards until a spacecraft is shot into space

Additional Resources

Skills Practice Book—page 4

Teacher's Resource Binder
    Reinforcement Activities—
        page 4
    Enrichment Activities—
        pages 9–10, 53–55

Using English in Social Studies

This activity demonstrates the relationship between our changing language and other cultures. It allows students to draw conclusions through word study about some of the cultures that have contributed to the vocabulary of English.

Exercise
American Indian: knowledge of plants, animals, and places
Spanish: interest in ranches and horses
French: knowledge of cooking, development of legal system
German and Dutch: knowledge of cooking, serving, or selling of food; development of the celebration of Christmas

---

Using English in Social Studies

▶ **Comprehension**

You have studied the cultures of many countries in your social studies class. Word study will also tell you about a people's culture.

You have learned that many of the words in English were borrowed from other languages. Usually, the borrowed words show the areas for which a certain culture was known or admired. For example, many of the words used in music—*largo, andante, violin, soprano*—were borrowed from the Italian language.

Exercise Telling About Culture from Borrowed Words

▶ **Analyzing/Drawing Conclusions**

Study the lists of borrowed words below. Look up any unfamiliar words in a dictionary. Briefly write what you can tell about each culture from the words English borrowed from each language. For what knowledge or abilities were the people known or admired?

See answers in margin.

American Indian	Spanish	French	German and Dutch
skunk	bronco	sauté	waffle
hickory	chaparral	boil	rathskeller
terrapin	corral	au gratin	pumpernickel
persimmon	lariat	court	delicatessen
sequoia	rodeo	witness	cookie
kayak	mesquite	crime	coleslaw
Minneapolis	stampede	castle	sleigh
Mississippi	mustang	baron	Santa Claus
Okeechobee	mesa	mansion	Kriss Kringle

14

Additional Resources

Skills Practice Book
Mixed Practice—page 5
Using Language Skills in Writing—page 6

Chapter 1 Review

A. Studying How Our Language Grows Here are six ways that words are added to the English language.

1. By borrowing
2. By making a word from initials
3. By using the name of a person or place
4. By using part of another word
5. By putting two words together
6. By using technical terms as common words

Decide how each of the following words came into our language. Write each word on your paper. After each word, write the number of the way that the word was added to our language. Use your dictionary for help.

holography	6	jerseys	3
ambulance	1	UNICEF	2
OPEC	2	spacewalk	5
sunrise	5	coyote	1
memo	4	mike	4
poinsettia	3	petite	1
gas	4	VISTA	2
SCUBA	2	lacrosse	1
saxophone	3	deb	4
salami	1	paisley	3

▶ Structured Application

B. Understanding Scientific Terms Write the definition for each of the following scientific terms. Use each word correctly in a sentence. Use your dictionary for help.

1. LASER a narrow intense beam of light strong enough to cut through solids
2. nose cone the front part of a rocket
3. holography a photographic technique using laser light to make images with a three-dimensional appearance
4. spacewalk an astronaut moving in space outside the spacecraft
5. liftoff the moment a spacecraft leaves the ground

15

Chapter Review

This review allows teachers to evaluate student understanding of the concepts presented in this chapter.

Additional Resources

Skills Practice Book
Review—page 7

Test Booklet
Mastery Test—pages 3–6

Chapter 2

Chapter Objectives

1. To recognize the difference between fragments and complete sentences
2. To identify the two parts of the sentence: subject and predicate
3. To identify the simple predicate, or verb
4. To identify the simple subject, or subject of the verb
5. To recognize subjects in unusual positions
6. To identify the four kinds of sentences
7. To use the correct end punctuation for each kind of sentence
8. To recognize subjects in different kinds of sentences
9. To identify and form compound subjects
10. To identify and form compound predicates

Motivating the Students

Write the following poem on the board. Point out that one way to recognize sentence types is by looking at the end punctuation. Have the students note the different kinds of sentences included in this short verse: a *question*, a *statement*, an *exclamation*, and an *imperative* sentence. Tell students that they will learn how to recognize and write all of these sentence types.

What Did?

What did the carrot say to the wheat?
"Lettuce rest, I'm feeling 'beet.'"
What did the paper say to the pen?
"I feel quite all 'write,' my friend."
What did the teapot say to the chalk?
Nothing you silly . . . teapots can't talk!
—Shel Silverstein
from *A Light in the Attic*

Remind students that a sentence is a group of words that expresses a complete thought. Explain that this chapter will help students to understand and write good, complete sentences. Read out loud and discuss the introduction on page 17. Stress the idea that effective communication relies on the speaker's or writer's ability to create good strong sentences. In this chapter, students will learn how to build this kind of sentence.

Week 2

Chapter Management Guidelines

This chart may be used to help structure daily lesson plans

Day 1	Day 2	Day 3	Day 4	Day 5
Chapter 2 Opener, p. 17; Part 1, "Sentences and Fragments," pp. 18–19	Part 2, "Subjects and Predicates," pp. 20–21	Part 3, "The Simple Predicate, or Verb," pp. 22–24	Part 4, "The Simple Subject," pp. 25–27	Part 5, "The Subject in Different Positions," pp. 28–29

Chapter 2

Writing and Understanding Sentences

Thousands of years ago, cave dwellers used pictures to express their ideas and record their history. Picture writing was a very simple way to record ideas. However, the pictures could have different meanings for different people. Often, only parts of ideas could be expressed with pictures.

Today, our writing is more precise. Words and sentences have replaced symbols and pictures. We are able to present complete thoughts by using words arranged in sentences. A sentence is a group of words that expresses a complete thought.

In this chapter, you will learn how to use four kinds of sentences to express different kinds of thoughts. You will also learn about the parts of a sentence and the many ways to arrange them. Most importantly, you will learn that whenever you speak or write, you must use complete sentences to make your ideas clear.

17

Special Populations

LD These students frequently write poor sentences. Remind them, as they work on this chapter, that every sentence must have a subject and a predicate. Periodically ask students to define the terms *subject, predicate,* and *sentence.* Encourage students to ask themselves *who* or *what* each sentence is about, and *what happens* or *what is.*

LD students often omit word endings and articles. Read over students' work with them and help them to identify their own mistakes. Do not penalize students for spelling errors. Instead, encourage students to refer to "Guide to Spelling" in the **Power Handbook**.

NSD Provide extra drill for these students. They must be exposed to well formed sentences using Standard English. Once they become accustomed to hearing proper sentence structure, students are more likely to use it.

Related Chapters

You may wish to refer to related material in other chapters as you teach the following concepts:

1. Nouns in the subject of the sentence, Chapter 3, "Nouns for Precise Meaning," page 45

2. Verbs and how they are used in a sentence, Chapter 4, "Verbs for Writing Power," page 61

3. Subject–verb agreement, Chapter 11, "Mastering Subject–Verb Agreement," page 195

4. Writing a variety of sentences, Chapter 15, "Revising and Combining Sentences," page 269

Additional Resources

Skills Practice Book—pages 8–19
Test Booklet—pages 7–12
    Pretest—pages 7–8
    Mastery Test—pages 9–12
Teacher's Resource Binder
    Reinforcement Activities—
      pages 5–17
    Enrichment Activities—
      pages 39–52
    Process of Writing Transparencies
    Ideas for Creative Teaching

eek 3

pter Management Guidelines   This chart may be used to help structure daily lesson plans.

Day 1	Day 2	Day 3	Day 4	Day 5
Chapter 2, Part 6, "Four Kinds of Sentences," pp. 30–31	Part 7, "Finding Subjects in Different Types of Sentences," pp. 32–33	Part 8, "Compound Subjects," pp. 34–35	Part 9, "Compound Predicates," pp. 36–37	Chapter Review and selected end-of-chapter activities

Part 1

Objective

To recognize the difference between fragments and complete sentences

Presenting the Lesson

 All Students

1. Read and discuss page 18. Make sure that students can define the words *sentence* and *fragment*.

2. Ask students to match the following sentence parts to form complete sentences. Do not discourage humorous combinations. They will help to reinforce the need for careful sentence composition in serious writing.

> that white rabbit
> the TV repairman
> cheered for the winning team
> many excited fans
> ran past the matador
> munched on a carrot
> bloomed in the garden
> a charging bull
> some yellow daisies
> fixed our broken television

3. Assign and discuss Exercises A, B, and C on page 19. Encourage students to use the process of writing when completing Exercise C. Refer them to the "Guidelines for the Process of Writing" in the **Power Handbook.** Tell students to determine what is in the package before they begin to write.

4. Use Exercise A on page 38 for additional practice if needed.

 Basic Students

Before assigning the exercises on page 19, ask students to tell whether these word groups are complete sentences or fragments. For each group of words, ask students *who or what is this about?* and *what happened?* Point out that if they can not answer both of these questions, the group of words is not a sentence.

1. Was counting his money. F
2. My sister is going to college. S
3. Shouted at the umpire. F
4. Our dog waited by the curb. S
5. The members of the club. F
6. Everyone likes a good sport. S

---

1 Sentences and Fragments

> ┌─ *Focus* ─────────────────────────
> A **sentence** is a group of words that expresses a complete thought.
> └──────────────────────────────────

▶ **Comprehension/Classifying**

Look at this group of words.

> The viceroy butterfly

This group of words, or phrase, is about the viceroy butterfly. It does not, however, tell what happens to the butterfly, or what the butterfly does. It is not a complete idea.

Now consider this phrase.

> lives in Canadian forests

This group of words tells you *what happens*. However, it does not tell *who* or *what* lives. This phrase also presents only part of an idea. A group of words that does not express a complete idea is called a **fragment**.

A **sentence** expresses a complete thought. Every sentence must tell *whom* or *what* the sentence is about. It must also tell *what happens*. Read the following group of words. It expresses a complete thought. It is a sentence.

> The viceroy butterfly lives in Canadian forests.

🔑 **Key to Writing** Make sure every sentence you write tells a complete thought. Do not leave your reader with only part of an idea.

18

Exercises　Recognizing Complete Sentences

▶ Classifying/Analyzing

A. Number your paper from 1 to 10. Label each group of words *Sentence* or *Fragment*.

1. A pocket of my jeans. F
2. Sold ten tickets. F
3. Two trucks blocked the intersection. S
4. The day before the race. F
5. We visited Mount Rushmore. S
6. Between the laundromat and the corner. F
7. Carefully climbed out on the roof. F
8. Louis was asleep. S
9. A fountain in Lincoln Park. F
10. Three pounds of hamburger. F

▶ Analyzing/Structured Application

B. Correct each fragment by adding words that make it a complete sentence. Write the complete sentences on your paper.

1. On Friday
2. All the bus drivers
3. Came at six o'clock
4. In the deep, dark night the mountain lion
5. Got stuck in the revolving door
6. Galloped across the bridge
7. Exploded in midair
8. Cautiously tried the ice on the pond
9. Too much water
10. Under a log

▶ Creative Application

C. Writing Look at this list of fragments. The fragments tell about a mystery bonus package that Terry ordered from a catalog. Use the list to write a brief paragraph about the arrival of the mystery package. Add words to make each fragment a complete sentence.

1. an unusual package
2. the top, bottom, and sides
3. the earsplitting noises
4. used all his strength
5. tore it open
6. had such an odd shape

19

Additional Resources

Skills Practice Book—page 8

Teacher's Resource Binder
　Reinforcement Activities—
　　page 5

Advanced Students

After the students have completed Exercises A and B, have them make complete sentences out of the sentence fragments in Exercise A. Then, ask students to complete each fragment in two or three different ways.

Special Populations

LD, NSD These students need extra drill on determining the difference between sentences and fragments.

Point out that *fragment* means "a piece or a part of something." It is not complete. Write the headings *Fragment* and *Complete Idea* on the board. Ask students to provide several examples of each. Have students identify a complete idea for each fragment. This exercise reinforces the difference between a fragment and the complete idea represented by a sentence. You might begin by discussing these samples with students.

Fragment	Complete Idea
button	shirt
toe	foot
bread	sandwich
fragment	sentence

Reinforcement

1. Have the students follow the directions for Exercise A on page 19 using these word groups:

1. Flew over the mouth of the Amazon River. F
2. Ellen reserved two theater tickets for Friday evening. S
3. In the final edition of today's newspaper. F
4. The salty smell of sea water. F
5. The sound of bike tires on the gravel. F
6. The green spaceships. F
7. Performed tricks of magic. F
8. The picture on the cover of the book. F
9. The stray cat purred. S
10. All the students in the class. F

2. Have students complete each of the fragments in the **Reinforcement** activity. Answers will vary.

Enrichment

For enrichment activities, see the Unit Projects in the Teacher Notes on page 3. One or more of these projects have special activities for gifted and talented students.

Part 2

Objective

To identify the two parts of the sentence: subject and predicate

Presenting the Lesson

All Students

1. Read and discuss page 20. Tell students to ask *whom* or *what* the sentence is about to find the subject. Ask what the subject *does* or *is* to find the predicate.

2. Stress that the usual sentence pattern is subject followed by predicate.

Examples:

Subject	Predicate
The large dog	scared my sister.
Thunderstorms	occur in spring.

3. Assign and discuss Exercises A, B, and C on page 21. Do part of Exercise A together as a group. Refer students to "Guidelines for the Process of Writing" in the **Power Handbook** before they begin Exercise C. Students should complete each fragment before they write the paragraph.

4. Use Exercise B on page 38 for additional practice if needed.

Basic Students

After discussing step 2 of **Presenting the Lesson,** provide further drill in recognizing sentence patterns by having the students identify the subject and predicate of the following sentences:

Subject	Predicate
The garage door	is open.
My father	vacuumed.
The car brakes	failed.

Do at least part of Exercise B as a group activity before assigning students to complete the work independently.

Advanced Students

Have students rewrite all of the sentences in Exercise A. They should write either a new subject or a new predicate for each sentence.

---

2 Subjects and Predicates

> **Focus**
>
> The **subject** of a sentence tells *whom* or *what* the sentence is about. The **predicate** tells what the subject *does* or *is*.

▶ Comprehension/Analyzing

Every sentence has two parts. The **subject** tells *whom* or *what* the sentence is about. The **predicate** tells what the subject *does* or *did*. The predicate can also tell what the subject *is* or *was*. Look at the subjects and predicates in these sentences.

Subject	Predicate
A small monkey (what)	chatters noisily at us. (what the subject does)
The old car (what)	lost its muffler. (what the subject did)
Angie Wood (who)	is the best artist in the class. (what the subject is)
The conch shell (what)	was large and pink. (what the subject was)

Notice that every sentence can be divided into two parts. All words in a sentence are part of either the subject or predicate.

Exercises   Finding Subjects and Predicates

▶ Analyzing

A. Copy each sentence. Draw one line under the subject. Draw two lines under the predicate.

1. The red sports car raced on the flats.
2. Thanksgiving falls on November 28 this year.
3. Charlie Brown walked the first batter.
4. Ducklings followed their mother around the barnyard.
5. A robin built her nest in the pear tree.
6. Jay's cat eats June bugs and other beetles.
7. The second-string players watched from the bench.
8. We paddled through the rough water.
9. Lisa took her hiking boots on the camping trip.
10. The blackout lasted six hours.

▶ Analyzing/Structured Application

B. Number your paper from 1 to 10. Label each group of words in italics *Subject* or *Predicate*. Then write a new sentence by changing the words in italics.

1. *Trivia* ^S *games* are very popular.
2. The Girl Scout troop *collected food for needy people*. ^P
3. *Bert's family* ^S visited Badlands National Park.
4. The art class *decorated the hallways for Halloween*. ^P
5. *Eighteen different planes* ^S performed at the air show.
6. *Montgomery and Lansing* ^S are both state capitals.
7. The jugglers on stage *delighted the audience*. ^P
8. Lovely green crystals *remained in the dish*. ^P
9. *Hanukkah and Yom Kippur* ^S are Jewish holidays.
10. Every snowflake *has six points*. ^P

▶ Creative Application

C. Writing Write a news story about a school science fair. Include the following groups of words in your story. Complete each fragment by adding a subject or a predicate.

walked among all the displays   crowded around
some plant and fungus exhibits   judges with notepads
made a lot of noise

21

Additional Resources

Skills Practice Book—page 9

Teacher's Resource Binder
  Reinforcement Activities—
    pages 6–7

Special Populations

LD Simplify the directions for Exercise A. Students will then be able to do the work independently. Have students copy each sentence, putting a slash mark between the subject and predicate. Help students to complete each of the fragments in Exercise C before they write their news stories.

ESL, NSD Students might do a listening activity. Tape record the sentences in Exercise A. Have students read the sentences as they hear them on the tape. Then have them complete Exercises A and B as directed in the text.

Reinforcement

1. Have the students follow the directions for Exercise A on page 21 using these sentences:

1. The mechanic oiled the gearshaft.
2. Hot gases surround the planet Venus.
3. The tiger ran across the plain.
4. My dad cooked spaghetti.
5. Horace watched the soccer match.
6. The bus moved slowly.
7. Angela plays the banjo.
8. The ancient Egyptians buried their pharoahs in pyramids.
9. The girls gathered firewood.
10. The truck driver drove to the loading dock.

2. Have the students write an interesting predicate for each of these subjects. Begin each sentence with the words given. Completed sentences will vary.

1. an iceberg
2. Cora's new bike
3. the last peanut butter cookie
4. three low-flying planes
5. most of my classmates

3. Have the students write an appropriate subject for each of these predicates: Completed sentences will vary.

1. plays the electric guitar.
2. drives a pickup truck.
3. live in the ocean.
4. won the baseball game.
5. flew at 10,000 feet above sea level.

Chapter 2   **21**

Part 3

Objective

To identify the simple predicate, or verb

Presenting the Lesson

 All Students

1. Read and discuss page 22. Stress that the *verb* and *simple predicate* are both names for the same thing. Point out that the verb is only a part of the complete predicate in most sentences.

2. If a student raises the question, explain that the verb may be more than one word. However, in the exercises in this lesson, all verbs are just one word. Students will learn more about multiple-word verbs in Chapter 4, "Verbs for Writing Power," pages 61–89.

3. Read and discuss page 23. Make sure that students thoroughly understand the difference between action verbs and state-of-being verbs.

4. When discussing verbs, give particular attention to the state-of-being verbs listed on page 23. Tell students that *look, feel,* and *taste* are sometimes used as action verbs. However, they will be used only as state-of-being verbs in this part.

5. Assign and discuss Exercises A, B, and C on pages 23–24. Refer students to the "Guidelines for the Process of Writing" in the **Power Handbook.** Before students begin Exercise C, ask them to recall the most frightening storm they have ever experienced.

6. Assign Exercise C on page 39 for reinforcement if needed.

Basic Students

Before assigning the exercises on pages 23–24, have the students identify the verbs in the following sentences:

1. The dinosaur is a prehistoric animal.
2. H.G. Wells wrote *The Time Machine.*
3. The three new students arrived early.
4. I am a photographer.
5. The cat's eyes are green.

When assigning Exercise A, make sure the students can identify the complete subject and complete predicate before locating the verb.

---

3 The Simple Predicate, or Verb

> **Focus**
>
> A **verb** is a word that tells about action, or that tells what someone or something *is.*

▶ Comprehension

You know that a sentence can be divided into two main parts. We call the subject part the **complete subject**. The complete subject includes all of the words that tell *whom* or *what* about the sentence.

The predicate part of the sentence is called the **complete predicate**. The complete predicate includes all of the words that tell what the subject *does* or *is.*

Read the following examples of complete subjects and predicates.

Complete Subject	Complete Predicate
The talented young archer	shot.
The talented young archer	shot an arrow.
The talented young archer	shot an arrow into a straw target.
The grizzly bear	hibernated.
The grizzly bear	hibernated in a cave.
The grizzly bear	hibernated in a cave all winter.

Look at each complete predicate above. What is the key word in each one? The most important word in the first three complete sentences is *shot.* The most important word in the last three sentences is *hibernated.*

The most important part of every complete predicate is the **verb.** It is sometimes called the **simple predicate.** In this book, we will call the simple predicate the *verb.*

22

Types of Verbs

▶ Classifying

There are two types of verbs. Some verbs tell about an action. These are **action verbs**.

> We *hurried* to the beach.
> Rachel and Shane *brought* their goggles.
> Tara *collected* shells.

Other types of verbs tell that something *is*. These are called **state-of-being verbs**.

> The party *is* over.
> The guests *seem* disappointed.

Here are some common state-of-being verbs.

am	was	has been	seem	become
are	were	have been	look	feel
is	will be	had been	appear	taste

You will learn more about verbs in Chapter 4.

Exercises   Understanding Verbs

▶ Recalling

A. Number your paper from 1 to 10. Write the verb in each sentence.

1. A pack of dogs runs loose in the Arizona ghost town.
2. Reggie performs daring stunts on his skateboard.
3. The first movies were silent.
4. In spring, northern farmers boil maple sap into syrup.
5. The bike marathon is an annual event.
6. The guide told our group about the state capitol.
7. One of my cousins writes for *Newsweek*.
8. The divers appeared happy after the competition.
9. Sacajawea guided Lewis and Clark through the Northwest Territory.
10. Esther's stories are unbelievable but true.

23

Advanced Students

Direct the students to the **Enrichment Activity**. Have them write similar sentences for these words. Students may use a dictionary or the "Thesaurus" in the **Power Handbook**.

watch	sample	trick
purchase	mark	

Reinforcement

Have the students follow the directions for Exercise B on page 24 using these sentences:

1. Sari wrote the correct answers on the chalkboard. AV
2. My father is president of the company. SOBV
3. Ross ran around the track. AV
4. Jill feeds the bird every day. AV
5. I attended the meeting at the church. AV
6. Sharona bit into the apple. AV
7. There was no explanation for the disaster. SOBV
8. Eat three well balanced meals a day. AV
9. This cloth feels scratchy. SOBV
10. Lori took the train downtown. AV

Enrichment

Each sentence pair below uses a particular word two ways. In one of the sentences, the underlined word is a verb. In the other, it is not. Have the students choose the sentence in each pair whose underlined word is a verb.

1. The charge for the meal was low.
   The cavalry charged up the hill. verb
2. Run home and get your baseball mitt. verb
   He scored a run in the first inning of the game.
3. That light is too bright.
   Light a match. verb
4. Please set the alarm clock. verb
   I bought a paint set.
5. They drive to Florida every year. verb
   The drive home seemed long.

Additional Resources

Skills Practice Book—page 10

Teacher's Resource Binder
Reinforcement Activities—
  page 8

B. Number your paper from 1 to 10. Write the <u>verb</u> in each sentence. Then label it *Action Verb* (AV) or *State-of-Being Verb* (SBV).

1. Queen Elizabeth I <u>ruled</u> England for forty-five years. AV
2. Water <u>freezes</u> at 0° C or 32° F. AV
3. Everyone <u>seemed</u> tired after the one-mile swim. SBV
4. My mother once <u>met</u> Pearl Bailey backstage. AV
5. Padre Island and the Alamo <u>are</u> tourist attractions located in Texas. SBV
6. Dale <u>found</u> a dollar bill in the parking lot. AV
7. Medicine Hat <u>is</u> the name of a town in Canada. SBV
8. The problems on the math test <u>look</u> difficult. SBV
9. The lightning storm <u>caused</u> static on the radio. AV
10. Charlie Chaplin and Mary Pickford <u>were</u> famous silent film stars. SBV

C. Writing Imagine that it is a beautiful day, and you are out walking. Suddenly, the sky turns dark, the wind howls, and you find yourself in the middle of a terrible storm. Write a short story that tells about the storm and what you do to find shelter. The storm may be a rain storm, blizzard, hurricane, or tornado. Use strong action verbs to tell your story.

24

4 The Simple Subject

> **Focus**
>
> The **subject of the verb** is the most important part of the complete subject.

▶ Comprehension/Analyzing

In a complete sentence, every verb has a subject.

Complete Subject	Verb
The train	departed.
The eight o'clock train	departed.
The eight o'clock train to the city	departed.
The clock	chimed.
The grandfather clock	chimed.
The grandfather clock in the front hall	chimed.

Look at each complete subject above. What is the key word in each one? The most important words in each group of subjects are *train* and *clock*.

The most important word in the complete subject is called the **simple subject** of the sentence. Another name for the simple subject is the **subject of the verb**.

To find the subject of the verb, first find the verb. Then ask *who?* or *what?* before the verb. The answer names the simple subject in the sentence.

Look at these examples.

> 1. The crowd at the rock concert cheered loudly.

Verb: *cheered*
Who or what *cheered*? *crowd*
Crowd is the subject of *cheered*.

25

Part 4

Objective

To identify the simple subject, or subject of the verb

Presenting the Lesson

 All Students

1. Read and discuss pages 25–26. Remind students that they are already familiar with subjects of sentences. Refer them back to part 2 of this chapter. Now they learn to identify the simple subject by finding the key word that tells *whom* or *what* about the predicate. Point out that in most sentences the subject comes before the verb, but other words may separate them.

2. Tell students that they can make their sentences more lively by building interesting subjects. To demonstrate this point, put the following chart on the board.

The tiger roared
The sleek tiger roared
The sleek tiger in the cage roared

3. Assign and discuss Exercises A, B, and C on pages 26–27. Before students begin Exercise C, explain what a photo safari is. Show students a picture of a wart hog in an encyclopedia.

4. Use Exercise D on page 39 for additional practice if needed.

 Basic Students

Discuss the following sentences with the students before assigning the exercises. Have them find the verb. Then have them find the simple subject by asking *who* or *what* about the verb.

1. Those berries are delicious.
2. My brother played soccer.
3. Anita will vote in the class election.
4. The table of contents is found at the beginning of a book.
5. My visitors from Michigan have arrived.

◆ **Advanced Students**

Discuss again the chart on page 25. Point out how, by adding descriptive words to the simple subject, the sentence becomes more interesting. After students finish Exercises A and B, have them revise sentences 1, 4, 7, and 10 in Exercise A by adding descriptive words to the simple subject.

Special Populations

LD Students might do Exercise C as a group activity. First, discuss a photo safari. Make sure students understand what each of the animals looks like and, generally, how it behaves. Talk about which other animals students might add to their story. Next, help students to develop a good topic sentence. It should be narrow enough so that it can be developed well in a single paragraph. As students create their story, write it on the board. When finished ask them to read the story and suggest changes. For reinforcement, students should copy the final, correct version on their papers.

ESL These students may be accustomed to different sentence structures than those used in English. The process for finding the predicate and subject of a sentence should be repeated often.

Reinforcement

Have the students follow the directions for Exercise A on page 26 using these sentences:

1. Nora ran in the 100-yard dash.
2. Ken's tomato plants grew several feet high in his garden.
3. Felix proudly rode his horse in the parade last week.
4. The largest ship in the world sailed from Japan to San Francisco.
5. The repairman fixed our air-conditioner.
6. The pterodactyl was a flying reptile.
7. A sailor expertly tied the rope into a slip knot.
8. Lindsay writes for the school paper.
9. An old crocodile with a long scar on its back swam slowly up the Nile River.

Enrichment

Divide the class into two groups. Have one group write six complete predicates, and the other group write six complete subjects. Then list these on the board. Now divide the class into groups of three or four. Each group should combine subjects and predicates on the board to write a silly story. Have each group share its story when complete.

> **2. After dinner, my whole family watched television.**

Verb: *watched*
Who or what *watched*? *family*
Family is the subject of *watched*.

> **3. Penguins are graceful in the water.**

Verb: *are*
Who or what *are*? *penguins*
Penguins is the subject of *are*.

🔑 **Key to Writing and Speaking**   Whenever you write or speak, try to place the subject and verb close together. This will help keep the meaning of your sentence clear.

Awkward: *Sharon*, in the tree house, *remained* alone until suppertime.

Better: *Sharon remained* alone in the tree house until suppertime.

Exercises   Finding the Verb and Its Subject

▶ Analyzing

A. Copy each sentence. Draw two lines under the verb. Draw one line under the subject of the verb.

1. The centaur disappeared into the forest.
2. Carol coached our soccer team.
3. Joel is a newspaper carrier.
4. Hornets buzzed angrily under the window.
5. Karen's new watch keeps accurate time.
6. Ripe wheat waved in the breeze.
7. The monster glowed green and gold in the dark.
8. The little people in *The Wizard of Oz* were Munchkins.
9. All three boys played the trumpet well.
10. The porcupine's eyes reflected the glow of the headlights.

26

▶ **Analyzing**

B. Number your paper from 1 to 10. Copy each sentence. Draw two lines under the complete predicate. Then draw one line under the complete subject. Finally, write the simple subject.

1. Heavy traffic frequently jams the Holland Tunnel. traffic
2. Colorful sailboats dotted the glassy lake. sailboats
3. The hedge behind our garage was full of flowers. hedge
4. Mr. Parker's class studied simple engines. class
5. The dinosaur skeletons at The Natural History Museum were very interesting. skeletons
6. The crispy lettuce in that salad tasted fresh. lettuce
7. My older brother built a clubhouse in our yard. brother
8. A rusty blue truck pulled into our driveway. truck
9. Indians in the Southwest used adobe for their houses. Indians
10. Pink and white dogwood trees lined the streets. trees

▶ **Creative Application**

C. Writing Write a short story about an African photo safari. Use each of these animals as the subject of one of the sentences in your story: zebra, wart hog, and giraffe. Add other sentences to complete your story.

Additional Resources

Skills Practice Book—page 11
Teacher's Resource Binder
  Reinforcement Activities—
    page 9

Part 5

Objective

To recognize subjects in unusual positions

Presenting the Lesson

 All Students

1. Read and discuss page 28. In working with subjects in unusual positions, emphasize that students should first locate the verb in the sentence.

2. Read and discuss the **Key to Writing and Speaking** on page 28. Stress the use of this technique in students' writing to make it more interesting.

3. Assign and discuss Exercises A and B on page 29. It may help to invert some of the sentences before analyzing them. For Exercise C on page 29, students should first draft a paragraph. Then, in the revising stage, they might change the position of the subjects in some sentences.

4. Use Exercise E on page 40 for additional practice if needed.

 Basic Students

Have the students find the subject in each of the sentences below. Encourage them to change the word order, placing the subject before the verb.

1. After the rain, flowers bloomed.
2. Through the woods raced the deer.
3. Here are the award-winning books.
4. Among the crowd appeared the winners.

Do Exercise A with the students. Have students write the subject and verb of each sentence in normal word order on their papers.

 Advanced Students

Have the students identify the sentences in Exercises A and B in which the subject comes after the verb. Ask them to rewrite these sentences so that the subject comes first, changing or dropping words where necessary.

Special Populations

LD Students with sequencing problems will have difficulty with this part.

---

5 The Subject in Different Positions

┌─ *Focus* ─────────────────────────────┐
The subject does not always come at the beginning of a sentence.
└─────────────────────────────────────┘

▶ Comprehension/Analyzing

In most sentences the subject comes at the beginning, before the verb. Sometimes, however, writers change the order of a sentence. They do this to add variety to a paragraph.

An owl perched on the highest branch.

On the highest branch, an owl perched. (The subject comes near the end of the sentence. It is still before the verb.)

On the highest branch perched an owl. (The order of the subject and verb are reversed.)

To find the subject in sentences with unusual order, first find the verb. Then ask *who*? or *what*? before the verb.

Who or what perched? An *owl* perched.
Owl is the subject of the sentence.

Sentences Beginning with *Here*, *There*, and *Where*

Many sentences begin with the word *Here*, *There*, or *Where*. In these sentences, the subject always follows the verb. Use the same steps as usual to find the subject.

There is your paintbrush.
Who or what is? *paintbrush*
Paintbrush is the subject of *is*.

 Key to Writing and Speaking Putting the subject in a different place can make a sentence more interesting.
The flooding river poured over the dam.
Over the dam poured the flooding river.

28

Exercise B
1. Through hoops jumped six lions.
2. Onto the shore crashed the waves.
3. Beneath our lawn tunneled a mole.
4. Here are the replacement parts for the bike.
5. Out of bounds fell the basketball.
6. Into its den darted the fox.
7. There is Mr. Fryer's house.
8. Above our mantle hangs my picture.
9. On the plains grazed the buffalo.
10. Here is your cab.

Exercises   Finding the Subject

▶ Analyzing

A. Number your paper from 1 to 10. Copy each sentence. Draw two lines under the verb. Draw one line under the subject of the verb.

1. There is a funnel cloud in the distance.
2. Into the pool plunged the diver.
3. Just before the storm, the girls zipped the tent flaps.
4. Where is the key to your locker?
5. Over the haunted house floated strange shapes.
6. There are many irritating commercials on that television program.
7. Under the bridge, the hikers rested.
8. Slowly, Sandy understood.
9. Across the black sky flashed the lightning.
10. Two hours after lights out, Kevin crept from his tent.

▶ Structured Application

B. Number your paper from 1 to 10. Rewrite each sentence so that the subject comes after the verb. *See answers at bottom of page 28.*

1. Six lions jumped through hoops.
2. The waves crashed onto the shore.
3. A mole tunneled beneath our lawn.
4. The replacement parts for the bike are here.
5. The basketball fell out of bounds.
6. The fox darted into its den.
7. Mr. Fryer's house is there.
8. My picture hangs above our mantle.
9. The buffalo grazed on the plains.
10. Your cab is here.

▶ Creative Application

C. Writing Write a paragraph describing your favorite place to be by yourself. Change the order of some of your sentences so that the verb comes before the subject.

> Example: A large *plant* hangs in the corner.
> In the corner hangs a large *plant*.

29

Help them to reword sentences in a more usual order.

ESL These students may have difficulty with this part. As students do the exercises, remind them that regardless of where the subject appears in the sentence, it will always answer the questions *who?* or *what?* about the predicate. It always tells what the sentence is about. The predicate always answers *what happened?* or *what is?*

Reinforcement

1. Have the students follow the directions for Exercise A on page 29 using these sentences:

1. Into the sunset rode the cowboy.
2. Where is the unopened box of nuts?
3. Here are the packages.
4. The television newscaster interviewed the President.
5. There are one thousand meters in a kilometer.
6. Abby smelled pie in the kitchen.
7. Where is the hardware store?
8. Into the gully rolled the stones.
9. Loudly Sara called to her brother.
10. Through the dark tunnel drove the truck driver.

2. Have the students follow the directions for Exercise B on page 29 using these sentences:

1. The baseball game continued into the evening.
2. The car drove into the desert.
3. The answers to the exercise are here.
4. Clouds hung over the field.
5. The keys dropped into the puddle.
6. Phil leaned over the railing.
7. The time is now.
8. Many students remained there.
9. The students walked quickly through the hall.
10. The rain beat against the window.

1 Into the evening continued the baseball game.
2 Into the desert drove the car.
3 Here are the answers to the exercise.
4 Over the field hung clouds.
5 Into the puddle, dropped the keys.
6 Over the railing leaned Phil.
7 Now is the time.
8 There remained many students.
9 Quickly through the hall walked the students.
10 Against the window beat the rain.

Additional Resources

Skills Practice Book—page 12

Teacher's Resource Binder
Reinforcement Activities—
pages 10–11

Part 6

Objectives

1. To identify the four kinds of sentences

2. To use the correct end punctuation for each kind of sentence

Presenting the Lesson

 All Students

1. Read and discuss page 30. Point out that students are probably familiar with different names for the four kinds of sentences.

declarative = statement
interrogative = question
imperative = command or request
exclamatory = exclamation

2. Do Exercise A on page 31 out loud with the class. Assign and discuss Exercises B and C. Refer students to the "Guidelines for the Process of Writing" in the **Power Handbook.** Stress the importance of careful end punctuation for sentences.

3. Use Exercise F on page 40 for additional practice if needed.

 **Basic Students**

After you do Exercise A with the students, ask them to explain why they chose each answer. For example, "The sentence is an imperative sentence because it makes a request."

◆ **Advanced Students**

After the students have completed the exercises, have them rewrite each sentence in Exercise A on page 31 as a different kind of sentence. They may have to add or change words around. Remind them to punctuate the new sentences correctly. For example, they might change the first, imperative sentence to an interrogative, *Can you measure the length of the table?*

Special Populations

LD These students might have difficulty remembering the four sentence types and the correct terms for each. Help students by putting the following information on a chart and posting it in the classroom.

---

6 Four Kinds of Sentences

> **Focus**
>
> There are four types of sentences: **declarative**, **interrogative**, **imperative**, and **exclamatory**.

 Comprehension/Classifying

Listen to people talking in your classroom. People state facts, ask questions, make requests, and show strong feelings. They use four types of sentences to express different kinds of thoughts and emotions.

1. A **declarative** sentence tells or states something. End a declarative sentence with a period.

The teratosaurus was a meat-eating dinosaur.

2. An **interrogative** sentence asks a question. Use a question mark after an interrogative sentence.

Did you march in the St. Patrick's Day parade?

3. An **imperative** sentence makes a request or gives an order. Use a period at the end of most imperative sentences. When an imperative sentence shows strong feeling, end it with an exclamation point.

Keep your eyes on the ball.   Don't be late!

4. An **exclamatory** sentence expresses a strong feeling, such as surprise, shock, or excitement. End an exclamatory sentence with an exclamation point.

Ted won first prize!

🔑 **Key to Writing and Speaking**   When you speak, you use all four kinds of sentences. Try to do the same when you write. Writing that is made up of only declarative sentences can be dull.

30

Exercise B
1. Declarative. Is there a hornets' nest under the front porch?
2. Interrogative. Please turn off the hose.
3. Interrogative. Jupiter is the largest planet.
4. Imperative. Will you finish your project?
5. Interrogative. The ukulele was first played in Portugal.
6. Declarative. Mark is a terrific skater!
7. Declarative. Did the ballernia wear toe shoes?
8. Interrogative. The half hitch is an easy knot to tie.
9. Imperative. Will you wait for the next elevator?
10. Exclamatory. Did we win?

Exercises   Identifying the Kinds of Sentences

▶ Classifying/Analyzing

A. Number your paper from 1 to 10. Copy each sentence and punctuate it correctly. Write *Declarative*, *Interrogative*, *Imperative*, or *Exclamatory* to show what type each sentence is.

1. Measure the length of the table.   Imperative
2. You're out!   Exclamatory
3. Birds' bones are hollow.   Declarative
4. Take a break.   Imperative
5. Do you have an eraser?   Interrogative
6. What a scary feeling I got!   Exclamatory
7. Is the pressure in the tires too high?   Interrogative
8. Ms. Minden's cat had a rabies shot.   Declarative
9. Does a chipmunk have a stripe down its back?   Interrogative
10. Tell me all about your problem.   Imperative

▶ Classifying/Structured Application

B. Tell whether each sentence is *Declarative*, *Interrogative*, *Imperative*, or *Exclamatory*. Rewrite each sentence by changing it to the type shown in the parentheses. Punctuate each sentence correctly.

See answers at bottom of page 30.

1. There is a hornets' nest under the porch. (interrogative)
2. Will you please turn off the hose? (imperative)
3. Is Jupiter the largest planet? (declarative)
4. Finish your project. (interrogative)
5. Was the ukulele first played in Portugal? (declarative)
6. Mark is a terrific skater. (exclamatory)
7. The ballerina wore toe shoes. (interrogative)
8. Is the half hitch an easy knot to tie? (declarative)
9. Wait for the next elevator. (interrogative)
10. We won! (interrogative)

▶ Creative Application

C. Writing Pretend that you can take a journey into the past. What year will you travel to? What will your first reaction be to this strange time? What will you say to the first person you meet? What questions will you ask? Write a paragraph about this trip. Use all four types of sentences in your paragraph. Punctuate each correctly.

31

Additional Resources

Skills Practice Book—page 13

Teacher's Resource Binder
  Reinforcement Activities—
    page 12

Declarative	Statement
Interrogative	Question ?
Imperative	Order
Exclamatory	Strong Feeling !

When students do the exercises, suggest that they identify sentence types by marking them with the initials *S*, *Q*, *O*, and *SF*, in addition to the punctuation marks. This activity will reinforce the correct use of end marks.

ESL Some students will have difficulty with end punctuation. In Spanish, question marks and exclamation points precede the sentence, and are inverted. Provide extra drill in punctuating sentences.

Reinforcement

Have the students follow the directions for Exercise A on page 31 using these sentences:

1. Take an ear of corn.   Imperative
2. May I borrow your pen?   Interrogative
3. Our president served two terms.   Declarative
4. How brilliant that diamond is!   Exclamatory
5. I rode in the fifty-mile bike race.   Declarative
6. Rake the leaves into a pile.   Imperative
7. Felix climbed the apple tree.   Declarative
8. Are Tammy's eyes brown or grey?   Interrogative
9. Focus the telescope on the moon.   Imperative
10. How good these ribs taste!   Exclamatory

Enrichment

Demonstrate the differences in the four kinds of sentences by reading each one out loud.

Declarative:
I want an apple.

Interrogative:
Do you want an apple?

Imperative:
Please give me an apple.

Exclamatory:
What a delicious apple!

Have students write other sentences, using the same form as the above example. Ask students to share some of their sentences with the class.

Part 7

Objective

To recognize subjects in different kinds of sentences

Presenting the Lesson

 All Students

1. Read and discuss page 32. Review imperative, interrogative, and exclamatory sentences. Refer students back to part 6, if necessary.

2. Remind students that the best way to find the subject of an interrogative or exclamatory sentence is to first change it into a declarative sentence. Then use the familiar procedure of asking *who?* or *what?* about the verb. The subject of an imperative sentence is always *you*.

3. Do Exercise A on page 33 with the class. Have the students identify each sentence by kind: interrogative, imperative, or exclamatory. Assign Exercises B and C to be done independently. Before students begin Exercise C, encourage them to discuss some of their favorite childhood stories, especially those with nonhuman characters.

4. Use Exercise G on page 41 for additional practice if needed.

 Basic Students

After doing Exercise A with the class, ask those students having difficulty to write the following sentences, changing the word order so that a subject comes before the verb. They may need to drop some words to make the sentences work. Then have them identify the verb and subject in each sentence.

1. Were the students quiet during the play?
   The students were quiet during the play.
2. Do these plants grow without water?
   These plants do grow without water.
3. How beautiful the colors of autumn are!
   The colors of autumn are beautiful.
4. Could the wind make that noise?
   The wind could make that noise.
5. Finish the exercise as quickly as possible.   You finish the exercise as quickly as possible.

 Advanced Students

After they have completed Exercise B, have the students write five questions about a favorite topic. Then ask them to exchange their questions with a partner

7 Finding Subjects in Different Types of Sentences

> **Focus**
>
> The subject in interrogative and exclamatory sentences may be difficult to find. First, rearrange the word order. Then follow the usual steps.
> In imperative sentences, the subject *you* is understood.

▶ Comprehension/Analyzing

You have learned that some sentences are not arranged in the usual subject-verb order. Interrogative, exclamatory, and imperative sentences may all have unusual organization.

To find the subject of an interrogative sentence, change it to a declarative sentence. Then find the verb and ask *who?* or *what?* before it.

Interrogative Sentence:	Is she happy about the news?
Declarative Sentence:	She is happy about the news.
	Who *is? She* is.
	She is the subject of the verb *is*.

To find the subject in an exclamatory sentence, change it to a declarative sentence. Then find the verb and ask *who?* or *what?* before it.

Exclamatory Sentence:	Was that movie boring!
Declarative Sentence:	That movie was boring.
	What *was? Movie* was.
	Movie is the subject of *was*.

An imperative sentence appears to have no subject.

Sit down.   Wait a minute.

In these sentences, *you* is understood as the subject.

(You) Sit down.   (You) Wait a minute.

32

Exercise B
1. You were the winner.
2. I am too early for the show.
3. (You) Give your collie a bath.
4. The moon looks orange.
5. Tony's tennis shoes are new.
6. (You) Take your time.
7. We saw a dark cave.
8. The athletes were tired after the game.
9. Your baby sister is tiny.
10. (You) Shovel the snow.

Exercises Finding Subjects and Verbs

▶ Analyzing

A. Copy these sentences. Draw two lines under each verb. Draw one line under the subject of the verb. Write the subject of imperative sentences in parentheses in the place where it is understood.

1. Is the story true?
2. Finish your game before supper. (You)
3. How bumpy this road is!
4. Give me your autograph, please. (You)
5. What a strange costume Ben wore!
6. Are you hungry yet?
7. Turn left at the first stoplight. (You)
8. Proceed with caution. (You)
9. Is the prickly pear a cactus?
10. What sharp fangs that snake has!

▶ Analyzing/Structured Application

B. Rewrite each sentence to show usual subject-verb order. You may need to leave out some words. Add (*You*) to imperative sentences. Then, underline the subject once and the verb twice.

See answers at the bottom of page 32.

Example: Is Karen the youngest in her family?
Karen is the youngest in her family.

1. Were you the winner?
2. Am I too early for the show?
3. Give your collie a bath.
4. How orange the moon looks! (Drop *How*.)
5. Are Tony's tennis shoes new?
6. Take your time.
7. What a dark cave we saw! (Drop *What*.)
8. Were the athletes tired after the game?
9. How tiny your baby sister is! (Drop *How*.)
10. Shovel the snow.

▶ Creative Application

C. Writing Do you remember stories you heard as a child? Trains could talk and bears asked owls questions. Write your own story or tale using nonhuman characters. Use all four types of sentences.

33

Additional Resources

Skills Practice Book—page 14

Teacher's Resource Binder
Reinforcement Activities—
page 13

and write statements using the same subjects and verbs as in the questions, but with the subject first.

Special Populations

LD, ESL Students will need extra practice. Provide a chart that shows the steps in finding the subject of an interrogative or imperative sentence. Post it in the classroom. Include the following information on your chart.

Finding Subjects

1. Change the sentence into a declarative sentence.
2. Find the verb.
3. Ask *who?* or *what?* about the verb. The answer to this question is the subject of the sentence.

Reinforcement

1. Have students change the following sentences into declarative sentences. They should underline the subject in each sentence.

1. Was that huge bird a condor?
   That huge *bird* was a condor.
2. What a good time we had!
   We had a good time.
3. Were you home last night?
   You were home last night.
4. How happy I am to see you.
   I am happy to see you.
5. Have you had dinner?
   You have had dinner.
6. Are we late for the meeting?
   We are late for the meeting.
7. What a cold month January is!
   January is a cold month.

2. Have the students follow the directions for Exercise A on page 33 using these sentences:

1. Should I water the violets?
2. How can a computer help us?
3. Has Gordon taken a picture of the Old Faithful geyser?
4. What a pretty planet Saturn is!
5. Can Donna sing the high notes?

Enrichment

Have each student find a short excerpt in a literature or social studies textbook that has examples of different kinds of sentences. Have the students copy the excerpt and identify each sentence type. Then have several students read their selections out loud.

Part 8

Objective

To identify and form compound subjects

Presenting the Lesson

 All Students

1. Read and discuss page 34. Stress that compound means "more than one."

2. Point out that the conjunctions *and* and *or* can both be used to form compound subjects, but that they have different meanings. Make sure that students understand the proper use of commas in compound subjects.

3. Assign Exercises A, B, and C on page 35. Discuss the various possible answers. Point out that sometimes words in addition to the simple subjects are included in the compound subject. For Exercise C, encourage students to list the items included in their sales before they begin to write their advertisement.

 Basic Students

Work at least three items in Exercises A and B as a group activity. Then assign the rest of the exercises and Exercise C to be completed independently.

◆ **Advanced Students**

For Exercise C, ask students to provide compound subjects with three parts in at least three of their sentences.

Special Populations

LD Students may have some difficulty with the placement of commas. Do not put too much emphasis on punctuation at this time. It is more important that students can recognize a compound subject and identify the simple subjects in each sentence.

ESL Simplify exercise sentences for ESL and LD students by eliminating the modifiers in the compound subjects.

8 Compound Subjects

┌─ Focus ──────────────────────────────┐
A **compound subject** has two or more parts.
└──────────────────────────────────────┘

▶ Comprehension/Analyzing

Notice that the subject in the sentence below has two parts.

Subject	Predicate
Rosemary and *Alan*	watched the hockey game.

When a subject has two or more parts, it is called a **compound subject**. *Compound* means "having more than one part."

The word *and* is used to join the parts of a subject. The word *or* can also be used to join parts of a subject. The words *and* and *or* are conjunctions. A **conjunction** is used to join the two parts of the subject.

Sometimes a subject has three or more parts. Then, use commas to separate the parts. Place a conjunction before the last part. Look at this example.

The trees, the bushes, and *the flowers* need rain.

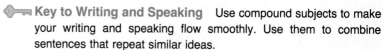 **Key to Writing and Speaking**   Use compound subjects to make your writing and speaking flow smoothly. Use them to combine sentences that repeat similar ideas.

Awkward: In the Middle Ages, *pages* trained to become knights.
In the Middle Ages, *squires* trained to become knights.
Better: In the Middle Ages, *pages* and *squires* trained to become knights.

34

Reinforcement

1. Have the students follow the directions for Exercise A on page 35 using these sentences:

1. Rhonda and Pamela entered the three-legged race.
2. Wilbur and Orville Wright flew the first airplane at Kitty Hawk, North Carolina.
3. The iron, the radio, and the television overloaded the circuit.
4. Stephanie and Carl have the same birthday.

Exercises Compound Subjects

▶ Analyzing

A. Copy the following sentences. Draw two lines under each verb. Then draw one line under each part of the compound subject.

1. Emily, Charlotte, and Anne Brontë wrote novels.
2. The Knicks or the Celtics are in the play-offs.
3. Shirley, Della, and Pat are best friends.
4. The comma, semicolon, and period have special meanings in computer programming.
5. Radishes, carrots, and potatoes grow underground.
6. A stuffed dog or a book of nursery rhymes is a good gift for the baby.
7. Tony Dorsett and O. J. Simpson won a trophy.
8. Marisa and Juan tied for first place in the contest.
9. Cereal, milk, juice, and toast make a good breakfast.
10. The Mohawks and four other tribes joined forces as the powerful Five Nations.

▶ Structured Application

B. Think of a compound subject for each sentence below. Copy the sentences. Fill in the blanks with a compound subject.

1. ____ and ____ are the busiest streets near us.
2. ____ or ____ whistled.
3. ____ or ____ tastes good on a baked potato.
4. ____ and ____ are my favorite sports.
5. ____, ____, and ____ rode down Cherry Street.
6. Many ____ and ____ grew in the greenhouse.
7. ____, ____, and ____ are months with thirty days.
8. ____ and ____ clung to the overturned boat.
9. ____ and ____ are my favorite singing groups.
10. Over-ripe ____ and day-old ____ were on sale.

▶ Creative Application

C. Writing Imagine that you are a grocery store, boutique, or hobby store manager. It is time for your big year-end sale. Write an advertisement for this sale. Name several specific items that will be marked at each sale price. Use compound subjects.

35

5. The flies and the ants came to our picnic.
6. Rome and Venice are cities in Italy.
7. Jimmy and Martha flew in a helicopter.
8. Steak and potatoes taste good together.
9. Penguins and polar bears live in cold climates.
10. Christine and Guy counted the number of chairs and desks in the school.

2. Have the students follow the directions for Exercise B on page 35 using these sentences: Answers will vary.

1. ____ and ____ have a common boundary.
2. ____, ____, and ____ are three beverages listed on the menu.
3. ____ and ____ play basketball on the school team.
4. Either ____ or ____ will go with us to the amusement park.
5. ____ and ____ starred in my favorite movie.

3. Have the students add a compound subject to each predicate below to make a complete sentence.
Answers will vary.
1. have eaten the apple pie.
2. play in the band.
3. were climbing the backyard tree.
4. enjoy roller skating.
5. grow in the vegetable garden.
6. found Indian arrowheads.
7. are constellations.
8. played tennis at the park.

Enrichment

Have the students rewrite each of the following sentence pairs as a single sentence with a compound subject.

1. Tom earned an A in math.
   Amy earned an A in math.
   Tom and Amy earned an A in math.
2. My aunt visited the Grand Canyon.
   My cousin visited the Grand Canyon.
   My aunt and my cousin visited the Grand Canyon.
3. The rabbit ate the lettuce.
   The gerbil ate the lettuce.
   The rabbit and the gerbil ate the lettuce.
4. Many rainstorms occur in April.
   Many windstorms occur in April.
   Many rainstorms and windstorms occur in April.
5. Sandwiches are served for lunch.
   Salads are served for lunch.
   Sandwiches and salads are served for lunch.

Additional Resources

Teacher's Resource Binder
Reinforcement Activities—
    pages 14–15

Part 9

Objective

To identify and form compound predicates

Presenting the Lesson

 All Students

1. Read and discuss page 36. Discuss how the different meanings of the conjunctions *and*, *but*, and *or* change the meaning of a sentence.

2. Do Exercise A on page 36 out loud with the class. Assign and discuss Exercises B and C. Point out that Exercise B asks the students to write both compound subjects and compound predicates. Before students begin Exercise C, discuss what they think a zookeeper's regular duties might include.

3. Use Exercise H on page 41 for additional practice if needed.

 Basic Students

After doing Exercise A with the class, have students work as a group to find appropriate compound subjects and compound predicates for Exercise B. Provide assistance as needed.

 Advanced Students

Have the students form five sentences of their own that each contain a compound subject and a compound predicate. Supply this example: "Laura and Rosalind rented a boat and fished all afternoon."

Special Populations

See the notes under **Special Populations** in part 8.

Reinforcement

1. Have the students follow the directions for Exercise A on page 36 using these sentences:

1. Marvin strapped on his parachute and jumped from the plane.
2. My father walks to the train station and rides the train to work.
3. A small frog hopped off the log and jumped into the pond.

---

9 Compound Predicates

> ┌─ *Focus* ───────────────────────────────
> A **compound predicate** has two or more parts.
> └──

 Comprehension

Notice that the predicate in the sentence below has two parts.

Subject	Predicate
The horse	*took the lead* and *won the race.*

When a predicate has two or more parts, it is called a **compound predicate**. When a predicate has three or more parts, use commas to separate the parts. Place the conjunction before the last part. Read this sentence.

Meg *went home, ate a snack,* and *started her homework.*

🔑 **Key to Writing and Speaking** Use compound predicates to make your writing and speaking flow smoothly. Use them to combine sentences with similar ideas.

Our class played lacrosse.
Our class won.
Our class played lacrosse and won.

Exercises   Finding Compound Predicates

▶ Analyzing

A. Copy the following sentences. Draw one line under the subject of each sentence. Then draw two lines under each part of the compound predicate. Remember to include the commas when you copy these sentences.

Example: Mary Lou Retton practiced long hours and became a top gymnast.

1. Elizabeth left the muffins in the oven too long and burned them.
2. Ice covered the streets and caused numerous accidents.

36

Exercise B

Everyone pitched in to plan a surprise farewell party for Mrs. Dawson. Janet, Sue, and Kay painted banners. Three boys collected money and bought a present. Scott ordered a big cake and bought other refreshments, too. I brought a camera and hid behind the door. I hoped to get a good picture. When Mrs. Dawson walked into the dark room, we flicked on the lights, threw confetti, and yelled, "Surprise!" That was one of the few times our teacher was speechless.

3. Lydia's family went to the Grand Canyon, rode burros down the trail, and spent the night at the bottom of the canyon.
4. The Angels scored four runs in the first inning and stayed ahead during the rest of the game.
5. Frederick Douglass escaped from slavery and became a speaker for anti-slavery groups.
6. Our class rented a bus and visited the Natural History Museum.
7. King Kong broke loose in New York City, climbed the World Trade Center, and fought off fighter planes.
8. On the field trip, you bring your lunch or buy a hot dog at the cafeteria.
9. Tracy saved her allowance and bought a new camera.
10. Hector came to bat, ignored three wide pitches, and smashed the fourth one into the stands.

▶ Structured Application

B. Rewrite the following paragraph. Use compound subjects and compound predicates to make this paragraph less choppy. See answers at bottom of page 36.

Everyone pitched in to plan a surprise farewell party for Mrs. Dawson. Janet painted a banner. Sue painted a banner. Kay painted a banner. Three boys collected money. The same three boys bought a present. Scott ordered a big cake. Scott bought other refreshments, too. I brought a camera. I hid behind the door. I hoped to get a good picture. When Mrs. Dawson walked into the dark room, we flicked on the lights. We threw confetti. We yelled "Surprise!" That was one of the few times our teacher was speechless.

▶ Creative Application

C. Writing Zany Zeke is a zookeeper at the San Diego Zoo. Zeke is going on vacation. Before he leaves, he must tell his assistant, Wanda, how to care for the animals. Write Zany Zeke's instructions. Include several compound predicates and compound subjects in your paragraph.

37

Additional Resources

Skills Practice Book—page 15
Teacher's Resource Binder
Reinforcement Activities—
pages 16–17

4. I switched on the flashlight but couldn't see through the fog.
5. Orlanda went to the microphone and spoke to the crowd.

2. Have the students complete each sentence below with a compound predicate. Answers will vary.

1. A duck in the lake _____ and _____ at the hikers.
2. The freshly baked bread _____ warm and _____ delicious.
3. Marco Polo _____ to China and _____ a book about the country.
4. Cindy _____ a quarter in the slot of the pay telephone and _____ her home phone number.
5. Carter _____ a wallet on the floor and _____ it to the lost-and-found.

3. Have the students think of a compound predicate for each subject listed below. Then have them write the complete sentence. Answers will vary.

1. the spaceship
2. waterfalls
3. a gardener
4. my older brother
5. six peaches

Enrichment

Have the students rewrite each of the following pairs of sentences as a single sentence with a compound predicate.

1. The poodle ran around the yard.
   The poodle jumped over the fence.
   The poodle ran around the yard and jumped over the fence.
2. Marcia cut out the dress pattern.
   Marcia sewed the dress.
   Marcia cut out the dress pattern and sewed the dress.
3. My pen rolled across the desk.
   My pen leaked all its ink.
   My pen rolled across the desk and leaked all its ink.
4. Eric called the restaurant.
   Eric ordered a pizza.
   Eric called the restaurant and ordered a pizza.
5. The Science Club held a contest.
   The Science Club awarded a prize.
   The Science Club held a contest and awarded a prize.

Exercises for Mastery

These **Exercises for Mastery** may be used for additional practice of the concepts presented in this section. Each exercise focuses on a single concept and should be used after the page number indicated in parentheses.

Writing and Understanding Sentences

▶ Recalling/Analyzing/Structured Application

A. Recognizing Complete Sentences Number your paper from 1 to 10. Label each group of words *Sentence* or *Fragment*. Then, complete each fragment to make it a sentence. (Use after page 19.)

1. Swooped from the sky. F
2. Peanut butter and jelly. F
3. Many airlines fly to Los Angeles. S
4. Quickly chose players for their teams. F
5. The lights of Broadway. F
6. Won a prize in the broad jump. F
7. We already mailed the contest entry blank. S
8. The satellite monitored the weather. S
9. Hovered just above the ground. F
10. The Colorado River flows through Arizona. S

B. Finding Complete Subjects and Predicates Copy these sentences. Draw one line under the complete subject of each sentence. Draw two lines under the complete predicate.
(Use after page 21.)

1. Campaign workers hung posters of both candidates all over downtown.
2. The seaplane revved up its motors.
3. A six-foot snowdrift covered our driveway.
4. South Africa has many diamond mines.
5. Our coach put the fourth relief pitcher on the mound in the ninth inning.
6. A huge brown eagle glided over the mountain top.
7. The book from Japan shows pearl divers.
8. Many old apple trees by the barn were toppled in the storm.
9. The woolly mammoth became extinct in prehistoric times.
10. A heavy fog hid the old lighthouse.

38

Additional Resources

Skills Practice Book
Mixed Practice—pages 16–17

C. Finding the Verb Number your paper from 1 to 10. Write the verb in each sentence. (Use after page 24.)

1. Sequoya <u>invented</u> the first Indian alphabet.
2. All the guests <u>brought</u> birthday presents.
3. Saturn <u>was</u> the Roman god of agriculture.
4. Clothing styles <u>change</u> every season.
5. Mrs. Figueroa <u>runs</u> a grocery store on South Homecrest Avenue.
6. The rug <u>had</u> a mysterious lump in it.
7. Jennifer <u>pitched</u> three scoreless innings.
8. Roger Bannister <u>ran</u> the first four-minute mile.
9. The empty car slowly <u>coasted</u> down the hill toward the lake.
10. The huge whale <u>surfaced</u> from the ocean like a great gray volcano.

D. Finding the Verb and Its Subject Number your paper from 1 to 10. Copy each sentence. Draw two lines under the verb. Draw one line under the subject of the verb. (Use after page 27.)

1. <u>Rain</u> <u><u>leaked</u></u> through the roof and down the walls.
2. <u>Eric</u> usually <u><u>takes</u></u> his flippers to the lake.
3. The first official United States <u>flag</u> <u><u>had</u></u> only thirteen stars.
4. The weary <u>joggers</u> <u><u>circled</u></u> the cinder track again and again.
5. The <u>foal</u> <u><u>stood</u></u> on long wobbly legs.
6. <u>Sunspots</u> <u><u>are</u></u> cooler than the other parts of the sun's surface.
7. The high iron <u>gate</u> <u><u>swung</u></u> silently on giant hinges.
8. <u>Rob</u> <u><u>water-skis</u></u> barefoot.
9. Nearly out of breath, <u>Sara</u> <u><u>dashed</u></u> across the finish line to take first place.
10. A <u>light</u> on the instrument panel <u><u>blinked</u></u> on and off.

39

Exercises for Mastery Continued

E. Finding the Subject in Different Positions Copy each sentence. Draw two lines under the verb. Then draw one line under the subject of the verb. (Use after page 29.)

1. Here comes Mark.
2. Under the eaves, several long icicles formed.
3. Where is the other magazine?
4. Here are the Yankees' mid-season statistics.
5. Out of nowhere came the sound of a siren.
6. After the argument, Holly left.
7. In the Mississippi River are many dangerous sandbars.
8. On our summer vacation, we went to Yosemite National Park.
9. In today's newspaper, there is an article about an unidentified flying object.
10. Over the city arched a double rainbow.

F. Identifying Kinds of Sentences Copy and correctly punctuate these sentences. Then write whether each sentence is *Declarative*, *Imperative*, *Interrogative*, or *Exclamatory*. (Use after page 31.)

1. What a good mood you're in! Exclamatory
2. Cotton cloth is cooler than polyester fabric Declarative
3. From the airplane the thunderheads look huge and frightening. Declarative
4. Can you repair the cuckoo clock? Interrogative
5. Call me at five o'clock. Imperative
6. Does Kim's jackknife have a can opener? Interrogative
7. Feed the dog only once a day. Imperative
8. Rustler is my cousin's horse. Declarative
9. How tall you're getting! Exclamatory
10. Hit the puck harder. Imperative

40

G. Finding Subjects and Verbs in Sentences Copy the sentences below. Draw two lines under the verb in each sentence. Draw one line under the subject of the verb. If the subject is understood, write it in parentheses. (Use after page 33.)

1. How strong she is!
2. Return these empty bottles for the deposit. (You)
3. How delicious that watermelon looks!
4. Were those rabbits in the garden again?
5. What exciting stories Nancy tells!
6. Is *The Floorwalker* a Charlie Chaplin comedy?
7. Look at that flash of lightning. (You)
8. What beautiful tulips and daffodils you have in your yard!
9. Ask the forest ranger for information on using the campgrounds. (You)
10. Are the songs from the movie on the record?

H. Writing Compound Subjects and Compound Predicates Use the fragments below to make complete sentences. Add a compound subject to each predicate. Add a compound predicate to each subject. Punctuate each sentence correctly. (Use after page 37.)

1. hibernate in winter
2. headed out to sea
3. six yellow ducklings
4. are countries in South America
5. Abraham Lincoln
6. the ping-pong ball
7. rain
8. fluttered around the streetlight
9. my Garfield telephone
10. should be oiled

41

Using Grammar in Writing

These challenging and enjoyable activities allow the students to see how the concepts of grammar, usage, and mechanics may be applied in actual writing situations. Each exercise is designed to give students practice in several of the skills they have acquired in this section. The activities also provide opportunities for students to write creatively about a wide variety of interesting and unusual subjects.

As students complete these activities, remind them to follow the process of writing. Be sure to allow adequate time for prewriting activities. Individual conferences or peer-group sessions may be used for help with drafting and revising.

Students might enjoy doing Exercise C as a small group activity. Tell students to use their imagination when writing about food combinations that make healthy snacks. However, their snacks should be legitimate, edible, healthy food combinations.

Using Grammar in Writing

▶ Creative Application

A. *Wonderkid Magazine* asked you to interview an important scientist. You chose Dr. Robert Jarvik, who designed the first artificial heart for humans.

Write the interview and include some of the questions you asked and the answers you received. Your interview should contain all four types of sentences.

B. You are opening a pet shop in town. To help shoppers make selections when they come into your shop, you need to make some signs. Write one sentence for each sign. The complete subject of each sentence should fully identify the animal. The compound predicate should tell two things the animal does.

Example: This colorful parrot sits on a perch and mimics voices.

C. Using Compound Subjects and Verbs in Health Mrs. Verde's sixth-grade health class was surprised to learn that some snack foods can be healthful sources of energy. To put their knowledge to use, the class prepared a "snack feast." Write a brief paragraph that tells about some of the food combinations the students might have created for snacks. Use some compound subjects such as *peanuts and raisins* or *bran muffins and wheat bread*. Use some compound predicates such as *popped some corn and seasoned it* or *cut and stuffed pita pockets*.

42

Additional Resources

Skills Practice Book
Using Sentences in Writing—
page 18

Chapter 2 Review

▶ Classifying

A. Recognizing Types of Sentences Write *Fragment* if the group of words is an incomplete sentence. If the group of words is a sentence, write the punctuation mark that each complete sentence needs. Finally, write *Declarative*, *Interrogative*, *Imperative*, or *Exclamatory* to tell what kind of sentence it is.

1. Is it difficult to learn a foreign language? Interrogative
2. What a frightful movie that was! Exclamatory
3. Understood all the directions Fragment
4. When was Alaska purchased from Russia? Interrogative
5. Cricket is a sport played with a ball and bat. Declarative
6. Choose a partner for the relay. Imperative
7. Dashed around the track at school Fragment
8. Louisiana is nicknamed the Pelican State. Declarative
9. Use an almanac to find the answers. Imperative
10. Waited anxiously for spring to come Fragment

▶ Analyzing

B. Finding the Subject and Verb Copy the following sentences. Underline the subject once and the verb twice. In sentences with compound subjects or compound verbs, be sure to underline each subject and verb. If the subject is not given, write it in parentheses in the place where it is understood.

1. The statues in the museum were marble.
2. Where are the charcoal and paints?
3. What talented skaters Kim and Dana are!
4. Try this delicious coconut bread. (You)
5. Anthony knew the story of *The Nutcracker* ballet.
6. Across the field trotted the ponies.
7. The receiver caught the pass, tumbled into the end zone, and scored a touchdown.
8. Lock the door and give the key to me. (You)
9. Chipmunks and squirrels live in wooded areas.
10. How foggy it was by the pond!

43

Additional Resources

Skills Practice Book
Review—page 19

Test Booklet
Mastery Test—pages 9–12

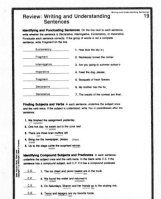

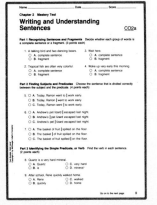

Chapter Review

These exercises provide review of the concepts presented in this section. Each exercise challenges the students to apply several of the skills they have acquired during previous study.

Because the "mixed" feature of these activities makes them more difficult, the teacher may wish to have basic students do the exercises orally or in small groups.

Chapter 3

Chapter Objectives

1. To define a noun
2. To differentiate between common nouns and proper nouns
3. To differentiate between singular and plural nouns
4. To form plural nouns correctly
5. To form possessive nouns correctly

Motivating the Students

Review the parts of a sentence with the students. One of the parts of speech used in all sentences is a noun. Read the following excerpt from *Handbook for Boys—Boy Scouts of America*. Ask the students to notice how precise nouns are used to tell the reader where each form of wildlife can be found.

> When rain or the blazing sun beats down, animals react very differently. Deer huddle around the base of a tree, where the needles or leaves keep off the rain. Woodchucks or marmots dive for a stone wall, or the shelter of rocks. Bobcats, or mountain lions crawl into caves, or under the overhang of a rocky ledge. Rabbits jump into a dense thicket, or down a hole. Squirrels and owls seek out their nests in a hollow tree. Snakes slither into a log—and beetles crawl under rocks or leaves—all to stay there till the weather is better for them.

Read and discuss with students the chapter introduction on page 45. Tell the students that in this chapter they will learn how to use precise nouns to make their writing clear.

Special Populations

LD Students will have difficulty remembering the spelling rules for plural and possessive nouns. Summarize these spelling rules in chart form and distribute one to each student, or make posters to put up around the classroom.

ESL Students will need assistance in identifying unfamiliar nouns that are unique to American culture. Especially watch for items related to sports, the media, and famous personalities.

NSD Students may speak dialects which have their own particular rules for forming plurals and possessives. They will need extra practice and should be encouraged to use Standard English.

Week 4

Chapter Management Guidelines This chart may be used to help structure daily lesson plans.

Day 1	Day 2	Day 3	Day 4	Day 5
Chapter 3 Opener, p. 45; Part 1, "What Are Nouns?" pp. 46–47; Part 2, "Common Nouns and Proper Nouns," pp. 48–49	Part 3, "Singular Nouns and Plural Nouns," pp. 50–52	Part 3, "Singular Nouns and Plural Nouns," pp. 50–52	Part 4, "Nouns That Show Possession," pp. 53–55	Chapter Review and selected end-of-chapter activities

Nouns for Precise Meaning

Related Chapters

You may wish to refer to related material in other chapters as you teach the following concepts:

1. Using nouns in sentences, Chapter 2, "Writing and Understanding Sentences," page 17

2. Nouns and words that replace nouns, Chapter 12, "Understanding Pronouns," page 209

3. Capitalizing proper nouns, "Guide to Capitalization" in the **Power Handbook.**

4. To find a variety of nouns that name one thing, the "Thesaurus" in the **Power Handbook.**

Additional Resources

Skills Practice Book—pages 20–26

Test Booklet—pages 13–16
   Pretest—pages 13–14
   Mastery Test—pages 15–16

Teacher's Resource Binder
   Reinforcement Activities—
      pages 18–24
   Enrichment Activities—
      pages 39–52, 57
   Process of Writing Transparencies
   Ideas for Creative Teaching

As you speak and write, you change the pictures and ideas in your mind into words. To help others see these same ideas and pictures, you use words that name people, places, things, and ideas. These words are called nouns.

In this chapter, you will learn to use specific nouns to express your ideas. If you choose nouns carefully, you will always say and write exactly what you mean.

45

Part 1

Objective

To define a noun

Presenting the Lesson

 All Students

1. Read page 46. Discuss the four types of nouns: those naming persons, those naming places, those naming things, and those naming ideas. Make sure that students understand that nouns are not limited to physical objects. Ask students to supply additional examples of all types of nouns.

2. In the Teacher Notes for part 4 in this chapter, there is a discussion of other ways to identify nouns. You may choose to refer to it now.

3. Assign and discuss Exercises A, B, and C on page 47. Encourage students to make a list of people, places, and things they will point out on their tour.

4. Use Exercise A on page 56 for additional practice if needed.

 Basic Students

Before assigning the exercises, remind students that they can identify a noun by asking, "Does the word name a person, place, thing, or idea?"

Work the first few sentences in Exercise A with students. Remind them that a word is a noun if it fits into any of the four categories.

 Advanced Students

Have students rewrite each of the sentences in Exercise A or Exercise B, replacing one or more of the nouns in each sentence with different nouns.

Special Populations

LD, ESL, NSD These students may not recognize some of the nouns in these exercises. Either define these words, or substitute words that are more familiar.

ESL You might substitute the following exercise for Exercise C in this part: Pretend that you are planning a visit to your native country. Where will you go? What will you see? Whom will you meet? On what days will you go and return?

---

1 What Are Nouns?

> ── *Focus* ──
>
> A **noun** names a person, place, thing, or idea.

▶ Comprehension/Classifying

There are many names that tell who you are. You may be an athlete, a musician, and a friend. These different names for you are nouns. Nouns are used to name persons, places, things, or ideas.

Many nouns name things that can be seen. Some examples are *secretary*, *village*, and *octopus*. Some nouns name things that can neither be seen nor touched. These include nouns such as *freedom*, *hope*, *shyness*, and *weakness*.

Here are some other examples of nouns.

Persons	Places	Things	Ideas
astronaut	desert	dinosaur	friendliness
dancer	ocean	robot	faith
Juanita	London	Eiffel Tower	intelligence
Paul	Africa	*Mayflower*	joy

🔑 **Key to Writing and Speaking** Choose the noun that names exactly what you mean. Do not say *boat* if you mean *canoe*. Do not write *bird* if you mean *canary*.

46

Exercises Identifying Nouns

▶ **Recalling**

A. Number your paper from 1 to 10. Find the nouns in the sentences below and list them on your paper.

1. Texas is the second largest state.
2. Did Mario have the courage to enter the haunted house again?
3. The tip of my ski is stuck under the log.
4. Mrs. Holmes kept her promise to the boys.
5. Crocodiles are found in many rivers in Africa.
6. An alert lifeguard sat on the platform at the beach.
7. Some cities have problems with pollution.
8. My older sister moved to Maine because of her job.
9. Aaron watched three porpoises jump out of the water.
10. What skills did Kelly learn in gymnastics?

▶ **Classifying**

B. List the nouns in each sentence. After each noun, tell whether it refers to a person, place, thing, or idea.

1. Alaska and Hawaii are not on the mainland.
2. The cheese on this pizza tastes funny.
3. There was excitement among the actors before the play.
4. A foil is a sword with a button on the point.
5. Mike and Brian have a strong friendship.
6. Sally was in Frontierland, looking at the old covered wagons.
7. People from Brazil speak Portuguese.
8. Beethoven is a famous composer.
9. The colonists wanted their freedom from England.
10. Mr. Martinez won't take any nonsense.

▶ **Creative Application**

C. Writing A student from Australia will be visiting your school for one day. You have offered to take your visitor on a tour of your neighborhood. Think about the most interesting people, places, and things to point out. Make a list of those people, places, and things. Then write a paragraph explaining what your tour will include.

47

Reinforcement

1. Have the students copy the following paragraph and underline all the nouns.

Tom rode his bike to the First National Bank in Hailey and applied for a job. Tom was a junior at Davis High School and Tom wanted to be a stock boy on Saturdays. Mr. Dexter gave Tom an application to fill out. Later that week, the manager asked Tom to start on the first Saturday in September.

2. Have students list the nouns in the following paragraph. After each noun, have them tell whether it refers to a person, place, thing, or idea.

Haiku is a form of verse that was first written in Japan. There are three unrhymed lines. The first and the third lines have five syllables each, while the second line has seven syllables. Most haiku tell about a subject in nature.

3. Ask students to list as many nouns as they can that refer to themselves.

Example:	Jim Davis	student
	boy	friend
	son	player

Enrichment

For enrichment activities, see the Unit Projects in the Teacher Notes on page 3. One or more of these projects have special activities for gifted and talented students.

Additional Resources

Skills Practice Book—page 20
Teacher's Resource Binder
  Reinforcement Activities—
    page 18

Part 2

Objective

To differentiate between common nouns and proper nouns

Presenting the Lesson

All Students

1. Read and discuss page 48.

2. Ask students to think of additional examples of multi-word proper nouns. Stress that proper nouns always begin with a capital letter.

3. You might do Exercise A on page 49 as a class activity. Assign and discuss Exercises B and C. As they begin Exercise C, encourage students to make lists of souvenirs they might collect.

4. Use Exercise B on page 56 for additional practice if needed.

Basic Students

For additional practice, write the following list of nouns on the board. Have students identify each noun as *Common* or *Proper*.

troop C	movie C	game C
Maryland P	car C	Bill Cosby P
Daniel Webster P	Pike's Peak P	ocean C

Do the first few items in Exercise B with students.

Advanced Students

Have the students write three sentences using common nouns. Then have them rewrite the sentences, replacing each common noun with a proper noun.

Special Populations

LD Students will need some extra drill in identifying nouns. Write several common nouns, such as *city, state,* and *actor* on 3"x5" note cards. Divide students into two teams. Each team draws a card from the stack. The team works together to list as many proper nouns for the common noun as they can. The team with the most correct items, written in one minute, wins.

ESL Students might use their native countries as the topic for Exercise C.

---

2 Common Nouns and Proper Nouns

> **Focus**
>
> A **common noun** is a general name for a person, place, thing, or idea. A **proper noun** names a particular person, place, thing, or idea.

▶ Comprehension/Classifying

When you call yourself a student, you are giving yourself a name that you share with all the boys and girls in your class. This name is common to a whole group of people. Many other nouns are also common to whole groups of people, places, or things. Some examples are *country, town, book,* or *animal.* These are called **common nouns.**

Some nouns name particular persons, places, or things. Names like *Pete Rose, Houston,* and *Washington Monument* are called **proper nouns.** Proper nouns are always capitalized. Look at these examples of common nouns and proper nouns.

Common Nouns	Proper Nouns
children	Jane Banks, Michael Banks
park	the Grand Canyon National Park
road	Jefferson Road
town	Richmond
continent	Asia
artist	Grandma Moses
building	the Sears Tower

Key to Writing and Speaking Use proper nouns to make your writing and speaking more specific.

General: The girl went to the store.
Specific: Marilyn went to Savemore Foods.

48

Exercises Finding Common and Proper Nouns

▶ Classifying/Analyzing

A. Divide a piece of paper into two columns. Label one column *Common Nouns* and one column *Proper Nouns*. Write each noun in the correct column. Be sure to capitalize proper nouns.

1. maria PN
2. lake ontario PN
3. cowboy CN
4. martin luther king, jr. PN
5. elmwood elementary school PN

6. harbor CN
7. soccer CN
8. canyon CN
9. parrot CN
10. appalachian mountains PN

▶ Structured Application

B. The following is a list of common nouns. Write a proper noun for each one.

Example: island—Oahu

1. author
2. tribe
3. war
4. woman
5. president

6. car
7. actor
8. country
9. holiday
10. magazine

▶ Creative Application

C. Writing You have just returned from a month-long trip. On this trip, you visited several cities and states. Think about the souvenirs you collected from each place that you visited. Make a list of those souvenirs. Write a paragraph describing the souvenirs and telling where each was collected. Underline all the common nouns once and the proper nouns twice in your paragraph.

49

Reinforcement

1. Have the students follow the directions for Exercise A on page 49 using these nouns:

1. eagle CN
2. vase CN
3. salt lake city PN
4. earthquake CN
5. tina turner PN
6. st. louis PN
7. airport CN
8. norway PN
9. apartment CN
10. han solo PN
11. riverbank CN
12. king arthur PN
13. california PN
14. dictionary CN
15. library of congress PN
16. devil's tower national monument PN
17. grapefruit CN
18. barbara PN
19. galaxy CN
20. fort worth PN

2. Have students copy these sentences. Have them capitalize the first word in each sentence and each proper noun.

1. this courtroom is used by judge fitzgerald.
2. ms. berkeley will teach our history class this year.
3. next month we will visit shanghai, peking, and hong kong.
4. one of the boys can run faster than eric.
5. that beautiful music was composed by johann sebastian bach.

3. Have the students follow the directions for Exercise B on page 49 using these nouns: Answers will vary.

1. planet
2. author
3. mayor
4. dog
5. friend
6. sister

7. state
8. singer
9. game
10. bank
11. restaurant
12. athlete

Enrichment

Ask students to bring short newspaper articles to class. Have them circle all proper nouns and underline all common nouns. If possible, duplicate one article for class discussion. Ask the students whether they can find any capitalization errors in the newspaper articles.

Additional Resources

Skills Practice Book—page 21

Teacher's Resource Binder
Reinforcement Activities—pages 19–20

Common Nouns and Proper Nouns

Finding Common and Proper Nouns (1)

Part 3

Objectives

1. To differentiate between singular and plural nouns
2. To form plural nouns correctly

Presenting the Lesson

 All Students

1. Read and discuss the rules on pages 50-51. Ask volunteers to name additional examples to support each rule. Make sure that students know the difference between a consonant and vowel. Review, if necessary.

2. Remind students that some nouns have only one form for both the singular and plural. Other nouns change forms completely. The nouns that change form, and the words that are exceptions to Rule 3, should be memorized.

3. Read and discuss the **Key to Writing and Speaking.** Encourage students to use a dictionary when they are unsure about how to form the plural of a noun.

4. Assign and discuss Exercises A, B, and C on page 52. Before students begin Exercise C, allow some time for them to discuss what items they would choose on a shopping spree.

5. Use Exercise C on page 57 for additional practice if needed.

 Basic Students

Work at least three of the sentences in Exercise A with the students. You might also ask the students to provide the number of the rule followed for each item of Exercise B. This activity will reinforce the spelling rules.

 Advanced Students

Have students look in a science, health, or social studies book for examples of singular and plural nouns. They should write eight to ten singular nouns and the same number of plural nouns from a page in the book. Students should then write the plural form of all singular nouns and identify the spelling rule that applies to each word.

---

3 Singular Nouns and Plural Nouns

> ┌─ *Focus* ─────────────────────────────
> A **singular noun** names one person, place, thing, or idea.
> A **plural noun** names more than one person, place, thing, or idea.
> └──────────────────────────────────────

▶Comprehension/Classifying

Some nouns name just one person, place, thing, or idea. *Camera*, for example, names one thing. It is a **singular noun**.

Other nouns name more than one thing. They are **plural nouns**. *Cameras* is a plural noun.

Here are seven rules for forming the plurals of nouns.

1. To form the plurals of most nouns, just add -s.

computers   streets   hamburgers   players

2. When the singular noun ends in s, sh, ch, x, or z, add -es.

glasses   bushes   crutches   taxes   waltzes

Player   Players

50

3. **When the singular noun ends in o, add -s.**

radios   tacos   pianos   Eskimos

Exceptions: For the following nouns ending in *o,* add *-es.*

echoes   heroes   potatoes   tomatoes

4. **When the singular noun ends in y with a consonant before it, change the y to i and add -es.**

army—armies   company—companies

5. **For most nouns ending in f or fe, add -s. For some nouns ending in f or fe, however, change the f to v and add -es or -s.**

chief—chiefs	elf—elves	loaf—loaves
roof—roofs	self—selves	calf—calves
dwarf—dwarfs	life—lives	knife—knives
cuff—cuffs	leaf—leaves	wolf—wolves
safe—safes	half—halves	shelf—shelves

6. **In some cases, the plural noun is the same as the singular.**

salmon   bass   scissors   news

7. **Some nouns form their plurals in special ways.**

ox—oxen   woman—women   goose—geese

Key to Writing and Speaking   Always check a dictionary when you are unsure about how to form the plural of a word. If the plural form is not listed in the dictionary, just add an *s* to the singular.

51

Special Populations

LD, ESL, NSD Students should have spelling rules available in chart form for quick reference. Make a permanent list and post it in the classroom.

ESL, NSD Practice the pronunciation of plural nouns listed under Rules 1 and 2. Nouns ending in *-s* have one of two end sounds; /s/ as in *streets* and /z/ as in *computers.* Nouns ending in *-es* have the end sound /əz/ as in *bushes.* Nouns listed under Rules 3 and 4 end in the /z/ sound, and those in Rule 5 that do not change their spellings to add *s* end in the /s/ sound.

Reinforcement

1. Have the students number their papers from 1 to 10. Ask them to write every plural noun in each sentence.

1. Leaves are turning shades of yellow, orange, and red.
2. The artists washed the paintbrushes in soap and water.
3. Jesse sharpened the knives and then cleaned both fish.
4. The people sunned themselves on the beaches along Lake Michigan.
5. Ponies pulled carts filled with potatoes to the market.
6. The shelves were stacked with radios and stereo record players.
7. Raymond herded sheep in the foothills of the Pyrenees Mountains.
8. Have the women completed their tournament games?
9. The babies were frightened by the honking of the geese.
10. Carmen sold boxes of grapefruit to the tourists.

2. Have the students form the plural for each of these nouns:

1. shoe	*shoes*	11. birthday	*birthdays*
2. wish	*wishes*	12. flamingo	*flamingos*
3. studio	*studios*	13. child	*children*
4. penny	*pennies*	14. dictionary	*dictionaries*
5. painting	*paintings*	15. perch	*perches*
6. elf	*elves*	16. lunch	*lunches*
7. grass	*grasses*	17. man	*men*
8. pinto	*pintos*	18. foot	*feet*
9. sky	*skies*	19. life	*lives*
10. half	*halves*	20. deer	*deer*

3. Have the students write the correct plural form for each sentence below.

1. Three (mouses/<u>mice</u>) ate the cheese.
2. Those (<u>leaves</u>/leafs) blew into the gutter.
3. Give the (toyes/<u>toys</u>) to the small child.
4. The weather warning covers four (<u>counties</u>/countys).
5. The bells of all the (churchs/<u>churches</u>) rang at noon.

Exercises   Forming Plurals

▶ Recalling

A. Number your paper from 1 to 10. Write the plural form for each noun below.

1. monkey   monkeys
2. cliff   cliffs
3. ax   axes
4. piano   pianos
5. deer   deer
6. child   children
7. alley   alleys
8. life   lives
9. candy   candies
10. halo   halos

▶ Analyzing

B. Number your paper from 1 to 15. Rewrite each sentence. Make each noun in italics plural.

1. The mail *carrier* delivered the *box*.   carriers, boxes
2. The *fly* were killed by the spray.   flies
3. The *woman* cut the *sandwich* on the *plate* in *half*.   women, sandwiches, plates, halves
4. In some *country*, even adults believe in *elf*.   countries, elves
5. There are *goose* hiding under the *bush* in the *marsh*.   geese, bushes, marshes
6. The farmer placed *potato* and *tomato* on the *table*.   potatoes, tomatoes, tables
7. The *child* played on the *beach*.   children, beaches
8. The *man* displayed the *radio* on the *shelf*.   men, radios, shelves
9. The paper uses *computer* to print the *news*.   computers, news
10. The *dairy* in the *city* suffered *loss*.   dairies, cities, losses
11. Tara sharpened the *knife* before she cut the *loaf* of bread and the *cheese*.   knives, loaves, cheeses
12. *Wolf* howled in the cold, clear night.   Wolves
13. The *cuff* on your pants are dragging in the mud.   cuffs
14. *Eskimo* spend most of their *life* surrounded by ice and snow.   Eskimos, lives
15. The *bell* of the *church* ring at noon.   bells, churches

▶ Creative Application

C. Writing You have just won a fifteen-minute shopping spree at your local department store. Think about it and write a list of the items you would select. Write a paragraph describing the items.

52

Additional Resources

Skills Practice Book—page 22

Teacher's Resource Binder
Reinforcement Activities—
    pages 21–22
Enrichment Activities—
    page 57

4 Nouns That Show Possession

Focus

A **possessive noun** shows who or what owns something.

▶ Comprehension

Everyone owns things, from clothes, to toys, to pets. When you wish to say that someone owns something, you use the **possessive form** of the noun.

Marion took a *week's* vacation. (The possessive form of *week* is *week's*.)

Ed borrowed *Becky's* skateboard. (The possessive form of *Becky* is *Becky's*.)

Making Singular Nouns Show Possession

To form the possessive of a singular noun, add an apostrophe and an *s*.

Singular Noun	Possessive Form
grandfather	grandfather's
Mrs. Wills	Mrs. Wills's

53

Part 4

Objective

To form possessive nouns correctly

Presenting the Lesson

All Students

1. Read and discuss pages 53–54.

2. Emphasize the importance of first deciding if a word is singular or plural before making it possessive.

3. In addition to the definition of a noun given in this chapter, there are other ways to identify a noun. The following chart, **Ways To Identify Nouns**, is based on the structure of a word and the order of words in a sentence. The chart may be used to point out additional ways in which nouns function.

Ways To Identify Nouns

1. Look for words that have a singular, plural, or possessive form.

Singular	Plural	Possessive
girl	girls	girl's

2. Look for words that follow *a, an* or *the.*

The *table* was made of pine.

3. Look for words that fit the blanks in one of these test sentences:

_____ are very important.

That is a _____.

See the _____.

Put it near the _____.

---

4. Assign and discuss Exercises A, B, and C on page 55. Before students begin Exercise C, have them discuss the kinds of items a person might bring to summer camp.

5. Use Exercise D on page 57 for additional practice if needed.

Basic Students

When discussing the last two paragraphs on page 54, write the following phrases on the board. Ask the students to explain how changing the place of the apostrophe changes the meaning of the possessive.

1. the dog's food
   the dogs' food
2. the bird's song
   the birds' song
3. the carpenter's tools
   the carpenters' tools

◆ Advanced Students

After the students have completed the exercises on page 55, ask them to write a story as silly as they like. They should use at least six of the phrases they wrote for Exercise B in their stories. Remind students to make sure they have written the possessive forms correctly.

Special Populations

LD, ESL, NSD Students should have available a chart with the rules for forming possessives. Either make a chart or write the rules on the board.

Discuss with students the frequently confused words *its* and *it's*. Point out that *its* is a possessive form. *It's* is a contraction, or shortened version, of the two words *it is*.

Reinforcement

1. Have the students follow the directions for Exercise A on page 55 using these sentences:

1. We applauded the *guitarist* performance. guitarist's
2. *Dr. Sawyer* patient chart was left in the examining room. Dr. Sawyer's
3. Several houses in the *tornado* path were damaged. tornado's
4. The *children* father paid the babysitter for her work. children's
5. The *tenants* landlord installed a smoke alarm in each apartment. tenants'
6. *Tracy* photographs of the Grand Canyon are sharp and clear. Tracy's
7. The factory *employees* quitting time was 3:30 P.M. employees'
8. This *computer* memory stores information on the weather. computer's
9. Most of my *uncle* house has been painted. uncle's
10. *Charles* sailboat is passing the lighthouse. Charles's

2. Have the students follow the directions for Exercise B on page 55 using these nouns:

Making Plural Nouns Show Possession

There are two rules to remember for forming the possessive of a plural noun.

1. If the plural noun ends in *s*, simply add an apostrophe.

Plural Noun	Possessive Form
pirates	pirates'
cats	cats'

2. If the plural noun does not end in *s*, add an apostrophe and an *s*.

Plural Noun	Possessive Form
children	children's
mice	mice's

🔑 **Key to Writing** Be careful to use punctuation correctly when you form possessives. Notice how changing the place of the apostrophe can change the meaning. *The student's pencils* means the pencils belong to one student. *The students' pencils* means the pencils belong to two or more students.

student's   students'

54

Exercises Writing Possessives

Recalling

A. Rewrite the following sentences. Use the possessive form for each word in italics.

1. The trainer took the *runner* pulse. runner's
2. Is that the *manager* phone number? manager's
3. The new *girl* hair was long and curly. girl's
4. Follow your *mother* advice. mother's
5. A parade honored the *astronauts* homecoming. astronauts'
6. We could see the *raccoons* tracks. raccoons'
7. The *sailors* yellow slickers protected them from the salty ocean spray. sailors'
8. The *actress* smile looked real. actress's
9. My *dogs* ears perked up. dogs'
10. *Tess* butterfly collection has at least two dozen different varieties. Tess's

Recalling/Structured Application

B. Write the possessive form of each of the following nouns. Then write another noun after each possessive form to show what the first noun might possess.

Example: Thomas Edison
Thomas Edison's invention

1. the mechanic 's
2. the secretaries '
3. Louise 's
4. the children 's
5. Albert Jones 's
6. your neighbors '
7. a monkey 's
8. some steel workers '
9. an automobile 's
10. an ostrich 's

Creative Application

C. Writing Several friends are spending the summer at Camp Wonderlake. One night raccoons open the campers' lockers and spill the contents all over the cabin floor. Make a list matching the spilled belongings to the owners. Write a brief paragraph describing what items belong to whom.

1. a giraffe's
2. Vera's
3. the farmers'
4. my brother's
5. Rover's
6. Officer Kaufman's
7. James's
8. America's
9. a sheep's
10. carpenters'
11. Julie's
12. books'
13. window's
14. player's
15. cities'
16. king's
17. lady's
18. oxen's
19. child's
20. children's

Enrichment

An important proofreading skill is knowing when a sentence requires a possessive form and when it does not. Ask students to select the correct word for each sentence.

1. Several (boys/boy's) played baseball in the park.
2. My (sisters/sister's) class went on a field trip yesterday.
3. The volume (control's/controls) are broken.
4. Seven (children/child's) won a prize in the contest.
5. Our (cats/cats') food dishes were empty.

Additional Resources

Skills Practice Book—page 23
Teacher's Resource Binder
Reinforcement Activities—
pages 23–24

55

These **Exercises for Mastery** may be
used for additional practice of the concepts presented in this section. Each
exercise focuses on a single concept,
and should be used after the page number indicated in parentheses.

Exercise B
1. French, Cadillac, Detroit
2. Day
3. Ellen
4. Vicker's Theater
5. Walkerville Public Library
6. Carlsbad Caverns
7. Morning Glory Pool, Yellowstone National Park
8. Vermont
9. Payless Drugstore
10. Death Valley, California

Exercises for Mastery Chapter 3

Nouns for Precise Meaning

▶ Recalling/Classifying/Analyzing

A. Finding the Nouns Number your paper from 1 to 10. Write
the nouns in each sentence below. (Use after page 47.)

1. The corn was stored in the silo.
2. My sister Tanya invited her classmates to a picnic
   in the park.
3. Robin Hood led the fight against the Sheriff of
   Nottingham.
4. Directions are on the back of the package.
5. The eagle is a symbol of freedom in America.
6. Barbara brought the class some delicious candy
   made from pecans and caramel.
7. Spring is my favorite season.
8. This thermometer is for the oven.
9. The librarian found the book about Tibet on the
   top shelf.
10. Coaches help athletes improve teamwork.

B. Finding Common Nouns and Proper Nouns Copy these
sentences. Capitalize each proper noun. Underline the common
nouns once and the proper nouns twice. Words to be capitalized are
shown in margin. (Use after page 49.)

1. A french explorer named cadillac founded detroit.
2. Memorial day is a national holiday.
3. My cousin ellen can change that tire.
4. Vicker's theater was showing a double feature.
5. Walkerville public library is the biggest library in
   the county.
6. My family visited carlsbad caverns.
7. Morning glory pool in yellowstone national park
   looks like a blue morning glory.
8. John bought this syrup in vermont.

56

Additional Resources

Skills Practice Book
Mixed Practice—page 24

9. Payless drugstore was running a special on all sunglasses.
10. Death valley in california receives less than three inches of rain yearly.

C. Forming Plurals Write the plural form of each noun. (Use after page 52.)

1. dish dishes
2. ox oxen
3. deer deer
4. buzz buzzes
5. loaf loaves
6. goose geese
7. box boxes
8. ratio ratios
9. lady ladies
10. series series
11. buoy buoys
12. sheep sheep
13. lobby lobbies
14. day days
15. dwarf dwarfs or dwarves
16. wheelchair wheelchairs
17. dress dresses
18. valley valleys
19. roof roofs
20. echo echoes

D. Writing the Possessive Form Write the correct possessive form of each word in italics. (Use after page 55.)

1. *Darcy* math book was on the table. Darcy's
2. My *uncle* cabin is in New Jersey. uncle's
3. Sue bandaged her *dogs* paws. dogs'
4. The *ladies* coats are in the next room. ladies'
5. Three *dentists* offices are on Shirley Street. dentists'
6. A goose was in the *magician* hat. magician's
7. Can you find your *puppy* leash? puppy's
8. My *grandmother* store is closed in July. grandmother's
9. The *boys* appetites were huge. boys'
10. *People* opinions vary. People's

57

Using Grammar in Writing

These challenging and enjoyable activities allow the students to see how the concepts of grammar, usage, and mechanics may be applied in actual writing situations. Each exercise is designed to give students practice in several of the skills they have acquired in this section. The activities also provide opportunities for students to write creatively about a wide variety of interesting and unusual subjects.

As students complete these activities, remind them to follow the process of writing. Be sure to allow adequate time for prewriting activities. Individual conferences or peer-group sessions may be used for help with drafting and revision.

Using Grammar in Writing

▶ Creative Application

A. Did you ever wonder how the streets in your neighborhood got their names? Streets are often named for important people, places, and things. Cherokee Road, Illinois Avenue, and Lake Street are three examples.

Imagine that the mayor has written you a letter asking you to name five new streets in your town. Answer the mayor's letter. In your reply, suggest five street names and give the reasons for your choices.

B. Using Nouns in Science All plants and animals can be grouped or classified. The classification becomes more specific as the group is narrowed down. The animal kingdom is first divided into groups: vertebrates (animals with backbones) and invertebrates (animals without backbones). Vertebrates are then broken down into seven classes. One class is Mammalia, or Mammals. There are eighteen orders in this class.

Use an encyclopedia to find the names of the orders in the Class Mammalia. Then choose three orders and find at least two species for each one.

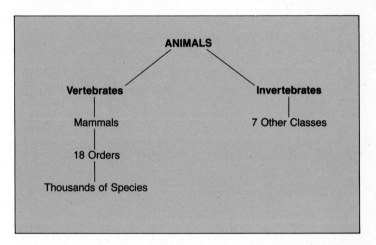

Additional Resources

Skills Practice Book
  Using Nouns in Writing—
    page 25

Using Nouns in Writing 25

Picture yourself as the first explorer to visit an unknown part of the earth. The place you explore might be a cave, a mountain, a swamp in the Everglades, a rain forest in the jungle, the ocean floor, or the North Pole. You are keeping a journal of your exploration. Write a paragraph describing all the strange and wondrous things you see. These things may be real or imaginary. Underline all the nouns in your paragraph. Remember to capitalize any proper nouns. Paragraphs will vary.

Chapter 3 Review

▶Classifying/Analyzing

A. Finding Common Nouns and Proper Nouns Make two columns on your paper. Label one column *Common Nouns* and the other *Proper Nouns*. Then read the paragraph below. Write each noun in its proper column. Remember to capitalize the proper nouns. If the same noun appears more than one time, you need to write it only once. Words to be capitalized are shown in margin.

The story of paul bunyan is a famous tale that began in the united states. For years, people all over america have told stories of a giant lumberjack who could perform great deeds. paul's strength and abilities were amazing! He could drive stumps into the ground with his bare fists. He could squeeze water out of boulders. paul dug the mississippi river and cleared the states of iowa and kansas for the farmers. With his companion, a blue ox named babe, paul cleared western pastures so cattle could graze. The adventures of paul bunyan are still enjoyed by americans.

B. Writing Singular, Plural, and Possessive Nouns Make four columns on your paper. Label them *Singular Noun*, *Plural Noun*, *Singular Possessive*, and *Plural Possessive*. Write each of the ten nouns listed below in the correct column. Then complete the chart by writing the three other forms of each noun in their proper columns.

Example:

Singular Noun ^{SN}	Plural Noun ^{PN}	Singular Possessive ^{SP}	Plural Possessive ^{PP}
astronaut	astronauts	astronaut's	astronauts'

1. guards' PP
   guard guards guard's
2. lizards PN
   lizard lizard's lizards'
3. hero SN
   heroes hero's heroes'
4. burro's SP
   burro burros burros'
5. ghosts' PP
   ghost ghosts ghost's

6. children PN
   child child's children's
7. ponies PN
   pony pony's ponies'
8. snakes' PP
   snake snakes snake's
9. firefighter SN
   firefighters firefighter's firefighters'
10. turtle SN
    turtles turtle's turtles'

59

Additional Resources

Skills Practice Book
Review—page 26

Test Booklet
Mastery Test—pages 15–16

Chapter Review

These exercises provide review of the concepts presented in this section. Each exercise challenges the students to apply several of the skills they have acquired during previous study. Because the "mixed" feature of these activities makes them more difficult, the teacher may wish to have basic students do the exercises orally or in small groups.

Exercise A
Paul Bunyan, United States, America, Paul's, Paul, Mississippi River, Iowa, Kansas, Babe, Paul, Paul Bunyan, Americans

Chapter 4

Chapter Objectives

1. To identify action verbs and state-of-being verbs

2. To differentiate between main verbs and helping verbs

3. To recognize direct objects in sentences

4. To identify linking verbs and the words they link in sentences

5. To recognize and form the simple tenses of verbs

6. To identify the three principal parts of common regular verbs

7. To identify the three principal parts of common irregular verbs

8. To choose the correct verb from these pairs that are often confused: *can, may; let, leave; lie, lay*

9. To choose the correct verb from these pairs that are often confused: *teach, learn; rise, raise; sit, set*

Motivating the Students

1. Chapter 2, "Writing and Understanding Sentences," pages 17–43, introduces the use of verbs in sentences. Briefly review the definitions of subjects and predicates. Then, read and discuss the chapter introduction on page 61.

2. Read aloud the following excerpt from *Where the Lilies Bloom.* Ask the students to point out words that describe an action. Then, point out how these words bring to life the mountain winds.

On the 30th day of October the dreaded winds that breed along mountain turrets around Trial Valley, exploding to life with the first real temperature change, came barreling into Trial Valley. Shivering the bare branches, pounding and shrieking, it sent the snakes and the groundhogs and all other wildlife scurrying to burrowed refuge. The tall, stout teasels out beside the cow enclosure bent low in its wake. Some of the loose shingles on our roof were pried and went sailing off into the raging air. Romey and I climbed up and had a look at the bald places. What was left seemed to me to be a mighty thin defense.

—Vera and Bill Cleaver

Special Populations

LD Since this is a long chapter, you will need to provide frequent review of

Week 5

Chapter Management Guidelines   This chart may be used to help structure daily lesson plans

Day 1	Day 2	Day 3	Day 4	Day 5
Chapter 4 Opener, p. 61; Part 1, "Kinds of Verbs," pp. 62–64	Part 2, "Main Verbs and Helping Verbs," pp. 65–67	Part 3, "Direct Objects of Verbs," pp. 68–69	Part 4, "Linking Verbs," pp. 70–71	Part 5, "Verb Tenses," pp. 72–74

Chapter 4

Verbs for Writing Power

When the director on a movie set yells "Action!" a make-believe world comes to life. Pirates leap from ship to ship. The posse gallops after the bandits. Astronauts float and tumble in zero gravity. Enemy aircraft explode in the sky.

The words *leap, gallops, float, tumble,* and *explode* tell about action. Words that tell about action are called verbs. In this chapter, you will learn about action verbs and state-of-being verbs. You will add helping verbs to main verbs to express different meanings. You will master the use of pairs of verbs that are often confused. You will enjoy working with the many verb forms that set your speaking and writing in motion.

61

previously learned concepts. Shorten or modify exercises as necessary.

Action verbs should not be a problem. State-of-being verbs, helping verbs, and linking verbs will be more difficult for students to conceptualize. Provide extra drill on these.

ESL Some students will be accustomed to conjugating verbs only in their own languages. Others will need guidance in recognizing singular and plural forms of verbs in various tenses. Some students will have difficulty with helping verbs for which there are no equivalents in their native languages. Provide extra assistance and drill in these areas.

NSD The forms of *be*, helping verbs, and tense will require special attention. These are frequently misused in dialects. Stress the importance of using standard English verb and tense forms in all written work.

Related Chapters

You may wish to refer to related material in other chapters as you teach the following concepts:

1. How verbs are used in sentences, Chapter 2, "Writing and Understanding Sentences," page 17, and Chapter 15, "Revising and Combining Sentences," page 269

2. Negatives and other adverbs, Chapter 17, "Adverbs for Clear Description," page 301

Additional Resources

Skills Practice Book—page 27–40
Test Booklet—pages 17–22
    Pretest—pages 17–18
    Mastery Test—pages 19–22
Teacher's Resource Binder
    Reinforcement Activities—
        pages 25–36
    Enrichment Activities—
        pages 39–52, 58
    Process of Writing Transparencies
    Ideas for Creative Teaching

Week 6

Chapter Management Guidelines   This chart may be used to help structure daily lesson plans.

Day 1	Day 2	Day 3	Day 4	Day 5
Chapter 4, Part 6, "The Principal Parts of Verbs," pp. 75–76	Part 7, "Irregular Verbs," pp. 77–79	Part 7, "Irregular Verbs," pp. 77–79	Part 8, "Confusing Pairs of Verbs," pp. 80–81; Part 9, "Other Confusing Pairs of Verbs," pp. 82–83	Chapter Review and selected end-of-chapter activities

Part 1

Objective

To identify action verbs and state-of-being verbs

Presenting the Lesson

All Students

1. Read and discuss pages 62–63.

2. Ask students to give additional examples of verbs that describe an action you can see and verbs that describe an action you can't see. Have them use these verbs in sentences.

3. Since action verbs are more easily understood and recognized than state-of-being verbs, additional practice with the latter may be needed. Ask students to identify the state-of-being verb in each of these sentences:

1. That award is a high honor.
2. We are happy with our new car.
3. The document was very important.
4. This problem seems impossible.
5. Hector's mother is a biologist.

Then, have students suggest sentences using all of the state-of-being verbs listed in this section.

4. When reading the **Key to Writing,** refer students to the "Thesaurus" in the **Power Handbook** as a source for finding more interesting verbs. Write the following sentence on the board. Have students substitute verbs that are more descriptive.

The dog ran down the street.

5. Assign and discuss Exercises A, B, and C on page 64. Before students begin Exercise C, have them decide what kinds of movies they would most like to direct.

6. Use Exercise A on page 84 for additional practice if needed.

Basic Students

Before assigning the exercises, have the students list several action verbs and then think of sentences for each one. Then, do the same for each of the state-of-being verbs listed on page 63. This could be done as a group activity.

1 Kinds of Verbs

> **Focus**
>
> **Verbs** are words that tell about action or state that something *is*.

▶ Comprehension/Classifying

You use two kinds of verbs when you speak or write. These are **action verbs** and **state-of-being verbs**.

Action Verbs

Some verbs tell about action you can see.

> Dale *skated* at the ice rink.
> Rosanne *painted* the stage scenery.
> Uncle Gerry *sings* in a barbershop quartet.

Other verbs tell about action you cannot see. That is, there is no physical movement.

> Nick *remembered* the answer.
> Brenda *wished* for a tournament win.
> Our class *planned* a field trip.

State-of-Being Verbs

Some verbs do not show action. They tell that something *is*. Such verbs are called state-of-being verbs. These are the most common state-of-being verbs.

am	are	were	being
is	was	be	been

Look at the state-of-being verbs in the following sentences.

Dr. Johnston *is* my dentist.
The sky *was* cloudy.
Whales *are* mammals.

Other familiar state-of-being verbs include these.

look	appear	become
feel	sound	remain
taste	smell	seem

The porcupine *seems* clumsy.
Burlap *feels* rough.
This milk *tastes* sour.

🔑 **Key to Writing**   Strong action verbs add interest and life to your writing. Choose the most descriptive verbs you can find.

Fireworks *exploded* in the black sky.

The grizzly *snatched* a trout from the cold stream.

63

◆ **Advanced Students**

After the exercises have been completed, have the students write new sentences using the verbs in Exercises A and B. Students should identify each verb as *action* or *state-of-being*.

Special Populations

LD, ESL Students may rely on common verbs, ones that are familiar and comfortable. Encourage them to use the "Thesaurus" in the **Power Handbook** for more specific verbs.

Allow time for students to make a "Dictionary of Verbs," with illustrations, to use as a personal reference source.

Reinforcement

1. Have the students follow the directions for Exercise A on page 64 using these sentences:

1. Our school held an art fair.
2. The mood at the party seemed happy.
3. Sharon remembered her umbrella.
4. Our dog, Wuffy, hates dog treats.
5. Today, the weather is hot and humid.
6. The snake shed its skin.
7. That car splashed mud on me.
8. My brothers were at that movie.
9. Hyacinths are fragrant flowers.
10. The game ended sooner than we expected.

2. Have the students follow the directions for Exercise B on page 64 using these sentences:

1. He won the skateboard contest. A
2. Stevie Wonder plays the piano and the guitar. A
3. The baby was just two weeks old. SB
4. I forgot the words to the song. A
5. Orlando is the best swimmer on the team. SB
6. You left the lights on again. A
7. Those yellow birds are canaries. SB
8. Ten years is a long time. SB
9. You ate all the popcorn again. A
10. Clark Kent is Superman. SB

Enrichment

1. Collect a set of interesting action pictures from newspapers and magazines. Number the pictures. Pass them around the room and ask students to think of one verb suggested by each picture. When all students have finished their lists, write all the suggestions for each picture on the board. Can each be used as a verb in a sentence about the picture? Discuss the verbs and sentences. Which ones most accurately tell about the action in the pictures?

2. For additional enrichment activities, see the Unit Projects in the Teacher Notes on page 3. One or more of these projects have special activities for gifted and talented students.

Exercises Finding Action Verbs and State-of-Being Verbs

▶ Recalling

A. Number your paper from 1 to 10. Write the verb in each sentence.

1. Good morning, I <u>am</u> your swimming instructor.
2. The yearling <u>seems</u> skittish.
3. Colorful ceramic pots <u>lined</u> the tables.
4. Your directions <u>were</u> very helpful.
5. The rand <u>is</u> a unit of money in South Africa.
6. Garth <u>slid</u> into home plate.
7. The burning hickory <u>smells</u> wonderful.
8. The vendors <u>displayed</u> their vegetables daily at the farmer's market.
9. It <u>feels</u> hot and humid today.
10. Delores <u>bowled</u> a strike.

▶ Recalling/Classifying

B. Number your paper from 1 to 10. Write the verb in each sentence. Then tell what kind of verb it is. Write *Action* or *State-of-Being*.

1. The rabbit's big, velvety ears <u>twitched</u>. A
2. This costume <u>looks</u> old. SB
3. Judy <u>loves</u> cheese on her hamburgers. A
4. <u>Listen</u> to the crickets in the basement. A
5. Your directions <u>seemed</u> very clear. SB
6. Suddenly, Sean's dark eyes <u>flashed</u>. A
7. I <u>know</u> the name of our senator. A
8. The first woman candidate for President <u>was</u> Victoria C. Woodhull. SB
9. The kingfisher <u>swallowed</u> a frog and two fish. A
10. Richard's bike accident <u>happened</u> last June. A

▶ Creative Application

C. Writing Imagine that you have just been chosen to direct a movie starring your favorite actor or actress. Write a paragraph that records the action as the filming begins. Then underline all the verbs in your paragraph.

64

Additional Resources

Skills Practice Book—page 27

Teacher's Resource Binder
Reinforcement Activities—
page 25

2 Main Verbs and Helping Verbs

┌─ *Focus* ─────────────────────────────────────┐
│   A verb may be a single word or a group of words. │
└──┘

▶ Comprehension

You know that many verbs are single words. Read these sentences.

> Eric *rides* a moped.   Melita *played* her cello.

Often, however, a verb is made up of two or more words. Look at these examples.

> Eric *is riding* a moped.   Melita *was playing* her cello.
> Eric *has been riding* a moped.   Melita *might have played* her cello.

When there are two or more words in the verb, the last word is the main verb. Other words are helping verbs.

Helping Verbs	Main Verbs	Verb
is	riding	is riding
has been	riding	has been riding
was	playing	was playing
might have	played	might have played

Forms of the verbs *be*, *have*, and *do* are the most commonly used helping verbs.

be—be, am, is, are, was, were
have—have, has, had
do—do, does, did

These helping verbs can also be used as main verbs.

Used as Helping Verb	Used as Main Verb
Bob *is* going.	Bob *is* the pitcher.
Sally *has* finished.	Sally *has* a cold.

65

Objective

To differentiate between main verbs and helping verbs

Presenting the Lesson

 All Students

1. Read and discuss pages 65–66. Give special attention to the difference between the use of verbs as helping verbs and as main verbs. In the examples showing *is* and *has* as helping verbs, point out the main verb as well. Use the following sentences for practice. Have the students tell whether the word in italics is a helping verb or a main verb. For those that are helping verbs, have the students find the main verbs in the sentence as well.

1. That tree <u>is swaying</u> in the breeze.
2. The winner <u>was</u> Mary McCann.
3. Everyone <u>did</u> the lesson perfectly.
4. My new pen <u>is</u> already dry.
5. I <u>have given</u> that idea some serious thought.

2. Discuss separated parts of verbs. Point out that *not* frequently separates parts of verbs. An interrogative sentence often begins with a helping verb, such as *did*, *are*, or *have*. The main verb follows the subject. Stress that interrupters such as *not* are not part of the verb.

3. Assign and discuss Exercises A, B, and C on page 67. After students complete Exercise C, have them revise their paragraphs, replacing all of the weak verbs with strong verbs. Refer students to the "Thesaurus" in the **Power Handbook.**

4. Use Exercise B on page 84 for additional practice if needed.

 Basic Students

Work through the first three or four items in Exercise A with the students. Have them first find all the verbs in the sentence. Then, remind them that, if there is more than one verb, the last one is the main verb.

Encourage students to examine the entire sentence when looking for verbs. They should not stop when they find one verb. This activity will also encourage students to look at the sentence as a unit rather than just as individual words. Make sure that students understand the special instances in which helping verbs and main verbs might be separated in a sentence.

 Advanced Students

Have the students write an action verb with each of the helping verbs listed at the top of page 66. Encourage students to combine two or three helping verbs with an action verb. The result will be a list of two, three, and four word verbs.

Special Populations

ESL In some languages there are frequently no equivalents to English helping verbs. Additional practice may be necessary for these students.

NSD The helping verb is dropped in many dialects, resulting in sentences such as, *What you doing?* Students might listen to tapes of correctly worded sentences in order to reinforce proper sentence structure.

ESL, NSD Students should practice turning questions with separated verb parts into statements. This will help students to recognize separated verbs when they appear in questions.

Students may find *do* especially difficult, when it is used as a helping verb in questions or for emphasis in statements. Encourage students to memorize the forms of *do*.

Reinforcement

1. Have the students follow the directions for Exercise A on page 67 using these sentences:

1. The pirates have seized the ship.
2. The scout meeting will be held next Tuesday.
3. My bowling ball has somehow rolled into a gutter.
4. Our jeep might have gotten a flat tire on that gravel road.
5. The bank teller will lock the safe every night.
6. Jerry had never seen that movie before.
7. Princess Aurora has been sleeping for nearly one hundred years.
8. Daryl should have played that song at the party.

Several other helping verbs can be used with main verbs.

be	must	will	should
being	can	would	may
been	could	shall	might

Separated Parts of the Verb

The main verb and its helping verbs are not always together. They may be separated by other parts of the sentence.

The batter *was* not *watching* the signals.
Andrea *has* never *missed* a band practice.
Did the kindergartners *make* popcorn today?
Frankenstein *could*n't *control* his monster.

Notice that *not* and the ending *n't* in the contraction are not verbs. Also notice that in questions, one or more words often come between the helping verb and the main verb.

66

Exercises   Finding Main Verbs and Helping Verbs

▶ Recalling/Classifying

A. Number your paper from 1 to 10. Make two columns. Head the first column *Helping Verbs*. Head the second *Main Verb*. Write the verbs for each of these sentences in the correct column.

1. The red wolf is becoming extinct.
2. The arm of an orangutan may be over three feet long.
3. The Bears were beating the Vikings, 7-0.
4. You should have eaten a nutritious breakfast.
5. Some words can be pronounced two different ways.
6. Will Momoko bring her skateboard?
7. Have you ever written a poem?
8. Curt could have joined the hockey team.
9. Computers are already performing many useful and important tasks.
10. The President can not be elected more than twice.

▶ Structured Application

B. Write the following sentences. Add one or two helping verbs to each sentence. Choose from the lists on pages 65-66.

Answers will vary. Suggested answers are given.

1. I _was_ not expecting your phone call.
2. The old chestnut tree _has been_ hit by lightning.
3. Where _can_ we find a book about marine life?
4. You _might have_ seen the flames.
5. This contest entry _may_ be too late.
6. The beach ball _had_ completely collapsed.
7. Skip _has_ never had the measles.
8. That bottle _has_ floated here from Greenland.
9. We _had_ already packed the picnic basket.
10. The team _has_ not been defeated.

▶ Creative Application

C. Writing Write one paragraph describing a funny incident you may have seen or heard about. Be sure to include several strong verbs that will help your reader picture the action you are describing. Underline the verbs in your paragraph.

9. Mules are slowly pulling the boat through the canal.
10. Arlette could probably answer your questions about submarines.

2. Have the students follow the directions for Exercise B on page 67 using these sentences: Answers will vary.

1. Every student _____ entered the contest.
2. One paragraph in my report _____ describe whales.
3. Scientists _____ testing that metal.
4. Thousands of people _____ see the show.
5. Elena _____ never eaten an apricot.
6. I _____ not feeling well last week.
7. Your invitation _____ not mailed on time.
8. These pants _____ not fit Marion.
9. My mother _____ not know your aunt.
10. Your dog _____ stop chasing my cat.

67

Additional Resources

Skills Practice Book—page 28

Teacher's Resource Binder
Reinforcement Activities—
pages 26–27

Part 3

Objective

To recognize direct objects in sentences

Presenting the Lesson

 All Students

1. Read and discuss pages 68–69. Emphasize that the direct object receives the action of a verb. Tell students that only an action verb can have a direct object. You may also wish to point out that a proper noun can be used as a direct object, as in this sentence.

Alexander applauded Marcia.

2. Assign and discuss Exercises A, B, and C on page 69. Before students begin Exercise C, have them discuss what kinds of things the scientist might invent. Students should decide on a specific item before they write.

3. Use Exercise C on page 85 for extra practice if needed.

 Basic Students

Write the following sentences on the board. Ask students to tell whether the sentence has a direct object. If it does, they should name it. Remind students to ask who? or what? after the verb to find the direct object.

1. Mario wrote a poem about summer.
   poem
2. Your plants are growing well. no D.O.
3. The wind is howling fiercely. no D.O.
4. Computers can solve difficult problems.
   problems
5. Many desert animals sleep during the day. no D.O.
6. Ella did not play in the finals. no D.O.
7. My brother collects rare stamps.
   stamps
8. The modern Olympic Games began in 1896. no D.O.

When assigning the exercises, do the first few sentences of each exercise together with the students.

 Advanced Students

Have the students use each of the following words as a direct object in a sentence.

pencil	sled	lawn
desk	book	table

---

3 Direct Objects of Verbs

> ### Focus
> The **direct object** is the noun or pronoun that receives the action of the verb.

▶ Comprehension/Analyzing

In some sentences, the subject and verb alone express a complete thought.

Subject	Verb
The audience	applauded.
Marilyn	coughed.
Everyone	laughed.

Other sentences, however, are not complete until a word or words are added after the verb.

Paul polished the *sailboat*.
Lucia dropped her *magazine*.

The noun or pronoun that completes the action of the verb is the **direct object** of the verb. *Sailboat* tells what Paul polished. *Magazine* tells what Lucia dropped. *Sailboat* and *magazine* are direct objects.

To find the direct object in a sentence, first find the verb. Then ask *whom*? or *what*? after the verb. The word that answers *whom*? or *what*? is the direct object. If you cannot answer the questions *whom*? or *what*? there is no direct object.

Christy likes salamanders.
Christy likes *what*? *salamanders*
The direct object is *salamanders*.

Julio exercises in the morning.
Julio exercises *whom*? Julio exercises *what*?
You cannot answer the questions *whom* or *what*? There is no direct object.

Key to Writing and Speaking
Use direct objects to give your reader or listener as much information as possible. Do not say, "Jim was painting," say "Jim was painting *the room*."

Exercises   Understanding Direct Objects

▶ Analyzing

A. Copy the following sentences. Draw one line under the verb. Draw two lines under the direct object.

1. The scuba diver found a shipwreck.
2. Two shepherds sheared the ewes.
3. The pilot steered his craft onto the airfield.
4. Eun Lee stenciled the frame.
5. The children have built a huge sculpture.
6. The Bureau of the Mint manufactures all coins.
7. Kathy will repair the brakes on her bike.
8. Delores likes yogurt with cinnamon and honey.
9. The United States exports grains to the Far East.
10. A kangaroo carries her young in a pouch.

▶ Structured Application

B. Number your paper from 1 to 10. Write a direct object to complete each of the following sentences.   Answers will vary.

1. Hamid planted ____ in his front yard.
2. The Cardinals scored a ____.
3. Newspapers littered the ____.
4. Jolita rode the ____ with ease.
5. The reporter wrote a sensational ____.
6. After the concert, the conductor left the ____.
7. Leroy wore a bright yellow ____.
8. Kristin put the ____ in her wallet.
9. My favorite radio station plays good ____.
10. Did you close the ____?

▶ Creative Application

C. Writing Write a story about a weird scientist. Perhaps the scientist is creating a computer that changes Mondays into Fridays. Use direct objects to complete some verbs in your story.

69

Special Populations

LD Review with students the definitions of *noun* and *pronoun*. Have students identify all the nouns in the Exercise A sentences. Then, they should find direct objects. This exercise will reinforce the concept that a direct object is always a noun or pronoun.

ESL Supply students with a list of simple two and three word sentences. For example, you might use *She eats*, and *He draws*. Have students add a noun or pronoun to each. Explain that they are adding direct objects to complete each sentence.

Reinforcement

1. Have the students follow the directions for Exercise A on page 69 using these sentences:

1. Rex is burying a bone in our backyard.
2. The mailman delivered a package to our house today.
3. We saw William Perry at the football game.
4. Louise has begun a new book.
5. Aaron plays the harmonica.
6. Tamara returned the book to the wrong library.
7. The factory manufactured microchips for computers.
8. I am writing my autobiography.
9. The wind blew leaves into the gutter.
10. A lone wolf hungrily eyed the unsuspecting sheep.

2. Have the students follow the directions for Exercise B on page 69 using these sentences: Answers will vary.

1. Agnes planted _____ in the garden.
2. My classmate, Melanie, chose the _____.
3. Have you read this _____?
4. A garage mechanic fixed our _____.
5. The mother robin brought _____ to her young.
6. After the play, my brother and I cleaned the _____.
7. The archaeologist discovered a large ancient _____.
8. Lenore raked the _____ into several neat piles.
9. We ate _____ for dinner last night.
10. I will visit _____ next summer.

Additional Resources

Skills Practice Book—page 29
Teacher's Resource Binder
Reinforcement Activities—
pages 28–29

Part 4

Objective

To identify both linking verbs and words they link in sentences

Presenting the Lesson

⬤ All Students

1. Read and discuss page 70. Emphasize that linking verbs are not action verbs. They simply tell that something *is*, or *exists*. They are always followed by an adjective, a noun, or a pronoun.

2. The text uses the term *adjective* here for the first time. Define it simply as a describing word. The adjective will be fully discussed in Chapter 16.

3. Thoroughly discuss the examples on page 70. Be sure that students understand the difference between direct objects and the predicate words that follow linking verbs.

Point out that in the first two sample sentences, *feel* and *taste* indicate a state of being. No action is being performed. *Ill* describes *I*. *Sour* describes *pickles*.

4. Stress that if the noun following a verb is receiving the action of the verb, it is a direct object, and the verb is an action verb. If the noun following the verb tells something about the subject, the verb is a linking verb.

5. Assign and discuss Exercises A, B, and C on page 71. Before students write their paragraphs for Exercise C, encourage them to list the names of the people they plan to include.

6. Use Exercise D on page 85 for practice if needed.

▶ Basic Students

Before assigning the exercises, have the students work together to identify both the linking verbs and the words they link. Write the following sentences on the board. Follow the directions for Exercise A.

1. A unicycle is difficult to ride.
2. Mother's rhubarb pie smells great.
3. Ben was a pirate in the play.
4. Johanna felt nervous on the plane.
5. The cutest kittens were orange.
6. The movie was funny.

---

4 Linking Verbs

> **Focus**
>
> Some state-of-being verbs are called **linking verbs**.

▶ Comprehension

Some verbs express a state of being. They usually link, or connect, the subject with a word in the predicate. That is why they are often called **linking verbs**. Read these sentences.

Carrie *is* tall.   Mountain lakes *are* cold.

In the examples, linking verbs connect *Carrie* with *tall* and *lakes* with *cold*. The words *tall* and *cold* tell about the subject. They are linked to the subject in each sentence by the linking verbs *is* and *are*.

The words *am*, *is*, *are*, *was*, *were*, *be*, *been*, and *become* are often used as linking verbs. The words *seem*, *look*, *appear*, *smell*, *taste*, *feel*, and *sound* can also be linking verbs.

The words that follow linking verbs and tell something about the subject can be adjectives, nouns, or pronouns. They are called predicate words because they appear in the predicate.

I *feel* ill. (*Ill* is an adjective.)

These pickles *taste* sour. (*Sour* is an adjective.)

Angela *is* my best friend. (*Friend* is a noun.)

A goat *became* our team mascot. (*Mascot* is a noun.)

Do not confuse nouns following linking verbs with direct objects of verbs. In the examples just given, you can see that *friend* and *mascot* tell something about the subject of each sentence. They do not receive action of the verbs, and are not direct objects. To identify a linking verb, decide whether the noun following the verb tells something about the subject of the sentence. If it does, the verb is a linking verb.

70

Exercises Mastering Linking Verbs

A. Draw three columns on your paper. Label them *Subject*, *Linking Verb*, and *Predicate Word*. Find these three parts in each sentence. Write them in the proper columns.

1. A young kangaroo is a joey.
2. That clown's hat looks ridiculous.
3. Christie Brinkley is a famous model.
4. The stew smells delicious.
5. Bullfighters seem brave.
6. Rachael's story sounds unbelievable.
7. The dungeon looks scary.
8. Under water, straight lines appear wavy.
9. Long John Silver is a character in *Treasure Island*.
10. The cast is quiet during the rehearsal.

> Recalling/Structured Application

B. Number your paper from 1 to 10. Write the linking verb in each sentence. Then write a new sentence by changing the word linked to the subject.

1. The queen bee is the largest bee in the hive.
2. Bobby Orr has been a famous athlete for many years.
3. Vacations are always too short.
4. The police detective felt uneasy in the dark warehouse.
5. That down quilt seems very cozy.
6. The sea was calm after the storm.
7. Eli Whitney was the inventor of the cotton gin.
8. The bill becomes a law on February 15.
9. Grace's costume looks bizarre.
10. Mopeds are efficient vehicles.

> Creative Application

C. Writing Did you know that there is a book titled *Who's Who in America*? It contains information about well-known people. Write a "Who's Who in Our School" paragraph. Name important people and their positions. Tell what each person does and what he or she is like. You might include the principal, secretary, and librarian.

Additional Resources

Skills Practice Book—page 30

Teacher's Resource Binder
Reinforcement Activities—
pages 30–31

 Advanced Students

Have the students write one sentence for each of the linking verbs they found in Exercise A.

Special Populations

LD, ESL The most difficult aspect of this part may be determining when the following words are linking verbs and when they are action verbs.

taste, smell, feel, look, sound
Provide extra practice with these verbs.

Reinforcement

1. Have the students follow the directions for Exercise A on page 71, using these sentences:

1. That foreign stamp is rare.
2. Your answer may be correct.
3. This record appears scratched.
4. Ludwig von Beethoven was a great composer.
5. Our cat looks graceful.
6. Simon has been my friend since first grade.
7. The newspaper cartoons are usually funny.
8. Stars appear bright in the night sky.
9. The fur collar feels soft.
10. This ear of sweet corn tastes fresh.
11. The angry crowd grew restless.
12. This pancake looks burned.

2. Have the students follow the directions for Exercise B on page 71 using these sentences: Sentences will vary.

1. The edge of this knife is dull.
2. My skates are becoming rusty.
3. The chili tastes fiery.
4. The fastest animal is the cheetah.
5. I don't feel sleepy.
6. The sequoia trees in California look huge.
7. Our country's oldest national park is Yellowstone.
8. The Vikings were Scandinavian pirates.
9. Mother must be very angry.
10. The most popular breed of dog is the cocker spaniel.

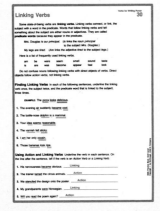

Part 5

Objective

To recognize and form the simple tenses of verbs

Presenting the Lesson

 All Students

1. Read and discuss pages 72–73. Give additional examples for each of the simple tenses. Have students create sentences for each. Make sure that students understand that the present tense has two forms: one used with singular subjects, ending in -s or -es, and one used with plural subjects, not ending in -s or -es. In the future tense, the main verb does not use the -s or -es for singular or plural subjects.

2. Demonstrate the natural formation of the regular verb past tense with a nonsense word example.

The teams *gronch* onto the field.
Yesterday the teams _____.
   (gronched)

Discuss the spelling changes that occur when the past tense of verbs is formed.

3. Assign and discuss Exercises A, B, and C on page 74. After students complete their paragraphs for Exercise C, have them proofread carefully to check the corrections and spelling of all verbs.

4. Use Exercise E on page 86 for additional practice if needed.

 Basic Students

Before assigning Exercises A and B, review the formation of simple tenses. Go over the first few sentences of each exercise with the group. Discuss the students' answers.

 Advanced Students

Have the students write three brief paragraphs: the first one about what they did last night; the second one about what they do every night; and a third about what they will be doing tonight. Ask them to underline the verbs in each paragraph.

---

5 Verb Tenses

> **Focus**
>
> Different forms of a verb are used to show time. These forms are called the **tenses** of a verb.

▶ Comprehension/Classifying

Verbs do more than tell of an action or a state of being. They also tell about time. They tell when something takes place. By changing their forms, verbs tell whether the action or state of being is past, present, or future.

The **present tense** tells about an action or a state of being happening now.

    I *work* at school. I *am* a student.

The **past tense** tells about an action or state of being that was completed in the past.

    I *worked* all last summer. I *was* a library aide.

The **future tense** tells about an action or a state of being happening in the future.

    I *will work* at the pool next year. I *will be* a lifeguard.

These three tenses are called the **simple tenses**. They are three of the most important tenses.

Tense changes are made in three ways.

1. By a change in ending: *look, looked*
2. By a change in spelling: *know, knew*
3. By a change in helping verbs: *did work, will work*

72

Forming the Present Tense

When the subject of a sentence is plural, use the basic form of the verb. The basic form of the verb has no endings or changes. Also, use the basic form of the verb with the pronouns *I* and *you*. Add *-s* or *-es* to the basic form when the subject is singular. Read these sentences.

I *ride.*   You *ride.*   He *rides.*   We *ride.*   They *ride.*

Forming the Past Tense

Form the past tense of most verbs by adding *-ed* to the present tense. Verbs that form the past tense by adding *-ed* to the basic form of the verb are called **regular verbs**.

laugh   laugh*ed*   tackle   tackl*ed*

Other verbs, called **irregular verbs**, change their spelling to show the past tense.

do   *did*   think   *thought*

There is also another way that you can show a change in tense. You can use a helping verb with the main verb.

smile   *had smiled*   ran   *had run*

Forming the Future Tense

Form the future tense by using the helping verbs *will* or *shall* with the present tense.

write   *will write*   sing   *shall sing*

Key to Writing   When you write, keep your verbs in the same tense. Do not switch tenses.
Incorrect: I *moved* to the door. I *open* it and *peek* out.
Correct: I *moved* to the door. I *opened* it and *peeked* out.

73

Special Populations

ESL Many students are accustomed to conjugating verbs in their own languages. Have them transfer this skill to English. Introduce several new verbs and have students conjugate each in the simple tenses. This will build and reinforce vocabulary.

NSD Students frequently have difficulty forming verb tenses correctly. Provide extra drill on this part.

Reinforcement

Have students follow the directions for Exercise A on page 74 using these sentences:

1. The bell will ring twice.   future
2. Sara wrote a letter every day.   past
3. The kitten nuzzled up to the Irish setter.   past
4. Juan hits the ball almost every time he bats.   present
5. All the ice melted in the hot sun.   past
6. The line went all the way around the block.   past
7. I will do my best.   future
8. Some jets travel faster than the speed of sound.   present
9. Hot bacon sizzled in the pan.   past
10. The stream dried up in the summer.   past

Additional Resources

Skills Practice Book—page 31
Teacher's Resource Binder
Reinforcement Activities—
page 32

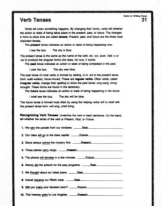

Exercises   Using Verb Tenses

▶ Recalling/Classifying

A. Number your paper from 1 to 10. Write the verb in each of the following sentences. Then write the tense of the verb. Write *Past*, *Present*, or *Future*.

1. The fans cheered loudly. Past
2. Sir Edmund Hillary climbed Mount Everest. Past
3. The committee will bring the streamers. Future
4. We saw a porpoise show at the zoo. Past
5. Clayton Moore played the Lone Ranger. Past
6. Everglades National Park is south of Homestead, Florida. Present
7. Tracy will meet you at the airport. Future
8. Pam Shriver plays professional tennis. Present
9. I will return this book to the library. Future
10. Native Americans first explored the Rocky Mountain wilderness. Past

▶ Analyzing

B. Number your paper from 1 to 10. Write the form of the verb asked for in each of the following sentences.

1. I (future of *read*) all of the Hardy Boys mysteries. will read
2. The lawyer (past of *argue*) her case. argued
3. Blake (present of *roast*) chestnuts in the fireplace. roasts
4. Tyrone (past of *carve*) a duck decoy. carved
5. The airplane (future of *land*) in a few minutes. will land
6. Gypsy moths (past of *devour*) countless trees. devoured
7. Evan and Teresa (past of *pick*) raspberries. picked
8. A cricket game (present of *confuse*) most Americans. confuses
9. Sponges (present of *live*) in the deep seas. live
10. The track team (future of *run*) in a meet tomorrow. will run

▶ Creative Application

C. Writing You are a bicycle racer. You have just finished the second lap of a race and your teammate has now taken over. She is reaching the halfway mark. In a brief paragraph, tell how your team has done so far, how your teammate is doing, and what you think the outcome of the race will be. Underline the action verbs you use.

74

6 The Principal Parts of Verbs

┌─ **Focus** ─────────────────────────────────┐
    All verb tenses are made from the three **principal parts** of
a verb: present, past, and past participle.
└───┘

▶ Comprehension/Classifying

    You have seen that every verb has many different forms. For example, you have the forms *talked, have talked, had talked, will talk, would have talked,* and others. All of these different forms of a verb are made from just three parts. For this reason, the three parts of any verb are called its **principal parts**.

    Look at the principal parts of the verbs below.

Present	Past	Past Participle
call	called	(have) called
climb	climbed	(have) climbed
hurry	hurried	(have) hurried
look	looked	(have) looked
paste	pasted	(have) pasted
stop	stopped	(have) stopped
talk	talked	(have) talked
walk	walked	(have) walked

    The **present** part of the verb is its present tense. Add *-s* to form the singular. The present part used with *will* or *shall* forms the future tense.

    The **past** part of the verb is its past tense.

    The **past participle** is always used with a helping verb such as *have*. Look at these other examples.

is called	was being called
has called	shall be called
have called	has been called
had called	will have called
was called	should have been called
were called	

75

Part 6

Objective

To identify the three principal parts of common regular verbs

Presenting the Lesson

 All Students

    1. Read and discuss pages 75–76. Make sure that students can identify the principal parts of regular verbs. They should know how to form each part.

    2. Emphasize that the past participle form of regular verbs is the same as its past form. The next part of this chapter will discuss the three forms of irregular verbs. Carefully go over the example of how the past participle is used with linking verbs to make other forms of the verb. Have the students suggest sentences for each of the forms. Add helping verbs to the other past participle forms listed on page 75 and have students suggest sentences for each.

    3. Assign and discuss Exercises A, B, and C on page 76. For Exercise C, divide the class into small groups. Have each group solve the mystery. Then, each student should write a news story.

    4. Use Exercise F on page 86 for additional practice if needed.

 Basic Students

    1. Before assigning Exercise A, review the concepts presented in this lesson. Then, do the first few items in Exercise A with the students. Review words that can be used as helping verbs.

    2. Before assigning Exercise B, do the first two items in the exercise together with the students.

◆ **Advanced Students**

    Have the students write three sentences for each of the example verbs in this part: *call, hurry, look, paste, stop, walk.* Each of the three sentences should use the past participle, with a different helping verb. Discuss with students how the change in helping verbs alters the meaning of the sentence.

Example: Jenny had called you earlier.
I have called you every day this week.
Louise should have called me.

Special Populations

LD, ESL Make a chart showing the conjugation of the verb *have*. Allow students to refer to the chart as they work on this part. Perfect tenses are difficult for Spanish-speaking students since the verb *have* has an equivalent in Spanish *(tener)*, but the helping verbs *have*, *has*, and *had* do not.

Reinforcement

1. Have the students follow the directions for Exercise A on page 76 using these verbs:

1. lift   lifted, (have) lifted
2. reveal   revealed, (have) revealed
3. smell   smelled, (have) smelled
4. call   called, (have) called
5. recite   recited, (have) recited
6. end   ended, (have) ended
7. explode   exploded, (have) exploded
8. hope   hoped, (have) hoped
9. cook   cooked, (have) cooked
10. jog   jogged, (have) jogged

2. Have the students follow the directions for Exercise B on page 76 using the following words:

1. create (past participle)   (have) created
2. skip (past)   skipped
3. bark (present)   bark
4. chew (past participle)   (have) chewed
5. wash (past)   washed
6. irritate (past participle)   (have) irritated
7. smother (past)   smothered
8. hope (past)   hoped
9. boil (past participle)   (have) boiled
10. touch (past)   touched

Notice that with regular verbs, the past participle is the same as the past form. This is not always true of irregular verbs. You will learn more about the principal parts of irregular verbs in part 7.

Exercises   Mastering the Principal Parts of Verbs

▶ Classifying

A. Divide your paper into three columns. Label one column *Present*, one column *Past*, and the third column *Past Participle*. Write each of the following words in the *Present* column. Then write the past and past participle forms in the proper columns. Use one or more helping verbs with the past participle.   Helping verbs will vary.

1. print   printed, (have) printed
2. decorate   decorated, (have) decorated
3. paste   pasted, (have) pasted
4. carry   carried, (have) carried
5. use   used, (have) used
6. help   helped, (have) helped
7. confuse   confused, (have) confused
8. list   listed, (have) listed
9. cover   covered, (have) covered
10. like   liked, (have) liked

▶ Structured Application

B. Number your paper from 1 to 10. Write the form of each verb asked for in parentheses. Then use each verb in a sentence. You may use one or more helping verbs with the past participle.

1. introduce (past participle)   introduced
2. protect (past)   protected
3. wobble (present)   wobble
4. add (past participle)   added
5. trade (past)   traded
6. sound (past participle)   sounded
7. develop (past)   developed
8. need (past participle)   needed
9. improve (past)   improved
10. organize (past participle)   organized

▶ Creative Application

C. Writing Reporter Ace Cunningham arrives on the scene. The assignment—to solve the mystery and break the story, fast! The clues—shattered glass, a grinning tabby cat, and a *very* soggy carpet. Ace solves the mystery. Write Ace's story. Use *have*, *has*, or *had* with some of the verbs in the story.

76

Additional Resources

Skills Practice Book—page 32
Teacher's Resource Binder
Reinforcement Activities—
page 33

Irregular Verbs

> **Focus**
>
> Some verbs form the past tense in special ways. These verbs are called **irregular verbs**.

Comprehension

You have learned that the past form of a regular verb is made by adding -*ed* to the present form.

    move—moved   block—blocked   tip—tipped

Some verbs, however, have special past forms. These verbs are **irregular verbs**. Here are some examples.

    sing—sang   give—gave   go—went

Sometimes, the past participle of an irregular verb is the same as the past form.

    brought—(have) brought   taught—(have) taught

Many irregular verbs have special past participle forms.

    rode—(have) ridden   flew—(have) flown

Remember these rules whenever you use irregular verbs.

1. The past form is used alone without a helping verb.

The camel *drank* the entire bucket of water.

2. The past participle must always be used with a helping verb.

The camel *had drunk* the entire bucket of water.

On page 78 there is a list of the principal parts of the most common irregular verbs. Study this list. Refer to it whenever you are unsure about the proper form of an irregular verb. In addition, the dictionary also lists the principal parts of irregular verbs under the present form.

77

Part 7

Objective

To identify the principal parts of common irregular verbs

Presenting the Lesson

 All Students

1. Read and discuss pages 77–78. Tell students that since irregular verbs do not follow a regular pattern in forming principal parts, it is important to become familiar with these verbs and their principal parts. Review the four rules for forming the past tense of irregular verbs. Point out that more than one helping verb can be used with past participles. When discussing the list of common irregular verbs, ask students to give sentences using the three forms of the verbs. Tell the students that the dictionary will also list the principal parts of irregular verbs.

2. Assign Exercises A, B, and C on page 79. After students complete their paragraphs for Exercise C, have them proofread their work. They should check the spelling and correct form of all irregular verbs.

3. Use Exercise G on page 87 for additional practice if needed.

 Basic Students

Before assigning Exercise A, review the rules for forming the past tense of irregular verbs. Remind the students to refer to the chart in this chapter when completing the exercises. Do the first two or three sentences with the students.

When assigning Exercise B, remind students that the past participle form always occurs with *have, has,* or *had.*

 Advanced Students

Have the students write ten original sentences, using the verbs in Exercise B.

Special Populations

LD, ESL, NSD A chart of irregular verbs and their principal parts should be posted. LD students find irregular verbs difficult because the parts must be memorized and often do not "sound" correct (rung, got, swum). Break the list into smaller sections so students learn only a few verbs at a time.

ESL Students may not be familiar with the idea of "irregular" verbs. Stress that these verbs do not follow the rules for forming principal parts and must be memorized.

NSD Students may be accustomed to using different forms of these verbs. Encourage them to refer to the chart often and to use these forms in their writing and speaking. They often leave out the helping verb *have*, resulting in sentences such as *I been walking*, *I done it*, and *I known it*. Provide extra drill and practice on the correct usage of this helping verb.

Reinforcement

1. Have the students follow the directions for Exercise A on page 79 using these sentences:

1. The customer (buy) the last newspaper from the newsstand.   bought
2. Louise (wear) an unusual outfit.   wore
3. I (speak) to my teacher about the assignment.   spoke
4. I (say) no such thing!   said
5. Cindy (fly) to Mexico and back in a weekend.   flew
6. That essay (give) us something to think about.   gave
7. Michael (eat) dinner early last night.   ate
8. They both (come) to the same conclusion.   came
9. Ajax (grow) to be a beautiful dog.   grew
10. Lester (do) all his homework in the library.   did

2. Have the students follow the directions for Exercise B on page 79 using these sentences: Helping verbs will vary.

1. The loaves of bread (past participle of rise).   (have) risen
2. Morgan (past of wear) his new coat for the first time today.   wore
3. Many people (past participle of teach) themselves to play an instrument.   (have) taught
4. Things (past participle of take) a turn for the worse.   (have) taken
5. We (past of run) out of paint before we could finish the posters.   ran
6. Clarissa (past participle of sing) in the chorus for years.   (has) sung
7. My father (past of see) *Star Wars* five times.   saw
8. I feel as if I (past participle of know) the Feldmans all my life.   (have known)
9. Muriel (past of go) for a long walk with her dog.   went
10. It looks like Clark (past participle of fall) off his bike.   (has) fallen

Principal Parts of Common Irregular Verbs

Present	Past	Past Participle
begin	began	(have) begun
break	broke	(have) broken
bring	brought	(have) brought
choose	chose	(have) chosen
come	came	(have) come
do	did	(have) done
drink	drank	(have) drunk
eat	ate	(have) eaten
fall	fell	(have) fallen
fly	flew	(have) flown
freeze	froze	(have) frozen
give	gave	(have) given
go	went	(have) gone
grow	grew	(have) grown
have	had	(have) had
know	knew	(have) known
lay	laid	(have) laid
lie	lay	(have) lain
ride	rode	(have) ridden
ring	rang	(have) rung
rise	rose	(have) risen
run	ran	(have) run
say	said	(have) said
see	saw	(have) seen
sing	sang	(have) sung
sit	sat	(have) sat
speak	spoke	(have) spoken
steal	stole	(have) stolen
swim	swam	(have) swum
take	took	(have) taken
teach	taught	(have) taught
wear	wore	(have) worn
write	wrote	(have) written

78

Additional Resources

Skills Practice Book—
pages 33–34, 204–220

Teacher's Resource Binder
Reinforcement Activities—
page 34
Enrichment Activities—
page 58

Exercises   Using Irregular Verbs

▶ Analyzing

A. Number your paper from 1 to 10. Rewrite each of the following sentences. Change the present form in parentheses to the past form.

1. The frisbee contest (begin) an hour ago. began
2. Our hoe (break), so we can't plant the garden. broke
3. Sue (write) the sign using calligraphy. wrote
4. Jack's beanstalk (grow) high into the clouds. grew
5. Seth (ride) his pony to the fiesta. rode
6. Carol (bring) helium balloons to the party. brought
7. Before breakfast, I (swim) ten laps. swam
8. On Christmas morning, all the churches in the village (ring) their bells. rang
9. The monarch butterflies (fly) from Canada to Mexico. flew
10. Coach Baily (teach) me to play soccer. taught

B. Number your paper from 1 to 10. Write the correct form of the verb in parentheses for each sentence. Helping verbs will vary.

1. Pete Rose (past of *steal*) second base. stole
2. Puffs of smoke (past of *rise*) from the chimney. rose
3. The ice on the skating pond is (past participle of *freeze*). frozen
4. The clues have (past participle of *fall*) into place. fallen
5. The Kahn family (past of *go*) to Jeckyl Island. went
6. My sisters have (past participle of *eat*) all the pizza. eaten
7. Becky has (past participle of *run*) in marathons. run
8. Nobody (past of *know*) where the treasure was. knew
9. The chickens had (past participle of *lay*) many eggs. laid
10. Dr. Hirasawa (past of *speak*) to our team about safety in sports. spoke

▶ Creative Application

C. Writing Imagine that you entered a time machine and noticed two red buttons marked *Plymouth Rock, 1620* A.D., and *The Moon, 1969* A.D. You pushed one and instantly moved back in time. Write a paragraph about what you saw and did. Use the past and past participle forms of verbs in your paragraph.

79

Part 8

Objective

To choose the correct verb from these pairs that are often confused: *can, may; let, leave; lie, lay*

Presenting the Lesson

 All Students

1. Read and discuss page 80. Discuss the right meaning of the examples and the wrong meaning that results from the wrong choice. Have the students give more examples of sentences correctly using these verbs.

2. Assign and discuss Exercises A, B, and C on page 81. Before beginning Exercise C, students may enjoy discussing "Miserable Mervin" and the possible problems he could cause.

 Basic Students

One way to avoid choosing the wrong verb is to read each sentence, using key words in the definition in place of the word. Have students substitute the key words in each of the example sentences in this lesson. Then, before assigning Exercises A and B, do the same for the first few questions in each exercise.

 Advanced Students

Have the students write two sentences for each of the following verbs: *can, may, leave, let, lie,* and *lay.* Have the students write their sentences on posters. Display the posters in the classroom. This will provide visual reinforcement of correct usage for other students.

Special Populations

NSD Many of these word pairs are commonly misused in dialects. Students need oral drill in order to recognize and use these verbs correctly.

Reinforcement

1. Have the students follow the directions for Exercise A on page 81 using these sentences:

1. (<u>May</u>, Can) I borrow your pencil?
2. The white mice were (<u>let</u>, leave) out of the cage.

---

8 Confusing Pairs of Verbs

> **Focus**
>
> Several pairs of verbs are often confused. These include *can* and *may*, *let* and *leave*, and *lie* and *lay*.

▶ Comprehension

Look at the correct way to use these confusing verbs.

Can and **May**
1. *Can* means "to be able."
2. *May* means "to allow" or "to permit."

Melissa *can* run the fastest.
You *may* go to the concert.

Let and **Leave**
1. *Let* means "to allow" or "to permit."
2. *Leave* means "to depart" or "to let stay or be."

Let me see your scrapbook.
What time do you *leave* for school?
Leave the dog in the yard.

Lie and **Lay**
1. *Lie* means "to rest" or "recline."
2. *Lay* means "to put or place something."

My cat often *lies* on the windowsill.
Lay paper on the floor before you paint.

Lay also means to produce eggs: A hen *lays* eggs.

Exercises Using Verbs Correctly

▶ Recalling

A. Number your paper from 1 to 10. Choose the right verb from the parentheses. Write it on your paper.

1. You're (lying, laying) on my towel.
2. (May, Can) Marcia and Fred really read that fast?
3. Certainly Jean (may, can) leave her bike in our garage.
4. (Let, Leave) the needle of the compass settle.
5. I like to (lie, lay) on the couch when I read.
6. (May, Can) we take Trudy to the boat races tomorrow?
7. Cindy always (lets, leaves) her coat on the sofa.
8. Bricklayers (lie, lay) bricks with a trowel.
9. The bus (lets, leaves) from Fountain Square hourly.
10. (May, Can) I carry those packages for you?

▶ Analyzing

B. Number your paper from 1 to 10. If a verb is incorrect, write the correct form. If the verb is correct, write *Correct*.

1. May I see your slides? Correct
2. The fishing net leaves all the minnows through. lets
3. The lions laid still in the heat. lay
4. Don't lay your coat on the chair. Correct
5. Can Chris and I go out in the canoe? May
6. Let your wet umbrella on the porch. Leave
7. The terrier lays on the front steps all afternoon. lies
8. Can you read the bottom line without glasses? Correct
9. Don't ever lie plastic dishes on the hot stove. lay
10. "Please leave me stay up late," begged Karen. let

▶ Creative Application

C. Writing You often baby-sit for your three-year-old neighbor, "Miserable" Mervin Malone, but you are unable to sit this Saturday. Mrs. Malone has asked you to write brief notes for Mervin's new sitter. Using the words below, write some of the important things the sitter will need to know.

can	lie	leave
may	lay	let

3. (Can, May) you draw a picture of that house on the corner?
4. Hannah will (lay, lie) the dishes on the kitchen table.
5. All of you (can, may) take a break now.
6. The legendary golden goose (lies, lays) golden eggs.
7. A fire can (let, leave) the house in ruins.
8. (May, Can) Becky and I collect the test papers?
9. (Let, Leave) me try to thread the sewing machine.
10. Nancy was (laying, lying) in her tent.

2. Have the students follow the directions for Exercise B on page 81 using these sentences:

1. Elena likes to lie on the rug.
   correct
2. Were you laying in the sun?
   lying
3. Beth's dog can catch a frisbee.
   correct
4. May I play the part of the prince?
   correct
5. Don't let your bike on the porch.
   leave
6. Lay your wet raincoat over the chair.
   correct
7. Mr. Costa is lying tile in the bathroom.
   laying
8. May this table seat eight people?
   Can
9. Let the cookies on the plate.
   Leave
10. Leave me finish my homework.
    Let

81

Additional Resources

Skills Practice Book—page 35

Teacher's Resource Binder
Reinforcement Activities—
page 35

Part 9

Objective

To choose the correct verb from these pairs that are often confused: *teach, learn; rise, raise; sit, set*

Presenting the Lesson

 All Students

1. Read and discuss page 82. Discuss the correct meaning of the examples given for each verb pair. Point out the wrong meaning that occurs with an incorrect choice. Ask the students to give additional examples of sentences using these verbs.

2. Assign and discuss Exercises A, B, and C on page 83. As students proofread their work for Exercise C, have them check for correct spelling and use of all verbs.

3. Use Exercise H on page 87 for additional practice as needed.

 Basic Students

Have students restate the exercise sentences using key words from the definitions in place of the verbs in order to determine the correct choice.

 Advanced Students

Have students expand the posters they began in part 8, adding sentences with the verbs in this part.

Reinforcement

1. Have the students follow the directions for Exercise A on page 83 using these sentences:

1. Mr. Giannini (teaches, learns) our gym class.
2. Smoke (raised, rises) from the cottage's chimney.
3. The seals (teach, learn) tricks from their trainers.
4. Tory (set, sits) the planter on the windowsill.
5. The mythical phoenix (rises, raises) from its own ashes.
6. The lion (set, sits) at the entrance of its den.
7. Debby is (learning, teaching) Paul to dance.
8. The movers will (rise, raise) the piano with a forklift.

---

9 Other Confusing Pairs of Verbs

> **Focus**
>
> Other verb pairs that are often confused are these: *teach* and *learn*, *rise* and *raise*, and *sit* and *set*.

▶ Comprehension

You have learned about some verbs that are often confused. Here are more of these verb pairs.

> **Teach and Learn**
>
> 1. *Teach* means "to show how" or "to explain."
> 2. *Learn* means "to understand" or "to gain knowledge."

Now I will *teach* you to play chess.
The kindergartners will *learn* to tie laces.

> **Rise and Raise**
>
> 1. *Rise* means "to move upward" or "to get up."
> 2. *Raise* means "to move something upward" or "to lift."

If we *rise* early enough, we can watch the sunrise.
Raise your hand and ask Mr. Kelly your question.

> **Sit and Set**
>
> 1. *Sit* means "to be in a seat" or "to rest."
> 2. *Set* means "to put or place something."

The captain *sits* in the cockpit.
Set the casserole on the table.

Exercises   Using the Right Verb

▶ Recalling

A. Number your paper from 1 to 10. Choose the correct verb from the parentheses. Write it on your paper.

1. (Teach, Learn) me how to make popcorn.
2. After the long hike, I wanted to (sit, set) and relax.
3. Kathy should (rise, raise) and take her place on stage.
4. (Sit, Set) still while I take your picture.
5. Ron will (teach, learn) me the basic swimming strokes.
6. Can Mr. Scot (rise, raise) the sail himself?
7. (Teach, Learn) Jessica and me how to throw a lasso.
8. The hockey stick was (sitting, setting) where I left it.
9. He was (teaching, learning) us to eat with chopsticks.
10. Did Jill (rise, raise) the flag this morning?

▶ Analyzing

B. If the verb in each of the following sentences is incorrect, write the correct form. If there is no error, write *Correct*.

1. Fay is learning her parakeet to talk.   teaching
2. Did the drum major rise his baton?   raise
3. Muff perked up his ears, wagged his tail, and set up.   sat
4. Will you learn me to play checkers?   teach
5. The huge, hot air balloon began to rise.   Correct
6. Mary climbed the rock and sat down.   Correct
7. Is the moon raising earlier or later?   rising
8. Angela would like to learn yoga.   Correct
9. Sit down your catcher's mitt and retrieve balls.   Set
10. I found Jud setting on a bench in the park.   sitting

▶ Creative Application

C. Writing You spent a month at Camp Thunderbolt. Using the ideas below, write three entries in your camp diary.

Day 1 - Describe waking in the morning. Use *rise* and *raise*.
Day 2 - Describe some camp activities. Use *teach* and *learn*.
Day 3 - Describe the preparations for a cookout. Use *sit* and *set*.

9. The jeweler (sits, sets) a diamond in the center of the ring.
10. The bread dough must (raise, rise) before we bake it.

2. Have the students follow the directions for Exercise B on page 83 using these sentences:

1. You have to sit still to fish.   correct
2. Do they raise only corn in Kansas?   correct
3. Louise didn't even rise her voice.   raise
4. Please learn me how to ski.   teach
5. Uncle Frank usually sets up waiting for me.   sits
6. The barometer is rising.   correct
7. Learn the students the new song.   teach
8. Raise that curtain a few inches.
9. Sit that vase over in the corner.   set
10. Agnes taught many people to knit.   correct

Enrichment

Write the following assignment on the board.

Imagine that you are taking flying lessons. You are, however, not learning how to fly a plane. You are learning to fly like a bird. Write a dialogue between your teacher and yourself. Correctly use the following verb pairs: *can* and *may*; *let* and *leave*; *sit* and *set*; *learn* and *teach*; *raise* and *rise*; and *lie* and *lay*.

83

Additional Resources

Skills Practice Book—page 36
Teacher's Resource Binder
Reinforcement Activities—
page 36

Exercises for Mastery

These **Exercises for Mastery** may be used for additional practice of the concepts presented in this section. Each exercise focuses on a single concept, and should be used after the page number indicated in parentheses.

Verbs for Writing Power

▶ Recalling/Classifying/Analyzing

A. Finding Action Verbs and State-of-Being Verbs Make two columns on your paper. Head one column *Action Verbs* (AV) and the other *State-of-Being Verbs* (SB). Find the verb in each sentence and place it in the right column. (Use after page 64.)

1. The spider web <u>was</u> delicate and lacy. SB
2. Catherine <u>considered</u> the question carefully. A
3. <u>Were</u> you at the bicycle shop this morning? SB
4. I <u>am</u> certain about the address. SB
5. The grandfather clock <u>chimes</u> every hour. A
6. Brian <u>knows</u> about the battle of Saratoga. A
7. <u>Are</u> you Doctor Cleveland? SB
8. The village <u>slept</u> under the stars. A
9. <u>Were</u> the coyotes near the campsite last night? SB
10. Ivy <u>clung</u> to the crumbling chimney. A

B. Mastering Main Verbs and Helping Verbs Number your paper from 1 to 10. Make two columns. Head the first column *Helping Verbs*. Head the second *Main Verb*. Write the verbs for each of these sentences in the correct column. (Use after page 67.)

1. <u>Did</u> you <u>watch</u> the eclipse of the moon?
2. A thermometer <u>will be</u> <u>needed</u> to check the temperature of the water.
3. The sales clerk <u>had been</u> wrong about the price of the jacket.
4. I <u>may have</u> <u>pushed</u> the wrong button.
5. What else <u>could</u> we <u>say</u>?
6. That delegate <u>may have</u> <u>voted</u> against me.
7. The children were just <u>pretending</u>.
8. The fire <u>could have</u> <u>destroyed</u> the entire block.
9. The river <u>has</u> <u>risen</u> fifteen inches this spring.
10. Carol and Diane <u>have been</u> <u>collecting</u> seashells.

84

Additional Resources

Skills Practice Book
Mixed Practice—pages 37–38

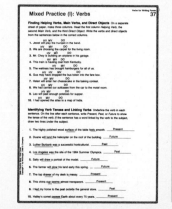

C. Recognizing Direct Objects Number your paper from 1 to 10. Write the verb in each sentence. Then write the direct object of the verb. (Use after page 69.)

1. Carrie delivers newspapers.
2. The kitten chased a slow, brown mole.
3. A snake can shed its skin.
4. The police have closed our street to traffic for the block party.
5. Spelunkers explore caves.
6. My aunt and uncle own a farm in Iowa.
7. I have been taking lessons in figure skating for three years.
8. Have you ever played rugby?
9. Joanna studied Portuguese before she took her trip to Brazil.
10. Pony Express riders changed horses every ten miles.

D. Finding Linking Verbs Number your paper from 1 to 10. Make two columns. Head the first column *Linking Verbs*. Head the second column *Action Verbs*. Write the verbs for each of these sentences in the correct column. (Use after page 71.)

1. The snail disappeared into its shell.
2. The trip seemed shorter on the way home.
3. This surprise party was my idea.
4. We remodeled our basement.
5. Ocean breezes always smell delightful.
6. The workers are building a new museum.
7. Yolanda collects shells of all kinds.
8. Hinduism is the major religion of India.
9. That noise in the attic sounds eerie.
10. Someone pulled the fire alarm.

85

Exercises For Mastery Continued

E. Recognizing Verb Tenses Number your paper from 1 to 10. Tell the tense of each verb in italics. Write *Present*, *Past*, or *Future*. (Use after page 74.)

1. Al and Jim *waited* for their bus. Past
2. My dog *chases* cats and squirrels. Present
3. A plane *lands* at the international airport every twenty-eight seconds. Present
4. The artist *splattered* paint all over his canvas. Past
5. We *watch* the news on television every night. Present
6. Mark *will call* by ten o'clock. Future
7. The marketplace *buzzes* with busy shoppers. Present
8. The peacock *will fan* his tail feathers for his mate to see. Future
9. I *looked* everywhere for my lost shoe. Past
10. Susan *will study* for an hour at the library. Future

F. Recognizing Principal Parts Number your paper from 1 to 10. Write the verb in each sentence. Then tell whether the verb is in the present, past, or past participle form. (Use after page 76.)

1. The carpenters have sanded all the desks. past participle
2. The excited pitcher waved the championship trophy high over his head. past
3. A monkey's tail curls tightly around a branch. present
4. Anita had finished her painting. past participle
5. Magnolia blossoms fall in the heavy rain. present
6. The bristle worms feed on coral. present
7. Four young sparrows begged for food. past
8. That waterfall has poured over the cliff for hundreds of years. past participle
9. Krista organized the scavenger hunt. past
10. King Arthur called together the Knights of the Round Table. past

86

G. Using Irregular Verbs Number your paper from 1 to 10. Write the form of the verb asked for in each of the following sentences. (Use after page 79.) Helping verbs with participles will vary.

1. The telephone (past of *ring*) three times and stopped. rang
2. Charlie Brown always (past of *lose*) the game. lost
3. The actor (past participle of *forget*) his lines. (has) forgotten
4. The choir (future of *begin*) caroling at the hospital on Sunday mornings. will begin
5. He (present of *know*) the answer to the riddle. knows
6. Miners (past participle of *dig*) in this ground for minerals. (have) dug
7. Charlayne (past of *go*) to see the penguins. went
8. Jenina (past of *catch*) a large salmon. caught
9. Alice (past of *shrink*) when she drank from the bottle. shrank
10. Sitting Bull (past of *fight*) in the Battle of Little Bighorn. fought

H. Choosing the Right Verb Number your paper from 1 to 10. Choose the right verb from the parentheses. Write it on your paper. (Use after page 83.)

1. (Rise, **Raise**) the lid and insert the tape.
2. Don't (sit, **set**) that brush on the wet paint.
3. Who (**teaches**, learns) the players to punt?
4. The spray (**rises**, raises) high above the falls.
5. (Let, **Leave**) the huckleberries that aren't ripe yet.
6. Mark can (lie, **lay**) tile as fast as his father.
7. The panther (**sits**, sets) quietly in a tree until his prey appears.
8. (**Let**, Leave) me help you put the train set together.
9. Eric likes to (**lie**, lay) on the beach on sunny days.
10. Gary, (can, **may**) I please see your stamp collection?

87

Using Grammar in Writing

These challenging and enjoyable activities allow the students to see how the concepts of grammar, usage, and mechanics may be applied in actual writing situations. Each exercise is designed to give students practice in several of the skills they have acquired in this section. The activities also provide opportunities for students to write creatively about a wide variety of interesting and unusual subjects.

As students complete these activities, remind them to follow the process of writing. Be sure to allow adequate time for prewriting activities. Individual conferences or peer-group sessions may be used for help with drafting and revision.

For Exercise C, bring to class a variety of resources on these three topics. Allow the students sufficient time to read before they begin to write.

Using Grammar in Writing

▶ Creative Application

A. Imagine that the World's Best Stuntperson Contest was held in your town. Write a paragraph describing what each of the three finalists did. Tell who won and explain why he or she was the best.

▶ Sequence/Creative Application

B. You and your friends are in the cave at Haggar Hill. You are trying to convince your friends not to be afraid because the cave is not haunted. Then you discover you are wrong. It *is* haunted! Write a story about your adventure.

First, explain why you agreed to go into the cave. Then, describe what you are seeing and doing in the cave at this time. Finally, tell how you will feel when you get out.

▶ Creative Application

C. Using Verbs in History Choose one of the following "firsts" in history. Read about it in an encyclopedia. Then write a brief paragraph in your own words. Tell about this famous first in history. Write your story in the past tense. Then write it in the present tense. Notice how the story comes alive when you give a present tense account.

1. Gold is discovered in California.
2. Orville and Wilbur Wright fly the first airplane.
3. Sir Edmund Hillary climbs Mt. Everest.

Additional Resources

Skills Practice Book
  Using Verbs in Writing—
    page 39

Chapter 4 Review

▶Classifying/Analyzing

A. Finding Verbs and Direct Objects Number your paper from 1 to 10. Write the <u>complete verb</u> in each sentence. Tell whether it is an action verb or a state-of-being verb. Then write the <u>direct object</u> of each action verb.

1. The glass ornaments <u>appear</u> fragile. state-of-being verb
2. The bird <u>might have hurt</u> its wing. action verb
3. <u>Grill</u> the steaks for fifteen minutes. action verb
4. Martin <u>is hanging</u> his coat in his locker. action verb
5. The cellar <u>smelled</u> musty. state-of-being verb
6. Sara <u>spiked</u> the volleyball over the net. action verb
7. Mexico and Canada <u>are</u> both neighbors of the United States. state-of-being verb
8. Black-and-white cows contentedly <u>chewed</u> their cuds among the daisies. action verb
9. The Pacific <u>may be</u> the deepest ocean. state-of-being verb
10. Ernie <u>could</u> never <u>have ridden</u> that wild horse. action verb

B. Using Verbs Correctly Number your paper from 1 to 10. Choose the correct verb from the parentheses. Write it on your own paper.

1. (Can, <u>May</u>) I borrow your tennis racket?
2. Ling will (<u>teach</u>, learn) me about Chinese food.
3. The bat (<u>lies</u>, lays) near the dugout.
4. The peanuts (been, <u>have been</u>) on the counter since dinner yesterday.
5. Carman had (ran, <u>run</u>) his remote control car.
6. The baby has (drank, <u>drunk</u>) all her pineapple juice.
7. The audience (<u>sang</u>, sung) along with the group of performers on stage.
8. Beth really (done, <u>did</u>) a double back flip!
9. Sandra, please (lie, <u>lay</u>) that carpet on the floor.
10. I (rise, <u>raise</u>) the shades every morning.

89

Additional Resources

Skills Practice Book
Review—page 40

Test Booklet
Mastery Test—pages 19–22

Chapter Review

These exercises provide review of the concepts presented in this section. Each exercise challenges the students to apply several of the skills they have acquired during previous study.

Because the "mixed" feature on these activities makes them more difficult, the teacher may wish to have basic students do the exercises orally or in small groups.

Chapter 5

Chapter Objectives

1. To understand the function of the paragraph and to recognize good paragraphs

2. To identify a topic sentence in a paragraph by its function

3. To write good topic sentences

Motivating the Students

1. Read and discuss page 91.

2. Have the students thumb through their texts. Point out that all of the lessons are divided into paragraphs.

3. Make copies or use an overhead projector to study the three paragraphs excerpted from *The Great White* by Jane and Paul Annixter. Point out that each paragraph is indented. Ask the students to identify the main idea of each paragraph. Ask if all sentences are related to the main idea. Answers will vary.

Moveless (the polar bear) waited, her narrow black-tipped muzzle pointed out across the swirling waters. On the edge of a big floe the dark form of a ringed seal stood out against the white. It was nearly a quarter of a mile away, but as usual the bear's keen wet nose told the story.

The bull seal was dim of sight. He trusted mainly to his acute hearing and to submarine vibrations for safety and for prey. In his element under water his microphone eardrums and the whole of his sensitized body were like a radar system, and he could track and swim down the fastest fish. It was on land or ice that he was handicapped.

Out in the open water to leeward of the seal's floe, many big ice pans and small ice cakes were floating. The smallest of these kept to the line of whitecaps breaking against the far side of the floe. Strangely, it was scarcely tossed by the waves but seemed to have a will of its own. When it was just abreast of the seal's flow, it suddenly sank. A few moments later, from out of the white smother of spray almost beneath the bull seal's nose, there rose the startling head and shoulders of a second polar bear.

—Jane and Paul Annixter

Week 7

Chapter Management Guidelines
This chart may be used to help structure daily lesson plans.

Day 1	Day 2	Day 3	Day 4	Day 5
Chapter 5 Opener, p. 91; Part 1, "What Is a Paragraph?" pp. 92–94	Part 2, "Good Topic Sentences," pp. 95–97	Chapter Review and selected end-of-chapter activities	Chapter 6 Opener, p. 101; Part 1, "Prewriting: Finding Ideas," pp. 102–103; Part 2, "Prewriting: Choosing and Limiting a Topic," pp. 104–105	Part 3, "Prewriting: Developing a Topic," pp. 106–107

Chapter 5

Learning About Paragraphs

Do you know how a car is put together on an assembly line? As the car moves along, more and more parts are added. All of these parts must work together. If a part is missing or misplaced, the car may not work well.

Writing a paragraph is somewhat like assembling a car. A paragraph is built with sentences. The sentences all work together to tell about one main idea. If any sentences in a paragraph are missing or out of place, the paragraph may not explain the main idea well.

In this chapter, you will study the basic parts of a paragraph—the topic sentence and supporting sentences. Knowing what a good paragraph should include is the first step to writing one yourself.

91

Special Populations

ESL Read example paragraphs out loud. Your inflections and tonal changes will aid their comprehension.

NSD Give students extra exercises. Some NSD students create "paragraphs" by extensive use of run-on or stringy sentences.

Related Chapters

You may wish to refer to related material in other chapters as you teach the following concepts:

1. Using the writing process, Chapter 6, "Choosing a Process for Writing," page 101

2. Writing that explains, Chapter 10, "The Process of Explaining *How*," page 177

3. Narrative writing, Chapter 13, "The Process of Narrative Writing," page 225

4. Description, Chapter 19, "Description and the Process of Writing," page 331

5. Writing to explain why, Chapter 22, "Writing About Opinions", page 379

Additional Resources

Skills Practice Book—pages 41–44

Test Booklet—pages 23–26
  Pretest—pages 23–24
  Mastery Test—pages 25–26

Teacher's Resource Binder
  Reinforcement Activities—
    pages 37–38
  Enrichment Activities—
    pages 1–2, 11, 39–52, 59–61
  Process of Writing Transparencies
  Ideas for Creative Teaching

Part 1

Objective

To understand the function of the paragraph and to recognize good paragraphs

Presenting the Lesson

 All Students

1. Read the text and the examples on pages 92–93. Emphasize that a *main idea* is what a paragraph is about, and that each paragraph should be about just one main idea. Each sentence in the paragraph must tell something about the main idea. Also point out that a paragraph is always indented.

Be sure the students understand why the first passage is not a good paragraph and the second one is. Have students tell the main idea of the second paragraph.

2. Assign and discuss the exercise on pages 93–94.

Paragraphs 1 and 3 are the good paragraphs. For these paragraphs, ask the students to state the main idea of each paragraph, and then ask them to list the supporting details. Paragraphs 2 and 5 are not good because they include sentences that do not tell about the main idea. Have the students identify those sentences. Paragraph 4 is not good because it presents several ideas, not one main idea.

 Basic Students

Do the exercises as a classroom activity.

Provide the students with examples of good paragraphs. Have them identify the main idea of each paragraph. (Either find a good selection of paragraphs from magazines or books, or use paragraphs taken from old reading texts or tests.)

 Advanced Students

Have the students rewrite paragraph 4, so that it will be a good paragraph. Explain that for paragraph 4 they must choose one main idea and then perhaps do some research. Point out that each sentence in paragraph 4 could be a main idea.

---

1 What Is a Paragraph?

┌─ *Focus* ─────────────────────────────┐

A paragraph is a group of sentences. The sentences all tell about one **main idea**.

└──┘

▶ Comprehension

A writer expresses ideas in sentences. The sentences are arranged in paragraphs. In a paragraph, all the sentences work together to tell one main idea. Read this paragraph.

> There was no price that could be put on Sounder's voice. It came out of the great chest cavity and broad jaws as though it had bounced off the walls of a cave. It mellowed into half-echo before it touched the air. It was louder and clearer than any purebred's voice. Each bark bounced from slope to slope in the foothills like a rubber ball. It was not an ordinary bark. It filled up the night and made music. —WILLIAM ARMSTRONG

▶ Drawing Conclusions

The first sentence of the paragraph says that Sounder's voice was special. This is the main idea of the paragraph. All of the other sentences tell about the main idea. They talk about the things that kept Sounder's bark from being ordinary.

Notice that the first line of the paragraph is indented. It begins a few spaces to the right. The first sentence in a paragraph is always indented.

The group of sentences below looks like a paragraph. However, it is not really a paragraph at all. See if you can tell why.

> Pigeons are good at living in the city. Some pigeons are brown, some are gray, and some are black. Once my brother caught a pigeon and tried to train it. Carrier pigeons have flown thousands of miles.

This group of sentences does not have one main idea. It has four. Each one of these sentences could be the main idea of a separate paragraph.

92

Now see how the paragraph could be improved.

Pigeons are good at living in the city. They can live in just about any sheltered place—under railroad tracks, tucked under the edges of roofs, in gutters, in garages. Loud city noises don't scare pigeons a bit. People don't frighten them, either. In fact, they like living near people because people often feed them.

Remember that a good paragraph has only one main idea. It is made up of complete sentences. All these sentences work together to tell about the main idea.

Exercise Studying Paragraphs

▶ Analyzing/Evaluating

Read the following paragraphs. Use what you have learned to decide if each is a good paragraph. Explain your reasons.

1. Baseball is truly an international sport. The major U.S. leagues include two teams in Canada. The sport is popular in many Latin American countries and is also a major sport in Japan. There, games sometimes attract more than 30,000 fans. good paragraph

2. Flapjack has strange habits for a parakeet. She likes to sleep late in the morning. I like to sleep late too, but Mom always wakes me. Flapjack's crabby all day if someone wakes her before ten. Last Saturday morning, I was crabby. I had to get up early and mow the lawn. Flapjack settles down after her usual breakfast of a pancake spread with peanut butter. Not a good paragraph; underlined sentences are not about the main idea.

3. Snack-sized pizzas are easy to make. First, toast and butter half an English muffin. Spread a thin layer of spaghetti or pizza sauce on the muffin. Add extras such as cooked hamburger, onions, olives, and mushrooms. Put mozzarella cheese on top. Broil three to five minutes or until the cheese is melted. good paragraph

93

Additional Resources

Skills Practice Book—page 41
Teacher's Resource Binder
Reinforcement Activities—
page 37
Enrichment Activities—
page 59

Special Populations

LD Some students may have difficulty locating the main idea. See the activity under **Basic Students**.

ESL For reinforcement, provide paragraphs on a slightly lower reading level. Let students identify the main ideas in each paragraph.

Reinforcement

Duplicate the following paragraphs for the students. Have the students identify the main idea of each paragraph and any sentences that do not refer to the main idea. (The sentences that do not belong are underlined.)

1. Wild chestnut was very plentiful in the mountains before the blight killed it all. It grew very straight, sometimes four to five feet in diameter, was fairly soft and light, easily split and worked, and lasted forever. In fact, the stumps of huge chestnuts cut fifty years ago still dot the mountain slopes. It was the favorite wood of the old timers, and it was used for almost everything.

—Eliot Wigginton

2. The surface of the planet Mercury is similar to our Moon. Both have many craters. There is no water or air on either of them. Someday I hope to go to the moon. It would be an exciting challenge to travel in space.

Enrichment

1. From a source outside the classroom, have each student provide an example of writing that is divided into paragraphs. These sources might include an encyclopedia, a favorite book, a magazine, or a newspaper. Have students underline the main idea in each paragraph. Assemble a bulletin board display around this theme: Paragraphs Are Everywhere.

2. For additional enrichment activities, see the Unit Projects in the Teacher Notes on page 3. One or more of these projects have special activities for gifted and talented students.

4. Wearing braces on your teeth has some good points. Three students in Mr. Chen's math class got braces the same week. New metals and ways of putting on braces mean that they work better in a shorter time. People with braces often feel shy about them at first. My Mom says it's better to have braces for a few years than to have crooked teeth your whole life. Not a good paragraph; there is no main idea.

5. The removal of the Cherokees from Georgia during the winter of 1838–39 is known as the Trail of Tears. That winter U.S. troops forced seventeen thousand men, women, and children to march through snow and bitter cold. Most were barefoot. All were hungry. <u>One famous Cherokee named Sequoya invented a system for writing the Cherokee language. The California redwood trees are called sequoias in honor of this leader.</u> Almost a fourth of the Cherokee people died on the Trail of Tears. Not a good paragraph; underlined sentences are not about the main idea.

94

2 Good Topic Sentences

Focus

A **topic sentence** presents the main idea of a paragraph.

▶ Comprehension/Making Inferences

The sentences in a paragraph work together to explain one idea. The main idea of a paragraph is often stated in a topic sentence. Usually the topic sentence is the first sentence in a paragraph. It lets the reader know what the rest of the sentences are going to be about.

Read the following paragraph. What is the topic sentence of this paragraph? What main idea does it express?

> Eskimos waste nothing and are geniuses at putting everything to use. Their winter clothes are made from the fur of several kinds of animals found in the region. Tough hides and a few strips of wood are fashioned into slim canoes, or kayaks, in which they paddle far out into the ice-filled seas to catch seals, walruses, and white whales. The raw, oily "blubber" of these great beasts is a favorite Eskimo food. When the blubber is heated, it yields oil, which used to be burned in stone lamps.
>
> —from *The Best in Children's Literature*

Writing Good Topic Sentences

A good topic sentence does two important jobs. First, it states the main idea of a paragraph. Second, the topic sentence must catch the reader's attention. Read the following topic sentences. Do they make you want to read more of the paragraphs that they begin?

> I'm going to write about Samantha, who was good at solving mysteries.
> This story is about a werewolf.

95

Objectives

1. To identify a topic sentence in a paragraph by its function
2. To write good topic sentences

Presenting the Lesson

 All Students

1. Read and discuss pages 95–96 up to **Limiting the Topic.** Emphasize that a topic sentence states the main idea of a paragraph and that the rest of the sentences develop the idea in the topic sentence. Study the example thoroughly. After the students identify the first sentence as the topic sentence, discuss how each of the other sentences in the paragraph supports the topic.

Mention that the topic sentence is not always the first sentence in a paragraph.

2. Discuss writing interesting topic sentences. Have the students change the following dull topic sentences into informative and interesting ones.

The baby was cute.

This is about skiing.

I'm going to write about Mike, who runs in marathon races.

Italian food is good.

3. Read **Limiting the Topic** on page 96. Ask the students if the following topic sentences are appropriate for a paragraph or if they should be more limited. Have students suggest ideas for supporting each topic sentence. Supporting details will vary.

a. The U.S. Congress is a branch of our government. too broad

b. Applying clown make-up is an art. appropriate

c. The marathon is a well-known Olympic event. appropriate

d. The aroma of dinner cooking drew me into the kitchen. appropriate

e. Snakes come in many varieties. too broad

4. Assign and discuss Exercises A and B on page 97.

Basic Students

To reinforce writing topic sentence skills, follow the directions for Exercise A on page 97 using the sentences below.

1. I am going to explain how to mow the lawn. dull
2. After the storm, we awoke to a scene of destruction. interesting
3. This paragraph is about early railroads. dull
4. The Cherokee Indians were the only tribe with a written alphabet. interesting

Advanced Students

Have the students find two examples, in their reading or another textbook, of paragraphs in which the topic sentence appears first and is followed by at least three supporting sentences that refer to the main idea stated in the topic sentence. Students should find one example paragraph in which the first sentence is not the topic sentence.

Special Populations

LD For students with severe reading difficulty, paragraphs could be tape recorded. Students could give topic sentences orally.

Reinforcement

Duplicate the following paragraphs for the students. Have them write an interesting topic sentence that states the main idea for each paragraph. Also have them explain what each supporting sentence adds to the main idea.

1. I walked down our street but couldn't find my dog. I called out his name but he didn't come. So I was becoming worried. Then I smelled barbecued steak being cooked in the Elliots' back yard. Patches loves meat, and I wondered if he had smelled the steak too. Sure enough, I found Patches by the grill, whining and begging Mr. Elliot for some meat.

Each of these topic sentences states the main idea of a paragraph. However, neither of them is interesting enough to catch the reader's attention. A good topic sentence never begins with such words as "I am going to write about . . ." or "My paragraph is about . . . ." An interesting topic sentence is written so that the reader wants to read on.

Look at these revised topic sentences.

> Samantha was a super sleuth.
> Part wolf, part man, the werewolf howled at the full moon.

These topic sentences present the main ideas and interest the reader. The reader wonders, "What mysteries has Samantha solved?" and "What is the werewolf about to do?" The reader wants to read the paragraphs to find the answers to these questions.

Limiting the Topic

As you write a topic sentence, think of it as an umbrella. It is one sentence that covers, or takes in, all the other sentences in the paragraph. However, be sure that the main idea expressed by the topic sentence can be covered in one paragraph. If necessary, narrow the main idea of a topic sentence. You should be able to tell about the idea in just one paragraph.

Guidelines for Writing a Topic Sentence

As you write topic sentences, keep the following important points in mind.

1. A topic sentence should tell what the paragraph is about.
2. A topic sentence should be interesting enough to catch the reader's attention.
3. A topic sentence should present an idea that is narrow enough to be covered in one paragraph.

Exercises Good Topic Sentences

▶ Analyzing/Structured Application

A. Read the topic sentences below. Tell which sentences are interesting and which are not. Then rewrite the dull sentences to make them more interesting.

1. Frightened and injured, the only survivor made his way through the thick jungle. Interesting
2. I'm going to tell you about my best friend. Dull
3. *Incredible* is the only word to describe Kareem Abdul-Jabbar. Interesting
4. I taught my pet dog some tricks. Dull
5. Coral, which comes in unusual shapes and delicate colors, is actually a type of skeleton. Interesting
6. This paragraph is about camping. Dull

▶ Structured Application

B. Here are three groups of sentences. Make them into paragraphs by writing a topic sentence for each group. Be sure that each topic sentence tells what the other sentences in the group are about.
Answers will vary. Sample sentences are provided.

1. Mexico has had a powerful influence on U.S. culture. The food of Mexico has become popular in all parts of the country. Many Mexican words have become part of the English language. Mexican music has influenced American music. Mexican designs have been used in American houses, especially in the Southwest.

2. The African lion was magnificent . His coat and mane were soft gold. He stood, straight and proud, looking over the grasslands. He gave a long, powerful roar. He was the master of the kingdom.

3. Jewelry has always played an important role in people's lives . Long ago the people of East Africa used jewelry as weapons. The Aztecs of Mexico used it to show a person's place in society. Jewelry has been worn for its magical powers and as a way of remembering people. For example, in the 1800's some British women wore bracelets made of the braided hair of dead relatives.

2. January had borrowed the winds of March and was using them overtime. Ice spewed out of the ground. Rags and paper were wrapped around faucets to keep them from freezing. Broken window panes were stuffed with rags. Window cracks were jammed with paper. Beds were weighted down with homemade quilts and old overcoats and clothes. Men and boys wore two pairs of trousers. Girls and old ladies bundled up like babes.

—Sylvester Leaks

Enrichment

Duplicate several one-paragraph news articles for the class. Have students read them out loud and tell which sentence served as the topic sentence. Ask students to write a headline which states the main idea of the article.

Additional Resources

Skills Practice Book—
pages 42–43

Teacher's Resource Binder
Reinforcement Activities—
page 38
Enrichment Activities—
pages 1–2, 11, 60–61

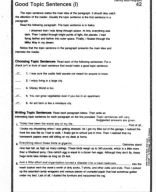

Using English in Health

This activity gives students an opportunity to recognize paragraph structure and to find the main idea in reading material for other subject areas.

Using English in Health

▶ Comprehension

Most Americans today are very concerned about their health. They exercise and try to eat healthy foods.

Advertisers and health groups have noticed this attitude. They are developing ads that teach people more about health. Often, these ads are catchy slogans that capture the main idea about a food or product. Here are some examples.

Have more milk 'cause milk does more.
The incredible, edible egg.

Exercise   Studying Paragraphs

▶ Analyzing/Structured Application

Look for the topic sentence in each paragraph below. Then read the rest of the sentences to see what information each adds about the main idea. Write the topic sentence of each paragraph. Then rewrite the topic sentence as a catchy slogan.

1.   A study done in Britain shows that eating cheese after a meal may be good for your health. Scientists have found that cheese may fight bacteria in your mouth that can cause cavities. Even if eating cheese does prevent tooth decay, the study warns that eating cheese will never replace brushing your teeth.

2.   Drinking milk is a habit that will keep you healthy throughout your life. Milk keeps your bones strong while you are growing. Scientists studied women who drank milk regularly as children and teen-agers. The bones of these women were stronger than those who did not drink as much milk. In addition, scientists noticed that some women continued to drink milk as adults. These women kept the good bone structure they had as children.

98

Chapter 5 Review

▶ Analyzing

Studying Paragraphs Use these two paragraphs to answer the questions below. <small>See answers in margin.</small>

1

Pueblo boys learned many things from their fathers. They learned to grow corn, squash, and beans. The Pueblos lived on the desert lands of the West and Southwest. The boys learned to weave beautiful designs into cloth. Also, the craft of painting designs on pottery was handed down from one generation to another. Boys learned to weave baskets for harvesting corn. They also learned to make silver jewelry and carve wooden dolls.

2

One howl shows that a wolf wants to "talk." Another type of howl signals a warning that danger is near. When the members of a pack gather to begin a hunt, they greet each other with howls. Then, a much wilder, more primitive howl signals the beginning of the hunt. A wolf howls sadly when a loved one dies or is injured.

1. What is the main idea of paragraph 1? of paragraph 2?
2. Which paragraph does not have a topic sentence?
3. What is the topic sentence of the other paragraph?
4. Write a topic sentence for the paragraph that does not have one.
5. Which paragraph has a sentence that does not tell about the main idea? Write the sentence.

Chapter Review

This review allows teacher to evaluate student understanding of the concepts presented in this chapter.

1. Paragraph 1—Pueblo fathers taught their sons many things Paragraph 2—Wolves communicate by howling.
2. Paragraph 2
3. Pueblo boys learned many things from their fathers.
4. A wolf's howl has many meanings for other wolves.
5. Paragraph 1. The Pueblos lived on the desert lands of the West and Southwest.

Additional Resources

Skills Practice Book
Review—page 44

Test Booklet
Mastery Test—pages 25–26

Chapter 6

Chapter Objectives

1. To become aware of writing as a process with stages that can be adapted for any form of writing

2. To develop techniques for choosing and limiting a topic

3. To gather information and develop a topic

4. To organize details in a logical order

5. To make a writing plan

6. To draft while following a writing plan

7. To revise and proofread

8. To make and share a final copy

Motivating the Students

1. Explain that the process writers use is similar to the processes used in many other occupations. Builders rely on blueprints; artists first sketch in pencil; cooks follow recipes and plan menus.

Stress that no writer actually sits down and produces a beautiful, polished article or story without forethought or revision.

2. First, read the following quotation by Joseph Heller. Explain that even professional writers may have dreamed about writing easily, with little effort.

> I wanted to be a writer when I was in the sixth grade—of course I wanted to be one without working at it.
>
> —Joseph Heller

Then read these words of Ernest Hemingway. Point out that professional writers go through many of the same procedures during writing that students do.

> I always rewrite each day up to the point where I stopped. When it is all finished, naturally you go over it. You get another chance to correct and rewrite when someone else types it, and you see it clean in type. The last chance is in the proofs. You're grateful for these chances. I rewrote the ending to *Farewell to Arms,* the last page of it, thirty-nine times before I was satisfied.
>
> —Ernest Hemingway

Week 8

Chapter Management Guidelines   This chart may be used to help structure daily lesson plans

Day 1	Day 2	Day 3	Day 4	Day 5
Chapter 6, Part 4, "Prewriting: Organizing Ideas," pp. 108–109	Part 5, "Drafting," pp. 110–111	Part 6, "Revising and Proofreading," pp. 112–115	Part 7, "Writing and Sharing the Final Copy," pp. 116–117	Chapter Review and selected end-of-chapter activities; Cumulative Review pp. 122–123

Chapter 6

Choosing a Process for Writing

Have you ever thought about what the world would be like without writers? There would be no books, magazines, or newspapers. There would be no movies or television.

Writing is certainly an important part of our lives. Almost everyone writes, yet no two people write in exactly the same way. The method each person uses changes depending on the type of writing being done. Most writers, however, follow a general pattern. They begin with an idea, make a plan, and write. Then they try to improve their writing. When they are satisfied with their work, they share it with others.

In this chapter, you will learn about the process of writing. You will learn to use the process of writing to become a better writer. You will discover how to complete each of the four stages in this process: prewriting, drafting, revising, and sharing. The choices in each stage make the process a little different for every writer and for every type of writing.

101

Explain that many writers think through much of the structure of a story before they begin to write. Stress that thinking is part of the process of writing.

Tell students that in this chapter they will learn about the stages in developing any form of writing. Tell them that when they use this process they will find writing easier, and they will be better writers. In later chapters, they will use this process to develop many kinds of writing.

Special Populations

LD, ESL Refer to pages T32–T35 at the front of this Teacher's Edition for additional special populations notes for the teaching of composition to these students. Additional demonstration and guided practice in using the steps in the process of writing may be necessary for some of these students. Pair ESL students with native speakers of English for help with explanations and exercises.

NSD Writing offers an opportunity for these students to use Standard English.

Related Chapters

You may wish to refer to related material in other chapters as you teach the following concepts:

1. Paragraph structure, Chapter 5, "Learning About Paragraphs," page 91

2. Word choice, Chapter 9, "Discovering the Dictionary and Thesaurus," page 161

3. Using specific nouns, verbs, adjectives, and adverbs, the "Thesaurus" in the **Power Handbook**

Additional Resources

Skills Practice Book—pages 45–51

Test Booklet—pages 27–32
Pretest—pages 27–28
Mastery Test—pages 29–32

Teacher's Resource Binder
Reinforcement Activities—
pages 39–43
Enrichment Activities—
pages 3, 39–52, 62–63
Process of Writing Transparencies
Ideas for Creative Teaching

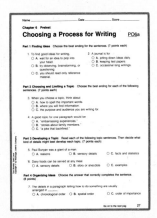

Part 1

Objective

To become aware of writing as a process with stages that can be adapted for any form of writing

Presenting the Lesson

 All Students

1. Read and discuss **Journal Writing** as a source for writing ideas. Explain that a journal can be private or public, (Many have been published, such as *Travels with Charley* by John Steinbeck and *The Diary of Anne Frank.)*

2. Read **Brainstorming** on page 102. Point out how the ideas in the cluster chart have been grouped. Tell students that they can "map" their brainstorming ideas in ways other than a cluster. For example, they can list ideas or develop more sequential outlines.

3. Read about discussions and interviews, reading and researching, observing, and questioning on page 103. Mention that observing can be used along with journal writing. Details that are observed can be noted in the journal. Writers often carry notebooks with them so that they can record their impressions. Stress the importance of new ways of looking at ordinary situations. Explain that these are all methods of getting ideas from outside sources. Suggest that students (with permission from all parties) tape record discussions, interviews, and questioning sessions.

4. Have the students begin writing folders in which they save examples of their work, both to remind themselves of what they have written, and to suggest ideas and areas of improvement. Have them keep all prewriting steps as well as final papers in these folders.

5. If you have not already done so, introduce students to the "Guidelines for the Process of Writing" and "Writing Topics" in the **Power Handbook.**

6. Assign Exercise A on page 103. Have volunteers draw their clusters on the board for class discussion. Then assign Exercise B. Remind students that both observation and reading can be sources for writing ideas they might wish to record in their journals.

1 Prewriting: Finding Ideas

Focus

Good ideas for writing can be found in many ways.

▶ Comprehension/Generalizing

Have you found that the hardest part of writing is getting started? Unless a topic is assigned by your teacher, do you just sit with a blank sheet of paper and wait for an idea to pop into your head? There is a better way to begin. The following methods may help you think of interesting ideas.

Journal Writing Write your ideas, thoughts, feelings, and experiences in a notebook. Write about everyday happenings as well as special moments in your life. Write in your journal often. It will be a good source for writing ideas.

Brainstorming Begin by thinking about one general idea. Then think of as many related ideas as possible. Jot down anything that comes to mind. Below is a **clustering chart** that one student made while she brainstormed. You might make a clustering chart like this one.

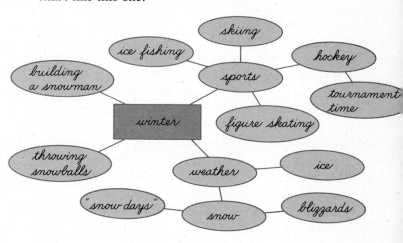

102

▶ **Basic Students**

Do several clustering charts as a class, recording the students' ideas on the board. Start with broad topics such as *food, holidays,* or *music.*

Have students observe one of the following: a grocery store, a post office, or school library. Then, have students work in groups and brainstorm ideas for writing. Guide them in making cluster charts or lists to group their ideas.

Discussion and Interviews Listen carefully to what other people say. Their stories and experiences might provide interesting ideas to write about.

Reading and Researching Flip through books, newspapers, and magazines. You will find an endless variety of topics. Encyclopedias and other resource books are also good sources of information. Save ideas in a writing folder or journal.

Observing Look at what goes on around you. Take notes on anything you see or hear that makes you curious or that you just find interesting.

Questioning Jot down a few questions and answer them. Question anything you would like to know more about. Questions might be about real or imaginary situations.

What people do I admire? Why?

What would a city be like without cars?

What would happen if people could become invisible whenever they wanted?

Exercises   Discovering Topics

▶ Creative Application

A. Brainstorming Write down the first person, place, and thing that come to mind. Then think of as many related ideas as you can for each. You may work alone or with a partner or group. Follow the example of the clustering chart on page 102. Save your ideas in a writing folder.

B. Journal Writing Begin a writer's journal. Write down one funny, eerie, or exciting experience that happened to you in the last year. Think of as many details as possible about the experience. Or, simply write in your journal every day for one week. Record your thoughts, feelings, ideas, and experiences. Some entries might be a few sentences. Others might be several paragraphs. Look over your journal at the end of the week. What ideas for topics do you find?

103

Additional Resources

Skills Practice Book—page 45
Teacher's Resource Binder
  Process of Writing Transparencies

Duplicate and distribute a page from a newspaper or magazine. Have students list as many ideas for writing as possible that the page suggests. Then discuss their lists in class.

Special Populations

LD Some students may need additional help with clustering. See the notes under **Basic Students.**

ESL Brainstorming offers an excellent opportunity for these students to make a positive contribution and gain confidence in oral speaking. Encourage students to draw on their cultural experiences for sources of writing topics.

Reinforcement

1. Have students brainstorm and then create cluster charts based on one of the following topics: *relatives, animals, friends,* or *clothes.*

2. Have students write journal entries about one happy or one sad experience that happened to them in the past year.

3. To help students write even when they think they have nothing to say, instruct the students to write continuously in their journals for a specified period of time. Make these writing sessions short at first, only a minute or two. They may write whatever they are thinking. No structure is necessary. Stress that the important thing is to keep writing. Have students save these papers to refer to for idea starters.

Enrichment

1. Bring in a scenic poster and have students list writing ideas based on the scene.

2. Play some music that strongly suggests a mood or setting, and have students list ideas based on that music.

3. For additional enrichment activities, see the Unit Projects in the Teacher Notes on page 3. One or more of these projects have special activities for gifted and talented students.

Part 2

Objective

To develop techniques for choosing and limiting a topic

Presenting the Lesson

 All Students

1. Read and discuss pages 104–105. Point out how the items on Jennifer's list are narrower than the general subject of *pets*. Also point out that students used brainstorming in part 1 as a way of finding ideas. Now they are using brainstorming along with questioning to choose and limit a topic.

2. Clarify the idea that a topic must be much more limited for a paragraph than for a composition. Do this by having students supply limiting questions for one of Jennifer's topics. Point out when the topic is narrow enough for a composition. Continue the questioning process and limit the topic further so that it is suitable for a paragraph.

3. Read and discuss **Purpose and Audience** on page 105. Help students understand how audience affects writing. Ask what Jennifer would have to consider if her composition were written for a group of biologists, or for young children who want a pet chameleon.

4. Explain that even though two writers are working with the same general subject, their limiting questions are unique, and thus they will produce very different products.

5. Assign and discuss Exercise A on page 105. Then assign Exercise B on page 105. Have students exchange papers and judge whether each classmate's topic has been sufficiently limited for a paragraph. Have them make suggestions for improvement.

 Basic Students

To help with recognizing broad and narrow topics, ask students to find the broadest topic in the following list.

Why New York is fun to visit
Places to visit in Chicago
The old trolleys of Detroit
Cities in the United States

---

2 Prewriting: Choosing and Limiting a Topic

> **Focus**
>
> Choose a general subject that interests you. Choose one that you would like to share with others. Limit your subject.

▶ *Comprehension/Critical Reasoning*

To find your own topic, use the methods that you studied in part 1. Try a few different methods until you find an idea that interests you.

After you have chosen a general subject, your next step is to narrow or limit it. This means you must make your subject more specific. Your subject must be very specific if you are writing just one paragraph. A composition, on the other hand, is several paragraphs about one topic. Topics for compositions can be broader than topics for single paragraphs.

How can you make your subject specific? Use the same methods that you used to discover writing ideas. You might brainstorm to find several smaller ideas that tie in to your general subject. Then you can ask questions about that specific idea until you discover a limited topic.

One student, Jennifer, began limiting her subject, *pets*, by brainstorming. She listed everything that came to mind.

the neighborhood pet shop	canaries that sing
caring for a pet	tropical fish
animals that make good pets	talking parrots
my pet chameleon	what to do with pets when
cocker spaniels	you are not at home

After looking over her list, Jennifer decided to write about her pet chameleon. To narrow her topic even more, Jennifer asked herself the questions at the top of the next page.

104

Who? my pet chameleon, Houdini	How? escapes from cage
What? causes problems, always in trouble	Why? doesn't like cage; maybe bad-tempered
When? all the time	Where? at home

The answers to these questions helped Jennifer narrow her topic. She decided to write about Houdini's frequent escapes from its cage. This topic is specific enough to cover well in a single paragraph.

Purpose and Audience

After you have limited your topic, you must consider your **purpose**, or reason for writing. Is it to tell a story or to describe a person, place, or thing? Do you want to give instructions or explain an opinion? Then you must consider your **audience**, or readers. Will they be students, your aunt, or the editor of your local newspaper? Answering these questions will help you choose the best information and the right kind of language for your readers.

Exercises   Limiting a Subject

Critical Reasoning/Structured Application

A. Limiting a General Subject Imagine that your teacher has assigned a paragraph on the subject of *magic*. Limit this subject so that it can be covered well in one paragraph. Use brainstorming and questioning to limit your subject. Write your purpose and tell who your readers will be. Share your specific topic with your classmates.

Critical Reasoning/Creative Application

B. Choosing and Limiting Your Topic Choose one topic from the list you wrote in part 1. You might also select a topic from the "Topics for Writing" in the **Power Handbook**, pages 464–466. Limit your topic so that it can be easily covered in one paragraph. Decide on your purpose for writing and tell who your audience will be. Save your notes in your writing folder.

105

Additional Resources

Skills Practice Book—page 46
Teacher's Resource Binder
Reinforcement Activities—
page 39
Process of Writing Transparencies

To give practice in questioning, have students orally answer the questions *who, what, when, where, why,* and *how* for the following subjects. Write the answers on the board.

a. my cousin Frank
b. my uncle's car

 Advanced Students

Have these students use the general subject *food* and give examples of limited topics for the following types of papers: to explain how something works, to express an opinion, to describe, and to give instructions.

Special Populations

LD Pair each student with a stronger writer for Exercise A. See the notes under **Basic Students.** For Exercise B, give additional help in the limiting process.

ESL For Exercises A and B, pair students with native speakers of English.

Reinforcement

1. Have students follow the directions for Exercise A on page 105 using the following topics:

a. seasons
b. childhood illnesses
c. vacations

2. Ask students to suggest how purpose and audience would affect each of the following topics. Have them test the following purposes with each topic: to tell a story, to describe a person or place, to give instructions or an opinion. Have students suggest possible audiences for each topic.

a. feeding cats
b. why seat belts are important
c. my uncle George

Enrichment

Bring in several large print advertisements from magazines aimed at a variety of audiences. Consider using magazines about sports, finances, computers, children, or cooking. Discuss with students the purpose and audience of each ad. Then, have students find ads on their own and identify the elements discussed. These could be posted in a bulletin board display.

Part 3

Objective

To gather information and develop a topic

Presenting the Lesson

 All Students

1. Read and discuss page 106. Stress that students should always take and keep notes during this prewriting step so that they have the information when they begin to write. Mention the importance of gathering more information than is needed so that the best can be used.

2. Test the students' understanding of the kinds of information that can be gathered. Have them suggest one example of each kind of information that might be used to support the topic sentence: Swimming regularly improves physical fitness.

3. Remind students about gathering the right kind of information for purpose and audience. For example, a letter to a cousin about the terrific place visited on vacation would come alive with stories and examples. That same vacation spot would be discussed in an encyclopedia with facts and statistics.

4. Assign and discuss Exercises A and B on page 107.

 Basic Students

Have students as a group list sensory details describing their classroom. Put their list on the board for discussion.

Have students list reasons that support each of the following opinions:

a. Spring is a pleasant season.

b. Jan Smith is the best candidate for student government president.

c. All students should learn a second language.

Give students individual help with Exercise B on page 107.

---

3 Prewriting: Developing a Topic

> **Focus**
>
> Gather information to support your topic.

▶ **Comprehension**

After limiting your topic, you must develop it. The first step is to gather information that supports or explains it.

There are several ways to gather information. You can talk to others, look through your journal, or brainstorm. You might also browse through the library, or simply observe your subject. You might analyze a situation. That is, you break down a problem into its parts. You might look at the causes and effects of a situation. You might look at the steps in a process, or at the important features of a new invention.

At times, it will be necessary to use more than one method of gathering information. The type of information you need will depend upon your purpose for writing. The following will help you decide what kind of information you need. It will also suggest ways to gather that information.

Sensory details appeal to the five senses of sight, sound, smell, touch, and taste. These details make the person, place, or thing you are describing seem real. Gather sensory details through observation, memory, or imagination.

Stories tell about real or imaginary experiences. A brief story, or **anecdote**, can help your readers understand an idea. A story can come from your experiences, from talking to others, from reading, or from imagination.

Examples help to develop a general idea. Imagine that you were writing a paper about some things a sixth grader could do over summer vacation. You might give examples of what you did on your vacation. Examples can come from your own experience, observation, reading, or research.

106

Facts and statistics can support an opinion or add important information to a report. Suppose you were writing a report about a famous hockey player. You might use facts and statistics to show how the player's performance compares to that of other hockey players. Facts and statistics can be proven true. Gather facts by researching your topic. Reference books, such as encyclopedias, atlases, and almanacs contain many facts and statistics.

Reasons are explanations that tell why you think your ideas are right. Reasons are often used to support an opinion or tell why something happened. For example, you might think your class should have a Mardi Gras celebration. You could support your opinion with these reasons. 1) It is a good way to celebrate the coming of spring. 2) The class has been working very hard all semester, and Mardi Gras would be a nice break. Look for reasons in your experience, reading, and research.

Exercises   Selecting and Developing Details

▶ **Analyzing/Structured Application**

A. Selecting Details Read the following list of topics. Decide on the types of details that might best be used to develop each topic. For some topics, more than one kind of detail might be useful. Then choose one of these topics and list several details you might use to develop it. Answers may vary.

Why girls should play Little League baseball   reasons, facts, examples

A bakery in my neighborhood   sensory details, anecdote

How I met my friend from Japan   anecdote

Why a certain television show should be cancelled   reasons, facts

Famous musicians of the 1980's   examples, facts

▶ **Critical Reasoning/Creative Application**

B. Developing Details Gather information and develop the details for the topic you selected in part 2. Use the methods presented in parts 1 and 3. Choose details that fit your purpose for writing. Save these notes in your writing folder.

107

Additional Resources

Skills Practice Book—page 47
Teacher's Resource Binder
Reinforcement Activities—
   page 40
Enrichment Activities—
   pages 12, 62
Process of Writing Transparencies

Have students select a topic from their journal entries or from writing topics suggested in the **Power Handbook.** You may wish to assign a topic, biking or vacation places for example. Have students develop a topic sentence and lists of examples and sensory details that could be used to develop the topic. Have them keep these lists in their writing folders.

Special Populations

LD Provide and discuss examples of paragraphs developed with each kind of information discussed in the lesson. See also the notes under **Basic Students.**

ESL Because the placement of modifiers in English differs from other languages, students may need to refer to Chapter 16, "Adjectives for Creative Expression," page 283 and Chapter 17, "Adverbs for Clear Description," page 301.

Reinforcement

1. Have each student list sensory details that describe his or her kitchen in the morning.

2. Have students list examples of ways they spend their free time (or ways they would like to).

3. Have students state three reasons for one of the following:

—providing music lessons for all students
—televising school sports

4. Have students follow the instructions for Exercise A on page 107, using the following topics: Answers may vary.

a. the radio of the future
   sensory details, facts, reasons
b. how to train a dog
   reasons, facts, examples
c. grandfather's childhood
   anecdote
d. the first blizzard of the year
   sensory details, anecdote, facts
e. why we should avoid junk food
   reasons, facts

Enrichment

Share with students examples of anecdotes and stories of famous people that you find in biographical collections in the library or in current newspaper and magazine articles.

Part 4

Objectives

1. To organize details in a logical order
2. To make a writing plan

Presenting the Lesson

■ All Students

1. Explain that when a writer organizes details, it is easier for a reader to follow the writer's thoughts.

2. Read **Chronological Order** on page 108. Explain that the word *chronological* is based on the root *chrono*, which means time. Introduce the idea that the method of organization chosen depends partly on the purpose for writing. For example, chronological order can be used to give step-by-step directions on how to do or make something (First put 1/3 cup of oil in the pan. Then put in three kernels . . . .) or for telling a story (When I awoke at 7, I heard a strange noise. I forgot about it until 8:30, when. . . .).

3. Read **Natural or Spatial Order** on page 108. Explain that natural order presents details in the order the writer wants them noticed by the reader. This way, the writer can lead up to a significant detail. The writer might also choose to present details as they would be seen by an observer of the object or scene. Have the students suggest a type of writing for which this organization would be used. (description of a scene, building, object, etc.)

4. Read **Order of Importance** on page 108. Stress that usually it is best to place the most important reason in an argument last because it remains in a reader's mind. Ask for what type of writing this organization is suited. (writing about an opinion)

5. Read **Making a Writing Plan** on page 108. Carefully examine Jennifer's writing plan. Point out that Jennifer did not at first write her details in the best order. She examined her details and then added the numbers. Because students will not read Jennifer's story until later in the chapter, it may be necessary for you to explain that Jennifer has chosen chronological order.

6. Read and discuss **Organizing a Composition** on page 109. Demonstrate the difference in grouping details for a paragraph and for a composition. Write a composition topic, three main ideas, and several details on the board. Have students suggest how details could be grouped under the main topics. For example, the broad topic of caves could be limited to "Mammoth Cave" for a composition and "My visit to Mammoth Cave" for a paragraph.

7. Assign the exercise on page 109. You may wish to have students exchange papers when they have completed their writing plans. Have them check that the way of ordering chosen is a logical one for the topic. Also have them look for any unrelated details that may remain.

---

4 Prewriting: Organizing Ideas

Focus

Look over your details and arrange them in a logical order. Then make a writing plan.

Organize Your Details

▶ Comprehension/Inferring Sequence

The final step in the prewriting process is to organize your information. Read your list of details and cross out any that do not support your main idea. Add any new ideas that will improve your writing.

Once you are satisfied with your list of details, put them into a logical order. You can organize ideas in several ways.

Chronological Order Details are arranged in the order in which they did or should happen. Use chronological order to tell a story. Also, use it to explain a process.

Natural or Spatial Order Details are arranged in the order in which you see them. This might be from side-to-side, top-to-bottom, or far-to-near. Arrange your details in natural order when you describe a person, place, or thing.

Order of Importance Details are arranged from the least to the most important idea, or from the most to the least important idea. Use order of importance to arrange reasons that tell why something is so or to plan a description.

Make a Writing Plan

As you decide on an order for your details, make a writing plan. A writing plan should include your topic, audience, and purpose. It should also show your details in the order in which you plan to write them.

108

Here is Jennifer's writing plan.

topic: my pet chameleon

purpose: to tell about the problems my pet causes

audience: classmates

details: *2* My chameleon is an escape artist.

           3 leaps off high tables

           4 travels fast

           ~~eats only live prey, such as crickets~~

           5 keeps trying to escape

           6 I bought him a heat lamp.

           7 My chameleon doesn't do much except sit on a rock.

           ~~Frogs are also difficult, unrewarding pets.~~

           1 chameleon's name — Houdini

...ld number ...details in ...rect order.

These details aren't important to the story.

Organize a Composition

As you organize your details, you may find that you have more than one main idea. In that case, you will write a composition. A composition is several paragraphs about the same topic.

When you write a composition, first decide what the main idea of each paragraph will be. Then, group together the details that support each main idea. Next, organize the ideas in each paragraph and then the paragraphs in a logical order.

Exercise   Making Your Own Writing Plan

▶ Creative Application

Make your own writing plan. Use the details and topic you developed in part 3. Save your writing plan in your folder.

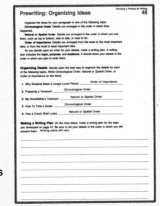

109

Basic Students

Duplicate an example of each kind of paragraph order (chronological, natural, order of importance) for the students. Have the class identify the order used in each case.

Have students rearrange the following group of ideas into logical order. Ask them to explain what order they followed. *natural (spatial) order*

   a. Beneath her bangs sparkled oval green eyes. *2*

   b. Her red hair was pulled into two tight braids. *1*

   c. Her smile revealed several missing baby teeth. She said, "Hello." *4*

   d. Her nose, red from the freezing cold, was sprinkled with freckles. *3*

Advanced Students

Ask students to find and identify an example of each kind of paragraph order. Suggest that they look through magazines, their own writing, and textbooks. Have the students share their paragraphs with the class.

Special Populations

LD Suggest that students put the parts of their writing plan and each detail on 3″ × 5″ note cards. Students can then add, eliminate, and rearrange without recopying. Also see the notes under **Basic Students.**

ESL Some students may have difficulty with expressing time order. Additional practice and review of prepositions, adverbs, and word placement may be helpful.

Reinforcement

Have students state the best type of paragraph organization for each of these topics.

   a. All children should learn to budget their allowances. *order of importance*

   b. Mom sighed as she surveyed my room. *natural (spatial) order*

   c. Yesterday was the worst day of my life. *chronological order*

Part 5

Objective

To draft while following a writing plan

Presenting the Lesson

 All Students

1. Read and discuss page 110. Stress the importance of concentrating on getting the ideas on paper. The mechanics of writing, punctuation, and form can be checked and corrected later during revision or proofreading. Students may also make changes in content before they are satisfied with their writing. Some writers write many drafts before the final product takes form. Point out that there are many styles. Encourage students to experiment with drafting styles until they find one or two they are comfortable with. The teacher may wish to suggest one of the following. These methods or variations seem to be among the most common.

Highly structured: The writer works from very complete prewriting notes.

Loosely structured: The writer works from rough notes, experimenting with ideas and organization during writing.

Bridges: The writer begins with two or three main points or situations to be covered, and concentrates on building logical bridges between the points during drafting.

Quick draft: The writer composes quickly, not stopping to refine ideas or rework copy until the revising stage.

Slow draft: The writer works meticulously, carefully drafting one sentence or paragraph at a time, revising continuously, and reworking the piece in its entirety when the draft is complete.

2. Read about using the right language on pages 110–111. Be sure students understand the terms *Standard English, Formal English* and *Informal English* and the appropriate situations for the use of each.

3. Have the students compare the first draft on page 111 with the prewriting notes on page 109. Have students notice how the ideas in the writing plan are worked into the draft. Allow time to study the changes Jennifer made and the reasons for those changes.

4. Assign the exercise on page 111. Stress the need to keep writing flowing as students draft.

5 Drafting

┌─ *Focus* ─────────────────────────────────┐

Let your writing plan guide you as you put your ideas into sentences and paragraphs.

└───┘

▶ **Comprehension**

Now that you have finished planning your writing, you are ready to begin drafting. Begin with your topic sentence. Then write down your details in the order you want to present them. Use your writing plan as a guide.

Do not be afraid to make changes or add new ideas. Be sure that these new ideas support your topic. Take out any unnecessary details as well. Try different ways of organizing your details until you find the best type of organization.

Do not try to express your ideas perfectly in the first draft. You may even write several drafts before you are satisfied.

Choose a Drafting Method

No two people write in exactly the same way. Everyone develops his or her own writing style. Some people start drafting and don't stop until they have all their ideas on paper. Others write a sentence or two and stop. They read over what they have written and make corrections. Then they continue writing. Still others combine these two methods. Use whatever style is most comfortable for you.

Use the Right Language

As you write, choose language that suits your audience. However, always use standard English. **Standard English** follows all of the rules of good grammar. It is understood by everyone who speaks the English language.

110

Standard English can be formal or informal. **Informal English** is the language of everyday speech. It is casual. It includes simple sentences and simple vocabulary. **Formal English** often uses longer sentences and an advanced vocabulary. Use informal English when writing to a friend or classmate. Use formal English in all serious writing, such as class papers, essay contests, and business letters.

A Sample Draft

Jennifer followed her writing plan as she wrote the first draft of her paragraph. Notice her thoughts as she wrote.

I got more than I asked for when I received
~~I felt very lucky when I got~~ a chamelon for my
That's when
birthday. ~~I~~ decided to name him Houdini. I had
such a small pet
figured that ~~a chamelon~~ would be no trouble. I was
leaped
wrong. A chamelon is an escape artist. He ~~jumped~~
out, jumped off the table, and went under a radiator. It took me a long time to catch him. From that
time on, he has tried to get out every time I feed
him. I tried to make him feel better. I bought him a
new cage and a lamp. It didn't help Houdini just
sits on his rock all day, looking for the nearest exit.

use idea er.

My topic sentence should be more interesting.

I need a more specific verb.

Exercise Writing a Draft

▶ Creative Application

Write a draft of the paragraph you have been planning. Keep your audience and purpose in mind. Follow your writing plan as you work. Remember, though, that you can make changes as you write. Add or take out details as your draft develops. You may need to write more than one draft. Save your work in your writing folder.

111

Ask the students to identify the standard form of the word or words in parentheses.

a. We (ain't got, don't have) any maga-zines.
b. The fireman doesn't want (any, no) help.
c. Rose (catched, caught) a fish.
d. We (be, are) the ones that made the team.
e. Those students (aren't, ain't) allowed to leave early.

Help the students individually as they write their first drafts or have them work in pairs. If their development during pre-writing was inadequate, have them look again at their details. Have them fill in missing information.

 Advanced Students

Suggest that students add two or three details as they draft. Also encourage them to experiment with various drafting styles. If a writer is usually a slow drafter and is getting bogged down with changes, suggest writing one draft straight through and reworking it later.

Special Populations

LD, ESL Stress the idea that perfection is not the goal at this stage. Give encouragement. Some students may need to dictate material to you or an aide. Make no corrections. The students will then work with what you have written for revision.

Reinforcement

Ask students to identify each sentence that is written in Standard and Formal English.

a. James and I saw the explosion.
   James and me saw the explosion.
b. "I can't hardly believe my eyes," said James.
   "I can hardly believe my eyes," said James.
c. The building be falling down.
   The building was falling down.
d. I knew we would have to discuss what we saw.
   I knew we were gonna have to talk about what we seen.
e. We had a blast yesterday.
   We had a good time yesterday.

Additional Resources

Skills Practice Book—page 49
Teacher's Resource Binder
  Reinforcement Activities—
    page 42
  Enrichment Activities—
    page 63
  Process of Writing Transparencies

Part 6

Objective

To revise and proofread

Presenting the Lesson

All Students

1. Read and discuss page 112. Review the concepts presented in the **Questions for Revising** on page 112. Point out that the order of importance for revising would be: clarity and interest; organization; and, finally, individual sentences and words in the piece of writing. Explain that revising is seldom orderly. Many changes may be made and sometimes a piece may be completely rewritten so that the final product is as good as possible. The questions in the guideline provide a valuable starting point for revising.

2. Read about working with a revising partner on page 113. Explain that the work of professional writers is usually edited by someone else. Explain that there are many methods of revision. Help students find a technique of revising that suits them and the type of writing they are doing. You may wish to discuss the following techniques for revising.

Editorial groups In pairs or small groups, students critique one another's writing.

Group questioning After one student in a group reads a piece of writing out loud, the other students ask questions focusing on what they still want to know about the subject.

Clinics In workshops, students with similar writing problems receive instruction from the teacher. This may involve completing prepared material, or working together to solve common problems.

Tutoring A student who is weak in some area is paired with a student who is stronger in the same area.

3. Read about proofreading on page 113. Discuss thoroughly the **Guidelines for Proofreading** on page 114. Point out that there is a difference between proofreading and revising. Revising involves changes in content and organization while proofreading is concerned with changes in grammar, mechanics, and spelling.

4. Read **Using Symbols for Revising and Proofreading** on page 114. Have the students examine the proofreading symbols and find examples of their use in the revised version of the sample paragraph. Allow time for students to study the changes that Jennifer made and the reasons for those changes.

5. Assign and discuss the exercise on page 115. Assign revising partners for this exercise.

---

6 Revising and Proofreading

Focus

Revise and proofread to improve your writing.

▶ **Comprehension/Analyzing**

You are now ready to begin the third stage of writing, **revising**. When you revise, you improve what you have written. You might add or take out details. You might also change the way you have organized your details. You add precise nouns, strong action verbs, and descriptive adjectives and adverbs. When you proofread, you look for mistakes in grammar, capitalization, punctuation, and spelling.

Try to plan writing assignments so that you have time to put your draft away for a few days. At least put it away for an hour or two. When you look at it again, you may see mistakes that you missed the first time. Another way to find mistakes is to read your draft out loud. You can also ask a friend or parent to read your draft and to offer suggestions. Follow these guidelines when you revise.

Guidelines for Revising

1. Does each paragraph begin with an interesting and informative topic sentence? Do all the sentences tell about the main idea?
2. Are the details specific? Should any be left out? Should any be added?
3. Are the details arranged in logical order?
4. Are the sentences in the best possible order? Should any sentences be moved?
5. Does my writing accomplish my purpose?
6. Does my language suit my audience?
7. Do I like what I have written? Will others enjoy reading it?

112

Basic Students

Give special attention to the guidelines for revising on page 112. Many students find it easier to spot errors in mechanics than to think through the organization of a piece of writing. Let the students know that you and the rest of their audience will be even more concerned with their ideas than with mechanics. Give guidance as the students revise.

Working with a Revising Partner

Sometimes it is difficult to find your own mistakes when you write. This is because you already know what you wanted to say. A revising partner can help. A revising partner might be a friend, classmate, brother, sister, or a parent. Choose someone who will take your writing seriously.

Ask your revising partner to read your paper carefully. Do your ideas make sense? Ask your partner to suggest ways to improve your writing. Ask for specific suggestions. You may want your partner to use the "Guidelines for Revising." Use your partner's suggestions to make changes.

Proofreading

As you revised your writing, you probably found mistakes in grammar, capitalization, punctuation, and spelling. Checking for these types of errors is called **proofreading**. Proofread your writing several times before making a final copy. Use the proofreading symbols found on page 114 to make corrections on your draft. Follow these guidelines when you proofread.

113

Review the proofreading symbols. Be sure students can use these on their own.

 Advanced Students

These students often view revision as a sign of imperfection. Stress that drafts only show what the writer has been thinking. More changes will be necessary during revision. Explain that if their first drafts were good, their revised drafts will be even better. Remind students to use the "Thesaurus" in the **Power Handbook** for specific word choice.

Special Populations

LD Some students may find using proofreading symbols too difficult. Allow these students to make corrections in a way that they are comfortable with.

ESL Pair students with native speakers of English for proofreading.

NSD Help these students check for the use of Standard English as they revise.

Reinforcement

Duplicate the following paragraph. Have students proofread and make corrections using proofreading symbols.

Early spring weather is never predictable. At least not in this state. The rain can be in 3 forms: snow, sleet, or water. The wind can make walking outside a dangerous activity. people have to watch out for flying objects, and sometimes have to hold on to telephone poles or street signs so they don't fly away theirselves! Worse, there is always the possibility of a tornado. Finally, the temperature itself range from freezing to uncomfortably hot. I'm not kidding! Somehow, our springs don't resemble the descriptions I read in my books when I was little.

Work with the students individually or in small groups as they revise their own paragraphs.

Additional Resources

Skills Practice Book—page 50

Teacher's Resource Binder
Reinforcement Activities—
  page 43
Enrichment Activities—
  page 3
Process of Writing Transparencies

Guidelines for Proofreading

1. Look for errors in grammar and usage. Use the grammar chapters in this text to help you correct any mistakes you find. For example, if you think you have used the wrong form of an irregular verb, see Chapter 4, pages 77-79.

2. Be sure you have capitalized correctly, including titles used with names and the titles of books, songs, movies, and so on. See the "Guide to Capitalization," pages 467-479 in the **Power Handbook.**

3. It is important to punctuate your writing correctly. If you are not sure when to use a comma or how to use apostrophes or quotation marks properly, see the "Guide to Punctuation," pages 480-499 in the **Power Handbook.** This guide also provides information on end marks, colons, and semicolons.

4. Check your work for spelling errors. Be sure to check the spelling of proper nouns, especially the names of any people you have mentioned. Use the "Guide to Spelling," pages 500-508 in the **Power Handbook,** or look up the word in a dictionary or encyclopedia.

5. Check the correctness of any dates or other figures you have used in your writing. Be sure your facts are stated clearly and accurately.

Using Symbols for Revising and Proofreading

Use the following symbols for revising and proofreading to change and correct your draft.

Symbols for Revising and Proofreading	
∧ Add letters or words.	— Take out letters or woerds.
⊙ Add a period.	¶ Begin a new paragraph.
≡ capitalize a letter.	∧ Then add a comma.
/ Make a capital Letter lowercase.	∩ Trade the position of letters or words.

A Sample Revision

Here is how Jennifer revised and proofread her paragraph. Notice her thoughts as she wrote. Also notice the kinds of errors she found as she proofread.

I got more than I asked for when I received a
chamel_eon for my birthday. I had figured that such
Little did I know that
a small pet would be no trouble. ~~I was wrong.~~ A
When I opened the door to his
chamel_eon is an escape artist. He leaped out, *cage,*
raced
jumped off the table, and ~~went~~ under a radiator. It
an hour
took me ~~a long time~~ to catch him. That's when I
decided to name him Houdini. From that time on,
make a getaway
he has tried to ~~get out~~ every time I feed him. I tried
more content by buying *big*
to make him feel ~~better. I bought~~ him a new cage
heat
and a lamp. It didn't help Houdini just sits on his
rock all day, looking for the nearest exit.

> *I should say what he leaped out of.*

> *I should use stronger verbs.*

> *This should be two sentences.*

Exercise   Revising and Proofreading

▶ **Creative Application**

Carefully read over the draft of your composition. Check the content and organization. Add or take out details as necessary. Improve your word choice. Use a revising partner to help you find weaknesses in your draft. Follow the "Guidelines for Revising" in this part or on page 462 in the **Power Handbook**.

When you are satisfied with the content and organization of your draft, proofread your writing. Use the "Guidelines for Proofreading" on page 114 in this part or on page 463 of the **Power Handbook** to help find your errors. Use proofreading symbols to make corrections on your draft.

115

Part 7

Objective

To make and share a final copy

Presenting the Lesson

 All Students

1. Read and discuss about preparing the final copy on page 116. Explain that readers often rate a piece of writing on its neatness. If a paper looks sloppy, it may not be read at all.

2. Before students make their final copies, inform them of additional manuscript requirements for your class. Whatever your preference, be sure specifications are clear.

3. Read about sharing writing on page 116. Discuss with students how they prefer their writing to be presented and shared.

Teachers may be interested to know that *The Writer's Market* (Writer's Digest Books) contains listings for several children's magazines. Students might wish to consider submitting work for publication. In additiion, professional journals often list contests students can enter, such as the "Spring Poetry Festival" in the *English Journal*. Civic and patriotic organizations also sponsor student writing contests. Check with the local Chamber of Commerce for a listing of such organizations.

4. Read the sample final copy on page 117. Ask students to list the ways Jennifer has revised her draft (on page 111). Explain that Houdini, an American magician who lived from 1874 to 1926, was known for his ability to escape from impossible cages and locks.

5. Assign the exercise on page 117.

 Basic Students

Stress that it is better to correct errors on a final copy than to hand in a neat but error-filled paper.

---

7 Writing and Sharing the Final Copy

Focus

Make a neat final copy of your writing. Find a way to share it with your readers.

Writing the Final Copy
▶ Comprehension

When you are satisfied with your writing, begin your final copy. First, choose a good title for your writing. Center your title at the top of the page. Leave a one-inch margin around your writing. Indent each paragraph.

When you have finished writing, proofread your final copy one more time. If you find a mistake, correct it neatly.

Sharing Your Writing

Now you will share your writing with your readers. There are several ways to do this.

Oral Presentations Read your work out loud to the class, or give oral presentations in small groups.

Skits Plan a skit to dramatize a narrative. You might also record your story on a cassette tape. Then you could start a **story tape library** in your school.

Writing Booklets Making writing booklets is another way to share your work. You and your classmates might make booklets on a single theme, such as "Our Hobbies."

Bulletin Boards and Posters Display your writing on the bulletin board in your room or on the school bulletin board. You might also make a poster to display your descriptive writing. Glue a neat copy of your writing on a piece of posterboard. Use photographs or drawings to illustrate your topic.

116

Models For a report on how something works, you might make a model of that object. To demonstrate the use of wind as an energy source, you might make a model windmill.

Class Discussions Your teacher may wish to make a copy of your writing or put it on the overhead projector. You could then have a class discussion about your work.

Contests Enter your writing in contests or send it to newspapers or magazines. Ask your teacher for details.

Sample Final Copy

Here is Jennifer's final copy. Compare it with her first draft. Notice how she has improved her writing.

My Escape Artist

I got more than I asked for when I received a chameleon for my birthday. I had figured that such a small pet would be no trouble. Little did I know that a chameleon is an escape artist. When I opened the door to his cage, he leaped out, jumped off the table, and raced under a radiator. It took me an hour to catch him. That's when I decided to name him Houdini. From that time on, he has tried to make a getaway every time I feed him. I tried to make him feel more content by buying him a big new cage and a heat lamp. It didn't help. Houdini just sits on his rock all day, looking for the nearest exit.

Exercise   Making and Sharing a Final Copy

reative Application

Make a final copy of your work. Write as neatly as possible. Be sure to include a title. Indent each paragraph. Leave a one-inch margin around your writing. Proofread your final copy one last time. Finally, decide on a way of sharing your writing.

117

Speaking and Listening

Objective

To use interview techniques to get information for a report.

Presenting the Activity

This activity gives special emphasis to the speaking and listening skill of interviewing. Students have learned that one stage in the process of writing involves gathering information. Point out that interviewing is one way to gather information. Explain that like writing, interviewing requires planning and preparation. Discuss questioning techniques with the students. You might wish to mention that an alternative to taking notes during an interview is tape recording what is said.

Explain that if they tape record an interview, they should first obtain permission from the interviewee. They should always write down the questions and answers. Refer students to the "Guide to Punctuation" in the **Power Handbook** to review rules on punctuating dialogue.

Speaking and Listening

Interviewing
▶ Comprehension

You know that you can get information for a report by reading, doing research, and brainstorming. Another good way to gather information is by talking to people.

In order to get the right information, you must ask the right questions. To discover the right questions, follow these steps.

1. Ask yourself what you want to know about a subject.
2. Make a list of this information.
3. Turn each item on your list into a question. Some questions might have more than one part.

Suppose you were interviewing someone about his or her career. You might ask some of these questions to learn specific details about the career.

What type of education is required?
Is there a special training program?
What is the salary range in this career?
What hours do you work?
Do you work alone or with other people?
What is the most enjoyable/challenging part of your career?

Exercise   Interviewing
▶ Creative Application

First, choose a career you would like to learn more about. Then choose a person to interview about the career. Do enough research to determine what kinds of questions you would like to ask.

Interview the person. Listen carefully to what he or she says. Take notes and ask questions if you do not understand something.

Creative Writing

Creative Writing

These activities provide opportunities for imaginative applications of the skills presented in this chapter. Remind students to use the process of writing when completing these exercises. Remind students that they might use spatial organization for the descriptive details in their paragraphs.

▶ Creative Application

A. According to the *Guinness Book of World Records*, the tallest person on earth in 1985 was Muhammad Aalam Channa, from Pakistan. He was 8 feet, 3 inches tall. Imagine that you are the tallest person on earth. How would your life be different from what it is today?

List the advantages and disadvantages of being 8 feet, 3 inches tall. Write a paragraph that tells whether your life would be easier or more difficult if you were that tall. Include reasons from your list to support your opinion.

B. Have you ever thought about being an architect? An architect designs buildings. If you were to design your own house, what would it look like? Make a list of all the special features that would be in your house. List the different rooms and the colors you would use to decorate each room. List the furniture you would put in each room. Finally, decide where your house would be located. Would it be a farm in North Dakota? Would it be in a high-rise in New York City? Then, in a few paragraphs, describe your house.

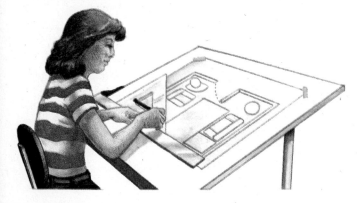

119

Using English in Other Subjects

This activity allows students to see the relationship between the process of writing and the process of thinking. You might wish to list the stages in the process of writing on the board. Then, list the steps in problem-solving so that they can see the correlation.

Tell students that following the steps in the problem-solving process will yield better results than will acting on impulse. Emphasize that adjustment is often a necessary part of the problem-solving process. The first solution reached may need some improvement. Tell students that trying out the solution and evaluating the results will let them see what improvements, if any, are needed.

As students complete the exercise on page 120, have them write down their thoughts as they go through each of the stages of the thinking process, using the sample on page 120 as a model. Have students share their problem-solving techniques with the class.

Using English in Other Subjects

▶ Comprehension/Critical Reasoning

The process of writing is really the process of thinking. First, you identify what you want to write about. Then, you consider and try different methods. Whenever you solve a problem, you use a similar process. First, you identify the problem. Next, you think about the choices. Third, you decide upon a solution and try it. Then, you evaluate the results and, finally, adjust your solution as necessary. Look at how Tim solved a problem.

Problem: My cat just gave birth to four kittens. There is not enough room in our apartment to keep them. What can I do?

Choices: Put an advertisement in the newspaper.
Give them to friends. I know Lisa wants a kitten.
Give them to my cousin who lives on a farm in Iowa.
Take them to a shelter.

Find a Solution: I think I'll give them to friends. Then I can see the kittens whenever I want.

Try Out the Solution and Evaluate the Results: Only two friends actually want kittens. I have four.

Adjust: I let Lisa and Washington pick out the kittens they wanted. Then I asked my mom if we could keep the other two until we visit my cousin this summer. My mom agreed.

Exercise Solving Problems

▶ Critical Reasoning/Structured Application

Read the following problems. Choose one. Tell how you would solve this problem. Use the five-step process for problem solving.

1. Summer is coming, and you'd like a new skateboard. You do not have quite enough money saved.
2. You hear classmates planning to cheat on a test.
3. Your gym class is learning how to work on gymnastics equipment, but you are afraid.

120

Chapter 6 Review

▶ Generalizing

A. Limiting a Topic Look over the general subjects that are listed below. Choose two of them. Then limit each topic so that it can be covered in a single paragraph.

food   cars   television
robots   hobbies   animals

▶ Classifying

B. Organizing Details Look over the following details about the praying mantis. Write the words *Appearance* and *Actions* at the top of two columns. Then write the details in the proper column.

App. = Appearance; Act. = Actions

Sits and waits until its victim is within reach   Act.

Lashes out and impales its victim on sharp spines   Act.

Claw at the top of each forelimb   App.

Powerful forelegs   App.

Small jaws and mouth   App.

Eats nothing but live food   Act.

Wide-spaced, bulging eyes   App.

Becomes the color, shape, and texture of its prey   App.

Prayerful posture   App.

Eats mostly insects such as bees, butterflies, and crickets   Act.

Cannibalism in the species is common   Act.

▶ Recalling

C. Identifying Parts of the Writing Process Look at the following list of writing activities. Tell whether each activity is most likely *Prewriting*, *Drafting*, *Revising*, or *Proofreading*.

1. correcting errors in spelling   Proofreading
2. gathering information   Prewriting
3. putting ideas in logical order   Prewriting
4. writing your ideas in paragraph form   Drafting
5. brainstorming   Prewriting
6. changing the order of details in your draft   Revising
7. working with a revising partner   Revising

121

Additional Resources

Skills Practice Book
Review—page 51

Test Booklet
Mastery Test—pages 29–32

Chapter Review

This review allows teachers to evaluate student understanding of the concepts presented in this chapter.

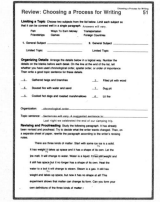

Cumulative Review

These exercises provide a cumulative review of the concepts presented in this unit. Each exercise challenges the students to apply several of the skills they have acquired while studying this unit.

Cumulative Review

Unit 1

Composition

▶ Recalling

A. Process of Writing Write the following sentences on your paper. Complete each sentence by filling in the blanks with the word or words necessary to make a correct statement about the process of writing.

1. Limiting your topic and organizing ideas are both part of the <u>prewriting</u>, or planning, stage.
2. When you <u>draft</u>, you put your notes in sentence and paragraph form.
3. Improving the content of your writing is called <u>revising</u>.
4. You should use details such as <u>fact</u>(s), <u>example</u>(s), and <u>reason</u>(s) to support your ideas.
5. If you describe your day from morning to evening, you would probably use <u>chronological</u> order.

▶ Structured Application

B. The Paragraph Read the following paragraphs. Write a topic sentence that tells the main idea of the paragraph.

<u>The young girl was excited about her role as a clown</u> . Joanne began by covering her entire face with white makeup. She drew blue stars around her eyes and outlined her lips to form an enormous smile. After fastening the red rubber nose, she covered her head with a curly orange wig. A floppy green hat made her costume complete.

<u>I felt so awkward on that first day at school</u> . My stiff new shoes made my feet feel like prisoners that wanted to be free. Nothing fit. The desk was too small, and the pencil was too fat. I didn't know another person in the room, and had no idea what might happen next. The teacher said we were "little ladies and gentlemen," and she was looking forward to the whole year together.

122

Grammar

▶ Analyzing

Sentences, Nouns, and Verbs Each of the following sentences contains two errors. Identify the errors. Write the sentences correctly. Suggested answers are given. Errors are shaded.

1. Can I borrow your book about Eskimoes? May, Eskimos
2. Eileen had took her camera to disneyland. taken, Disneyland
3. Leroy throwed the bone to his dog, rover. threw, Rover
4. Janes brothers have went to the hockey tournament. Jane's, gone
5. Both men's stores on denver Street. were, Denver
6. Studied the beliefs of the indians. We, Indians
7. The coachs choosed teams for the volleyball game. coaches, chose
8. I never knowed that ostriches were the largest birds in africa. knew, Africa
9. Seths forgotten toys laid outside in the thunderstorm last night. Seth's, lay
10. Watched the sun raise over the treetops. I, rise
11. Jeromes skateboard been outside all night. Jerome's, has been
12. The salmons swimming upstream. salmon, are swimming
13. The childrens' toys left in the kitchen. children's, were left
14. The scout's will rise the flag. scouts, raise
15. Can you learn me how to play Katies harmonica? teach, Katie's

Related Skills

Classifying

Word History On your paper, write a definition for each of the five terms. Then look at the list below to find two examples for each term. Write the two examples after the definition. See answers in margin.

1. clipped word   3. compound word   5. blended
2. borrowed word   4. acronym   word

motel	plane	SCUBA	bouquet	smog
LASER	printout	alligator	hatchback	gym

123

(These Unit Projects are continued from T. E. page 3.)
a weekly deadline and day for distribution. They should discuss production and budget and should devise a means of covering costs with the teacher.

Computer Activity: Computers and Writing

Help students see that computers can be used effectively during several stages in the writing process. Depending upon computer accessibility, students might try one or more of the following activities:

Have students keep their journal entries on floppy disks. Each student should have a disk. Students can enter ideas at any time they might have access to a computer. Before a writing assignment, they would run a printed copy of the contents of their journal disks. This printed copy will provide ideas for writing.

During drafting or revision, have students experiment with moving blocks of text by using a simple word processing program. Suggest that they try changing the placement of a topic sentence, or moving a paragraph in the body to a different position in the text. Direct them to print both versions of their writing. Then with a peer editor or writing partner, have them study and discuss each version to see which placement is best.

Exercise for Related Skills
1. A clipped word is a shortened form of a long word. *Plane* and *gym* are clipped words.
2. A borrowed word is a word taken from another language. *Alligator* and *bouquet* are borrowed words.
3. When two or more words are put together to make a new word, the new word is called a compound word. *Printout* and *hatchback* are compound words.
4. When the initials of a group of words are put together to make a new word, the new word is called an acronym. *LASER* and *SCUBA* are acronyms.
5. When two words are put together to make a new word and some of the letters are dropped, the new word is called a blend. *Motel* (*motor* + *hotel*) and *smog* (*smoke* + *fog*) are blends.

UNIT 2

Introducing the Unit

1. Organization of the Unit Read and discuss the list of chapters, the unit title, and the introduction on page 124. Point out how all the chapters in the unit work together to improve both study and language skills. Be sure students see how the dictionary and thesaurus are useful to vocabulary improvement and how an improved vocabulary is helpful for both test-taking and writing. Discuss the two kinds of writing covered in the unit and talk about the purposes for each.

Continue the lesson with **Motivating Through Literature,** below.

2. Use the **Unit Management Guidelines** below to help you develop your weekly lesson plan. An optional week 9 has been provided to allow for variations in the length of grading periods. The teacher may wish to use this week for review, additional practice, and the presentation of selected special feature pages. Teachers who work on four- or six-week grading periods may adapt the chart accordingly.

Motivating Through Literature

Have the students read silently as you read aloud "So Will I," on page 125. Explain that before the invention of writing, a storyteller was often appointed to remember and retell important events. Briefly discuss the idea of family history being passed along from one generation to another. Use the following questions to stimulate discussion of the poem. Suggested responses are given but answers may vary.

1. What two people does the poem mention? a grandfather and grandchild
2. What do the grandfather's memories describe? many of the beauties of nature in an unspoiled world
3. What are some things that can be learned from listening to someone from an older generation? what the world was like at an earlier time
4. Who will tell the children twenty or thirty years from now about today's world? the students' generation

UNIT 2

Building Memories

In Unit 2 you will continue to learn how your language works. Your vocabulary will grow as you learn new words. You will discover two useful writing tools—the dictionary and the thesaurus. You will use new writing skills to explain how to do something or how something happens. Finally, you will explore the process that is used to write a story.

Language makes it possible to record what is going on around you. You can share childhood memories of a snowfall, a meadow teeming with wildflowers, or a picture of a special summer sky with others. Your words can give generations yet to come a picture of your world.

Unit Management Guidelines

Week 10	Week 11	Week 12	Week 13	Week 14
Unit 2 Opener, pp. 124–125; Chapter 7, Parts 1–7, pp. 126–145	Chapter 8, Parts 1–4, pp. 146–159	Chapter 9, Parts 1–5, pp. 160–175	Chapter 10, Parts 1–6, pp. 176–193	Chapter 11, Parts 1–4, pp. 194–207

SO WILL I

My grandfather remembers long ago
    the white Queen Anne's lace that grew wild.
He remembers the buttercups and goldenrod
    from when he was a child.

He remembers long ago
    the white snow falling falling.
He remembers the bluebird and thrush
    at twilight
    calling, calling.

He remembers long ago
    the new moon in the summer sky
He remembers the wind in the trees
    and its long, rising sigh.
And so will I
        so will I.

—CHARLOTTE ZOLOTOW

125

Tell them that this unit will help them to become the storytellers who will pass on ideas to the next generation.

Unit Projects

Independent Activity: Mystery

To strengthen skills in the planning and organization of the elements of a narrative, and to sharpen thinking skills, ask each student to read a mystery twice: first for enjoyment, then to analyze and take notes on the way the author hid clues to the solution of the mystery.

As preparation for writing their own mysteries, have students talk about characters, settings, and plot ideas in the mysteries they read. Students should develop and makes notes on these elements for their own stories. Suggest that the students make an idea chain similar to the one on page 231.

Direct students to write their first drafts. Have some students share their plot ideas with the class. Discuss how these students have hidden the clues that lead to the solution. Suggest better ways to introduce the clues and make their stories more difficult to solve. Allow sufficient time for revision. Have students make a final copy and share their stories with the class. Discuss what has been learned about mystery writing.

For Gifted and Talented Students Suggest that these students write and produce their mysteries in play form.

Group Activity: Explaining How

To give students experience with writing clear explanations, have the class create project activity boxes. Divide the class into groups. Assign each group a topic, such as art, science, or music. First, the group will collect ideas for simple projects. Then, they will write an explanation for each activity on an index card. On the index card, they should include materials needed and steps to completion. The cards can be filed in an (Unit Projects are continued on T. E. page 247.)

Week 15	Week 16	Week 17	Week 18
Chapter 12, Parts 1–4, pp. 208–223	Chapter 13, Parts 1–5, pp. 224–235	Chapter 13, Parts 6–8, pp. 236–245; Cumulative Review, pp. 246–247	Additional Review, Reinforcement, and Enrichment. See number 2 under **Introducing the Unit.**

Chapter 7

Chapter Objectives

1. To manage an assignment
2. To make a study plan
3. To gather information by skimming and scanning
4. To use the SQ3R method of study
5. To use the parts of a book to gather information
6. To develop memorization skills
7. To develop test-taking skills
8. To recognize and answer different types of test questions

Motivating the Students

1. Ask the students if they have ever received a poor grade on a test that they thought they had done well on. Discuss some of the reasons why that might happen. Talk about some of the ways in which students can learn things. Ask students to name things that can be easily learned, such as names, and things that can only be learned through practice and study, such as a history lesson.

2. Read and discuss the chapter introduction on page 127. Point out that study skills can also be useful outside of school. Because test-taking and studying are both skills, they can be practiced and improved. In this chapter, students will learn how to improve these skills.

Special Populations

LD Overlearning the SQ3R study method will help students to compensate for a variety of reading and learning disabilities. Habitually poor test scores and class performance can be improved. Provide extra practice, frequent review, and reminders to use this method of study in all subjects.

ESL Some students may not be familiar with American textbooks and tests. This chapter is especially important for them. Make sure that students understand both terminology and process in this chapter. Provide definitions or simplify vocabulary whenever necessary.

Week 10

Chapter Management Guidelines   This chart may be used to help structure daily lesson plans.

Day 1	Day 2	Day 3	Day 4	Day 5
Unit and Chapter Openers pp. 125–127; Part 1 "Managing Assignments," pp. 128–130	Part 2, "Skimming and Scanning," pp. 131–132; Part 3, "Using the SQ3R Method," pp. 133–135	Part 4, "Using the Parts of a Book," pp. 136–137; Part 5, "Memorizing," pp. 138–139	Part 6, "Preparing for and Taking Tests," pp. 140–141; Part 7, "Types of Test Questions," pp. 142–143	Chapter Review and selected end-of-chapter activities

Chapter 7

Study and Test-Taking Skills

Would you stop reading a good book halfway through? Would you listen to only part of a tour guide's explanation? Of course not. You would never settle for just a little information. Neither should you settle for just part of what is available to you in school. Good study and test-taking skills can help you to understand and learn everything you want to know.

In this chapter, you will learn how to develop good study and test-taking skills. You will learn to manage assignments, to skim and scan, to memorize, and to use the SQ3R study method. You will learn how to use the parts of a book and how to make a study plan. Finally, you will learn how to answer many types of test questions.

127

Related Chapters

You may wish to refer to related material in other chapters as you teach the following concepts:

1. Gathering information, Chapter 6, "Choosing a Process for Writing," page 101

2. Thinking and reasoning skills, Chapter 21, "Clear Thinking and Communication," page 367

3. Using the parts of a book to find information, Chapter 23, "Developing Library and Research Skills," page 397

Additional Resources

Skills Practice Book—pages 52–57

Test Booklet—pages 33–40
   Pretest—pages 33–34
   Mastery Test—pages 35–40

Teacher's Resource Binder
   Reinforcement Activities—
      pages 44–48
   Enrichment Activities—
      pages 14, 39–52, 64
   Ideas for Creative Teaching

Part 1

Objectives

1. To manage an assignment
2. To make a study plan

Presenting the Lesson

● All Students

1. Read and discuss page 128. Emphasize the importance of answering the four questions about any assignment. Make sure that the students understand the terms *product* and *materials*. Urge the students to ask questions about any assignment that seems unclear. Have them keep an assignment notebook, either as a section of their notebook, or as an individual notebook.

2. Read and discuss page 129. Have students distinguish between short-term and long-term goals, giving examples of each. Then, have them examine the sample study plan and identify each stage in the long project.

3. Assign and discuss Exercises A and B on page 130.

▶ Basic Students

Before assigning Exercise A, have students answer the four questions on page 128 for each assignment in the exercise. Then, help the students set up the columns for recording the exercise. You may wish to work out the first assignment on the board before having the students complete the second one on their own.

Before assigning Exercise B, help the students select an assignment. Encourage students to include family and recreational activities in their plans.

◆ Advanced Students

Ask the students to look through textbooks to find three examples of short-term and long-term assignments. Ask the students to make a study plan for one long-term assignment. Some students might explain to the class how they analyzed and scheduled the steps in the project.

---

1 Managing Assignments

> **┌─ Focus ──────────────────────────────┐**
> To complete an assignment, you must first understand it. You can then plan your time to finish it at home.
> **└───────────────────────────────────────┘**

▶ Comprehension

To complete study projects successfully, you must develop a plan. Follow the steps below to develop a plan for managing your assignments.

Understand the Assignment

To complete any assignment successfully, you must first understand exactly what you are expected to do. You must be able to answer four key questions.

1. What type of assignment is it? Is the assignment drawing a diagram, answering questions, or writing a composition?

2. What should the final product be? Should it be a written report, a skit, or answered questions?

3. What materials are needed? Do you need textbooks, a notebook, tools, or art supplies?

4. When is the assignment due? Is the work due the next day? Do you have time to complete it in stages?

Record the Assignment

Once you understand the assignment, write it in a special section of your notebook or in a separate assignment notebook. Record these details.

1. The subject or class
2. The exact assignment, including special instructions
3. The date the assignment is given
4. The date the assignment is due

128

Set Goals

In order to complete an assignment by its due date, you must learn to plan your study time wisely. The first step in planning is learning to set long- and short-term goals.

A **short-term assignment** can be completed in one study session. Reading a poem, working several math problems, and reading a social studies assignment are short-term projects.

Long-term assignments require several days or weeks to complete. They must be broken into smaller tasks, each of which can be completed in one session. Writing a computer program or a three-page paper on a poet are long-term projects.

Make a Study Plan

A study plan is a tool for planning your study time. It is helpful to have a study plan for long-term projects.

To make a study plan, draw seven columns on a large piece of paper, one for each day of the week. First, put on the chart activities that have already been planned. Sports practices and recreation activities should be included. Daily homework and household chores should also be listed.

Next, take the long-term project and divide it into smaller, manageable parts.

The study plan below was made by a student who had one week to complete a science project. Notice how this long-term assignment was broken down into several manageable tasks.

Monday	Tuesday	Wednesday	Thursday	Friday	Saturday	Sunday
After school— go to library for books Take notes	Piano Lesson 3:30	Practice piano 4:30-5:30 → 4:00 Dentist		Help decorate for J.J.'s party	Clean porch J.J.'s party 1:00-4:00	Dinner at Grandma's Make final copy
Homework— 6:30-7:30	Take notes	Organize notes	First draft		Revise first draft	Homework— 6:30-7:30

129

Additional Resources

Skills Practice Book—
  pages 52–53
Teacher's Resource Binder
Reinforcement Activities—
  page 44
Enrichment Activities—
  page 64

Special Populations

LD Students with organizational deficiencies will have difficulty with this part. Supply a printed study plan grid for students to use in the exercises. Have a supply of these grids for students to use in other classes. Help students to organize their study plans. Point out that they should first put into a plan any regular activities. Then they should add the more flexible items, scheduling them in the order of their importance, from the most to least important.

Reinforcement

1. Have the students follow the directions for Exercise A on page 130 using these assignments.

1. Read Chapter 5, 'The World of Minerals,' in your science book. Look over the list of terms at the end of the chapter, and write the definitions of these words. Be sure to have this assignment finished by Monday.
2. Make an illustration of the solar system, showing the orbit of each planet. Turn in your drawings on Wednesday.

2. For each of the following assignments have students make a study plan.

1. Choose one musical instrument, and research its history. Give a three-minute talk to the class on Monday about that instrument.
2. After you read Chapter 4, write a short skit that portrays a disagreement between Thomas Jefferson and Alexander Hamilton. The skit is due on Tuesday.
3. Keep a log of the kinds of exercise you get each day for five days. Then, write a summary of your exercise habits and ways you might improve them. This assignment is due in one week.

Enrichment

For enrichment activities, see the Unit Projects in the Teacher's Notes on page 125. One or more of these projects have special activities for gifted and talented students.

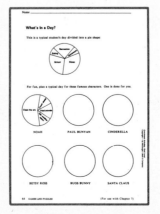

Exercises Recording Assignments and Making a Study Plan

▶ Inferring Sequence/Structured Application

A. Imagine that your teacher has given you the following assignments. Read each assignment carefully. Then divide your paper into four columns: *Subject*, *Assignment*, *Date Given*, and *Date Due*. The *Assignment* column should be wider than the others. Write the information for each assignment as you would record it in an assignment notebook.

1. "Here is a worksheet that will test your skill at multiplying fractions. The worksheet gives directions for making invisible ink. It lists how much of each ingredient you need. Next to the list, write the amount of each ingredient you need to make half the basic recipe. Then list the amount of each ingredient needed for one-and-a-half times the recipe. Today is Wednesday. Have the worksheet finished by Friday."

2. "Today you studied the importance of colorful, precise verbs. For homework, look for lively verbs in newspaper headlines. Copy each headline and underline the verb. You should find at least ten examples. This assignment is due tomorrow."

▶ Inferring Sequence/Creative Application

B. Make a one-week study plan that includes the completion of a long-term project. Choose a long-term project that has been assigned in one of your classes, or pretend that you have been assigned a particular long-term project. Your study plan should include your daily chores, homework, and any other planned activities. Then break down the long-term project into smaller tasks, and assign them specific time slots in your study plan. Your study plan should be similar to the model plan on page 129.

130

Skimming and Scanning

> **Focus**
>
> **Skimming** and **scanning** are important reading and study skills.

▶ Comprehension

Usually you read books and assignments word for word. Sometimes, however, you need to read quickly to find certain types of information. **Skimming** and **scanning** are two types of reading that help you gather information quickly.

Skimming

Skimming is one type of fast reading. Use skimming to get a general idea of what a book, chapter, or article is about. To skim, let your eyes travel quickly down the page. Do not read every word. Pay special attention to the following items.

Titles	Key words	Pictures and
Headings	Topic Sentences	captions

Scanning

Scanning is also a type of fast reading. It is used to find specific information. To scan, quickly glance down the page. Keep reading in this way until you notice key words and phrases that show you are near the information you need. Then slow down and read more carefully.

To understand the importance of scanning, imagine how difficult it would be to find a number in the phone book if you had to read every name! Suppose you had to find out the year in which Abraham Lincoln became a lawyer. How long would it take to find the information if you had to read an entire encyclopedia article? Scanning would make both tasks faster.

131

Part 2

Objective

To gather information by skimming and scanning

Presenting the Lesson

◼ All Students

1. Read and discuss pages 131–132. Stress that skimming and scanning are used to discover a general idea or to find specific information quickly, but that a closer reading is necessary for deeper understanding.

2. Emphasize that the purpose of skimming is to find the main idea. Point out the usefulness of titles, headings, topic sentences, key words, pictures, and captions.

3. Emphasize that the purpose of scanning is to find specific information. Discuss with students situations in which scanning would be a useful skill. For example, they might use scanning to look for a particular movie listing in the newspaper.

4. Assign and discuss Exercises A and B on page 132.

▶ Basic Students

Have students practice skimming and scanning with the following paragraph. They should skim to find the main idea of the paragraph, then scan to answer these questions.

Bones come in many shapes. Some of the bones in your body are round and some are flat. The bones on your head are flat. So are your hip bones. Some of your bones are very long. Others, like the bones in your fingers, are short. But all 206 of your bones have one thing in common: they are strong!

1. What is the subject of this paragraph? bones
2. How many bones are in your body? 206
3. What is the shape of your hip bones? flat

◆ Advanced Students

Have the students write a paragraph about themselves. They should tell about some of their favorite things. Then, have the students exchange papers and scan to find the information as quickly as possible. Students should list each item as they locate it in the paragraph.

Special Populations

LD, ESL Students will need some additional work on skimming and scanning skills. Define the terms presented in this part. You might post these terms and definitions on the board: *titles*—names; *headings*—words or phrases in dark print; *topic sentence*—main idea of paragraph; *captions*—words that tell about a picture; *key words*—special words.

Skimming and scanning require drawing conclusions about context from key words. Scanning requires an ability to discriminate between what is important and supporting details.

Reinforcement

1. Have the students follow the directions for Exercise A on page 132 using the following article.

2. Then have the students scan the article and answer these questions.

1. What is the snapping turtle's best defense? its powerful jaws

2. What is the carapace? the upper, arched part of a turtle's shell

3. Which kind of turtle provides tortoise shell? the hawksbill turtle

All turtles have a shell. Some of them, such as the box turtle, can draw the head, legs, and tail inside the shell, and tightly close the upper and lower halves. The snapping turtle, however, has a small lower shell which does not begin to cover it. Its powerful jaws are its best defense. Sea turtles likewise are unable to retreat inside their shells.

The upper arched part of the shell is called the *carapace.* The flat lower part is the *plastron.* The upper shell is made up of the backbone and ribs, which have grown together with plates of bone. The lower shell is fused with the breastbone. In the hard-shelled turtles the bone is covered with horny shields. The markings and colors differ with each kind and may be very beautiful. The hawksbill turtle, which lives in warm seas throughout the world, provides the tortoise shell from which ornamental articles are made.

Exercises Practicing Skimming and Scanning

▶ Analyzing/Generalizing

A. Skim the article below in Exercise B. What is it about? Write the answer on your paper. the cooling process in a refrigerator

▶ Analyzing/Drawing Conclusions

B. Scan the article. Write the answers to these questions.

1. What is a thermostat? a temperature regulator

2. Where does freon go when it leaves the storage tank? to the condenser coils

3. Is freon in a gas or a liquid form at the end of the cooling cycle? liquid

Freon and the Cooling Process

The cooling process of a refrigerator takes place in a cycle.

Stage 1 — The cooling cycle begins when the **thermostat**, the temperature regulator, signals that the refrigerator is too warm. The signal starts the pump which pushes a coolant, liquid **Freon**, at high pressure through a small hole in a long tube.

Stage 2 — After the liquid has passed through the small hole into the **evaporator coils**, it is no longer under pressure. Therefore, the Freon evaporates and becomes a gas. As it evaporates, the Freon absorbs heat from the refrigerator.

Stage 3 — Next, the Freon travels to the **compressor**, which forces the Freon under pressure into the **condenser coils**. In these coils, the Freon changes back into a liquid and releases heat into the air outside the refrigerator. The cooling cycle is now complete.

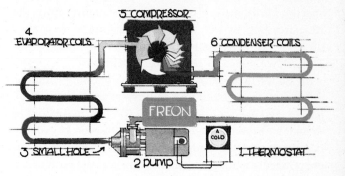

132

Additional Resources

Skills Practice Book—page 54

Teacher's Resource Binder
  Reinforcement Activities—
    page 45

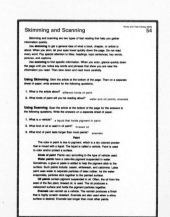

Using the SQ3R Method

┌─ *Focus* ───────────────────────────────────┐
│ Use the **SQ3R study method** to discover, understand, and │
│ remember important information in your reading. │
└──┘

▶ Comprehension

For most of your assignments, you need to read and study written information. One way to help yourself learn the material is to use a study method called the **SQ3R method**. SQ3R stands for the five steps of the method: *Survey, Question, Read, Record,* and *Review.*

Here is an explanation of this study plan.

┌──┐
│ **The SQ3R Study Method** │
│ │
│ **Survey** Quickly look over the material to get a general idea │
│ of the contents. Read the titles and subtitles. Look │
│ at any pictures, maps, tables, or graphs. Read the │
│ introduction or the first few paragraphs. Look at │
│ the final paragraph. │
│ │
│ **Question** Look at any study questions presented at the end │
│ of the material or given to you by your teacher. │
│ These questions will help you pick out information │
│ as you read. │
│ │
│ **Read** Read carefully. Identify the main ideas in each │
│ section. Look for answers to the study questions. │
│ │
│ **Record** After reading, write the answers to the questions. │
│ Make brief notes to help you remember the an- │
│ swers and any other important ideas. │
│ │
│ **Review** Read the questions again. Try to answer them │
│ without looking at your notes. If you can't, review │
│ the material to find the answers. Then study your │
│ notes so that you will be able to recall the informa- │
│ tion at a later time. │
└──┘

133

Part 3

Objective

To use the SQ3R method of study

Presenting the Lesson

All Students

1. Read and discuss pages 133–134. Make sure the students can name and identify the purpose of each step in the SQ3R method. Carefully discuss the note-taking process and the importance of putting the main ideas into students' own words.

2. Assign and discuss the exercise on pages 134–135. Read the directions out loud and encourage students to ask questions until they understand the assignment. Check students' notes to make sure they found the answers to the review questions.

Basic Students

Before assigning the exercise, demonstrate each of the SQ3R steps, using a different article or textbook chapter. Give the students group practice in taking notes, helping them to pick out the most important ideas from the article or chapter. You may wish to work with some students individually when practicing the SQ3R method.

Advanced Students

Have students find an interesting and informative article in a news or science magazine. They should use the SQ3R method to read and study the article. After surveying the article, they should list three questions that cover the main ideas of the article. Have students answer these questions after they have completed the reading step of the SQ3R method.

Special Populations

LD It is important that students overlearn the SQ3R method. It can then be a valuable tool for reading and studying in all classes. Put the steps of the SQ3R method on a poster. You might also provide students with several individual copies of these steps so that they can check off each point as they complete it. This procedure is especially helpful to those students with difficulties in sequencing. Work through the exercise on pages 134–135 with students. Repeat the process with a selection from their science or social studies books.

ESL If students have difficulty with the vocabulary in the selection on page 135, have them first use the process on an article or selection with more basic vocabulary.

Reinforcement

Using an actual class reading assignment, have the students use the SQ3R method. Then have them answer the four questions found in the exercise on page 134. Check students' notes for main ideas and rephrasing in the students' own words.

Exercise

1. Titles and subtitles, the first paragraph.
2. Joseph Merlin invented the roller skate about 1760. People can roller skate in a curve. Roller skates have two major parts: the boot and the skate assembly. Wheels made of polyurethane revolutionized roller skating.
3. See review questions.

For Your Review

1. About 1760. In 1863 James Plimpton designed a roller skate that enabled people to skate in a curve.
2. The boot and the skate assembly.
3. Polyurethane wheels are lighter and quieter. Skaters can move faster on them. They provide smoother, more comfortable skating.

The notes you take as you study should be in your own words. They should consist of key words and phrases that relate to main ideas. Notes need not be written in complete sentences, but they should be clear enough for you to understand later.

Keep your notes in a notebook with sections for each subject. Write the subject and the date at the top of each page of notes. Add other headings that will help you to locate your notes easily when you need to refer to them. These notes will provide you with a brief summary of everything you study. They can be used when you need to find information quickly or when you are reviewing for a test.

Exercise   Using a Study Method
▶ Analyzing/Drawing Conclusions

Read the article about roller skates, using the SQ3R method. Look at the review questions at the end of the article before you begin. They will help you study correctly. Answer the following questions when you have finished reading. See answers in margin.

1. Where should you look for clues about the contents of the article? What clues do you find?
2. Take notes as you read each paragraph. What are the main ideas in the article?
3. Write the answers to the three review questions on your own paper.

ROLLER SKATES

Joseph Merlin, a Belgian musician, invented the roller skate about 1760. James Plimpton, an American inventor, designed an improved roller skate in 1863. Plimpton's "rocking skate" enabled people to roller skate in a curve by simply leaning to one side. Skating in curves had previously been possible only on ice skates.

Most roller skates have two major parts, the *boot* and the *skate assembly*.

134

Additional Resources

Skills Practice Book—page 55

The Boot is made of leather. Boots worn for recreational and artistic skating have high tops and are laced up the front to a point above the ankle. Speed skaters wear boots with low-cut tops. The boots of all roller skates should fit snugly and hug the heel firmly.

The Skate Assembly is a metal structure attached to the sole of the boot. The main parts of the assembly are the *plate*, two *truck assemblies*, the *toe stop*, and four wheels. The truck assemblies, which are mechanisms attached to the front and back of the plate, contain movable parts that enable skaters to turn corners. The toe stop is a device at the front of the skate that allows skaters to stop quickly and to perform maneuvers.

Two wheels are attached to axles at the front and two at the back of the skate. Early roller skate wheels were made of clay or wood. In the mid-1970's, roller skating was revolutionized by the introduction of wheels made of hard plastic called *polyurethane*. Such wheels are lighter and quieter than those made of clay or metal, and skaters can move faster on them. Polyurethane wheels also provide smoother, more comfortable skating.

Some people wear *clamp-on skates*, which are skate assemblies that they attach to their shoes.

For Your Review   See answers in margin.

1. When was the first roller skate invented? One hundred years later, the design was improved. How?
2. What two parts make up most roller skates?
3. Why are polyurethane wheels superior to clay or wood wheels?

— *The World Book Encyclopedia*

135

Part 4

Objective

To use the parts of a book to gather information

Presenting the Lesson

 All Students

1. Read and discuss page 136. Make sure every student can find the table of contents and index of this text. Ask them to check each of their textbooks to find which ones have glossaries.

2. Using an index is a skill that requires practice. Discuss with students the concept of cross-referencing. They should take advantage of suggestions to check other topics for information they might be able to use. Also encourage students to check alternative entries, even if none are suggested. List some topics on the board and ask students what other entries they might check for each: tractors (farm equipment, machinery), roses (plants, flowers, perennials), diamonds (coal, gems, South Africa).

3. Assign and discuss Exercises A and B on page 137.

 Basic Students

Have students use their books to answer the following questions. They should tell whether they will find the answers by looking in the index or the table of contents or both.

1. On what page will you find spelling rules? index, table of contents,
2. What is a card catalog? index or table of contents
3. In what chapter can you learn about the process of writing? table of contents

 Advanced Students

Have the students make a glossary for the article on roller skates in the exercise on page 135. Tell them to first identify the words that may be difficult in the passage, and then to define them and write the definitions in alphabetical order. Students might work in pairs or small groups on this project.

---

4 Using the Parts of a Book

> **Focus**
>
> Use the parts of a book to help you find information quickly.

▸ Comprehension

Nonfiction books are useful when you are gathering information on a particular topic. However, there are many books on most topics. How can you find those that will be most useful to you? How can you quickly find information in the books you choose? There are three special parts of a book that can help you answer these questions: The **table of contents**, the **index**, and the **glossary**.

You will find a **table of contents** at the front of most nonfiction books. It lists the title of each chapter in the book and the page on which it begins. It may also list the main topics that each chapter discusses. Check to see whether the topic you are looking for is listed. Locate and study the table of contents in this book.

At the back of most nonfiction books, you will find an **index**. Every important topic that is discussed in the book is listed in alphabetical order in the index. Each topic is followed by the numbers of the pages on which it is discussed. Locate and study the index in this book.

The index is a good place to look for specific terms. Look for broader topics in the table of contents.

Another useful part of some nonfiction books is a **glossary**. A glossary lists difficult words in alphabetical order, and defines them according to the way they are used in the field discussed in that book. A glossary is especially handy in books that use many unfamiliar terms or familiar terms that are used in specialized ways.

136

Special Populations

LD Before doing the exercises, review alphabetical order so that students can use the index efficiently. Do Exercise A

Exercises   Using Parts of the Book

▶ Recalling

A. Look for each of these terms in the table of contents and the index of this book. Tell the part of the book that lists each term. Some terms can be found in both places. Some can be found in only one place.

1. suffixes TOC, IND
2. pronouns TOC, IND
3. card catalog TOC, IND
4. topic sentences TOC, IND
5. verbs TOC, IND
6. conjunctions TOC, IND
7. reference books IND
8. ZIP codes IND

▶ Analyzing

B. Look at the following table of contents. Then answer the questions below it.

		Guide to Home Repair	
Chapter 1		Basic Tools and How To Use Them	4–21
	Part 1	Hammers	4
	Part 2	Saws	8
	Part 3	Screwdrivers	13
	Part 4	Wrenches and Pliers	16
Chapter 2		Fasteners	22–34
	Part 1	Glue	22
	Part 2	Nails, Brads, and Staples	25
	Part 3	Screws and Bolts	30
Chapter 3		Finishing Materials	35–45
	Part 1	Paints, Stains, and Varnishes	35
	Part 2	Brushes	41

1. Does this book give directions for building a go-cart? no
2. In what chapter and part would you find information on a Phillips screwdriver? Chapter 1, Part 3
3. What is a brad? Name two similar devices. a device for fastening things; nails, staples
4. In what chapter and part would you find information on what type of stain to use on wood patio furniture? Chapter 3, Part 1
5. Where would you find information on camel's hair paint brushes? Chapter 3, Part 2

orally with students. Then you might assign additional topics for students to work on independently.

Reinforcement

Have the students follow the directions for Exercise A using these topics:

1. adjectives TOC, IND
2. skimming TOC, IND
3. prepositions TOC, IND
4. thank-you notes IND
5. metaphors IND
6. quotation marks TOC, IND
7. sentences, fragments of TOC, IND
8. spelling TOC, IND
9. encyclopedias IND
10. rhyming TOC, IND

Enrichment

If the school has a library, give each student a research question. Send them in small groups to check out books in which they might find the answers. Have them share the books and information with the class. Also have students tell which parts of the books they used to find information. Possible questions are:

1. How tall is the Statue of Liberty?
2. What is the distance from the pitcher's mound to the plate in major league baseball?
3. Who wrote *Little Women*?
4. In what year did Marie Curie win the Nobel Prize in Physics?
5. What is a marsupial?

Additional Resources

Skills Practice Book—page 56

Teacher's Resource Binder
Reinforcement Activities—
    page 46
Enrichment Activities—
    page 14

Part 5

Objective

To develop memorization skills

Presenting the Lesson

 All Students

1. Read and discuss pages 138–139. Go over each memorizing method discussed in this part. Ask students to think about which method might work best for them. Have them explain their answers. Try each method in class, using words from the dictionary, math formulas, or random lists of items that are provided by the students.

Stress the importance of trying all methods. Students will find that some work better for them than others. Also point out that some skills will prove more effective in one subject area than in another. Students must be flexible enough to experiment until they discover what works best for them.

2. Assign and discuss Exercises A and B on page 139.

 Basic Students

When you assign Exercise A, you may wish to have the students write each word on a piece of paper in the order they appear in the book. Then, have them put the paper away and try to write the words as they remember them.

Do Exercise B with the students as a group activity.

 Advanced Students

Challenge students to memorize a list of items. For how many months can they memorize the official birthstone, flower, and one famous historical event?

Special Populations

LD Students should overlearn the skills presented in this part. This can be accomplished with sufficient practice and repetition. Begin by providing a study sheet that lists the skills in a simplified way. Assign a specific list of items or details for students to learn for use with each memory skill presented in this part. In each case, show students how to use the skill.

---

5 Memorizing

> **Focus**
>
> **Memorizing** is a study skill that can be learned and improved with practice.

▶ Comprehension

Memory makes it possible to learn information once, then recall and reuse it again and again. In school, you might memorize important dates in history, spelling words, or math formulas. At home, you might memorize a friend's phone number or a favorite recipe.

The first step in memorizing is to make sure you understand the material. If necessary, ask your teacher, a parent, or a friend to help you.

There are many ways to memorize. Since people learn in many different ways, try these to find the methods that work best for you.

1. Recite out loud. If you read a list of words silently, you may remember several words. If you read the list out loud, you are likely to remember several more words. The sound of your own voice often helps you remember. Walking back and forth, or pacing, while reciting out loud may help you remember even more.

2. Write the material. Just as the sound of your voice can help you remember, the action of moving a pen or pencil on paper is a memory booster. Seeing what you have written also helps the material stay in your mind.

3. Connect ideas. It is easier to remember a list of facts if you can connect, or associate, them in some way. When you associate things, you think of some way they fit together. You might remember history dates by first putting them in the order in which they happened. You might remember a list of science vocabulary words by putting them in alphabetical order. A shopping list could be divided into categories: dairy products, fruits and vegetables, breads and cereals, and meat.

4. Use memory games. There are countless memory tricks and games that you may find helpful. You may try visualizing what you want to remember. To visualize, close your eyes and try to picture the items you want to remember. Then, to recall your list, visualize the same picture.

Here is a popular game that uses letters rather than pictures. Take the first letter of each word you want to memorize. Then think of a phrase that uses each of those letters as a first letter of a word in the phrase. For example, the notes on the lines of a musical staff are *E, G, B, D,* and *F.* You might remember these notes on the lines of a staff by learning this phrase: *"Every Good Boy Does Fine."* Remember the names of the planets with this phrase: *"My Very Educated Mother Just Served Us Nine Pizzas."* The planets are *Mercury, Venus, Earth, Mars, Jupiter, Saturn, Uranus, Neptune,* and *Pluto.*

5. Repeat and review the material. Repeat your list or memory game several times. Repeat it at different times of the day for several days until you can easily call it to mind.

Exercises Improving Memory Skills

▶ Structured Application

A. The following list names the parts of an octopus. Read the list out loud several times. Close your book. Then write as many words as you can remember.

trunk	skirt	eye	suckers
head	tentacles	siphon	

▶ Creative Application

B. Make a memory game that will help you remember the list of words in Exercise A. Can you write a sentence in which each word begins with the first letter of a word in the list? Write your sentence. Now can you recite the words in the list?

139

Have the students follow the directions for Exercises A and B using this list of players and positions for a softball team:

Fletcher—catcher
Renee—first base
Agnes—second base
Marie—shortstop
Leona—third base
Jordan—right field
Sabrina—center field
Nelson—left field
Richard—pitcher

Additional Resources

Teacher's Resource Binder
Reinforcement Activities—
   page 47

Part 6

Objective

To develop test-taking skills

Presenting the Lesson

 All Students

1. Read and discuss **Preparing for a Test** on pages 140–141. Discuss each of the guidelines. Ask students how these guidelines might help them prepare for a test. Ask them if they sometimes feel nervous or unprepared for a test. Tell them that proper study methods and test-taking skills can help them do better on tests.

2. Read and discuss **Taking a Test** on page 141. Carefully go over each guideline. Stress the importance of time-management when taking a test.

3. Assign and discuss the exercise on page 141.

 Basic Students

Help the students prepare the study plan for the exercise. In the days before the test, review the study plan and help the students follow the guidelines. The day before the test, remind students to eat well and get plenty of rest. Right before the test, review the guidelines for taking a test. After the test, ask students whether they felt that they did better on the test than they would have without the study plan. Encourage them to keep using this method on their own.

 Advanced Students

Have the students that consistently perform well on tests write about their test-taking strategies and advise other students on how to prepare for a test. Share the strategies with the class.

Special Populations

LD Students with organizational deficiencies will need some help in preparing their study plans. Provide students with a test preparation checklist that they might use each time they prepare for a test. Walk students through each step in preparing for a test they will be taking.

---

6 Preparing for and Taking Tests

┌─ *Focus* ─────────────────────────────────┐
    Learning and using test-taking skills can help you improve your test results.
└──┘

▶ Comprehension

Knowing how to prepare for and take tests can improve your test scores. Use these guidelines to help you improve your test-taking skills.

Preparing for a Test

1. Know what to study. If you have questions about what the test will cover, ask your teacher before you begin to prepare. Focus your studying on the information the test will cover.

2. Make a study plan. Study on a daily basis. Do not wait until just before the test. Determine how much time you will need to prepare for the test. Plan ahead for that time.

3. Organize your study materials. Keep a notebook. Organize lists of vocabulary and spelling words, completed assignments, and quizzes. These are your tools for review.

4. Review. Skim reading assignments and carefully reread class notes. Review the study questions and answers you wrote as you used the SQ3R study method. Complete and study any review guides or worksheets received in class.

5. Memorize important facts. Use the memorizing skills you learned in part 5 to remember important names, dates, events, or vocabulary terms. Have someone quiz you.

6. Be rested and alert. Plenty of sleep and good nutrition help you do your best. Now relax. You are ready to take the test.

Follow these guidelines for taking a test.

140

Taking a Test

1. Skim the test. Look at the length of the test and the types of questions. Plan your time accordingly.

2. Read all directions before you begin. Ask questions if you do not understand the directions. Follow directions exactly.

3. Answer easy questions first. Then go back to the longer or more difficult questions. Allow extra time for these questions.

4. Review the test. Look for missing answers, confusing answers, and messy handwriting. Make the necessary changes. Make sure all questions are answered.

Taking a Standardized Test

You have probably taken several standardized tests in the past few years. These tests compare your level of learning to that of other students. You cannot study for these tests. A good night's sleep before the test is the best preparation.

Most standardized tests measure the number of correct answers you write in a limited time period. If a question is very difficult and is taking too long, skip it and go to the next. If you finish the test early, return to the unanswered questions.

Follow directions carefully. Some standardized tests have sections on several subjects, such as reading comprehension, vocabulary, math, science, and social studies. Be sure that you are putting your answers under the correct test heading on the answer sheet.

Exercise   Preparing for and Taking a Test

▶ Creative Application

Choose a test that you will be taking soon. Develop a study plan to prepare for this test. Use the guide on page 129 to write your plan. Prepare for this test by following your study plan.

When it is time to take the test, follow the guide on this page.

141

Repeat these steps for their next several tests in a variety of subjects. Write the four steps for taking a test on their test papers. Students will then be able to use the skills that they have learned and practiced.

Reinforcement

Have students discuss whether or not the study plans they made and used for the exercise were effective. Ask students to comment on which were the most helpful steps in preparing for a test.

Part 7

Objective

To recognize and answer different types of test questions

Presenting the Lesson

All Students

1. Read and discuss pages 142–143. Discuss each question type and the strategies given for answering them. You may wish to give examples of each type of question, using tests from this textbook and others. When discussing standardized tests, you may wish to show students a sample answer sheet and discuss the importance of marking it correctly.

2. Assign and discuss the exercise on page 143.

Basic Students

Integrate the concepts covered in this part into their daily curriculum. Practice with a variety of test item formats. Do the exercise as a group activity, making sure that the students understand the structure of each test question type. Then, assign the reinforcement activity on page 143 of these Teacher Notes, having the students work independently.

Advanced Students

Write a list of essay questions on the board. You might take questions from recently studied science or social studies material. Ask students to select a topic and write an outline of the points they would discuss in answering the question. Make sure that the outline includes a statement of the main idea.

Special Populations

LD Students should have extra practice in working all types of test questions. Concentrate especially on true-false and multiple choice questions. Use a variety of key words in each so that students can see how these affect the answer. Demonstrate how to handle choices such as *All of the above* or *None of the above* in multiple choice questions.

7 Types of Test Questions

> **Focus**
>
> There are many types of test questions. Know how to answer each kind.

▶ Comprehension/Classifying

Improve your test scores by learning how to master the different types of test questions.

1. True-False A true-false question is written as a statement. You must decide whether the statement is correct or incorrect. If *any part* of the statement is incorrect, the entire statement is false. Words such as *all*, *never*, *always*, and *none* are often found in false statements. Words such as *some*, *most*, *many*, and *usually* often signal true statements.

2. Multiple Choice A multiple choice question has three or more possible answers, usually identified with such small letters as *a*, *b*, *c*. Before answering, read all of the possible choices. Eliminate the incorrect choices. Then pick the best answer from those that remain. Pay special attention to choices such as *all of the above* and *none of the above*.

3. Matching In this exercise, you match numbered items in one column with lettered answers in another. You place the letter of the correct answer next to the question. In some cases, you will use a letter more than once, or not at all.

4. Fill-in-the-Blank In this type of question, you add a missing word or words to a sentence. Sometimes you will be given a list of words to choose from. Remember to use proper capitalization and punctuation.

5. Short Answer Write your answer to this type of question in one or two sentences. Make sure sentences are complete. Use proper capitalization and punctuation.

6. Essay Most essay questions are answered in paragraph form. To organize your answer, follow a simple process of writing. Jot down ideas, organize the ideas in logical order, and write. Again, capitalize and punctuate correctly.

7. Questions for Standardized Tests Standardized tests are used to compare the progress of students in specific areas, such as school districts or states. Most standardized tests are multiple choice. To take these tests, follow the guidelines you learned above for taking multiple choice tests.

Standardized tests, as well as some class tests, may use separate answer sheets. To mark the correct answer, you fill in small circles, ovals, or squares with your pencil. You must mark answers carefully, because these answer sheets are read by machines. Fill in circles completely. Erase stray marks which may otherwise be read as an answer.

Exercise   Understanding Different Types of Test Questions

▶ Structured Application

Look carefully at the statement below. Then write four test questions based on that statement. Write one of each type: true-false, multiple choice, fill-in-the-blank, and short answer.

The deepest spot in the Atlantic Ocean is near Puerto Rico. It is 30,246 feet deep—almost six miles.

143

Additional Resources

Teacher's Resource Binder
Reinforcement Activities—
    page 48

Reinforcement

Have the students follow the directions for the exercise on page 143 using these statements:

1. The Escorial is a monastery and palace in central Spain, located 26 miles west of Madrid. It was built by King Philip II.
2. The Library of Congress is the national library of the United States. It is located in Washington, D.C., and contains more than 70 million items.

Enrichment

Have students research a variety of subjects in an encyclopedia. Then, have them make up test questions about those subjects. Have them write at least one example of each of the types of questions discussed in this part. Check to see that the answer choices for multiple choice and matching questions include a correct answer. Have students work in small groups.

Using English in Math

This activity may be used to demonstrate how to use study skills in math. Read and discuss page 144 with students. Make sure they understand how to apply the SQ3R method to a word problem in math before they try the exercise.

For additional reinforcement, use the example below.

Look how Karen used this study method to solve a word problem.

Survey   Karen read this problem. Most mornings, Juan runs 2.5 miles. This week he ran every day except Friday. How many miles did Juan run this week?

Question   "What do I have to find out?" Karen has to find out how many miles Juan ran this week.
"What information am I given?"
Karen knows that Juan ran 6 days this week. He ran 2.5 miles each day.
"What process should I use?"
Karen decides that multiplication is the correct process to use.

Compute   Karen multiplies 6 × 2.5

$$\begin{array}{r} 2.5 \\ \times\ \ 6 \\ \hline 15.0 \end{array}$$

Record   Karen writes the answer.
15

Review   Karen reworks the problem to make sure it is correct.

Using English in ▶ Math

Using English in ▶ Math

▶ Comprehension

You are now familiar with many different study skills. One of the most useful is the SQ3R study method. It will help you learn and understand many types of new materials.

You can create similar study methods for specific areas. One area where a study method might be especially helpful is math. Try the five steps of this study method to solve a word problem in math.

Survey: Read the math problem or word problem.

Question: Ask yourself these questions.
"What do I have to find out?"
"What information am I given?"
"What process should I use to solve the problem?"

Compute: Work the math problem.

Record: Write the answer.

Review: Check over your work. Make sure that your answer is correct.

Exercise   Using a Study Method for Math

▶ Structured Application

Use a study method to solve this word problem.

Ed's delivery truck can carry 2,700 pounds of produce. Ed is delivering cabbages to several supermarkets. Each cabbage weighs about 3 pounds. Approximately how many cabbages can Ed's truck carry in one load? $2{,}700 \div 3 = 900$

144

Chapter 7 Review

▶ Classifying/Analyzing

A. Mastering Study Skills Write the answers to the following "test" questions on your own paper. Then tell what type of question the items in each part are.

Part 1 Write *True* or *False* for each statement. True-False questions

1. Short-term assignments can be completed in only a few weeks. False
2. To complete an assignment correctly, you must first understand the directions. True
3. A study plan should allow time for your regular chores and activities. True

Part 2 For each question, write the letter of the correct answer. Multiple Choice questions

1. Which of the following is part of the SQ3R study method? __a__
   - a. Record   b. Repeat   c. Rest
2. What should class notes not contain? __c__
   - a. your own words   c. complete sentences
   - b. key words and phrases

Part 3 Match the word in column 1 with its definition in column 2. Write the correct letter next to each number. Matching questions

__b__ 1. index
__c__ 2. glossary
__a__ 3. table of contents

a. list of titles and subheadings
b. alphabetical listing of topics
c. alphabetical list of terms and definitions

▶ Creative Application

B. Using Memory Skills Try to make up two memory tricks to complete the following assignment. Describe each memory device in a paragraph.

Assignment: Memorize the names of the seven continents of the world: Asia, Europe, Antarctica, North America, Africa, Australia, and South America.

145

Chapter Review

This review allows teachers to evaluate student understanding of the concepts presented in this chapter.

Additional Resources

Skills Practice Book
Review—page 57

Test Booklet
Mastery Test—pages 35–40

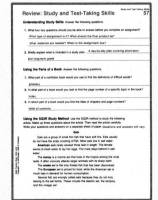

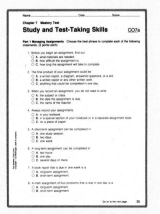

Chapter 8

Chapter Objectives

1. To use definition, restatement, and examples in context to discover word meanings

2. To identify base words

3. To recognize common prefixes and use them to discover meanings of unfamiliar words

4. To recognize common suffixes and use them to discover meanings of unfamiliar words

Motivating the Students

1. Write these words on the board: *nonfactual, unanswerable.* Have students identify the parts that can be removed from the beginning and end of the words, and still leave a meaningful word. As you erase the word part, point out how the meaning of the word changes when beginnings and endings are removed. Tell students that getting to the main part of a word is one way to unlock the meaning of an unfamiliar word. Add that they will learn other ways in this chapter to understand new words.

2. Explain that sometimes words and sentences around an unfamiliar word will give clues to what the unfamiliar word means. Ask students to listen for clues that help define the word *tranquil* after you read this passage.

> Ruth stared at the pond. Not a ripple could be seen; the water was like glass. A butterfly lit briefly on a branch in front of her. Even the birds were quiet. Whenever Ruth was upset, she came to this tranquil place.

Ask a volunteer to define *tranquil.* Then, have students identify the details that helped to define *tranquil.*

3. Read and discuss the introductory paragraphs on page 147. Tell the students that knowing how to decipher context clues and learning the meanings of different word parts will help them understand and learn many new words.

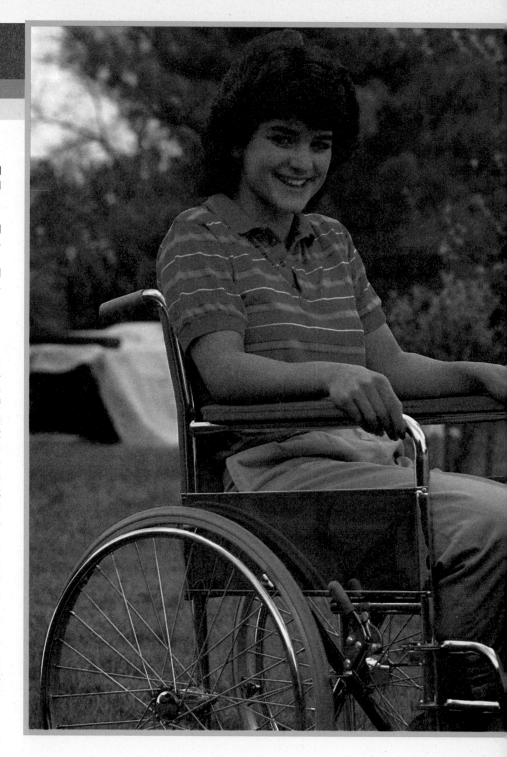

Week 11

Chapter Management Guidelines This chart may be used to help structure daily lesson plans.

Day 1	Day 2	Day 3	Day 4	Day 5
Chapter 8 Opener, p. 147; Part 1, "Using Context Clues: Definition, Restatement, and Example," pp. 148–149	Part 2, "Using Word Parts: Base Words," pp. 150–151	Part 3, "Using Word Parts: Prefixes," pp. 152–153	Part 4, "Using Word Parts: Suffixes," pp. 154–155	Chapter Review and selected end-of-chapter activities

Chapter 8

Building Your Vocabulary

As you read a story or a magazine article, you may come across an unfamiliar word. If a dictionary is not handy, you can become a special kind of detective—a word detective. You can use word clues to solve the mystery of what the unfamiliar word means.

One kind of clue you can look for is a context clue. The context is the words and sentences that surround the unfamiliar word. You can also look for clues in the meanings of different word parts.

In this chapter, you will learn ways to unlock the meanings of new and unfamiliar words. Each new word that becomes familiar to you helps your vocabulary grow.

147

Special Populations

LD Provide additional oral exercises to reinforce the vocabulary concepts presented in this chapter.

ESL This chapter is especially important for ESL students as they build their knowledge of the structure of English.

NSD Students may increase their standard English vocabulary by learning new words through context clues. Provide extra practice as needed.

Related Chapters

You may wish to refer to related material in other chapters as you teach these concepts:

1. Scanning and skimming, Chapter 7, "Study and Test Taking Skills," page 127

2. Word meaning, Chapter 9, "Discovering the Dictionary and Thesaurus," pages 161

Additional Resources

Skills Practice Book—pages 58–65

Test Booklet—pages 41–46
  Pretest—pages 41–42
  Mastery Test—pages 43–46

Teacher's Resource Binder
  Reinforcement Activities—
    pages 49–52
  Enrichment Activities—
    pages 15–16, 39–52
  Ideas for Creative Teaching

Name _____ Date _____ Score _____

Chapter 8 Pretest
Building Your Vocabulary   PO8a

Part 1 Using Context Clues: Definition, Restatement, and Example Read each of the following sentences and decide the meaning of the underlined word. Then tell which kind of context clue helped you understand the meaning of the word. (10 points each)

The stew was made from mutton, in other words, from an adult sheep.

1. The word closest in meaning to the underlined word is:
   ○ A. stew
   ○ B. meat

2. The context clues in this sentence
   ○ A. defined or restated the word
   ○ B. helped explain the word by example

The pool was filled with large carp and other fish.

3. The word closest in meaning to the underlined word is:
   ○ A. pool
   ○ B. fish

4. The context clues in this sentence
   ○ A. defined or restated the word
   ○ B. helped explain the word by example

Part 2 Using Word Parts: Base Words For each item, choose the correct base word. (8 points each)

5. fearlessly
   ○ A. fear
   ○ B. less
   ○ C. ear

6. untruthfully
   ○ A. full
   ○ B. truth
   ○ C. under

7. dishonesty
   ○ A. dish
   ○ B. honest
   ○ C. nest

Go on to the next page   41

Part 1

Objective

To use definition, restatement, and examples in context to discover word meanings

Presenting the Lesson

 All Students

1. Read and discuss pages 148–149. Be sure students understand the idea of *context*. Discuss the three techniques described for finding the meaning of unfamiliar words in context. Emphasize the role of key words and punctuation marks in finding context clues. As you read the examples, have students tell which words in the sentences help to define the unfamiliar words.

2. Stress that using examples to find meanings requires both imagination and logical thinking. The reader must be able to understand the category to which the given example belongs. Then the reader will be able to see why the new word belongs to that category. For example, a reader must recognize crabs and lobsters before understanding that they are crustaceans.

3. Assign and discuss Exercises A and B on page 149.

4. Use the exercise on page 156 for additional practice if needed.

 Basic Students

Before assigning the exercises, give the students extra practice in recognizing definition, restatement, and example in context by having them develop an example of each on their own. Write the words *beverage, tool,* and *sandal* on the board. Have the students suggest a sentence for each one, using the techniques of definition, restatement, and example to provide context clues for a reader who does not know the meaning of the words. Write their suggestions on the board.

When assigning the exercises, do the first few items with the students before having them work on their own.

1 Using Context Clues: Definition, Restatement, and Example

> **Focus**
>
> You can use **context clues** to unlock the meaning of an unfamiliar word in a sentence. A context clue may define, restate, or give an example of an unfamiliar word. Context is the words or sentences around a particular word.

Definition and Restatement

▶ Comprehension

A writer may define an unfamiliar word or restate it in a different way. Read these examples.

> Lindsay bought an *aspidistra*—a type of lily with stiff, glossy leaves. (definition)
>
> I just want a *morsel*, a tiny piece, of your delicious banana bread. (restatement)

Example

An example in a sentence may also help to explain an unfamiliar word. Read this sentence.

> *Crustaceans*, like crabs and lobsters, are plentiful in these waters. (example)

The context tells you that crabs and lobsters are examples of *crustaceans*. This helps explain the meaning of *crustaceans*.

Sometimes the unfamiliar word itself is the example. Then you can use the general term to decide what the word means.

> Woodworking tools, like the *lathe* and saw, should be a part of every workshop.

The context tells you that a *lathe* is a woodworking tool.

148

Certain key words and punctuation marks signal that a writer is giving a context clue.

Key Words Signaling Definition or Restatement

also known as	that is	or
in other words	which is	also called

Punctuation Marks Signaling Definition or Restatement

dashes, commas, and parentheses

Key Words Signaling an Example

and other	for example	like
especially	for instance	such as

Exercises   Mastering Context Clues

Analyzing/Making Inferences

A. Use the context clues in each sentence to write a definition for the word in italics. Check your definition in a dictionary.

1. The *joey*, or baby kangaroo, lives in its mother's pouch.
   baby kangaroo
2. Some seasonings have a strong flavor, especially *curry*.
   a seasoning
3. The magician's cape was *magenta* (purplish red).
   purplish red
4. The cages held *quetzals* and other tropical birds.
   a tropical bird
5. Cindy likes Greek desserts—*baklava*, for example.
   a Greek dessert
6. Melody is *ambidextrous*; that is, she can use both hands with equal ease. able to use both hands with equal ease
7. *Pit vipers*, like rattlesnakes, are poisonous. snakes
8. A vaccine against *pertussis*, also known as whooping cough, is given to infants. whooping cough
9. The report contained many *visual aids*, such as graphs and charts. illustrative material to help the reader
10. Some insects, *locusts*, for example, appear in cycles. an insect

Creative Application

B. Look up the following words in a dictionary. Use each word in a sentence that contains a context clue to explain the meaning of the word.

rebus	marmoset	awl	brocade	herbivorous

149

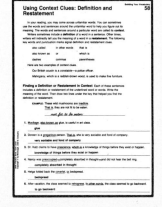

Additional Resources

Skills Practice Book—
pages 58–59

Teacher's Resource Binder
Reinforcement Activities—
page 49
Enrichment Activities—
pages 15–16

Advanced Students

Have the students choose two words from the following list, look up the meaning of each word in a dictionary, and use each word in two original sentences that reveal the meaning of that word in context. One sentence should use restatement, and the other should use example clues.

conifers	fowl
mammal(s)	vehicle
gem(s)	

Special Populations

ESL, NSD Pronunciation variations may make locating words in the dictionary difficult. Review some basic letter-sound relationships and alphabetizing rules with the students.

Reinforcement

Have the students follow the directions for Exercise B, using these words:
Answers will vary.

1. vertigo	4. fatigue
2. sanguine	5. buttress
3. rigid	

Enrichment

1. Find and reproduce a newspaper article, or other short reading selection, that uses either definition, restatement, or example in context to reveal the meanings of unfamiliar words. Ask students to circle each unfamiliar word and to underline the surrounding words and sentences that give clues to its meaning. Encourage students to find all the examples in the passages.

2. For additional enrichment activities, see the Unit Projects in the Teacher Notes on page 125. One or more of these projects have special activities for gifted and talented students.

Part 2

Objective

To identify base words

Presenting the Lesson

 All Students

1. Read and discuss page 150. Make sure students understand the meaning of the term *base word* and can interpret the development of the examples, *agree* and *thought*. After discussing the examples, write the following words on the board: *unthinkable, harmless, unable, wonderment*. Have students find the base words. Then, have them think of new words that can be made by adding different word parts to the base words.

2. Assign and discuss Exercises A and B on page 151.

3. Use Exercise B on page 157 for additional practice if needed.

 Basic Students

Before assigning the exercises, make sure that students understand what a base word is and that not all words contain added parts. Write the list of words below on the board. As a group activity, have the students decide which are base words with added parts and which have no added parts. For those with added parts, have students find the base words.

uncaring   care   misread   read   reuse   use
under   mist   reason

 Advanced Students

Have students underline and define the base words in the following list. Then, have the students tell how the meaning of the whole word differs from the base word.

unreal   true   mindful   thought
prewash   to clean   performance
soundless   noise   display-act

2 Using Word Parts: Base Words

> **Focus**
>
> A word part can be added to the beginning or end of a base word to form a new word.

▶ Comprehension/Analyzing

Many words are made up of several parts. Often, there is a **base word**, or main word. One or more word parts may be added to the beginning or end of the base word. Sometimes, you can unlock the meaning of an unfamiliar word by studying the parts.

When a word part is added to a base word, a new word is formed. For example, the word part *dis-* is added to the beginning of the base word *agree* to form *disagree*. Adding the word part *-ment* to the end makes the word *agreement*.

What base word is in these three words?

thoughtless   rethought   unthoughtful

The base word is *thought*. The word part *-less* was added to make *thoughtless*. The word part *re-* was added to make *rethought*. Two word parts, *un-* and *-ful*, were added to make *unthoughtful*. What is the base word in each of these two sets of words?

preshrink   repay
shrinkable   payment
unshrinkable   prepayment

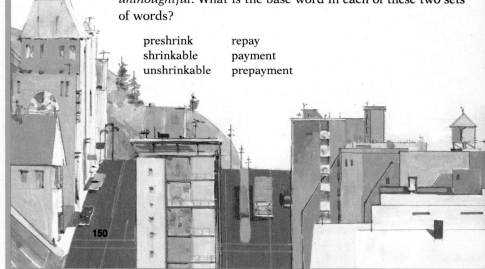

150

Exercises   Building on Base Words

▶ Recalling/Analyzing

A. Copy each of the following words on a sheet of paper. Find and write the base word after each word.

1. senseless sense
2. mouthful mouth
3. unreadable read
4. preview view
5. restatement state
6. misfit fit
7. thunderous thunder
8. incomplete complete
9. kicker kick
10. nonprofit profit
11. happiness happy
12. successful success
13. unlucky luck
14. helper help
15. redo do
16. prewrite write
17. inhuman human
18. penniless penny
19. spoonful spoon
20. colorless color

▶ Structured Application

B. Add a word part to the beginning or the end of each of the following base words. If you wish, add word parts to both places. Write the new words you have made on your paper. Tell what the new word means.

1. flaw
2. move
3. heat
4. speak
5. wonder
6. lock
7. worth
8. paint
9. spell
10. joy

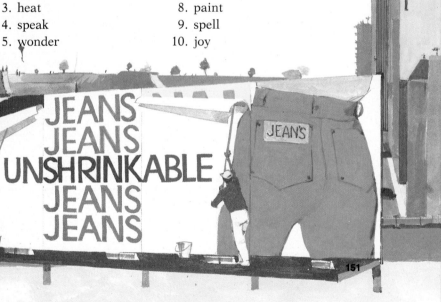

151

Special Populations

LD Be sure students understand the meanings of the base words before doing the exercises.

ESL Some students may speak a Romance language. Capitalize on the fact that they will probably be familiar with Latin root words. Encourage students to share additional examples. Oriental students may have difficulty distinguishing the base word from other word parts. Give these students additional examples of words with similar bases.

Reinforcement

Have the students follow the directions for Exercise A on page 151 using these words:

1. unbearable bear
2. respectful respect
3. misshapen shape
4. conductor conduct
5. infringement infringe
6. unclear clear
7. breathless breath
8. watcher watch
9. infallible fallible
10. ponderous ponder

Enrichment

Divide the class into groups. Provide the following list of base words. Have the groups make as many new words as possible by adding prefixes and suffixes. Set a time limit. Answers will vary.

law   like
hope   happy
turn

Additional Resources

Skills Practice Book—page 60

Teacher's Resource Binder
Reinforcement Activities—
page 50

Part 3

Objective

To recognize common prefixes and use them to discover meanings of unfamiliar words

Presenting the Lesson

 All Students

1. Explain that the word *prefix* is made up of the prefix *pre-* meaning *before* and the base word *fix* meaning to place. The word *prefix* means "to place before." Discuss pages 152–153. Write the headings *Prefix*, *Base Word*, and *New Word* on the board. Ask students to build additional words by using all of the prefixes discussed in this part.

2. Emphasize that when words begin with the letters found in these prefixes, the letters are not necessarily a prefix. Besides the words *under* and *missile*, have the students suggest other words that begin with the letters in common prefixes but that do not actually contain a prefix. (read, must, unify, press)

3. Assign and discuss Exercises A and B on page 153.

 Basic Students

Before beginning the exercises, give students added practice in distinguishing words with and without a prefix by testing the following words:

miser	pre|shrunk	re|apply
mis|quote	preach	reach
non|sense	union	
none	un|known	

Also, review the meanings of all the common prefixes defined in this part. Then, work the first few items in each exercise with the students before having them complete the rest on their own.

---

3 Using Word Parts: Prefixes

> **Focus**
>
> A **prefix** is a word part added to the beginning of a word.

▶ **Comprehension**

When you add a prefix to a base word, you create a new word. The new word has a different meaning. By knowing the meanings of common prefixes, you can often understand the meaning of the new word. Look at this example.

Prefix	Base Word	New Word
non-	+ stop	nonstop

The prefix *non-* always means "not." The base word *stop* means "to halt or bring to an end." Therefore, the new word means "to go on without halting or stopping."

Here are other commonly used prefixes.

im-, in-	These prefixes mean "not." *Impossible* means "not possible." *Inaccurate* means "not accurate."
mis-	The prefix *mis-* means "wrong." *Mislead* means "to show the wrong way." You give the wrong information when you *misinform* someone.
pre-	This prefix means "before." To *preheat* an oven means "to heat an oven before putting food into it."
re-	This prefix has two meanings. It may mean "back." To *recall* means "to call something or someone back." *Re-* may also mean "again." To *recopy* means "to copy again."
un-	This prefix sometimes means "not." *Unwashed* means "not washed." *Un-* may also mean "the reverse of." *Unlock* means the reverse of *lock*, or "to open or release."

152

When you look at a new word, try to break it into prefix and base word. Remember that not all beginning letters that look like prefixes are prefixes. For example, the letters *un* are not a prefix in the word *under*, nor are the letters *mis* in *missile*. That is because neither *der* nor *sile* are base words.

Remember that the spelling of the base word never changes when a prefix is added to it.

Exercises   Adding Prefixes to Base Words

▶ Analyzing

A. Answer these questions.

1. If a *mature* plant is fully grown, what is an *immature* plant? a plant that is not fully grown
2. If an *essential* ingredient in a recipe is necessary, what is a *nonessential* ingredient? an ingredient that is not necessary
3. Write today's *date*. What is a time that *predates* today? a time that came before today
4. If a goal is *attainable*, it can be reached. What is an *unattainable* goal? a goal that is not reachable
5. If you *dye* fabric, you color it. What do you do when you *redye* it? color it again

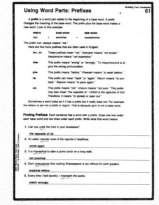

▶ Integrating

B. Here are lists of prefixes and base words. Find and match the prefix that can be combined with each base word. Build as many new words as you can. Not all of the base words and prefixes will go together. Check your new words in the dictionary. Tell what each new word means. Suggested answers are: imperfect, incorrect, misspell, nonstop, precooked

Base Words	Prefixes
spell	im-
perfect	in-
correct	mis-
cooked	non-
stop	pre-

Additional Resources

Skills Practice Book—page 61

Teacher's Resource Binder
    Reinforcement Activities—
    page 51

Part 4

Objective

To recognize common suffixes and use them to discover meanings of unfamiliar words

Presenting the Lesson

 All Students

1. Read and discuss page 154. Explain that the endings students added in earlier parts of the chapter are suffixes. Also mention that suffixes can change the meanings of words. Have students suggest words ending in -less. Show how the meaning changes in these words. Put the headings *Base Word, Suffix,* and *New Word* on the board. Ask students to build additional words by using all of the commonly used suffixes discussed in this part. Mention that a suffix can be added to another suffix as in *restlessness.*

2. Discuss the spelling changes that can occur when suffixes are added. Refer students to the "Guide to Spelling" in the **Power Handbook.** Test students' understanding by having them work with *sense, sensible,* and *flip, flipper.*

3. Assign and discuss Exercises A and B on page 155.

4. Use Exercise C on page 157 for additional practice if needed.

 Basic Students

After the students have studied the common suffixes and their meanings, have them correctly add one or more of the following suffixes to the base words listed below: -er, -or, -able, -ible
Answers will vary.

paint	collapse
inspect	laugh
conduct	train
light	reduce

Point out that they should check a dictionary to learn if these endings can be added to a base word.

---

4 Using Word Parts: Suffixes

┌─ *Focus* ─────────────────────────────┐
│ A **suffix** is a word part added at the end of a base word. │
└──┘

▶**Comprehension**

When you add a suffix to a base word, you create a new word. The new word has a different meaning than the base word. By knowing the definitions of common suffixes, you can often understand the meanings of new words.

Base Word	Suffix	New Word
hazard	+ -ous	hazardous
glory	+ -ous	glorious

The suffix *-ous* means "full of" or "having." A *hazardous* trip is full of hazards or dangers. A *glorious* celebration is one that is full of glory. Here are some other common suffixes.

-able, -ible	These suffixes have two meanings. They can mean "can be." A *washable* sweater can be washed. *Digestible* food can be digested. The suffixes can also mean "having this feature." For example, a *valuable* necklace has value.
-er, -or	These suffixes mean "a person or thing that does something." A *baker* bakes and a *demonstrator* demonstrates. The suffix *-er* may also mean "more." *Stronger* means "more strong."
-ful	This suffix has two meanings. One is "full of." A *fistful* of pennies means "a fist that is full of pennies." The suffix *-ful* can also mean "having." A *peaceful* country has peace.
-less	The suffix *-less* means "without." *Speechless* means "without speech."

154

Exercise A
1. beauty + -ful; full of beauty
2. courage + -ous; full of courage
3. mercy + -less; without mercy
4. worry + -er; one who worries
5. sing + -er; one who sings
6. spine + -less; without a spine
7. stress + -ful; full of stress
8. danger + -ous; full of danger
9. sense + -ible; having good sense
10. laugh + -able; able to be laughed at

Sometimes the spelling of a base word changes when a suffix is added. Look at these examples.

value + -able = valuable   fat + -er = fatter

Review the spelling rules for adding suffixes on pages 503–505. When in doubt about how to add a suffix, refer to your dictionary.

Exercises   Adding Suffixes to Base Words

▶ Analyzing

A. Copy these words. After each word, write the base word and the suffix that was added. Remember that sometimes the spelling of the base word has been changed. Then write the meaning of each word.

See answers at bottom of page 154.

Example: driver = drive + -er; one who drives

1. beautiful
2. courageous
3. merciless
4. worrier
5. singer
6. spineless
7. stressful
8. dangerous
9. sensible
10. laughable

▶ Analyzing/Critical Reasoning

B. Answer these questions.

1. If *indicate* means "to point out," what is an *indicator*? a person or thing that points something out
2. If *spite* means "a feeling of anger or annoyance toward someone," what is a *spiteful* person? a person full of anger toward someone
3. If *rest* is "peace or ease," what does *restless* mean? without peace
4. If a *cavern* is "a cave," what does *cavernous* mean? full of space like a cave
5. If *flame* means "the blaze of a fire," what does *flammable* mean? able to catch on fire

155

Exercises For Mastery

The **Exercises for Mastery** may be used for additional practice of the concepts presented in this section. Each exercise focuses on a single concept, and should be used after the page number indicated in parentheses.

Exercises for Mastery   Chapter 8

Building Your Vocabulary

▶ Making Inferences/Analyzing

A. Using Context Clues Number a sheet of paper from 1 to 15. Use context clues to write a definition for each word in italics. Use a dictionary to check your definitions. (Use after page 149.)

1. The *cobbler* who mended these shoes always does excellent work. one who mends shoes
2. Monique enjoys *croissants*, eclairs, and other French pastries. a French pastry
3. The homes of the Pueblo Indians are made of *adobe*, or sun-dried brick. sun-dried brick
4. The *cyclamen*—a plant of the primrose family— made a lovely centerpiece. a plant of the primrose family
5. The *plantain*, unlike other bananas, is eaten as a cooked vegetable. a kind of banana
6. Cheryl has such *zeal*, or enthusiasm, for ballet that she practices willingly. enthusiasm
7. *Nocturnal* animals like owls, raccoons, and bats sleep during the day. animals that sleep during the day
8. You can grow *basil* and other herbs in pots. an herb
9. The *pterodactyl*, a prehistoric reptile, looks like an enormous ugly bird. a prehistoric reptile
10. The knight was on a *quest*, a search, for dragons. a search
11. Those drops make the pupils of your eyes *dilate*, or become larger. become larger
12. The *centaur* and other imaginary creatures appear frequently in Greek and Roman myths. an imaginary creature
13. The *petrel*, a truly seagoing bird, will die if only fresh water is available to drink. a seagoing bird
14. The pirates searched the cave without finding the *cache*—hiding place—of the treasure. hiding place
15. I am often confused by *homophones*, or words that sound the same. words that sound the same

156

Additional Resources

Skills Practice Book
Mixed Practice—page 63

B. Finding Base Words Copy each of the following words on a piece of paper. Write the base word after each word. (Use after page 151.)

1. gracious   grace
2. rebid   bid
3. unwashable   wash
4. beautiful   beauty
5. immeasurable   measure

6. nonsmoker   smoke
7. effortless   effort
8. reusable   use
9. previewer   view
10. misprint   print

C. Finding Meaning from Word Parts Answer the following questions. (Use after page 155.)

1. If a *significant* fact is important, what is an *insignificant* fact?   a fact that is not important
2. If a *ferrous* metal contains iron, does a *nonferrous* metal?   no
3. If *daunt* means "to discourage," what is a *dauntless* person?   a person who is not discouraged
4. If a *peer* is an "equal," what does *peerless* mean?   without equal
5. Do *preflight* instructions help a pilot to take off or to land?   take off
6. If a *shorn* sheep has no wool left, what does an *unshorn* sheep look like?   a sheep with all its wool
7. If a *mobile* fixture can be moved, can an *immobile* fixture?   no
8. To *trespass* is to go onto another's property without permission. What is a *trespasser*?   a person who goes onto another's property without permission
9. If *immerse* means "to plunge into a liquid," what can you do with an *immersible* coffee pot?   you can plunge it into water to wash it
10. If *stenography* is the skill of writing in shorthand, what is a *stenographer*?   a person who writes in shorthand

157

Using English in Science

This activity gives students an opportunity to apply what they have learned about defining words from context and word parts to the decoding of scientific terms. The activity also provides an opportunity for students to use descriptive writing skills in a subject other than English. During prewriting, have students list the parts of the shell in the order that they will be describing them. Point out that this will help them to organize their details later when they draft.

Using English in ▶ Science

▶ **Comprehension**

Much of the study of science involves carefully observing the world around us. Scientists describe and label the things they observe. In this way, scientists make the information they gather useful to everyone.

Often, the terms scientists use as their labels and in their descriptions are very technical. That is why scientists sometimes use context clues in their writing. When context clues are included with technical vocabulary words, the technical terms are easier to understand.

Exercise   Using Technical Terms To Describe

▶ **Creative Application**

Study the labeled diagram of the shell below. Write a description of the shell that you could read aloud to the class. Use context clues that will make the labeled terms easier to understand. You may want to look up the terms in a dictionary first. Include enough detail so that your listeners will be able to picture the shell. It will be helpful if you begin the description at one point on the shell and then describe the parts around the shell. End at the point where you began.

Example:

The outer lip, or outside edge of the shell, forms a round opening.

Univalve Shell

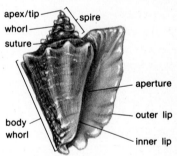

apex/tip
spire
whorl
suture
aperture
outer lip
inner lip
body whorl

158

Additional Resources

Skills Practice Book
Using Vocabulary Skills in Writing—page 64

Using Vocabulary Skills in Writing   64

You are a scientist who has just discovered a remarkable potion. Write a news report for a television station about your new discovery. Make up at least three new words in which you name your potion and explain its benefits. Be sure to include context clues that explain the meaning of each new word.   Answers will vary.

Chapter 8 Review

▶ Making Inferences/Analyzing

A. Using Context Clues Read the following sentences. Write a definition for each word or phrase in italics on your paper.

1. The *gecko*, an insect-eating lizard, is found in the Hawaiian Islands. an insect-eating lizard
2. Flounder, sole, and *orange roughy* were on sale at the fish market. a kind of fish
3. Mrs. Lopez likes *chamomile* tea as well as other herb teas. an herb
4. Syd played the *recorder*, which is an early form of the flute. an early form of the flute
5. The photographer put the camera on a *tripod*, a three-legged stand. a three-legged stand
6. *Notions* like needles, thread, buttons, and pins are in that top drawer. small items used in sewing
7. Several times a day, the crier called the people to prayer from the *minaret* (a tower that is attached to a Moslem mosque). a tower attached to a Moslem mosque
8. *Backgammon*, like chess and checkers, is a popular board game. a board game
9. The Viking ship sailed through the *fiord*, which is a narrow inlet of sea bordered by steep cliffs. a narrow sea inlet
10. The elf costumes were a combination of *chartreuse* and other shades of green. a shade of green

▶ Analyzing

B. Identifying Word Parts Copy the following words. Find the base word and write it on your paper. Then write any prefixes or suffixes used with it. Tell what each word means. See answers in margin.

Example: misspell   spell, mis-; to spell wrongly

1. nonporous
2. reapply
3. unbreakable
4. employer
5. incurable
6. refillable
7. venomous
8. reversible

159

Chapter Review

This review allows teachers to evaluate student understanding of the concepts presented in this chapter.

Exercise B
1. pore, non-, -ous; without pores to let air or fluid through
2. apply, re-; apply again
3. break, un-, -able; not able to be broken
4. employ, -er; someone who employs workers
5. cure, in-, -able; something that cannot be cured
6. fill, re-, -able; able to be filled again
7. venom, -ous; full of venom or poison
8. reverse, -ible; able to be reversed

Additional Resources

Skills Practice Book
  Review—page 65

Test Booklet
  Mastery Test—pages 43–46

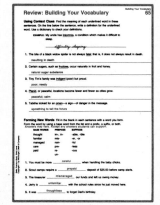

Chapter 9

Chapter Objectives

1. To find words in the dictionary by using alphabetical order
2. To know the function of guide words
3. To read and understand a dictionary entry
4. To differentiate among the multiple meanings in a dictionary entry for a single word
5. To understand the purpose of a thesaurus
6. To know how to use a thesaurus

Motivating the Students

1. Read the introduction on page 161 orally. Remind the students that dictionaries and thesauri help them to learn more about words. The more they know about words and their meanings, the more colorful and more precise their vocabularies will be.

Develop the idea that the necessity to know about words extends beyond school. Students will need to know and use new words in their work and hobbies. The dictionary is and will continue to be a very useful tool.

2. Read the following passage to the students. Talk about "browsing" in dictionaries. What can be learned? Point out that in one way the dictionary does contain stories—it tells the story of where each word came from. Tell students that in this chapter they will be learning more about what dictionaries have to offer.

One morning a sixth grader went to his school library and borrowed a dictionary. The same afternoon he returned it.

"Something wrong?" the librarian asked.

"It's a very interesting book," he told her, "but I didn't read it. The stories are too short."

The sixth grader was mistaken about finding stories in the dictionary, but he was right about something else.

Although every school and library and most homes own a dictionary, no one ever reads it—at least not page by page, like a mystery story or a science book.

The fact that no one reads the dictionary doesn't surprise the people who make dictionaries. "A dictionary is hardly a book to read," one dictionary maker said, "but it's a marvelous book to browse in."

Week 12

Chapter Management Guidelines This chart may be used to help structure daily lesson plans

Day 1	Day 2	Day 3	Day 4	Day 5
Chapter 9 Opener, p. 161; Part 1, "Locating the Word You Need," pp. 162–163; Part 2, "Using Guide Words," pp. 164–166	Part 3, "The Parts of a Dictionary Entry," pp. 167–169	Part 4, "Multiple Meanings," pp. 170–171	Part 5, "Using a Thesaurus," pp. 172–173	Chapter Review and selected end-of-chapter activities

Chapter 9

Discovering the Dictionary and Thesaurus

An artist uses many tools to create a painting. Various brushes, knives, canvasses, and carefully mixed paints may all be necessary.

Writers use tools to shape their ideas, too. Two important tools that writers use are the dictionary and the thesaurus.

A dictionary is a reference book that lists words and gives the meanings, pronunciation, and history of each word. A thesaurus contains lists of synonyms and antonyms. Writers sometimes overuse a word. A thesaurus contains other words that can be used to replace an overused word.

This chapter will show you how to use the dictionary and thesaurus. You will find these tools useful as you write.

161

Browse means "to nibble at, to glance here and there through a book."
—Robert Kraske

Special Populations

LD Give extra practice on alphabetizing

LD, ESL These students may find multiple meanings confusing. Provide many examples.

ESL Finding words in a dictionary according to pronunciation will be difficult for these students. Provide help as needed.

Related Chapters

You may wish to refer to related material in other chapters as you teach the following concepts:

1. Using nouns, Chapter 3," Nouns for Precise Meaning," page 45
2. Using verbs, Chapter 4, "Verbs for Writing Power," page 61
3. Vocabulary, Chapter 8, "Building Your Vocabulary," page 147
4. Using adjectives, Chapter 16, "Adjectives for Creative Expression," page 283
5. Using adverbs, Chapter 17, "Adverbs for Clear Description," page 301

Additional Resources

Skills Practice Book—pages 66–71

Test Booklet—pages 47–52
  Pretest—pages 47–48
  Mastery Test—pages 49–52

Teacher's Resource Binder
  Reinforcement Activities—
    pages 53–58
  Enrichment Activities—
    pages 17–18, 39–52, 65
  Ideas for Creative Teaching

Part 1

Objective

To find words in the dictionary by using alphabetical order

Presenting the Lesson

All Students

1. Read and discuss page 162. Be sure students can alphabetize words that start with the same letter or the same first two letters. Work with additional examples if necessary. Have the students insert each of these words in the proper place in lists 1–4: *bright*, *wave*, *cheap*, and *interlock*.

2. Assign and discuss Exercises A and B on page 163.

Basic Students

Provide drills in using alphabetical order. If necessary, allow the students to write out the alphabet and keep it on their desks during the drills.

Drill 1: Call out a letter of the alphabet at random and instruct the students to open their dictionaries to that letter. Continue calling letters until the students become proficient at opening their dictionaries to the right place.

Drill 2: Have dictionary relay races. Assign each row of students a list of words. The first student will look up the first word in the dictionary, write down the page number on which it appears, and pass the list to the next person. That student will do the second word, and so on.

Advanced Students

Have the students make two alphabetical lists of the names of the Presidents of the United States. One list should be a list of the first names, and the other should be a list of the last names.

Special Populations

LD, ESL, NSD Provide additional practice with alphabetizing to the second and third letter.

ESL Reassure students they are not expected to know the meanings of all the words they are alphabetizing.

---

1 Locating the Word You Need

> **Focus**
>
> The words in a dictionary are always arranged in alphabetical order.

▶ Comprehension

It is easy to use a dictionary. Words are listed alphabetically. This helps you quickly locate the information you need.

Using Alphabetical Order

The words listed on a dictionary page are called **entry** words. The entry words are usually listed in two columns in alphabetical order. The first words in a dictionary begin with *a*. The last ones begin with *z*.

Two words may begin with the same letter. When that happens, they are alphabetized by the second letter. *Pinto* comes before *punt* because *i* comes before *u*. Many words have the same first and second letters. Then, the words are alphabetized by the third letter. For example, *dormouse* comes before *double* because *r* comes before *u*. This process can continue to the fourth and fifth letters and even beyond.

Here are some groups of words that are arranged in alphabetical order.

1	2	3	4
amateur	whitefish	channel	interchange
bridge	wigwam	cheese	interfere
nighthawk	wool	chickadee	intermediate
shiver	worm	chimney	intern
unicorn	wreath	chowder	international
visor	wrinkle	church	interruption
X-ray	wrist	churn	intersection

162

Exercises Using Alphabetical Order

▸ Inferring Sequence

A. Below are three columns of words in alphabetical order. Insert the additional words in the correct place in each column. Then rewrite the new columns.

1	**2**	**3**
magic	plateau	skycap
magnify	platypus	skydiver
mockingbird	pleats	skylight
mosquito	plenty	skywrite

1.	2.	3.
magic	plastic	skycap
magnify	plateau	skydiver
math	platform	skylark
Merlin	platypus	skylight
meteor	pleats	skyline
mockingbird	pledge	skyrocket
mosquito	plenty	skywalk
moss	plunge	skyward
mustang	plywood	skywrite

Words To Add

1. Merlin, math, mustang, moss, meteor
2. plastic, plywood, pledge, plunge, platform
3. skylark, skyrocket, skyward, skywalk, skyline

▸ Structured Application

B. Create your own mini-dictionary of words you learn in science. Collect about ten terms. List them in alphabetical order. Use a dictionary and give a short definition for each term. Here are a few to get you started.

albumen	The white of an egg
biology	The study of living things
cell	The simplest unit in the structure of living matter

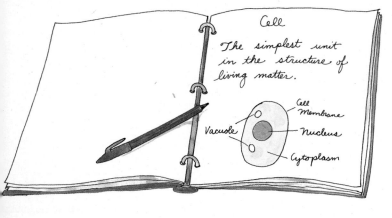

163

Reinforcement

1. Have the students correctly alphabetize the lists of words below.

1	**2**	**3**	**4**
4 never	4 top	1 drain	5 chill
2 every	1 table	4 drown	2 chicken
1 charity	2 terrible	3 drip	4 chili
5 zoo	5 turn	2 dream	3 children
3 marble	3 tip	5 drug	1 Chicago

2. Follow the directions for Exercise A on page 163 using the words below:

Words To Add

7 boulevard	9 slush	5 intern
10 bush	2 slather	9 intrude
1 balloon	8 sluggish	3 interest
4 beast	4 sleet	8 intricate
5 book	5 slide	6 interview

1	**2**	**3**
2 barley	1 slack	1 intake
3 bear	3 sled	2 intention
6 botulism	6 slight	4 intermediate
8 boundary	7 slope	7 into
9 bunting	10 sly	10 intrust

Enrichment

1. Explain to the students the difference between an *abridged* dictionary and an *unabridged* dictionary. Bring an unabridged dictionary to class for the students to examine. Then have the students examine five different dictionaries. Ask them to write down the title, the number of pages included, and the number of entries for each dictionary.

2. For additional enrichment activities, see the Unit Projects in the Teacher Notes on page 125. One or more of these projects have special activities for gifted and talented students.

Additional Resources

Skills Practice Book—page 66

Teacher's Resource Binder
Reinforcement Activities—
pages 53–54

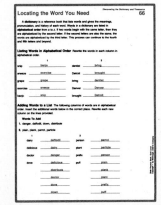

Part 2

Objective

 To know the function of guide words

Presenting the Lesson

All Students

1. Read and discuss page 164. Stress that guide words are a useful aid for quickly locating words in the dictionary only if alphabetizing skills have been mastered.

2. Practice finding guide words in classroom dictionaries. Begin by calling out page numbers and asking the students to give the guide words for that page. Then progress to giving words and asking for the guide words for the page on which each word appears.

3. Assign and discuss Exercises A and B on page 166.

Basic Students

Do the first half of Exercise A orally. Allow the students to work in pairs to complete the exercise.

For reinforcement, provide a number of additional items similar to those in Exercise B if needed.

Advanced Students

Have students compete to see who can complete Exercise B most quickly. Time the students as they work.

Special Populations

LD Display a large chart of the alphabet in the classroom for these students to refer to.

Reinforcement

1. Have the students decide on which page they would find the following words if these were the guide words:

page 751—sustain/swarm
page 752—swarthy/sweepstakes
page 753—sweet/swing

752 swear	753 swelling	751 swaddle
753 swindle	752 swatch	753 swerve
751 suture	751 swap	752 sweep

2 Using Guide Words

> ### Focus
>
> **Guide words** tell the first and last entry words on a dictionary page. Guide words are printed in heavy black type at the top of the page.

▶ Comprehension

Look at the sample dictionary page on page 165. Look at the two words printed in heavy black print at the top of each page. These words are called guide words. **Guide words** help you quickly locate the entry word and information you need.

The guide word on the left tells you the first entry word on the page. The guide word on the right tells you the last entry word on the page. The guide words on page 165 are *pliers* and *plumate*. Now look at the word entries on that page. The word *pliers* is the first entry on the page. The word *plumate* is the last entry on that page. All of the other entry words fall between *pliers* and *plumate*.

·ers (plī'ərz) *n.pl.* [< PLY¹] small pincers for gripping small objects, bending wire, etc.

ight¹ (plīt) *n.* [< Anglo-Fr. *plit*, for Fr. *pleit*, a fold] a condition or tate of affairs; esp., an awkward, sad, r dangerous situation [the *plight* of he men trapped in the mine]

ight² (plīt) *vt.* [OE. *plihtan*, to pledge *pliht*, danger] to pledge or prom-e, or bind by a pledge —**plight one's roth** to make a promise of marriage

im·soll mark (or **line**) (plim'sɔl, sȯl, -sȯl) [after S. *Plimsoll* (1824–98), ng. statesman] a line or set of lines n the outside of merchant ships, howing the water level to which they nay legally be loaded

plink (pliŋk) *n.* [echoic] a light, harp, ringing or clinking sound —*vt., vi.* **1.** to make such ounds on (a piano, banjo, etc.) **2.** to shoot at (tin cans, etc.)

inth (plinth) *n.* [< L. < Gr. *plinthos*, a brick, tile] **1.** the quare block at the base of a column, pedestal, etc. **2.** the base n which a statue rests

in·y (plin'ē) **1.** (L. name *Gaius Plinius Secundus*) 23–79 .D.; Rom. naturalist & writer: called *the Elder* **2.** (L. name *iaius Plinius Caecilius Secundus*) 62?–113? A.D.; Rom. writer & tatesman: called *the Younger*: nephew of *Pliny the Elder*

i·o·cene (plī'ə sēn') *adj.* [< Gr. *pleōn*, more + *kainos*, new] esignating or of the last epoch of the Tertiary Period in the enozoic Era —**the Pliocene** the Pliocene Epoch or its rocks: ee GEOLOGIC TIME CHART

Pli·o·film (plī'ə film') [< PLIABLE + FILM] *a trademark for a* heeting of rubber hydrochloride used for raincoats, as a cover-ng for packages, etc.

is·sé, plis·se (pli sā') *n.* [< Fr. < pp. of *plisser*, to pleat] . a crinkled finish given to cotton, nylon, etc. with a caustic oda solution **2.** a fabric with this finish

od (pläd) *vi.* **plod'ded, plod'ding** [prob. echoic] **1.** to walk or nove heavily and with effort; trudge [the old horse *plodded* long the street] **2.** to work steadily and monotonously; rudge [to *plod* away at one's work] —*n.* **1.** the act of plodding . the sound of a heavy step —**plod'der** *n.* —**plod'ding·ly** *adv.*

·loid (ploid) [< Gr. -*ploos*, -fold + -OID] *a combining form* *meaning* of or being a (specified) multiple of the basic (haploid) number of chromosomes characteristic of a group of related or-anisms [*diploid*]

onk (pläŋk, ploŋk) *vt., vi., n.* same as PLUNK

op (pläp) *vt., vi.* **plopped, plop'ping** [echoic] **1.** to drop with a ound like that of something flat falling into water **2.** to drop eavily —*n.* the act of plopping or the sound made by this —*adv.* with a plop

o·sive (plō'siv) *adj.* [< (EX)PLOSIVE] *Phonet.* produced by topping and then suddenly releasing the breath, as the sounds f *k, p,* and *t* when used at the beginning of words —*n.* a plosive ound

ot (plät) *n.* [OE., a piece of land] **1.** a small area of ground [a arden *plot*] **2.** a chart or diagram, as of a building or estate . a secret, usually evil, scheme **4.** the plan of action of a play, novel, etc. —*v.* **plot'ted, plot'ting 1.** *a)* to draw a plan of (a hip's course, etc.) *b)* to mark the position or course of on a nap **2.** to make secret plans for [to *plot* a robbery] **3.** to plan he action of (a story, etc.) **4.** *a)* to determine the location of (a oint) on a graph by means of coordinates *b)* to represent (an quation) by joining points on a graph to form a curve **5.** to lan together secretly; scheme [to *plot* against the king] — lot'less *adj.* —**plot'less·ness** *n.* —**plot'ter** *n.*

YN.—*plot* is used of a secret, usually evil, project or scheme the details of which have been carefully worked out [a *plot* to keep him from getting his inheritance]; *intrigue*, implying more complicated scheming, suggests hid-en, underhanded dealing often of an illegal nature [the *intrigues* of the oyal court]; *machination* emphasizes trickery and slyness in forming plots ntended to harm someone [the *machinations* of the villain]; *conspiracy* uggests a plot in which a number of people plan and act together secret-y for an unlawful or harmful purpose [a *conspiracy* to seize the hrone]; *cabal* suggests a small group of persons involved in a political ntrigue

ough (plou) *n., vt., vi.* chiefly Brit. sp. of PLOW

plov·er (pluv'ər, plō'vər) *n., pl.* **plov'ers, plov'er:** see PLURAL, II, D, 1 [< OFr., ult. < L. *pluvia,* rain] a shore bird with a short tail, long, pointed wings, and a short beak

PLOVER
(to 11 in. high)

plow (plou) *n.* [ME. *ploh* < Late OE.] **1.** a farm implement used to cut and turn up the soil ☆**2.** anything like this; specif., a SNOW-PLOW —*vt.* **1.** to cut and turn up (soil) with a plow **2.** to make fur-rows in or as with a plow **3.** to make as if by plowing [he *plowed* his way through the crowd] **4.** to cut a way through (water) —*vi.* **1.** to use a plow in tilling the soil **2.** to cut a way (*through* water, etc.) **3.** to go forward with effort; plod **4.** to begin work vigorously (with *into*) **5.** to strike against forcefully (with *into*) —**plow back** to reinvest (profits) in the same business en-terprise —**plow up 1.** to remove with a plow **2.** to till (soil) thoroughly —**plow'a·ble** *adj.* —**plow'er** *n.*

plow·boy (plou'boi') *n.* **1.** formerly, a boy who led a team of horses drawing a plow **2.** a country boy

plow·man (plou'mən) *n., pl.* -**men 1.** a man who guides a plow **2.** a farm worker

plow·share (-sher') *n.* the share, or cutting blade, of a mold-board plow

ploy (ploi) *n.* [? < (EM)PLOY] an action or maneuver intended to outwit or confuse another person in order to get the better of him

pluck (pluk) *vt.* [OE. *pluccian:* for IE. base see PILE²] **1.** to pull off or out; pick [to *pluck* an apple from a tree] **2.** to drag or snatch; grab [he *plucked* a burning stick from the fire] **3.** to pull feathers or hair from [to *pluck* a chicken, *pluck* eyebrows] **4.** to pull at (the strings of a musical instrument) and release quickly to sound tones **5.** [Slang] to rob or swindle —*vi.* **1.** to pull; tug; snatch (often with *at*) [he *plucked* at his long mus-tache] **2.** to pluck a musical instrument —*n.* **1.** a pulling; tug **2.** courage to meet danger or difficulty; fortitude —**pluck up** to stir up one's (courage); take heart —**pluck'er** *n.*

pluck·y (pluk'ē) *adj.* **pluck'i·er, pluck'i·est** brave; spirited; de-termined —see SYN. at BRAVE —**pluck'i·ly** *adv.* —**pluck'i·ness** *n.*

plug (plug) *n.* [MDu. *plugge*] **1.** an object used to stop up a hole, drain, etc. **2.** *a)* a cake of pressed tobacco *b)* a piece of chewing tobacco **3.** a device, as with prongs that stick out, for fitting into an electric outlet, etc. to make electrical contact **4.** *same as: a)* SPARK PLUG *b)* FIREPLUG **5.** [Colloq.] a defec-tive or shopworn article ☆**6.** [Slang] an old, worn-out horse ☆**7.** [Colloq.] a boost, advertisement, etc., esp. one slipped into the entertainment part of a radio or TV program, a magazine article, etc. —*vt.* **plugged, plug'ging 1.** to stop up (a hole, etc.) with a plug (often with *up*) **2.** to insert (something) as a plug [he *plugged* the putty in the hole] **3.** [Colloq.] *a)* to promote (a song) by frequent performance ☆*b)* to promote with a plug (*n.* 7) **4.** [Slang] to shoot a bullet into —*vi.* [Colloq.] to work or study hard and steadily; plod —**plug in** to connect (an electrical device) with an outlet, etc. by inserting a plug in a socket or jack —**plug'ger** *n.*

☆**plug hat** [Old Slang] a man's high silk hat

☆**plug·o·la** (plug'ō lə) *n.* [PLUG, *n.* 7 + (PAY)OLA] [Slang] the paying of a bribe, or a bribe paid, for the dishonest promotion of something or someone on radio or TV

☆**plug·ug·ly** (-ug'lē) *n., pl.* -**lies** [Old Slang] a ruffian or gang-ster

plum (plum) *n.* [OE. *plume*] **1.** *a)* any of various small trees bearing a smooth-skinned fruit with a flattened stone *b)* the fruit eaten as food **2.** a raisin, when used in pudding or cake [*plum* pudding] **3.** the dark bluish-red or reddish-purple color of some plums **4.** something excellent or desirable [the new contract is a rich *plum* for the company]

plum·age (plōō'mij) *n.* [MFr. < L. *pluma,* a feather] a bird's feathers

plu·mate (-māt, -mit) *adj.* [< L. *pluma,* a feather] *Zool.* resem-bling a feather, esp. in structure

t, āpe, cär; ten, ēven; is, bīte; gō, hôrn, tōōl, look; oil, out; up, fur; get; joy; yet; chin; she; thin, then; zh, leisure; ŋ, ring; for *a* in *ago, e* in *agent, i* in *sanity, o* in *comply, u* in *focus*; ' as in *able* (ā'b'l); Fr. bál; ë, Fr. coeur; ö, Fr. feu; Fr. mon; Fr. coq; ü, Fr. duc; r, Fr. cri; H, G. ich; kh, G. doch; ‡foreign; ☆ Americanism; < derived from. See inside front cover.

---

2. Follow the instructions for Exercise B on page 166 using these words:
Answers will vary depending on dictionary used.

debris	cutlet	invention
smirk	excess	mahogany
guest	adverb	tatami
video	petal	recruit

Enrichment

Show the students several specialized dictionaries. Explain that although the subject matter may be different, all dic-tionaries are arranged in alphabetical order, and that they use guide words to help the reader locate an entry faster.

Next have the students look at an encyclopedia volume. Point out that en-cyclopedias, too, are arranged in alpha-betical order. Note the guide words on the pages in the encyclopedia.

Additional Resources

Skills Practice Book—page 67

Teacher's Resource Binder
Reinforcement Activities—
page 55

Exercises Using Guide Words

▶ Analyzing

A. Number your paper from 1 to 10. In the list below are ten sets of guide words. After each set of guide words is another word. Decide whether you would find that word on a page before the guide words, on the page with the guide words, or on a page after the guide words. Write *Before*, *With*, or *After* beside each number on your paper. Look at the following example.

Guide Words		Other Word
obtain	ocean	occupant

The word *occupant* comes between *obtain* and *ocean* in the alphabet. Therefore, you would find *occupant* on the page with the guide words *obtain* and *ocean*. *With* is the correct answer.

	Guide Words		Other Word	
1.	rap	rat	rant	Before
2.	steep	step	stereo	After
3.	enlist	enter	enough	With
4.	jubilee	jukebox	judge	With
5.	nip	noble	nobleman	After
6.	cafeteria	calcium	cafe	Before
7.	diffuse	dilemma	diminish	After
8.	grew	gripe	grief	With
9.	preservative	presume	present	Before
10.	self-reliant	Seminole	spinet	After

▶ Structured Application

B. Remember that the purpose of guide words is to help you find words more quickly. Find the following words in a dictionary. Copy the guide words from the page where you find each word.

ladybug	millepede	narwhal
kiwi	falcon	lamprey
pheasant	sailfish	snake
goat	trawler	bat
iguana	gazelle	cricket

The Parts of a Dictionary Entry

> **Focus**
>
> The information a dictionary gives about a word is called the **entry**. The entry may contain many parts.

Comprehension/Analyzing

You can learn a great deal about a word from reading the entry. The entry for the word *plot* contains six parts. Look at the information in each of these parts.

Entry Word

> plot

The first part of an entry is the word. In most dictionaries, it is divided into syllables. This is done with a space or a centered dot. For example, the word *pliers* would be printed like this: **pli·ers**.

Pronunciation

> (plät)

The next part of an entry is the pronunciation. In most dictionaries, the pronunciation is printed in parentheses. When you pronounce a two-syllable word, one syllable gets a stronger emphasis than the other. The emphasis is shown in a dictionary by using accent marks (′).

> **pli·ers** (plī′ərz)   **plum·age** (ploo′mij)

Notice that in the pronunciations, the words have been respelled. This kind of spelling is a way of showing the sounds in the word. In the word *plot*, the letter *o* has the short *o* sound as in the words *hot* and *top*. The dictionary shows this sound as

Part 3

Objective

To read and understand a dictionary entry

Presenting the Lesson

 All Students

1. Read and discuss each of the subdivisions of Part 3, on pages 167–169.

2. Entry Word: Clarify the difference between an *entry* and an *entry word*. Ask the students to count all of the entry words on page 165. How many entry words are there in all? (32)

3. Pronunciation: Have the students read several of the words in the pronunciation key on page 165. After each word, point out the special marks or letters used in it. Ask for other words with the same sound. Write the following words on the board and ask the students to determine their pronunciation from the entries on page 165: *Pliocene, plisse, plough, ploy, plumage.*

4. Parts of Speech: Point out that some words can function as more than one part of speech. A dictionary entry will show the parts of speech that a word can have and the meaning for each.

5. Word Origin: The original language is usually given in an abbreviation. Make sure students are familiar with these abbreviations:

OE (Old English)   L (Latin)
ME (Middle English)   Gk (Greek)
OFr (Old French)   Sp (Spanish)

Make sure, also, that the students understand the meaning of the symbol < (is derived from). Mention that some dictionaries list this information at the last part of the entry.

6. Synonyms: Explain that synonyms are words that have similar meanings. Their meanings are never exactly the same, however. Read through the list of synonyms for *plot*.

Are students familiar with all the synonyms given there? Caution them against using synonyms whose meaning they do not understand. Mention the thesaurus as a source for synonyms. Tell students they will study more about the "Thesaurus" later in this chapter.

7. Assign and discuss Exercises A and B on page 169.

Basic Students

To help familiarize students with the process of applying the information from the pronunciation key to the actual pronunciation of a new word, try the following exercise. Students should use the sample dictionary page.

Which word in the pronunciation key tells how to pronounce each of the following vowel sounds?

1. The *i* in pliers (bite)
2. The *u* in plug (up)
3. The *o* in plop (car)
4. The *oy* in plowboy (oil)
5. The *y* in Pliny (even)

◆ **Advanced Students**

Have the students use the pronunciation key on page 165 to translate the phonetic spelling of these words to their regular spelling.

1. ig zam' ə nā' shən
2. ek' s'lənt
3. ôt'ə mat' ik
4. kən trib'yōōt
5. kwes ch ə ner'

Special Populations

See notes under **Basic Students.**

Reinforcement

1. Follow the directions for Exercise A on page 169.

1. What is the slang use of the word *pluck*? to rob or swindle
2. Does the first syllable of *plumage* rhyme with the word *plum*? no
3. Which synonym of *plot* implies complicated scheming and suggests hidden and underhanded dealings? intrigue
4. What is the meaning of the phrase "to plight one's troth"? make a promise of marriage
5. What parts of speech can the word *plow* be? noun and verb

2. Follow the instructions for Exercise B on page 169.

1. lieu (lōō), n., place
2. knave (nāv), n., a male servant or a man of humble status
3. mnemonic (nē män' ik), adj., helping or meant to help, the memory
4. yacht (yät), n., a large boat or v., to sail in a yacht

ä. At the bottom of the right-hand pages of most dictionaries there is a **pronunciation key**. This explains the sound of each letter in the respellings.

Part of Speech

After the pronunciation, the dictionary gives the part of speech. Most dictionaries use these abbreviations.

n. = noun **v.** = verb **adj.** = adjective	**pro.** = pronoun **adv.** = adverb **prep.** = preposition	**conj.** = conjunction **interj.** = interjection

Some words may be used as more than one part of speech. Each part of speech is followed by the appropriate definition. The word *plot* is defined as a noun (**n.**), then as a verb (**v.**).

Word Origin

Next comes the origin of the word. This tells what language first used the word.

[OE., a piece of land]

OE. stands for Old English. The dictionary contains a list of the abbreviations used and tells what each one means.

Definition

The definition is an explanation of the meaning of a word.

plot (plät) **n.** [OE., a piece of land] **1.** a small area of ground [a garden *plot*] **2.** a chart or diagram, as of a building or estate. **3.** a secret, usually evil, scheme **4.** the plan of action of a play, novel, etc.— **v. plot'ted, plot'ting 1.** *a)* to draw a plan of (a ship's course, etc.) *b)* to mark the position or course of on a map **2.** to make secret plans for [to *plot* a robbery] **3.** to plan the action of (a story, etc.) **4.** *a)* to determine the location of (a point) on a graph by means of coordinates *b)* to represent (an equation) by joining points on a graph to form a curve **5.** to plan together secretly; scheme [to *plot* against the king]—**plot'less adj.—plot'less·ness n.—plot'ter n.**

168

Synonyms

A list of synonyms is found in some dictionaries. The list is usually found at the end of an entry. It can help you choose words that will make your writing more precise.

> **SYN.—plot** is used of a secret, usually evil, project or scheme the details of which have been carefully worked out *[a plot to keep him from getting his inheritance]*; **intrigue,** implying more complicated scheming, suggests hidden, underhanded dealing often of an illegal nature *[the intrigues of the royal court]*; **machination** emphasizes trickery and slyness in forming plots intended to harm someone *[the machinations of the villain]*; **conspiracy** suggests a plot in which a number of people plan and act together secretly for an unlawful or harmful purpose *[a conspiracy to seize the throne]*; **cabal** suggests a small group of persons involved in a political intrigue

Exercises   Using the Dictionary Entry

▶ Analyzing

A. Use the sample dictionary page on page 165 to answer the following questions.

1. From what language did the word *plissé* come? What does the word mean? French, a fabric with a crinkled finish
2. Divide the word *plumate* into syllables. plu·mate
3. Write a synonym for *plot* that means "a group of people working together secretly." conspiracy
4. What parts of speech can the word *plod* be? verb, noun
5. What do the words *plough* and *plow* have in common? Plough is the British spelling of *plow*.

▶ Structured Application

B. Use your dictionary to learn how each of the following words is pronounced. Be prepared to pronounce each one in class. Then write down the definition of each word and its part of speech.

xenon   psyche   gnu   err   pneumatic

Enrichment

If possible, the teacher should make a copy of the *Oxford English Dictionary* available for class examination. Explain its use and importance to English. Let students look up a few words. Suggested entries: *eavesdrop*, *nice*, and *fang*.

Additional Resources

Skills Practice Book—page 68
Teacher's Resource Binder
Reinforcement Activities—
  page 56
Enrichment Activities—
  pages 17–18

Part 4

Objective

To differentiate among the multiple meanings in a dictionary entry for a single word

Presenting the Lesson

All Students

1. Read and discuss page 170. Note the differences in the meanings of the word *pluck* in each of the sentences on the page. Explain that a change in meaning can occur because the word can be more than one part of speech.

2. Assign and discuss the exercise on page 171.

Basic Students

Before assigning the Exercise on page 171, have the students open their dictionaries to the entry for *run*. Have volunteers read the different meanings aloud. Then have the students identify the definition that fits each of these sentences. Answers will vary according to dictionary used.

1. He will *run* around the track three times.
2. The train *runs* from Chicago to Kansas City.
3. There was a *run* on the bank.
4. The player scored a *run* in the last inning of the game.
5. There is a *run* in the nylon material.

Advanced Students

After the students complete the exercises, have them write five sentences with the entry word *plot*, using a different meaning in each sentence.

Special Populations

ESL Point out that in English a word may function as more than one part of speech and the word may not show a change in form.

Reinforcement

1. Have students find the numbered definition for the following words on page 165. Use each word in a sentence in a way that fits the numbered definition. Answers will vary.

---

4 Multiple Meanings

Focus

A dictionary may list several meanings for an entry word.

▶ Comprehension

Information about the meanings of a word makes up the largest part of a dictionary entry. Many English words have more than one meaning. When you look up a word, you have to choose a meaning that matches how the word is being used.

Look up the word *go* in your dictionary. How many definitions are given for it? The Student Edition of *Webster's New World Dictionary of the American Language* gives forty definitions for this one word!

Look at the definitions for the word *pluck* on page 165. Notice that each definition is numbered. Notice also that for most of the definitions there is a sentence or phrase given as an example. These examples show how the word is used for a particular definition. Sometimes these examples are as much help to you as the definitions themselves.

In each of the following sentences, the word *pluck* has a different meaning. Can you find the definition on page 165 that matches each use?

John *plucked* at his long mustache.
I felt a *pluck* at my sleeve.
Sandy *plucked* an apple from the tree.
It took *pluck* to rescue the drowning girl.

170

Exercise Using the Multiple Meanings of a Word

▶ Analyzing/Drawing Conclusions

Number your paper from 1 to 10. Use the following dictionary entry for the word *front*. Write the number of the definition that fits each sentence at the bottom of the page. Choose from the first fifteen definitions in the entry.

Dictionary Entry for *front*

front (frunt) **n.** [< OFr. < L. *frontis*, genitive of *frons*, forehead] **1.** outward behavior or appearance, esp. when merely pretended [to put on a bold *front*] **2.** the part of something that faces forward; most important side **3.** the first part; beginning [toward the *front* of the book] **4.** the place or position directly before a person or thing **5.** a forward or leading position or situation ☆**6.** the first available bellhop, as in a hotel **7.** the land bordering a lake, ocean, street, etc. **8.** the most forward area, where actual fighting is going on in a war **9.** a specified area of activity [the home *front*] **10.** a broad movement in which different groups are united in order to achieve certain political or social aims ☆**11.** a person who serves as a public representative of a business, group, etc., as because of his prestige ☆**12.** a person, group, etc. used to cover up some activity, esp. an illegal one [the barber shop was a *front* for the numbers racket] **13.** a stiff shirt bosom, worn with formal clothes **14.** a face of a building; esp., the face with the principal entrance **15.** *Meteorol.* the boundary between two masses of air that are different, as in density —**adj. 1.** at, to, in, on, or of the front **2.** *Phonet.* sounded toward the front of the mouth [i in *bid* and e in *met* are *front* vowels] —**vt. 1.** to face; be opposite to [our cottage *fronts* the ocean] **2.** to be before in place **3.** to meet; confront **4.** to defy; oppose **5.** to supply or be a front to [white stone *fronts* the building] —**vi. 1.** to face in a certain direction ☆**2.** to be a front (senses 11 & 12) (with *for*) —**in front of** before; ahead of

All numbers in answers refer to the noun definition.

1. The directions were in the *front* of the pamphlet. 3
2. Stephanie is at the *front* of all class activities. 5
3. Mr. Montgomery built his house on the ocean *front*. 7
4. The weather report said that a warm *front* is coming. 15
5. When my grandfather was in the Army, he was stationed at the *front*. 8
6. People on the home *front* joined the Civil Defense. 9
7. The *front* of the church had caved in. 2
8. The senator is a *front* for farmers. 11
9. When the desk clerk saw all the luggage I had, she called, "*Front*!" 6
10. He puts up a *front* to hide his nervousness. 1

171

1. plug def. 3, noun
2. plod def. 2, verb
3. plot def. 4, noun
4. plum def. 3, noun
5. plow def. 1, noun

2. Have the students use their classroom dictionaries to look up each underlined word in the following sentences. Then have them write the definition that best fits each sentence. Also have them state the part of speech of each underlined word.

1. Never <u>resort</u> to violence to solve a problem. v., to turn to for help, support
2. Mark <u>jumped</u> Julie's last king and won the checkers game. v., to capture an opponent's piece
3. The jockey checked her <u>mount</u> before beginning the race. n., horse
4. It took three weeks to build the <u>set</u> for the play. n., scenery for a play
5. The <u>review</u> of the play was complimentary. n., a report telling about a play and giving an opinion about it

Enrichment

Remind students that the specific meaning of a word is called its *denotation* and that the general meaning of a word is called its *connotation*. The connotation of a word often includes certain feelings about that word. Ask students to explain the difference in connotation for each of these pairs of synonyms. Answers will vary.

house/home   punish/discipline
skinny/thin   crowd/mob

Additional Resources

Skills Practice Book—page 69

Teacher's Resource Binder
  Reinforcement Activities—
    page 57
  Enrichment Activities—
    page 65

Part 5

Objectives

1. To understand the purpose of a thesaurus
2. To know how to use a thesaurus

Presenting the Lesson

 All Students

1. If you have not already done so, introduce the students to the "Thesaurus" in this text.
2. Read and discuss page 172. Emphasize that even though synonyms have similar meanings, they are rarely interchangeable. Remind students that the synonym they choose must be the same part of speech as the word being replaced.
3. Turn to the sample thesaurus included in this text. Have students examine index pages 510–511. To check the students' ability to use the index, ask if each of these words is an entry word or a synonym within another entry. Then have them find each word in the thesaurus.

group (entry)   poor (synonym)
enjoy (synonym) small (entry)

4. Return to page 173. Assign and discuss the exercise.

 Basic Students

Provide additional group practice using the thesaurus in this book before assigning the exercises. Have the students find these words in the thesaurus. Ask them to name a synonym for each one. Discuss the shades of difference between the meanings of the synonyms.
Answers will vary.

make   get   furious
little   see   wonderful

 Advanced Students

Have the students rewrite this conversation replacing the words in italics with more specific synonyms. Ask them to use the "Thesaurus".
Answers will vary.

"The apartment is *big*," *said* the real estate agent. "It has a *good* view of the lake from the living room, and it has a *beautiful* fireplace. Would you like to *see* it?" she *asked*.

"Sure," Laura *said*. "It sounds *great* compared to the *many* apartments I've seen so far."

---

5 Using a Thesaurus

─ Focus ─

A **thesaurus** is a book of synonyms and antonyms. **Synonyms** are words with similar meanings. **Antonyms** are words with opposite meanings.

▶ Comprehension

Writers find that the thesaurus is a helpful reference book. It lists commonly used words and some synonyms and antonyms for these words. A thesaurus can help a writer find lively and specific words to replace words that are dull or general.

Some thesauri are arranged alphabetically. Others have an index you must use to locate a word. The index contains a listing of all the words and synonyms in the thesaurus and the location of each word. For example, if you look up the word *tiny* in a thesaurus index, you will see that you can find that word in the entries for *little* and *small*.

Read this sentence.

The chef cooked the muffins.

Cook is a very general word that means "to prepare food." If a writer wished to replace *cook* with a more specific verb, the thesaurus would be helpful. Read this sample thesaurus entry for the word *cook*.

> *V.* **cook,** boil, coddle, parboil, steam, precook, poach, scald; heat, warm, prepare, fix (*colloq*.); broil, sizzle, barbecue, grill, fry, frizzle, brown, braise, griddle, roast, rotisserie, sauté, pan-fry, sear, stew, simmer, fricassee, bake, escallop, pressure-cook, autoclave.
> *Adj.* **cooked,** boiled, etc. (see *Verbs*); well-cooked, well-done; overcooked, overdone; undercooked, underdone, rare; uncooked, raw; underbaked, half-baked, doughy.
> [*pert. to cooking*] culinary.
> See also **CONTAINER, FIRE, FOOD, HEAT.**

172

Try substituting *bake* for *cook*.

The chef baked the muffins.

The word *baked* tells exactly how the muffins were cooked. *Baked* is more specific than *cooked*.

Choose synonyms carefully when you use a thesaurus. Synonyms are similar in meaning, but they are not exactly the same. Sometimes a synonym will not fit the situation. Check a dictionary to see if *poached* is used correctly in this sentence.

The chef *poached* the steak.

Poach means to cook in a simmering liquid such as water or milk. *Poach* does mean "to cook," but it would not be a good choice in this sentence.

When you use a thesaurus, be careful to look up the correct part of speech. For example, *cooked* was used as a verb in the sample sentence. Look again at the sample thesaurus entry. *Cooked* can also be an adjective. Choose the synonym that is the same part of speech as the word it replaces.

Note that there is a thesaurus in this book on pages 510–524. It is arranged a bit differently than the ones described. It provides extra help for student writers. The introduction on pages 510–511 will tell you how to use this special thesaurus.

Exercise   Using a Thesaurus
▶ Analyzing/Drawing Conclusions

Look up each word in italics in the special thesaurus on pages 510–524. Rewrite the sentences using suitable synonyms.
Possible synonyms are given.

1. Mr. Barclay *asked* about job openings at the new computer factory. inquired
2. Jenny *broke* her glasses playing touch football. shattered, smashed
3. The candidate *ended* his speech with a reminder to vote. closed
4. Julie *saw* a cave deep in the woods. spotted
5. A *group* of birds was attracted by the birdfeeders. flight

173

LD, ESL, NSD Emphasize the fact that synonyms are not really interchangeable. Give additional examples of inappropriate synonym replacement. Provide additional practice with using synonyms.

Using a thesaurus will help students to expand their vocabulary. Provide additional practice as needed.

Reinforcement

1. Use the "Thesaurus" to find two synonyms for six of the following words. Use each synonym in a sentence to show its meaning.   Answers will vary.

| smart | teach | bad | walk |
| brave | angry | run | wrong |

2. Follow the directions for the exercise on page 173.

1. Karen *likes* Mr. Adamle's sports broadcasts. enjoys
2. The nurse *helped* the doctor with the patient. assisted
3. The immigrant finally *got* a work permit. obtained
4. The mice *ran* across the kitchen floor. scampered
5. "It's a home run!" *said* the announcer. exclaimed

Enrichment

Have the students examine several full-size thesauri. Point out that some have indexes and some do not. Also, point out that most thesauri do not define the synonyms. Therefore, a thesaurus should be used along with a dictionary. Instruct the students to look up the meaning of a synonym before using it in a sentence.

Additional Resources

Skills Practice Book—page 70
Teacher's Resource Binder
  Reinforcement Activities—
  page 58

Using English in Sports

The activity on this page helps the students see that knowing how to use a dictionary and thesaurus is useful in other subjects. This activity focuses on sports. You may wish to have your students suggest other subjects in which dictionary and thesaurus skills would be useful.

Using English in → Sports

▶ **Comprehension**

Sports like football and soccer burst with action and excitement. That is why sports reporters and writers look for verbs that will keep their writing especially active. For example, a reporter would not write, "The Celtics defeated the Hawks with a score of 90 to 49." Instead, the line might read, "The Celtics destroyed the Hawks with a score of 90–49." Larry Bird didn't "make" a basket, he "drilled" one from the floor.

Often, you will want to write about or tell about an exciting game you saw. Always imagine that you, too, are a reporter. Look for words that will re-create the game for others.

Exercise   Using the Right Word
▶ **Creative Application**

Use a dictionary and a thesaurus to rewrite the following article. Replace commonplace words with active, lively words. Take special care with verbs. Make the reader see what is happening.

Rockets Beat Edgewood

The Rockets won their second game this season. They beat Edgewood 24–8 Tuesday on the home court.

Rich Rupeg led the offense with twelve points. Rich made four baskets in four tries in the first half. Jon Greeb helped the offense by making five points.

In the second half, Edgewood fought back. Kurt Wolf ran down the court and made a spectacular shot. Berg, Herbeth, and Beck all scored, too.

The effort was too late. The Rockets scored and held the lead. The crowd cheered as the winning basket lit up the scoreboard.

Chapter 9 Review

▶ Analyzing/Structured Application

A. Using Guide Words Below are the guide words for ten dictionary pages. Copy the guide words on your paper. Beside each pair, write a word that you would find on that page.

anther	antidote	one	ooze
drill	drop	prize	procession
fisher	fix	rondo	rose
immune	impel	stir	stock
matted	maximum	vanilla	various

B. The Multiple Meanings of a Word Read the sentences below. Each of the words in italics is used in an unusual way. Use your dictionary to find the meanings.

1. My mother allowed me to get a *hunch* of pineapple. a chunk
2. Men and women have not worn *ruffs* since the seventeenth century. a high, frilled collar
3. Aaron is Lauren's *spark*. boyfriend
4. He tried to *cow* us by telling a scary story. make timid and meek
5. The movie cameraman *panned* the crowd looking for celebrities. move a camera back and forth to scan the scene
6. Because the ship was always *listing,* many of the passengers were sick. tilting to one side
7. In the attic was an old *fell* rug. made from an animal's hide
8. John used a *spinner* to catch that large bass. a fishing lure

▶ Creative Application

C. Using the Thesaurus Look in the thesaurus on pages 510–524 to find a synonym for each of the following words. Select three synonyms for each word. Using the words correctly, write a sentence using each synonym.

    quiet   bad   run   strange   important

Chapter Review

This review allows teachers to evaluate student understanding of the concepts presented in this chapter.

Additional Resources

Skills Practice Book
Review—page 71

Test Booklet
Mastery Test—pages 49–52

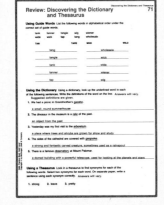

Chapter Objectives

1. To analyze paragraphs that explain a process

2. To select and research a topic

3. To organize details in time order and develop a writing plan

4. To draft an explanation

5. To revise and proofread an explanation

6. To make a final copy and share it with others

Motivating the Students

1. Read Shel Silverstein's poetic "how-to" explanation.

How to Make a Swing
With No Rope
or Board or Nails

First grow a moustache
A hundred inches long,
Then loop it over a hick'ry limb
(Make sure the limb is strong).
Now pull yourself up off the ground
And wait until the spring—
Then swing!

—Shel Silverstein
from *A Light in the Attic*

2. Ask the students if all of the steps in the process are clear and in the proper order. Explain that, although the example is ridiculous, the poet does present a clear explanation of how to make a swing. Now read this poem.

Recipe for a
Hippopotamus Sandwich

A hippo sandwich is easy to make.
All you do is simply take
One slice of bread,
One slice of cake,
Some mayonnaise,
One onion ring,
One hippopotamus,
One piece of string,
A dash of pepper—
That ought to do it.
And now comes the problem . . .
Biting into it!

—Shel Silverstein
from *Where the Sidewalk Ends*

3. Point out that this explanation needs improvement. It does not explain what to do with the ingredients. Steps in the process are omitted.

Week 13

Chapter Management Guidelines This chart may be used to help structure daily lesson plans

Day 1	Day 2	Day 3	Day 4	Day 5
Chapter 10 Opener, p. 177; Part 1, "Thinking About Writing To Tell How," pp. 178–179; Part 2, "Prewriting: Planning an Explanation," pp. 180–181	Part 3, "Prewriting: Organizing Information," pp. 182–183; Part 4, "Drafting Your Explanation," pp. 184–185	Part 4, "Drafting Your Explanation," pp. 184–185	Part 5, "Revising Your Explanation," pp. 186–188; Part 6, "Making and Sharing the Final Copy," p. 189	Chapter Review and selected end-of-chapter activities

Chapter 10

The Process of Explaining *How*

Have you ever explained to a friend how to do your favorite craft project? Have you ever read a magazine article about how icebergs are formed? Have you ever listened to a weather forecaster tell how hurricanes are born? In each of these situations, a step-by-step process is explained. Each process tells how to do something or how something happens.

In this chapter, you will learn the process of writing to explain *how*. You will discover interesting topics to explain. You will also learn how to present a topic in a clear, step-by-step way.

177

4. Read and discuss the introduction on page 177. Ask the students for examples of explanations that they encounter at home or in school. Tell students that in this chapter they will learn how to write a clear, organized explanation.

Special Populations

LD Students' primary difficulties will be with the activities that involve detailing and sequencing. Provide extra practice and reinforcement in these parts. Keep all topics simple and limited.

ESL Because of limited vocabulary, students will benefit from a demonstration of each of the steps in presenting or writing an explanation. Make sure that students understand each step before going on to the next step. Simplify vocabulary as necessary. LD students will also benefit from this approach.

NSD Stress the importance of using Standard English so that directions and explanations are clearly understood.

Refer to the suggestions on pages T32–T35 at the front of this Teacher's Edition for additional notes on teaching composition to special populations.

Related Chapters

You may wish to refer to related material in other chapters as you teach the following concepts:

1. Writing paragraphs, Chapter 5, "Learning About Paragraphs," page 91

2. The process of writing, Chapter 6, "Choosing a Process for Writing," page 101

3. Researching topics for writing, Chapter 24, "The Process of Writing a Report," page 421

Additional Resources

Skills Practice Book—pages 72–76

Test Booklet—pages 53–58
    Pretest—pages 53–54
    Mastery Test—pages 55–58

Teacher's Resource Binder
    Reinforcement Activities—
        pages 59–61
    Enrichment Activities—
        pages 4, 19, 39–52
    Process of Writing Transparencies
    Ideas for Creative Teaching

Name _____ Date _____ Score _____

Chapter 10 Pretest
The Process of Explaining *How*   P10a

Part 1 Thinking About Explanations Read each topic sentence below. Decide what the paragraph will be about. (10 points each)

1. Most people never get to see a snake shed its skin.
   ○ A. how to care for a pet snake
   ○ B. the process a snake goes through to shed its skin

2. It is easy to play the word game called "Mischmasch," which was invented by the writer Lewis Carroll
   ○ A. how to play "Mischmasch"
   ○ B. how Lewis Carroll wrote

Part 2 Planning an Explanation Choose the correct answer to each question. (10 points each)

3. Once you have decided on a topic, what should you do?
   ○ A. Make sure that no one else is using the same topic.
   ○ B. Make notes about what you want to cover in your explanation.

4. What should the notes about your topic include?
   ○ A. an outline of your paper
   ○ B. all the steps in the process you are explaining and all the materials needed

5. What is wrong with this writing plan?

   How To Make Water Bells
   1. Put different amount of water in each glass.
   2. Tap each with a spoon to hear the sound.
   3. Arrange the glasses in order from highest sound to lowest.

   ○ A. There are no materials listed.
   ○ B. The steps do not give enough information
   ○ C. The order of steps is not clear.

Go on to the next page.   53

Part 1

Objective

To analyze paragraphs that explain a process

Presenting the Lesson

All Students

1. Read and discuss pages 178–179. Have students look at Example 1 on page 178. Ask them to list the equipment Rosa needed. Then, list the steps on the board explaining how to make rain. After students have a chance to think about the questions under **Think and Discuss,** have them discuss their responses. Point out that the steps are listed in chronological order—that is, in time order. Explain that if the steps were not in proper order, or if a step were omitted, the experiment would not work.

2. Read and discuss Example 2. List the steps in the process on the board. Point out the similarities between the two examples. Also point out the differences. Even though one paragraph tells how to do something, and the other tells how something works, the order of steps in both is important.

Explain that there is a direct relationship between the steps in a process and the end result. Have students suggest what might happen if a process were carelessly explained or followed. For example, what would happen if you left "two eggs" out of the list of ingredients for making banana bread?

3. Read **Now It's Your Turn** on page 179. Tell students to start thinking about topics for explanations that tell *how.*

Basic Students

Give the students practice in listing the steps in a process. Select several simple tasks and have the students list all of the steps involved in completing each process. You might use these topics: *polishing shoes, peeling an orange, addressing a letter, opening a locker.*

Advanced Students

Have students write several examples of common daily routines that require following a process. Then have them list

---

1 Thinking About Writing To Tell *How*

> **Focus**
>
> Writing that tells *how* explains how to do something. It may also explain how something works or happens.

When people want to know more about their world, they often begin by asking *how*. *How* does a car engine work? *How* are railroad tunnels built? *How* can you fix a leaky faucet?

Pretend that your teacher asked everyone in the class to write a report telling how to do a science project. How would you write your explanation?

Example 1

▶ Analyzing/Evaluating

Read and Think. Rosa wrote these directions telling how to make rain using common household materials. Look for the steps she uses to explain the process. Notice their order.

> When cold air and a humid cloud meet, the cold air changes the humidity into rain. To make a model showing how this happens, first fill a kettle with water. Heat the water. In the meantime, fill a long-handled metal saucepan with ice. Then, place a short glass mug or cup under the spout of the kettle. Hold the pan of ice five inches above the steaming spout. "Rain" from the steam will begin to collect on the bottom of the pan. Soon, rain will begin to drop into the mug or cup.

Think and Discuss. Read the following questions. Think about how to answer them. Discuss your ideas with your classmates.

1. Are all the steps included in Rosa's explanation?
2. Are the steps for making rain presented in any special order? Can you describe that order?
3. What might happen if the order of the steps were changed?
4. What might happen if Rosa left out some steps?

178

Example 2

▶ Analyzing/Evaluating

Read and Think. Rosa's paragraph explained how to do something. Now read these paragraphs that explain how something works.

The alarm sounds at the fire department headquarters in Phoenix, Arizona. A member of the staff rushes over to the computer terminal and punches some figures on its keyboard. Within a few seconds, symbols and words appear on the video screen. The peculiar images pinpoint the location of the burning building by showing the streets that surround it.

Next, the information on the fire is relayed to the computer terminals in all the fire stations in Phoenix. This fire happens to be in an area that Company No. 7 is responsible for. At Company No. 7's station house, an official locates the fire on a wall map and gets a printout from the computer. The officer in charge speeds with a firefighting crew to the blaze, armed with the printout of information about the burning building.

—JAMES A. BAGGETT

Think and Discuss. Read the following questions. Then, reread the paragraphs above. Find answers to the questions. Talk about your ideas with your classmates.

1. Do you now understand how firefighters respond to a fire?
2. Describe the order of the steps telling how firefighters respond to a fire.
3. Is each step stated clearly and simply?

▶ Generalizing

Now It's Your Turn

You have read and thought about two explanations that tell *how*. Each explanation uses clear, simple steps to explain how to do something or how something happens or works. In this chapter, you will learn to share your knowledge and special interests with others. You will learn to write an explanation that tells *how*.

179

Additional Resources

Teacher's Resource Binder
Reinforcement Activities—
page 59

the steps in at least three routines. Students might list the steps in their routine for getting ready for school every morning. This activity will prepare students for the prewriting activities presented later in this chapter.

Special Populations

LD, ESL, NSD Some students will have difficulty following the steps in one or both of the sample paragraphs. The problem may stem from either sequencing difficulties or the level of vocabulary. Help students make the paragraph more manageable by numbering the steps in each. You might have students actually do the experiment outlined in the first paragraph.

Reinforcement

Ask students to analyze this paragraph. It explains how to use an apple to print a T-shirt. Are the directions clear? Has anything been left out? Are the steps arranged in logical order?

You can make your own stenciled T-shirt. All you need are a plain T-shirt, an apple, a stiff paintbrush, and textile paints in your favorite colors. You should also have an old piece of cloth to practice on. First, slice the apple in half, from stem to bud. Brush a thick layer of paint over the cut side of one apple half. Then press the apple, paint side down on the old cloth. Practice until you have the desired effect. Finally, make the stencil print on your T-shirt.

Enrichment

1. Have the students find examples of writing to explain *how* in newspapers or magazines. Have the students identify each article as an example of either how to do something or how something works. Read and discuss their examples in class. Ask students which articles are clear explanations and which are not clear.

2. For additional enrichment activities, see the Unit Projects in the Teacher Notes on page 125. One or more of these projects have special activities for gifted and talented students.

Part 2

Objective

To select and research a topic

Presenting the Lesson

All Students

1. Read and discuss pages 180–181. Encourage students to keep their topics fairly simple. A broad or complicated topic will be too difficult to cover adequately in a single paragraph. You might wish to refer students to Chapter 6, "Choosing a Process for Writing," page 101, for more information on choosing and limiting a topic.

2. Remind students that skimming and scanning are valuable tools for gathering information. Refer students to Chapter 7, "Study and Test-Taking Skills," page 127, to review these useful reading skills.

3. Emphasize the need to include all steps of the process in their lists. Remind students that this is the planning stage of their paragraphs. Stress that without careful planning, they will not have good paragraphs.

4. Assign and discuss Exercises A and B on page 181.

Basic Students

Work with the students individually on Exercise B. Help each one to select an appropriate topic. Then have the students list the steps in the process that they are explaining. Have each student choose a partner and exchange papers. Ask the students to see if they can understand the process to be explained from the list of steps. If not, have them make suggestions for improvement.

Advanced Students

Students will find it more interesting to write about a topic that is new to them. Encourage them to choose topics from the lists they developed for Exercise A on page 181.

Special Populations

LD Students need additional practice in gathering information and listing steps. Help students to select a topic from the "Topics for Writing" in the **Power**

---

2 Prewriting: Planning an Explanation

> **Focus**
>
> Before you write, decide exactly what you want to explain. Then list all the steps and information needed to explain your topic.

Choosing a Topic

▶ Comprehension

Sometimes the topic for an explanation is chosen for you. A friend sees you swimming. She asks you how to do the sidestroke. Your teacher assigns you to write a report on how a thermometer works.

At other times, you can select your own topic. Your choice may be something you already know well. For example, if your hobby is rock collecting, you might explain how crystals are formed. You can also select a topic you want to learn more about. You might want to find out how a solar eclipse occurs.

Gathering Information

Once you have a topic, make some notes about what you want to cover in your explanation. What do you already know about your topic? What do you need to research?

If you know your topic well, the information in your notes will come from your own knowledge. If your topic is one you want to learn more about, you will have to get your information from outside sources. There are many outside sources for information. You might read magazines, newspapers, books, or an encyclopedia article. You might also talk to someone who is an expert on your topic. For more ideas about getting information from outside sources, see Chapter 23, "Developing Library and Research Skills."

Listing Important Steps

As you write notes about your topic, make sure to list all the steps in the process you are explaining. State each step simply and clearly. As you do, pretend you are writing for someone who knows nothing about your topic. Make sure that you have included every step in a logical order. Otherwise, your reader will be confused.

If you are telling how to do something, instructions for gathering necessary materials should be included in the list of important steps. These materials should include tools, ingredients, and any other supplies that may be necessary.

Exercises Choosing a Topic and Gathering Information

▶ Structured Application

A. Thinking of Topics Complete each of the following activities. They will give you ideas for writing topics. Keep these ideas in your writing folder.

1. Read several articles in a newspaper. Cut out any articles that explain how to do or make something. Look in the food, sports, and home life sections.
2. Complete the following sentence in ten different ways. "I wish I knew how _____ works."
3. Imagine that you have been asked to teach a class of kindergartners a simple skill. List five skills that you might teach this class.

▶ Creative Application

B. Choosing a Topic Select a process that you would like to explain. You may choose your own topic, a topic from Exercise A, or one listed in the **Power Handbook** on pages 464–466. Then, begin gathering information, making notes as you go. Write down all the steps in the process. If you are explaining how to do something, include any necessary materials.

181

Handbook. Brainstorm with students to discover the materials and steps needed for this topic. Write these details on the board in logical order. Then repeat this process as students work on their own topics.

ESL Encourage students to choose a topic with which they are familiar. They are more likely to have better command of the vocabulary for a familiar topic than for an unfamiliar one. This is a good opportunity for students to discuss and explain a custom, craft, or other topic associated with their native countries.

Reinforcement

Have students exchange the lists they developed for Exercise B on page 181. Students should then evaluate the lists they receive and make suggestions for reorganizing information, adding or taking out steps, or whatever other changes might be needed to make the steps and processes clearer.

Additional Resources

Skills Practice Book—page 72

Part 3

Objective

To organize details in time order and develop a writing plan

Presenting the Lesson

 All Students

1. Read and discuss pages 182–183. Emphasize the importance of using time order to explain a process. Stress the importance of completing each step before moving on to the next step. For example, Damon should list all of the materials needed for making the volcano in one step. He should not add something after he has begun to explain how to make the volcano.

2. Have students study Damon's sample writing plan. Point out the revisions that Damon made after rereading his plan. Discuss the problems in Damon's original plans and the changes his thoughts suggest.

3. Assign and discuss Exercises A and B on page 183.

 Basic Students

Have students work in pairs to complete Exercise A. Walk around the room and guide students as they identify the logical order of the steps. For Exercise B, have students use the writing plan presented under **Special Populations.**

 Advanced Students

Have students work with individual basic students, helping them to analyze and organize the steps in their lists.

Special Populations

LD Students will need additional practice in sequencing. Refer back to the steps that the students developed for item 3 in Exercise A on page 181. Write these steps on the board. Then, work with students to number these steps in chronological order. Finally, help students to number the steps of their individual topics.

---

3 Prewriting: Organizing Information

> **Focus**
>
> Use **time order** to arrange the steps in an explanation that tells *how*.

▶ Comprehension/Inferring Sequence

When you take swimming lessons, you first learn floating and breath control. If you did not master these skills first, you would certainly have trouble learning how to do the crawl or butterfly strokes. The order in which you learn swimming skills is important.

Order is also important when you explain a process. To help the reader understand your explanation, arrange the steps in time order. **Time order** is the order in which the steps happen.

Arranging Your Details

Look at your notes. Write a *1* beside the step that happens first. Put a *2* beside the second step. Continue until all your steps are numbered. Your finished list is your **writing plan**.

If you are explaining how to do something, your first step should include instructions to gather the necessary materials. Your last step should state the final product or result.

After you have listed and numbered all the steps, check your work. Have you left out any steps? If so, add them. Are any steps in the wrong order? Make any necessary corrections.

A Sample Writing Plan

Damon did a project for geography class when his class was studying the volcanoes of Hawaii. His writing plan tells how to make a model volcano. Notice how he numbered his steps. Notice, also, his thoughts as he looked over his notes.

182

---

4   Put baking soda in cup

1   Materials needed: ^{6-ounce} paper cup, modeling clay,

                4 tablespoons baking soda,

                ½ cup vinegar, newspaper

I should say what size cup.

2   Cover table with newspapers

3   Form clay around sides of cup *right side up* to look like a mountain

5   Add vinegar to baking soda in cup

I forgot to say which way the cup goes.

Exercises   Arranging Details

▶ Analyzing/Inferring Sequence

A. Organizing Your Steps Imagine you want to explain how a balloonist flies a hot-air balloon. The notes you have made are listed below. Number your details in a step-by-step order.

3   To take off, the balloonist lights the propane burner under the nylon bag. This heats the air in the balloon. Because hot air rises, the balloon will go up.

5   To land, the balloonist turns down the burner to cool the air, or opens the vent in the top of the balloon to let out some hot air.

2   Two people may get into the basket.

1   A hot-air balloon is made up of a large nylon bag, or balloon, attached to a basket and a propane burner under the balloon.

4   To make the balloon go higher, the balloonist turns up the heat in the burner.

▶ Inferring Sequence/Creative Application

B. Making a Writing Plan Look at the list of steps you wrote in part 2 for your paragraph telling *how*. Now make a writing plan. Number your details in time order. Check your work. Add any missing details. If you have unnecessary details, take them out.

183

LD, ESL, NSD Provide a sample writing plan for students. You might use this form.

Materials needed:
   Step 1 —
   Step 2 —
   Step 3 —
Result:

Reinforcement

Write the following sentences on the board. Have students reorganize these sentences so that they are in a logical time sequence.

   Here are five easy steps to great photographs.[1] Then, examine the subject through your camera's viewfinder.[4] Put yourself at least four feet away from the subject.[3] Finally, press your shutter button, while holding the camera steady.[6] First, you must choose an interesting subject.[2] Next, aim your camera carefully.[5]

Enrichment

Have students make a bulletin board display of explanations that tell *how*. They might include articles from newspapers or magazines, instruction manuals, game instructions, and recipes.

Additional Resources

Skills Practice Book—page 73
Teacher's Resource Binder
  Reinforcement Activities—
    page 60

Part 4

Objective

To draft an explanation

Presenting the Lesson

All Students

1. Read and discuss pages 184–185. Remind students that the order of steps in their writing plans is the same order that should appear in their final paragraphs. If necessary, they can reorganize some of the steps at this time to make the process clearer.

2. Discuss Damon's sample draft. Ask students whether or not the paragraph is well organized. Ask students to comment on how Damon's changes have improved his paragraph. What other changes might he make to improve it even more?

3. Explain that the purpose of signal words is to point out steps and to help the explanation flow smoothly. Discuss the use of signal words in Damon's paragraph. Do the signal words accomplish what they should?

4. Assign and discuss Exercises A and B on page 185.

▶ Basic Students

Before assigning Exercise B, have each student write appropriate signal words in the margin of his or her writing plan. Then have the students complete the exercise in class. Students should closely follow their writing plans as they work. Walk around the room giving assistance as needed.

◆ Advanced Students

After students complete Exercise B, have them number the steps in their paragraphs. Then, have them insert signal words where appropriate. Caution students that when signal words are overused, they become ineffective. Have students rewrite their paragraphs, using different signal words in different places. Then ask students to evaluate the paragraphs to decide which use of signal words is more effective.

---

4 Drafting Your Explanation

> **Focus**
>
> Now that you have a writing plan, use it as a guide for drafting your explanation.

▶ **Comprehension/Analyzing**

A good writing plan is the skeleton of your final paragraph or composition. Use your writing plan as the outline of your first draft. As you work on this draft, continue thinking about your topic. Try to make each step clear. Make sure each step flows smoothly from the step before it.

You may make changes at this point in the writing process. However, do not be concerned if your draft is not perfect at this time. Later, when you revise, you will have a chance to make your explanation even better and to correct any errors you may have made.

A Sample Draft

Damon used his writing plan to write a draft of his explanation telling how to make a model volcano. Notice his thoughts as he wrote.

You can make a model volcano in your own kitchen! First, you'll need to get some newspapers, a 6-ounce paper cup, some modeling clay, 4 tablespoons baking soda, and ½ cup vinegar. Cover the table with *4 layers of* newspaper. Put the cup, right side up, on the table. Form the clay around the *sides of the* cup. Next, put the baking soda in the cup. Add ¼ cup vinegar. *You can add another ¼ cup vinegar if you want to.*

I should be more specific.

The clay must touch the sides the cup.

I'd better tell the how to keep the volcano going.

184

As he wrote, Damon thought about his explanation. He added two details and another step. Damon will make more changes as he continues the writing process.

Signal Your Steps

Certain words and phrases "signal" a new step. For example, Damon used *first* and *next* to signal steps in his draft. Here are some common signal words which you can use to help your reader understand the steps in your explanation.

Signal Words

first, second, next, last, finally,
then, now, when, while, until, during,
after that, the next step, at the same time

Exercises   Drafting Your Explanation

▶ Analyzing/Structured Application

A. Adding Signal Words Rewrite the following sample draft. As you do, add two or three signal words to help a reader follow the steps more easily.

> If you can't sink a toy boat in the bathtub, how does a craft as big as a submarine stay under water? The secret is in its special storage tank. The submarine takes water into this tank. Water pushes the air out of the storage tank. Because water is heavier than air, the submarine sinks. When the crew wants to surface, air is blown into the tank, forcing the water out. The submarine rises to the surface.

▶ Creative Application

B. Writing Your First Draft Write a first draft of your explanation. Follow your writing plan, adding or rearranging your ideas if necessary. Remember to use signal words to help your reader to follow the steps more easily.

185

Special Populations

LD, ESL Students will need close supervision as they draft. Talk through the process before they begin. Remind students to follow their writing plans as they work. Provide assistance as needed.

NSD Stress the importance of using Standard English when writing an explanation. In order for an explanation to be effective, the audience must clearly understand the steps in the process.

Reinforcement

Have students follow the instructions for Exercise A on page 185 using this paragraph: Signal words may vary.

A Trick with a Mobius Strip

Would you like to play a trick on a friend? All you need is a piece of newspaper, a scissors, and tape. Cut a strip of newspaper two inches wide. Twist the end of the paper once. Tape the ends together. You have a Mobius strip. Tell your friend to cut down the middle of the strip to make two loops. When your friend is done, there will still be only one loop—but it will be twice as long!

Additional Resources

Skills Practice Book—page 74

Teacher's Resource Binder
Reinforcement Activities—
page 61

Part 5

Objective

To revise and proofread an explanation

Presenting the Lesson

All Students

1. Read and discuss pages 186–188. Tell students that they can check to see whether or not they have written a clear explanation by actually following the steps. In this way they will be able to pinpoint unclear directions or missing steps. Point out the questions Damon's friend had about the experiment. Ask students if they have any other questions about the process. Then, discuss the thought bubbles and Damon's reasons for changes.

2. Stress the importance of careful proofreading for all written work. Review proofreading symbols with students. You might make a chart of the symbols presented in Chapter 6, "Choosing a Process for Writing," page 114, and display it in the classroom.

3. Assign and discuss Exercises A and B on page 188.

Basic Students

Give students extra practice and assistance in the revising process. Have students work with advanced students as revising partners, or divide them into small groups. Encourage students to discuss their work with their partners or groups as they work. Stress content revision over proofreading at this time.

Advanced Students

Students who have mastered the process of writing an explanation should work on improving their writing by making it more lively and interesting. They can do this by reordering some sentences and adding descriptive words.

Advanced students sometimes see the need for revision as the sign of poor work or failure. Assure students that all good writers, including professionals, revise their work.

---

5 Revising Your Explanation

> **Focus**
>
> Check to make sure your explanation is simple, clear, and complete as you revise your first draft.

▶ Comprehension

Writing that tells *how* must be well organized and easy to follow. Otherwise, the reader will become confused.

As you revise your draft, think about the following questions. They will help you to write a clear, precise explanation.

> **Guidelines for Revising a *How* Explanation**
>
> **1.** Did I include all the required materials and any other necessary information?
> **2.** Have I stated all the steps of the process?
> **3.** Are my steps stated simply and clearly?
> **4.** Are my steps in the right order?
> **5.** Have I used signal words to make the steps easy to follow?

A good way to test your explanation is to have some friends read it. See if they can follow your directions or understand your explanation. If they have any trouble, mark your draft at that point. Go back later and rework that part of your draft.

A Sample Revision

Damon tested his explanation on a friend. At the end, Damon's surprised friend had a few questions.

"What should people expect when they mix vinegar and baking soda? You never really say."

"How quickly should you pour the vinegar into the cup?"

"Why would you add more vinegar later?"

Because Damon did not want any of his other readers to be surprised, he thought about his friend's questions. Then, he revised his paragraph. Notice his thoughts as he worked.

You can make a model volcano ^erupt in your own kitchen! First, you'll need to get some newspapers, a 6-ounce paper cup, some modeling clay, 4 table-spoons baking soda, and ½ cup vinegar. Cover the table with 4 layers of newspaper. Put the cup, right side up, on the table. Form the clay around the sides of the cup ^so it looks like a mountain. Next, put the baking soda in the cup. ^Quickly Add ¼ cup vinegar ^and watch the eruption. You can add another ¼ cup vinegar if you want to ^make another eruption.

I need to say what the volcano will do.

...ould ...how ...to ...r.

I'd better say what happens here.

Special Populations

LD, ESL Avoid overstressing grammar, mechanics, and usage. Students should concentrate primarily on content revision at this time.

NSD Again, stress the importance of using Standard English. As part of the revision process, students should check their explanations to make sure they have used only Standard English.

Reinforcement

Work with students to develop a list of questions to use in the revising process. The list should include the questions in the box on page 186 as well as some of their own. Put these questions on a chart and post it in the classroom so students may refer to it as they work.

Enrichment

Invite a typist who works on a word processor to speak to the class. Have the expert explain to the students that many professional writers use word processors now. Also have the expert explain the advantages of a word processor in the revision process. The speaker might also point out special features that help in revising, such as built-in dictionaries.

187

Additional Resources

Skills Practice Book—page 75
Teacher's Resource Binder
  Enrichment Activities—
    pages 4, 19

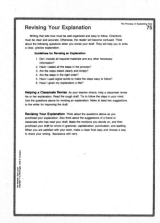

Proofreading Your Explanation

Before you make a final copy of your explanation, proofread it carefully. Look for mistakes in grammar, capitalization, punctuation, and spelling. Use the proofreading symbols you learned in Chapter 6, page 114, to mark corrections on your paper.

When Damon proofread his paragraph, he remembered that numbers under 100 are not written as figures. Instead, they are written out. So he changed his paragraph like this.

You'll need to get some newspapers, a *six* ~~6~~ ounce paper cup, some modeling clay, *four* ~~4~~ table-spoons baking soda, and *one-half* ~~½~~ cup vinegar. Cover the table with *four* ~~4~~ layers of newspaper.

Exercises   Revising an Explanation

▶ Analyzing/Evaluating

A. Helping a Classmate Revise As your teacher directs, help a classmate revise his or her explanation. Read the rough draft. Try to follow the steps in your mind. Also keep in mind the questions in the box on page 186. Make at least two suggestions to the writer for improving the draft based on any questions you had as you read.

▶ Creative Application

B. Revising Your Explanations Use the questions on page 186 to revise your explanation. Also, use the suggestions of a friend or classmate who has read your draft. Finally, proofread your explanation. Make any necessary corrections.

188

6 Making and Sharing the Final Copy

> **Focus**
>
> Choose an interesting title for your explanation. Then make a clean, final copy. Proofread your final copy and correct any errors neatly.

Your final copy should show off your best work. Make sure it is clean and neat. Choose a title that names the topic being explained.

Here is Damon's final copy. Notice how he added the ideas from his friend.

Making a Model Volcano

You can make a model volcano erupt in your own kitchen! First, you'll need to get some newspapers, a six-ounce paper cup, some modeling clay, four tablespoons baking soda, and one-half cup vinegar. Cover the table with four layers of newspaper. Put the cup, right side up, on the table. Form the clay around the sides of the cup so it looks like a mountain. Next, put the baking soda in the cup. Quickly add one-fourth cup vinegar and watch the eruption. You can add another one-fourth cup vinegar if you want to make another eruption.

Exercise   Making and Sharing the Final Copy

▶ **Creative Application**

Think of an interesting title for your work. Then, make a neat, clean, final copy. Check your final copy for any errors. Make any necessary corrections neatly. Finally, turn to pages 116–117 and choose a method of sharing your writing with your classmates.

189

Part 6

Objective

To make a final copy and share it with others

Presenting the Lesson

 All Students

Read and discuss page 189. Have students complete the exercise and turn in their final copies. Use the following criteria to evaluate student work.

Guidelines for Evaluation

Strong The most successful explanatory paragraphs will display the following characteristics: (5 points)

1. will include all necessary steps in the process, including the gathering of materials if necessary
2. will list steps in sequential order
3. will describe each step fully
4. will present steps in clear, specific language
5. will use transitional words or phrases necessary to establish coherence
6. will contain no more than two or three minor errors in grammar, usage, and mechanics

Average A paragraph of average quality will meet most of the criteria of the successful response but may display two or three of the following problems: (3 points)

1. may be missing a minor step of the process
2. may not fully develop each step of the process
3. may be somewhat lacking in coherence
4. may display several errors in grammar, usage, and mechanics

Weak A weak paragraph will display only one or two of the characteristics of a successful response. It will also be characterized by several of the following problems: (1 point)

1. missing steps
2. a lack of organization and coherence
3. vague or ambiguous language
4. numerous errors in grammar, usage, and mechanics

Speaking and Listening

This page gives special emphasis to the speaking and listening skill of explaining a process. This activity may be used to show students how the concepts presented in this chapter may be applied in an oral context.

Objective

To present an oral explanation of how something happened, how something is made, or how to do something

Presenting the Activity

Allow students some time to research their topics before they begin to prepare their tour presentations. You might also have students practice their presentations in small groups before they present them to the class.

Speaking and Listening

Giving a Tour
▶ Comprehension

Tour guides give explanations every day. A tour guide in a printing plant might explain how the pages for a book are printed and how color pictures are processed. A guide in an automobile factory might explain how a car or small truck is assembled. A guide in a bakery might explain how giant mixers knead dozens of loaves of bread in a single batch.

All of these four guides use the same methods you learned to explain *how*. First, they think about the process they are going to explain. Next, the guides gather details about the process and then put them in a logical order. Finally, they may make some note cards to help them practice the talk they will give during the tour.

Exercise   Conducting a Tour
▶ Creative Application

Imagine that you have volunteered to take a group of younger students on a tour of a museum. You may choose to give a tour and presentation about how something happened, such as how dinosaurs became extinct. You may choose to explain how something is made, such as how fossils are formed. Your third choice is to explain how to do something. For example, you may explain how to identify certain varieties of birds or snakes. Choose the topic for your explanation. List the steps in the process. Put these steps in logical order. Finally, put your presentation on note cards. When you have finished writing, practice your presentation out loud. Ask your friends or family for suggestions on how to make it better.

Remember to end your tour by asking if there are any questions. You may also wish to use posters or other visual aids to add interest to your presentation.

190

Creative Writing

Creative Writing

These activities provide opportunities for imaginative applications of the skills presented in this chapter. Students might enjoy doing either Exercise A or B as a group project.

▶ Creative Application

A. Pretend your cousin who lives in a different state visited you last summer. He taught you how to do the Green Frog, the latest dance at his school. It is so fantastic that you decide to teach the Green Frog to your friends. Write an explanation telling how this new dance step is done. For fun, ask your classmates to see if they can follow your instructions.

B. Imagine that you are a reporter who has just been assigned to cover an exciting discovery that may help feed the world's populations. In addition to the already-known unusual substances that can serve as food such as seaweed, acorns, and the fiber inside cattails, a new discovery has been made. Your news article will tell what the new discovery is, where it is found, how it is prepared, and what nutrition it offers.

C. You have always wanted a Bingle Box. Before your parents will let you have one, they want to know more about it. Write a paragraph explaining what a Bingle Box is and how it works.

191

Using English in Computer Studies

This activity may be used to emphasize the relationship between explaining a process and programming a computer. Have students put their flow charts on poster board and display them in the classroom or school library.

Using English in Computer Studies

▶ Comprehension

In this chapter, you learned to explain *how* to do something and *how* something works. When you program a computer, you have to explain *how* to the computer.

The directions you give a computer are called a **program**. Sometimes the computer programmers make a map of the program as they write it. This map is called a **flow chart**. The flow chart might show how the computer will do a math function or where the computer makes decisions about the next step in the program.

Look at the flow chart below. It explains how to blow your nose. Notice that this flow chart has a *start* position and an *end* position. It also has *yes* and *no* options for each step. All steps finally lead to the end step, "BLOW NOSE."

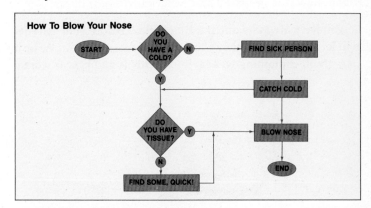

Exercise   Making a Flow Chart
▶ Creative Application

Choose any simple process such as combing your hair, brushing your teeth, or making a sandwich. Then make a humorous flow chart showing how to do this task. Use the flow chart above to guide you.

Chapter 10 Review

▶ **Inferring Sequence**

A. Organizing an Explanation Look at the following notes telling how to make eight tacos. Copy the notes on your paper. Number them in the correct order.

3 Put cooked hamburger in taco shells.

6 Eat and enjoy.

1 Ingredients needed: frying pan, one pound of hamburger, one large onion, salt and pepper, eight hard taco shells, two medium tomatoes, one small head of lettuce, six ounces of cheddar cheese, one bottle of taco sauce.

4 Top hamburger with chopped tomatoes, shredded lettuce, and shredded cheese.

2 Fry hamburger with onion, salt and pepper; drain grease.

5 Top lettuce, tomatoes, and cheese with taco sauce.

▶ **Analyzing**

B. Finding Signal Words Read the following paragraph and answer the questions at the end. See answers in margin.

A rocket is launched in one direction by pushing in the opposite direction. First, fuel is burned inside the rocket. The burning fuel then produces hot gas inside the rocket. At the same time, the heat makes those gases swell. Soon, the gases grow to the point where they need to escape. The only place the gases can escape is through an opening in the back of the rocket. Finally, the gases force their way out, pushing against the earth. This pressure forces the rocket into the air.

1. What are the steps in this process?
2. Make a list of the signal words used in this paragraph.
3. What order is used in this paragraph?

193

Chapter Review

This review allows teachers to evaluate student understanding of the concepts presented in this chapter.

Exercise B

1. Fuel is burned inside the rocket. Burning fuel produces gas. The gases swell and escape through an opening in the back of the rocket. They push against the earth, forcing the rocket into the air.
2. First, then, At the same time, Soon, Finally
3. Time order

Additional Resources

Skills Practice Book
Review—page 76

Test Booklet
Mastery Test—pages 55–58

Chapter 11

Chapter Objectives

1. To make the subject and the verb in a sentence agree in number

2. To avoid errors in agreement between subjects and verbs that have special forms

3. To make subjects and verbs agree in number in sentences beginning with *there, where,* or *here*

4. To use verbs that agree in number with compound subjects

5. To avoid errors in agreement with a subject that is separated from the verb by a prepositional phrase

6. To avoid errors in subject-verb agreement when certain pronouns are used as subjects

Motivating the Students

1. Read the introduction on page 195 orally. Review the definition of a sentence, and emphasize that every sentence needs a subject and a verb. Explain that like the key and the lock in the example, the subject and the verb in a sentence must "fit," or agree, in order to work well.

2. Read this humorous poem.

The Eel

I don't mind eels
Except as meals.
And the way they feels.
     —Ogden Nash

Explain that poets often use incorrect spelling or grammar to achieve humor. This is called *poetic license*. Point out to the students that although incorrect usage may be acceptable in Ogden Nash's humorous poems, it is not acceptable in their writing. Then see if they can find the agreement error in "Eels." Explain that since *they* is plural, it should be used with the plural verb *feel*.

3. Read "The Octopus" by Ogden Nash. Have the students find the agreement errors in the poem.

Tell me, O Octopus, I begs,
Is those things arms, or is they legs?
I marvel at thee, Octopus;
If I were thou, I'd call me Us.

Tell students that what they learn in this chapter will help them use subjects and verbs that agree.

Week 14

Chapter Management Guidelines   This chart may be used to help structure daily lesson plans.

Day 1	Day 2	Day 3	Day 4	Day 5
Chapter 11 Opener, p. 195; Part 1, "Making the Subject and Verb Agree," pp. 196–197	Part 2, "Making Special Verbs Agree," pp. 198–199	Part 3, "Agreement in Special Situations," pp. 200–201	Part 4, "Making Verbs Agree with Certain Pronouns," pp. 202–203	Chapter Review and selected end-of-chapter activities

Mastering Subject-Verb Agreement

What happens when you try to open a lock with the wrong key? Of course, the lock does not open. The notches in the key must fit the notches of the lock. Language works in a similar way. The subjects and the verbs must work together to make good sentences.

In this chapter, you will learn how to make the subjects and verbs of your sentences work together. You will learn how to do this even when using special subjects, compound subjects, or prepositional phrases between the subject and the verb. Studying this chapter carefully will give you an important key to using language correctly.

195

Special Populations

ESL Students may need some review. The concepts of *singular* and *plural* will be familiar, but their application to English may require extra explanation.

NSD Some dialects contain non-standard subject-verb agreement structures. Use extra examples and practice as necessary.

Related Chapters

You may wish to refer to related material in other chapters as you teach the following concepts:

1. Sentences, Chapter 2, "Writing and Understanding Sentences," page 17

2. Pronouns, Chapter 12, "Understanding Pronouns," page 209

3. Words that show relationships, Chapter 20, "Using Prepositions and Conjunctions," page 349

Additional Resources

Skills Practice Book—pages 77–83

Test Booklet—pages 59–62
    Pretest—pages 59–60
    Mastery Test—pages 61–62

Teacher's Resource Binder
    Reinforcement Activities—
        pages 62–65
    Enrichment Activities—
        pages 39–52, 66–67
    Process of Writing Transparencies
    Ideas for Creative Teaching

Part 1

Objective

To make the subject and the verb in a sentence agree in number

Presenting the Lesson

 All Students

1. Read and discuss page 196. Emphasize the -s ending as the mark of the singular form of most verbs.

2. Ask the students to suggest a number of verbs. Write them on the board. Have the students identify the verbs as singular or plural. Then ask the students to create a sentence for each verb. Have the students point out the subject and verb in each sentence. Ask them if the subjects and verbs agree in number.

3. Assign and discuss Exercises A and B on page 197.

4. Assign Exercise C on page 197. Remind students to use the process of writing when completing the assignment. Ask the students to share their paragraphs with the class.

5. Use Exercise A on page 204 for additional practice if needed.

 Basic Students

Before assigning the exercises, provide additional practice in recognizing number in nouns and verbs. Ask them to identify each of these verbs as singular or plural and then to write sentences that use each verb. Remind them that the subject must agree in number with the verb.

dives (s)   enter (p)   play (p)   hatch (p)
bakes (s)   paints (s)   rely (p)   controls (s)

 Advanced Students

Point out that the problem of subjects and verbs agreeing in number does not occur in either the past tense or the future tense.

John *walked* home.
The girls *walked*, too.
John *will go*.
The girls *will go*, too.

---

1 Making the Subject and Verb Agree

┌─ *Focus* ─────────────────────────────┐
│ The subject and the verb in a sentence must agree. │
└──┘

▶ **Comprehension**

A singular noun stands for one person, place, thing, or idea.

game   fox   coin   trust

A plural noun stands for more than one person, place, thing, or idea.

games   foxes   coins   joys

Verbs also have singular and plural forms. In a sentence, the verb must **agree in number** with its subject. A subject and verb agree in number when they are both singular or both plural.

Singular	Plural
One *cloud floats* in the sky.	Many *clouds float* in the sky.
The *movie starts* soon.	The *movies start* soon.

The *s* at the end of verbs such as *floats* and *starts* shows that the verbs are used with singular nouns. *Floats* and *starts* are singular verbs.

When the noun is plural, the *s* is dropped from the verb. The noun *clouds* is plural. Therefore *float* does not have an *s*. *Movies* is plural, so *start* does not end in *s*. *Float* and *start* are plural verbs.

Most singular verbs are formed by adding *s*. However, there are some exceptions to this rule. To form singular verbs, follow the same spelling rules that you learned on pages 50–51 about forming the plurals of nouns. Read these examples.

Plural	Singular	Plural	Singular
wat*ch*	watch*es*	his*s*	hiss*es*
hurr*y*	hurr*ies*	go	go*es*

196

Exercises Making Subjects and Verbs Agree

▶ Analyzing/Classifying

A. Make three columns on your paper. Label the columns *Subject*, *Verb*, and *Number*. For each sentence, write the subject and verb in the correct column. Then, write *Singular* or *Plural* in the last column.

1. My sister studies at Tulane University. Singular
2. The teacher keeps supplies in the metal cabinet. Singular
3. Rico's airplane lands at Gate H. Singular
4. Frogs hibernate in the mud. Plural
5. Children play in the vacant lot on Fifth Street. Plural
6. Wombats make affectionate pets. Plural
7. Some students learn foreign languages in school. Plural
8. Ivy covers the north side of the brick house. Singular
9. Heavy rainstorms cause erosion. Plural
10. My parrot says twenty different words. Singular

▶ Recalling/Analyzing

B. Number your paper from 1 to 10. Choose the correct verb from the parentheses. Write it on your paper.

1. Keiko always (finishes, finish) practice before dinner.
2. Fireworks (flashes, flash) on Independence Day.
3. Spiders (spins, spin) silky webs.
4. That robot (moves, move) its arms and legs.
5. Lifeguards (learns, learn) to handle emergencies.
6. Big plows (clears, clear) our snowy streets in winter.
7. That restaurant (serves, serve) unusual sandwiches.
8. Archaeologists (digs, dig) for artifacts.
9. The concert (starts, start) earlier than I thought.
10. Hugh (mows, mow) lawns to earn money.

▶ Creative Application

C. Writing Write a one-paragraph story in the present tense. Use three or more phrases from the list below as subjects in your sentences. Be sure the verbs agree in number with the subjects.

a haunted house	a hundred bats
a creaky door	thick, sticky spider webs
a ghostly figure	a musty odor

197

Additional Resources

Skills Practice Book—page 77
Teacher's Resource Binder
Reinforcement Activities—
page 62

However, point out that the problem does occur when the participle form of a verb is used. The helping verb must agree in number with the subject.

> Jane *is eating* dinner.
> The twins *are eating* dinner.
> Larry *has eaten* dinner.
> The boys *have eaten* dinner.

Special Populations

ESL Third person singular verbs and plural nouns both end in *-s*. ESL students may find this confusing. Give additional practice using fill-in sentences.

Reinforcement

1. Follow the directions for Exercise A on page 197 using these sentences:

1. The conductor collects the train tickets. singular
2. Gloria's dog barks loudly. singular
3. Cats drink milk. plural
4. Ballet dancers practice daily. plural
5. Mr. Davis carves animals from bars of soap. singular
6. Only physicians can write prescriptions. plural

2. Follow the directions for Exercise B on page 197 using these sentences:

1. Myra never (ask, asks) questions.
2. Lightning (flash, flashes) across the sky.
3. That machine (fill, fills) perfume bottles.
4. Lightning bolts (flash, flashes) across the sky.
5. Chemists (create, creates) products.
6. Ants (build, builds) elaborate tunnels.

Enrichment

1. Have the students "listen" for errors in subject-verb agreement for several days. Ask them to record each sentence that contains an error. They may find the errors in TV shows, on the radio, or in everyday conversations. Discuss the faulty sentences in class. Have the students correct them.

2. For additional enrichment activities, see the Unit Projects in the Teacher Notes on page 125. One or more of these projects have special activities for gifted and talented students.

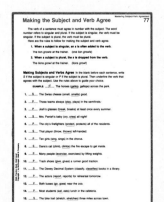

Part 2

Objectives

1. To avoid errors in agreement between subjects and verbs that have special forms

2. To make the subjects and verbs agree in number in sentences beginning with *there*, *where*, or *here*

Presenting the Lesson

 All Students

1. Read **Special Forms of Certain Verbs** on page 198. Put the following chart on the board and discuss it.

	Singular	Plural
Present Tense	is	are
	has	have
	does	do
Past Tense	was	were
	had	had
	did	did

Also discuss the negative contractions of the words on the chart (such as *isn't* and *hasn't*). Ask the students which of the verbs and negative contractions may be used with *he*, *she*, *we*, and *they*.

2. Read and discuss **There Is, Where Is, and Here Is** on page 198. Help the students to find the subjects in additional sentences. *(Where is my kazoo? There is a rainbow. Here is your change.)*

3. Assign and discuss Exercises A and B on page 199.

4. Assign Exercise C. Refer students to the "Guide to Punctuation" in the **Power Handbook** for rules on punctuating dialogue. Ask students to share their conversations with the class.

5. Use Exercise B on page 204 for additional practice if needed.

2 Making Special Verbs Agree

Focus

Some verbs have special forms. Follow the rules of agreement for these verbs.

Special Forms of Certain Verbs

▶ Comprehension

A few verbs have special forms. Make sure to choose the verb form that matches your subject in number.

Is, Was, Are, Were The verb forms *is* and *was* are singular. The forms *are* and *were* are plural.

> Singular: Carlos *is* here. Carlos *was* here.
> Plural: The boxes *are* here. The boxes *were* here.

Has, Have The verb form *has* is singular. *Have* is plural.

> Singular: Pam *has* a plan.
> Plural: They *have* a plan.

Does, Do The verb form *does* is singular. *Do* is plural.

> Singular: Joe *does* the cooking.
> Plural: They *do* the cooking.

There Is, Where Is, Here Is

Many sentences begin with *There*, *Where*, or *Here*. These words are never subjects of sentences. To decide whether to use a singular or plural form of a verb in such a sentence, first find the subject by asking *who?* or *what?* before the verb.

> There is the Big Dipper.
> *Who* or *what* is? The Big Dipper is.
> *Big Dipper* is the subject.
> *Big Dipper* is singular. Use the singular verb *is*.

198

Exercises   Using the Right Verb Form

▶ Recalling

A. Number your paper from 1 to 10. Choose the right form of the verb from the parentheses. Write it on your paper.

1. Two ski poles (was, <u>were</u>) standing in the drift.
2. Several owls (is, <u>are</u>) hooting in the woods.
3. Where (<u>is</u>, are) everybody?
4. (<u>Doesn't</u>, Don't) a rhea look like an ostrich?
5. Toni's knee (<u>was</u>, were) swollen.
6. Here (<u>is</u>, are) one of the oars for the canoe.
7. Native American war bonnets (was, <u>were</u>) made with long feather tails.
8. Where (does, <u>do</u>) these bike paths lead?
9. The locker rooms (is, <u>are</u>) newly painted.
10. There (was, <u>were</u>) three coconuts on the palm tree.

▶ Recalling/Analyzing

B. Number your paper from 1 to 10. For each sentence, write the correct verb form. Use the present tense of the verb in parentheses.

1. There (be) no salt in the salt shaker.   is
2. Jack and Fred (have) directions for the scavenger hunt.   have
3. Max (do) warm-up exercises before jogging.   does
4. The stores on Central Street (be) always closed on holidays.   are
5. The noises in this cave (have) weird echoes.   have
6. There (be) many reasons for the President's action.   are
7. Where (do) the twins go to camp?   do
8. Molly (have) a collection of baseball pennants.   has
9. Where (do) the books on the table belong?   do
10. Here (be) four more pieces for the puzzle.   are

▶ Creative Application

C. Writing After months of working with your invention, you have succeeded in communicating with life on a distant planet. Write a brief account of your conversation. Include information such as "Life here is . . ." or "Things there are . . ." or "Where is . . . ."

199

Additional Resources

Skills Practice Book—page 78
Teacher's Resource Binder
   Reinforcement Activities—
      page 63

Basic Students

Before assigning Exercises A and B, have the students find the subject in each sentence. Then do the first half of each exercise orally. Have students complete the rest of each exercise independently.

Advanced Students

There are two other subjects that may cause problems in agreement of subject and verb: 1) words giving amounts are usually considered singular, and 2) a title of a book or organization, even when plural, is considered singular. After the students have completed the exercises, write these sentences on the board and discuss them with the students.

1. Three yards (is, are) enough material for this outfit.
2. Sixty cents (is, are) not enough for hot lunch.
3. The Women's Club (is, are) meeting tonight at our house.
4. *Great Buildings of the World* (is, are) a book on architecture.

Special Populations

NSD Give extra practice for agreement of subjects with a variety of state-of-being verbs.

Reinforcement

1. Have the students follow the directions for Exercise A on page 199 using these sentences:

1. Mae (has, have) the correct change for the bus fare.
2. The walls in the kitchen (<u>have</u>, has) been painted yellow.
3. The baskets on the truck bed (<u>were</u>, was) full of pears.
4. (Do, Does) they want blueberries on their waffles?
5. That wind (<u>does</u>, do) sound awful.

2. Have the students choose the correct form of the verb for each of the following sentences:

1. Where (are, <u>is</u>) the sock that matches this one?
2. There (is, are) a secret compartment in this desk.
3. Here (is, are) a sample of the coconut milk.
4. Where (does, <u>do</u>) penguins winter?
5. There (<u>were</u>, was) many reasons for the fall of the Roman Empire.

Part 3

Objectives

1. To use verbs that agree with compound subjects

2. To avoid errors in agreement with a subject that is separated from the verb by a prepositional phrase

Presenting the Lesson

 All Students

1. Read and discuss **Compound Subjects** on page 200. Stress the difference between *and* and the other conjunctions used in a subject. Be sure students understand the use of *either-or* and *neither-nor*.

2. Read **Prepositional Phrases After the Subject** on pages 200–201. Point out that the best way to decide which verb form to use is to read the sentence omitting the prepositional phrase.

3. Assign and discuss Exercises A and B on page 201.

4. Assign Exercise C. Remind students to use the process of writing when completing the assignment. After they have drafted their paragraphs, let classmates read them and make suggestions for revisions.

5. Use Exercise C on page 205 for additional practice if needed.

 Basic Students

Deal with each subject in isolation. After reading **Compound Subjects,** do items 3, 4, 6, 9, and 10 of Exercise A orally. Then assign items 2, 4, 6, 8, and 10 of Exercise B to be done independently. Other items in each exercise can be completed by students working in pairs.

Next, read **Prepositional Phrases After the Subject.** Do items 1, 2, 5, 7, and 8 of Exercise A orally. Then assign items 1, 3, 5, 7, and 9 of Exercise B for independent work.

---

3 Agreement in Special Situations

> **Focus**
>
> Pay special attention to compound subjects and prepositional phrases when you make subjects and verbs agree.

Compound Subjects

 Comprehension/Analyzing

When two or more parts of a compound subject are joined by the conjunction *and*, use the plural form of the verb.

> The mayor and the police chief *were* in the parade.
> Speed skating and downhill skiing *are* two Olympic sports.

When the parts are joined by *or, either-or,* or *neither-nor*, use the form of the verb that agrees with the nearer subject.

> Carol or Janet *is* singing.
> Neither Matthew nor his brothers *are* coming.
> Either six pencils or one pen *costs* a quarter.

Prepositional Phrases After the Subject

Be careful with prepositional phrases that come between the subject and the verb. Do not confuse the subject of the verb with the object of the preposition. Look at this sentence.

> The *gate* near the pines *makes* squeaky noises.
> The verb is *makes*. Who or what makes? *Gate*
> *Gate* is the subject of the sentence.
> *Gate* is singular, so you use the singular verb *makes*.
> *Near the pines* is a prepositional phrase. The verb must agree with the subject, not with the prepositional phrase.

🔑 **Key to Writing and Speaking** Do not rely on what "sounds right" to make subjects and verbs agree. Follow the rules of subject-verb agreement.

Exercises   Choosing the Right Verb Form

▶ **Classifying/Analyzing**

A. Make two columns on your paper. Label them *Subject* and *Verb*. Write the subject and verb for each sentence in the correct column.

1. Many new recruits for the Army are women.
2. The customer at the counter needs service.
3. The corn and buns for the picnic cost six dollars.
4. Radio and television inform people about the news.
5. Many students from Harper School audition today.
6. Skiers and snowmobilers wait for big snowfalls.
7. In autumn, smoke from burning leaves fills the air.
8. The road through the countryside is narrow.
9. Neither the clay nor the paint for your project is here.
10. Gina or Joan plays badminton every weekend.

▶ **Analyzing**

B. Number your paper from 1 to 10. Choose the correct verb from the parentheses in each sentence. Write it on your paper.

1. Some trees with thick bark (survives, survive) fires.
2. Kermit or Miss Piggy (is, are) my favorite Muppet.
3. My friends from Tampa (visits, visit) me often.
4. Grandma and Grandpa often (calls, call) me.
5. The onions in the salad (tastes, taste) strong.
6. Either the swimmers or their coach usually (accepts, accept) the trophy.
7. This camera bag with two pockets (seems, seem) best.
8. Yellowstone and Yosemite (is, are) national parks.
9. Three men on horseback (leads, lead) the parade.
10. Neither the lights nor the phone (works, work).

▶ **Creative Application**

C. Writing Imagine that one day you find a strange coin. You pick it up, turn it over three times, and a genie appears. You are granted three wishes. You may make two things disappear from the world and one thing appear. In a paragraph, explain your choices. Use several compound subjects.

201

Have the students write five original sentences with compound subjects. Tell the students to vary the conjunctions. Then have them write five sentences with the subject separated from the verb by a prepositional phrase. Discuss these sentences in class.

Special Populations

ESL, NSD Compound subjects and indefinite pronouns may require extra practice. Encourage their use in classroom conversation. Offer extra drill as needed.

Reinforcement

1. Follow the directions for Exercise A on page 201 using these sentences:

1. Many old cars in that garage are rusty.
2. In our village, policemen and firemen take physical fitness tests.
3. The aroma of baking bread fills the air.
4. The path through the garden is muddy.
5. Sailboats and small fishing boats use the lake.
6. The models from the agency posed for the photographs.
7. The oranges and lemons in the groves are ripe.

2. Follow the instructions for Exercise B on page 200 using these sentences:

1. Bob and Jerry (run, runs) a mile daily.
2. Either Dr. Warren or one of the interns (is, are) in the emergency room.
3. Neither Rhonda nor her classmates (are, is) going to the camp until June.
4. Naomi or Samantha (deliver, delivers) the newspaper.
5. Mason or his sister (tell, tells) a ghost story every Halloween.
6. Either Luigi or John (sing, sings) the solo part.

Enrichment

Using newspapers as a source, have the students find examples of sentences with compound subjects and sentences with subjects and verbs separated by prepositional phrases. Discuss the sentences in class. Have the students find the subject and verb in each sentence.

Additional Resources

Skills Practice Book—page 79
Teacher's Resource Binder
  Reinforcement Activities—
  page 64

Part 4

Objective

To avoid errors in subject-verb agreement when certain pronouns are used as subjects

Presenting the Lesson

All Students

1. Read and discuss page 202. Remind students to disregard any prepositional phrases following a subject when they are choosing the correct verb to use in a sentence.

2. Assign and discuss Exercises A and B on page 203.

3. Assign Exercise C. Remind students to use the process of writing when completing the assignment. As the students draft, they may wish to organize their details in chronological order.

4. Use Exercise D on page 205 for additional practice if needed.

Basic Students

Do Exercise A orally. Then help the students select the subject in each sentence in Exercise B. Have the students complete Exercise B independently.

Advanced Students

Have the students write ten sentences with indefinite pronouns as subjects. Read the sentences out loud in class to check for subject–verb agreement.

Special Populations

NSD Give extra examples to illustrate the indefinite pronouns that can be used as either singular or plural pronouns.

---

4 Making Verbs Agree with Certain Pronouns

> **Focus**
>
> Follow special rules of agreement with certain pronouns.

I and *You*

▶ Comprehension

The pronoun *I* stands for a single person. However, the only singular verb forms used with it are *am* and *was*.

> I *am* in my room.   I *was* here yesterday.

Otherwise, the plural form of the verb is always used.

> I *do* my work.   I *have* a cold.   I *throw* a good fastball.

Although *you* can be singular or plural, always use a plural verb with this pronoun.

> "You *were* late," the coach said to the player.
> "You *were* late," the coach said to the seven players.

Special Pronouns

The pronouns below are singular. They use singular verbs.

either	each	everyone	anyone
neither	one	everybody	nobody

> Either *is* right.   Neither *was* famous.

In the sentences above, a singular verb follows a singular subject. When a prepositional phrase follows one of these pronouns, the verb must still agree with the pronoun subject.

> Either of the answers *is* right.
> Neither of the scientists *was* famous.

202

Exercises Choosing the Correct Verb Form

▶ Classifying/Analyzing

A. Make three columns on your paper. Label the columns *Subject*, *Prepositional Phrase,* and *Verb.* Find these three parts in each sentence. Write them in the correct column.

1. Nobody in our class swims a full pool length.
2. One of the propellers was bent.
3. Either of those skaters needs more practice.
4. Neither of the cats sleeps silently.
5. One of the bathroom faucets leaks.
6. Everyone on the scavenger hunt walks with a partner.
7. Neither of the digital clocks tells perfect time.
8. Anyone from Montana knows what a blizzard is.
9. Each of the displays is ready to be presented.
10. Nobody at the picnic wants a hammock.

▶ Recalling/Analyzing

B. Number your paper from 1 to 10. Choose the correct form of the verb for each sentence. Write it on your paper.

1. You (was, were) ready, (wasn't, weren't) you?
2. I (am, is, are) going for a walk.
3. Each of the girls (has, have) five minutes for her act.
4. With your new bike, you (rides, ride) faster than ever.
5. Of all the library aides, I (am, is, are) the youngest.
6. Each of the uniforms (has, have) the sponsor's name.
7. (Has, Have) you brought in the flag?
8. Everybody from both classes (was, were) invited.
9. (Was, Were) you afraid?
10. My mother and I (am, is, are) going to the flea market.

▶ Creative Application

C. Writing Imagine that you are a bowling ball. A group of friends has arrived at the alley to bowl. The person who appears to be the most awkward and least experienced bowler is heading for you. Write a paragraph about what happens next. Use at least three of these pronouns in your story: *either, neither, each, one, everyone, everybody, anyone, nobody, I, you.*

203

Reinforcement

1. Copy these sentences leaving a space for the verb. Draw a circle around the prepositional phrase. Then choose the right form of the verb and write it.

1. Each (of the lunch boxes) (contains, contain) a sandwich and an apple.
2. One (of the students) (ride, rides) a motorcycle (to school).
3. Neither (of the boys) (want, wants) to give away the kittens.
4. Everyone (in the music class) (hope, hopes) to be selected (for the band).
5. Anyone (among those actors) (are, is) suitable (for the part).
6. Nobody (in this one-hundred-year-old photograph) (are, is) smiling.
7. Each (of the bottles) (was, were) labeled and sealed.
8. Neither (of the girls) (are, is) going downtown tomorrow.

2. Have the students follow the directions for Exercise B on page 203 using these sentences:

1. (Don't, Doesn't) you know the answer?
2. (Is, Are, Am) you ready for lunch?
3. You (was, were) telling us about the erupting volcano.
4. Both you and I (was, were) in the first grade that year.
5. You baton-twirlers (march, marches) after the band and before the horses.

Additional Resources

Skills Practice Book—page 80

Teacher's Resource Binder
Reinforcement Activities—
page 65
Enrichment Activities—
pages 66–67

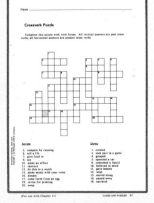

Exercises for Mastery

These **Exercises for Mastery** may be used for additional practice of the concepts presented in this section. Each exercise focuses on a single concept, and should be used after the page number indicated in parentheses.

Exercises for Mastery

Mastering Subject-Verb Agreement

▶ Recalling/Analyzing

A. Using the Right Verb Form Number your paper from 1 to 10. Choose the correct form of the verb from the parentheses. Write it on your paper. (Use after page 197.)

1. Many horses (huddles, huddle) in the shade.
2. One large furnace (heats, heat) the entire apartment building.
3. Termites often (hides, hide) under old logs.
4. An old umbrella (stands, stand) in the closet.
5. Two secretaries (works, work) in our school office.
6. Police officers (protects, protect) our citizens and our community.
7. A kangaroo (carries, carry) her young in a pouch.
8. That pianist (plays, play) very well.
9. Scary movies (makes, make) me shiver.
10. Calculators (adds, add) numbers both quickly and accurately.

B. Writing the Correct Verb Form Number your paper from 1 to 10. Write the correct form of the verb in parentheses.

(Use after page 199.)

1. (Was, Were) the three of you too hot?
2. How (does, do) Corrine get to school?
3. The equipment (has, have) been moved to the attic of the civic center.
4. My four pet fish (doesn't, don't) need a lot of attention or care.
5. Here (is, are) some larger pieces of fabric.
6. Our book order (is, are) in the mail.
7. Where (does, do) Mrs. Baker keep the stapler?
8. (Isn't, Aren't) there any tomatoes left?
9. There (has, have) been many warm days in October.
10. The muffins (was, were) toasted in the oven.

Additional Resources

Skills Practice Book
   Mixed Practice—page 81

C. Choosing the Right Verb Form Number your paper from 1 to 10. Choose the correct form of the verb for each sentence. Write it on your paper. (Use after page 201.)

1. Dan and Joanie (takes, <u>take</u>) turns on the rope swing hanging from the tree.
2. The man in the corral (<u>looks</u>, look) scared.
3. Neither the apples nor the pears (tastes, <u>taste</u>) ripe.
4. Posters and mobiles (decorates, <u>decorate</u>) our room.
5. The monkeys in that cage (is, <u>are</u>) amusing.
6. Either Raymond or Rita (<u>collects</u>, collect) newspaper money this week.
7. Balloons and streamers (hangs, <u>hang</u>) from the ceiling of the gym.
8. The antique glass figures in this display case (breaks, <u>break</u>) very easily.
9. Neither the scouts nor their leader (<u>sees</u>, see) the bear inside the cave.
10. The wheels on the hay wagon (needs, <u>need</u>) oil.

D. Making Verbs Agree with Certain Pronouns Number your paper from 1 to 10. For each sentence, write the correct present form of the verb in parentheses. (Use after page 203.)

1. Everyone usually (crowd) the stadium entrance before the game. crowds
2. Each of the egg baskets (look) full. looks
3. Nobody on the camping trip (have) a compass. has
4. I usually (come) home by four o'clock. come
5. Nobody on the basketball team (practice) free throws every day. practices
6. You always (be) welcome at my house. are
7. Neither of the crepes (be) blueberry. is
8. You and I (be) going with Audrey. are
9. Sometimes, one of the ferrets (get) loose. gets
10. Everyone in the theater (cry) during that movie. cries

205

Using Grammar in Writing

These challenging and enjoyable activities allow the students to see how the concepts of grammar, usage, and mechanics may be applied in actual writing situations. Each exercise is designed to give students practice in several of the skills they have acquired in this section. The activities also provide opportunities for students to write creatively about a wide variety of interesting and unusual subjects.

As students complete these activities, remind them to follow the process of writing. Be sure to allow adequate time for prewriting activities. Individual conferences or peer-group sessions may be used for help with drafting and revision.

You may wish to have the class compose one or two sentences together before they begin writing individually. Remind students that details in a narrative are usually arranged in chronological order.

Using Grammar in Writing

▶ **Creative Application**

A. Imagine that your pen pal from Italy is visiting. Take him or her on a tour of your town. What interesting sights would you point out? In a paragraph, write what you would say to your pen pal. Begin some of your sentences with phrases such as "Here is . . ." or "There is . . . ."

B. Combine one or two of the following noun phrases and verb phrases to make sentences. Use the sentences in a story. Add more sentences to complete the story. Make sure that subjects and verbs agree in number.

Noun Phrases
the cat and the kangaroo
green spots on the wall
a frog with three eyes
an eagle and a mouse
the jack-o'-lantern with the crooked smile
a family of raccoons

Verb Phrases
knock(s) loudly on the door
eat(s) spaghetti with a ruler and pliers
jump(s) onto my bed thinking it is a trampoline
hop(s) down to the basement in search of spider webs
race(s) out the door as the clock strikes 11:59

C. Using Subject-Verb Agreement in Computer Studies Write a paragraph on the function of parts of a computer. Use these computer terms as subjects of some sentences.

disks	monitor	printer
function keys	disk drive	keyboard

Use an encyclopedia or textbook if necessary. Make sure that your subjects and verbs agree.

206

Additional Resources

Skills Practice Book
Subject-Verb Agreement in Writing—page 82

Chapter 11 Review

▶ Recalling/Analyzing

A. Making Subjects and Verbs Agree Number your paper from 1 to 10. Choose the correct verb from the parentheses. Write it on your paper.

1. Either football or rugby (is, are) my favorite sport.
2. Steam from the geysers (fills, fill) the air.
3. Where (has, have) you been?
4. One of the film projectors (makes, make) clicking sounds when it is turned on.
5. There (was, were) five pigeons on our roof.
6. I (have, has) the answer to the puzzle.
7. You (draws, draw) the funniest cartoons.
8. The glass ornaments in this box (is, are) shattered.
9. Cindy or Lauren (takes, take) tap-dancing lessons.
10. Everybody (thinks, think) you (is, are) right.

B. Choosing the Correct Verb Number your paper from 1 to 10. Write the correct present tense form of the verb in parentheses.

1. Our neighbors or my aunt (feed) our hamster when we're away. feeds
2. The instructions for my new tape recorder (seem) confusing. seem
3. Where (do) this maze begin? does
4. Neither those stores nor that restaurant (open) on Sundays or Mondays. opens
5. "There (go) my allowance!" Sammy said. goes
6. The coins in Meghan's collection (be) valuable. are
7. Near the White House (be) a famous monument, the Lincoln Memorial. is
8. Either three small pizzas or one large pizza (serve) six people. serves
9. The dogs on our block (bark) every morning. bark
10. The musicians in the orchestra and the actors (have) a dress rehearsal tonight. have

207

Additional Resources

Skills Practice Book
Review—page 83

Test Booklet
Mastery Test—pages 61–62

Chapter Review

These exercises provide review of the concepts presented in this section. Each exercise challenges the students to apply several of the skills they have acquired during previous study. Because the "mixed" feature of these activities makes them more difficult, the teacher may wish to have less-advanced students do the exercises orally or in small groups.

Chapter 12

Chapter Objectives

1. To define pronouns and to identify pronouns in sentences

2. To use pronouns correctly as subjects of sentences

3. To use pronouns correctly after state-of-being verbs

4. To use pronouns correctly as objects in sentences

5. To identify possessive pronouns and use them correctly

6. To distinguish between possessive pronouns and contractions that are spelled similarly

Motivating the Students

Copy the following paragraphs about Marco Polo on the board. Underline all the pronouns. Have students identify what noun each underlined word replaces. Tell students that the underlined words are pronouns, and that pronouns take the place of nouns.

MARCO POLO (1254–1324) Seven hundred years ago Venice was a great center of trade. *Her* merchants traveled far and wide to buy and sell.

In 1255 two of *her* merchants had journeyed far into Asia. *They* had gone beyond the Black Sea. These merchants were brothers—Nicolo and Maffeo Polo. As *they* turned toward home *they* met an ambassador on *his* way to the court of the great Kublai Khan. Kublai Khan was the ruler of a very large part of Asia. *His* court was in a city of Cathay, the land *we* now call China. The Polos decided that *they,* too, would go to Cathay.

It took them a year to reach the court of Kublai Khan. There *they* were well treated. When, after several years, the Polos started back to Venice, the Khan invited *them* to return. *He* hoped *they* would bring teachers with *them* when *they* came again.

—Golden Book Encyclopedia

Explain that there are several kinds of pronouns in this paragraph. In this chapter, students will learn about these pronouns and how to use them correctly in sentences.

Now read and discuss with students the introduction on page 209.

Week 15

Chapter Management Guidelines   This chart may be used to help structure daily lesson plans.

Day 1	Day 2	Day 3	Day 4	Day 5
Chapter 12 Opener, p. 209; Part 1, "What Are Pronouns?" pp. 210–212	Part 2, "Using Subject Pronouns," pp. 213–215	Part 3, "Using Object Pronouns," pp. 216–217	Part 4, "Possessive Pronouns," pp. 218–219	Chapter Review and selected end-of-chapter activities

Chapter 12

Understanding Pronouns

It is the bottom of the ninth inning, and the score is tied. You are the coach. Your next batter hasn't had a hit in the last eight times at bat. He seems to be tired. It is time for a change. What do you do? Of course! You send in a pinch hitter to replace the regular batter!

In language, pronouns act something like pinch hitters in baseball. A pronoun is sometimes used to replace a noun.

In this chapter, you will learn how to use pronouns correctly in place of nouns. You will learn how to use pronouns as subjects of sentences, objects of verbs, and possessives.

209

Special Populations

LD Permit students to refer to charts of singular, plural, and possessive pronouns. Display these charts in the room. Provide extra practice whenever possible. Students will have some difficulty determining when to use subject pronouns and when to use object pronouns. Review Chapter 2, "Writing and Understanding Sentences," on page 17.

ESL This chapter may be difficult for some students. The use of pronouns varies greatly from one language to another. Be sure that students understand the concepts being taught before they attempt the exercises.

NSD Many dialects have their own systems for determining pronoun usage. Allow students to refer to charts of singular, plural, subject, object, and possessive pronouns when doing the exercises in this chapter. Stress the importance of using standard English in writing and speaking.

Related Chapters

You may wish to refer to related material in other chapters as you teach the following concepts:

1. Using pronouns in sentences, Chapter 2, "Writing and Understanding Sentences," page 17.

2. Using nouns in sentences, Chapter 3, "Nouns for Precise Meaning," page 45

3. Pronouns as objects of prepositions, Chapter 20, "Using Prepositions and Conjunctions," page 349

Additional Resources

Skills Practice Book—pages 84–90

Test Booklet—pages 63–68
  Pretest—pages 63–64
  Mastery Test—pages 65–68

Teacher's Resource Binder
  Reinforcement Activities—
    pages 66–70
  Enrichment Activities—
    pages 20, 39–52, 68
  Process of Writing Transparencies
  Ideas for Creative Teaching

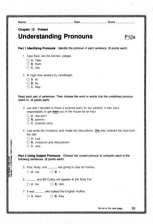

Part 1

Objective

To define pronouns and to identify pronouns in sentences

Presenting the Lesson

■ All Students

1. Read and discuss pages 210–211. Write the three uses of pronouns on the board.

2. Discuss **Key to Writing and Speaking.** Explain that the use of too many pronouns makes sentences dull and repetitious. Also point out that too many pronouns can be confusing. The listener or reader might not be able to determine to whom or to what the pronoun refers.

3. Assign and discuss Exercises A, B, and C. After students complete Exercise C, have them underline the pronouns in their paragraphs. Ask the students to share their paragraphs with the class.

4. Use Exercise A on page 220 for additional practice if needed.

▶ Basic Students

Do Exercise A as a group activity. Then allow the students to work in pairs to complete Exercise B.

Give the students practice in using pronouns. Have them revise the following paragraph using pronouns in place of overused nouns.

Sharon wrote a story about Sharon's cat. Sharon took the story to school. Sharon hoped that Sharon's teacher would like the story and would give Sharon a good grade.

◆ Advanced Students

Have students make posters of singular and plural pronouns to display in the classroom for both basic and special populations students.

Special Populations

LD Students should review the definition of a noun before they begin this part. Encourage students to refer to the lists of singular and plural pronouns for review as they do the exercises.

1 What Are Pronouns?

Focus

A **pronoun** is a word used in place of a noun.

▶ Comprehension

Read this paragraph.

> Fireflies get the fireflies' name from the flashes of light the fireflies give off. The light is not really fire. The light is a heatless chemical reaction.

What is wrong with this paragraph? Reading the nouns *fireflies* and *light* so many times is boring. The repetition may even get in the way of your understanding of the paragraph. Now read this paragraph.

> Fireflies get their name from the flashes of light they give off. The light is not really fire. It is a heatless chemical reaction.

What is different about the second paragraph? The words *their, they,* and *it* replace the nouns *fireflies* and *light* in several places. The paragraph is now more interesting and easier to read. Words like *their, they,* and *it* are pronouns. **Pronouns** are words used in place of nouns.

When you speak and write, pronouns can be used to refer to the following persons and things.

1. To yourself: *I* asked *my* cousin to play badminton with *me*.
2. To someone you are talking to: *You* can leave *your* puppy here.
3. To other persons, places, or things: *She* sold vegetables from *our* garden to *them*.
   He gave *Carla* the prize. *She* thanked *him*.

Notice that a pronoun can replace a noun from the same sentence or from an earlier sentence. A pronoun can also refer to another pronoun. In the last example, *him* refers to *he*.

210

Pronouns take many forms. Like nouns, pronouns can be either singular or plural. Look at the pronouns in this chart.

Singular Pronouns			
Person Speaking:	I	my, mine	me
Person Spoken To:	you	your, yours	you
Other Persons, Places, and Things:	he	his	him
	she	her, hers	her
	it	its	it

Plural Pronouns			
Person Speaking:	we	our, ours	us
Person Spoken To:	you	your, yours	you
Other Persons, Places, and Things:	they	their, theirs	them

Key to Writing and Speaking Do not overuse pronouns. Sometimes, you can replace a noun with a synonym instead.

> Example: Robert E. Lee was respected by his soldiers. *He* was fair, and *he* was intelligent. *The general* was also a brilliant soldier.

Exercises   Recognizing Pronouns

▶Recalling

A. Number your paper from 1 to 10. Write all the pronouns from each sentence.

1. Donna promised she would loan me both her mask and her snorkel.
2. I watched the swan preen its snowy feathers.
3. We couldn't wait to tell them about our bulldozer ride.
4. Will you find Jesse's marbles and return them to him?

211

Reinforcement

1. Have the students follow the directions for Exercise A on page 211 using these sentences:

1. My gerbil escaped from its cage.
2. We laughed at Nora's jokes and asked her for more.
3. Earth rotates on its axis.
4. Your older sister is watching her favorite T.V. program.
5. Jim and he drew pictures of our car.
6. She heard an album of their latest songs.
7. Will he meet them at the picnic?
8. The elephant picked up the peanuts with its trunk.
9. They are coming to our team's basketball game.
10. Does she know your new telephone number?

2. Have the students list the ten pronouns in the following paragraph. Next to each pronoun they should write the word that the pronoun replaces.

Sandy is learning how to play the mandolin. Her(1) parents gave it(2) to her(3) last month for her(4) birthday. She(5) likes the sound of the instrument. She(6) finds it(7) easy to play. It(8) has steel strings, so the tips of her(9) left fingers have grown callouses. She(10) has joined the school orchestra.

1. Sandy	6. Sandy
2. mandolin	7. mandolin
3. Sandy	8. mandolin
4. Sandy	9. Sandy
5. Sandy	10. Sandy

Enrichment

For enrichment activities, see the Unit Projects in the Teacher Notes on page 125. One or more of these projects have special activities for gifted and talented students.

Additional Resources

Skills Practice Book—page 84
Teacher's Resource Binder
  Reinforcement Activities—
  page 66

Exercise B
1. his, Cory
2. He, Cory; it, letter
3. He, Cory
4. he, Cory; them, contests
5. he, Cory; I, Cory
6. He, Cory
7. no pronouns
8. it, trip (or First prize)
9. their, people
10. them, people; they, people

5. We watched the army helicopters approach their landing pads.

6. Have you ever seen a snake shed its skin?

7. Your tomatoes are much riper than ours.

8. He coaxed the chickens out of their coop.

9. Tara will help us fire our pottery in her kiln.

10. Did Mr. Wong ask you to help him move his computer?

▶ Analyzing

B. Number your paper from 1 to 10. List the pronouns in each sentence of the following story. One sentence has no pronouns. Beside each pronoun, write the noun it replaces. See answers in margin.

1. Cory went to the post office to mail his letter. 2. He hoped it would arrive on time. 3. He had entered contests many times before. 4. Unfortunately, he had never won any of them. 5. The contest rules said he must write a paragraph called "Why I want to go to Washington, D.C." 6. He could send only one contest entry. 7. First prize was a trip to the capital of the United States. 8. Cory hoped very much to win it. 9. At the post office, other people hurried to mail their letters. 10. Cory watched them and wondered if they were entering the contest, too.

▶ Creative Application

C. Writing You saw an exciting magic show. The featured performers were Zena Zodiac, Waldo the Wonderful, and the comedy team of Porke and Beanes. In a paragraph, describe each performer and his or her act. Include at least five pronouns in your paragraph.

212

2 Using Subject Pronouns

Focus

The **subject pronouns** are *I, you, he, she, it, we,* and *they*. Use them as subjects of sentences and after state-of-being verbs.

▶Comprehension

Use only subject pronouns as the subject of a verb.

Look at these sentences.

> Nicole saw the ball coming.
> *She* snatched *it* from the air.

In the first sentence, *Nicole* is the subject. In the second sentence, *She* is the subject. Only the pronouns *I, you, he, she, it, we,* or *they* can be used as the subject of a verb. For example, you would never say, *"Her snatched it from the air."*

You probably have no trouble choosing the correct pronoun when it appears by itself in the subject. Sometimes, however, one or more pronouns appear in a compound subject. Read these sentences.

> Jeff and (he, him) grilled fish over the campfire.
> She and (I, me) hiked four miles.

The pronouns appear in the subject parts of these sentences. Therefore, you use the subject pronouns *he, She,* and *I*. If you are unsure about what pronoun to use, try dividing the compound subject into two parts.

> *Jeff* grilled fish over the campfire.
> *He* grilled fish over the campfire.

Then put the parts together, using the same pronoun.

> Jeff and *he* grilled fish over the campfire.

213

Part 2

Objectives

1. To use pronouns correctly as subjects in sentences
2. To use pronouns correctly after state-of-being verbs

Presenting the Lesson

 All Students

1. Review the subject-predicate pattern for sentences. Students will easily recognize a noun in the subject position. Make it clear that pronouns, as substitutes for nouns, may take over this function.
2. Read and discuss pages 213–214. Stress that the pronoun that is correct in a simple subject is also correct in a compound subject. Have students try each pronoun by itself as the subject of a sentence. The students should have no trouble accepting the rule that covers which pronouns should be used as subjects and which should not.
3. Review the definition of state-of-being verbs as discussed in Chapter 4, "Verbs for Writing Power," page 61. Make sure that students understand that a subject pronoun always follows a state-of-being verb.
4. Assign and discuss Exercises A, B, and C on page 215. Encourage students to use the process of writing when completing Exercise C. After students finish writing, have them check their choices of pronouns by using the tests suggested in this part.
5. Use Exercise B on page 220 for additional practice if needed.

▶ **Basic Students**

Give the students group practice in applying the technique illustrated in the lesson, testing each part of the compound subject by itself, using these sentences:

1. Sabrina and (me, <u>I</u>) talked.
2. (<u>We,</u> Us) girls talked.
3. Mr. Mazany and (<u>they,</u> them) talked.
4. Gerald and (<u>she,</u> her) talked.
5. The coaches and (him, <u>he</u>) talked.
6. My parents and (<u>I,</u> me) talked.

Advanced Students

Have the students write two sentences for each of the subject pronouns listed in the **Focus** box on page 213. In one sentence, the pronoun should be used as the subject. In the other sentence, the pronoun should come after a state-of-being verb.

Special Populations

LD, ESL Do Exercise A orally with students. Make sure they understand why the subject pronoun is used in each sentence. If ESL students have not yet memorized the list of subject pronouns, allow them to refer to the list on page 213, or to the posters on display in the classroom.

NSD Some students will automatically use the pronouns they are accustomed to hearing. Stress the importance of always using a subject pronoun as the subject of a sentence and following a state-of-being verb.

Reinforcement

1. Have the students follow the directions for Exercise A on page 215 using these sentences:

1. Linda and (me, I) need new tennis shoes.
2. (We, Us) fans hope our team is in the play-offs.
3. (Him, He) and (I, me) walked along the winding creek.
4. Can (her, she) bring the sled back up the hill?
5. (They, Them) have told Willie where the secret hideout is.
6. The winners of the diving competition were Teresa and (I, me).
7. The people in the old photograph are my great-grandfather and (her, she).
8. The fishermen were Jules and (they, them).
9. This team's best pitchers are (we, us) southpaws.
10. The doctors in the emergency room were Dr. Delon and (he, him).

2. Have students choose the correct pronoun from the parentheses and write it on their papers.

1. (We, Us) boys planted a pine tree.
2. Ms. Tandy and (we, us) came on the bus at Elm Street.
3. The third graders and (me, I,) were drenched.

Follow the same steps to choose pronouns for the following example.

> (She, Her) and (I, me) hiked four miles.
> *She* hiked four miles. *I* hiked four miles.
> *She and I* hiked four miles.

Sometimes a pronoun is followed by a noun in the subject of a sentence. To know which pronoun is correct, use the steps listed above.

> (We, Us) girls swam across the lake.
> *We* swam across the lake.
> *The girls* swam across the lake.
> *We girls* swam across the lake.

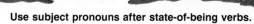

Use subject pronouns after state-of-being verbs.

Look at these sentences.

> *He* was the highest scorer.
> The highest scorer was *he*.

Both sentences mean the same thing. The pronoun following *was* can be made the subject without changing the meaning of the sentence. Any pronoun that follows a state-of-being verb can be made the subject of the sentence without changing the meaning of the sentence. Therefore, only a subject pronoun can be used after a state-of-being verb.

 Key to Writing and Speaking Subject pronouns are often used as linking words to connect the ideas in two sentences.

> Example: My running shoes are light-weight and sturdy. *They* help prevent injuries.

214

Exercises Identifying Subject Pronouns

▶ Recalling

A. Number your paper from 1 to 10. Choose the correct pronoun from the parentheses in each sentence. Write it on your paper.

1. (<u>They</u>, Them) sent us a bill for the plumbing.
2. (Him, <u>He</u>) and (<u>I</u>, me) both ran to answer the phone.
3. The fastest swimmers were Dwight and (<u>she</u>, her).
4. When did (<u>he</u>, him) last see the missing red shirt?
5. (Her, <u>She</u>) and Juanita both love your monster stories.
6. Hurry! (Us, <u>We</u>) are late for their Halloween party!
7. (Them, <u>They</u>) always laugh at our jokes.
8. (Us, <u>We</u>) neighbors often have a cookout on July 4.
9. Seth and (me, <u>I</u>) peered through our telescopes.
10. The team captains are Amy and (<u>he</u>, him).

▶ Analyzing

B. Number your paper from 1 to 10. Rewrite the second sentence after each number, using a pronoun to replace the repeated words.

1. Homer played checkers frequently. Homer often won. He
2. Bob and Cara were late. Bob and Cara had been studying all afternoon. They
3. The branch was dead. The branch cracked and fell. It
4. Pam sang scales to warm up. Pam sang loudly. She
5. Cal and Ann called. Cal and Ann want to see us. They
6. A treasure hunt is today. A treasure hunt is fun. It
7. Hope and I ran through the rain. Hope and I got wet. We
8. Sam fell asleep in his chair. Sam had been up late. He
9. Omar and Dave are doing magic tricks. Omar and Dave will put on a show. They
10. Herb and I fell. Herb and I slipped on the ice. We

▶ Creative Application

C. Writing Write a paragraph about your favorite music group. Include the members' names and the instruments they play. Use subject pronouns in your paragraph. Try to include a subject pronoun after a state-of-being verb.

4. Did you find two blue mittens? (Them, <u>They</u>) are mine.
5. (<u>They,</u> Them) and the other cans are behind the garage.
6. The raft and (us, <u>we</u>) girls got stuck under Daw's Bridge.
7. My dog and (me, <u>I</u>) went outside to take a look.
8. (<u>He,</u> Him) and (us, <u>we</u>) clocked the runners at the race.
9. Bryan and (<u>she</u>, her) found the Little Dipper last night.
10. (<u>We,</u> Us) are in a hurry.

215

Additional Resources

Skills Practice Book—page 85

Teacher's Resource Binder
Reinforcement Activities—
pages 67–68

Part 3

Objective

To use pronouns correctly as objects in sentences

Presenting the Lesson

● All Students

1. Review action verbs and direct objects. Refer to Chapter 4, "Verbs for Writing Power," on page 61.
2. Read and discuss **Pronouns After Action Verbs** on page 216.
Have the students refer once more to the pronouns listed on page 216 and try each one by itself as the object of a verb.
3. Many students will insist on the incorrect pronoun choice *I* when selecting the first person pronoun used in a compound object. *Me* somehow seems less formal. Encourage students to use the test suggested in this part. They should try each pronoun in a compound object separately. Ask the students for original sentences using *me* correctly.
4. Read and discuss **Pronouns After Prepositions** on page 216.
It is not important for students to understand prepositions completely at this time. Prepositions are studied in Chapter 20. You might write the following list of prepositions on the board for reference.

Prepositions

about	around	beside	in	past
above	at	between	into	to
across	before	by	near	toward
after	behind	down	of	under
against	below	for	on	up
along	beneath	from	over	with

5. Assign and discuss Exercises A, B, and C on page 217. After they complete exercise C, have the students share their "wills" with the class. Make sure that students understand the meaning of "wills" and "misers."
6. Use Exercise C on page 221 for additional practice if needed.

▶ Basic Students

When discussing **Pronouns After Action Verbs,** ask the students to break down each of the following into three sentences, as in the example on page 216. They should then write the sentences using correct pronouns.

---

3 Using Object Pronouns

> **Focus**
>
> The **object pronouns** are *me*, *you*, *him*, *her*, *it*, *us*, and *them*. Use them as the objects of verbs or prepositions.

Pronouns After Action Verbs

▶ Comprehension

A noun does not change its form when it is used as the object of a verb. Pronouns, however, have special object forms.

The object pronouns are *me*, *you*, *him*, *her*, *it*, *us*, and *them*. *You* and *it* can be used as both subject and object pronouns. Look at the object pronoun used in this sentence.

The lifeguard warned *us* about the jellyfish.

Pronouns are sometimes part of a compound object. If you are not sure which pronoun to use, try each part separately.

Have you seen (he, him) or (she, her)?
Have you seen *him*? Have you seen *her*?
Have you seen *him* or *her*?

Pronouns After Prepositions

One kind of word always has a noun or pronoun after it and shows a relationship between that noun or pronoun and the rest of the sentence. This kind of word is called a **preposition**. The noun or pronoun that follows a preposition is called the **object of the preposition**. Object pronouns are used as objects of prepositions. Look at these sentences.

We waited for *Zach* and *Ramona*. We waited for *them*.

You will learn more about prepositions in Chapter 20. To find a list of common prepositions, see page 350.

216

Exercises   Mastering Object Pronouns

▶ Analyzing

A. Some sentences below have both object and subject pronouns. Write only the object pronouns from each sentence on your paper.

1. We left for the picnic and Carla followed behind <u>us</u>.
2. The last time I was at bat, the ball almost hit <u>me</u>.
3. Sasha played the mandolin for Yuri and <u>them</u>.
4. The ranger led the bird watchers and <u>us</u> to the nest.
5. The parrot's answer amused <u>him</u>.
6. She will bake the muffins if you will bring some of <u>them</u> to the brunch.
7. Magicians' tricks always amaze <u>her</u>.
8. We recognized <u>him</u> from the artist's sketch.
9. Call <u>me</u> when the grill is hot.
10. Liz ate the nuts while the monkeys chattered at <u>her</u>.

▶ Recalling/Analyzing

B. Number your paper from 1 to 10. Choose the correct pronoun from the parentheses in each sentence. Write it on your paper.

1. Slowly, the bear lumbered toward (I, <u>me</u>).
2. The sultan ruled (<u>them</u>, they) long and wisely.
3. Do you believe Irma or (she, <u>her</u>)?
4. Ms. Lee complimented the class and (he, <u>him</u>).
5. Uncle Burt chased (we, <u>us</u>) out of the barn.
6. Don't tell (I, <u>me</u>) the answer. Let (I, <u>me</u>) guess.
7. Sharp stalactites hung all around (we, <u>us</u>).
8. The puppy curled up beside (<u>him</u>, he) and fell asleep.
9. This relay race depends on Francine and (<u>her</u>, she).
10. The skunk just ignored Toby and (they, <u>them</u>).

▶ Creative Application

C. Writing A farmer finds a tiny safe in his field. In the metal box is a yellowed piece of paper titled "The Miser's Will." Write what the farmer reads in this very unusual will. Include at least three object pronouns. Here is the first line to get you started. "To my cat, Pinky, I leave a silver bell for his collar. I leave *it* to *him* for his years of loyalty."

217

Additional Resources

Skills Practice Book—page 86
Teacher's Resource Binder
  Reinforcement Activities—
  page 69

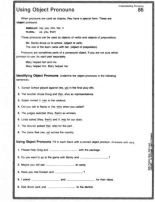

1. José invited (she, <u>her</u>) and (<u>me</u>, I).
2. Mr. Park forgot (<u>them</u>, they) and (I, <u>me</u>).
3. Mrs. Yen had promised (<u>him</u>, he) and (I, <u>me</u>) a ride to the library.

When discussing **Pronouns After Prepositions,** have the students rewrite these sentences with the correct pronouns. Have them use the same test they used in the first exercise to determine the correct pronouns.

1. Herbert came with Dana and (I, <u>me</u>).
2. I sent letters to my mother and (<u>him</u>, he).
3. Put the bag of chips near Janice and (<u>her</u>, she).

◆ **Advanced Students**

Have the students write two sentences with each object pronoun. In one sentence the pronoun should be a direct object. In the second sentence it should be the object of a preposition.

Special Populations

LD Allow students to work on Exercise C in small groups. Encourage students to discuss what unusual items this eccentric person might have included in his will. Help students to correctly use object pronouns in their sentences.

ESL Make sure that students understand the meaning of *will* and *miser* before they begin this exercise.

Reinforcement

1. Have the students follow the directions for Exercise B on page 217 using these sentences:

1. The paramedics carried (he, <u>him</u>) in a stretcher to the ambulance.
2. The magician entertained (we, <u>us</u>) for an hour.
3. Detective Poole called (<u>me</u>, I) from upstairs.
4. Christopher woke Vi and (I, <u>me</u>) at six o'clock this morning.
5. Their art teacher gave Rona and (they, <u>them</u>) some pastel chalks.
6. The huge black bat flew toward Lope and (I, <u>me</u>).
7. I decided to go with Ann and (they, <u>them</u>) to the beach.
8. Don't the Clarks live on the floor above (she, <u>her</u>)?
9. The Houston Oilers played against (<u>them</u>, they) in Cincinnati.
10. Sara will do the parachute jump after Doug and (<u>him</u>, he).

Part 4

Objectives

1. To identify possessive pronouns and use them correctly
2. To distinguish between possessive pronouns and contractions that are spelled similarly

Presenting the Lesson

All Students

1. Read and discuss page 218. Provide examples of nouns showing possession. Have the students change the nouns into pronouns. Point out that although a noun shows possession by adding an apostrophe, possessive pronouns never include apostrophes.

Janet's cat	=	her cat
Mike's bike	=	his bike
the dog's dish	=	its dish

2. Tell students that if they are unsure about whether a word is a contraction or a possessive pronoun, they can ask themselves this question: Does the word have an apostrophe? Remind students that possessive pronouns never have apostrophes.

3. Assign and discuss Exercises A, B, and C on pages 218–219. After students complete Exercise C, have them share their paragraphs with the class.

4. Use Exercise D on page 221 for additional practice if needed.

Basic Students

Review the possessive forms of nouns with students before studying this part. Refer students to Chapter 3, "Nouns for Precise Meaning," page 45.

Do the first half of each exercise orally. Students can complete the remainder independently.

Advanced Students

Have the students write original sentences with *its, it's, your, you're, whose, who's, their,* and *they're.* Display these sentences in the classroom.

Special Populations

LD Students should work with a reference sheet or list of possessive pro-

---

4 Possessive Pronouns

> ### Focus
> The **possessive pronouns** are used to show ownership.

▶ **Comprehension**

Possessive pronouns are used to show ownership. The possessive pronouns are *my, mine, his, her, hers, its, our, ours, their, theirs, your,* and *yours.*

> *My* kite has a longer tail than *your* kite.
> *His* beagle and *her* hound chase squirrels.

In the first sentence, the pronouns *my* and *your* tell whom the kites belong to. *His* and *her* point to the owners of the dogs in the second sentence.

To make a noun show possession, you add an apostrophe and an *s.* Pronouns, however, have special possessive forms. Possessive pronouns never use apostrophes.

Possessive pronouns may be confused with contractions that are spelled similarly. Look at the difference in these pairs.

> Possessive Pronoun: The dog licked *its* paw.
> Contraction: *It's* going to snow today. (It is)

> Possessive Pronoun: *Their* costumes are in the wardrobe.
> Contraction: *They're* moving to Nebraska. (They are)

> Possessive Pronoun: *Your* film is being developed.
> Contraction: *You're* next for the floor exercise. (You are)

Exercises   Using Possessive Pronouns

▶ **Analyzing**

A. Write the correct pronoun to replace the noun in parentheses.

> 1. Anna entered (Anna's) Irish setter in the dog show.   her
> 2. Dave thought that (Dave's) was the best carving.   his

3. The Plishkas painted (the Plishkas') antique rocking
   horse blue. *their*
4. The male peacock is brightly colored and (the
   peacock's) mate is brown. *his*
5. Sam hoped the winning name would be (Sam's). *his*
6. Do you know the Reeds? This family crest is (the Reeds'). *theirs*
7. Sue looked at the watch and said it was not (Sue's). *hers*
8. The raccoon is washing (the raccoon's) food. *its*
9. The players wore (the players') new uniforms. *their*
10. Aunt Jan tasted (Aunt Jan's) freshly baked bread. *her*

▶ **Recalling/Analyzing**

B. Number your paper from 1 to 10. Choose the correct word from
the parentheses in each sentence. Write it on your paper.

1. Did you say (you're, your) learning Morse code?
2. (It's, Its) a question of whose tale you like better.
3. Is this (you're, your) record or mine?
4. The swallow is going to build (it's, its) nest.
5. Wendy said (you're, your) hammer was broken.
6. I like (they're, their) special cheese sauce.
7. (You're, Your) beetle collection is on display at the
   science fair.
8. (They're, Their) lost oar washed up on shore.
9. The cricket makes a sound with (it's, its) wings.
10. (They're, Their) the new dance teachers.

▶ **Creative Application**

C. Writing At Camp Winona the evening activities are planned by
the campers. In a paragraph, tell what item related to music, crafts, or
games each of the campers brought. Tell how each camper entertained the group. Use possessive pronouns in your paragraph.

219

nouns. You might write these on the
board. Allow students to refer to the list
during discussion and as they complete
the exercises.

NSD In some dialects, the subject pronoun *they* is often substituted for the
possessive pronoun *their*. It's *they*
house. Give them *they* keys. Provide
extra drill so that students have the opportunity to practice the correct form.

Reinforcement

1. Have students follow the directions
for Exercise A on page 218 using these
sentences:

1. The Dorans put aluminum siding on (the
   Doran's) house. *their*
2. Avi got a perfect score on (Avi's) math
   test. *his*
3. Marion put on (Marion's) sunglasses at
   the ballgame. *her*
4. I would prefer to drive (the speaker's)
   car. *my*
5. A hummingbird moves (the hummingbird's) wings rapidly. *its*
6. That camera is (the McCoy's). *theirs*
7. Granny tasted the cookies and said
   that the recipe was not (Granny's). *hers*
8. I think that that pen is (the speaker's). *mine*

2. Have students follow the instructions for Exercise B on page 219 using
these sentences:

1. (It's, Its) too early for the store to open.
2. Is that (you're, your) computer?
3. (Who's, Whose) going to run for Congress from our district?
4. You will recognize the car by (it's, its)
   dented fender.
5. (They're, Their) report was about the
   Irish potato famine.
6. (You're, Your) the tallest player on the
   team.
7. (Who's, Whose) mittens are these?
8. The flower looks as if (it's its) dying.

Enrichment

Ask the students to write several sentences introducing one of the following
people to some friends. The sentences
must use at least six pronouns: two as
subjects, two as objects of sentences,
and two showing possession.

1. Count Dracula
2. Cinderella
3. E.T.
4. Mary Poppins
5. Han Solo

Additional Resources

Skills Practice Book—page 87
Teacher's Resource Binder
  Reinforcement Activities—
    page 70
  Enrichment Activities—
    pages 20, 68

Exercises for Mastery

These **Exercises for Mastery** may be used for additional practice of the concepts presented in this section. Each exercise focuses on a single concept, and should be used after the page number indicated in parentheses.

Exercises for Mastery   Chapter 12

Understanding Pronouns

▶ Recalling/Analyzing

A. Recognizing Pronouns Number your paper from 1 to 10. Write all the pronouns in each sentence. (Use after page 212.)

1. My aunt called us long distance from Alaska.
2. If your calculator doesn't work, use mine.
3. Tell Kevin to invite Maggie when he sees her.
4. Mark's new shoes crunched his toes.
5. The Jacobs didn't fly their seaplane.
6. I saved my allowance but she spent hers.
7. Jon took our binoculars on his hike.
8. Throw your best slider and watch me hit it.
9. The Plains Indians pitched their teepees near water.
10. The peacock turned toward me and fanned its tail.

B. Mastering Subject Pronouns Number your paper from 1 to 10. Choose the correct pronoun from the parentheses and write it on your paper. (Use after page 215.)

1. (He, Him) and (me, I) put decals on our new skateboards.
2. (We, Us) students voted for a picnic at the beach.
3. The marchers and (them, they) lined up with the band at 8:30.
4. Davy, (her, she), and (I, me) rode in the helicopter.
5. The winner was (she, her).
6. When Val put on her mask, we could not tell it was (her, she).
7. (He, Him) came early and (us, we) weren't ready.
8. For our art project, (we, us) girls made colorful animal posters.
9. Did you know that the winning pitcher was (me, I)?
10. The shuttle astronauts are (they, them).

220

Additional Resources

Skills Practice Book
Mixed Practice—page 88

C. Using Object Pronouns Number your paper from 1 to 10. Write the correct pronoun from the parentheses in each sentence. (Use after page 217.)

1. Mrs. Nohr introduced (we, <u>us</u>) to the choir director.
2. Ramon wrestled (he, <u>him</u>) for the championship.
3. You've convinced (I, <u>me</u>) that I need a haircut.
4. Wash the berries and put (they, <u>them</u>) in a bowl.
5. For the exhibit, Frank helped (he, <u>him</u>) build a model of a windmill.
6. The storm caught (we, <u>us</u>) by surprise.
7. Aunt Liz took (we, <u>us</u>) to see the musical *Cats*.
8. Please feed the baby and put (she, <u>her</u>) to bed.
9. Put the pages in order and number (<u>them</u>, they).
10. Ellen would not take the ski lift because it frightened (she, <u>her</u>).

D. Using Possessive Pronouns Number your paper from 1 to 10. For each sentence, write the correct possessive pronoun to replace the word in parentheses. (Use after page 219.)

1. Todd shook (Todd's) head in amazement. his
2. This is Bob's notebook and (Bob's) compass. his
3. Michelle always gives away the punch line of (Michelle's) jokes. her
4. The river had shrunk to (the river's) original depth. its
5. The comet seemed to lose (the comet's) tail as it neared Earth. its
6. The Chins left (the Chins') house keys with Kim when they went on vacation. their
7. Evelyn gave (Evelyn's) report clearly. her
8. The dragon roared and flames sprang from (the dragon's) mouth. its
9. Molly and I cleaned up (Molly's and my) room. our
10. The balloon slipped (the balloon's) mooring. its

221

Using Grammar in Writing

These challenging and enjoyable activities allow the students to see how the concepts of grammar, usage, and mechanics may be applied in actual writing situations. Each exercise is designed to give students practice in several of the skills they have acquired in this section. The activities also provide opportunities for students to write creatively about a wide variety of interesting and unusual subjects.

As the students complete these activities, remind them to follow the process of writing. Be sure to allow adequate time for prewriting activities. Individual conferences or peer-group sessions may be used for help with drafting and revision.

Allow students some time to research their character before they begin writing Exercise C. You might refer students to Chapter 25, "Writing Letters and Filling Out Forms," page 443 for information on proper format for letters.

Using Grammar in Writing

▶ Creative Application

A. Choose a sport such as soccer, baseball, track, or swimming. You are the coach. Before the big game or meet, you give your team a pep talk. Write the speech you give to your team. Use several pronouns in your talk. Here is a line to get you started. "The game is *ours*, team. Now, go out there and show *them* what *you* can do."

B. Imagine you are a movie director. Choose a book or short story you wish to make into a movie. Write a paragraph explaining what actor or actress you will cast to play the main character. Tell why you chose this person. Be sure to use both subject and object pronouns in your paragraph.

C. Using Pronouns To Write About History Choose a character from history and write a letter to this person. Begin by briefly introducing yourself and telling something about you or your family. Tell the historical character how the world is different now from when he or she lived. Include details that would interest this person. For example, Ben Franklin might like to know how we use electricity in today's world.

Use several pronouns in your letter. Your letter may include some of the following phrases.

my name is	*it* has	*we* like
I live	*your* invention	how did *he*
in *our* town	*their* ideas	*she* began

222

Additional Resources

Skills Practice Book
Using Pronouns in Writing—
page 89

Chapter 12 Review

▶ Recalling/Analyzing

A. Choosing the Correct Pronoun Number your paper from 1 to 10. Write the correct pronoun from the parentheses in each sentence.

1. Did Marnie or (they, them) show you the fossils they found?
2. It was (he, him) in the Dracula costume.
3. The horse nibbled my hand when I fed (he, him) the carrot.
4. It was (her, she) and (them, they) who volunteered.
5. (We, Us) hikers made it to the top of the mountain!
6. The Kominskis and (we, us) vacation at the seashore every year.
7. The firefighter saved (them, they) and their pets.
8. Don't (I, me) have an appointment with the dentist this morning?
9. Surely you don't believe (she, her)!
10. If Ryan doesn't finish, Clark will help (he, him).

B. Mastering Possessive Pronouns Number your paper from 1 to 10. Write the correct word from the parentheses in each sentence.

1. (It's, Its) raining more in July than it did in June.
2. (They're, Their) smoke alarm went off accidentally.
3. Does the cat see (it's, its) reflection in the mirror?
4. (You're, Your) setting up the tent, aren't you?
5. The baby wren broke (it's, its) wing learning to fly.
6. (Who's, Whose) radio is turned up so loud?
7. (They're, Their) canoe is an aluminum twelve-footer.
8. (Who's, Whose) feeding the tropical fish?
9. (They're, Their) telling a story to the class.
10. Do Sharon and you write (you're, your) own poetry?

223

Chapter Review

These exercises provide review of the concepts presented in this section. Each exercise challenges the students to apply several of the skills they have acquired during previous study. Because the "mixed" feature of these activities makes them more difficult, the teacher may wish to have Basic students do the exercises orally or in small groups.

Additional Resources

Skills Practice Book
Review—page 90

Test Booklet
Mastery Test—pages 65-68

Chapter 13

Chapter Objectives

1. To understand the elements of a narrative

2. To identify the parts of a longer narrative

3. To recognize sources for story ideas

4. To make a plot outline

5. To expand a plot outline into a story

6. To indicate sequence through transitional words and phrases

7. To use description and dialogue to create interest in narrative writing

8. To recognize the need to revise and to implement revisions

9. To proofread a narrative

10. To make and share a final copy

Motivating the Students

1. Read the following passage to the class.

> Wilbur sighed. It had been a busy day—his first day of being terrific. Dozens of people had visited his yard during the afternoon, and he had had to stand and pose, looking as terrific as he could. Now he was tired. Fern had arrived and seated herself quietly on her stool in the corner.
>
> "Tell me a story, Charlotte!" said Wilbur, as he lay waiting for sleep to come. "Tell me a story!"
>
> So Charlotte, although she, too, was tired, did what Wilbur wanted.
>
> "Once upon a time," she began . . .
>
> —E. B. White

2. Have the students read the introduction to the chapter on page 225. Ask what stories they enjoy. Discuss why these are favorites. Discuss some stories they might write about.

Special Populations

Refer to the suggestions on pages T32 to T35 at the front of this Teacher Edition for special populations notes for the teaching of composition.

Week 16

Chapter Management Guidelines   This chart may be used to help structure daily lesson plans

Day 1	Day 2	Day 3	Day 4	Day 5
Chapter 13 Opener, p. 225; Part 1, "Thinking About Narrative Writing," pp. 226–227	Part 2, "Parts of a Narrative," pp. 228–229	Part 3, "Prewriting: Finding and Developing Ideas," pp. 230–231	Part 4, "Prewriting: Organizing a Story," pp. 232–233	Part 5, "Drafting a Story," pp. 234–235

The Process of Narrative Writing

Related Chapters

You may wish to refer to related material in other chapters as you teach the following concepts:

1. Using the writing process, Chapter 6, "Choosing a Process for Writing," page 101

2. Using adjectives, Chapter 16, "Adjectives for Creative Expression," page 283

3. Using adverbs, Chapter 17, "Adverbs for Clear Description," page 301

Additional Resources

Skills Practice Book—pages 91–97

Test Booklet—pages 69–74
　Pretest—pages 69–70
　Mastery Test—pages 71–74

Teacher's Resource Binder
　Reinforcement Activities—
　　pages 71–72
　Enrichment Activities—
　　pages 5, 21–22, 39–52
　Process of Writing Transparencies
　Ideas for Creative Teaching

The phrases "Once upon a time" and "Tell me a story" exist in many languages. Just about everyone loves a good story. Stories take us to worlds filled with people, sights, and sounds we might otherwise never experience.

Narrative writing is writing that tells a story. Narratives are not written only by professional writers. You write narratives, too. If you write a tale about imaginary characters, that is narrative writing. You are also writing a narrative when you record your experience at the state fair in your diary. If you tell the story of the soccer playoffs for the school newspaper, that is narrative writing, too.

In this chapter, you will learn to use the process of narrative writing to create a story of your own. You will also learn skills that will help you to act out a story with others.

225

Chapter Management Guidelines　This chart may be used to help structure daily lesson plans.

Day 1	Day 2	Day 3	Day 4	Day 5
Chapter 13, Part 6, "Using Description and Dialogue," pp. 236–237	Part 7, "Revising a Narrative," pp. 238–240	Part 8, "Writing and Sharing a Final Copy," p. 241	Chapter Review and selected end-of-chapter activites	Cumulative Review, pp. 246–247

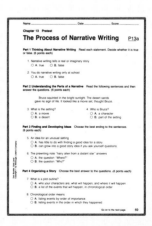

Part 1

Objective

To understand the elements of a narrative

Presenting the Lesson

 **All Students**

1. In part 1 of this chapter, both student and professional samples are shown. Part 1 sharpens the students' ability to analyze and evaluate while stressing individual styles of writing.

2. Have the students read the introduction and Example 1 on page 226.

3. For the questions under **Think and Discuss,** always allow students time to think through the material independently before discussing it as a class. Ask them to support their answers with examples from the narrative.

4. Use the procedure explained in steps 2 and 3 with Example 2 on page 227. After students have read Example 2, discuss which of the stories seems real and which seems imaginary.

5. Read and discuss **Now It's Your Turn** on page 227.

 **Basic Students**

To reinforce understanding of the elements of a narrative, have students name some movies they have seen. Then discuss and identify the elements of each narrative.

◆ **Advanced Students**

Show the students how to do a simple annotated bibliography listing author, title, and a brief statement about what was good or bad about a book. Have the students compile simple annotated bibliographies for five books that they have read and enjoyed.

Special Populations

LD Before proceeding further, have students read the two example stories orally. Be sure they can tell the main idea of each and can sequence the events.

---

1 Thinking About Narrative Writing

┌─ *Focus* ─────────────────────────────┐
│ A **narrative** is a real or imaginary story. │
└──┘

Imagine you and your classmates have just returned from a field trip to a nearby aquarium. After talking about all the real fish you saw, your teacher asks you to write a story about an imaginary sea creature. What would your story be like?

Example 1

▶ Interpretation/Making Inferences

Read and Think. Jorge wrote a story about a sea creature. As you read Jorge's story, try to decide what makes it interesting.

> The water of Santa Rosa lagoon was bright blue. My friend Maria and I decided to go snorkeling. We wanted to find an angelfish for Maria's aquarium. We put on our fins and masks and began to search underwater. Suddenly, a large sea monster swam toward me. It was shiny black, with two arms and two long flipper legs. There were two silver humps on its back and one large eye in the middle of its face. As it swam, thousands of bubbles came out of its silver humps. I came to the surface quickly and ripped off my mask.
>
> "Maria," I screamed. "Get out of the lagoon! There's a horrible sea monster!"
>
> As I reached the shore, I heard Maria's laughter. I turned around to see Maria standing with the horrible creature. I began laughing, too. My sea monster turned out to be our neighbor, Mr. Velásquez, who had gone scuba diving.

Think and Discuss. Read Jorge's story again. Then discuss the following questions with your classmates.

1. Who are the characters in Jorge's story?   Maria, Jorge, Mr. Velásquez
2. Which sentence tells you where the story takes place?   the first
3. What happens first in the story? How does the story end?
   Maria and Jorge go snorkeling. Jorge's "monster" turns out to be Mr. Velásquez.

226

Example 2

▶ Interpretation/Making Inferences

Read and Think. Here is another example of narrative writing. This was written by a professional writer.

> Fear gripped the animals as they watched the battle. The serpent wound himself like steel bands about the unicorn's hind legs. A fierce war-cry came from the unicorn as he struggled to free himself. His nostrils flared, and he reared up with his forelegs thrashing. Sharp cloven hooves came crashing down upon the serpent, whose strong hold began to weaken. The unicorn was gigantic in his mighty splendor. His spirit was ruthless, and his mane flowed like windswept flames. Over and over he screamed and struck until the viper was overwhelmed and powerless.
>
> Whirling around, the unicorn drew back and faced his enemy. Then his blue eyes caught the serpent's, and the evil one felt shame pierce his cold heart for the first time. He slithered away in fear, knowing that one of his own kind would have never spared his life. —MARIANNA MAYER

Think and Discuss. Think about these questions. Discuss your ideas with your classmates.

1. Who are the characters in this narrative? *the serpent and unicorn*
2. What is the unicorn like? What tells you this? *brave, strong, forgiving* *He wins and lets his enemy live.*
3. How are the events of the story arranged? *in time order*
4. Is the story based on a real or an imaginary event? *imaginary*

▶ Drawing Conclusions/Generalizing

Now It's Your Turn

Now you have read narratives based on both real and imaginary experiences. Each narrative has a set of characters and a setting where the action occurs. Each narrative tells the events in the order they happened.

In this chapter, you will learn how to write your own narrative. You may want to reread these two stories as you plan and write your own story.

227

ESL If example stories are too difficult, substitute stories at a lower reading level. Have students answer questions similar to those in the text.

Reinforcement

Briefly review and discuss some well-known fairy tales, folktales, and fables. Break the students into small groups. Have each group choose a fairy tale, folktale, or fable. Direct them to update the elements of setting, character, and plot to fit a modern day situation. Allow time for groups to share their creations with the class.

Enrichment

1. To make students aware that narratives come in many forms, have the class bring and study some comic strips. Have them identify the elements of a narrative present in each.

2. For additional enrichment activities, see the Unit Projects in the Teacher Notes on page 125. One or more of these projects have special activities for gifted and talented students.

Part 2

Objective

To identify the parts of a longer narrative

Presenting the Lesson

 **All Students**

1. Read and discuss page 228.

2. Make three charts, one for each part of a narrative. Have the students suggest some good settings, characters, and plots. Write them on the appropriate chart. Students can refer to these when brainstorming for story ideas.

3. Assign and discuss the exercise on page 228. Explain that the story was written by a young Apache Indian girl. She got the story idea from some of her tribe's legends. After students have read the story and before they complete the questions, discuss the identity of Coyote. Is he an animal, as in a fable, or a human character?

▶ **Basic Students**

Work through the exercise on page 228 orally with the students. If students have difficulty identifying the parts of a longer narrative, provide additional practice using a selection from a reading or literature text.

◆ **Advanced Students**

Ask the students to select a narrative sample. Let them write five original questions about their sample. Then, ask them to give the sample and questions to another student to read and answer.

Special Populations

LD Provide a study sheet that lists the story elements in outline form, such as I. Story, A. Place, B. Time and so on. Students can fill in the details after reading the story. For students with severe reading difficulty, tape the story.

ESL Encourage students to share folk stories from their native cultures. Have them point out the story elements. If the exercise story is too difficult, provide a story on a lower reading level.

2 Parts of a Narrative

Focus

All narratives have three parts: a **setting**, **characters**, and a **plot**.

▶ Comprehension

When you write a story, you must create an imaginary world for your readers. To do this, you must make sure your story has a setting, characters, and a plot.

Setting The setting of a story tells where and when the action takes place. A writer may choose a real setting or create an imaginary one. A writer usually describes the setting early in the story so the reader can picture the action.

Characters Characters are the people or animals that the story is about. Characters may be based on real people, or they may come from the writer's imagination. **Main characters** play a greater part in the story than the others do.

Plot The events that happen in the story make up the plot. The writer usually tells about these events in the same order that they occurred. The story builds until the most exciting part, or **climax**, of the story is reached. After that, the author directs the details toward the end, or conclusion.

Exercise   Understanding the Parts of a Narrative

▶ Interpretation

Read the narrative below. Answer the questions that follow.

COYOTE AND THE MONEY TREE

Coyote had some money, just a few dollars. He was walking down a road trying to figure out how to change those dollars into something more valuable.

Coming toward him were some American prospectors with their horses and mules and blankets and guns and bags of food.

Coyote had a brilliant thought. He put his money up in the branches of a tree that was growing beside the road. Then he just sat there watching the tree.

When the prospectors rode up, they asked him, "What are you doing?"

"I am watching this tree. It is very valuable," Coyote said.

"Why is it valuable? What is in that tree?" the prospectors asked.

"Money grows on that tree," Coyote said. "When I shake it, money falls out."

The prospectors laughed at him. So Coyote shook the tree a little, and one of his dollars fell out.

Now the men were very interested. "Sell us that tree," they said.

"No," Coyote said, pretending to be angry. "This is the only tree in the world that grows money."

The prospectors said to him, "We will give you everything we have . . . our horses and mules and everything else. We'll just climb down, and you'll own everything."

Coyote still pretended not to want to, and the prospectors tried to persuade him.

But after a while Coyote let them persuade him. "All right," he said. "I will sell you the tree. There's only one thing."

"Anything at all," they said.

"See those blue mountains over there? Well, you will have to wait until I get there. If you shake the tree before that, nothing will come out, and you will spoil it forever."

The prospectors agreed. So Coyote jumped on one of the horses and rode away with everything they had.

When he reached the blue mountains, the men shook the tree. Only one dollar fell out, though they shook and shook and shook. That was the last dollar Coyote had put there.

Over by the blue mountains, Coyote was laughing.

—TINA NAICHE

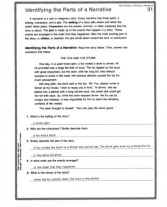

1. **What is the setting of the story?** a road in the old West or Southwest near a mountain range
2. **Who are the characters?** Coyote and the prospectors
3. **Briefly describe the plot of the story.** Coyote wants to make his two dollars worth more. He tricks prospectors into thinking that money grows on a tree. They trade all their belongings for the tree.

Additional Resources

Skills Practice Book—page 91

Reinforcement

Read this excerpt from *Lassie Come Home* to the students. Then have them answer the questions that follow.

"Thy mother and me have decided upon it that Lassie shall stay here till she's better. Anyhow, nobody could nurse her better than us. But the day that the duke comes back, then back she goes, too. For she belongs to him, and that's honest, too. Now tha has her for a while, so be content."

. . . The boy knew how short it was one morning as he went to school and saw the duke's motorcar driven by Priscilla.

. . . It was hard to pretend to listen to lessons in school that morning. There was only waiting for noon. Then the boy ran home.

"Mother! The duke is back and he's coming to take Lassie away."

"Eigh, drat my buttons. Never no peace in this house. Is tha sure?"

"Aye. He stopped me. He said tell father he'll be round at five. Can't we hide her? Oh, mother."

"Nay, thy father—"

"Won't you beg him? Please, please. Beg father to—"

"Young Joe, now it's no use. So stop thy teasing! Thy father will not lie. That much I'll give him. Come good, come bad, he'll not lie."

—Eric Knight

1. Who are the characters in the story?
   parents, Joe, duke
2. What does the use of dialect terms such as *thy* and *nay* tell you about the setting? It may not be in present time and possibly not in America.
3. Briefly list the events in the order they happened. Lassie can stay awhile. The duke comes. The boy pleads but father won't lie.

Enrichment

1. Ask the school librarian for a time the class might visit. Then have each student check out a fiction book of his or her choice. Bring the books back to the classroom and set up a story corner. Whenever the students have a spare moment, they can spend time reading the stories they and their classmates enjoy.

2. For additional enrichment activities, see the Unit Projects in the Teacher Notes on page 125. One or more of these projects have special activities for gifted and talented students.

Part 3

Objective

To recognize sources for story ideas

Presenting the Lesson

All Students

1. Read and discuss pages 230–231.
2. Refer to Teacher Notes in "Choosing a Process for Writing." Go over the sources for discovering ideas listed on page 230. Help the students suggest a sample story idea for each source. Refer the students to the story samples given in part 1. Ask the students what sources the writers might have used for ideas. Point out that narratives about experiences are real. Those that come from a writer's imagination are not.
3. Help the students understand how Ellen developed her story idea from a possible setting. Point out the additional ideas listed on page 231 that Ellen did not use. Suggest the following situation: *a lonely looking man on a bus.* Have the students develop an idea chain. Record their suggestions on the board. Discuss which ideas might be developed further and which might be discarded.
4. Assign and discuss Exercises A and B on page 231. Emphasize that this is the time to jot down as many ideas as possible. Students are not writing a story yet, but they may use one of these ideas to develop a narrative as they continue with the chapter.

Basic Students

Go back to the ideas on the board. Develop these with more suggestions. Show students how to group ideas about characters, setting, and plot that might make a story. Provide individual help as the students begin to develop their own story idea in Exercise B.

Advanced Students

Have the students make an idea chain like the one on page 231 using the following setting:

a submarine at the bottom of the ocean

---

3 Prewriting: Finding and Developing Ideas

> **Focus**
>
> Ideas for stories may come from your experiences. They can also come from your imagination or what you read.

Finding a Topic

▶ Comprehension

All stories start with a writer's ideas. Look at the world around you. Explore your imagination for ideas.

Finding Story Ideas in Your Experience You can discover ideas for stories in your own life. There may be a story in the first time you rode a horse, or your first day at dance class. You can also write about people you know. Think about the time your friend thought he saw a ghost, or the summer your neighbors found a family of raccoons in their attic.

Looking for Ideas When You Read A friend's letter about a fishing trip may contain a story idea. A newspaper or magazine article may suggest something to write about. Perhaps an entry in your journal could be developed into a story.

Thinking Creatively Sometimes your imagination is the best place to begin a story. Ask yourself "What if . . . ?" For example, think about an apple orchard. What if the apples were magical? What would happen if you ate one? Think of other periods in time, other worlds, or unusual people.

Exploring Your Ideas

Your first brainstorming session may not give you all the ideas you need. For example, you may have an idea for a terrific character or an unusual setting. However, that may be all you have. Now you must help this idea grow into a story.

230

Ask yourself some questions to make your idea grow. Ask *Who? When? Where? What happened? Why?* and *How?*

Write down all your questions and several possible answers for each one. Then choose the answers you like best. These will become part of your prewriting notes.

One student, Ellen, remembered a deserted cabin that she had seen on vacation. The cabin seemed like a good setting for a story. Now Ellen had to come up with the other elements for her story. After Ellen asked her questions, she put the answers into the form of an idea chain. Here is how the chain looked. The answers she chose are marked with a star.

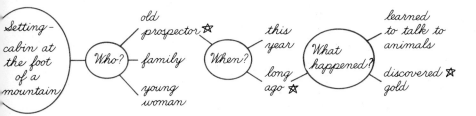

Next Ellen will decide how the prospector looked. Then she will ask herself what happened after he found the gold.

Exercises   Finding and Developing Story Ideas

▶ **Structured Application**

A. Finding Ideas Think about something you have always wanted to be, such as an explorer, the President, or a composer. Join a group of three or four other classmates. Brainstorm and share ideas for a story that tells about your one day as _____. Write a list of the ideas that you like. Choose the best idea to develop further. Save the other ideas in your notebook.

▶ **Creative Application**

B. Developing an Idea Use the idea you chose from Exercise A, or find an idea in the **Power Handbook**, pages 464-466. Ask questions to develop your idea. Begin with an idea chain similar to the one shown in the lesson. Include as many details as possible.

231

Special Populations

LD Allow students to work in pairs or groups to brainstorm and list story ideas. Some students may need specific story suggestions.

ESL Encourage students to draw on their native cultural experiences for different story ideas.

Reinforcement

Ask the students to imagine themselves as an animal. Then, have them brainstorm in groups of three or four. They should make a list or idea chain of ideas for a story that would tell about a day as the animal they have chosen.

Enrichment

Have the students read some myths and fables from other cultures. Have them keep a list of the story elements from myths in their writing folders. These can be used as story idea-starters.

Additional Resources

Skills Practice Book—page 92

Part 4

Objective

To make a plot outline

Presenting the Lesson

All Students

1. Read and discuss the introduction through the section titled **Making a Story Contract.** Point out how a contract can help the students begin their plot outlines.

2. Read and discuss **Making a Plot Outline.** Analyze Jill's outline with the students. Define *chronological order* if necessary. Point out that this is the way Jill organized her details. Discuss the fact that details for narrative writing are often arranged this way. Ask students why this is so. Have the students explain why Jill made the changes she did.

3. Refer to the long narrative sample in part 2 again. As a whole group, make a plot outline for the sample.

4. Assign and discuss Exercises A and B on page 233. Have the students schedule story conferences with a partner after they complete Exercise B. Partners should offer some suggestions for further improving the plot outline.

Basic Students

Pair students with stronger writers for Exercise A. Then, ask each pair to explain the reasoning behind their order of events.

Schedule conferences with students after they complete Exercise B on page 233. Discuss their plot outlines and suggest any necessary changes.

Advanced Students

Have students read the following introductory paragraph. Then have students list a possible series of events this story could have. The events should be listed in chronological order in the form of a plot outline.

One afternoon last summer my sister Heidi and I decided to take the canoes out on the Brule River by ourselves. Our family was camping at the state park. I climbed in, and Heidi waded into the water, pushed us

---

4 Prewriting: Organizing a Story

> ┌─ *Focus* ─────────────────────────────────
> You write a **plot outline** to organize ideas in your story.
> └───

▶ Comprehension

The answers to your prewriting questions have provided details for your story. The next step is to make a story contract. Then you must decide how to organize your ideas.

Making a Story Contract

A **story contract** is a brief statement of who your characters are, what will happen in the story, and where the events will take place. Making a contract helps you keep ideas in focus.

Look again at the questions and notes you wrote as you developed your story idea. Try to sum them up in one or two sentences.

Here is how a student, Jill, wrote her story contract.

> I will write a story about trying to solve a mystery. It will take place in my neighborhood. The characters in it will be Miss Hayes and me.

Making a Plot Outline

Next, you will organize the events in a story. You will do this by making a **plot outline.** In part 2, you learned that a plot is the series of events in a story. A plot outline lists these events in the order in which they happened. In other words, they are listed in **chronological order.** The first event is listed first. The second event is listed second, and so on.

Jill wrote a plot outline as she prepared to write her story. Jill listed the events in chronological order. She studied her plot outline. Note her thoughts as she makes changes.

232

1. My neighbor, Miss Hayes, comes home on

   the bus. (happens every Monday)

2. I'm curious about the package she carries.

3. *She always carries a box wrapped tightly with string.*

~~4.~~ 3. I follow her to her house.

~~5.~~ 4. I fall in the bushes.

These two ideas are out of order.

~~6.~~ 5. I try to look in her window.

~~7.~~ 6. Miss Hayes comes out and yells at me.

~~7. There are many interesting people in my~~

   ~~neighborhood.~~

I forgot to tell about the package.

This has nothing to do with my story.

Note that when Jill studied her outline, she saw that she had left out some information. She had listed two events in the wrong order and included a detail that was not needed. As you get ready to write, be sure to reread your outline.

Exercises   Organizing Story Events

▶ Analyzing/Inferring Sequence

A. Organizing Events Imagine that you are writing a story about training your dog. The plot outline of your story is shown below. Put it in correct time sequence.

5 He got away and rolled in a mud puddle.

1 My dog, Alfie, was a dog in need of training.

4 Then I tried to teach him to roll over.

3 Instead of shaking hands, he jumped on me.

6 As I gave Alfie a bath, I decided that maybe he was better off not trained.

2 First, I tried to teach him to shake hands.

▶ Inferring Sequence/Structured Application

B. Making a Plot Outline Choose one of the story ideas you developed on page 231. Make a plot outline for it. Remember to study it and make changes if you need to.

off, and hopped in. We paddled quietly for about a mile, and then we heard rushing water. That's when I remembered we had left our life jackets on the riverbank back at the park.

Special Populations

LD To reinforce the concept of time order, provide simple stories that are incorrectly sequenced and have the students put the events in order.

ESL Pair students with native speakers of English for Exercise B.

Reinforcement

As a class activity, have students develop a plan for one of the following story ideas. Tell them to choose characters, setting, and plot. List their plot outline on the board.

While working with her computer, Juanita discovers that she has accidentally managed to communicate with beings from outside our solar system.

What appears to be a costume jewelry necklace purchased at a garage sale turns out to be very valuable.

Enrichment

Explain the idea of flashbacks in longer narratives. Explain that an event from the past may temporarily interrupt the chronological flow. Have students suggest story situations when this technique would be effective.

Additional Resources

Skills Practice Book—page 93

Teacher's Resource Binder
  Enrichment Activities—
    page 21

Part 5

Objectives

1. To expand a plot outline into a story
2. To indicate sequence through transitional words and phrases

Presenting the Lesson

 All Students

1. Read and discuss page 234 through the section titled **A New Direction.** Define the terms, *drafting, introduction, body,* and *conclusion.* Emphasize the function of the introduction, body, and conclusion. Explain why every story must have all three parts.

2. Be sure students understand the relationship between items on their plot outlines and paragraphing their stories. Explain that the introduction can form one paragraph. Each main event on their plot outlines may become a paragraph main idea.

3. Analyze Jill's sample draft with the students. Have them suggest reasons why Jill made the changes she did. Point out that Jill has already started revising. Discuss different drafting styles. Refer to notes in "Choosing a Process for Writing" in this Teacher's Edition.

4. Go over the time words listed on page 235. Explain the importance of using time words to keep a story moving. Have students suggest additional examples that could be added to the list in the text. Make a chart of time words and post it in the room. Remind the students to refer to the chart when writing.

5. Assign and discuss Exercises A and B on page 235. Have students separate desks as much as possible for quiet composing time.

 Basic Students

Do Exercise A as a group activity.

Discuss with the students how they plan to develop their plot outlines into paragraphs. Have students suggest and list time words that could be used. Then assign Exercise B. Circulate around the room to offer individual help with drafts as needed.

---

5 Drafting a Story

> **Focus**
>
> When you draft your narrative, you change the ideas in your plot outline into paragraphs and sentences.

Drafting Your Story

▶ Comprehension

Now you are ready to draft your story. You can put your ideas into sentence and paragraph form. Your narrative should have an introduction, a body, and a conclusion.

A story begins with an **introduction**. This is usually where the author introduces the characters and describes the setting. The action of the story may begin in the introduction.

Most of the action of the story takes place in the **body**, or the middle part of the story. It is in the body of the story that the action builds to the climax, or most exciting part.

The writer then brings the story to an end, or **conclusion**. At the conclusion, the loose ends are tied up and the story is brought to a close. Some narratives are only a paragraph or two. Others must be longer to tell the story. Your plot outline will help you tell how long your story should be.

Paragraphs in Your Draft Your plot outline can also help you break your story into paragraphs. You know that a paragraph has one main idea. Your introduction may be a paragraph by itself. Each main event in your plot outline can also become a main idea for a paragraph. Then, write your conclusion.

A New Direction Sometimes as you draft a narrative, new ideas may come to you that were not part of your plot outline. You may find your story going off in unexpected directions. These ideas are often better than those in your plot outline. Do not be afraid to try to use these new ideas.

234

Jill began to draft her story. She made some changes in the introduction as she wrote. Her thoughts are shown in blue.

I always thought there was something mys- *Maybe it was the long black cape* terious about Miss Hayes.∧Every Monday she *she wore.* came home on the four o'clock bus. She carried a big brown box wrapped tightly with *had to know* *package* string. I ~~wish I knew~~ what was in that ~~box~~.

> *I need to tell why she was mysterious.*

> *The last sentence is boring.*

Jill thought carefully as she worked on her draft. You will see later how she made further improvements.

Using Time Words

A writer uses time words and phrases to make events flow smoothly from one to another. These time words help the reader to follow the events in a story.

Jill's introduction contains the time phrases "every Monday" and "four o'clock." These tell you when Miss Hayes appeared. Here are some other time words.

> **Time Words and Phrases for Narrative Writing**
>
> first, next, always, once long ago, every summer, the first time, by morning, after lunch, that evening, soon, later, in a while

Exercises   Drafting a Story

▶ Analyzing

A. Creating Paragraphs Look at Jill's prewriting notes in part 4. Explain how you would break her ideas into paragraphs.

▶ Creative Application

B. Drafting Write a rough draft for your story. Work the events in your plot outline into an introduction, a body, and a conclusion. Use time words to make the events flow smoothly.

235

Encourage students to explore new directions their drafts can take as they expand their outlines. Have them consider new ideas, perhaps even new endings for their narratives.

Special Populations

LD Some students may have difficulty getting their drafts on paper or making changes. If possible, allow students to draft at the board and then recopy. They might also use a computer and a very simple word processing program. Using a tape recorder is another possibility.

Reinforcement

Provide copies of the following narrative or read it aloud. Have students identify the time words and phrases used.

On moving day we packed all of our belongings into huge boxes. Then, we labled each box. When we had loaded all the boxes on the van, we noticed that our cat, Whiskers, was missing. For about an hour, we searched the entire neighborhood. We couldn't find Whiskers. Finally, we decided to leave without him. We arrived across town at our new home at about noon. Before lunch, we started to unpack the boxes. To our surprise, out of the carton marked food jumped Whiskers.

Enrichment

The teacher should obtain sample drafts of famous writers. Many libraries have these available. Reproduce the drafts or use an overhead projector to share them with the class. Point out the changes made and the possible reasons for those changes.

Additional Resources

Skills Practice Book—page 94
Teacher's Resource Binder
  Reinforcement Activities—
  page 71

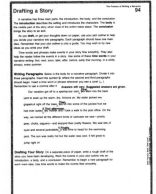

Part 6

Objective

To use description and dialogue to create interest in narrative writing

Presenting the Lesson

All Students

1. Read and discuss the material on page 236 through **Using Description.** Have the students point out the descriptive words in Jill's narrative. Ask the students what mood these words help to create. Students should get the idea that using vivid description is a way to make a picture with words. The teacher may wish to have students refer to part 2 of Chapter 19, "Description and the Process of Writing," on page 331, that discuss gathering sensory details.

2. Read and discuss the rest of part 6. Refer students to the "Guide to Punctuation," in the **Power Handbook** to review the rules for correct punctuation of dialogue. Point out that a new paragraph begins when the speaker changes.

3. Assign and discuss Exercises A and B on page 237. Tell students that a good way to judge dialogue is to hear it. They might want to read it aloud to help them judge what they have written. For Exercise B, point out that dialogue will not work for some stories, those with only one character for example. Description, however, is always appropriate. Suggest using the "Thesaurus" on page 509 of the **Power Handbook** to aid with word choice for vivid description.

Basic Students

Have the students work in pairs for Exercise A on page 237. Ask them to do each situation orally first, each one taking on the role of one of the characters in the situation. Then, have them write the dialogue. Remind students to check the punctuation and capitalization.

Schedule a story conference with each student. Have the students show you the areas where they plan to add description and dialogue. Then assign Exercise B.

Advanced Students

Choose a short scene from a play. Give students the script and have them read the scene aloud. Explain the placement of dialogue next to the character's names and the stage directions. Have students rewrite the scene in the form of a narrative, with dialogue.

Special Populations

LD, ESL Provide an adjective, adverb word bank that gives words in context. Make this accessible to students to use as they write.

NSD Students should discuss dialect and its usefulness in narrative writing. Encourage the use of dialect, their own or another dialect, as part of the dialogue in their stories.

---

6 Using Description and Dialogue

> ### Focus
> Dialogue and description make a narrative come to life.

Using Description

▶ Comprehension

Writers use description to help the reader picture, feel, hear, taste, or smell what is happening in a story. Realistic description makes the reader feel as if he or she is part of the story. As Jill worked on her draft she wrote this.

> Miss Hayes lived in the house next door.

Jill realized that her readers could not tell much about Miss Hayes's house, so she added some description.

> Miss Hayes lived in the house next door. It was an old white house with peeling paint. Its shutters creaked whenever the wind blew. Tall, scraggly bushes grew beneath each window.

Jill's descriptive details make the house seem mysterious. Readers feel that something spooky may be about to happen.

Using Dialogue

When characters talk together, their conversation is called **dialogue.** Dialogue keeps the action moving in a story. It is a more interesting way of showing what is happening than just telling about the action. You can also use dialogue to help your readers learn about a character. Writers show what a character is like by showing what the character says and how he or she talks. Before you use dialogue in your story, check the **Power Handbook** for important rules about writing dialogue correctly. Notice that a new paragraph begins each time the speaker changes.

236

As Jill continued drafting her story she wrote this.

> I could hear Miss Hayes talking to someone inside her house.
> But Miss Hayes lived all alone!

Jill saw that if she added dialogue she could make her readers feel some uneasiness about Miss Hayes. This is what she wanted to accomplish. She changed her draft to read:

> Inside, Miss Hayes was talking. I could hear her raspy voice as she said, "And how are you today, my little ones?"
> Who could she be talking to? Miss Hayes lived alone!

Now Jill's readers can hear Miss Hayes for themselves. Miss Hayes seems more real and the readers feel that they are a part of the story.

Exercises Using Description and Dialogue

▶ Structured Application

A. Writing Dialogue Rewrite the statements below as dialogue. Capitalize and punctuate them correctly. See answers in margin.

1. I told Ron that I couldn't help him. He was angry.
2. Ruth said that we must put mushrooms on the pizza. Eric told Ruth that he didn't like mushrooms.
3. The lifeguard shouted at us to get off the pier. We said we would.
4. Julie asked Carlos to hang a picture. He told her that he would do it if he could find a hook.
5. Mrs. Ling told Ian not to mow where the newly seeded grass was. Ian forgot. Mrs. Ling asked him why he hadn't listened to her.
6. Sue wanted to know where Nancy was. Denise told her that Nancy had an appointment with the dentist.

▶ Creative Application

B. Adding Description and Dialogue Carefully study the draft of your story. Add description and dialogue where needed.

237

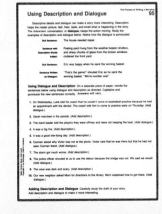

Reinforcement

Have the students follow the directions for Exercise A on page 237 using the following statements.

1. The forest rangers shouted at us to get away from the bear's cave. We said we would.
2. Mr. Worrell asked Ryan where his science homework was. Ryan said his dog ate it.
3. Betsy asked Nan how she liked her new house. Nan said she was lonely for her old one.
4. The dentist told Eduardo that he had no cavities. Eduardo was glad.
5. Chang's grandparents asked him if he would like to spend the weekend at their house. Chang said he would, if his parents would let him.

1. "Get away from that cave. There's a bear in there!" shouted the forest rangers.
  "We will," we replied.
2. "Where is your science homework?" inquired Mr. Worrell.
  "My dog ate it," mumbled Ryan.
3. "Nan, how do you like your new house?" asked Betsy.
  "I'm lonely for my old one," Nan responded.
4. "Eduardo, you have no cavities," announced the dentist.
  "Terrific!" shouted Eduardo.
5. "Would you like to come over to cook out and stay over for the weekend, Chang?" offered Grandpa.
  "I'd love to!" Chang answered. "Let me see if it's ok with Mom and Dad."

Exercise A
1. "Ron," I said, "I can't help you."
  "I'm angry," Ron said.
2. "We must put mushrooms on the pizza," Ruth said.
  "I don't like mushrooms," Eric protested.
3. The lifeguard shouted at us. "Get off the pier!" she screamed.
  "We will! We will!" we cried.
4. "Would you hang this picture, Carlos?" Julie pleaded.
  "I will if I can find a hook," Carlos responded.
5. "Ian, I told you not to mow where the newly seeded grass is," Mrs. Ling said. "Why didn't you listen to me, Ian?" Mrs. Ling asked.
  "I forgot," replied Ian.
6. Sue asked, "Where is Nancy?"
  "She has an appointment with the dentist," Denise replied.

Enrichment

To illustrate the use of dialect in narrative writing, read aloud, or obtain recordings of some Jack Tales or Joel Chandler Harris's stories about Brer Rabbit. You might wish to read a passage from *Huckleberry Finn* or another work by Mark Twain that illustrates use of dialect. Discuss the use of regional dialect in these stories and what this adds to each story.

Part 7

Objectives

1. To recognize the need to revise and to implement revisions
2. To proofread a narrative

Presenting the Lesson

 All Students

1. Discuss why putting a draft aside for awhile might be a good idea.
2. Read and discuss the introduction and **Guidelines for Revising a Story** on page 239. As you read the Guidelines, ask the students to suggest why each might be important in producing a good narrative.
3. Read and discuss the section titled **Sample Revision** on page 238. If possible, project the draft of the body of Jill's story on an overhead transparency. Make another overhead that shows the changes she made. Place it over the original draft. Guide students in analyzing the changes and the reasons for these changes.
4. Read and discuss **Proofreading Your Narrative** on page 240. Remind students to refer to the "Guide to Capitalization," the "Guide to Punctuation," and the "Guide to Spelling" in the **Power Handbook** as they proofread their papers.
5. Assign and discuss Exercises A and B on page 240.

 Basic Students

Review the rules for punctuation in the **Power Handbook.** Then, complete Exercise A as a group activity.

 Advanced Students

As students revise their drafts, have them write down their thoughts, much like the thought bubbles in the lesson. Have them explain each decision for a change in their writing. Have them identify what was ineffective in the original version and explain why they think the revision is better.

7 Revising a Narrative

Focus

Before making a final copy, revise your story carefully.

▶ Comprehension/Analyzing

Put the draft of your story aside for awhile. Think about what you have written. Then reread it carefully. Decide what changes might improve your story.

Sample Revision

Here is the draft of the body of Jill's story.

Last Monday,
∧ I hid under those bushes. I was determined to discover what was in the mysterious package.

I didn't tell when.

Inside, Miss Hayes was talking. I could hear her raspy voice as she ~~said~~ *croaked,* "And how are you, my little ones?" Who could she be talking to? Miss Hayes lived alone!

I can use more powerful verbs.

As I stood up to ~~look~~ *peek* in Miss Hayes's window, I ~~went~~ *tumbled* backward.

Miss Hayes came out and asked what had happened. She was angry, but what she said explained the mystery of the package.

I haven't told what the mystery was.

I felt silly that night.

As Jill studied her draft, she noticed some problems. Then she thought of ways she could improve her work and add interest and excitement to her story.

Problem: I need more detail. I didn't tell how I fell.

Result: As I stood up to peek in Miss Hayes's window, my foot got tangled in a bush. I fell backwards and yelled, "Help!"

Problem: The part where Miss Hayes comes out should be more exciting. I could use dialogue.

Result: Miss Hayes rushed out. "What are you doing in my bushes?" she shouted. "You scared me to death! There I was, quietly repairing my antique dolls, when I heard screaming. I nearly cracked one doll's arm off. Get on home with you!"

Problem: My last paragraph needs to let the reader know the mystery is solved and the story is over.

Result: Discovering that Miss Hayes carried old dolls in her mysterious package did not make my cuts and bruises feel any better. I think I will leave detective work to the professionals.

Read the final copy of Jill's story on page 241. Notice that Jill's revisions made her story more interesting.

As you revise your own narrative, ask yourself the following questions.

Guidelines for Revising a Story

1. Can my readers clearly picture the characters and setting?
2. Will my plot hold the reader's interest?
3. Does my story have an introduction, a body, and a conclusion?
4. Do the events in the story follow chronological order?
5. Would adding description and dialogue make my story seem more real to the reader?
6. Have I chosen powerful verbs, precise nouns, and the adjectives and adverbs I need?

239

Special Populations

LD, ESL To help students develop an "eye" for proofreading, use an overhead projector to display sample compositions. Have students identify errors and suggest corrections.

NSD Stress the importance of using Standard English.

Reinforcement

Have students exchange papers and make suggestions for improvement or correction of mechanical errors on the classmate's paper. Allow time for students to implement the suggestions.

Additional Resources

Skills Practice Book—page 96
Teacher's Resource Binder
  Enrichment Activities—
    page 5

Exercise A

"I think I would like to be an astronaut someday,"
Beth told her best friend, Simone.

"Why an astronaut?" Simone asked.

Beth said, "It would be fun to visit other planets.
I'm interested in science and space. I'd be a good
astronaut."

Simone smiled and said, "You probably would."

Proofreading Your Narrative

You have worked hard to make your story interesting. Now you want to make certain that it contains no errors. Before you make your final copy, proofread your writing carefully, using the proofreading symbols on page 114. Look for any mistakes you may have made in grammar, capitalization, punctuation, and spelling. Ask another person to read your writing. Sometimes someone else can see errors you may have missed.

Look very carefully at the punctuation of dialogue. You may want to check the rules for punctuating and capitalizing direct quotations in the **Power Handbook**. Study the examples and rules there as you proofread your own writing.

Exercises   Revising a Narrative

▶ Structured Application

A. Punctuating Dialogue On your paper, copy the following conversation from a story. Add the punctuation that is needed.

See answers in margin.

I think I would like to be an astronaut someday, Beth told her best friend, Simone. Why an astronaut, Simone asked. Beth said it would be fun to visit other planets. I'm interested in science and space. I'd be a good astronaut. Simone smiled and said, You probably would.

▶ Judging/Evaluating

B. Working with a Classmate To Revise Exchange narratives with a classmate. Read each other's story. Use the "Guidelines for Revising a Story" on page 239 to make suggestions for improvement. Then, follow your classmate's suggestions and revise your own story.

8 Writing and Sharing a Final Copy

Focus

Proofread your story and make a final copy.

▶ Comprehension

Now, you can give your story a title. A good title hints at what the story is about without giving away too much.

Here is Jill's final copy.

Monday's Mystery

I always thought there was something mysterious about Miss Hayes. Maybe it was the long black cape she wore. Every Monday she came home on the four o'clock bus. She carried a big brown box wrapped tightly with string. I had to know what was in that package.

Miss Hayes lived in the house next door. It was an old white house with peeling paint. Its shutters creaked whenever the wind blew. Tall, scraggly bushes grew beneath each window. Last Monday, I hid under those bushes. I was determined to discover what was in the mysterious package.

Inside, Miss Hayes was talking. I could hear her raspy voice as she croaked, "And how are you, my little ones?" Who could she be talking to? Miss Hayes lived alone!

As I stood up to peek in Miss Hayes's window, my foot got tangled in a bush. I tumbled backwards and yelled, "Help!"

Miss Hayes rushed out. "What are you doing in my bushes?" she shouted. "You scared me to death! There I was, quietly repairing my antique dolls, when I heard screaming. I nearly cracked one doll's arm off. Get on home with you!"

Discovering that Miss Hayes carried old dolls in her mysterious package did not make my cuts and bruises feel any better. I think I will leave detective work to the professionals.

Exercise   Writing and Sharing a Final Copy
▶ Creative Application

Make a final copy of your story. Add a title. Proofread your story again. Then choose a way of sharing your story with your class.

241

Part 8

Objective

To write and share a final copy

Presenting the Lesson

 All Students

Read and discuss Jill's final copy on page 241. Assign and discuss the exercise on page 241. Use the guidelines to judge a narrative.

Guidelines for Evaluation

Strong The narratives will display the following characteristics: (5 points)
1. will include the elements of characters, setting, and plot
2. will develop these elements with appropriate details
3. will contain a definite introduction, body, and conclusion
4. will use chronological order
5. will use transitional words and phrases to maintain coherence and establish sequence
6. will use precise, vivid language to tell the story
7. will use description or dialogue as appropriate to enhance the story
8. will contain no more than two or three minor errors in grammar, usage, and mechanics

Average A narrative of average quality will meet most of the criteria of the successful response but will display two or three of these problems: (3 points)
1. may lack full development of characters, setting, or plot
2. may lack a satisfactory ending
3. may lack some coherence
4. may display several errors in grammar, usage, and mechanics

Weak A weak narrative will be characterized by these problems: (1 point)
1. inadequate development of character, setting, or plot
2. confused sequence of events; abrupt, confusing shifts in time or location; lack of necessary transitional words and phrases
3. no definite beginning and ending
4. vague, imprecise language
5. grammar, usage, and mechanics errors

Speaking and Listening

Objective

To develop techniques for reading and presenting a short dramatic scene

Presenting the Activity

This page gives special emphasis to the speaking and listening skill of acting in a play. This activity may be used to show students how the concepts presented in this chapter may be applied in an oral context.

Speaking and Listening

Drama

▶ Comprehension

A play is a story that is written to be acted out before an audience. A play, like a narrative, contains characters, a setting, and a plot. However, in a play, the story is told through the actions and dialogue of the characters. The audience learns what happens from what the characters do or from what they say.

The playwright, or author, often includes special directions to help the actors. These are called **stage directions**. Stage directions are never read out loud. Instead, they tell the actor how to say a line or how to move on stage. For example, stage directions may tell an actor to pause at a certain point to show the audience that the character is uncertain about what to do.

In a way, members of the audience participate in a play, too. They must listen and think carefully, so that they can understand the relationships between characters and actions. They must think about what is going to happen next. An audience must be quiet in order to listen. Talking is rude. It is a distraction to other members of the audience and to the actors on the stage.

Exercise   Acting in a Play

▶ Creative Application

Work with a group of classmates to choose a short scene from a play that can be presented to the class. Choose a play from your literature book, or one your teacher suggests. Decide who will play each character. Practice reading the character's parts in your group. Create simple costumes and scenery if you wish. When you are ready, present the scene before the class.

242

Creative Writing

Creative Writing

These activities provide opportunites for imaginative applications of the skills presented in this chapter.

▶ Creative Application

A. Choose one of the pictures below. Create a story, using that picture as your idea starter. Use the writing process that you have learned in this chapter as you write your narrative.

B. Write dialogue for one of the following situations. Capitalize and punctuate the dialogue correctly.

1. One slice of pizza speaks to another as hungry teen-agers approach the table.
2. Imagine that you have a Siamese cat. What would your cat tell your sister's new puppy?
3. Imagine that you can talk to any famous person from the present or past. Write your conversation.

243

Using English in Science

This activity shows the relationship between narrative fiction and scientific fact. You may wish to further discuss science fiction authors and topics before beginning the exercise. The teacher may wish to check with the school librarian to obtain a list of science fiction books available in the school library or establish a "sci-fi" reading corner in the classroom. Some possible authors might include Ray Bradbury, Robert Heinlein, and Ursula LeGuin.

▶ Comprehension

Scientific knowledge and narrative writing can blend to form a special kind of fiction that is called **science fiction**. Some knowledge of science is necessary to write science fiction. In fact, many authors of science fiction are both scientists and writers. They have accurate knowledge about what is true in science today. They use this information to write about a world in which scientific possibilities have become scientific fact. For this reason, science fiction is often set in the future.

Because science fiction has such a strong base in real scientific fact, it often comes true. Many years ago some science fiction authors wrote about things that exist in our world today. Jules Verne wrote about an atomic-powered submarine. Arthur C. Clarke described communication satellites and space stations.

WELCOME, EARTH CREATURES

Exercise   Blending Narrative Writing and Science

▶ Creative Application

Choose one of the scientific inventions from the following list, or find one of your own choice. Use an encyclopedia or other reference source to learn about the invention. Take some notes on what you learn. Then, imagine how this invention or its use might change in the future. Now, write a narrative that uses the information you found and the ideas your imagination has supplied. Follow the steps you have learned in this chapter to write an exciting science-fiction narrative.

LASER beams   computers and artificial intelligence
antibiotics   freeze-dried food

244

Chapter 13 Review

▶ **Inferring Sequence**

A. Using Time Order Read the following story events. Put them in the correct sequence.

3 After a long time, the boy surfaced on the other side of the swimming pool.

1 Pedro stood poised on the high dive as he studied the water beneath him.

4 He spouted water as he let the air out of his lungs.

5 The watching crowd applauded and cheered wildly.

2 His dark figure lifted off the platform, shot downward, and sliced through the water.

▶ **Structured Application**

B. Punctuating Dialogue Rewrite the following dialogue. Insert the correct capitalization and punctuation. Remember to begin a new paragraph each time the speaker changes.

See answers in margin.

I'm going downstream and try the hole by the bank. I think Big Old Sam is just waiting for my lure Kyle said. You're kidding, Faye replied. You mean you believe what those guys told us about Old Sam? Sure I do answered Kyle. They've been fishing this stream for years he pointed out. Haven't you ever heard of teasing asked Faye. I think they were really putting us on. But you go ahead and try if you want to. I will insisted Kyle. I'll even share Old Sam with you at dinner he boasted.

C. Using Time Words and Phrases Copy the paragraph below. Fill in each blank with a suitable time word or phrase. Use the time words and phrases on page 235 or others that you think of.

Possible answers in blanks.

<u>Each summer</u>, just when school gets out, the Posts fly to their cabin in Canada. They buy their tickets <u>three months</u> early <u>The weekend</u> before they leave, they pack their suitcases. <u>Early</u> on the day of the flight, they leave for the airport. Their plane leaves the runway and their adventure <u>finally</u> begins.

245

Chapter Review

This review allows teachers to evaluate student understanding of the concepts presented in this chapter.

Exercise B

"I'm going downstream and try the hole by the bank. I think Big Old Sam is just waiting for my lure," Kyle said.

"You're kidding," Faye replied. "You mean you believe what those guys told us about Old Sam?"

"Sure I do," answered Kyle. "They've been fishing this stream for years," he pointed out.

"Haven't you ever heard of teasing?" asked Faye. "I think they were really putting us on. But you go ahead and try if you want to."

"I will," insisted Kyle. "I'll even share Old Sam with you at dinner," he boasted.

Additional Resources

Skills Practice Book
Review—page 97

Test Booklet
Mastery Test—pages 71–74

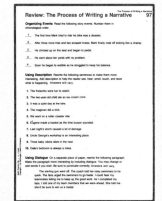

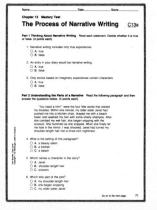

Cumulative Review

These exercises provide a cumulative review of the concepts presented in this unit. Each exercise challenges the students to apply several of the skills they have acquired while studying this unit.

To evaluate the explanatory writing in Exercise A, see the Guidelines for Evaluation in the Teacher Notes on page 189.

To evaluate the narrative writing in Exercise B, see the Guidelines for Evaluation in the Teacher Notes on page 241.

Exercise C
1. You scan to get specific information.
2. SQ3R stands for survey, question, read, record, and review.
3. A study plan shows all planned activities, including lessons, sports, recreation, daily homework, household chores, and long-term projects.
4. Most standardized tests are multiple choice.
5. Writing a report is an example of a long-term assignment.

Cumulative Review

Composition
▶ Creative Application

A. Explaining *How* Write brief, clear instructions on how to do one of the following: 1) bathe the dog; 2) start the power lawn mower; 3) load and run the dishwasher; 4) play a favorite game such as Scrabble, dominoes, or rummy. Choose another topic if you wish.

B. Writing Narratives Tell a story about 1) the time the sun didn't rise; 2) you followed a gnome underground; 3) you were proud of yourself. You may also look in the **Power Handbook,** pages 464-466, for other writing ideas.

Grammar
▶ Recalling/Analyzing

Pronouns and Subject-Verb Agreement Number your paper from 1 to 10. Write the correct word from the parentheses.

1. (She, Her) and (I, me) saw a mountain goat when we toured in Canada.
2. Hygrometers (measure, measures) humidity.
3. (Whose, Who's) ski jacket is this?
4. Both lanes of the highway (is, are) closed.
5. Will (they, them) help Maria and (I, me) inflate the helium balloons?
6. (Is, Are) you still working on the mural?
7. Everyone in my family (like, likes) granola cereal for breakfast.
8. Neither the fabric nor the buttons (cost, costs) over a dollar.
9. Mario and (he, him) told (we, us) students all about Groundhog Day.
10. A raccoon uses (it's, its) front paws the way we use our hands.

246

Related Skills

▶ Making Inferences

A. Vocabulary Development and Dictionary Skills Use context clues to learn the meaning of each underlined word below. Write the word and its meaning. Next, use a dictionary to find another meaning for that word. Write that meaning.

Second meanings will vary.

1. Finding the treasure was a <u>fluke</u>. In other words, it was a stroke of luck. fluke—a stroke of luck

2. Builders will <u>revamp</u>—or remodel—the apartments. revamp—remodel

3. Making the tree house look like a spaceship was a <u>novel</u> (original and clever) idea. novel—original and clever

4. I enjoyed watching the flightless birds, especially the <u>kiwi</u>, at the zoo. kiwi—a flightless bird

5. The tailor used <u>ferret</u>, which is narrow cotton, silk, or wool tape. ferret—narrow cotton, silk, or wool tape

B. Using a Thesaurus Use the thesaurus at the back of this book to replace each of the underlined words below.

Answers will vary.

1. That <u>big</u> glacier stretches for five miles.
2. Returning the lost wallet was the <u>good</u> thing to do.
3. We watched wild horses <u>run</u> up and down the hills.
4. Do you notice anything <u>strange</u> about that house?
5. With her backpack, Julia <u>walked</u> up the steep hill.

▶ Structured Application

C. Study and Test-Taking Skills Read the following statements. Rewrite the statements correctly on your paper. See answers in margin.

1. You scan to get a general idea of what a book or chapter is about.
2. SQ3R stands for select, question, remember, record, and revise.
3. A study plan shows only homework assignments.
4. Standardized tests usually contain essay questions.
5. Writing a report is a short-term assignment.

247

(These Unit Projects are continued from T. E. page 125.) activity box. Designate time occasionally for an activity period. Allow students to draw an activity from the various categories in the box and prepare and demonstrate the project for the class.

Computer Activity: Test Practice

Give students experience with computer programs designed to increase test-taking skills in vocabulary, analogy, and comprehension. These programs often present the material in a game format that students find challenging. Specific titles of such programs can be found in directories, such as the *Instructor's Computer Directory for Schools* which is available from *Instructor Magazine*. Programs are categorized by subject and the directory will often comment on the quality of the programs.

Provide time for students to use these kinds of programs in class or in the school computer facility.

For Gifted and Talented Students Encourage these students to use programs such as those written for high school students to prepare for the SAT tests.

Additional Resources

Test Booklet

UNIT 3

Introducing the Unit

1. Organization of the Unit Have the students read the chapter titles, the unit title, and the introduction to the unit on page 248. Explain that this unit will improve their ability to carefully observe and accurately describe the people, places, things, and events around them. Tell the students that they will also see how description can be used to picture the world of their imagination.

Continue the lesson with **Motivating Through Literature,** below.

2. Use the **Unit Management Guidelines** below to help you develop your weekly lesson plan. An optional week 9 has been provided to allow for variations in the length of grading periods. The teacher may wish to use this week for review, additional practice, and the presentation of selected special feature pages. Teachers who work on four- or six-week grading periods may adapt the chart accordingly.

Motivating Through Literature

Have the students read silently as you read "Paint Box" on page 249. As you read the poem, be sure your voice clearly indicates the two speakers in the poem. Describe the colors cobalt, umber, and ultramarine for the students before discussing the poem. Briefly talk about how artists represent things. Discuss how paintings differ from photographs. Use the following questions to stimulate discussion of the poem. Suggested answers are given but answers may vary.

1. How many speakers are there in the poem? How can you tell when each is speaking? two speakers—Each set of quotation marks indicates the words of a speaker.
2. What are some of the animals named in the second stanza and what colors are they? What is strange about these descriptions? crimson and white tiger, blue camel, purple panther—The animals named are not really these colors.
3. What have the ideas for these colors come from? the artist's imagination
4. What is the artist asked to paint now? an imaginary world with imaginary people

Painting with Words

In Unit 3 you will gain the skills you need to tell about the world around you. You will discover how to use adjectives and adverbs in clear descriptive sentences. You will grow to appreciate poetry as a special way to see, to describe, and to use language. Finally, you will see how descriptive writing becomes a part of many other kinds of writing.

The skills you gain will help you express yourself clearly when you speak and write. With these skills you can share your picture of the world around you. You can also share the world your imagination creates. You will discover new people, places, and experiences. Then you can paint them with colors no one else has seen.

Unit Management Guidelines

Week 19	**Week 20**	**Week 21**	**Week 22**	**Week 23**
Unit 3 Opener, pp. 248–249; Chapter 14, Parts 1–3, pp. 250–257	Chapter 14, Parts 4–7, pp. 258–267	Chapter 15, Parts 1–4, pp. 268–281	Chapter 16, Parts 1–5, pp. 282–299	Chapter 17, Parts 1–4, pp. 300–315

THE PAINT BOX

"Cobalt and umber and ultramarine.
Ivory black and emerald green—
What shall I paint to give pleasure to you?"
"Paint for me somebody utterly new."

"I have painted you tigers in crimson and white."
"The colors were good and you painted aright."
"I have painted the cook and a camel in blue
And a panther in purple." "You painted them true."

"Now mix me a color that nobody knows,
And paint me a country where nobody goes.
And put in it people a little like you.
Watching a unicorn drinking the dew."

—E. V. RIEU

249

5. How are the people watching the uni-corn? The unicorn is an imaginary creature. Both the people watching it and the artist must use their imaginations.

Stress the point that creativity allows the artists, inventors, and scientists in the world to see things that no one else does and to bring these things into the world for the rest of us.

Point out that the poet has used de-scriptive skills so well that we can clearly picture the imaginary world in the poem. Remind the students that this unit will help them write so that others can pic-ture what they describe.

Unit Projects

Independent Activity: Poetry

Help students construct a nicely bound "blank book" in which they can record finished copies of their own poems or descriptive passages. Stu-dents will need several sheets of blank paper folded in half and strong sewing thread or yarn. They can use two pieces of light cardboard covered with fabric or contact plastic for the cover. The paper is stitched down the fold and through the cover to form a spine for the book.

To encourage unique subjects for the poems, suggest that the students begin some writing sessions in the library look-ing for unusual topics in science books, biographies, stories, histories, and cur-rent periodicals.

Allow class time to write poetry. Have writing conferences with each student. Require that students do revisions of their poems on notebook paper before finished poems are copied into the spe-cial books.

Display the finished "poetry books" and decide on a way for students to share their poetry.

For Gifted and Talented Students Require that these students write poetry following a specific form, haiku, cinquain, or son-nets for example. Provide instructions, explanation, and examples of each kind of poetry to be written.

(Unit Projects are continued on T. E. page 344.)

Week 24	Week 25	Week 26	Week 27 (optional)
Chapter 18, Parts 1–3, pp. 316–325	Chapter 18, Part 4, pp. 326–329; Chapter 19, Parts 1–2, pp. 330–335	Chapter 19, Parts 3–4, pp. 336–343; Cumulative Review, pp. 344–345	Additional Review, Reinforcement, and Enrichment. See number 2 under **Introducing the Unit.**

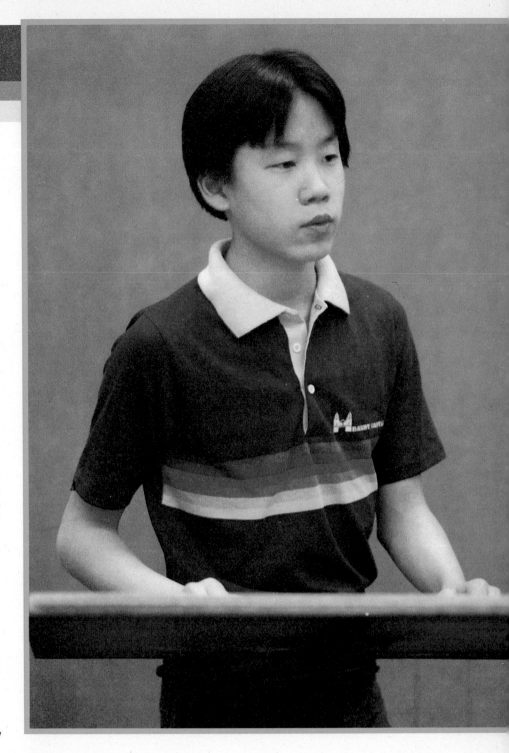

Chapter 14

Chapter Objectives

1. To use note cards to prepare a talk
2. To practice presenting a talk
3. To effectively present a talk
4. To identify and overcome communication barriers
5. To develop critical listening skills
6. To evaluate a talk
7. To effectively participate in a conversation
8. To effectively participate in a discussion
9. To effectively lead a discussion
10. To identify nonverbal messages, motive, point of view, and bias
11. To fairly evaluate a group discussion

Motivating the Students

Read the following poem to the students. Discuss with the students the need for effective communication. In this poem, the party is ruined because someone did not listen carefully. Ask students if they can think of other more serious situations in which clear communication, both speaking and listening, is crucial.

Spaghetti

Spaghetti, spaghetti, all over the place,
Up to my elbow—up to my face,
Over the carpet and under the chairs,
Into the hammock and wound round the
　　stairs,
Filling the bathtub and covering the desk,
Making the sofa a mad mushy mess.
The party is ruined, I'm terribly worried,
The guests have all left (unless they're all
　　buried).
I told them, "Bring presents." I said, "Throw
　　confetti."
I guess they heard wrong
'Cause they all threw spaghetti!

　　　　　　　—Shel Silverstein
　　　　　　　from *Where the*
　　　　　　　Sidewalk Ends

Now read and discuss the introduction to the chapter on page 251. Ask the students to share some anecdotes about times they have misheard information or said something incorrectly. What was the outcome of this breakdown in communication? Tell students that in this chapter they will learn how to become better listeners and better speakers.

Week 19

Chapter Management Guidelines This chart may be used to help structure daily lesson plans.

Day 1	Day 2	Day 3	Day 4	Day 5
Unit and Chapter Openers, pp. 248–251	Part 1, "Preparing a Talk," pp. 252–253	Part 2, "Presenting a Talk," pp. 254–255	Part 2, "Presenting a Talk," pp. 254–255	Part 3, "Becoming a Good Listener," pp. 256–257

Chapter 14

Sharpening Speaking and Listening Skills

Imagine what life would be like if you could neither speak nor listen. You would not be able to take part in discussions and conversations. You could not learn about the world through television or radio news shows. Sharing your feelings and ideas would become much more difficult. Listening and speaking are important parts of your everyday life.

This chapter explores several important listening and speaking skills. You will learn how to prepare and deliver an interesting, well-organized talk. You will also learn how to take part in and lead a discussion. These skills will help you to become a better listener and a more effective speaker.

251

Related Chapters

You may wish to refer to related material in other chapters as you teach the following concepts:

1. How to present ideas, Chapter 21, "Clear Thinking," page 367

2. The process of organizing and writing the talk, Chapter 6, "Choosing a Process for Writing," page 101

3. Organizing and writing a particular talk, Chapter 10, "The Process of Explaining *How*," page 177, and Chapter 24, "The Process of Writing a Report," page 421

Additional Resources

Skills Practice Book—pages 98–100

Test Booklet—pages 85–90
  Pretest—pages 85–86
  Mastery Test—pages 87–90

Teacher's Resource Binder
  Enrichment Activities—
    pages 23, 39–52, 69
  Ideas for Creative Teaching

Week 20

Chapter Management Guidelines   This chart may be used to help structure daily lesson plans.

Day 1	Day 2	Day 3	Day 4	Day 5
Chapter 14, Part 4, "Listening to and Judging Talks," p. 258–259	Part 5, "Conversations and Discussions," pp. 260–262	Part 6, "Critical Listening in Discussions," p. 263	Part 7, "Evaluating Group Discussions," pp. 264–265	Chapter Review and selected end-of-chapter activities

Part 1

Objectives

1. To use note cards to prepare a talk
2. To practice presenting a talk

Presenting the Lesson

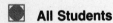 **All Students**

1. Read and discuss the introduction on page 252.
2. Read **Using Note Cards** on page 252. Remind students that it is often difficult to remember all they want to say in front of others. That's why note cards are important. Discuss the sample note card on page 252. Point out the outline form used on the card.
3. Read **Practicing Your Talk.** Discuss the importance of being well prepared when speaking in front of others. Go over the guidelines on page 253. Have the students give reasons why each is important.
4. Assign and discuss Exercises A and B on page 253.

▶ **Basic Students**

Give students plenty of time to gather details. Then help them to prepare note cards. Suggest key words and main ideas that will focus their presentations.

◆ **Advanced Students**

Have students practice their talks before a limited audience, such as parents, and to note suggested changes. Students should again practice their talks, keeping in mind the suggested changes. Have students discuss how an objective evaluation helped them improve their presentations.

---

1 Preparing a Talk

> **Focus**
>
> To prepare a talk, use the process of writing. Then prepare note cards and practice your talk.

▶ Comprehension

Writing is only one way to communicate ideas. Speaking is another form of communication.

Often, you will be asked to prepare a short speech, or talk. In Chapter 6, you learned about the stages in the process of writing. You can use most of these steps to prepare a talk. You will choose a topic and purpose, gather ideas, and organize your material. You will not write your talk word for word, however. Instead, you will make note cards and practice presenting your talk out loud.

Using Note Cards

Your talk will be more effective if you do not read it word for word. Note cards can help you remember ideas and keep you on the subject. Use $3'' \times 5''$ note cards. They are easy to hold and each one can be set aside after it is used. Write only enough information to jog your memory—a fact or two on each card. Study this example of a note card. Notice that it is in outline form.

> II. Setting of American musicals
> A. The Music Man-small town Iowa
> B. South Pacific-tropical island
> C. West Side Story-New York City

Practicing Your Talk

After you have prepared your talk, it is a good idea to practice it out loud. This will make you more comfortable with the material when you give your talk. Follow these guidelines when you practice your talk.

Guidelines for Practicing a Talk

1. **Read and reread your notes.** Know your material.
2. **Practice giving your talk in front of a mirror.** Practice standing straight, making appropriate gestures, and looking directly at your audience.
3. **Practice your talk out loud.** If possible, record yourself on a tape recorder. Try to speak clearly. Be careful not to hurry through your material. Stress important points.
4. **Give your talk in front of family members or friends.** They may have useful suggestions for you.
5. **Practice until you feel relaxed and confident.**

You will learn more about delivering your talk in part 2 of this chapter.

Exercises   Preparing and Practicing a Talk

▶ Creative Application

A. Prepare a short talk on something interesting that you have seen. It could be an unusual animal, a "talking" cash register, a robot, a tornado, or any other unusual thing or event. Follow the process of writing to prepare your talk. Write notes on 3″ × 5″ note cards. These notes should remind you of what you want to say.

▶ Evaluating

B. Practice in a group of four or five students. Comment on each talk presented in your group. Give at least two helpful suggestions for each talk. The "Guidelines for Delivering a Talk," which are presented in part 2, may give you additional help.

253

Special Populations

LD Students should be encouraged to choose a topic with which they are familiar. Students may need to read their entire speeches. In this case, allow them to write out their speeches on note cards. They should frequently refer to the guidelines for practicing as they work on their talks.

ESL, NSD These students will need extra guidance in choosing a topic, preparing note cards, and correcting pronunciation. Have students practice their talks in front of small groups. For NSD students, stress the importance of using Standard English so that they can be easily understood by everyone.

Reinforcement

Have students practice the process they have just learned by preparing a one-minute talk on one of the topics listed below. Students should prepare note cards on their topics and practice giving their talks in small groups. After students have a chance to practice, ask them to evaluate their notes. Were the cards detailed enough? Did they write too much? Students should keep these points in mind when they prepare their note cards for future talks.

Topics

a personal hero or heroine
a favorite vacation spot
an interesting hobby
a book others should read

Enrichment

1. Bring to class a book of famous speeches. Ask for volunteers to prepare and read part of one speech each day the class is working on this chapter. In addition to giving students examples of well written speeches, this exercise will allow students to become accustomed to speaking in front of the class before they present their own talks.

2. For additional enrichment activities, see the Unit Projects in the Teacher Notes on page 249. One or more of these projects have special activities for gifted and talented students.

Part 2

Objective

To effectively present a talk

Presenting the Lesson

▧ All Students

1. Read and discuss page 254. Stress the importance of the delivery of a talk. A good talk can become less effective if the delivery is poor. Tell students that they can greatly improve their talks by incorporating the points in the guidelines on page 254.

2. Read and discuss **Using Your Voice Effectively** on page 255. Make sure that students understand each of the terms presented in this part. Point out that the voice is a speaker's most important tool. If possible, bring to class recordings of well known speeches. Point out examples of good articulation, phrasing, and stressing.

3. Assign and discuss Exercises A and B on page 255.

▷ Basic Students

Allow students to practice their talks in small group situations. Point out areas that need improvement. Again, refer students back to the guidelines for review, if necessary.

◆ Advanced Students

Discuss with students the idea that newscasters deliver speeches every day on television. These speakers have learned to use all the steps covered in the guidelines for delivering a talk that students have just learned. Have students each write a short news story about something that is happening in school. After they practice their stories, have students present them to the class.

2 Presenting a Talk

┌─ *Focus* ─────────────────────────────────┐

How you present a talk is as important as what you say in the talk.

└──┘

▶ Comprehension

Your report may be interesting and well prepared. However, you must present it in an appealing way. Otherwise you will not reach your listeners. You need to think about your voice, your posture, your eye contact, and your gestures. Here are some suggestions to help you put across your ideas.

Guidelines for Delivering a Talk

1. **Be aware of your posture.** Stand tall and still, but not stiffly. Taking a deep breath will help you relax.

2. **Look at your listeners.** Make each person in the audience feel that you are talking directly to him or her. This is called *eye contact.*

3. **Use your hands and face in a meaningful way.** You can send your message with gestures as well as with words. If you are talking about something sad, do not smile. On the other hand, do not look glum if you are presenting a funny talk. Do not make distracting hand motions.

4. **Use your voice effectively.** Speak clearly and at a comfortable rate for you and your listeners. Be sure to speak loudly enough to be heard. You will learn more about using your voice in the section below.

5. **Use visual aids.** If they help make your talk clearer, include maps, charts, and pictures. Be sure they are large enough to be seen by everyone.

Using Your Voice Effectively

You know that **volume**, the power of your voice, is important. To make the most of your talk, you must also pay attention to the **rate** at which you speak. If you speak too slowly, the audience may become bored. If you speak too quickly, the audience may not understand you.

Articulation is the way sounds are joined to form separate words. A dictionary will help you with the standard American pronunciation of words. Always speak clearly and distinctly. People in different parts of the country may pronounce words in other ways. These differences are called **dialects**.

To get your meaning across, you must phrase your ideas correctly. **Phrasing** is putting together words into meaningful groups. This often requires **stressing**, or emphasizing, different words. Look at the following sentences. Then say them out loud. Who is the great swimmer in each sentence?

> The boy says his sister is a great swimmer.
> "The boy," says his sister, "is a great swimmer."

You can see how phrasing affects the meaning of these sentences. Be aware of how you phrase sentences when you give a talk.

Exercises Delivering a Talk

▶ Analyzing/Interpretation

A. Show the difference in meaning as you say these pairs of sentences.

> "You hope," she said, "too much."
> You hope she said too much.
>
> Ms. Sanders, our teacher, was late.
> Ms. Sanders, our teacher was late.

▶ Creative Application

B. Present the talk you planned and practiced in part 1. Follow the guidelines presented in this lesson.

255

Part 3

Objectives

1. To identify and overcome communication barriers
2. To develop critical listening skills

Presenting the Lesson

▪ All Students

1. Read and discuss pages 256–257. Make sure that students understand what it means to be a good listener. Stress that effective communication results only when the listener is as skilled and attentive as the speaker.

2. To encourage the development of listening skills, use several of the following lists. Have students listen as you read a complete list. Then ask them to write down as many of the items as they can remember. Note that lists with abstract words are more difficult to remember than lists of objects, and that lists of related objects are the simplest to recall.

run	sandwich	apple
cloud	oatmeal	pear
love	apple	grape
finger	cheese	orange
receive	soup	banana
bell	broccoli	peach

3. Read and discuss each item in the chart on page 256. Ask students to rate themselves in each area, using this evaluation scale.

1—always a poor listener
2—often poor
3—sometimes poor, sometimes good
4—often good
5—always a good listener

Discuss practical ways to become a better listener.

4. Make sure that students understand the difference between fact and opinion. Stress the importance of avoiding overgeneralizations. For further discussion on this topic, refer students to Chapter 21, "Clear Thinking," page 367.

5. Assign and discuss Exercises A and B on page 257.

---

3 Becoming a Good Listener

┌─ **Focus** ─────────────────────────────┐
│ To be a good listener, you must overcome communication barriers and develop good listening skills. │
└──┘

▶ Comprehension

A communication barrier is something that interferes with the messages between the speaker and the listener. Some barriers are created by listeners. For example, a listener might daydream or might refuse to accept new ideas. Other barriers are created by speakers. For example, a speaker might present confusing ideas or make distracting gestures.

This chart lists some communication barriers. It also tells how good listeners deal with these barriers.

Barriers to Communication	
Barrier	**Overcoming the Barrier**
Distractions	Good listeners pay attention. They save daydreaming for quiet moments alone. They tune out distractions and concentrate on what the speaker is saying.
Information overload	Good listeners sort information. They remember main ideas and devote less effort to remembering details.
Lazy listening	Good listeners work hard to get the most out of what they hear. They pay attention even when what they hear does not seem especially important.
Hasty conclusions	Good listeners are careful not to jump to conclusions or to get carried away with words or ideas. They make thoughtful judgments at the end of a presentation.
Narrow thinking	Good listeners are open to new ideas.

256

Basic Students

Tape record or videotape several commercials and play them for students. Discuss these commercials, having students identify several facts, opinions, and overgeneralizations.

Advanced Students

To help the students recognize words meant to stir the emotions and promote one point of view, read the following statements. Have the students tell which was spoken by a fan and which by an impartial observer. Ask them to identify the emotion-packed words.

Critical Listening

A **fact** is a statement about something that has really happened or is true. It can be proved. An **opinion** is one person's idea about something or someone. Opinions cannot be proved.

Every speaker uses a mixture of facts and opinions. A good listener must be alert to separate them. Watch out especially for overgeneralization.

A **generalization** is a statement of fact based on details. For example, imagine that fifteen out of twenty students in your class say that the Ferris wheel is their favorite ride. You could generalize that most of the class likes the Ferris wheel best. An **overgeneralization** is a statement that is too broad to be true. If you said that the favorite ride of *all* students is the Ferris wheel, that would be an overgeneralization. To spot overgeneralizations, listen for words such as *everyone*, *always*, *never*, *every*, *nobody*, *everybody*, *all the time*, and *no one*.

Exercises   Using Listening Skills

▶ Creative Application/Analyzing

A. In pairs, act out the following situations. Discuss the communication barriers that you notice between the characters.

1. A student comes home from school two hours late and meets a parent at the door.
2. A brother and sister both believe it is the other's turn to do the dishes.
3. One student has lost another student's book. The second student did not even know the first had borrowed the book.

B. With a partner, make up a commercial to sell a product. Present your commercial for the class. The class should do the following:

1. Point out facts that were presented in the commercial.
2. Identify opinions.
3. Identify any generalizations and overgeneralizations.

257

Version 1

In a ridiculous exhibition, Wainwright High scraped by the hard-fighting Rangers of Southern. In the final minute, Wainwright dropped a wild shot and squeezed out the lucky win.

Version 2

In a hard-fought game, Wainwright won a 75 to 74 victory over Southern last night. With only a few seconds to play, Wainwright shot the winning basket while the stands erupted in excitement.

Version 3

Coming from behind, the never-say-die players from Wainwright upset the overconfident Rangers of Southern 75 to 74. The magnificent shot by star Al Stronghart secured the win and provided a spectacular victory for the cheering fans.

Special Populations

LD Students may be poor listeners because they are easily distracted. Try to minimize distractions in the classroom. Do not let students have unnecessary materials on their desks. Have them work in small groups whenever possible.

Reinforcement

Read out loud short stories or excerpts from longer works. Prepare questions for students to answer at the conclusion of the reading. Be sure to include questions concerning main idea, sequence, and details.

Enrichment

Have students keep a notebook for at least a week of arguments they hear in commercials, political campaigns, from assembly or other speakers, or from special interest groups. Students should note these three points:

1. who was speaking
2. what the speaker's motive was
3. any words or details in the speaker's argument that indicated the speaker's bias or attempted to sway the listener

After the observation period, have the students discuss their findings.

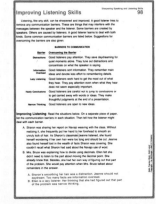

Additional Resources

Skills Practice Book—page 98
Teacher's Resource Binder
Enrichment Activities—
pages 39–52

Part 4

Objective

To evaluate a talk

Presenting the Lesson

 All Students

1. Read and discuss pages 258–259. Make sure the students understand that *content* is the information being presented and *presentation* is how it is said.

2. Discuss the **Guildelines for Listening to a Talk.** Tell students that the key to being a good listener is concentration.

3. Discuss the **Guidelines for Evaluating a Talk.** Point out the importance of each guideline. Have the students make a list of these guidelines. Then, as they listen to a talk, they can check off, or comment on, the speaker's content and the presentation.

4. Assign and discuss the exercise on page 259.

 Basic Students

Have the students play the game "Going to New York." The first person says, "I went to New York and I took my raincoat." Each student repeats the objects in order and adds another object. This exercise requires the student to concentrate on what is being said.

 Advanced Students

Have the students play a game of "telephone." The group lines up and a message is whispered down the line. No one may say the message more than once. Have the last person state the message. Then have the first person state the message as he or she heard it. Discuss the difference between the two. Point out the importance of concentrating and listening carefully, even to simple messages.

4 Listening to and Judging Talks

Focus

There are two parts to every talk: the **content** and the **presentation**. Use listening skills to fairly evaluate both parts of the talk.

▶ Comprehension

Listening is a skill just as speaking is a skill. A good listener gets much more out of a talk than does a lazy listener. Follow these guidelines for listening to talks.

Guidelines for Listening to a Talk

1. **Be sure you can see and hear the speaker.**

2. **Look directly at the speaker.** Show that you are interested.

3. **Listen closely to the speaker's opening statements.** They will give you an idea of what the speaker is going to talk about.

4. **Listen for the main ideas.** Important ideas often follow signal words such as *first, next, finally, therefore, however,* and *for example.* Also look for ideas that are repeated or stressed.

5. **Listen to the speaker's final statements.** They may highlight important ideas or summarize the main points. Sometimes you must do more than listen to a talk. You might be asked to evaluate or comment on someone else's talk. To do this, you must listen carefully to the content of the talk. You must also watch the presentation.

258

When your classmates give talks, you may be asked to evaluate their presentations. Being a good listener will allow you to make fair and helpful comments. Learning what to listen for in someone else's talk will also help you plan your own presentation.

Follow these guidelines when you evaluate a talk.

Guidelines for Evaluating a Talk

Content

1. **What was the topic of the talk?** Did the speaker make the topic clear and easy to understand?
2. **Was there enough information?**
3. **Did the information appear to be correct and to the point?**
4. **Was the information organized well?** Was the talk clear and easy to follow?

Presentation

1. **Did the speaker look directly at the audience?** Did he or she make eye contact with everyone in the audience?
2. **Did the speaker look relaxed, yet stand tall?**
3. **Was the speaker easy to hear and understand?** Did he or she speak slowly and clearly?
4. **Were the speaker's gestures helpful and natural?**

Exercise   Listening to and Evaluating a Talk
▶ Analyzing/Evaluating

Listen to someone give a talk. It may be a coach giving a pre-game pep talk, or a newscaster on a television news program. Evaluate the talk by answering the questions in the "Guidelines for Evaluating a Talk." How might the talk have been improved?

259

Special Populations

LD, ESL, NSD Students may have difficulty managing the language and evaluating a talk at the same time. Provide students with an evaluation form that they can use to check off points as they listen to a talk. They can add comments after the talk is completed, if they wish. You might use the following form.

	Excellent	Good	Needs Work
Posture			
Eye Contact			
Voice			
Gestures			
Visual Aids			

Comments:

Additional Resources

Skills Practice Book—page 99

Teacher's Resource Binder
Enrichment Activities—
pages 23, 39–52, 69

Part 5

Objectives

1. To effectively participate in a conversation
2. To effectively participate in a discussion
3. To effectively lead a discussion

Presenting the Lesson

◼ All Students

1. Read and discuss pages 260–261. Stress the importance of respecting other speakers. In both conversations and discussions, it is important to listen, think, and evaluate. Encourage students to be open-minded and receptive to new ideas. They should not choose a particular stand and stick to it regardless of points made by other speakers.

2. Make sure that students understand the role of the discussion leader. The leader does not do all the talking. He or she is responsible for keeping the discussion orderly and on the topic. The leader should make sure that everyone in the group has a chance to participate.

Ask students what they know from experience happens when a discussion group is lacking a good leader. Emphasize that this does not have to happen. A discussion can be constructive and purposeful if properly guided.

3. Assign and discuss Exercises A and B on page 262. Allow students sufficient time to prepare for the role playing situations in Exercise B.

▶ Basic Students

For Exercise B, pair each student with a more advanced student. Encourage each pair to first discuss the problem, and then decide on the best course of action. Remind students to refer back to the guidelines for participating in a discussion on page 261.

---

5 Conversations and Discussions

┌─ Focus ─────────────────────────────────
│   Conversations and discussions are good ways to share
│ ideas. You can learn how to prepare for a good conversa-
│ tion and discussion.
└──

▶ Comprehension

You have conversations and discussions every day, both in and out of school. You talk on the phone, answer questions, and share stories with friends and family. Most **conversations** are unplanned and unstructured.

You also have more formal, planned **discussions**. You can have a discussion to plan an event, solve a problem, or discuss a school subject. For example, a group of students might set a time for a meeting to plan a hallway mural or to decide the rules of a contest.

In both conversations and discussions, participants must be polite and respect other speakers. They must be ready to suggest ideas and solutions. In other words, to take part in any exchange of ideas, you must listen and think as well as speak.

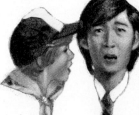

260

Follow these guidelines when you take part in a discussion. Most points also apply to a conversation.

> **Taking Part in a Discussion**
>
> 1. **Prepare for the discussion.** Gather information on the topic that others may not know.
> 2. **Listen carefully.** Respond to other participants. You may either support what is said or disagree.
> 3. **Add ideas.** Offer positive suggestions.
> 4. **Ask questions for these specific reasons:**
>   a. to clarify a point;
>   b. to get more information;
>   c. to move the discussion forward.
> 5. **Be polite.** Respect and accept ideas that are different from yours. When you disagree with a point, do not interrupt. Wait your turn and then explain why.
> 6. **Pay attention to the reactions of your listeners.**

Leading a Discussion

One person in a discussion group acts as the leader, or chairperson. He or she makes sure that the discussion is orderly. The leader keeps the participants on the subject and sees that everyone has a chance to contribute ideas.

> **Duties of a Discussion Leader**
>
> 1. **State the problem or ask another participant to do so.**
> 2. **Draw participants into the discussion through questions.** Make sure everyone takes turns talking. If a speaker strays from the subject, gently remind the group of the issue being discussed.
> 3. **Ask questions to clarify points.**
> 4. **Sum up what has been discussed or decided.**

 Advanced Students

Organize students into a group and have them discuss a problem or controversial issue at school. In this discussion, students must argue in favor of the side or point of view they do not really support. This exercise will force students to stop and think before they speak. It will also encourage them to use fact, rather than opinion, to support an issue.

Special Populations

LD As an alternative to Exercise B, have students participate in an actual discussion. They might plan an after-school softball game and picnic.

Reinforcement

Divide the class into small groups. Assign each group a topic of interest. Allow five to ten minutes for discussion. At the end of this time, have the group leader report back to the class on what the group has accomplished.

261

Exercises   Talking in Groups

▶ Analyzing

A. Imagine that your student council wants to organize a faculty baseball game to raise money for new bleachers. Read the following comments by a discussion leader. Which of these comments seem out of place? Which show the qualities of a good discussion leader? Be prepared to discuss your answers in class.

1. We are trying to decide if a faculty baseball game to raise money for new bleachers is a good idea. Are there any comments? good qualities
2. Can't you talk about anything except the Detroit Tigers? Let's get back to *our* game. out of place
3. Alex, we haven't heard from you. How would you organize the ticket sales? good qualities
4. That's an interesting idea, Sandy. What do you mean by winner's circle? good qualities
5. Did you see the football game last night? out of place

▶ Creative Application

B. Choose a partner. Act out a solution for each of the following problems.

1. One person has been talking for several minutes.
2. One person has listened carefully but has not talked.
3. You and another person speak at the same time.
4. Someone makes a statement you know to be incorrect.
5. Someone begins to change the topic before the original topic has been completed.

262

6 Critical Listening in Discussions

> **Focus**
>
> A speaker communicates in many ways. Learn to recognize and interpret a speaker's **nonverbal messages**, **motive**, **point of view**, and **bias**.

▶ Comprehension

You are always sending messages, even when you do not speak. **Nonverbal messages** include body movements such as a handshake or a smile.

Most communication is a mixture of verbal and nonverbal signals. A good speaker sends the same verbal and nonverbal signals. When you smile as you say, "I'm so glad to see you!" you are sending similar messages. A careful listener will notice if nonverbal signals do not match what is being said and think about what it means.

Good listeners also focus on the aims of a speaker. **Motive** is a person's reason for saying something. A speaker may want to inform, persuade, or contribute a new idea.

Point of view, including a person's likes and dislikes, may also affect the speaker's message. For example, two members of the school board discuss the purchase of new equipment for the football team. One enjoys football; the other does not. Each person's point of view will affect the decision.

Bias is an example of a strong point of view. A person may feel so strongly about an issue that he or she ignores important facts. The speaker presents only one side of the issue.

Exercise   Using Critical Listening Skills
▶ Analyzing/Creative Application

Pretend you are a reporter for your local newspaper. If possible, attend a PTA, city council, or school board meeting. You could also listen to a discussion on television. Write a brief report on the discussion. Give the speakers' motives, points of view, and any bias you can detect.

263

Part 6

Objective

To identify nonverbal messages, motive, point of view, and bias

Presenting the Lesson

All Students

1. Read and discuss page 263. Make sure that students understand nonverbal messages, motive, point of view, and bias. Provide additional examples of each, if necessary.

2. Stress the importance of being observant. Remind students that a speaker presents himself or herself as well as information. Tell students that with a little practice, they will become skilled at picking up nonverbal messages and will have a better idea of the speaker's total message.

3. Assign and discuss the exercise on page 263.

Basic Students

Have the students work on the exercise in groups of two or three. Help students to change their statements to fit each purpose.

Advanced Students

Have the students bring examples from a newspaper or magazine that demonstrate motive, point of view, and bias. Students might put these examples on a poster and display them around the classroom.

Special Populations

LD, ESL, NSD Identifying motive, point of view, and bias depends, to some extent, on recognizing subtleties in language. If students are having difficulty with this part, have them follow the directions under **Basic Students.**

Reinforcement

Have the students follow the directions for the exercise on page 263 using these subjects:

science fiction books   family vacations
bicycles   situation comedies

Part 7

Objective

To fairly evaluate a group discussion

Presenting the Lesson

 All Students

1. Read and discuss page 264. Assign students to play the parts in the sample discussion. Before reading, remind students of the guidelines for good discussion. Ask them to watch for speakers who do and those who do not follow these guidelines.

2. Assign and discuss the exercise on page 265.

 Basic Students

Do the exercise as a group activity. Make sure that students understand why Wendy is a good discussion leader and why Matt is not.

 Advanced Students

Some advanced students have a tendency to dominate a discussion. They are uncomfortable if there is a pause in the discussion. Because they are very capable, these students jump in to fill the void. Emphasize that a lull in the discussion is acceptable. Other students might need a little more time to organize their thoughts. It is important that everyone has a chance to participate.

Special Populations

LD Some students may have difficulty with the analytical skills required in this lesson. Do the exercise orally, helping them along as necessary.

Reinforcement

Have students continue the discussions they began for **Reinforcement** in part 5. Remind students to follow the guidelines for good discussion. They should work until they find a solution that is acceptable to the entire group.

---

7 Evaluating Group Discussions

> **Focus**
>
> A good discussion depends on the skill of the participants and the leader.

▶ Comprehension

Students at McDowell School are not using the school library often enough. The student council discusses the problem. Present are Wendy, Salina, Matt, Lisa, Paul, and Fred. You learned about the guidelines for discussion in part 5. Keep those guidelines in mind as you read this discussion.

WENDY: Mrs. García, the new librarian, would like your ideas about ways she can encourage library use. Are there any suggestions?

SALINA: I think that the library should be open later. Now, kids have to go to the public library where they can stay . . .

MATT: Ha! Who wants to hang around after school?

SALINA: Not you, that's for sure!

WENDY: Matt, Salina, we all have different ideas about ways to spend after-school time. Let's get back on the track. Salina has a good idea—lengthening library hours. Paul, have you come up with any ideas since we talked last?

PAUL: Many students don't know their way around the school library. Could Mrs. García arrange for small groups to visit the library?

LISA: Mrs. García might be willing, but what about the teachers? Would they let groups of students leave their classes?

MATT: Nah, teachers never let students out.

WENDY: Lisa, I think that's a good question. I'll ask Mr. Rehage today. We have to stop now. We do have two good ideas here: lengthening the library's hours and arranging library tours. Tomorrow, let's talk about the kinds of books you think should be added to the library's collection.

264

Exercise   Evaluating a Discussion

▶ Analyzing/Evaluating

Look over the guidelines for discussion in part 5. Number your paper from 1 to 8. Then, answer the following questions about the sample discussion. See answers in margin.

1. How does Wendy get the discussion off to a good start?
2. Which three comments do not follow the guidelines? Explain your answer.
3. Why is Salina's first comment important?
4. How could Wendy encourage Fred to participate?
5. Which participant most needs to improve his or her discussion skills? Why?
6. Which participant keeps the discussion moving?
7. How does Wendy end the discussion?
8. How should Wendy open the next discussion of this same subject?

265

Additional Resources

Skills Practice Book—page 100

Teacher's Resource Binder
Enrichment Activities—
pages 39–52

Using English in Health

Use this activity to demonstrate how discussion skills can be used to solve problems in many areas, both in and out of school.

The issue raised in this exercise is an important one. Students who have these concerns often do not know where to turn. If the school does have support groups, this discussion will point them out. If the school does not have such groups, the discussion becomes a constructive vehicle for identifying needs and possible ways to meet those needs.

Using English in ▶ Health

▶ Comprehension

You have just learned a very valuable skill—how to take part in and lead a group discussion. You will be able to use this skill both in and out of school.

Health is a topic that comes up in many classes. It is discussed in science, in gym, and in health class itself. It is a frequent topic of newspaper and magazine articles.

There are two areas of health that are often discussed: physical health and mental or emotional health. Physical health discussions may focus on topics such as illness, eating right, and exercise. Emotional health topics may include feeling good about yourself, your role as a family member, or how you relate to friends.

Support groups are often formed to help people deal with emotional health concerns. Everyone in the group takes part. Group members tell how they have handled a situation. They also listen to the experiences of others. By sharing ideas, the members support and help each other.

Exercise   Participating in a Group Discussion

▶ Creative Application/Critical Reasoning

Meet with three or four other students. Choose a discussion leader. Discuss what kinds of help-groups might be formed in your school. Also discuss the following questions.

1. What are some of the special needs of the students?
2. What topics are of special concern?
3. What would be the best way to start a help-group?
4. What teacher or administrator might help organize and sponsor a help-group?
5. What would be the best time and place to meet?
6. What might be accomplished by forming a group?

266

Chapter 14 Review

▶ Analyzing

A. Giving Talks and Participating in Group Discussions

Read the following statements. Number your paper from 1 to 10. If the statement is correct, write *True* on your paper. If it is incorrect, write *False*. Be ready to explain what is wrong with the statement.

1. Prepare a talk by using the steps in the process of writing. True

2. When you prepare a talk, you should use note cards with your entire speech written out. False. Write only a fact or two on each card.

3. State all of your information in the same tone of voice when you give a talk. False. Variety adds interest and emphasis.

4. When you give a talk, you should look at your notes the entire time so you do not forget anything. False. Look at your listeners.

5. When giving a talk, you should use natural gestures and expressions. True

6. A good listener should try to pick out the main ideas of the talk. True

7. You should judge the content and presentation. True

8. You should not gather extra information before a group discussion. This will give you an unfair advantage over other group members. False. You should be prepared to contribute ideas others haven't thought of.

9. When you disagree with someone in a group discussion, keep your opinion to yourself. False. Give your opinion, but be polite.

10. The leader of a discussion should always keep the discussion on the topic. True

▶ Creative Application

B. Giving a Talk
Choose one of the following topics. Prepare, practice, and present a one- to two-minute talk on this topic. Use the guidelines in this chapter to help you with each step.

1. Something new at school
2. A hobby
3. Your pet
4. Something funny that happened to you
5. An important game that you participated in

Chapter Review

This review allows teachers to evaluate student understanding of the concepts presented in this chapter.

Additional Resources

Test Booklet
Mastery Test—pages 87–90

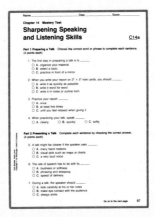

Chapter 15

Chapter Objectives

1. To recognize and correct run-on and stringy sentences

2. To join two related sentences using *and, but,* or *or*

3. To combine two sentences by joining related sentence parts

4. To combine sentences by adding a word from one sentence to another

5. To combine sentences by adding a group of words from one sentence to another

Motivating the Students

1. Write the following paragraphs on the board. Ask students to point out what is wrong with these paragraphs.

Kino lived on a farm that lay on the side of a mountain in Japan, the mountain rose so steeply out of the ocean that there was only a strip of sandy shore at its foot and upon this strip was a small fishing village where Kino's father sold his vegetables and rice and bought fish.

Kino often looked down upon the thatched roofs of the village and the village houses faced one another, and those which stood beside the sea did not have windows toward it and since Kino enjoyed looking at the waves, he often wondered why the village people did not, but he never knew until he came to know Jiya, whose father was a fisherman. Jiya's house did not have a window toward the sea either.

2. Ask students why these paragraphs are confusing. Ask for suggestions on how to improve them. Make corrections on the board according to students' suggestions. Then write the original paragraphs on the board. (See below.) Tell students that they are by the author Pearl S. Buck who is known for her simple and straightforward writing style. Tell students that in this chapter they will learn to improve their own writing by making it clear, direct, and easy to understand. They will learn to avoid the kinds of problems that appear in the first paragraphs on the board.

from "The Big Wave"

Kino lived on a farm that lay on the side of a mountain in Japan. The mountain rose so steeply out of the ocean that there was only a strip of sandy shore at its foot. Upon this strip was a small fishing village where Kino's father sold his vegetables and rice and bought fish.

Kino often looked down upon the thatched roofs of the village. The village houses faced one another, and those which stood beside the sea did not have windows toward it. Since Kino enjoyed looking at the waves, he often wondered why the village people did not, but he never knew until he came to know Jiya, whose father was a fisherman. Jiya's house did not have a window toward the sea either.

Read and discuss the introduction on page 269. Remind students that revision is part of the process of writing. In this chapter students will learn how to improve their writing by revising and combining sentences.

Chapter 15

Revising and Combining Sentences

A professional photographer arranges a scene carefully. The photographer may adjust the lighting or change the position of subjects. If one element is wrong, the picture will not be good.

Writers must work just as carefully to get the effects they want. Each sentence must be clear and well written. Then the reader understands exactly what the writer means.

This chapter will show you how to improve your writing by improving your sentences. You will see how to combine related ideas within a sentence. You will also learn to revise sentences so that your writing is clear and flows smoothly.

269

Special Populations

LD Conceptually disabled students who have difficulty classifying and categorizing may have problems recognizing related thoughts in the sentence combining activities. Be sure that students understand the single thoughts that make up each sentence before they combine sentences. Work through several sentences from each exercise with students.

ESL Some students may have difficulty with the longer sentences in this chapter, or be confused by the changing sentence patterns resulting from sentence combining. Make sure students understand the rules for sentence combining before they do the exercises.

NSD Some students may be accustomed to using stringy sentences in speaking. Stress the importance of using standard English in writing.

Related Chapters

You may wish to refer to related material in other chapters as you teach the following concepts:

1. Sentence structure, Chapter 2, "Writing and Understanding Sentences," page 17

2. Using modifiers to extend a sentence, Chapter 16, "Adjectives for Creative Expression," page 283, and Chapter 17, "Adverbs for Clear Description," page 301

3. Using conjunctions, Chapter 20, "Using Prepositions and Conjunctions," page 349

Additional Resources

Skills Practice Book—pages 101–108

Test Booklet—pages 91–94
   Pretest—pages 91–92
   Mastery Test—pages 93–94

Teacher's Resource Binder
   Reinforcement Activities—
      pages 73–79
   Enrichment Activities—
      pages 39–52, 70
   Process of Writing Transparencies
   Ideas for Creative Teaching

Week 21

Chapter Management Guidelines   This chart may be used to help structure daily lesson plans.

Day 1	Day 2	Day 3	Day 4	Day 5
Chapter 15 Opener, p. 269; Part 1, "Avoiding Run-on and Stringy Sentences," pp. 270–271	Part 2, "Combining Sentences and Sentence Parts," pp. 272–273	Part 3, "Combining Sentences by Adding Words," pp. 274–276	Part 4, "Combining Sentences by Adding Groups of Words," pp. 277–278	Chapter Review and selected end-of-chapter activities

Part 1

Objective

To recognize and correct run-on and stringy sentences

Presenting the Lesson

All Students

1. Read and discuss pages 270–271.

2. Review the concept of a good sentence. A good sentence expresses a complete idea. Point out that a run-on sentence is a jumble of many ideas. To avoid run-ons, students should think of each idea separately, separating the ideas with appropriate end punctuation.

3. Make sure that students understand the difference between run-on and stringy sentences. A run-on sentence is two or more complete ideas that are not separated by end punctuation or capital letters. A stringy sentence is several ideas joined by conjunctions, usually *and*.

4. Do Exercise A on page 271 orally. In addition to identifying the run-on and stringy sentences, ask the students to correct them.

5. Assign and discuss Exercise B on page 271.

6. Use Exercise A on page 279 for additional practice if needed.

Basic Students

When you work on Exercise A on page 271 with the students, have them identify the simple subject and verb of each sentence. Make sure they can recognize that run-on sentences and stringy sentences have more than one simple subject and verb.

Advanced Students

When discussing page 270, point out that a run-on sentence combines sentences that are not related and, therefore, must be rewritten separately. Explain that if a sentence combines two related ideas without a conjunction to join them, it may be corrected simply by adding the appropriate conjunction.

Four of the following sentence groups should be combined into one sentence using a conjunction to connect them

1 Avoiding Run-on and Stringy Sentences

> **Focus**
>
> Run-on and stringy sentences combine ideas incorrectly.

▶ **Comprehension**

A sentence is a group of words that expresses a complete thought. If you put too many thoughts into a sentence, you have written a **run-on sentence** or a **stringy sentence.**

Avoiding Run-on Sentences

Read this group of words.

Alex is washing the dishes *it is his turn to clean the kitchen.*

Notice that the example contains two complete thoughts. There is no period at the end of the first idea. There is no capital letter to mark the beginning of the second idea. The two ideas are run together. The example is a **run-on sentence**. It should be written as two separate sentences.

Alex is washing the dishes. It is his turn to clean the kitchen.

Avoiding Stringy Sentences

Read this sentence.

We read about planets and the next day we watched a movie about Venus and Mars and then we went to the planetarium.

This sentence strings too many ideas together with the word *and*. This is a **stringy sentence**. Each complete thought in a stringy sentence should be written in a separate sentence.

We read about planets. The next day we watched a movie about Venus and Mars. Then we went to the planetarium.

270

(sentences 1, 3, 4, and 5). The others are run-on sentences and should be separated (sentences 2 and 6). Direct the students to rewrite all the sentences correctly.

1. I got a new haircut my mother doesn't like it.
2. The new student in our class is the team's captain he's from New Jersey.
3. There's a new restaurant in our town they have the best ribs I've ever tasted.
4. People visiting Mackinac Island must walk they may ride a bike.
5. The girls gathered around the campfire they told ghost stories.
6. The Camerons toured the Grand Canyon they were on their way to Phoenix.

Notice that *and* correctly joins two sentence parts that are alike, *Venus* and *Mars*. Sometimes, it is correct to put together sentences and sentence parts with *and*. You will learn how to do this in part 2.

Exercises   Finding and Correcting Run-on and Stringy Sentences

▶ Classifying

A. Number your paper from 1 to 10. Label each sentence as a *Run-on Sentence*, a *Stringy Sentence*, or *Correct*.

1. Beth found her library book and she finished reading the story and then she went to bed.   Stringy
2. Chris uncovered the treasure he jumped for joy.   Run-on
3. Alan and Zoe learned how to cast a fly rod today.   Correct
4. Doug ate a large pizza for lunch he was still hungry.   Run-on
5. Some herb tea contains cinnamon and nutmeg.   Correct
6. We made popcorn and told ghost stories.   Correct
7. Sunday, we played soccer my team won.   Run-on
8. The wind howled outside and an owl hooted in the distance and the boards in the old house creaked.   Stringy
9. Jake thought the animal was an alpaca it was a llama.   Run-on
10. Emma uses a computer and she wrote a program to draw pictures and she prints them in color.   Stringy

▶ Structured Application

B. Rewrite these run-on and stringy sentences as separate sentences. Each sentence should contain only one complete thought.
See answers at bottom of page

1. The doorbell rang Mr. Montrose was at the door.
2. I had a dream about *Alice in Wonderland* and I thought I was Alice and I chased the White Rabbit.
3. Last January was the coldest month of the year there were twenty-two days of below-zero weather.
4. The koala is not a bear it is a marsupial.
5. Blue smoke rose from the chimney and light glowed from the windows and we could smell supper cooking.

271

Additional Resources

Skills Practice Book—page 101
Teacher's Resource Binder
    Reinforcement Activities—
    pages 73–74

Special Populations

LD Before they do the exercise students should review the rules for capitalization at the beginning of a sentence and end punctuation.

Reinforcement

1. Have students follow the directions for Exercise B on page 271 using these sentences:
  1. The roof leaked. buckets were placed around the cabin to catch the dripping water.
  2. Marla chose a date for her party. and she wrote the invitations. and then she bought the party favors.
  3. Jason dunked the basketball. he scored the winning goal.
  4. It snowed all night. snowdrifts blocked the driveway.
  5. Ako is visiting from Japan. and she attends the American school on weekdays. and she goes to a Japanese school on Saturdays.

2. Have the students rewrite the following paragraph, breaking it into shorter sentences.

  This book was written by Johanna Spyri. it is about a girl named Heidi and her grandfather. Heidi is happy living in the Alps with her grandfather. then she has to go to the city. she has many difficulties there, but finally returns to her mountain home.

Enrichment

For enrichment activities, see the Unit Projects in the Teacher Notes on page 249. One or more of these projects have special activities for gifted and talented students.

Exercise B
1. The doorbell rang. Mr. Montrose was at the door.
2. I had a dream about *Alice in Wonderland*. I thought I was Alice. I chased the White Rabbit.
3. Last January was the coldest month of the year. There were twenty-two days of below-zero weather.
4. The koala is not a bear. It is a marsupial.
5. Blue smoke rose from the chimney. Light glowed from the windows. We could smell supper cooking.

Part 2

Objectives

1. To join two related sentences using *and*, *but*, or *or*
2. To combine two sentences by joining related sentence parts

Presenting the Lesson

 All Students

1. Read **Joining Complete Sentences** on page 272. Provide additional pairs of sentences and have the students choose appropriate conjunctions to join each pair. Then have volunteers rewrite each pair of sentences as a single sentence. You might use the following sentences:

The basketball team was short.
They were fast.

Christa takes piano lessons.
She plays beautifully.

For exercise we take long walks.
We ride our bicycles.

Remind students to use a comma before the conjunction when joining complete sentences.

2. Assign and discuss Exercise A on page 273.

3. Read and discuss **Joining Sentence Parts** on pages 272–273. Have students practice joining sentence parts using these sentences.

Kevin reads science fiction.
Kevin reads mysteries.

Should I write in ink?
Should I write in pencil?

Joe can speak French.
He can not speak Italian.

4. Assign and discuss Exercise B on page 273.

5. Use Exercise B on page 279 for additional practice if needed.

 Basic Students

Work the first few sentences in each exercise orally with students. Have them work in pairs to complete the remaining sentences in each exercise.

 Advanced Students

Have the students join these sentences. Tell them to use their own judgment about the best way to combine them.

---

2 Combining Sentences and Sentence Parts

> ― *Focus* ―
>
> You can join sentences and sentence parts with **conjunctions**. The words *and*, *but*, and *or* are conjunctions.

▶ Comprehension

Sometimes you will want to join ideas that are related. Conjunctions join related sentences and sentence parts.

Joining Complete Sentences

Two sentences may often contain ideas that are alike. These related sentences can be joined by a comma and the word *and*.

Arthur wrote the story. Anna drew the illustrations.
Arthur wrote the story, **and** Anna drew the illustrations.

Sometimes two sentences are on the same topic but contain ideas that are different. These sentences can be joined by a comma and the word *but*.

The pea soup looked terrible. It tasted delicious.
The pea soup looked terrible, **but** it tasted delicious.

Two related sentences can show a choice between ideas. These sentences can be joined by a comma and the word *or*.

Is the tire inflated? Does it need air?
Is the tire inflated, **or** does it need air?

Joining Sentence Parts

Sometimes, ideas in two sentences are so closely related that words are repeated. By combining such sentences, the repeated words can be left out.

272

Exercise A
1. Leroy is afraid, but he won't admit it.
2. Will Kathy help us, or does she have other work to do?
3. Thunder rumbled in the distance, but the sun was shining here.
4. Jesse wanted to buy the album, but he didn't have enough money.
5. Michael planted the rosebushes, and Becky watered each one.

Exercise B
1. Adam and Meg watched the eclipse.
2. Jane can leave on Friday or Saturday.
3. The stove is old but reliable.
4. Steve nodded to the catcher and pitched the ball.
5. We carried sleeping bags and cooking utensils.

And is used to join sentence parts that show ideas are alike.

> Brian plays the drums. *Brian plays* the guitar.
> Brian plays the drums **and** the guitar.

When sentences contain ideas that are different, the related parts can usually be joined by *but*.

> Chris will write the music. *He will* not *write* the words.
> Chris will write the music **but** not the words.

Sentence parts that show a choice between ideas can usually be joined by *or*.

> Should Bonnie paint the dresser? *Should she* varnish it?
> Should Bonnie paint the dresser **or** varnish it?

Exercises   Combining Sentences

▶ **Analyzing/Structured Application**

A. Join each pair of sentences. Follow the directions in parentheses. See answers at bottom of page 272.

1. Leroy is afraid. He won't admit it. (Join with **, but.**)
2. Will Kathy help us? Does she have other work to do? (Join with **, or.**)
3. Thunder rumbled in the distance. The sun was shining here. (Join with **, but.**)
4. Jesse wanted to buy the album. He didn't have enough money. (Join with **, but.**)
5. Michael planted the rosebushes. Becky watered each one. (Join with **, and.**)

B. Join the related parts of the sentences. Leave out words in italics. See answers at bottom of page 272.

1. Adam watched the eclipse. Meg *watched the eclipse.*
2. Jane can leave on Friday. *She can leave on* Saturday.
3. The stove is old. *It is* reliable.
4. Steve nodded to the catcher. *He* pitched the ball.
5. We carried sleeping bags. *We carried* cooking utensils.

273

Additional Resources

Skills Practice Book—page 102
Teacher's Resource Binder
Reinforcement Activities—
pages 75–76

1. Carmen baked the cake, ,and ,Luis frosted it.
2. Will John be at the dance, ,or ,Does he have to work?
3. It was 20° below zero, ,but ,we were warm inside.
4. Clark is studying algebra, and ,chemistry. ,or
5. Would you prefer spaghetti? ,lasagne? ,or

Reinforcement

1. Have the students follow the directions for Exercise A on page 273 using these sentences.

1. Gary cleared the dishes off the table, ,and Carolyn washed and dried them. (Join with **,and.**)
2. Carlos finished his math assignment, He didn't have time for his science project. ,but (Join with **,but.**)
3. We arrived at the movie early, The seats were all taken. (Join with **,but.**) ,but
4. The temperature fell below freezing, Ice formed on the roads. (Join with **,and.**) ,and
5. Did Pamela save any money? Did she spend it all on her trip? (Join with **,or.**) ,or

2. Have the students follow the directions for the Exercise B on page 273, using these sentences and leaving out the underlined words.

1. My mother planted tomatoes, *She planted* peppers. (Join with **and.**) and
2. Oranges ,and bananas are fruit. Bananas ~~are~~ fruit. (Join with **and.**)
3. We'll have the picnic at the park, *We'll have it* at the beach. (Join with **or.**) or
4. The trip to the mountains was scenic. *The trip was* too long. (Join with **but.**) but
5. Will Mr. Martin arrive tonight? ~~Will he~~ arrive in the morning? (Join with **or.**) or

Enrichment

Provide the students with a variety of printed material, including books, magazines, and newspapers. Have them locate sentences in which two complete ideas have been combined by using ,and, but, or ,or.

Part 3

Objective

To combine sentences by adding a word from one sentence to another

Presenting the Lesson

 All Students

1. Read and discuss part 3 on pages 274–275. Have the students read the example sentences and explain why the first sentence in each pair is more important than the second one. Note how an idea from the main-idea sentence is repeated in the words in italics in the second sentence, even though the words may differ from those of the main-idea sentence. Explain that these words can, therefore, be eliminated. Ask the students to tell which details were added to the main-idea sentence when the sentences in each example were combined.

2. Emphasize the importance of using a dictionary to check the spelling of a word when its form is changed. Explain that when a word changes form according to regular spelling rules, the new form will not be listed in the dictionary (ie., *walk* to *walked*). However, when a change does not follow the rules, the new form will be listed after the entry word. Have the students look up *easy* in the dictionary. Ask them how the suffix *-ly* is added to the word. Also refer students to the "Guide to Spelling" in the **Power Handbook** for rules on spelling changes resulting from the addition of a suffix to a root word.

3. Assign and discuss Exercises A and B on pages 275–276.

4. Use Exercise C on page 280 for additional practice if needed.

 Basic Students

Do Exercise A orally. Then allow the students to work in pairs to complete Exercise B. Review the exercises after students have completed the work. Make sure they understand why sentences are combined in a particular way.

◆ **Advanced Students**

Have the students write an original sentence to be added to each group in Exercise A. On their papers, they should

---

3 Combining Sentences by Adding Words

> ── Focus ──
> You can combine two related sentences by adding a word from the second sentence to the first sentence.

▶ Comprehension

Sometimes the main ideas of two sentences work together, but one idea is more important than the other. There may be only one word in the second sentence that is really important. Read this example.

Sam dropped the pan. *The pan was* hot.

You can add the important word, *hot*, to the first sentence. Drop the rest of the second sentence. The new sentence is a shorter, better way of presenting the idea. Notice that the words in italics were left out.

Sam dropped the **hot** pan.

You can sometimes combine several sentences this way. Here are some examples.

The bus was full of commuters. *The bus was* creaky. *The commuters were* tired.
The **creaky** bus was full of **tired** commuters.

The motorboat rocked on the water. *The motorboat was* sleek. *The water was* choppy.
The **sleek** motorboat rocked on the **choppy** water.

Sometimes you will have to use a comma when you add more than one word to a sentence. Notice where the comma is added when the following sentences are combined.

Mrs. Gómez stroked the kitten. *The kitten was* frightened. *The kitten was* shivering.
Mrs. Gómez stroked the **frightened, shivering** kitten.

Adding Words That Change

Sometimes you must change the form of the word before you can add it to another sentence. You may have to add -*y*.

> Please repair those faucets. *They* leak.
> Please repair those **leaky** faucets.

Sometimes you will have to add -*ing* or -*ed*.

> I like to hear the thunder. *It crashes.*
> I like to hear **crashing** thunder.

> Vera replaced the plate. *It had a* crack.
> Vera replaced the **cracked** plate.

Sometimes you will have to add -*ly*.

> We painted the porch furniture. *We were* careful.
> We **carefully** painted the porch furniture.

Sometimes the word ending in -*ly* can go in more than one place in the sentence.

> We painted the porch furniture **carefully**.

When you make changes in the form of a word, check the dictionary to see that you have spelled the word correctly.

Exercises Combining Sentences by Adding Words

▶ Analyzing/Structured Application

A. Combine each pair of sentences into one sentence. Follow instructions in the parentheses. Leave out words in italics. See answers in margin.

1. The watch ran on a battery. *The battery was* tiny.
2. Around the turn came the horses. *They* galloped. (End the important word with -*ing*.)

275

write first the original sentence for each group, and then the combined sentence, with all three sentences joined. For item 1, a student might add the sentence *The watch was gold.* The combined sentence would read, *The gold watch ran on a tiny battery.*

Special Populations

LD, ESL, NSD Students should review the correct placement of adjectives and adverbs in sentences before they work the exercises. Remind students that an adjective that follows a linking verb can also be used before a noun. For example, *The battery was tiny* becomes *the tiny battery*.

Reinforcement

1. Have the students combine each pair of sentences into one sentence. Leave out unnecessary or repeated words.

1. Nathan received a~homemade mobile for his birthday. The mobile was homemade.
2. The ~healthy plants grew rapidly. The plants were healthy.
3. The hot travelers welcomed the~cool, gentle breeze. The breeze was cool. The breeze was gentle.
4. Kathryn put on her faded blue jeans. She did it quickly. The jeans were faded.
5. The galloping horse jumped over the wooden fence. The horse was galloping. The fence was wooden.

2. Have the students follow the directions for Exercise B on page 276, using these sentences.

1. Throw out that moldy piece of bread. It has mold on it.
2. The barking dog raced after the thief. The dog barked.
3. The clerk counted all the change correctly. She was correct.
4. We stood in the crowded lobby of the auditorium. There was a crowd in it.
5. The slow truck started up the steep hill. The truck was slow.

Enrichment

Have the students rewrite this paragraph combining sentences by adding words to make the paragraph sound smoother. Answers will vary.

Our trip to the beach was perfect. The sand glistened in the sun. The sand was hot. The sand was white. The ocean gently lapped the shore. The ocean was blue-green. Seagulls circled overhead. The seagulls were noisy. Pelicans dove into the water to catch their dinner. The pelicans were swift. What a wonderful place to spend the day!

Have students share their paragraphs. Point out how sentences can be combined in many different ways.

Exercise A
1. The watch ran on a tiny battery.
2. Around the turn came the galloping horses.
3. The frisky puppy scampered along the deserted beach.
4. The mare nuzzled the small, wobbly colt.
5. Please oil those squeaky hinges.
6. Deanna cautiously opened the door.
7. The child held tightly to the worn, tattered bear.
8. I bandaged my brother's sprained ankle.

Exercise B
1. One small boy sat in the huge waiting room.
2. Barbara skated gracefully over the smooth ice.
3. Danielle slipped silently into the empty hall.
4. The clever raccoons were able to open the covered garbage cans.
5. The hungry campers ate the crusty wheat bread.
6. The clown skillfully put on the sticky makeup.
7. The rusty lock suddenly snapped open.
8. The fire spread quickly to the abandoned warehouse.
9. Sophie carefully cut the red silk fabric.
10. Ken used green markers to make the pep rally signs.

---

3. The puppy scampered along the beach. *The puppy was* frisky. *The beach was* deserted.
4. The mare nuzzled the colt. *The colt was* small. *The colt was* wobbly. (Use a comma.)
5. Please oil those hinges. *They* squeak. (End the important word with *-y*.)
6. Deanna opened the door. *She opened it* cautiously.
7. The child held tightly to the bear. *The bear was* worn. *The bear was* tattered. (Use a comma.)
8. I bandaged my brother's ankle. *It was* sprained.

▶ Analyzing/Structured Application

B. Combine the sentences in each group. Add the important words from the second and third sentences to the first. You may have to change the endings of some words. See answers in margin.

1. One boy sat in the waiting room. The boy was small. The waiting room was huge.
2. Barbara skated over the ice. The ice was smooth. She was graceful.
3. Danielle slipped into the hall. She slipped silently. The hall was empty.
4. The raccoons were able to open the garbage cans. The raccoons were clever. The garbage cans were covered.
5. The campers ate the bread. The bread was crusty. The campers were hungry.
6. The clown put on the makeup. The clown put it on skillfully. The makeup was sticky.
7. The lock snapped open. The lock had rust on it. It snapped suddenly.
8. The fire spread to the warehouse. The warehouse was abandoned. The fire spread quickly.
9. Sophie cut the fabric. The fabric was red silk. Sophie cut it carefully.
10. Ken used markers to make the signs. The markers were green. The signs were for the pep rally.

276

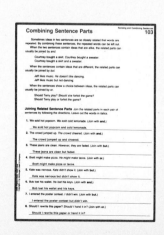

Additional Resources

Skills Practice Book—
pages 103–104

Teacher's Resource Binder
Reinforcement Activities—
pages 77–78

4 Combining Sentences by Adding Groups of Words

> **Focus**
>
> One sentence may contain a group of words that can be added to another sentence.

▶ Comprehension

Sometimes a group of words in one sentence can add important information to another sentence. The two sentences may be combined. Here is an example.

> The people tossed coins. *They tossed them* into the fountain.
> The people tossed coins **into the fountain**.

Sometimes the group of words in the second sentence tells about a person or a thing in the first sentence. These words should be added near the name of that person or thing in the first sentence.

> The bruise was painful. *It was* on my shoulder.
> The bruise **on my shoulder** was painful.

> The boy has practiced for weeks. *The boy is* playing the violin now.
> The boy **playing the violin now** has practiced for weeks.

When the group of words describes an action, place the group of words near the words that tell the action.

> My dog was waiting. *She was* at the end of the driveway.
> My dog was waiting **at the end of the driveway**.

Sometimes the group of words may be put in more than one place in a sentence.

> Our electricity went off **at ten o'clock**.
> **At ten o'clock**, our electricity went off.

277

Part 4

Objective

To combine sentences by adding a group of words from one sentence to another

Presenting the Lesson

All Students

1. Read and discuss pages 277–278. Have the students explain how the second sentence in each example is related to the first. Point out that the second sentence adds information to the first sentence. By changing some words and combining the sentences, repetition is avoided. However, the words in the second sentence must be placed near the person or thing in the first sentence that they tell about. Otherwise the meaning of the sentence may be unclear.

> I saw a monkey hanging from a tree. (meaning clear)
> Hanging from a tree, I saw a monkey. (meaning unclear)

2. Assign and discuss Exercises A and B on page 278.

3. Use Exercise D on page 280 for additional practice if needed.

Basic Students

Do the first few sentences of Exercise A orally. Have students complete the exercise on their own. Then read through the sentences in Exercise B. Have the students identify the main-idea sentence in each pair. Then, have them select the words that should be added to each main-idea sentence. Finally, have the students write out the combined sentences. Discuss their completed work.

Advanced Students

For Exercise A on page 278, ask the students to write a third sentence for each pair. Direct them to join the original sentence to the combined sentence using any of the techniques described in this chapter.

Special Populations

LD, NSD Students may not understand why some phrases may be added to only one spot in a sentence. Using the example sentences at the top of page 278, point out the meaning that results from incorrectly placed phrases. Stress the importance of clear writing and speaking so that the correct message is understood.

ESL Students may be confused by the clauses and verbal phrases resulting from sentence combining. Point out the verbs in the example sentences and show how the main verb in a simple sentence may become a verbal or part of a clause in the combined sentence.

Reinforcement

1. Have the students follow the directions for Exercise A on page 278 using these sentences and leaving out the words in italics:

1. She wore a diamond ring. *The ring was* on her finger.
2. For this assignment, follow the directions. *The directions are* at the top of the page.
3. The president gave a speech to the class. *The speech was* about choosing careers.
4. Mr. Clark left his wallet. *It was* lying on the table.
5. The bookstore was having a huge sale. *The bookstore is located* on Main Street.

2. Have the students follow the directions for Exercise B on page 278 using these sentences:

1. That book was very interesting. It was about choosing careers.
2. The girl is staying with us over the holidays. She is from Brazil.
3. Mark went to the museum. He went after he ate lunch.
4. Read the words at the bottom of the page. The words are printed in italics.
5. Mrs. Farrell planted petunias last summer. She planted them along her sidewalk.

Exercise A
1. The arrow in the target is Matt's.
2. Jane spotted a wallet lying under the car.
3. The band was playing a march.
4. All the wood by the fireplace is cut.
5. The snow blocking our door was two feet deep.

Exercise B
1. Those footprints in the mud are important clues!
2. There is a new box of cereal in the cabinet.
3. The wind blew the dust into my eyes.
4. Jamie hit a long fly deep into center field.
5. The design on the new tray was hand-painted.
6. My favorite was the fish cooked on the grill.
7. Uncle Jake phoned before we left.
8. Our group collected the syrup from maple trees.

Sometimes, however, words can be added to only one place to make a sensible sentence. Study these sentences.

> Mom asked me to wash the dog *three times today*. (Did she want you to give the dog three baths?)
>
> As I looked, I saw a plane fly *out the window*. (Did the plane crash through the window?)

After you combine two sentences, always read the new sentence carefully. Be sure it is clear and makes sense.

Exercises   Adding Groups of Words

▶ Analyzing/Structured Application

A. Combine the sentences in each pair. Add a group of words from the second sentence to the first sentence. Leave out the words in italics. Write the new sentence on your paper.   See answers in margin.

1. The arrow is Matt's. *The arrow is* in the target.
2. Jane spotted a wallet. *It was* lying under the car.
3. The band was playing. *It was playing* a march.
4. All the wood is cut. *It is* by the fireplace.
5. The snow was two feet deep. *It was* blocking our door.

B. Combine each pair of sentences. Add the important words from the second sentence to the first sentence.   See answers in margin.

1. Those footprints are important clues! The footprints are in the mud.
2. There is a new box of cereal. It is in the cabinet.
3. The wind blew the dust. It blew into my eyes.
4. Jamie hit a long fly. It went deep into center field.
5. The design was hand-painted. The design was on the new tray.
6. My favorite was the fish. It was cooked on the grill.
7. Uncle Jack phoned. He phoned before we left.
8. Our group collected the syrup. The syrup was from maple trees.

278

Additional Resources

Skills Practice Book—page 105
Teacher's Resource Binder
   Reinforcement Activities—
      page 79
   Enrichment Activities—
      page 70

Combining Sentences by Adding Groups of Words

Exercises for Mastery   Chapter 15

Revising and Combining Sentences

▶ Analyzing/Structured Application

A. Avoiding Run-on and Stringy Sentences Rewrite all run-on or stringy sentences. If the sentence is correct, write *Correct*.
See answers in margin. (Use after page 271.)

1. My sister is acting in the play I am working on the scenery.
2. I ordered a salad and I split a sandwich with Sam and I forgot to bring home a hamburger for Billy.
3. The wheat is tall and ripe.
4. The Good Witch waved her wand then Dorothy wore the ruby slippers.
5. She built the bookcase and she cleaned up the workshop and then she bought some paint.
6. Mr. Cory dug worms and put them in his bait box.
7. Explain the directions to Tony and Lisa they will understand.
8. Emma takes flute lessons Kate is Emma's teacher.

B. Joining Sentences and Sentence Parts Combine each pair of sentences. Follow the directions in the parentheses. Leave out words in italics.   See answers in margin. (Use after page 273.)

1. Arlene wore her hair long last winter. Now it is cut short. (Join sentences with **, but**.)
2. Ramona measured three boards. *Ramona* cut *three boards*. (Join sentence parts with **and**.)
3. Ted and Janet can hurry to catch the noon train. They can wait for the one o'clock bus. (Join sentences with **, or**.)
4. Steve collects rare postage stamps. Ivy *collects rare postage stamps*. (Join sentence parts with **and**.)
5. Sharon will dive for the shells. Tyrone will dive for the shells. (Join sentence parts with **or**.)

279

Exercises for Mastery

These **Exercises for Mastery** may be used for additional practice of the concepts presented in this section. Each exercise focuses on a single concept and should be used after the page number indicated in parentheses.

Exercise A
1. My sister is acting in the play. I am working on the scenery.
2. I ordered a salad. I split a sandwich with Sam. I forgot to bring home a hamburger for Billy.
3. Correct
4. The Good Witch waved her wand. Then Dorothy wore the ruby slippers.
5. She built the bookcase. She cleaned up the workshop. Then she bought some paint.
6. Correct
7. Explain the directions to Tony and Lisa. They will understand.
8. Emma takes flute lessons. Kate is Emma's teacher.

Exercise B
1. Arlene wore her hair long last winter, but now it is cut short.
2. Ramona measured and cut three boards.
3. Ted and Janet can hurry to catch the noon train, or they can wait for the one o'clock bus.
4. Steve and Ivy collect rare postage stamps.
5. Sharon or Tyrone will dive for the shells.

Additional Resources

Skills Practice Book
Mixed Practice—page 106

Chapter 15   **279**

Exercise C
1. Thick mugs of steaming soup warmed the skiers.
2. On each plate were several plump, juicy tomatoes.
3. The watchdog snarled fiercely.
4. The trees have large, shiny lemons.
5. The old chest contained a wrinkled document.

Exercise D
1. The fingerprints on the cane are evidence.
2. That man wearing a cape is the orchestra conductor.
3. Many people on vacation sent post cards to friends.
4. The divers wearing masks and snorkels studied the reef.
5. A lighthouse by the shore warned approaching ships.

Exercises for Mastery   Continued

C. Combining Sentences by Adding Words Combine the sentences by adding important words from the other sentences to the main idea sentence. Follow directions in parentheses. Leave out words in italics. See answers in margin. (Use after page 275.)

1. Mugs of soup warmed the skiers. *The mugs were* thick. *The soup was* steaming.
2. On each plate were several tomatoes. *They were* plump. *They were* juicy. (Use a comma.)
3. The watchdog snarled. *The snarl was* fierce. (End the important word with -*ly*.)
4. The trees have lemons. The lemons are large. They shine. (End the important word with -*y*. Use a comma.)
5. The chest contained a document. *The chest was* old. *The document had* wrinkles. (End the important word with -*ed*.)

D. Combining Sentences by Adding Groups of Words Combine the following pairs of sentences by adding the important words from the second sentence to the first sentence. Leave out the words in italics. See answers in margin. (Use after page 278.)

1. The fingerprints are evidence. *The fingerprints are* on the cane.
2. That man is the orchestra conductor. *That man is* wearing a cape.
3. Many people sent post cards to friends. *The people were* on vacation.
4. The divers studied the reef. *The divers were* wearing masks and snorkels.
5. A lighthouse warned approaching ships. *The lighthouse was* by the shore.

280

Additional Resources

Skills Practice Book
Using Sentence Combining in Writing—page 107

Chapter 15 Review

▶ Analyzing/Structured Application

A. Correcting Run-on and Stringy Sentences On your paper rewrite each of the following stringy and run-on sentences as two or three sentences. Use correct capitalization and punctuation. See answers in margin.

1. We climbed that steep hill we weren't even tired.
2. Steve got out the rake and he looked for his gloves and then it started to rain.
3. Brent started to walk to Kathy's house and he stopped to talk to Charlie and he stayed for a game of checkers.
4. Arlyn's head ached she had the flu.
5. Dorothy unwrapped the yarn she put it slowly into the dye.

B. Combining Sentences Join each of the following sets of sentences. Leave out the words in italics. Follow any directions in parentheses. See answers in margin.

1. My friends and I saw a movie. *It was* scary. *My friends and I saw the movie* yesterday.
2. New Jersey is small in size. It has a large population. (Join sentences with **, but.**)
3. An object landed in the sand. *The object had a* glow. (End the important word with *-ing*.)
4. You can buy the book at Anderson's Bookstore. You can borrow it from the Edgewater Library. (Join sentences with **, or.**)
5. Today I decided to buy the seed. *I decided to* plant the garden. (Join sentence parts with **and**.)

281

Chapter 16

Chapter Objectives

1. To understand the function of adjectives as words that modify nouns or pronouns

2. To correctly identify adjectives in sentences

3. To tell whether an adjective tells *what kind*, *how many*, or *which one* about a noun or pronoun

4. To identify and use articles

5. To identify and use demonstrative adjectives

6. To identify and use predicate adjectives in a sentence

7. To correctly form and use comparative and superlative forms of adjectives

Motivating the Students

Read the following poem to the students. Then discuss what information about adjectives the poem includes. If possible project or duplicate the poem so that students can appreciate the use of the adjective forms and the subtle play with words. Tell students that this chapter will help them understand and use adjectives.

Adjectives

Adjectives tell you the quality of a person,
    place or thing
As, *pretty* girl, *big* city, *fast* horse, *golden*
    ring.
Some adjectives increase their strength
By going on to greater length:
As, *"pretty"* when you're *positive* she's fair,
But *"prettier"* whenever you *compare,*
And see a second more exquisite face
Among the members of the human race.
But, *"prettiest"* is where you reach the
    top—
Superlative—and there you have to stop.
            —Mary O'Neill

Special Populations

LD Some students may have difficulty with exercises that require generating sentences. Do these as group exercises.

ESL Students may experience difficulty due to lack of gender and adjective

Week 22

Chapter Management Guidelines   This chart may be used to help structure daily lesson plans

Day 1	Day 2	Day 3	Day 4	Day 5
Chapter 16 Opener, p. 283; Part 1, "What Are Adjectives?" pp. 284–285; Part 2, "Kinds of Adjectives," pp. 286–287	Part 3, "Articles and Demonstrative Adjectives," pp. 288–290	Part 4, "Predicate Adjectives," pp. 291–292	Part 5, "Making Comparisons with Adjectives," pp. 293–295	Chapter Review and selected end-of-chapter activities

Adjectives for Creative Expression

placement in English. Provide extra explanation and practice as necessary.

NSD Comparative and superlative form usage may be difficult for these students. Allow additional oral and written practice.

Related Chapters

You may wish to refer to related material in other chapters as you teach the following concepts:

1. Using nouns, Chapter 3, "Nouns for Precise Meaning," page 46

2. Using verbs, Chapter 4, "Verbs for Writing Power," page 61

3. Pronouns, Chapter 12, "Understanding Pronouns," page 209

Additional Resources

Skills Practice Book—pages 109–116

Test Booklet—pages 95–100
  Pretest—pages 95–96
  Mastery Test—pages 97–100

Teacher's Resource Binder
  Reinforcement Activities—
    pages 80–84
  Enrichment Activities—
    pages 39–52, 71
  Process of Writing Transparencies
  Ideas for Creative Teaching

Annual Car Show
Civic Auditorium
January 16–18

You can hardly wait for the car show. You are curious about what you will see. What will the cars look like? Will they have sleek lines or square designs? Will colors be bright or dark? Will small Japanese cars still be popular or are larger American models coming back? These questions can be asked and answered by using adjectives.

In this chapter, you will learn how using adjectives can make your writing and speaking more specific and colorful. You will also learn how to use adjectives to make comparisons. You will discover that using adjectives effectively can brighten your language and make writing more fun.

283

Part 1

Objectives

1. To understand the function of adjectives as words that modify nouns or pronouns

2. To correctly identify adjectives in sentences

Presenting the Lesson

⬛ All Students

1. Read and discuss page 284. You may wish to review the definitions of nouns and pronouns before beginning the lesson. When discussing proper adjectives, make sure that students understand the capitalization rules. Refer to the "Guide to Capitalization" in the **Power Handbook**.

2. Write the following sentence on the board. Ask students to suggest adjectives that will make the sentence more interesting.

The cat slept on the chair.

3. Point out additional ways adjectives function.

Ways To Identify Adjectives

1. Adjectives have more than one form. They change form to show comparison. Adjectives of more than two syllables usually show comparison by using the words *more* and *most*.

new	newer	newest
good	better	best
awful	more awful	most awful

2. Adjectives are often preceded by words such as *very*, *quite*, or *much*.

very bright   quite good
much better

3. Adjectives usually occur before nouns.

Rosa has a *beautiful* ring.
Juan has the *best* idea.

---

4. Assign and discuss Exercises A, B, and C on page 285. Remind students to follow the process of writing when completing Exercise C. As students proofread, refer them to the "Guide to Punctuation" in the **Power Handbook** to check their dialogue for correct punctuation.

---

1 What Are Adjectives?

> **─ Focus ─────────────────────**
> An **adjective** is a word that modifies a noun or pronoun.

▶ Comprehension/Classifying

Look at these sentences.

A giraffe roams the plains.
A graceful, spotted giraffe roams the hot, African plains.

What words in the second sentence tell you more about the giraffe and the plains than the first sentence? *Graceful* and *spotted* describe *giraffe*. *Hot* and *African* tell about the *plains*. Each word adds more specific information to the sentence.

These words are **adjectives**. Adjectives describe, or modify, nouns and pronouns.

One or more adjectives may be used before the noun or pronoun being modified. Very often, when we use two or more adjectives together, we separate them with commas.

The *hot, thick, sticky* lava poured from the volcano.

Adjectives may also follow the word being modified.

I met Al, *tired* and *hungry*, at the top of the canyon trail.

Proper Adjectives

Some adjectives, such as *African*, are made by adding endings to proper nouns. These are called **proper adjectives**. Always begin a proper adjective with a capital letter.

Australia + -n = Australian   Vietnam + -ese = Vietnamese

Other proper adjectives do not have special endings.

Hitchcock thriller   Thanksgiving dinner

284

▶ Basic Students

Have students use adjectives to describe common objects in the classroom. Then, do the first few items in Exercises A and B with the students before having them work on their own. When the students find the adjectives in Exercise A, have them also identify the modified nouns or pronouns. Point out that adjectives usually occur before nouns in sentences.

Exercises Identifying Adjectives

▶Recalling

A. Number your paper from 1 to 10. Find the adjectives in each sentence. Write them on your paper.

1. Michael avoided the murky swamp.
2. The yellow and white daffodils are in bloom.
3. Sandy rode in the red Blazer go-cart.
4. A Newfoundland dog can pull heavy sleds.
5. The fisherman wore tall rubber boots in the stream.
6. I ordered Cantonese food at the Chinese restaurant.
7. José needs a new reed for the clarinet.
8. The poinsettia is a tropical American shrub.
9. The raccoon in the tree looks as if it is wearing a black, furry mask.
10. Tonya collects European and African coins.

▶Structured Application

B. Number your paper from 1 to 10. Write an adjective for each blank in the following sentences.

1. Charlie Brown has a ____ dog named Snoopy.
2. Walking along the beach, I found a ____ starfish.
3. ____ sounds came from the attic.
4. Karen just got a ____ telephone for her room.
5. The plate shattered when it hit the ____ floor.
6. Superman is my ____ hero.
7. ____ bikes are the best!
8. I always write letters in ____ ink.
9. Lana spent the entire evening reading a ____ book.
10. In the telescope, Tim could see ____ stars.

▶Creative Application

C. Writing One day, Amy was sitting on a log watching a colony of ants. After a short time, one of the ants came over and started talking about itself and the colony. In a paragraph, describe Amy and the ant colony. Use adjectives to make your description lively and precise.

285

Part 2

Objective

To tell whether an adjective tells *what kind, how many,* or *which one* about a noun or pronoun

Presenting the Lesson

 All Students

1. Read and discuss **Some Adjectives Tell *What Kind.*** Point out the endings often added to such adjectives. Ask students to suggest sentences that contain adjectives with the adjective endings given in the examples.

2. Read and discuss **Some Adjectives Tell *How Many.*** Point out that adjectives can tell *how many* in countable amounts (one, sixteen) or in general amounts (few, several). Have students suggest other examples of adjectives that tell *how many.*

3. Read and discuss **Some Adjectives Tell *Which Ones.*** Point out that these adjectives do not describe the nouns they modify but serve to point out the nouns.

4. Point out and discuss the **Key to Writing.** Give students additional examples of sentences using adjectives that tell number, size, shape, color, and age.

5. Assign and discuss Exercises A, B, and C on page 287. Remind students to follow the process of writing when completing Exercise C. In prewriting, students may wish to list all the words describing their subject, and then begin to draft.

6. Assign and discuss Exercise A on page 296 for additional practice, if needed.

 Basic Students

Work two to four of the items in Exercises A and B on page 287 with the students before having them complete the remaining items on their own.

 Advanced Students

Have the students rewrite the sentences in Exercise A on page 287, changing each adjective.

---

2 Kinds of Adjectives

> **Focus**
>
> An **adjective** can tell *what kind, how many,* or *which one* about the word it modifies.

▶ Comprehension/Classifying

Every adjective has one of three functions. It may tell *what kind, how many,* or *which one.* Using all three types of adjectives makes your writing and speaking clear and precise.

Some Adjectives Tell *What Kind*

Some adjectives describe by telling *what kind.*

Susan wore a *red* sweater and a *plaid* skirt.

Many adjectives that tell *what kind* are formed by adding an adjective ending to a noun.

rain*y*   danger*ous*   care*less*   color*ful*   comfort*able*

Some Adjectives Tell *How Many*

Some adjectives limit by telling *how many.*

Five boys ate *fifteen* hamburgers and *many* potatoes!

Some Adjectives Tell *Which One*

Adjectives point out specific nouns or pronouns by telling *which one* or *which ones.* An adjective that tells *which one* always comes before the word it modifies.

This end of the pool is deeper than *that* end.

286

Key to Writing   Adjectives that tell number, size, shape, color, and age often do not require commas.

>   Incorrect: I made the small, gray stone skip across the pond.
>   Correct: I made the small gray stone skip across the pond.

Exercises   Using Adjectives

▶ Classifying

A. Divide your paper into three columns. Label the columns *What Kind*, *How Many*, and *Which One*. Find all of the adjectives in each sentence and write them in the correct columns.

1. That bright light signaled to some people on shore.
2. Many people like this popular brand of creamy yogurt.
3. Those trucks have eighteen wheels.
4. That channel broadcasts dozens of commercials.
5. Is this English saddle for Sara?
6. These blue cards belong to that game.
7. Janet used this small wrench to fix that leaky faucet.
8. We ordered rye bread from that German bakery.
9. These encyclopedias have several colorful illustrations.
10. Few people have traveled to all fifty states.

▶ Structured Application

B. Number your paper from 1 to 5. Supply the kind of adjective asked for in parentheses.

1. A(n) ____ howl made Rich shiver. (what kind)
2. The boys found ____ coins when they cleaned the car seats. (how many)
3. All of the ____ darts belong to Belinda. (what kind)
4. Peculiar squeaky sounds came from the ____ closet. (which one)
5. The campers quickly added twigs to their ____ campfire. (what kind)

▶ Creative Application

C. Writing Describe one of the following unbelievable sights for a friend: the Loch Ness monster, a creature from outer space, or an underwater city. Use different types of adjectives.

287

Additional Resources

Skills Practice Book—page 110

Teacher's Resource Binder
  Reinforcement Activities—
  page 81

Special Populations

ESL Make sure students understand the concepts of *which one* and *what kind*. Agreement in gender and number between an adjective and the noun it modifies is much simpler in English than in many languages. Point out that usually, English does not require distinct forms for gender and number. However, the demonstrative adjectives *this, that, these* and *those* do reflect agreement in number.

Reinforcement

Have the students follow the directions for Exercise A on page 287 using these sentences:

1. That jeep has needed frequent repairs.
2. Those deer were running from the fire.
3. This robin has laid several eggs.
4. Will those drapes be hung in the living room?
5. A few clouds drifted across the sky.
6. Is this pop bottle returnable?
7. We have traveled through ten states.
8. Nona carefully ironed the ruffles on this blouse.

Enrichment

Have students rewrite the following passage. Add and label the types of adjectives discussed in the lesson.

>   Caterpillars are swarming on the tree. They are building cocoons. Soon there will be butterflies.

Part 3

Objectives

1. To identify and use articles
2. To identify and use demonstrative adjectives

Presenting the Lesson

 All Students

1. Read and discuss **Articles** on page 288. Point out that *the* can be used with either beginning consonant or vowel sounds whereas *a* is used before words beginning with consonant sounds and *an* is only used with words beginning with vowel sounds. You may wish to point out, however, that the article *a* is used before the long *u* sound, as in "a uniform."

Point out that articles are special adjectives that specify nouns but do not describe them. They are never used with pronouns.

2. Read and discuss **Demonstrative Adjectives** on page 288. Ask students to suggest phrases using the four demonstrative adjectives. Make sure the students realize that *this* and *these* refer to objects that are close at hand, while *that* and *those* refer to objects that are at a distance.

3. Read and discuss **Adjectives or Pronouns?** on page 289. Carefully go over the example sentences. Ask students to give examples of sentences using *this*, *these*, *that*, and *those* as both adjectives and pronouns. Make sure that students understand that the word *them* is always an object pronoun.

4. Assign and discuss Exercises A, B, and C on page 290.

5. Assign and discuss Exercise B on page 296 for additional practice if needed.

 Basic Students

Before assigning the exercises, review the concepts covered in this lesson. Then, do the first few items in Exercises A and B with the students before having them work independently. See notes under **LD** in **Special Populations**.

---

3 Articles and Demonstrative Adjectives

> **Focus**
>
> *A*, *an*, and *the* are special adjectives called **articles**.
> *This*, *that*, *these*, and *those* are **demonstrative adjectives**.

Articles

▶ Comprehension/Classifying

The words *a, an,* and *the* are **articles**. Because these words always modify nouns, they are also adjectives.

Use *a* before words beginning with consonant sounds.

> a moth   a kilt   a rose   a horse   a cup

Use *an* before words beginning with vowel sounds.

> an apple   an egg   an island   an ostrich   an umbrella

Some words begin with a silent *h*. When you pronounce these words, you do not say the *h* sound. Instead, you begin the word with the vowel sound after the *h*. Therefore, you follow the rule given above and use *an*.

> *an* heiress   *an* hourglass   *an* honest answer

The article *the* may be used before either a singular or a plural noun.

Demonstrative Adjectives

This, that, these, and *those* are called **demonstrative adjectives**. They are used to point out specific things. Use *this* and *that* with singular nouns. Use *these* and *those* with plural nouns.

> *This* peach tastes sweeter than *that* one.
> *These* notebooks cost only a quarter each. *Those* notebooks cost a dollar.

288

Demonstrative adjectives are often paired with the nouns *kind* and *sort*. Both *kind* and *sort* are singular words. Therefore, we say *this kind* and *this sort*. We use *these* and *those* only with the plurals: *these kinds* or *those sorts*.

> *This kind* of book lets you pick your own ending.
> *Those sorts* of illnesses are caused by poor nutrition.

Adjectives or Pronouns?

▶ *Analyzing*

Demonstrative words can play two roles. They are sometimes adjectives. Other times they are pronouns. A demonstrative word is an adjective if it answers the question *which one?* about a noun. A demonstrative word is a pronoun if it takes the place of a noun. Look at these examples.

Adjective: *This* bug is a beetle. (*This* tells which bug.)
Pronoun: *This* is a beetle.

Adjective: *These* greens are fresh. (*These* tells which greens.)
Pronoun: *These* are fresh.

Adjective: I bought *that* poster. (*That* tells which poster.)
Pronoun: I bought *that*.

Adjective: We gathered *those* shells. (*Those* tells which shells.)
Pronoun: We gathered *those*.

Them is always a pronoun. It is never used as an adjective. It is always used as an object, never as the subject of a sentence.

Incorrect: *Them* model airplanes are mine.
Incorrect: *Them* are my model airplanes.
Correct: *Those* are my model airplanes. I built *them* myself.
     (*Them* is a pronoun. It replaces the noun *airplanes*.)

🔑 **Key to Writing and Speaking**   Demonstrative adjectives tell you if the object they are pointing out is near or farther away.
    Near: this, these
      Far: that, those

289

Additional Resources

Skills Practice Book—page 111
Teacher's Resource Binder
  Reinforcement Activities—
    page 82

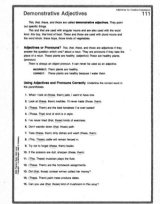

◆ Advanced Students

Have the students write two sentences for each of these words: *those* as an adjective, *those* as a subject pronoun, and *them* as an object pronoun.

Special Populations

LD To help students understand demonstrative adjectives, have students role play situations requiring their use—store clerk and patron for example.

NSD Some students make frequent errors in pronunciation and use of demonstrative adjectives. Errors are especially common in the usage of *those* and *them*. Provide additional examples and drill.

Reinforcement

1. Have the students follow the directions for Exercise A on page 290 using these sentences:

1. I can only use (those, that) brand of ribbon with my typewriter.
2. Why did you have to bring (them, those) old flower pots into the house?
3. Maria likes (that, this) record over there.
4. I told Louise about (these, this) curtains, yesterday.
5. Yolanda will never wear (them, those) glasses.

2. Have the students follow the directions for Exercise B on page 290 using these nouns: Answers will vary.

1. elbow	5. car	9. sofa
2. book	6. corn	10. bandage
3. carpet	7. garage	11. dust
4. cabbage	8. library	12. cushion

Enrichment

Giving directions often involves the use of adjectives that point out and describe. *Use the large spoon for the gravy and this spoon for the jelly*, for example. Have students write brief directions for a simple task. Have them underline the adjectives they use.

Exercises Using Demonstrative Adjectives and *Them*

A. Number your paper from 1 to 10. Choose the correct word from the parentheses. Write it on your paper.

1. Bill needs (<u>that</u>, those) kind of car to finish his model train set.
2. (Them, <u>Those</u>) unusual flowers are snapdragons.
3. Do you like (<u>this</u>, these) kind of art?
4. (<u>These</u>, Them) girls with me are my cousins.
5. (Them, <u>These</u>) muffins have chopped walnuts.
6. Lois often buys (this, <u>these</u>) sorts of rings.
7. (Them, <u>These</u>) are illustrations by Wanda Gág.
8. I think (this, <u>these</u>) kinds of crackers are the best.
9. (Them, <u>They</u>) are great photographs!
10. Can you see (<u>those</u>, them) geese flying south?

▶ Structured Application

B. Twelve nouns are listed below. Write six sentences, using two of the nouns in each sentence. Use an adjective in front of each noun. You may also add articles and demonstrative adjectives.

1. boat	4. rain	7. lighthouse	10. sea
2. sails	5. minnows	8. rocks	11. lightning
3. wind	6. fish	9. storm	12. thunder

▶ Creative Application

C. Writing Your school is having a rummage sale to raise money for the United Way. The following items are on the sporting goods counter. Write five sentences using articles and demonstrative adjectives that explain the value and the price of the items.

1. Two baseball pennants (both are close to you)
2. One basketball
3. Two catcher's mitts (one is near and one is far away)

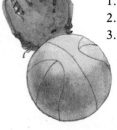

4 Predicate Adjectives

> **Focus**
>
> A **predicate adjective** is an adjective that follows a state-of-being verb. It describes the subject of the sentence.

▶ Comprehension

When an adjective follows a state-of-being verb, it is part of the predicate. Therefore, it is called a **predicate adjective**. A predicate adjective modifies the subject.

The crocodiles are hungry.
The rock climbers look tired.

A predicate adjective is different from the adjectives you have studied. Unlike most other adjectives, it comes after the word it modifies. It also is separated from the word it modifies by a state-of-being verb.

Here are some common state-of-being verbs that often come before predicate adjectives.

am	was	become	look
are	were	feel	seem
is	appear	grow	smell

Exercises Predicate Adjectives

▶ Analyzing

A. Copy the following sentences. In each sentence, draw one line under the predicate adjective. Then draw two lines under the word it modifies.

1. The full <u>moon</u> looks <u>bright</u>.
2. Before their entrance, the <u>dancers</u> became <u>jittery</u>.
3. The <u>team</u> was <u>happy</u> about its victory.
4. <u>Pat</u> looks <u>stronger</u> than any other weight lifter.
5. <u>I</u> am <u>sleepy</u> this morning.

291

Part 4

Objective

To identify and use predicate adjectives in a sentence

Presenting the Lesson

 All Students

1. Briefly review linking verbs (Chapter 4 pages 70–71). Remind students that linking verbs connect the subject with a word in the predicate.

2. Read and discuss page 291. Be sure that students understand that the predicate adjective must modify only the subject. For example, in *The flower is a yellow daisy*, the adjective yellow modifies the predicate noun, daisy. However, in the sentence, *The flower is yellow*, the adjective yellow modifies the subject flower. Therefore, it is a predicate adjective.

3. Have students suggest some sentences using the linking verbs on page 291 and containing some predicate adjectives.

4. Assign and discuss Exercises A, B, and C on pages 291–292. As students organize their details for Exercise C, they may wish to arrange them as they would be seen, from close up to far away.

5. Assign and discuss Exercise C on page 297 for additional practice if needed.

 Basic Students

Before assigning Exercises A and B, work the first two or three items with the students. Then, have them complete the remaining items on their own.

 Advanced Students

Have the students tell whether the underlined adjective is a predicate adjective. If it does not modify the subject, what noun does it modify?

1. My favorite sweater is <u>beige</u>. PA
2. The dog was a <u>gray</u> poodle. poodle
3. Bill's uncle is <u>friendly</u>. PA
4. The explorers were <u>restless</u>. PA
5. Several parents were <u>present</u>. PA

Special Populations

ESL Give many examples of predicate adjectives. Draw arrows from the predicate adjective to the subject to illustrate the descriptive relationship.

Reinforcement

Have the students follow the directions for Exercise B using these sentences:
Answers will vary.
1. Lemons are _____.
2. Before a test, we are very _____.
3. The boys were _____ after their victory yesterday.
4. Every day at noon, I am _____.
5. The sky was _____ this morning.
6. With the new addition, the house will be _____.
7. You are _____ than any other student here today.
8. This rose is _____.
9. Ann will be _____ when she sees your present.
10. From far away, the bell sounded _____.

6. The old Irish <u>castle</u> seems <u>enormous</u>.
7. <u>Buffalo</u> are <u>calm</u> in the afternoon heat.
8. The <u>lemonade</u> tasted <u>sour</u>.
9. <u>Marilyn</u> was <u>speechless</u> when she saw your present.
10. The <u>bell</u> sounded <u>faint</u>.

▶ Structured Application

B. Number your paper from 1 to 10. Write each sentence. Complete it with a predicate adjective. Then draw a line under the word it modifies.

1. The <u>flight</u> to Los Angeles will be _____.
2. The early <u>settlers</u> became very _____.
3. The hermit <u>crab</u> looks _____.
4. That mystery <u>book</u> was _____.
5. The week-old <u>milk</u> smells _____.
6. Without water, the <u>plants</u> will become _____.
7. Vincent's <u>violin</u> sounds _____.
8. This <u>apple</u> tastes _____.
9. The <u>sandpaper</u> feels _____.
10. The <u>pictures</u> of our vacation were _____.

▶ Creative Application

C. Writing Imagine that you are a scout for a group of explorers. Because you travel ahead of the others, you are the first to reach the peak of a mountain. You are all alone.

Describe the scene from the mountain peak. What do you see all around you? How do you feel? Use some linking verbs and predicate adjectives to write a paragraph about this experience.

292

Additional Resources

Skills Practice Book—page 112
Teacher's Resource Binder
Reinforcement Activities—
page 83
Enrichment Activities—
page 71

5 Making Comparisons with Adjectives

> **Focus**
>
> Use the **comparative form** of an adjective to compare two things.
> Use the **superlative form** of an adjective to compare three or more things.

▶ Comprehension/Classifying

A bear is big. A hippopotamus is big. An elephant is big.

All of these animals are big, but they are not the same size. We can show the differences in size by using special forms of adjectives.

We can use the word *bigger* to compare two things. We call *bigger* the **comparative form** of *big*.

The hippopotamus is *bigger* than the bear.

We can use *biggest* to compare three or more things. We call *biggest* the **superlative form** of *big*.

The elephant is the *biggest* of the three animals.

Follow these rules to make the comparative and superlative forms of adjectives.

1. Use the comparative form to compare two things. To make the comparative form of most short adjectives, add *-er*.

2. Use the superlative form to compare three or more things. To make the superlative form of most short adjectives, add *-est*.

Adjective	Comparative Form	Superlative Form
calm	calmer	calmest
big	bigger	biggest
cute	cuter	cutest
noisy	noisier	noisiest

293

Part 5

Objective

To correctly form and use comparative and superlative forms of adjectives

Presenting the Lesson

All Students

1. Read and discuss pages 293 and 294. Make sure that students understand the difference between the comparative form and the superlative form. Test the students' understanding by having them suggest adjectives and give the comparative and superlative form of each.

2. Refer students to the **Power Handbook** for additional reinforcement on spelling the forms of adjectives used for comparison.

3. In discussing *more* and *most*, tell students that a long adjective is one with more than two syllables.

4. Ask students to suggest sentences using the comparative and superlative forms of *good* and *bad*. Tell students that the dictionary will show comparative and superlative forms of adjectives that do not follow the regular patterns.

5. Point out and discuss the **Key to Writing and Speaking.**

6. Assign and discuss Exercises A, B, and C on page 295. Remind students to use the process of writing when completing Exercise C. Allow time for students to share their commercials with the class.

7. Assign and discuss Exercise D on page 297 for reinforcement if needed.

▶ Basic Students

To reinforce the students' understanding of the material presented, ask the students to use the comparative and the superlative forms of these adjectives in original sentences.

powerful   more, most powerful
good   better, best
dangerous   more, most dangerous
important   more, most important
bad   worse, worst
great   greater, greatest

Advanced Students

Have the students design simple crossword puzzles using the comparative and superlative forms of adjectives. You may wish to have students work in pairs or groups.

Special Populations

LD, ESL, NSD Have these students make a chart of the rules for comparative and superlative forms for reference.

ESL Provide ample illustration with explanation of the use of comparative and superlative forms. (*That chair over there is smaller than this one over here.*)

NSD Students often use *more* and *most* along with *-er* and *-est* endings. Provide oral and written practice for correction.

Reinforcement

Have the students follow the directions for Exercise A using these sentences:

1. A balanced meal is (better, gooder) for your health than junk food.
2. Name brands are usually (expensiver, more expensive) than generic brands.
3. My fever is (worse, more worse) than before.
4. That is the (funnier, funniest) show of the season.
5. Between Andrea and Luis, Luis is the (taller, tallest).
6. The elephant is (enormouser, more enormous) than the bison.
7. The first copy of my book report is the (worst, baddest) one.
8. Popeye is (hungrier, hungriest) for spinach than I am.
9. We chose the (most fat, fattest) cat in the litter.
10. Pecos Bill rode horses (gooder, better) than other cowboys.

Enrichment

Bring a copy of the *Guinness Book of World Records* to the class. Read a few of the records to the class that feature superlative adjectives, i.e. the fastest, the smallest, etc. Then have students work in small groups to make a poster illustrating some of the more interesting records.

Notice that when an adjective ends in a single consonant following a single vowel, such as *big*, you must double the final consonant before adding the ending. When the adjective ends in silent *e*, such as *cute*, drop the *e* before adding the ending. When the adjective ends in a *y* following a consonant, such as *noisy*, change the *y* to *i* before adding the ending.

Using *More* and *Most*

The comparative and superlative forms of some adjectives are not made by adding *-er* or *-est*. For longer adjectives, use the word *more* before the adjective to make the comparative form. Use the word *most* before the adjective to make the superlative form.

Adjective	Comparative Form	Superlative Form
difficult	more difficult	most difficult
noticeable	more noticeable	most noticeable
careful	more careful	most careful

The Forms of *Good* and *Bad*

The comparative and superlative forms of some adjectives are completely new words. Here are the forms of *good* and *bad*.

Adjective	Comparative Form	Superlative Form
good	better	best
bad	worse	worst

 Key to Writing and Speaking Never use the *-er* ending and the word *more*. Never use the *-est* ending and the word *most*.

Incorrect: This pillow is *more softer* than that one.
Correct: This pillow is *softer* than that one.

294

Additional Resources

Skills Practice Book—page 113
Teacher's Resource Binder
Reinforcement Activities—
page 84

Exercises Making Comparisons with Adjectives

▶ Recalling

A. Number your paper from 1 to 10. Choose the correct form of the adjective from the parentheses. Write it on your paper.

1. Claire is the (more careful, <u>most careful</u>) skier I know.
2. "Tomorrow will be (<u>colder</u>, more colder) than today," predicted the forecaster.
3. Of the two kickers, Bill scored (<u>more</u>, most) points.
4. The snow was (<u>worse</u>, worser) in the parking lot.
5. The Sky Harbor weather is (badder, <u>worse</u>) than ours.
6. Have you heard the (<u>latest</u>, most late) announcement?
7. Otis was the (friendlier, <u>friendliest</u>) of the three dogs.
8. Cindy has the (newer, <u>newest</u>) guitar in our group.
9. Of all the contestants, Kelly is the (less, <u>least</u>) nervous.
10. My boots were (<u>muddier</u>, more muddier) than yours after our long hike.

▶ Analyzing

B. Number your paper from 1 to 10. Write each sentence. Use the comparative or superlative form of the adjective in parentheses.

1. This puppy is (frisky) than that one. friskier
2. I tried all the flavors and this one tastes (good). best
3. Eric's jokes were (original) than Ed's. more original
4. Tuesday was the (warm) day of the week. warmest
5. This stew is the (salty) I have ever tasted. saltiest
6. Seventy was Sarah's (bad) bowling score. worst
7. These scissors are (dull) than those. duller
8. The subway train was (crowded) than the bus. more crowded
9. The cherries were the (tasty) of the three desserts. tastiest
10. That is the (wonderful) news I have heard all day! most wonderful

▶ Comparison-Contrast/Creative Application

C. Writing Imagine that you write television commercials. You are going to show how great your product is by comparing it to another brand. Make up a product and give it a name. Then write an ad that will persuade audiences that your product is the best!

295

Exercises for Mastery

These **Exercises for Mastery** may be used for additional practice of the concepts presented in this section. Each exercise focuses on a single concept, and should be used after the page number indicated in parentheses.

Exercises for Mastery

Chapter 16

Adjectives for Creative Expression

▶ Classifying/Analyzing

A. Using Adjectives Make three columns on your paper. Label the first column *What Kind*, the second column *How Many*, and the third column *Which One*. Number your paper from 1 to 10. Find all of the adjectives in each sentence and write them in the correct columns. Do not include articles. (Use after page 290.)

1. That lake has a sandy beach.
2. There are nine planets in the solar system.
3. Those Canadian coins fell out of my back pocket.
4. For several miles, we drove in dense, soupy fog.
5. That heavy rain saved many Russian wheat crops.
6. Babe Zaharias won important tournaments in several different sports.
7. These four months are named for Roman gods.
8. Strong west winds bent those willow trees.
9. Tonight, Kim killed twenty pesky mosquitoes.
10. That experimental model made many trial flights.

B. Using Articles and Demonstrative Pronouns Number your paper from 1 to 10. Choose the correct word from the parentheses. Write it on your paper. (Use after page 290.)

1. Mr. Redlin gave the sketch pads back to (those, them) art students.
2. A figure with eight sides is (a, an) octagon.
3. Many people like (that, those) kind of music.
4. Mary Poppins always carried (a, an) umbrella.
5. (A, An) huge crowd turned out for the fireworks.
6. Joanne listened to (those, them) tapes all afternoon.
7. The governor's visit is (a, an) honor for our school.
8. I'll wash the windows. (Them, They) are streaked.
9. (That, Those) kinds of shoes are not for hiking.
10. I can eat (them, those) pieces of pizza.

296

Additional Resources

Skills Practice Book
Mixed Practice—page 114

C. Mastering Predicate Adjectives Copy these sentences. In each sentence, draw one line under the predicate adjective. Then draw two lines under the word it modifies. (Use after page 292.)

1. The custard is still warm.
2. The water in the mountain lake feels icy.
3. Most of your answers are correct.
4. The ambulance siren sounded shrill.
5. Burning leaves smell fragrant.
6. After the parade, the streets looked littered.
7. California oranges are sweet.
8. Courtney will look very tall on those stilts.
9. Cajun food is far too spicy for me.
10. The whale looked monstrous to the sailors.

D. Making Comparisons with Adjectives Number your paper from 1 to 10. Choose the correct form of the adjective from the parentheses. Write it on your paper. (Use after page 295.)

1. Of the two sisters, Jean sings (better, best).
2. Elena is our (fastest, most fast) swimmer.
3. One path is (closer, more close) than the other.
4. Mr. Jensen is the (most honest, most honestest) person I know.
5. This is the (better, best) of the three shows.
6. My alarm clock has a (louder, more loud) buzzer than yours.
7. You should use a (lighter, more light) bowling ball than that one.
8. Teresa's skates are (newer, more new) than mine.
9. Sean has the (baddest, worst) temper in the family.
10. Mandy bought the (freshest, most freshest) fish in the market.

297

Using Grammar in Writing

These challenging and enjoyable activities allow the students to see how the concepts of grammar, usage, and mechanics may be applied in actual writing situations. Each exercise is designed to give students practice in several of the skills they have acquired in this section. The activities also provide opportunities for students to write creatively about a wide variety of interesting and unusual subjects.

As students complete these activities, remind them to follow the process of writing. Be sure to allow adequate time for prewriting activities. For Exercise C, during prewriting, students may wish to make a cluster chart of their details. Ideas about color could be grouped together, details about texture grouped, and so on. Individual conferences or peer-group sessions may be used for help with drafting and revision.

Using Grammar in Writing

▶ **Creative Application**

A. During the night, a UFO landed in your backyard. The visitors from space took you into their ship and gave you a tour. Write a paragraph about the spaceship. Use adjectives to describe all the unusual things inside. Try to use demonstrative adjectives to point out things that are near and farther away.

▶ **Evaluating/Creative Application**

B. Write a brief restaurant review for a restaurant that serves ethnic foods. It might be Japanese, Mexican, East Indian, Italian, French, Greek, or Scandinavian. Then describe several items you might find on the menu of the restaurant. Tell what you think is the best dish on the menu and what is the least appetizing. Finally, rate the restaurant from one to four stars.

C. Using Adjectives in Art Look at the painting below. Do you like it? Try to describe it to a friend. Use adjectives to describe such things as color, size, texture, shape, and design. Also, give reasons why you do or do not like it.

Sunflowers, 1887, VINCENT van GOGH.   Collection: State Museum Kröller-Müller, Otterlo, the Netherlands.

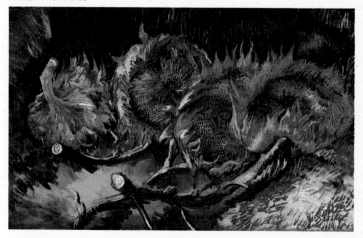

298

Additional Resources

Skills Practice Book
Using Adjectives in Writing—
    page 115

Chapter 16 Review

▶Classifying

A. Identifying Adjectives Number your paper from 1 to 10. After each number, write the adjectives that modify each italicized noun. After each adjective, write *What Kind*, *How Many*, or *Which One*. Do not include articles. <small>See answers in margin.</small>

1. This *whistle* makes a shrill *noise*.
2. Many *people* crowded into the tiny *elevator*.
3. The judges gave that *painting* a blue *ribbon*.
4. Ken studied in a peaceful *room*.
5. Eileen jogs two *miles* every *day*.
6. Judy has black wavy *hair*.
7. Put these thirteen *candles* on Frank's cake.
8. A manx is a tailless *cat*.
9. The newspaper *photographer* took several *pictures* of the mayor.
10. Are those *girls* waiting to buy some *tickets*?

▶Analyzing

B. Using Adjectives Correctly Number your paper from 1 to 10. Choose the correct adjective from the parentheses. Write it on your paper.

1. Our bus was (a, <u>an</u>) hour late yesterday afternoon.
2. Dennis bought (<u>this</u>, these) kind of gym shoes.
3. We rode on the (<u>faster</u>, fastest) of the two trains.
4. Is the United States postal system the (more reliable, <u>most reliable</u>) postal system in the world?
5. I ordered (this, <u>these</u>) kinds of foods at the international restaurant.
6. Nora and Molly used (them, <u>those</u>) computers to write their programs.
7. The domestic cat is the (<u>gentlest</u>, most gentle) of all.
8. Please put your ballots in (a, an) sealed envelope.
9. Mr. Scott prefers (<u>that</u>, those) kind of chili.
10. Of all sports, Glen thinks football is (more exciting, <u>most exciting</u>).

299

Additional Resources

Skills Practice Book
Review—page 116

Test Booklet
Mastery Test—pages 97–100

Chapter Review

These exercises provide a review of the concepts presented in this section. Each exercise challenges the students to apply several of the skills they have acquired during previous study. Because the "mixed" feature of these activities makes them more difficult, the teacher may wish to have less-advanced students do the exercises orally or in small groups.

Exercise A
1. This - whistle - Which One
   shrill - noise - What Kind
2. Many - people - How Many
   tiny - elevator - What Kind
3. that - painting - Which One
   blue - ribbon - What Kind
4. peaceful - room - What Kind
5. two - miles-How Many
   Every - day - How Many
6. black - wavy - hair - What Kind
7. these - candles - Which One
   thirteen - candles - How Many
8. tailless - cat - What Kind
9. newspaper - photographer - What Kind
   several - pictures - How Many
10. those - girls - Which One
    some - tickets - How Many

Chapter 17

Chapter Objectives

1. To understand that an adverb is a word that modifies a verb, an adjective, or another adverb

2. To identify adverbs in sentences

3. To use the comparative and superlative forms of adverbs correctly

4. To differentiate between adjectives and adverbs

5. To eliminate double negatives from writing and speaking

Motivating the Students

1. Tell the students that adverbs, like adjectives, are words that describe. Tell the students to listen for the describing words that tell *how, when, where,* and *to what extent* as you read the following passage. Explain that these are adverbs and that they will learn more about these words as they study this chapter.

Long ago, sailors had very adventurous lives. They would bravely head out to sea, never knowing what might happen. When a storm blew up, things could get really exciting. Immediately, everyone would go to work. Several of the sailors would quickly let the sails down so that the fiercely blowing wind would not tear the canvas. Often, the ship was pitching up and down so hard that the men found it quite difficult just to walk across the deck. Sometimes, sailors were thrown overboard. Later, when the excitement and the voyage were over, the men were always glad to be back in port.

Read the passage to the students again, pointing out the adverbs.

2. Read and discuss the chapter introduction on page 301.

Special Populations

ESL Students may confuse adverbs and predicate adjectives. Focus on the words modified and give ample time for practice.

NSD Students often use incorrect forms of comparative and superlative adverbs. Provide extra examples of correct usage and additional practice.

Week 23

Chapter Management Guidelines   This chart may be used to help structure daily lesson plan

Day 1	Day 2	Day 3	Day 4	Day 5
Chapter 17 Opener, p. 301; Part 1, "What Are Adverbs?" pp. 302–303	Part 2, "Making Comparisons with Adverbs," pp. 304–306	Part 3, "Adjective or Adverb?" pp. 307–309	Part 4, "Using Negatives Correctly," pp. 310–311	Chapter Review and selected end-of-chapter activities

Adverbs for Clear Description

Related Chapters

You may wish to refer to related material in other chapters as you teach the following concepts:

1. Using verbs, Chapter 4, "Verbs for Writing Power," page 61

2. Using adjectives, Chapter 16, "Adjectives for Creative Expression," page 283

3. Using modifiers, Chapter 19, "Description and the Process of Writing," page 331

Additional Resources

Skills Practice Book—pages 117–124

Test Booklet—pages 101–104
   Pretest—pages 101–102
   Mastery Test—pages 103–104

Teacher's Resource Binder
   Reinforcement Activities—
     pages 85–88
   Enrichment Activities—
     pages 24, 39–52, 72–73
   Process of Writing Transparencies
   Ideas for Creative Teaching

Imagine living in a world where no one could jump high, walk slowly, sing well, or grow taller. What would it be like if you could laugh but never laugh harder? What if you could be happy but never very happy. This is how life would be in a world without adverbs.

In this chapter, you will learn all about adverbs. You will learn to use adverbs to describe and to make comparisons. Finally, you will learn how to use negatives correctly.

301

Part 1

Objectives

1. To understand that an adverb is a word that modifies a verb, an adjective, or another adverb
2. To identify adverbs in sentences

Presenting the Lesson

All Students

1. Read and discuss pages 302–303. Discuss the sentences in the examples. Ask students to suggest other adverbs for each example. Stress the four ways that adverbs modify verbs.
2. Ask students to form adverbs by adding -*ly* to the adjectives in this list: sure, fair, slow, joyful, correct. Have them use each adverb in a sentence.
3. Assign and discuss Exercises A and B on page 303.
4. Assign and discuss Exercise A on page 312 for additional practice if needed.

Basic Students

After discussing the first paragraph on page 302, ask the students to rewrite these sentences twice by placing the adverb in different positions.

1. The man fixed the car quickly.
2. The baby cried often.
3. My sister read the letter carefully.

Advanced Students

As a group activity, have the students discuss whether each adverb they found in Exercise B describes a verb, an adjective, or another adverb. Ask them if the adverb answers one of these questions about the word it modifies: *how, where, when,* or *to what extent.*

Special Populations

LD Substitute the term *how much* for *to what extent* in exercises determining adverb function.

ESL Give extra practice on distinguishing adverbs from adjectives, especially predicate adjectives.

---

1 What Are Adverbs?

> **┌─ Focus ─**
>
> An **adverb** modifies a verb, an adjective, or another adverb.

▶ Comprehension/Classifying

In Chapter 16, you learned how adjectives can help you add excitement and clarity to your language. Adverbs can also help you improve your language by making it more precise.

An **adjective** modifies a noun or pronoun.

An **adverb** modifies a verb, an adjective, or another adverb.

> Cats pounce *silently.* (*Silently* modifies the verb *pounce.*)
>
> The train was *almost* late. (*Almost* modifies the adjective *late.*)
>
> Camille sings *very* well. (*Very* modifies the adverb *well.*)

An **adverb** tells *how, when, where,* or *to what extent* about the word it modifies.

> The whistle blew *loudly.* (*Loudly* tells *how* the whistle blew.)
>
> The Washington County Dog Show begins *tomorrow.* (*Tomorrow* tells *when* the show begins.)
>
> Three carpenters are working *upstairs.* (*Upstairs* tells *where* the carpenters are working.)
>
> My sand sculpture is *nearly* finished. (*Nearly* tells *to what extent* the sand sculpture is finished.)

An adverb that modifies an adjective or another adverb often comes before the word it modifies.

> *completely* clean   *very* slowly

An adverb that modifies a verb may be found in one of several positions.

> He smiled *often.*   He *often* smiled.   *Often,* he smiled.

302

Many adverbs are formed by adding -ly to adjectives.

careful — carefully   usual — usually   quiet — quietly

Other common adverbs include such words as *there, now, never, almost,* and *too.*

🔑 **Key to Writing and Speaking** Make your writing and speaking specific. Use adverbs to tell more about the time, place, and extent of the action.

Exercises   Using Adverbs

▶ **Classifying**
A. Number your paper from 1 to 12. Write each adverb and tell whether it answers *How, When, Where,* or *To What Extent.*

1. poorly How
2. later When
3. very Extent
4. inside Where
5. almost Extent
6. totally Extent
7. sometimes When
8. cautiously How
9. too Extent
10. recently When
11. up Where
12. merrily How

▶ **Analyzing**
B. Number your paper from 1 to 10. Write the adverb in each sentence below. Then write the word each adverb modifies. Some sentences have more than one adverb.

1. Roberto quit early. early, quit
2. Marcy played the same song twice. twice, played
3. My two calico cats often play. often, play
4. Vacation always ends too soon. always, ends; too, soon; soon, ends
5. The firefighters responded quickly. quickly, responded
6. We went to the game yesterday. yesterday, went
7. Hummingbirds' wings move very rapidly. very, rapidly; rapidly, move
8. The explosion happened quite suddenly. quite, suddenly; suddenly, happened
9. Please step forward. forward, step
10. Nancy rode the train downtown. downtown, rode

303

Additional Resources

Skills Practice Book—page 117
Teacher's Resource Binder
   Reinforcement Activities—
   page 85

Reinforcement

1. Have the students follow the directions for Exercise A on page 303 using these words:

1. much to what extent
2. now when
3. greatly to what extent
4. poorly how
5. clumsily how
6. correctly how
7. then when
8. inside where
9. loudly how
10. openly how

2. Have the students follow the directions for Exercise B on page 303 using these sentences:

1. Nancy is almost always late. almost, always; always, late
2. The coach cheered hoarsely. hoarsely, cheered
3. The bus is probably coming later. probably, coming; later, coming
4. Incredibly, the cat survived the fall. incredibly, survived
5. Paula waited impatiently. impatiently, waited
6. Coldly, he nodded at my greeting. coldly, nodded

Enrichment

1. Explain to students that the modern practice of adding the -ly ending to adverbs started a long time ago. In Old English spoken from the years 400 A.D. to 1100 A.D., there was an expression "in a manner." When people wanted to use that expression, they added -lice to a word. Over the years, -lice gradually became -ly. For example, Old English *slawlice* became our word *slowly.*

2. For additional enrichment activities, see the Unit Projects in the Teacher's Notes on page 249. One or more of these projects have special activities for gifted and talented students.

Part 2

Objective

To use the comparative and superlative forms of adverbs correctly

Presenting the Lesson

All Students

1. Read and discuss pages 304 and 305. Point out the similarities between the adjective and the adverb forms of comparison. Have students suggest sentences using the adverbs in the examples. Stress understanding of the adverbs that change completely to form the comparative and superlative.

2. Assign and discuss Exercises A, B, and C on pages 305–306. When completing Exercise C, students might wish to list their ideas before beginning to draft their paragraphs.

3. Assign and discuss Exercise B on page 312 for additional practice if needed.

Basic Students

Have the students write two more sentences for each of the following, first using the comparative form of the adverb and then the superlative form.

Example: Ginger poured the juice carefully.
Cindy poured the juice more carefully than Ginger.
Joel poured the juice the most carefully of the three.

1. Herbert played tennis badly.
2. My little sister woke up early.
3. Jonathan finished his work quickly.
4. Alicia did well on the last test.

Advanced Students

Have the students use both the comparative and superlative forms of the last five adverbs in Exercise A in original sentences.

Special Populations

LD, ESL Have students make a study sheet for reference that shows the three ways adverbs change to show comparison. Be sure adverbs that change form completely are listed.

---

2 Making Comparisons with Adverbs

> ─ *Focus* ─
>
> Use the **comparative form** of an adverb when you compare two actions.
>
> Use the **superlative form** of an adverb when you compare three or more actions.

▶ **Comprehension/Classifying**

Since adverbs, like adjectives, are words that describe, they can be changed to the comparative or superlative form.

Use the **comparative form** when you compare two actions.

The zebra ran *faster* than the rabbit.

Use the **superlative form** when you compare three or more actions.

Of all wild animals, the cheetah runs *fastest*.

304

NSD Students often use *more* and *most* with adverbs as an emphatic statement (most best). Provide extra examples of correct usage.

The comparative and superlative forms of adverbs are formed in three different ways.

1. Some short adverbs add -*er* to form the comparative. They add -*est* to form the superlative.

Adverb	Comparative	Superlative
late	later	latest
high	higher	highest
soon	sooner	soonest

2. Most adverbs that end in -*ly* form the comparative with the word *more*. They form the superlative with *most*.

Adverb	Comparative	Superlative
recently	more recently	most recently
brightly	more brightly	most brightly
cheerfully	more cheerfully	most cheerfully

3. Some adverbs change completely to form the comparative and superlative.

Adverb	Comparative	Superlative
well	better	best
badly	worse	worst
much	more	most
little	less	least

Exercises Using Adverbs To Compare

▶ Recalling

A. Number your paper from 1 to 12. Make three columns. Copy the words below in the first column. Write the comparative form of the adverb in the second column and the superlative form in the third.

See answers in margin.

1. often	7. gently
2. sweetly	8. bravely
3. carefully	9. much
4. late	10. early
5. well	11. hard
6. easily	12. little

Additional Resources

Skills Practice Book—page 118

Teacher's Resource Binder
Reinforcement Activities—
page 86

Reinforcement

1. Have the students follow the directions for Exercise A on page 305, using these words:

1. highly	4. far
2. loud	5. strangely
3. gently	6. little

Exercise 1
1. highly, more highly, most highly
2. loud, louder, loudest
3. gently, more gently, most gently
4. far, farther, farthest
5. strangely, more strangely, most strangely
6. little, less, least

2. Have the students follow the directions for Exercise B on page 306 using these sentences:

1. The morning star shines (more brightly, most brightly) than the others.
2. Of the three boys, Bart walked (farther, farthest).
3. Jeffrey ice skates (more safely, most safely) since he saw the safety film.
4. The evil witch was acting (more strangely, most strangely) than before.
5. We thought (more highly, most highly) of the hero than of the villain.
6. Our car ran (better, best) after the spark plugs were replaced.
7. Needa wakes up (earlier, earliest) on school days than Saturdays.

3. Have the students use each of the words in Exercise A on page 305 in a sentence. They should identify whether the adverbs tell *how*, *when*, *where*, or *to what extent*.

Enrichment

Have students collect examples of advertisements that make product comparisons. They should underline the adverbs and tell whether each is in the comparative or superlative form.

Exercise A
1. more often, most often
2. more sweetly, most sweetly
3. more carefully, most carefully
4. later, latest
5. better, best
6. more easily, most easily
7. more gently, most gently
8. more bravely, most bravely
9. more, most
10. earlier, earliest
11. harder, hardest
12. less, least

B. Number your paper from 1 to 10. Write the correct form of the adverb in the parentheses.

1. Theresa pitches (fast) than Sylvia.   faster
2. Gayle skis (carefully) than Ken.   more carefully
3. Of these two kinds of soup, I like pea soup (well).   better
4. The swift flies (rapidly) of all birds.   most rapidly
5. That stunt driver is driving (recklessly) than before. more recklessly
6. Of the three light bulbs, the 150-watt burns (bright). brightest
7. Chad is the (little) noisy person in the room.   least
8. I did (badly) than you on the test.   worse
9. I like bran flakes (well) than oatmeal.   better
10. Of all the letters in the English language, *e* is used (much) often.   most

▶ Comparison-Contrast/Creative Application

C. Writing A wizard has just cast a spell. You and your best friend will be fish for the next twenty-four hours. You will be a shark and your friend will be a goldfish. Write a brief paragraph telling who has the better time and why. Use several adverbs in the comparative form in your paragraph. For example: As a shark, I can swim *more quickly*. However, the goldfish fits into a bowl *better* than I do.

306

3 Adjective or Adverb?

Focus

An **adjective** describes a noun or pronoun.
An **adverb** modifies a verb, an adjective, or another adverb.

▶ Comprehension/Analyzing

Look at these lists of words.

Adjective	Adverb
playful	playfully
nice	nicely
slow	slowly
cautious	cautiously
easy	easily
cheerful	cheerfully

Adjectives and adverbs are both modifiers. Because adverbs are often formed from adjectives, they look very much alike. For these reasons, it is sometimes difficult to know when to use each type of word.

To decide whether to use an adjective or an adverb in a sentence, ask yourself what word is being modified.

Read this example.

Emanuel removed the sliver very (careful, carefully).

Which word is correct? In this case, the verb *removed* is being modified. Therefore, choose the adverb *carefully*.

Now look at this sentence.

Snow Treasure is a (real, really) good book.

Which word did you choose? In this sentence, the adjective *good* is being modified. Therefore, the adverb *really* is the correct choice.

307

Part 3

Objective

To differentiate between adjectives and adverbs

Presenting the Lesson

 All Students

1. Read and discuss the first section of Part 3, pages 307 and 308. Place particular emphasis on the difference in the questions answered by adjectives, *which one, what kind,* and *how many,* and those answered by adverbs, *how, when, where,* and *to what extent.* Ask students to give example sentences using the sample adjectives and adverbs from the list in the lesson.

2. Read **Using *Good* and *Well, Bad* and *Badly,*** on page 308. Make sure the students understand the meaning and use of each word. Discuss the **Key to Writing and Speaking** on page 308. Make sure that students understand that *well* is an adjective when it means "healthy." Ask students to suggest sentences that use *well* as an adverb and then as an adjective.

3. Assign and discuss Exercises A, B, and C on page 309. Remind students to use the process of writing when completing Exercise C. Remind students that events in a story are usually arranged in chronological order.

4. Assign and discuss Exercise C on page 313 for additional practice, if needed.

▶ **Basic Students**

Before assigning Exercise A, have the students decide whether the italicized words in the following sentences are adverbs or adjectives. Ask them to tell which words are modified.

1. My brother is a *faster* runner than Luis.
   Adj. runner
2. Beth wrote *faster* than I did.
   adv. wrote
3. The weather is *better* today.
   adj. weather
4. A monkey climbs *better* than a cat.
   adv. climbs

Do the first few questions in Exercises A and B with the students. Then, have them complete the exercises independently.

Advanced Students

After the students complete the exercises, have them use the words *well*, *better*, and *best* in two original sentences each: first as an adjective and then as an adverb.

Special Populations

LD, ESL, NSD Students would benefit from additional drill on *good, well/bad, badly*.

NSD Some students make errors with the *-ly* form of adverbs. (*She skates real nice.*) Provide additional drill as needed.

Reinforcement

1. Have the students follow the directions for Exercise A using these sentences:

1. That hat doesn't look (good, <u>well</u>) with your outfit.
2. You are (unusual, <u>unusually</u>) talkative today, Pedro.
3. (Surprising, <u>Surprisingly</u>), Sandra ate the whole pizza!
4. Rick was (real, <u>really</u>) surprised at the party.
5. Two eagles flew (majestic, <u>majestically</u>) over the mountain.
6. The cat's eyes shone (bright, <u>brightly</u>).

2. Have the students follow the directions for Exercise B on page 309 using these sentences:

1. That was a real beautiful dive.   *really*
2. The runners sped swift past the finish line.   *swiftly*
3. I drank the milk slow.   *slowly*
4. Nancy cleaned the barn thorough.   *thoroughly*
5. The flowers smelled sweetly.   *sweet*
6. Ten years passed quick.   *quickly*

> **Remember these rules:**
>
> **Adjectives** tell *which one*, *what kind*, or *how many* about nouns and pronouns.
>
> **Adverbs** tell *how*, *when*, *where*, or *to what extent* about verbs, adjectives, and other adverbs.

Using *Good* and *Well*, *Bad* and *Badly*

Good and *well*, *bad* and *badly* are often confused.
The words *good* and *bad* are adjectives. They tell *what kind*.

> Those peaches look *good*. (*Look* is used as a linking verb here. Therefore, *good* modifies *peaches*.)
> I feel *bad* about this. (*Feel* is a linking verb. *Bad* is a predicate adjective.)

The words *well* and *badly* are adverbs. Use them to modify verbs. *Well* and *badly* tell *how* something is done.

> Jon behaved *badly*. (*Badly* tells *how* Jon behaved.)
> Ellen dances *well*. (*Well* tells *how* Ellen dances.)

 Key to Writing and Speaking   Here is an exception to the rule about using *good* and *well*. *Well* is an adjective when it describes a noun or pronoun and means "healthy."

> Thomas does not feel well.

308

Additional Resources

Skills Practice Book—
   pages 119–120
Teacher's Resource Binder
   Reinforcement Activities—
      page 87
   Enrichment Activities—
      page 24

Exercises   Choosing the Correct Modifier

▶ Recalling

A. Number your paper from 1 to 10. Choose the correct modifier from the parentheses. Write it on your paper.

1. I performed (bad, <u>badly</u>) in the finals.
2. In training camp, the football players eat (good, <u>well</u>).
3. Ted speaks (slow, <u>slowly</u>) and clearly.
4. The hot air balloon rose (silent, <u>silently</u>) into the sky.
5. The Doberman turned (sudden, <u>suddenly</u>) and growled.
6. The hawk screeched (shrill, <u>shrilly</u>) as it swooped to snatch its prey.
7. Kelly plays tennis (real, <u>really</u>) well.
8. The child blushed (shy, <u>shyly</u>).
9. The plants grow (bad, <u>badly</u>) in dim light.
10. Do you feel (good, <u>well</u>) enough to play?

▶ Analyzing

B. Number your paper from 1 to 10. Find the error in each sentence. Then write each sentence correctly.

1. Karen didn't look real sure.   really
2. Dan pitched wild.   wildly
3. The fire alarm rang loud.   loudly
4. The actor sang too poor to get the role.   poorly
5. The barn looked spookily in the moonlight.   spooky
6. Lightning flashed bright in the distance.   brightly
7. I didn't feel too good when I had a fever.   well
8. The frog's tongue darts quick in and out.   quickly
9. The teams were matched fairly even.   evenly
10. Our telephone rang prompt at ten.   promptly

▶ Creative Application

C. Writing   In old television westerns, the good cowboys wore white hats and rode white horses. The bad cowboys wore black hats and rode black horses. In movies about King Arthur and Sir Lancelot, good knights wore white armor and bad knights wore black armor.

Write a short story about the cowboys or the knights. Compare the good guys and the bad guys. Use both adjectives and adverbs.

309

Part 4

Objective

To eliminate double negatives from writing and speaking

Presenting the Lesson

All Students

1. Read and discuss page 310. Ask students to suggest sentences for the negative words given as examples. Carefully discuss the avoidance of double negatives in speech and writing. Stress the importance of careful use of language and the difference between Standard and nonstandard English.

2. Assign and discuss Exercises A, B, and C on page 311. Remind students to use the process of writing when completing Exercise C. In prewriting, students may wish to make two lists of the events that happen with and without the ring. Allow time for students to share their writing.

3. Assign and discuss Exercise D on page 313 for additional practice if needed.

Basic Students

Carefully review the correct use of negatives in sentences. Then, do the first few items in exercises A and B with the students before having them complete the exercises on their own.

Advanced Students

Have the students write an original sentence for each of the negative words listed on page 310, making sure to avoid double negatives.

Special Populations

ESL Double negatives are required in some languages. Compare the form in the ESL student's language and mark out the extra negative to show the difference in English.

NSD Many non-standard dialects use double negatives. Repetition and practice can correct this linguistic habit.

4 Using Negatives Correctly

┌─ *Focus* ─────────────────────────────────┐
│   │
│   Never use a **double negative** when you write or speak.   │
│   │
└──┘

▶ Comprehension

The word *not* is an adverb that often causes problems. It is a negative. A negative is a word that says "no."

You remember that many contractions end in *-n't*. The *-n't* ending is a shortened form of *not*. Therefore, contractions that use *-n't* are negatives. Look at this list of negatives.

was + not = wasn't	would + not = wouldn't
have + not = haven't	can + not = can't
does + not = doesn't	are + not = aren't

Not all negatives are contractions. Look at these examples of negatives. They are easy to remember because most of them contain the word *no*.

no	no one	nothing	not
none	nobody	nowhere	never

When two negatives appear in one sentence, they result in a **double negative**. Avoid double negatives in both your writing and speaking.

Wrong: Tim *never* has *nothing* to do on Saturday.
Right: Tim *never* has anything to do on Saturday.
Right: Tim has *nothing* to do on Saturday.

Wrong: Marcia *didn't* have *nowhere* to sit.
Right: Marcia *didn't* have anywhere to sit.
Right: Marcia had *nowhere* to sit.

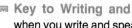 **Key to Writing and Speaking** Avoid using double negatives when you write and speak. Using double negatives makes you appear to be a careless user of language.

310

Exercises   Mastering Negatives

▶ Recalling

A. Number your paper from 1 to 10. Choose the correct word from the parentheses. Write it on your paper.

1. Gary can't think of (nobody, <u>anybody</u>) else to ask.
2. Don't you want (<u>any</u>, no) corn?
3. Sue won't take her cat (nowhere, <u>anywhere</u>).
4. Albert will not climb (<u>any</u>, no) ladder.
5. We aren't going (nowhere, <u>anywhere</u>) this summer.
6. I don't (never, <u>ever</u>) want to eat this again.
7. Sara never goes (<u>anywhere</u>, nowhere) without her dog.
8. I haven't heard (nothing, <u>anything</u>) about the accident.
9. We haven't (no more, <u>any more</u>) string for our kites.
10. Nina wouldn't like (no, <u>any</u>) macaroni.

▶ Analyzing

B. Each of the following sentences contains a double negative. Number your paper from 1 to 10. Write each sentence correctly. Some sentences may be corrected in more than one way.

See answers in margin.

1. Larry didn't never return my basketball.
2. Isn't there no more time to finish?
3. Violets can't grow in no direct sunlight.
4. Kevin and Yoshi aren't never late for gym.
5. Katherine couldn't find her missing locket nowhere.
6. Aren't you going to the mall with nobody?
7. No, thank you. I don't want none.
8. The mayor doesn't know nothing about the blackout.
9. Maria and Nancy weren't nowhere near the alarm.
10. Marty hasn't nothing to say.

▶ Comparison-Contrast/Creative Application

C. Writing Imagine that you bought a big rhinestone ring at a garage sale. When you wear it, some parts of your day go really well. When you do not wear it, life is bleak. Write a brief paragraph telling what happens when you wear the ring. In a second paragraph, tell what happens when you do not wear it. Use negatives correctly.

311

Additional Resources

Skills Practice Book—page 121

Teacher's Resource Binder
  Reinforcement Activities—
    page 88
  Enrichment Activities—
    pages 72–73

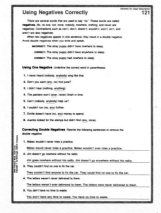

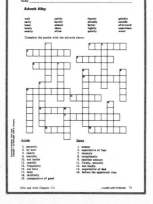

Exercises for Mastery

These **Exercises for Mastery** may be used for additional practice of the concepts presented in this section. Each exercise focuses on a single concept, and should be used after the page number indicated in parentheses.

Adverbs for Clear Description

▶ Recalling/Classifying/Analyzing

A. Finding Adverbs Number your paper from 1 to 10. Write each adverb and the word it modifies.   (Use after page 303.)

1. The elephant contentedly ate grass.   contentedly, ate
2. Come here quickly.   here, Come; quickly, Come
3. Brian plays outside every day.   outside, plays
4. That old tomcat has fought too many battles.   too, many
5. Janelle rarely spoke in the library.   rarely, spoke
6. We had so many choices for lunch today.   so, many; today, had
7. Jim and Cora left the game first.   first, left
8. The race ended here.   here, ended
9. Kevin has told that story very often.   very, often; often, told
10. Tammy saw only six doctors at the hospital.   only, six

B. Using Adverbs Correctly Number your paper from 1 to 10. Choose the correct adverb from the parentheses. Write it on your paper.   (Use after page 306.)

1. Meg sings (more better, <u>better</u>) after she warms up.
2. Of the four sisters, which one looks (more, <u>most</u>) like her mother?
3. Brenda worked (more hard, <u>harder</u>) than Bob.
4. Of all the goalies on the team, Jeremiah kicked the ball (farther, <u>farthest</u>).
5. In the forest, the fawn stood (<u>more quietly</u>, quieter) than the rabbit.
6. Sally likes bird watching (<u>less</u>, lesser) than Bill.
7. Of these two books, I like *Rascal* (<u>better</u>, best).
8. Does the robin or cardinal fly (<u>higher</u>, highest)?
9. Does Mark or Tony sleep (<u>less</u>, least)?
10. I run (more slow, <u>slower</u>) in cold weather than in warm weather.

312

Possible answers are:
1. Carter didn't need anything from the grocery store.
2. I won't have any glue left when I finish this kite.
3. Wanda never went anywhere without her best friend.
4. Didn't you bring a present either?
5. None of us knew anyone at the first troop meeting.
6. Walt is never going camping again.
7. The sky diver doesn't have a spare parachute.
8. Due to the rain, there wasn't anyone at the park.
9. Please don't use any more tape on the streamers.
10. Hal didn't have any balsa wood to carve a sailboat.

C. Choosing the Right Word Choose the right modifier, and write it on your paper. Next, write the word it modifies. Then write *Adjective* or *Adverb* to show how the modifier is used. (Use after page 309.)

Example: The soloist sang very (soft, softly).
softly, sang, Adverb

1. The actors knew their parts (perfect, <u>perfectly</u>). knew, Adv.
2. The goal line was drawn (uneven, <u>unevenly</u>). was drawn, Adv.
3. That (<u>sudden</u>, suddenly) storm surprised us. storm, Adj.
4. Was the baby sleeping (sound, <u>soundly</u>)? was sleeping, Adv.
5. You must eat right to feel (good, <u>well</u>). feel, Adv.
6. The mountains are (real, <u>really</u>) gigantic. gigantic, Adv.
7. The ocean seemed (<u>calm</u>, calmly). ocean, Adj.
8. The dragonfly hovered (silent, <u>silently</u>). hovered, Adv.
9. Mr. Steven's lesson was very (<u>good</u>, well). lesson, Adj.
10. Red Hawk and his brothers work together (good, <u>well</u>) as a team. work, Adv.

D. Using Negatives Correctly Number your paper from 1 to 10. Rewrite each of the sentences correctly. Some of the sentences may be corrected in more than one way. (Use after page 311.) See answers in margin.

1. Carter didn't need nothing from the grocery store.
2. I won't have no glue left when I finish this kite.
3. Wanda never went nowhere without her best friend.
4. Didn't you bring no present either?
5. None of us knew no one at the first troop meeting.
6. Walt is not never going camping again.
7. The sky diver doesn't have no spare parachute.
8. Due to the rain, there wasn't no one at the park.
9. Please don't use no more tape on the streamers.
10. Hal didn't have no balsa wood to carve a sailboat.

313

Additional Resources

Skills Practice Book
Mixed Practice—page 122

Using Grammar in Writing

These challenging and enjoyable activities allow the students to see how the concepts of grammar, usage, and mechanics may be applied in actual writing situations. Each exercise is designed to give students practice in several of the skills they have acquired in this section. The activities also provide opportunities for students to write creatively about a wide variety of interesting and unusual subjects.

As students complete these activities remind them to follow the process of writing. Be sure to allow adequate time for prewriting activities. Remind students that since they are writing to explain how, they may wish to organize their details in chronological order. Individual conferences or peer-group sessions may be used for help with drafting and revision.

Using Grammar in Writing

▶ **Creative Application**

A. Imagine that you are Maria's gym shoes. On her way home after track practice one night, you drop out of her gym bag. Before you can do anything about it, Maria is gone. You finally are reunited with Maria three days later. In diary form, write the story of your three-day struggle to find Maria. Use adverbs to tell *when*, *where*, and *how* the action takes place.

B. Imagine that your school's basketball team is playing in the Holiday Tournament. Because this is a very special event, you (the principal) have decided to give the students a "Guide for Tournament Dress and Sportsmanship." Write this announcement. Be sure to use negatives correctly.

C. Using Adverbs in Health In health class, you learn how important it is to take care of yourself. Now, put that knowledge to work. In a paragraph, explain how to do one of the following: eat healthful meals, handle stress, take your pulse, exercise safely, take care of your teeth, or help a choking victim. You may refer to your health text or an encyclopedia to help you with this exercise. Use adverbs correctly.

314

Additional Resources

Skills Practice Book
Using Adverbs in Writing—
page 123

Chapter 17 Review

▶ Analyzing/Drawing Conclusions

A. Identifying Adverbs Copy the following paragraph on your paper. Underline the ten adverbs. Then draw an arrow from each adverb to the word it modifies. Can you guess the name of this mystery animal? See answers below.

    This animal has a large, flat head. Its eyes almost never move, but it can see farther than most animals. It has good ears and hears well. It flies silently and swoops down quickly to catch its food. This animal often hoots softly as it sits high on its perch. owl

▶ Analyzing

B. Using Adverbs Correctly Number your paper from 1 to 10. Each of the following sentences has an error in adverb usage. Rewrite each sentence so that it is correct.

1. Paul does back flips easier than Lauren does. more easily
2. Of the three girls on the camping trip, Patty could see more clearly in the dim light. most clearly
3. Does the cat Garfield or his pal Odie trick Jon most often? more
4. Manuel won't never agree with Erin. will
5. The logger chopped near six cords of wood. nearly
6. Tina never did none of her homework. any
7. A gopher has real large cheek pouches. really
8. Of the six chess players, Ricardo is less patient. least
9. No one didn't want to ride in the old, rickety hay wagon. wanted
10. The octopus silently wrapped its tentacles tight around its prey. tightly

Exercise A
almost, never; never, move; farther, see; well, hears; silently, flies; down, swoops; quickly, swoops; often, hoots; softly, hoots; high, sits

315

Chapter Review

    These exercises provide review of the concepts presented in this section. Each exercise challenges the students to apply several of the skills they have acquired during previous study. Because the "mixed" feature of these activities makes them more difficult, the teacher may wish to have less-advanced students do the exercises orally or in small groups.

Additional Resources

Skills Practice Book
  Review—page 124

Test Booklet
  Mastery Test—pages 103–104

Chapter 18

Chapter Objectives

1. To identify lines and stanzas in poems

2. To recognize how the shape of a poem can be related to its meaning

3. To become aware of the sound patterns in poems created by rhyme, rhythm, and alliteration

4. To recognize that the sound of a poem is related to its meaning

5. To identify and understand sensory images, similes, and metaphors

6. To identify the mood of a poem

Motivating the Students

1. Read and discuss the chapter introduction on page 318. You may wish to bring a kaleidoscope to show the class. Ask the students to describe in words what they see in the kaleidoscope. Write their responses on the board in the shape of a poem.

2. Ask students to try to define poetry. Put suggested definitions on the board. Then read the following definitions given by well-known people.

"Poetry is the best words in their best order." Samuel Taylor Coleridge.

Discuss what this means and how it relates to the definitions suggested by the students. Then talk about the way poetry makes you feel. Tell students that Emily Dickinson wrote in a letter once that if she read something that made her feel "So cold no fire can warm me" and if the words made her feel as though "the top of my head were blown off," then she knew she was reading poetry.

Discuss how this definition relates to the ones the students suggested. Explain that because poetry involves both certain technical skills and the feelings of the poet and the reader, it is very difficult to form a perfect definition.

3. Point out that poetry can be enjoyed without formal study. One can respond to the image the poem suggests or enjoy the sound patterns without knowing about how they were created. You can also enjoy a painting or a musical selection without artistic or musical training. However, if you have some idea of the difficulties the artist

Week 24

Chapter Management Guidelines
This chart may be used to help structure daily lesson plans.

Day 1	Day 2	Day 3	Day 4	Day 5
Chapter 18 Opener, p. 317; Part 1, "Shape in Poetry," pp. 318–319	Part 2, "Sounds in Poetry," pp. 320–322	Part 2, "Sounds in Poetry," pp. 320–322	Part 3, "Pictures in Poetry," pp. 323–325	Part 3, "Pictures in Poetry," pp. 323–325

Appreciating the Language of Poetry

Have you ever looked into a kaleidoscope? As you turn one end, the bits of colored glass can tumble together to form lovely designs. Words, too, can be arranged in special patterns. A poet carefully chooses and arranges words and sounds. Then the reader can see an ordinary subject in a new and unusual way.

This chapter will help you understand and enjoy the language of poetry. You will study the sounds, pictures, and moods that can be found in poetry. When you understand and use the special language of poetry, you can make all your writing more interesting and exciting.

faces or even try to paint or play a musical instrument yourself, then a painting or musical selection has deeper meaning and importance. You appreciate it because you really understand it.

Related Chapters

You may wish to refer to related material in other chapters as you teach the following concepts:

1. Using modifiers, Chapter 16, "Adjectives for Creative Expression," page 283

2. Using more modifiers, Chapter 17, "Adverbs for Clear Description," page 301

3. Locating a variety of words, the "Thesaurus," in the **Power Handbook**

4. Capitalizing and punctuating, the "Guide to Capitalization," and the "Guide to Punctuation," in the **Power Handbook**

Additional Resources

Skills Practice Book—pages 125–129

Test Booklet—pages 105–110
  Pretest—pages 105–106
  Mastery Test—pages 107–110

Teacher's Resource Binder
  Reinforcement Activities—
    pages 89–92
  Enrichment Activities—
    pages 18, 25, 39–52
  Process of Writing Transparencies
  Ideas for Creative Teaching

317

Week 25

Chapter Management Guidelines This chart may be used to help structure daily lesson plans.

Day 1	Day 2	Day 3
Part 4, "Mood," pp. 326–327	Part 4, "Mood," pp. 326–327	Chapter Review and selected end-of-chapter activities

Part 1

Objectives

1. To identify lines and stanzas in a poem

2. To recognize that the shape of a poem can be related to its meaning

Presenting the Lesson

All Students

1. Read and discuss the introductory paragraphs on page 318. Emphasize the importance of paying attention to punctuation signals in a poem. Have students identify the beginnings and ends of sentences in the poem. Ask students to answer the questions in the text about the number of lines and stanzas. Mention that the three stanzas in this poem each contain a different number of lines. Explain that not all poems are structured in this way. A stanza may contain any number of lines. Mention that in some poems, all the stanzas are all the same length.

2. Read and discuss the section on concrete poems. Compare the way a concrete poem looks to the way a more conventional poem might look. Discuss the punctuation of the poem. Ask students what the shape of the poem suggests. Point out that the poet has arranged the words in this way so that they have a special visual effect.

3. Assign and discuss Exercises A and B on page 319. When the original poems are completed, display them.

Basic Students

Before assigning Exercise B, draw the shape of a skateboard on the board. Then fill in the lines of the concrete poem in the text. As you do so, point out how the lines of the poem are fitting into the shape of the skateboard. Then list several objects on the board that can be found in the classroom. Have the students discuss which of these objects might suggest good shapes for poems. Let the students use these objects for their concrete poems, if they wish. You may also wish to distribute several patterns in simple shapes such as a circle, diamond, etc. Have students fill in these

---

1 Shape in Poetry

> ─Focus─
>
> A poem is written in lines. The **lines** are grouped together to form **stanzas**.

▶ Comprehension/Interpretation

Poetry is different from other forms of writing. Most writing is made up of sentences that are arranged to form paragraphs. A poem, however, is written in **lines**. The lines are grouped together to form **stanzas**. How many stanzas make up the following poem? How many lines are in each stanza?

THE GARDEN HOSE

In the gray evening
I see a long green serpent
With its tail in the dahlias.

It lies in loops across the grass
and drinks softly at the faucet.

I can hear it swallow.

—BEATRICE JANOSCO

This poem has three stanzas. Each stanza is a different length. The period at the end of each stanza tells you that the stanza is a complete sentence. It is important to notice punctuation in poetry. When you read poetry, a comma tells you where to slow down and a period tells you where to stop.

Concrete Poems

A poet can arrange words in certain shapes. Sometimes, the shape of a poem can reflect the ideas in a poem. A **concrete** poem takes on the shape of its subject. What does the shape of the poem at the top of the next page make you think of? How is the shape related to what the poem is about?

318

shapes with words that give meaning to the shape, such as words describing a wheel or a baseball diamond.

Advanced Students

Have students write "Diamonte Poems." Begin by choosing a one word subject that forms the first line of the poem. The second line contains two words which describe the subject. The third line contains three verbs ending in

-ing that tell what the subject does. The fourth line contains two more describing words. The fifth line is a synonym for the subject in the first line.

THE SIDEWALK RACER
OR, ON THE SKATEBOARD

Skimming
an asphalt sea
I swerve, I curve, I
sway; I speed to whirring
sound an inch above the
ground; I'm the sailor
and the sail, I'm the
driver and the wheel
I'm the one and only
single engine
human auto
mobile

—LILLIAN MORRISON

Exercises   Recognizing the Shape of Poetry

▶ Comprehension/Interpretation

A. Read the following poem and answer the questions.

A DRAGONFLY

When the heat of the summer
Made drowsy the land,
A dragonfly came
And sat on my hand.

With its blue-jointed body,
And wings like spun glass,
It lit on my fingers
As though they were grass.

—ELEANOR FARJEON

1. How many lines does the poem contain? How many
   sentences? How many stanzas? *eight, two, two*
2. When you are reading the poem, where should you
   pause? Where should you come to a complete stop? *Pause*
   at the commas; come to a complete stop at the periods.

▶ Creative Application

B. Pick an object with a simple shape. Write a short concrete poem
about the object.

319

ESL Suggest that students share a
poem from their native language with the
class. Have them explain the subject of
the poem, or, if possible, give a simple
translation. Have the students explain
where lines and stanzas end as in the
lesson discussion.

Reinforcement

Read the following poem to the class
and have them answer the questions
that follow.

Balloons!

A balloon
is a wild
space animal,

restless pet
who bumps and butts
its head
on the cage walls
of a room—

bursts
with a bellow,
or escapes slowly
with sighs
leaving a limp skin.

Balloons
on the street
fidget
in the fresh air,
strain
at their string
leashes.

If you loose
a balloon,
it bolts home
for the moon.
        —Judith Thurman

1. How many stanzas does the poem contain?
   5
2. How many lines make up the poem?
   24
3. How many sentences are in the poem?
   3
4. After what word in the third stanza
   should you come to a complete stop?
   skin

Enrichment

For enrichment activities, see the Unit
Projects in the Teacher Notes on page
249. One or more of these projects have
activities for gifted and talented students.

Additional Resources

Skills Practice Book—page 125
Teacher's Resource Binder
  Reinforcement Activities—
  page 89

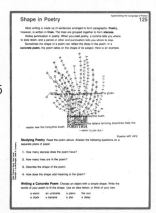

Part 2

Objectives

1. To become aware of the sound patterns in poems created by rhyme, rhythm, and alliteration

2. To recognize that the sound of a poem is related to its meaning

Presenting the Lesson

◼ All Students

1. Read the opening paragraph on page 320. Then read and discuss the section on rhyme. Be sure that the poems in this section are read out loud. The teacher may read the poems out loud before analysis and then have one or more student volunteers read the poems again after analysis. Ask students to suggest pairs of rhyming words.

2. Read and discuss the section on rhythm. Have students clap to the rhythm of "Rain Song" and to that of "Moonlight." Ask students why they think the rhythm of each poem is appropriate.

3. Read and discuss **Alliteration** on page 321. Point out that the alliteration in the poem helps to suggest the idea of the windshield wipers. The repeated rhythmic sound is related to the subject of the poem. Remind students of the tongue twisters they may have tried, such as "Sally sells sea shells at the sea shore." Ask students to suggest other phrases that use alliteration.

4. Have a student read the exercise poem out loud. Then assign and discuss Exercises A and B on page 322.

▶ Basic Students

Make sure that students understand that rhyming patterns may vary. Compare the rhyme pattern of "Rain Song" on page 320 to that of "A Dragonfly" on page 319.

Emphasize the musical quality of rhythm. Ask the students for the words of a popular song. Use the song lyrics to help the students find the rhythm.

Have students work in groups or pairs to list alliterative words before they complete Exercise B.

2 Sounds in Poetry

> **Focus**
>
> Poets use **rhyme**, **rhythm**, and **alliteration** to make special sound patterns.

▶ Comprehension/Analyzing

Sound is an important part of poetry. That is why the best way to read poetry is aloud. Poets carefully choose words to create certain sound patterns and effects. These effects give additional meaning to the words of the poem.

Rhyme

Words that **rhyme** have the same end sound. *Kite* and *right* are examples of rhyming words. In a poem, rhyming words are often used in a pattern. See if you can find the pattern of rhyme in the following poem.

RAIN SONG

The rain goes rushing down the street.
Soft gusts of sound it utters.
It sings a spring song cool and sweet
And chuckles in the gutters.

—REBECCA McCANN

The rhyming words are *street* and *sweet*, *utters* and *gutters*. Notice that the poet has planned where the rhyming words will be. The last words in the first and third lines rhyme. So do the words in the second and fourth lines.

Rhythm

Poems usually have a **rhythm**, or pattern of strong beats. The reader can feel the strong beats in each line.

320

The strong beats in the first two lines of "Rain Song" are marked here. Read the lines, stressing the marked words.

The rain goes rushing down the street.
Soft gusts of sound it utters.

The rhythm of the following poem is different from the steady beat in "Rain Song." The smooth, free-flowing rhythm in "Moonlight" makes you think of the graceful movements of a cat and the quiet beauty of moonlight. Notice, too, that there is no pattern of rhyme to limit that feeling.

MOONLIGHT

Like a white cat
Moonlight peers through windows,
Listening, watching.
Like a white cat it moves
Across the threshold
And stretches itself on the floor;
It sits on a chair
And puts white paws on the table.
Moonlight crouches among shadows,
Watching, waiting
The slow passing of night.

—MAUD E. USCHOLD

Alliteration

Rhyme is one way that poets repeat sounds. Another way is called **alliteration**. Alliteration is the repetition of a consonant sound at the beginning of words. Here is an example.

*W*indshield *w*ipers *w*ipe the *w*indshield

Repetition of sounds and words can emphasize the meaning of a poem. In the poem on the next page, repetition of *s* and *w* creates the sound of a windshield wiper.

321

 Advanced Students

Advanced Students

Explain to the students the system of identifying rhyme scheme by labeling each rhyming ending with a different letter. Help them to work out the *abab* rhyme scheme of "Rain Song." Then, after completing Exercise A, have them work out the rhyme scheme of "Windy Nights."

Special Populations

LD Point out that rhyming words are not always spelled alike, such as *doors* and *roars* in "Windy Nights." See also notes under **Basic Students.**

ESL Have students write a simple poem that contains rhyme in their native language. Have them read the poem out loud and then copy it on the board. Have them point out the words that rhyme. If possible, also have them identify the accented syllables. Point out that the sound qualities of poetry exist in all languages.

Reinforcement

Read this poem to the class and have them answer the questions that follow. If students have difficulty recognizing sound devices, put the poem on the board and mark places where repeated sounds occur.

Four Little Foxes

Speak gently, Spring, and make no sudden
    sound;
For in my windy valley, yesterday I
    found
New-born foxes squirming on the ground—
    Speak gently. —Lew Sarett

1. Which words in the poem rhyme?
   sound, found, ground
2. How many lines does the poem contain?
   4
3. How many sentences does the poem contain? 1
4. What sound is repeated to form alliteration? s
5. In what line of the poem does this occur? first
6. What words contain this sound?
   Speak, Spring, sudden, sound

Enrichment

Read the following riddle/poems to the class. Ask them to guess the answers. Then, using these riddles as a model, ask students to write original riddles. Each riddle/poem should consist of four lines and have some sort of rhyme pattern. Encourage students to use alliteration as much as possible. When the riddle/poems are complete, have students read them to the class. Let the class try to guess the answers.

Riddle me, riddle me,
What is that:
Over the head
and under the hat? (hair)

Tall and thin,
red within,
Nail on top
and there it is. (finger)

As round as a saucer,
As plump as a ball,
Can climb up the steeples,
And churches, and all. (the sun)

Windshield wipers wipe the windshield
   Wipe the water off the pane
This way   That way
This way   That way
This way   That way
    In the rain

—MARY ANN HOBERMAN

Exercises   Sounds in Poetry

▶ Drawing Conclusions/Analyzing

A. Read this poem. Answer the questions that follow.

WINDY NIGHTS

Rumbling in the chimneys,
   Rattling at the doors,
Round the roofs and round the roads
   The rude wind roars;
Raging through the darkness,
   Raving through the trees,
Racing off again across
   The great grey seas.

—RODNEY BENNETT

1. What are the rhyming words in this poem? doors/roars; trees/seas
2. Read the poem aloud to sense the rhythm. Where do the strong beats fall in the first two lines? Copy the first two lines and mark the strong beats. See poem.
3. What consonant sound is repeated in the first seven lines? Think about the subject of the poem. Explain why the poet may have chosen this consonant sound. r; because it imitates the sound of the wind
4. Find and write an example of alliteration in the last line of the poem. great grey

▶ Creative Application

B. Write a rhyming poem of at least four lines. One line should contain an example of alliteration. Try to cause a reader to hear the sounds that could be made by the subject of the poem.

322

Additional Resources

Skills Practice Book—page 126

Teacher's Resource Binder
  Reinforcement Activities—
    page 90

3 Pictures in Poetry

> **Focus**
> Poets create pictures with words by making comparisons and using sensory images.

▶ *Comprehension/Interpretation*

The language of poetry is filled with pictures. Poets have many ways of helping the reader see the pictures that the words of poetry create.

Sensory Images

Poets want readers to use their senses to understand and experience poetry. Often, poets appeal to the senses by using sensory words. Those words make the reader feel he or she can see, touch, taste, hear, or smell what is in the poem. The pictures and feelings these words create are called **sensory images**. Read the following poem. What images or pictures does your mind see as you read? To what senses is the poet appealing?

Butterflies beware!
Needles of pines can be sharp
in a gusty wind.

—SHOSEN

The reader sees fragile butterflies and can imagine touching the sharp needles. The reader can almost feel the gusty wind.

One way that poets create word pictures is by comparing one thing to another. The comparison helps readers see how things are similar but in a new or different way.

323

Part 3

Objective

To identify and understand sensory images, similes, and metaphors

Presenting the Lesson

All Students

1. Read and discuss the section on sensory images. Be sure students understand the term *sensory images*. List the five senses on the board as headings. Tell students to imagine that they are at a baseball game. Have them suggest sensory images for each sense category. Write these under the appropriate heading on the board.

2. Read and discuss the section on similes. Be sure the students can identify the similes in the poem and can tell what two things are being compared. Discuss how the sensory images and similes are related to the meaning of the poem "Some People." How do the images of brown leaves and shiny fireflies help to convey the meaning? Paraphrase the poem without similes or sensory images. Ask students to explain how poetic language helps make the poem's meaning more vivid.

3. Read and discuss the section on metaphor. Emphasize the differences between similes and metaphors. Discuss the specific ways in which the poem compares clouds to elephants. Ask the students why the poet may have chosen this comparison. Will it make them look at clouds a little differently?

4. Read the exercise poem out loud. Be sure students understand the meaning of *impinge*. Define any other unfamiliar words. Assign and discuss Exercises A and B on page 325. For Exercise B, encourage students to include sensory images as well.

Basic Students

Emphasize that similes use *like* or *as;* metaphors do not use these words to compare. Before assigning Exercise A, read through the questions and review the concepts that have been developed.

Advanced Students

For Exercise B, challenge students to write a poem that contains an extended metaphor.

Special Populations

LD For students that have difficulty with similes, give some very simple examples, such as "hard as a rock" or "stubborn as a mule."

ESL Discuss the fact that sensory images, similes, and metaphors exist in all languages. If possible, have students provide examples from their native languages to share with the class.

Reinforcement

Read the following poem and answer the questions that follow:

Flashlight

My flashlight tugs me
through the dark
like a hound
with a yellow eye,

sniffs
at the edges
of steep places,

paws
at moles'
and rabbits'
holes,

points its nose
where sharp things
lie asleep—

and then it bounds
ahead of me
on home ground.
—Judith Thurman

1. What does the poem compare a flashlight to? a hound dog with a yellow eye
2. Is this a simile or a metaphor? simile
3. Find an example where the poet appeals to the sense of touch.
   paws at sharp things
4. Find an example where the poet appeals to the sense of smell.
   sniffs at the edges
5. In your own words, explain how the poet says the flashlight and the dog are alike.
   Answers will vary. sniffs, paws, points its nose, bounds ahead

Enrichment

Explain the meaning of cliché to the class. Read the clichés at the top of the next column to the class:

Simile

A **simile** is a comparison that uses *like* or *as*. In the following poem, the poet uses two similes. In the first stanza, thoughts are compared to shriveled leaves. In the second stanza, thoughts are compared to shiny fireflies. The first simile uses *like*. The second simile uses *as*.

SOME PEOPLE

Isn't it strange some people make
   You feel so tired inside,
Your thoughts begin to shrivel up
   Like leaves all brown and dried!

But when you're with some other ones,
   It's stranger still to find
Your thoughts as thick as fireflies
   All shiny in your mind!

—RACHEL FIELD

Metaphor

A **metaphor** also compares one thing with another. However, a metaphor does not use *like* or *as*. A metaphor says that one thing *is* another.

Read the following poem. Can you find the metaphor?

THE DARK GRAY CLOUDS

The dark gray clouds,
the great gray clouds,
the black rolling clouds are elephants
going down to the sea for water.
They draw up the water in their trunks.
They march back again across the sky.
They spray the earth again with the water,
and men say it is raining.

—NATALIA M. BELTING

324

The specific metaphor is stated in the third line. The entire poem, however, compares the actions of clouds to the actions of elephants. Therefore, the poem is an extended metaphor. An **extended metaphor** continues the comparison throughout the poem. It shows more than one similarity between the things being compared.

Exercises   Recognizing Sensory Images, Simile, and Metaphor

▶ Interpretation/Analyzing

A. Read this poem. Then answer the questions that follow.

See answers in margin.

THE SKATERS

Black swallows swooping or gliding
In a flurry of entangled loops and curves,
The skaters skim over the frozen river.
And the grinding click of their skates as they impinge*
    upon the surface,
Is like the brushing together of thin wing-tips of
    silver.

—JOHN GOULD FLETCHER

*impinge, to strike or hit on or against something

1. What does the poet compare the skaters to? Is this a simile or a metaphor?
2. In the last four lines, what two things are being compared? Is this a simile or a metaphor?
3. Write one of the images your mind pictures as you read the poem.
4. Find an example that appeals to the sense of sight.
5. Find an example that appeals to the sense of sound.
6. Is the same comparison continued throughout the poem? What kind of metaphor is the poem?
7. Find and write an example of alliteration in the poem.

▶ Creative Application

B. Write your own poem. Include one simile or one metaphor.

325

fit as a fiddle
sly like a fox
hard as a rock
strong as an ox
dead as a mackerel
happy as a lark
cool as a cucumber

Point out to students that many such sayings are really similes that have been overused. Ask the class to think of more expressions like these. Write all of the clichés on the board. Then ask the class to change the clichés by creating new similes. Have the students use the dictionary and/or a thesaurus, if they wish.
Answers will vary.

Exercise A
1. black swallows; metaphor
2. skate blades and swallows' wing-tips; simile
3. birds swooping and gliding; skaters skating on a river; skates on the ice; birds touching wing-tips as they fly
4. birds flying; skaters skating
5. the click of skates on the ice; the whisper of wing-tips brushing each other
6. yes; extended metaphor
7. swallows swooping; skaters skim

Additional Resources

Skills Practice Book—page 127
Teacher's Resource Binder
  Reinforcement Activities—
    page 91
  Enrichment Activities—
    page 6

Part 4

Objective

To identify the mood of a poem

Presenting the Lesson

⬤ All Students

1. Read and discuss page 326. Discuss how the repetition of the phrase "One dark windy night" helps to set up the mood by helping to build suspense. Remind students that the setting of most horror movies is a stormy night.

Ask what the lines "I heard something . . . . A footstep, a whisper" suggest. (There is something to fear.)

2. Read "Cynthia in the Snow" on page 327. In addition to pointing out the words that contribute to mood that are discussed in the lesson, also point out the use of sound. Call attention to the alliteration in *laughs* and *lovely* and in *whitely* and *whirs*. Mention that the sounds suggested by the poem add to the lightness of the mood.

3. Discuss the rhythm of the poems on these pages. Ask which poem uses a steady beat and which one has a more free-flowing rhythm. ("Cynthia in the Snow" is more free-flowing.) Explain how this also helps to convey the moods of the poems. Ask students to point out any metaphors, similes, or other sensory images that they find in the poems. Ask how these sensory images help to reinforce the mood of the poems.

4. Assign and discuss Exercises A and B on page 327. Students might wish to brainstorm and list ideas for Exercise B before they begin to write. Encourage the students to use a thesaurus for precise word choice.

▷ Basic Students

Before assigning Exercise A, read through the questions and review the concepts that have been developed. Use some of the other poems in the chapter to help students identify the mood of a poem. Before assigning Exercise B, tell students to decide what mood their chosen place creates. Then, help students make a list of words that help to convey that mood. Have them use some of these words in the poem that they write.

---

4 Mood

> **Focus**
>
> **Mood** is the feeling the reader has when he or she reads a poem.

▶ Comprehension/Interpretation

Sometimes a poet wants the reader to feel a certain way. The feeling the reader experiences is called **mood**. A poet carefully chooses words to create a special mood. For example, if the mood of a poem is to be cheerful and lighthearted, the poet will use happy-sounding words such as *joy* or *laughter*. If the mood is to be sad, the poet could use words such as *dreary*, *weep*, or *gray*. Read the following poem. What is the mood? What words make you feel that way?

DARK WINDY NIGHT

When I was out walking
One dark windy night
I heard something behind me
One dark windy night
A footstep, a whisper
One dark windy night
A shadow before me
One dark windy night
Moonlight behind me
One dark windy night.
I shivered, I shook,
I did get a fright
When I was out walking
One dark windy night.

—ANNE ENGLISH

The poet wants you to experience an uneasy, spooky feeling. The repeated line "One dark windy night" and the words *shivered*, *shook*, and *fright* create the mood.

In this poem, the words *flitter-twitters*, *laughs*, and *whitely whirs* suggest a light, upbeat feeling. The words *lovely* and *beautiful* help the reader feel the quiet beauty of the snow.

CYNTHIA IN THE SNOW

It SHUSHES.
It hushes
The loudness in the road.
It flitter-twitters,
And laughs away from me.
It laughs a lovely whiteness,
And whitely whirs away,
To be
Somewhere otherwhere,
Still white as milk or shirts.
So beautiful it hurts.

—GWENDOLYN BROOKS

Exercises   Identifying the Mood of a Poem

▶ Interpreting/Drawing Conclusions
A. Read the following poem and answer the questions.

FOGHORNS

The foghorns moaned
   in the bay last night
so sad
so deep
I thought I heard the city
   crying in its sleep.

—LILIAN MOORE

1. What is the mood of the poem? sad
2. Why did the poet describe the sound as a *moan?*
                             to emphasize the sadness
3. What verbs contribute to the mood? What adjectives?
                         crying, moaned; sad, deep

▶ Creative Application
B. Write a poem about a place you know well. Try to choose words that create a certain mood.

327

Suggest that students start a "mood dictionary." As the students think of words that suggest a particular mood, or encounter such words in their reading, they should make a list of these. They can refer to the list when they write poetry or do other writing.

Special Populations

LD See notes under **Basic Students.**

NSD Suggest that students experiment with including dialect or colloquial phrases in their poems if appropriate to the subject. Provide samples by Langston Hughes, Gwendolyn Brooks, or Nikki Giovanni as models if possible.

Reinforcement

Read the following poem and answer the questions that follow:

Snow Toward Evening
Suddenly the sky turned gray,
The day,
Which had been bitter and chill,
Grew intensely soft and still.
Quietly
From some invisible blossoming tree
Millions of petals cool and white
Drifted and blew,
Lifted and flew,
Fell with the falling night.
         —Melville Cane

1. What mood do the words *gray*, *better*, and *chill* suggest? lonely, cold, depressing
2. Where in the poem does the mood begin to change? 4th line
3. What is the mood in the final lines of the poem? peaceful
4. What is the "invisible blossoming tree" and the "millions of petals cool and white"? snow
   Is this a simile or a metaphor? metaphor
5. What verbs in the last three lines help to establish the mood in this part of the poem? drifted, blew, lifted, flew
6. What sensory image in the seventh line contributes to the mood? cool white petals

Additional Resources

Skills Practice Book—page 128
Teacher's Resource Binder
Reinforcement Activities—
   page 92
Enrichment Activities—
   page 25

Using English in History

This activity allows students to see poetry not only as a literary form but as a means of recording history. It demonstrates that poetry is a very old form of literature.

In addition, this actively acquaints students with the fact that poetry has been used to record the history of our country.

Using English in History

▶ Comprehension

Poetry is one of the oldest forms of literature. Throughout time, people have used poetry and song to tell about important persons and events in history. For example, *The Iliad* and *The Odyssey* are very long poems that tell about the war between Greece and Troy in 1200 B.C..

The history of the United States, too, has been recorded in poems and songs. Many students have learned about the American Revolutionary War as they read these familiar lines from Henry Wadsworth Longfellow's well known poem "Paul Revere's Ride."

> Listen, my children, and you shall hear
> Of the midnight ride of Paul Revere.

Ballads that tell about the deeds of Daniel Boone, Davy Crockett, and John Luther Jones, better known as Casey Jones, are all poems set to music. People are still writing songs about important events. In the 1970's, the sinking of a Canadian ore ship on Lake Superior provided Gordon Lightfoot, a Canadian singer and composer, with the idea for the song "The Wreck of the *Edmund Fitzgerald*."

Exercise   Writing Poetry About History
▶ Creative Application

Choose an event in history that interests you. You may wish to take a new look at an old event, such as George Washington crossing the Delaware River. You may be interested in a more recent event, such as the American astronauts landing on the moon. Before beginning to write your poem, be sure you have the historical facts correct. You may want to do some research first. If you choose, you may set your poem to music. If you cannot compose a tune, try writing new lyrics that fit a familiar tune.

328

Chapter 18 Review

▶ Interpretation/Drawing Conclusions

Understanding Poetry Read "Lullaby" by Alan Bold and answer the questions that follow. See answers in margin.

LULLABY

Close your eyes gently
  And cuddle in
Keep yourself snug, a
  New day will begin.

Have pleasant dreams about
  Those things you love,
Sleep is an island
  Waiting above.

Night is a blanket
  Keeping you warm
If you close your eyes you can
  Come to no harm.

Dreams are like journeys
  Drifting along
Rest is a present
  Keeping you strong.

—ALAN BOLD

1. Write the words in the poem that rhyme. What pattern do you notice?
2. Find and write one example of alliteration.
3. Write the simile. What is being compared?
4. Find and write an example of a sensory image. To what sense is the poet appealing?
5. Find and write a metaphor from the poem. What is being compared?
6. Describe the mood of the poem. Write two words from the poem that contribute to this mood.

329

Chapter Review

This review allows teachers to evaluate student understanding of the concepts presented in this chapter.

Review Exercise

1. The words at the ends of the second and fourth lines in each stanza rhyme.
2. Close, cuddle, keep; your, yourself; those, things; keeping, close, can, come; you, you, your, you; Dreams, drifting
3. Dreams are like journeys; dreams and journeys
4. cuddle in (touch); blanket Keeping you warm (touch)
5. Sleep is an island—sleep and an island; Night is a blanket—night and a blanket; Rest is a present—rest and a present
6. restful, safe; lullaby, cuddle in, snug, pleasant, love sleep, blanket, warm, no harm, dreams, drifting, rest

Additional Resources

Skills Practice Book
Review—page 129

Test Booklet
Mastery Test—pages 107–110

Chapter 19

Chapter Objectives

1. To use descriptive language to create a clear picture of a subject

2. To use details that appeal to the senses

3. To organize details in a logical order

4. To use descriptive adjectives and adverbs, precise nouns, and strong verbs in a description

5. To use similes and metaphors to describe

Motivating the Students

1. Read the following passage from "The Man Who Was Thursday" to the students. Ask them to try to picture the scene that is being described. Define *gilded* before reading.

> When Syme went out into the starlit street, he found it for the moment empty. Then he realized (in some odd way) that the silence was rather a living silence than a dead one. Directly outside the door stood a street lamp, whose gleam gilded the leaves of the trees that bent out over the fence behind him. About a foot from the lamp-post stood a figure almost as rigid and motionless as the lamp-post itself. The tall hat and long frock-coat were black; the face, in an abrupt shadow, was almost as black.
>
> —G. K. Chesterton

After reading the passage, have students describe what they can remember. Discuss what words and phrases the writer used to make this possible. Discuss the mood or feeling the writer has created.

2. Read and discuss the chapter introduction on page 331. Have students point out the descriptive details in the passage by Marguerite Henry. Talk about the senses that Ms. Henry has appealed to.

Week 25

Chapter Management Guidelines This chart may be used to help structure daily lesson plans

Day 4	Day 5
Chapter 19 Opener, p. 331; Part 1, "Thinking About Descriptions," pp. 332–333	Part 2, "Prewriting: Gathering Details, pp. 334–335

Description and the Process of Writing

What do good writers do to make their stories and articles come to life? Read this paragraph by Marguerite Henry.

> The boy's dreams spun themselves out until there was nothing left of them. He slept a deep sleep. The candle in the lantern sputtered and died. The new moon rode higher and higher. Bats and nighthawks were flying noiselessly in the velvet night. They went about their business, swooping insects out of the air. With the gray light of morning, they vanished, giving way to the jangling chorus of the crows.

Notice how Marguerite Henry uses bright, descriptive words and sensory details to make her paragraph sparkle. Vivid description makes any story, letter, or report more interesting to read. In this chapter, you will learn how to make strong description a part of all your writing.

331

Special Populations

Refer to pages T32–T35 at the front of this Teacher's Edition for additional special populations notes for the teaching of composition.

Related Chapters

You may wish to refer to related material in other chapters as you teach the following concepts:

1. Using the writing process, Chapter 6, "Choosing a Process for Writing," page 101

2. Word replacement, Chapter 9, "Discovering the Dictionary and Thesaurus," page 161

3. Revising sentences, Chapter 15, "Revising and Combining Sentences," page 269

4. Using descriptive words, Chapter 16, "Adjectives for Creative Expression," page 283 and Chapter 17, "Adverbs for Clear Description," page 301

5. Using similes and metaphors, Chapter 18, "Appreciating the Language of Poetry," page 317

Additional Resources

Skills Practice Book—pages 130–133

Test Booklet—pages 111–116
  Pretest—pages 111–112
  Mastery Test—pages 113–116

Teacher's Resource Binder
  Reinforcement Activities—
    pages 93–94
  Enrichment Activities—
    pages 7, 39–52, 74–75
  Process of Writing Transparencies
  Ideas for Creative Teaching

Chapter Management Guidelines

This chart may be used to help structure daily lesson plans.

Day 1	Day 2	Day 3	Day 4	Day 5
Chapter 19, Part 3, "Prewriting: Organizing Details for a Description," pp. 336–337	Part 3, "Prewriting: Organizing Details for a Description," pp. 336–337	Part 4, "Revising To Improve Description," pp. 338–339	Chapter Review and selected end-of-chapter activities	Cumulative Review, pp. 344–345

Part 1

Objective

To use descriptive language to create a clear picture of a subject

Presenting the Lesson

 All Students

1. Both students and professional writing samples are included in part 1 for student analysis and evaluation. These samples illustrate varied styles of writing. They also show students what they can accomplish as well as showing how professionals write.

2. Read and discuss Example 1 on page 332. For **Think and Discuss,** always allow students time to think through the material independently before discussing it as a class. As students suggest details in response to the **Think and Discuss** questions, write them on the board. Point out that the description is organized from top to bottom.

3. Read and discuss Example 2 on page 333. Then answer the questions. Have the students use context clues to define the words *saturate* and *diffuse*. Have students point out specific details that appeal to sight, sound, and other senses. Discuss how each adds to the reader's picture of the scene. Note—The passage by Truman Capote has been edited slightly.

4. Students have now analyzed both student and professional writing samples. Explain that they will have an opportunity to write their own descriptions later in this chapter.

 Basic Students

Review adjectives and adverbs as descriptive words. Also, discuss precise nouns and exact verbs. Provide practice in writing precise descriptions. Supply photographs of still lifes or landscapes for the students. Have them list the items in the picture as headings on their papers. Beneath each heading, they should list descriptive details. Then, they can compose ten descriptive sentences. Encourage the use of all the senses.

---

1 Thinking About Descriptions

> ─ *Focus* ─
> A good descriptive paragraph paints a picture with words.

In your speaking and writing, you often describe people, places, and things. You use **sensory details** that tell how things look, sound, taste, feel, and smell. Imagine that you are writing a letter. You want to describe the costume you wore to a Halloween party. What would you write?

Example 1

▶ *Analyzing/Making Inferences*

Read and Think. Maggie wrote this paragraph in a letter to her cousin. Look for vivid words and phrases as you read.

> My hobo costume was outstanding. No one recognized me behind my dirt-smudged face. I even pulled a bashed-in old felt hat over my head so that no one could see my hair. I wore one of Dad's old corduroy suits. The ripped, patch-covered jacket hung down to my knees. Underneath the jacket was a bright red sweatshirt. I held the baggy pants up with a frayed rope. From the rope hung a tin plate and cup that clinked when I walked. Old army combat boots provided the final touch.

Think and Discuss. Carefully reread the paragraph. Then discuss the following questions with your classmates.

1. What are some of the details that help the reader know what the costume looks like? *Details will vary.*
2. Can you describe how Maggie has arranged the details in her paragraph? *Natural order; from top to bottom*
3. Which senses does Maggie appeal to in this description? *Sight, touch, sound*
4. Why do you think using sensory details is important in descriptions? *Answers will vary.*

332

 Advanced Students

Have students find examples of good descriptive writing in books, magazines, or newspapers. Have them share the examples with the class.

Example 2

Read and Think. In this paragraph, the writer describes a Christmas memory about baking fruitcakes. What descriptive words and phrases does he use to create a vivid picture?

> The black stove, stoked with coal and firewood, glows like a lighted pumpkin. Eggbeaters whirl, spoons spin round in bowls of butter and sugar, vanilla sweetens the air, ginger spices it. Melting, nose-tingling odors saturate the kitchen, suffuse the house, drift out to the world on puffs of chimney smoke. In four days our work is done. Thirty-one . . . cakes bask on window sills and shelves. —TRUMAN CAPOTE

Think and Discuss. Discuss these questions in class.

1. What sensory details does this paragraph include? To what senses do they appeal? Details will vary. Sight, sound, smell
2. What sense does Truman Capote appeal to first? second? third? Sight, sound, smell
3. What simile does the author use? Stove glows like a lighted pumpkin.

▶ Drawing Conclusions/Generalizing

Now It's Your Turn

You have looked at and thought about two descriptive paragraphs. Both use vivid words and phrases to create a picture for the reader. The details in each paragraph are organized in a logical order. Both paragraphs also create a mood. Now it is your turn to learn how to write descriptions.

333

Special Populations

LD, ESL, NSD Review nouns and verbs. Then review the words that describe the nouns and verbs. Point out that adjectives usually precede nouns while adverbs may occur in a variety of places. Also, see the notes under **Basic Students.**

Reinforcement

Have the students read the description below taken from *Go Tell It on the Mountain* and answer the questions that follow. Tell students to read through the passage once. Then, they should go back and read it again, pausing at the commas. Tell students to form a mental picture of what each phrase suggests and then go on to the next.

> To sweep the front room meant, principally, to sweep the heavy red and green and purple oriental-style carpet that had once been that room's glory, but was now so faded that it was all one swimming color, and so frayed in places that it tangled with the broom. John hated sweeping this carpet, for dust rose, clogging his nose and sticking to his sweaty skin, and he felt that should he sweep it forever, the clouds of dust would not diminish, the rug would not be clean.
>
> —James Baldwin

1. Give examples of sensory details that this passage contains. Tell what sense each appeals to.

2. The first sentence describes a thing. What is it?

3. What action is described in the second sentence?

Enrichment

1. Beauty in nature is a frequent subject of descriptions. Start a nature bulletin board. Have students collect photographs and artwork, either from magazines or their own original work. Ask them to find a written description from a poem, short story, or novel to accompany each illustration. Students may also write their own descriptions.

2. For additional enrichment activities, see the Unit Projects in the Teacher Notes on page 249. One or more of these projects have special activities for gifted and talented students.

Part 2

Objective

To use details that appeal to the senses

Presenting the Lesson

All Students

1. Read and discuss **Using Sensory Details** on page 334. After reading the example sentences, have students point out the sensory details that have been added to the example sentences. Have them tell which sense each detail appeals to. Write the following sentence on the board: The cat slept in the basket. Have students suggest several sensory details that can be added to appeal to the senses.

2. Read and discuss **Gathering Details** on pages 334–335. Practice each of the methods of gathering details. For example, have students observe and list details about the classroom. Have students list details of something from memory —perhaps the celebration of a recent holiday. Then, have them imagine details of a place or person they have never seen. They might picture a trip down the Amazon or a ride on a camel.

3. Read and discuss **Creating a Mood** on page 335. Ask students to suggest additional details for the examples.

4. Assign and discuss Exercises A and B on page 335.

Basic Students

Before assigning Exercise A, it may help to bring in pictures of an amusement park or carnival. Discuss the sights and sounds and smells that the picture or pictures evoke. Then, have the students complete Exercise A.

Advanced Students

Have the students write a descriptive poem using the details that they have listed about the carnival in Exercise A. Have students review techniques discussed in Chapter 18, "Appreciating the Language of Poetry," if necessary.

---

2 Prewriting: Gathering Details

> **Focus**
>
> When writing a description, use details that appeal to the senses.

Using Sensory Details

▶ Comprehension

You experience the world through your senses. For example, when you eat an orange, you taste the tangy juice. You also see the bright orange color and smell the special fragrance. You feel the smooth pulp on your tongue.

Whenever you write, use sensory details like these that appeal to sight, hearing, taste, and smell. Let the reader experience what you are describing. Read the following sentences. Sensory details have been added to the second sentence in each set.

> The girl wore a sweater over her dress.
> The frail girl wore a faded sweater over her crumpled dress.
>
> Ramon bit into the apple.
> Ramon crunched into the tart, cold apple.

Gathering Details

Sensory details are the building blocks of descriptive writing. You can gather the details you need in three ways.

First, you can **observe** your subject carefully. For example, imagine that you are watching a lion at the zoo. Study him closely. Is he yellow, golden, or the color of wheat? Does he walk, swagger, or prance? Is his mane woolly or silky? How would you describe his roar?

334

Sometimes details can be gathered from your **memory**. Suppose that you want to describe your first camping trip. Searching your memories of that trip can provide details of itchy insect bites, a cool mountain lake, and the smoky smell of a campfire.

Your **imagination** is another good place to find details. In your imagination, anything can happen. You can create new and unheard of details such as purple zebras and chocolate-covered broccoli. You can find bells that hum and a flower with ice-cold petals.

Creating a Mood

Choose details to create a specific mood or feeling. For example, imagine that you want to create a calm, relaxed mood in a description of a woodland setting. You might use phrases like *filtered sunlight, leaves ruffled by a gentle breeze,* or *the still pond.* To create a feeling of noisy confusion as you describe a thunderstorm, you might use phrases like *the crack of thunder* or *hail pounding the canvas tent.* You could help the reader see *wind beating saplings to the ground* and feel *the driving force of the rain.*

Exercises   Gathering Details

▶ Creative Application

A. Imagine that you are at an amusement park or carnival. Write a description of this scene. What would you see? Think about the smells and sounds that would surround you. What textures can you tell about? Include a variety of sensory details in your description.

B. Create an imaginary place. Brainstorm with some classmates to think of descriptive details. Record ideas on a chart. Write each of the five senses (sight, sound, taste, touch, smell) across the top of a paper. Under each heading, list details suggested by brainstorming. Save this chart.

335

Special Populations

LD For Exercise A, students whose motor skills make writing frustrating might tape record their descriptioins.

LD, ESL Pair students with stronger writers and native speakers of English for work on Exercise B.

Reinforcement

Have the students choose one topic from each of the following categories. Students should write the topic as a heading on their papers. Then, they should list as many details as they can think of for each topic. Remind students to check to see that they have included details from the five senses in their lists.

  a. observations of the school library
     observations of the school cafeteria at lunchtime
  b. remembering last night's supper
     the memory of your first day at school
  c. imagine seeing a volcanic eruption
     imagine meeting a dinosaur

Enrichment

Have students imagine that they are writing a pen pal in a foreign country. They will describe their town or community. Have them list details that describe some local attractions.

Additional Resources

Skills Practice Book—page 130
Teacher's Resource Binder
  Reinforcement Activities—
  page 93

Part 3

Objective

To organize details in a logical order

Presenting the Lesson

 All Students

1. Read and discuss pages 336–337. Discuss each method given for organizing details. Make sure that students see how the organizational methods are applied in the examples given. Have students suggest subjects that might be suitable for each method. Then list details describing the classroom and discuss how they might be arranged according to each method presented in the lesson. Have students suggest how the details in the first example passage might be rearranged so that the creature is described from top to bottom.

2. Provide additional paragraphs and discuss their organization as needed.

3. Assign and discuss the exercise on page 337.

 Basic Students

Bring in a picture of a somewhat uncommon animal, such as an armadillo or a tadpole. As a group activity, have the students suggest details that describe the animal, and then have them list the details in natural order. Then, have the students work independently on the exercise.

 Advanced Students

To further develop the concept of mood, divide these students into two groups. Both groups will brainstorm and list details for a scene in which they are in a small boat on a large body of water. Tell one group to list details indicating they feel peaceful and happy. Tell the other group to list details indicating they feel lonely, isolated, and fearful. Have the groups share their lists with the class. Point out how the choice of details creates different moods.

---

3 Prewriting: Organizing Details for a Description

┌─ *Focus* ─────────────────────────────────┐

Make your descriptions clear by organizing details in a logical order.

└──┘

▶ Comprehension/Inferring Sequence

The first step in writing a description is to make a list of sensory details. Next, you must arrange them in a logical order. This will help your readers clearly picture what you are describing. Here are some good ways to organize a descriptive paragraph.

Natural Order

Often, you arrange details in the same way that you would notice them. Then you are using **natural order**. Natural order is sometimes called **spatial order**. Natural order is one of the most common ways to arrange details. For example, you might look at a skyscraper by starting at the bottom and working your way to the top story. When you board a bus, you might notice the passengers from the front of the bus to the back. These are natural orders. Read the following paragraph. The details are arranged in natural order, from front to back.

> I thought at first that it was a rat or something that had broken the egg and eaten it. After I got a good look though, I could see that it wasn't any rat. It was about the size of a squirrel. It didn't have any hair, and its head—well, I couldn't believe my eyes when I saw it. It didn't look like anything I'd ever seen before. It had three little knobs sticking out of its head and sort of a collar up over its neck. It was a lizardy-looking critter. It kept moving its thick tail slowly back and forth in the nest. —OLIVER BUTTERWORTH

336

Order of Importance

Another way to organize your description is either to begin or end with the detail that impressed you the most. This is called the **order of importance**. For example, if your waitress at a restaurant had green hair on St. Patrick's Day, you might want to begin describing her with that striking detail. However, some details are more powerful if they are left for the end of a description.

Grouping by Senses

A third way to organize a description is by describing with one type of sense detail at a time. To describe a florist's shop, you might begin by using details that appeal to the sense of smell. Then you could continue with details that appeal to the sense of sight, and so on. Notice how the details in this description are grouped by senses.

> Confusion reigned in the restaurant kitchen. The strong odor of boiled corned beef and cabbage fought with the garlic of the spaghetti sauce. The rich, heavy odor of roasted duck completed a menu of aromas. Huge kettles were banged against steel counters. Chefs shouted to each other over the noise. In the background was the steady whack, whack of a butcher knife hitting the cutting block.

There are many ways to develop and organize a description. Choose the way that best suits your topic.

Exercise   Writing a Description

▶ Creative Application

Use the details you wrote for either Exercise A or B in part 2 to write a descriptive paragraph. Use natural order, the order of importance, or grouping by senses to arrange the details. Then write a draft of your descriptive paragraph.

337

Part 4

Objectives

1. To use descriptive adjectives and adverbs, precise nouns, and strong verbs in a description

2. To use similes and metaphors to describe

Presenting the Lesson

 All Students

1. Read and discuss **Using Adjectives and Adverbs** on page 338. First, read the example paragraph without the added adjectives and adverbs. Then, read it with the revisions. Discuss the effect of the revisions. Talk about the lonely feeling or mood that words such as *muddy*, *rusty*, *gray*, and *moldy* suggest. Stress that the addition of too many descriptive words can be confusing for the reader.

2. Read **Using Strong Verbs and Precise Nouns** on pages 338–339. Emphasize the importance of using action verbs, where appropriate, rather than state-of-being verbs in a description. Have students suggest some more precise verbs that could be used in place of *walk*. Discuss the examples of general and precise nouns mentioned in the lesson. Ask students to suggest other examples of more precise nouns for the following words: *animal*, *hat*, *house*. Talk about Helena's changes. How do the new words add to the reader's picture of the scene?

3. Read **Using Similes and Metaphors** on page 339. Make sure that students understand the difference between a metaphor and a simile. You may wish to refer to Chapter 18, "The Language of Poetry," page 317, to review the definitions and provide students with additional examples of similes and metaphors. Read the final revision. Have students look again at Helena's first draft on page 338. Discuss how the revisions have improved her letter.

4. Assign and discuss the exercise on page 339. Remind students to use the "Thesaurus" in their **Power Handbook** to find strong action verbs and precise nouns.

You may wish to use the following criteria to evaluate descriptive writing.

---

4 Revising To Improve Description

> **Focus**
>
> Improve description by carefully revising your writing.

Using Adjectives and Adverbs

▶ Comprehension

As you have learned, adjectives describe nouns and pronouns. Adverbs describe verbs, adjectives, and other adverbs. Use adjectives and adverbs to make your writing more vivid.

Helena wrote about her visit to friends in the country. As she reread her draft, she saw that by adding some adjectives and adverbs her readers would see the barn as she did.

The building was alone in a field. The paint had turned ˄*muddy* brown, and the door moved ˄*slowly* on one ˄*rusty* hinge. Sunlight came through the holes in the ˄*crumbling* roof. Cats chased ˄*gray field* mice through the ˄*moldy* straw on the floor.

Helena added only enough descriptive words to make her paragraph more interesting. A paragraph can be difficult to understand if too many descriptive words are used.

Using Strong Verbs and Precise Nouns

You have learned that there are two kinds of verbs. **Action verbs** are words such as *galloped*, *chase*, and *laughs*. **State-of-being verbs** are words like *is* and *became*. Whenever possible, use action verbs in your writing. Action verbs are stronger and more exact than state-of-being verbs.

Also pay special attention to the nouns in your descriptive writing. Replace general nouns such as *shoes*, *flower*, and *bear* with more precise nouns like *sneakers*, *tulip*, and *grizzly*.

As Helena continued the revision of her paragraph, she replaced weak verbs with strong action verbs. She also made some nouns more precise. She chose words that would create the mood she wanted.

The ~~building was~~ *barn stood* alone in a field. The paint had turned muddy brown, and the door ~~moved~~ *swung* slowly on one rusty hinge. Sunlight ~~came~~ *struggled* through the holes in the crumbling roof. Cats chased gray field mice through the moldy straw ~~on~~ *in* the ~~floor~~ *stalls*.

Using Similes and Metaphors

Use similes and metaphors to make comparisons. Similes and metaphors can make your writing clearer and more interesting. Helena added this simile to her description.

> The paint had turned muddy brown, and the door swung slowly on one rusty hinge like an autumn leaf about to fall.

Now read Helena's revised paragraph. Notice how much clearer and more interesting it is than her first draft.

> The barn stood alone in a field. The paint had turned muddy brown, and the door swung slowly on one rusty hinge like an autumn leaf about to fall. Sunlight struggled through the holes in the crumbling roof. Cats chased gray field mice through the moldy straw in the stalls.

Exercise   Using the Language of Description
▶ Creative Application

Look again at the description you wrote in part 3. Revise your paragraph. Replace weak verbs with strong action verbs. Replace general nouns with precise nouns. Add adjectives and adverbs for detail. Add a simile or metaphor if it fits. After you finish the revision, make a final copy and share it with your classmates.

339

Additional Resources

Skills Practice Book—page 132
Teacher's Resource Binder
  Enrichment Activities—
    pages 7, 74–75

Guidelines for Evaluation

Strong The most successful descriptions will display the following characteristics: (5 points)
1. will use sensory details to develop the topic
2. will use strong verbs, precise nouns, and appropriate modifiers to create a vivid picture in the mind of the reader
3. will demonstrate a sound organizational strategy, showing the relationship of one feature to another
4. will maintain a consistent mood
5. will contain no more than two or three minor errors in grammar, usage, and mechanics

Average A description of average quality will meet most of the criteria of the successful response but may display one or two of these problems: (3 points)
1. may include only one type of sense detail when more are needed and appropriate
2. may not create a definite mood
3. may use a vocabulary that is not vivid or precise
4. may display several errors in grammar, usage, and mechanics

Weak A weak description will display only one or two of the characteristics of a successful response. It will also be characterized by several of the following problems: (1 point)
1. lack of appropriate sensory details
2. rambling, illogical organization
3. a vague or imprecise vocabulary
4. numerous errors in grammar, usage, and mechanics

▶ Basic Students

Practice using the "Thesaurus" with the students. Remind them to choose words that match the meaning that they intend. Pair students with stronger writers for the revision process.

◆ Advanced Students

Have students work as a group and brainstorm for comparisons that are fresh and surprising to complete the following phrases.

fierce as   a mud puddle is like
sticky as   a moonbeam is like
slimy as   frost is like

Speaking and
Listening

Objective

To use listening skills to gather sensory details for a description

Presenting the Activity

This page gives special emphasis to the skill of listening for sensory details. Before assigning the activity, you may wish to practice listening skills with the class by having them close their eyes as you make various sounds. Then, ask them to describe the sounds in writing.

Speaking and Listening

Listening To Describe
▶ Comprehension

In a world filled with noise pollution, it is easy to tune out some sounds. However, sound is important to description. To describe accurately, writers must listen carefully to the sounds around them. In fact, writers often carry notebooks so that they can record sense details anytime and anywhere. In this way, a writer can build a storehouse of sense impressions. This is the raw material the writer uses to create similes, metaphors, and other descriptive images.

Exercise Listening To Describe
▶ Creative Application

Spend one morning carefully listening to the sounds around you. Begin as you awake. Try to hear and absorb every sound. Tune in to each separate sound. Record what you hear on paper as accurately as you can. Ask yourself what a certain sound might be compared to. In this way, you may create similes or metaphors. For example, you might describe the horn of a large truck on the highway as a trumpeting elephant. After your listening session, write a sentence that describes each sound with the details you recorded. Your morning of listening should produce many sentences.

340

Creative Writing

A. Imagine that you own a restaurant. Plan a new menu. Write a brief description of four menu items that would make your customers' mouths water. Remember, too many adjectives can spoil a description. Choose your adjectives carefully.

B. Use the following "recipe" to write a description in the form of a poem.

1. Write a noun.
2. Write two words describing the noun.
3. Write three words ending in *-ing* telling what the noun does.
4. Write two more new words describing the noun.
5. Write a synonym for the noun.

Look at this example.

dragon
fiery, hungry
roaring, lunging, crunching
ornery, scaled
monster

341

Creative Writing

These activities provide opportunities for imaginative applications of the skills presented in this chapter. As students complete Exercise A, tell them that although they will be dealing primarily with the sensory details of sight and taste, they should include other kinds of sensory details as well.

Using English in Geography

This activity provides an opportunity for students to combine map reading skills with what they have learned about descriptive writing. You may wish to emphasize the need to translate the information provided by the map into a mental picture of what the country looks like. Students should list their details during prewriting and decide on an appropriate method of organization.

Using English in ▶ Geography

▶ Comprehension

One way to describe a place is to draw a map of it. Different kinds of maps can show different types of facts. One kind of map, a topographical map, shows what the surface of the land is like. Usually, colors are used to show the various features. Green areas are low, yellow areas are higher, and brown areas are very elevated or mountainous. Other geographic details such as rivers and lakes are shown on this kind of map, too.

Exercise   Using Descriptive Details from a Map
▶ Creative Application

Study the topographical map of Italy shown below. Use the details on the map to write a description of what the country looks like.

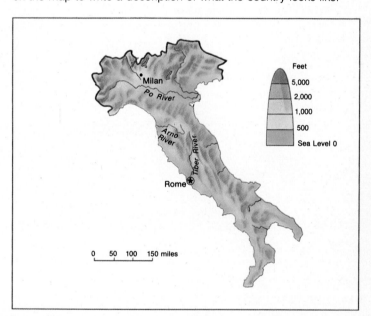

Chapter 19 Review

▶ Analyzing/Drawing Conclusions

A. Analyzing a Description Read this paragraph. Then answer the questions that follow. See answers in margin.

The bull ring or Plaza de Toros was a big, tawny brick amphitheatre standing at the end of a street in an open field. The yellow and red Spanish flag was floating over it. Carriages were driving up and people were getting out of buses. There was a great crowd of beggars around the entrance. Men were selling water out of big terra cotta water bottles. Kids sold fans, canes, roasted salted almonds in paper spills, fruit, and slabs of ice cream. The crowd was gay and cheerful but all intent on pushing toward the entrance. Mounted civil guards with patent leather cocked hats and carbines slung over their backs sat their horses like statues, and the crowd flowed through.

—ERNEST HEMINGWAY

1. List the descriptive words and phrases in this paragraph that help you get a clearer picture of the scene.
2. What comparison did the author use?
3. Describe the order used in this description.

▶ Structured Application

B. Using Descriptive Language Improve these sentences. Add the kinds of words described in the parentheses.

1. The shark ate the smaller fish. (Use a stronger verb and better adjective.)
2. The Halloween costume was unusual. (Use a stronger verb and an adjective.)
3. The bank president looked at the empty safe. (Use a stronger verb; add an adjective and adverb.)
4. The pillow was soft. (Use a simile or metaphor.)
5. The nurse walked quietly down the hall. (Use a stronger verb and an adjective.)

343

Additional Resources

Skills Practice Book
Review—page 133

Test Booklet
Mastery Test—pages 113–116

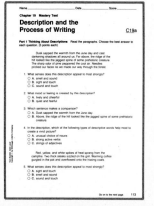

Cumulative Review

These exercises provide a cumulative review of the concepts presented in this unit. Each exercise challenges the students to apply several of the skills they have acquired while studying this unit.

To evaluate the descriptive writing in Exercise A, see the Guidelines for Evaluation in the Teacher Notes on page 339.

Exercise A
1. Write only a fact or two on each note card.
2. Practice giving your talk many times.
3. Eye contact means that you make each person in the audience feel that you are talking directly to him or her.
4. Ask questions for specific reasons and be polite when you disagree during a group discussion.
5. Use visual aids to help clarify your talk.

(These Unit Projects are continued from T. E. page 249.)

Group Activity: Description

Use this group activity to sharpen students' descriptive abilities and to give them practice in conceptualizing.

Break the class into groups. Give each group pictures and/or books showing artists' conceptions of inventions, housing, transportation, of the future. You may wish to limit each group to a specific topic, inventions, for example. Suggested books to use include the following: *The World of the Future Robots, The World of Future Cities,* and *The World of Future Star Travel* by Kenneth Gatland and David Jefferies and *The Kid's Whole Future Catalog* by Paula Taylor.

Each group should use the pictures and books as a springboard to generate their own idea of something that they think will be used in the future. They should write a description of their item. Have the groups brainstorm a list of adjectives that the students might use in describing their objects. Stress the need for rich, descriptive detail. Tell them to include explanations of how the object will be used, how it is constructed, and what special features it will have.

Then, have the groups prepare a poster, model, or diorama of their creations to accompany their description. Hold an Exposition of the Future. Have students display their own creations and view the work of other groups. Provide evaluation forms. Have each student describe and evaluate the creations of the other groups. Invite other classes to view the displays, if possible.

Composition
▶ Creative Application

Writing Descriptions Write a brief description of one of the following. Include well-chosen sensory details. Try to include a simile or metaphor.

   a. the first snowfall   c. the beach at noon
   b. your yard in summer   d. a setting of your choice

Grammar
▶ Recalling/Analyzing

Adjectives and Adverbs Choose the correct word from the parentheses. Write it on your paper.

1. Jacob did not pronounce the French words (good, well) during his oral exam.
2. (Those, Them) gorillas were the (largest, more large) animals in the circus parade.
3. Sam lettered the poster (carefuler, more carefully) than Christina did.
4. Coach Bentley gave (a, an) award to the player who scored the (greater, greatest) number of points.
5. These seeds grow into (this, these) kind of flower.
6. Suzanne did very (good, well) at the relay races.
7. The sun will melt the icicles (quick, quickly).
8. The aftershock caused (worse, worser) damage than the earthquake itself.

Related Skills
▶ Structured Application

A. Speaking and Listening The following statements are incorrect. Write each correctly on your paper. See answers in margin.

1. Write your speech out word for word on note cards.
2. Practice giving a talk only once.

344

3. Eye contact means you keep your eyes on your notes.
4. It is not a good idea to disagree or ask questions during a group discussion.
5. Do not use visual aids. They distract your listeners.

B. Revising and Combining Sentences Improve and rewrite the following sentences. Follow the directions in the parentheses. Leave out words in italics. See answers in margin.

1. An Indian paintbrush is an orange flower *and* it is Wyoming's state flower *and* it blooms in summer.
2. Penguins live on South Georgia Island. Elephant seals *live on South Georgia Island*. (Join sentence parts with **and**.)
3. I could smell the bacon. *It was* sizzling. *The bacon was* in the kitchen.
4. It started to rain. The team did not cancel the game. (Join the sentences with **, but**.)
5. The fenders on the bike are new. *The fenders* shine. (End the important word with *-y*.)

▶ Making Inferences/Analyzing

C. Poetry Read the poem below and answer the questions.
See answers in margin.

The night is a big black cat,
    The moon is her topaz eye,
The stars are the mice she hunts at night,
    In the field of the sultry sky.

—G. ORR CLARK

1. If you wrote another stanza for this poem, in which lines would you put the rhyming words?
2. Find and write two examples of alliteration.
3. Find and write an example of a sensory image. To what sense does it appeal?
4. Find and write an example of a simile or metaphor.

345

Computer Activity: Thesaurus

It is especially helpful to have a rich and varied word bank from which to choose details for descriptive writing. To aid students in building such a resource and to help them sharpen word selection skills, have students create a computer thesaurus that can be used as a supplement to the thesaurus in this text. Since the computer thesaurus will serve as a supplement, have students limit entries to words that are not included in the thesaurus in the **Power Handbook.**

Students should label each word with its part of speech, and give cross-reference words:

PLACE.—n. location, site
        v. locate, put
SITE.—n. location, place

Students can add entries to the thesaurus throughout the year. If possible, make several copies of the class thesaurus available during writing assignments. Encourage students to use them.

Exercise B
1. An Indian paintbrush is an orange flower. It is Wyoming's state flower. It blooms in the summer.
2. Penguins and elephant seals live on South Georgia Island.
3. I could smell the bacon sizzling in the kitchen.
4. It started to rain, but the team did not cancel the game.
5. The shiny fenders on the bike are new.

Exercise C
1. the second and fourth
2. big, black; sultry sky
3. big black cat—sight and touch; topaz eye—sight; stars, mice—sight; field, sky—sight
4. night is a big black cat—metaphor; moon is her topaz eye—metaphor; stars are the mice—metaphor; field of the sultry sky—metaphor

Introducing the Unit

1. Organization of the Unit Have students read the chapter titles, the unit title, and the introduction to the unit on page 346. Point out that everything the students do in and out of school involves some type of thinking. Also mention that much of what they do in and out of school involves analyzing discovering answers, and applying what has been learned. Explain that this unit will sharpen their thinking skills and their fact-finding skills. These skills are necessary for forming opinions and reporting information. Point out that no matter what students choose to do when they finish school, they will need to think clearly, form sound opinions, and express their ideas logically.

Continue the lesson with **Motivating Through Literature,** below.

2. Use the **Unit Management Guidelines** below to help you develop your weekly lesson plan. An optional week 9 has been provided to allow for variations in the length of grading periods. The teacher may wish to use this week for review, additional practice, and the presentation of selected special feature pages. Teachers who work on four- or six-week grading periods may adapt the chart accordingly.

Motivating Through Literature

Have students read silently as you read aloud the poem on page 347. Point out that the poet is Papago Indian. Mention that Indian literature often uses creatures in nature to teach important lessons about life. Use the following questions to stimulate discussion about the poem. Suggested answers are given, but answers may vary.

1. What creatures are mentioned in the poem and what are the qualities of each? owl, wise and knowing; eagle, powerful and bold; dove, peaceful and gentle
2. If a human behaved like these creatures, what qualities would the human have? wisdom, courage, peace

Explain that what the students are learning in school is helping them pre-

UNIT 4

Going Forth

In Unit 4 you will build on everything you have learned in this book. You will learn how clear thinking skills can help you to see relationships among facts. Clear thinking skills will also help you avoid some common errors that lead to poor reasoning. More research skills will help you gather facts so that you can write about your opinions or write a report. You will gain experience in filling out forms and writing letters.

Your clear thinking skills will help you when you solve a mystery you are reading or decide how to do a math problem. Your research and report writing skills will be useful in almost any subject.

You gain and improve skills in school so that you will be ready to explore the world. The greater your wisdom, the more confident you will be.

Unit Management Guidelines

Week 28	Week 29	Week 30	Week 31	Week 32
Unit 4 Opener pp. 346–347; Chapter 20, Parts 1–6, pp. 348–365	Chapter 21, Parts 1–4, pp. 366–377	Chapter 22, Parts 1–5, pp. 378–390	Chapter 22, Part 6, pp. 391–395; Chapter 23, Parts 1–5, pp. 396–411	Chapter 23, Parts 6–8, pp. 412–419; Chapter 24, Parts 1–2, pp. 420–425

I GO FORTH TO MOVE ABOUT THE EARTH

I go forth to move about the earth.
I go forth as the owl, wise and knowing.
I go forth as the eagle, powerful and bold.
I go forth as the dove, peaceful and gentle.
I go forth to move about the earth
    in wisdom, courage, and peace.

—ALONZO LOPEZ (Papago Indian)

347

pare for the place they will take in the world. Have a discussion about what the students want to do after they finish school. Point out that the skills they have gained from this and earlier units will help them to become whatever they choose.

Unit Projects

Independent Activity: Fact and Opinion

To help students see how fact and opinion are used in advertising, ask the students to keep a television commercial viewing diary for two weeks. Provide students with daily forms to fill out, headed as follows: *Product Name, Facts Given, Opinions Given.* As students view each commercial, they will indicate the product advertised, the facts given about the product, and statements of opinion about the product. Students should list any support given for opinions. Encourage students to view a variety of commercials.

After a two-week period, ask the students to analyze their data. Students should try to determine whether one type of product, such as cosmetics for example, relies on opinion while another type, food items, stresses facts. Students should also notice which products adequately support stated opinions and which give unsupported opinions.

Students may present their findings and conclusions to the class.

Group Activity: Local History

Help students develop their research and reporting skills by investigating the history of their local neighborhood. Direct them to gather information from resources such as the Chamber of Commerce, the library, even the cemetery. Encourage students to collect photos of the area from earlier times.

Suggest that students work in pairs to interview several older local residents in their neighborhood. Guide students in the careful preparation of open-ended interview questions.

(Unit Projects are continued on T. E. page 458.)

Week 33	Week 34	Week 35	Week 36 (optional)
Chapter 24, Parts 3–5, pp. 426–431	Chapter 24, Parts 6–8, pp. 432–441	Chapter 25, Parts 1–5, pp. 442–457; Cumulative Review, pp. 458–459	Additional Review, Reinforcement, and Enrichment. See number 2 under **Introducing the Unit.**

Chapter Objectives

1. To understand the function of the preposition

2. To identify prepositions in sentences

3. To identify nouns and pronouns as objects of prepositions

4. To identify prepositional phrases in sentences

5. To use the correct pronoun forms as objects of prepositions

6. To differentiate between prepositions and adverbs

7. To correctly use *between* and *among*

8. To use conjunctions to combine sentences

9. To recognize a word used as various parts of speech

Motivating the Students

Set up a display in the front of the room. Use a table as the focal point. Place objects on, under, over, around, and near the table. Then ask students to point out the relationship of each object to the table. As students use prepositions to state the relationship, write the prepositions on the board. Identify the words as prepositions. Point out to students that they already use these words in speaking and writing and that they will learn more about them in this chapter.

Read and discuss the introduction to the chapter on page 349. Emphasize the point that although words such as prepositions and conjunctions are small, they are important because they show relationships between words or combine ideas.

Special Populations

LD Review the terms *noun, pronoun, adverb, phrase, object,* and *modifier* before you begin this chapter.

This chapter will be difficult for students with visual-spatial perception difficulties. Prepare a reference chart of prepositions divided into these groups: direction, time, position, and manner.

ESL It is easiest for these students to learn and practice prepositions in pairs of opposites: *above* and *below, over* and

Week 28

Chapter Management Guidelines This chart may be used to help structure daily lesson plans

Day 1	Day 2	Day 3	Day 4	Day 5
Unit and Chapter Openers, pp. 346–349; Part 1 "What Are Prepositions?" pp. 350–351; Part 2, "Using Prepositional Phrases," pp. 352–353	Part 3, "Pronouns after Prepositions," pp. 354–355; Part 4, "Special Problems with Prepositions," pp. 356–357	Part 5, "What Are Conjunctions?" pp. 358–359	Part 6, "Using Words as Different Parts of Speech," pp. 360–361	Chapter Review and selected end-of-chapter activities

Using Prepositions and Conjunctions

Some small words in English may seem to have little meaning or importance. Yet look what happens when those words are missing.

"Jack ____ Jill"
____ *the World* ____ *Eighty Days*
"I've Been Working ____ the Railroad"
"The Night ____ Christmas"

The missing words are prepositions and conjunctions. These words are important because they show relationships and combine ideas. These two parts of speech help the other words in the sentence work together. The correct use of prepositions and conjunctions in your writing helps your reader see clear relationships between the words in your sentences.

349

under, up and *down, before* and *after.*

Some Spanish prepositions, such as *de* and *en,* have several meanings. Students will have to learn each of the prepositions that take the place of *de* and *en* and the meanings for these prepositions.

Related Chapters

You may wish to refer to related material in other chapters as you teach the following concepts:

1. Using prepositions in sentences, Chapter 2,"Writing and Understanding Sentences," page 17

2. Nouns and their position in sentences, Chapter 3, "Nouns for Precise Meaning," page 45

3. Object pronouns, Chapter 12, "Understanding Pronouns," page 209

4. Conjunctions, Chapter 15, "Revising and Combining Sentences," page 269

5. Adverbs, Chapter 17, "Adverbs for Clear Description," page 301

Additional Resources

Skills Practice Book—pages 134–142
Test Booklet—pages 117–120
  Pretest—pages 117–118
  Mastery Test—pages 119–120
Teacher's Resource Binder
  Reinforcement Activities—
    pages 95–102
  Enrichment Activities—
    pages 39–52, 76
  Process of Writing Transparencies
  Ideas for Creative Teaching

Part 1

Objectives

1. To understand the function of the preposition
2. To identify prepositions in sentences
3. To identify nouns and pronouns as objects of prepositions

Presenting the Lesson

 All Students

1. Read and discuss page 350. Make sure the students understand how the relationship stated in the sample sentence changes as the preposition changes. Ask students to substitute other prepositions from the list to see additional relationships.
2. As a class exercise, have students take turns making up sentences using prepositions from the list on page 350. Be sure that they use the words as prepositions and not as adverbs.
3. Make sure that students understand that the object of a preposition is always a noun or a pronoun.
4. Assign and discuss Exercises A, B, and C on page 351. Before students begin Exercise C, make sure they know what stalagmites and stalactites are.
5. Use Exercise A on page 362 for additional practice if needed.

 Basic Students

Before students do the exercises on page 351, help them to complete the following sentences by adding prepositional phrases. Encourage the group to change the meaning of each sentence by changing the prepositional phrase.

1. The mother quail ran _____.
2. The water _____ is very cold.
3. My little brother hid _____.
4. Mrs. Redondo told a story _____.

 Advanced Students

Have the students change the sentences in Exercise A by changing the preposition in each sentence.

---

1 What Are Prepositions?

┌─ **Focus** ─────────────────────────────

A **preposition** is a word that relates its object to some other word in the sentence. The noun or pronoun following the preposition is called the **object of the preposition**.

└──

▶ Comprehension

Prepositions relate the words following them to the words before them. Read these sentences.

The groceries are *in* the trunk.
Four fire engines zoomed *past* our house.

In and *past* are prepositions. They show the relationship between the groceries and the trunk and between the fire engines and the house.

The noun or pronoun following a preposition is called the **object of the preposition**. In the sentences above, *trunk* and *house* are the objects of prepositions.

You can change the relationship between words in a sentence by changing the preposition. These prepositions show different ways of relating the sheepdog and Anthony.

The sheepdog walked *behind* Anthony.
The sheepdog walked *around* Anthony.

Here is a list of words often used as prepositions.

about	before	down	of	to
above	behind	during	off	toward
across	below	for	on	under
after	beneath	from	onto	underneath
against	beside	in	out	until
along	between	inside	outside	up
among	beyond	into	over	upon
around	but (except)	like	past	with
at	by	near	through	without

350

Exercises   Finding Prepositions

▶ Recalling

A. Number your paper from 1 to 10. Write the preposition in each of the following sentences.

1. A tugboat pushed barges <u>down</u> the river.
2. There is gum stuck <u>on</u> my shoe.
3. The pinch hitter drove the ball deep <u>into</u> left field.
4. This portrait <u>of</u> George Washington is two hundred years old.
5. Louisa May Alcott wrote <u>about</u> her own times.
6. The kitten crawled out <u>onto</u> the limb and mewed.
7. Mom's tire was sliced <u>by</u> some broken glass.
8. The Plains Indians depended greatly <u>upon</u> the buffalo.
9. <u>Under</u> the new rules, our team can't compete.
10. <u>After</u> dinner, we will sing carols.

▶ Analyzing

B. Number your paper from 1 to 10. Write the <u>preposition</u> in each of the sentences below. After the preposition, write the <u>object</u> that follows the preposition. Write *None* if there is no preposition.

1. B. J.'s hamster was running <u>on</u> a <u>treadmill</u>.
2. Cornelia heard a creaking noise <u>in</u> the <u>hall</u>.
3. Tommy and Michael played basketball yesterday.   None
4. Jeff opened his book <u>to</u> the <u>index</u>.
5. Who put the butter <u>near</u> the <u>oven</u>?
6. Don't swim <u>beyond</u> that <u>sign</u>.
7. Paul washed and waxed the van.   None
8. We found these coins <u>under</u> the <u>bookcase</u>.
9. Did Marge park her bike <u>beside</u> the <u>fence</u>?
10. The apples <u>on</u> this <u>tree</u> aren't ripe.

▶ Creative Application

C. Writing Your science class is taking a field trip to visit a cave. Write a brief paragraph telling about your adventures with stalagmites, stalactites, and bats. Use prepositions to show relationships of people and objects in the cave.

351

Special Populations

LD After students complete Exercise A, do Exercise B orally with them. Remind students that every preposition must have an object. A noun or pronoun must follow every preposition.

ESL These students might begin a "Dictionary of Prepositions" with illustrations that show how each preposition relates one group of words to another. This exercise is especially helpful for students whose native language does not have an exact English equivalent for a particular preposition.

Reinforcement

1. Have the students follow the directions for Exercise A on page 351 using these sentences:

1. We planted the rose bushes <u>beside</u> the house.
2. An ant crawled <u>inside</u> the picnic basket.
3. The squirrel darted <u>underneath</u> the parked car.
4. Like a cat, Frank climbed <u>up</u> the tree.
5. <u>Without</u> gasoline, I can't start the lawnmower.
6. <u>During</u> the basketball game, Melanie scored twenty points.

2. Have the students follow the directions for Exercise B on page 351 using these sentences:

1. The light shone <u>on</u> my <u>face</u>.
2. The story is <u>about</u> a <u>magician</u>.
3. <u>After</u> <u>lunch</u>, we will go to the <u>museum</u>.
4. Kevin rode his bike <u>around</u> the <u>block</u>.
5. Kira hid her diary <u>under</u> the <u>bed</u>.
6. The explorers will hike <u>into</u> the <u>jungle</u>.
7. <u>Beneath</u> the <u>tree</u>, James found a bird's nest.

Enrichment

For enrichment activities, see the Unit Projects in the Teacher Notes on page 349. One or more of these projects have special activities for gifted and talented students.

Additional Resources

Skills Practice Book—page 134

Teacher's Resource Binder
  Reinforcement Activities—
    page 95
  Enrichment Activities—
    page 76

Part 2

Objective

To identify prepositional phrases in sentences

Presenting the Lesson

 All Students

1. Read and discuss page 352. Have the students share sentences that describe the picture. Write these sentences on the board. Underline the prepositional phrases. Make sure that students can recognize a prepositional phrase as a unit beginning with a preposition and ending with a noun or pronoun.

2. Read **Key to Writing and Speaking** out loud. Have the students give directions for locating various rooms in the school, the library, the lunchroom, or the gym. Point out the prepositional phrases used in each statement.

3. Assign and discuss Exercises A, B, and C on page 353. Remind students to use the process of writing when completing Exercise C.

4. Use Exercise B on page 362 for additional practice if needed.

 Basic Students

Do Exercise A orally with the group. Then ask students to replace one of the prepositional phrases in each sentence with another prepositional phrase that makes sense in that sentence.

 Advanced Students

Ask the students to write a "nonsense story" using at least five of the prepositional phrases from Exercise B on page 353. Prepositional phrases must be used correctly in sentences.

Special Populations

LD Do the first few sentences in Exercise A with students. Remind them that every prepositional phrase begins with a preposition and ends with a noun or pronoun.

ESL Students may have difficulty recognizing the object when it is separated from the preposition by adjectives. Provide additional practice using sentences

---

2 Using Prepositional Phrases

┌─ *Focus* ─────────────────────────────────┐
│   │
│   A **prepositional phrase** is a group of words that begins │
│ with a preposition and ends with its object. │
│   │
└──┘

▶ Comprehension/Interpretation

Look at this picture.
Think of two sentences that
describe what is happening.

A magician is standing *on the stage*.
He is pulling a rabbit *from his pocket*.

Your sentences probably contain phrases like the ones in italics. Look at the second italicized phrase. The phrase starts with a preposition. It ends with a noun, *pocket*, that is the **object of a preposition**. The preposition, its object, and all the words that modify the object combine to form a **prepositional phrase**. If a preposition has a compound object, all the parts of the object are included in the prepositional phrase.

> Weeds grew *in the lawn, the flower garden, and the vegetable garden.*

 Key to Writing and Speaking   Prepositional phrases are especially useful when you are describing or giving directions. They help you say exactly what you mean.

> Example: Go *down* the street and *around* the corner *to* the building *on* the left.

352

Exercises Finding the Prepositional Phrases

▶ Recalling

A. Number your paper from 1 to 10. Write all the prepositional phrases in each of the following sentences.

Example: The yarn was stuck to the paper with glue.
to the paper, with glue

1. The doll beside the lamp has a dress with red buttons.
2. Both of us heard the footsteps in the attic.
3. Draw a line under the word that begins with a vowel.
4. Maria played on the beach for hours.
5. On Sundays, there is music in the gazebo at the park.
6. The acrobat fell into the net from the tightrope.
7. Mary Ann waited near the theater until four o'clock.
8. Alone in the room, Shawn listened to his stereo.
9. The house across the street has been empty for a month.
10. I hung a clock with a flower design above the door.

▶ Analyzing/Structured Application

B. Number your paper from 1 to 10. Use each of the prepositional phrases below in a sentence. Underline the object or objects in each prepositional phrase.

1. past Mars, Jupiter, and Saturn
2. for her cousin
3. from El Paso
4. along the bank of the river
5. in Stacy's play
6. after the hurricane
7. outside my window
8. on the menu
9. among the new members
10. near the airport

▶ Creative Application

C. Writing To surprise your friend on his birthday, you hired a clown to deliver balloons and a singing telegram. The clown confused the addresses and arrived at your front door by mistake. Give the clown directions to get across town to your friend's house.

353

with long prepositional phrases and sentences that contain two or more prepositional phrases.

Reinforcement

1. Have the students follow the directions for Exercise A on page 353 using these sentences:

1. Adrienne read every book written by Marilyn Sachs. [prep / obj]
2. Underneath this huge mess were the lost letters. [prep / obj]
3. Cars parked beyond this line will be ticketed. [prep / obj]
4. Fortunately, the price of gasoline is falling. [prep / obj]
5. Pro football teams practice during the summer. [prep / obj]

2. Have the students follow the directions for Exercise B on page 353 using the following phrases:

1. for the baby
2. near the apple tree
3. after the school play
4. behind the space ship
5. beneath my bed
6. inside the classroom
7. without a sound
8. beyond the stars

Additional Resources

Skills Practice Book—page 135
Teacher's Resource Binder
  Reinforcement Activities—
  page 96

Part 3

Objective

To use the correct pronoun forms as objects of prepositions

Presenting the Lesson

● All Students

1. Read and discuss page 354.

2. Remind students that pronouns replace nouns, so objects of prepositions can be both nouns and pronouns. Discuss how the sample sentences on page 354 could be changed by substituting a noun for each object pronoun.

3. Read the following sentences. Ask the students to state the correct object pronoun for the noun in each prepositional phrase.

1. Go with Lisa.
2. This gift is for Darrell.
3. Did you talk to John and Fabian?

4. Make sure the students understand how to determine the correct pronoun form in a compound object. Ask them whether they have ever heard someone corrected for usng a sentence like *Ann and me are friends.* Point out that *Ann and me* is not always incorrect. It is correct when used as a compound object of a preposition, as in the sentence *Come to the park with Ann and me,* because *me* is an object pronoun.

5. Assign and discuss Exercises A, B, and C on page 355. For Exercise C, have students list prepositional phrases that they might use in their paragraphs, before they begin writing.

6. Use Exercise C on page 362 for additional practice if needed.

▶ Basic Students

Do the first few sentences of Exercises A and B with students. Remind students to first locate the preposition, and then its object. Also, remind them that an object pronoun is always used after a preposition, whether it is alone or used with another noun or pronoun.

◆ Advanced Students

Have the students write original sentences using each of the object pro-

---

3 Pronouns After Prepositions

> **Focus**
>
> When a pronoun is used as the object of a preposition, its object form must be used.

▶ Comprehension

Object forms of pronouns must be used as objects of prepositions. Here are the object forms.

> me   you   him   her   it   us   them

Notice the pronouns used as objects in these sentences.

> Mary Kay took an umbrella with *her*.
> Was there a message for *me*?
> Three swans were gliding toward *them*.

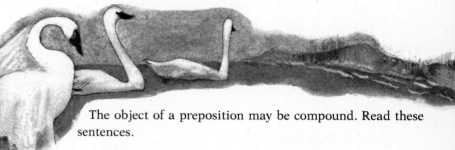

The object of a preposition may be compound. Read these sentences.

Simple Object	**Compound Object**
Study with *her*.	Study with *Darren* and *her*.
We stood beside *him*.	We stood beside *Jackie* and *him*.
Give that basket to *me*.	Give that basket to *her* and *me*.

If you are confused about which pronoun form to use, say the sentence with the pronoun alone following the preposition. Then say the complete sentence.

> All the team members played but Reba and (we, us).
> All the team members played but *us*.
> All the team members played but Reba and *us*.

354

Exercises   Using Pronouns After Prepositions

▶ Classifying

A. Make two columns on your paper. Head one column *Preposition* and the other *Object*. For each sentence write the preposition and the pronoun used as its object.

1. Joanna hit the baseball between us.
2. A letter from him arrived Thursday afternoon.
3. The lava oozed toward them.
4. Is my puppy following behind me?
5. A hummingbird is hovering above you.
6. The article about her is very interesting.
7. The race started without me.
8. Did you hide her present underneath it?
9. Lenny is performing the stunt with him.
10. We divided the reward among us.

▶ Recalling/Analyzing

B. Choose the correct pronoun from the two given in parentheses.

1. My dog likes to follow my friends and (I, me).
2. The roof over Marcia and (them, they) started to leak.
3. The coach called on Leo and (I, me).
4. A firecracker exploded in the sky over Timothy and (we, us).
5. My advice to Norita and (him, he) was ignored.
6. The howling of wolves echoed around Thompson and (they, them).
7. Bob and John will play tennis against you and (she, her) this morning.
8. Packages for Felipe and (she, her) came today.
9. Big, fluffy snowflakes fell upon Ricardo and (me, I).
10. Did the bicyclists race past Jamie and (they, them)?

▶ Creative Application

C. Writing Write a paragraph about playing Monopoly with three friends. Tell who played and where each person sat. Include phrases that have pronouns as objects of prepositions.

355

nouns listed at the top of page as objects of prepositions.

Special Populations

LD, ESL, NSD Write the object pronouns on the board. Encourage students to refer to this list as they do the exercises in this part. After students complete the exercises, have them read the sentences out loud. This reinforces use of the correct object pronouns after prepositions.

Reinforcement

Have the students follow the directions for Exercise A on page 355 using these sentences:

1. The story was written about her.
2. This secret is just between us.
3. Did Laura peek inside it?
4. Take your turn after me.
5. The show began without him.
6. Everyone liked the soup but you.
7. Their dog walked behind them.

Additional Resources

Skills Practice Book—page 136
Teacher's Resource Binder
  Reinforcement Activities—
  page 97

Part 4

Objectives

1. To differentiate between prepositions and adverbs

2. To correctly use *between* and *among*

Presenting the Lesson

All Students

1. Read and discuss page 356. Stress that a preposition must be followed by an object, either a noun or pronoun. Prepositions must be part of a phrase. Point out that several words in the list of prepositions can also be used as adverbs. These words are adverbs only when they are not followed by an object noun or pronoun.

2. Make sure that the students understand that *between* is used when speaking of two persons or things and *among* is used for three or more.

3. Discuss the **Key to Writing and Speaking** on page 356. Have the students give examples that illustrate this rule.

4. Assign and discuss Exercises A and B on page 357. Students might enjoy working on Exercise B in pairs or small groups.

5. Use Exercise D on page 363 for additional practice if needed.

Basic Students

After reading page 356, have the students do this exercise as a group activity. Have them use each of the following words in two sentences, first as the preposition in a prepositional phrase and then as an adverb.

under	by	off
above	across	in

Advanced Students

Explain to the students that when a prepositional phrase modifies a noun or a pronoun it is called an adjective phrase. When it modifies a verb, an adverb, or an adjective, it is called an adverb phrase. Ask the students to underline the prepositional phrases in these sentences and to write *adjective* or

---

4 Special Problems with Prepositions

> ― *Focus* ―
> Sometimes prepositions require special attention.

▶ Comprehension/Analyzing

Several words that are used as prepositions also are used as adverbs. Some examples are *up*, *down*, *around*, *in*, and *out*.

> We looked *up*. (adverb)
> We looked *up* the chimney. (preposition)
>
> The children ran *around*. (adverb)
> The children ran *around* the track. (preposition)

If you are not sure whether a word is an adverb or a preposition, look at how it is used. If it begins a phrase, it is probably a preposition. If it is used alone, it is probably an adverb.

Using *Between* and *Among*

You may hear the prepositions *between* and *among* used as if there were no difference between them. You should know the difference between them so that you can use them correctly.

We use *between* when we speak of two persons, things, or groups. We use *among* when we speak of three or more. Here are examples.

> Choose *between* these two programs.
> The next game is *between* the Jefferson team and us.
>
> We will divide the jobs *among* Nancy, you, and me.
> Honey bees darted *among* the jasmine blossoms.

 Key to Writing and Speaking   Avoid using a preposition when one is not necessary.

> Incorrect: **Where is my pencil at?**
> Correct: **Where is my pencil?**

Exercises   Special Problems with Prepositions

▶Recalling

A. Number your paper from 1 to 10. Write the correct word from the parentheses.

1. This is a secret (between, among) you and me.
2. Confetti was scattered (between, among) all the seats in the stadium.
3. In our solar system, Saturn is (between, among) Jupiter and Uranus.
4. The prize money was divided (between, among) Mario, Seth, and Anna.
5. There was a feeling of loyalty (between, among) the five friends.
6. The championship game was (between, among) the Dolphins and the Falcons.
7. I live (between, among) the Smiths and the Olsens.
8. (Between, Among) all the dishes on the menu, lasagna is my favorite.
9. Our car was difficult to find (between, among) all the others in the parking lot.
10. Is Elm Street (between, among) Park Avenue and Gregory Road?

▶Creative Application

B. Writing When you were in your favorite toy store, a kangaroo from the local zoo wandered through the door. The store manager shrieked. The kangaroo became frightened and started hopping throughout the store. Tell what happened as the manager chased the kangaroo up and down the aisles trying to catch it. Use the following words in your story.

1. down (adverb)
2. underneath (adverb)
3. outside (adverb)
4. between (preposition)
5. among (preposition)
6. over (preposition)

357

Additional Resources

Skills Practice Book—page 137

Teacher's Resource Binder
Reinforcement Activities—
page 98

adverb above the phrase. Then have them draw an arrow to the word the phrase modifies.

1. My cousin from Canada visited in the spring. Adj., cousin; Adv., visited
2. The movie about super heroes is showing in our town. Adj., movie; Adv., is showing
3. The man with a cane walked across the street. Adj., man; Adv., walked
4. I sat near a pond and watched the ducks with their young. Adv., sat; Adj., ducks
5. Someone in the crowd tripped over a barrier. Adj., someone; Adv., tripped

Reinforcement

1. Have the students follow the directions for Exercise A on page 357 using these sentences:

1. Choose one dress from (among, between) these three.
2. Hang up your coat (between, among) mine and Jenny's.
3. The election for class president will be (between, among) Willie and Beth.
4. (Between, Among) all of my friends, Mai is the only one who can tap-dance.
5. It is difficult to choose one (between, among) these delicious cookies.

2. In each of the following pairs of sentences, one word is used both as an adverb and a preposition. Have students identify that word in each sentence pair, and then tell where it is used as an adverb and where it is used as a preposition.

1. Look above! Look above the trees. *Adv. / Prep.*
2. Jim is inside. Jim is inside the house. *Adv. / Prep.*
3. Beyond, there is nothing but forest. *Adv.* Beyond the Sloan's cabin, there is nothing but forest. *Prep.*
4. They peeked below. They peeked below the dock. *Adv. / Prep.*
5. Stan drove around town. Stan drove around. *Prep. / Adv.*

Enrichment

Have each student bring to class a magazine or newspaper ad that contains one or more prepositional phrases. Ask them to circle each phrase. They should be prepared to present their findings to the class. The ads can then be used to create an interesting "real world" bulletin board display.

Chapter 20   **357**

Part 5

Objective

To use conjunctions to combine sentences

Presenting the Lesson

 All Students

1. Read and discuss page 358. Analyze each of the sentences on page 358. Make sure students can identify the words being connected by the italicized conjunction, and the role of those words in the sentence.

2. Stress that a comma is used in a compound sentence to signal the end of one idea and the beginning of another. The comma is always placed before the conjunction. Tell students that a comma is not always necessary if the ideas being joined by the conjunction are very short.

3. Assign and discuss Exercises A, B, and C on page 359. Before students begin Exercise C, put this on the board.

I'd like to talk to the giraffe
But I'm not tall
It's fun to hear the monkeys laugh
Or see them skim a wall
To know the wonder of the zoo
And gaze at a gnu.

4. Use Exercise E on page 363 for additional practice if needed.

 Basic Students

Review page 358 with the students before assigning Exercise B. Then, work through the exercise with them. Have the students read each sentence out loud. Point out the places where commas are needed.

Do Exercise C as a group activity.

 Advanced Students

After students complete the exercises on page 359, have them write original sentences following these directions:

1. Use *or* to join two interrogative sentences.
2. Use *and* to join two imperative sentences.
3. Use *but* to join two declarative sentences.
4. Use *and* to join two exclamatory sentences.

---

5 What Are Conjunctions?

> **Focus**
>
> A **conjunction** is a word that connects words or groups of words.

▶ Comprehension

A conjunction is a word used to join sentence parts or whole sentences. The words *and*, *but*, and *or* are conjunctions. The conjunctions in these sentences are joining sentence parts.

Glenna *and* her sister sped down the hill on saucer sleds.
(joins subjects)

The forward shot for the basket *but* missed it.
(joins predicates)

Buy some raisin bread *or* some muffins.
(joins direct objects)

The orchestra performed for the faculty *and* parents.
(joins objects of a preposition)

You have learned that *compound* means "having more than one part." In the example sentences above, conjunctions are used to join compound sentence parts. Conjunctions may also join whole sentences that are closely related in meaning.

The theater lights dimmed. The curtain went up.
The theater lights dimmed, *and* the curtain went up.

The princess had to guess Rumpelstiltskin's name.
He would take her first-born child.
The princess had to guess Rumpelstiltskin's name, *or* he would take her first-born child.

Notice that a comma is used at the end of the first sentence, before the conjunction. The comma alerts the reader to the end of one idea and the beginning of a second. Commas are not used to join sentence parts. Also, you may leave out the comma when the two sentences that you join are very short.

358

Exercises   Using Conjunctions

▶ Analyzing

A. In each sentence below, there is a compound subject, a compound predicate, or a compound object. Write which of the three you find. Underline the conjunction.

1. (Gary <u>and</u> his brother) dug for clams this morning.   CS
2. For breakfast, Lorraine likes (eggs <u>or</u> oatmeal.)   CO
3. The wind (shook the roof <u>and</u> rattled the door.)   CP
4. Glue (the string <u>and</u> the toothpicks) to the cardboard.   CO
5. Astronomers study (planets <u>and</u> stars.)   CO
6. Gerald (takes piano lessons <u>but</u> doesn't practice.)   CP
7. The puppy (yawned <u>and</u> shook himself.)   CP
8. (Football <u>and</u> soccer) are Lennie's favorite sports.   CS
9. Trudy splashed (Doug <u>and</u> me) with her paint.   CO
10. (The snow <u>and</u> ice) made the roads impassable.   CS

▶ Structured Application

B. Combine the following pairs of sentences into one sentence. Join related sentence parts. Choose a conjunction and use commas where necessary. Leave out words in italics.

See answers at bottom of page 358.

1. The theater was crowded. I could not find a seat.
2. Wendy watched the eclipse of the moon. John *watched the eclipse of the moon*.
3. The fiddler crabs climbed over the rocks. *The fiddler crabs climbed over the* branches.
4. Nancy liked riding the Ferris wheel best. Kirsten preferred driving the bumper cars.
5. Pedro washed the dishes. *Pedro* dried *the dishes*.
6. Lena called the office. There was no answer.
7. The tacos were spicy. *The tacos were* delicious.
8. The window isn't open. I feel a draft.
9. Did you lose your gloves? *Did you lose your* scarf?
10. Sue predicted the Braves would win. She was right.

▶ Creative Application

C. Writing Write a short poem in which every other line begins with a conjunction.

Reinforcement

1. Have the students follow the directions for Exercise A on page 359 using these sentences:

1. The dolphins and the seals performed at Sea World. comp. subj.
2. A tornado knocked over the fence and broke the windows. comp. pred.
3. Barney told jokes and riddles all evening. comp. obj.
4. The flight attendant served beverages and dinner. comp. obj.
5. George paid his bus fare and found an empty seat. comp. pred.
6. The Mississippi River and the Ohio River join here. comp. subj.
7. These homes and offices shake with each passing train. comp. subj.
8. Caroline leaned over and tied her shoelaces. comp. pred.
9. The jury may convict the defendant or may set him free. comp. pred.
10. Christopher Wren designed churches and government buildings. comp. obj.

2. Have the students follow the directions for Exercise B on page 359 using these sentences:

1. The food wasn't fancy, ˏbut We liked it.
2. I'd never seen a ballet before, ˏbut I enjoyed *The Nutcracker.*
3. Joe dodged the shortstop, ˏand He slid into third base.
4. The blob in the picture is a UFO, ˏor The photographer is fooling us.
5. Paula's guitar string snapped, ˏso She bought a new one.
6. Sit down, ˏand I'll help you.
7. The rain started, ˏand Everyone ran for cover.
8. The movie was good, ˏbut I liked reading the book better.

Additional Resources

Skills Practice Book—page 138
Teacher's Resource Binder
  Reinforcement Activities—
    pages 99–100

Part 6

Objective

To recognize a word used as various parts of speech

Presenting the Lesson

 All Students

1. Read and discuss page 360. Ask the students whether they can give examples of a word that can be used as various parts of speech. You might use the word *plant* as an example.

a. The farmer will *plant* the seedlings. (verb)

b. The *plant* grows best in sunlight. (noun)

c. My father is a plant *foreperson*. (adjective)

Encourage students to use a dictionary for examples of words used as more than one part of speech. Have them look especially for sample sentences in entries for such words.

2. Read and discuss the **Key to Writing and Speaking.**

3. Assign and discuss Exercises A, B, and C on page 361. Students might work in pairs when completing Exercise C.

4. Use Exercise F on page 363 for additional practice if needed.

 Basic Students

When discussing page 360, have the students suggest other words that can be various parts of speech that they are likely to use in their own conversations. Suggestions include: *dance* (noun and verb), *crowd* (noun, verb, and adjective), and *bike* (noun, verb, and adjective). Help students to use each of these words in a sentence for each part of speech indicated in parentheses.

 Advanced Students

Write the following words on the board and discuss the different pronunciations and meanings for each one when used as a noun and a verb. Have the students use each word in two sentences, first as a noun and then as a verb. Ask them to use the dictionary for help if necessary.

project	convict
conduct	record

---

6 Using Words as Different Parts of Speech

> **Focus**
>
> Sometimes the same word may be used as several parts of speech. When a word is used as a certain part of speech, it follows the rules for that part of speech.

▶ **Comprehension/Analyzing**

In part 4 of this chapter, you learned that the same word could be used as more than one part of speech. For example, the word *book* may be used in these three ways.

As a noun
This is my English *book*.

As a verb
The travel agent *booked* a seat for us on that flight.
The travel agent *will book* a seat for us on that flight.

As an adjective
Trudy gave a *book* report in class today.

Remember the rules for each part of speech when using words in different ways. For example, when you use *book* as a noun, you form the plural by adding *-s*: *books*. When you use it as a verb, you form the past tense by adding *-ed*: *booked*. When you use *book* in the future tense, you add the helping verb *will*.

There is only one sure way to decide what part of speech a word is. You must see how the word is used in the sentence.

Key to Writing and Speaking Take care when you use a word that can be more than one part of speech. The results can be confusing and even funny. Note this fashion designer's comment.

"Next season, women's dresses will be longer and there will be little change in women's purses."

Exercises   Identifying the Part of Speech

▶Analyzing

A. Number your paper from 1 to 10. Write what part of speech each word in italics is. The word may be a *Noun*, *Verb*, *Adjective*, *Adverb*, or *Preposition*.

1. My *down* jacket keeps me very warm.   Adj.
2. Do you *bat* right-handed or left-handed?   Verb
3. There was a *calm* before the terrible storm.   Noun
4. Uncle Stan taught me a *magic* trick.   Adj.
5. Put your bike *inside* before it rains.   Adv.
6. The scouts pitched camp *near* the Grand River.   Prep.
7. A *guide* explained the Eskimo exhibit.   Noun
8. Our teacher *charts* our progress in math.   Verb
9. Laurie listened to *rock* music.   Adj.
10. Mr. Marcum will *judge* the pogo stick contest.   Verb

▶Analyzing

B. In each pair of sentences that follows, one word is used as two different parts of speech. Number your paper from 1 to 5. After each number, write a. and b. After each letter, write the word in italics and tell what part of speech it is.

1. a. The class president *chaired* the meeting. b. This *chair* is too hard.   a. Verb b. Noun
2. a. A lyric soprano sings *high* notes. b. The team's fortunes have reached a new *high*.   a. Adj. b. Noun
3. a. My family moved to a new *house*. b. The school will *house* the visiting athletes.   a. Noun b. Verb
4. a. Vince went *outside* for a walk. b. We saw several deer *outside* the cabin.   a. Adv. b. Prep.
5. a. Ms. Taylor made a *pencil* sketch of the waterfall. b. I have to sharpen my *pencil*.   a. Adj. b. Noun

▶Creative Application

C. Writing Write two sentences for each word below. Use the word as the parts of speech shown in the parentheses.

1. well (Noun, Adverb)
2. walk (Noun, Verb)
3. cold (Adjective, Noun)
4. fly (Noun, Verb)

361

Additional Resources

Skills Practice Book—page 139
Teacher's Resource Binder
　Reinforcement Activities—
　　pages 101–102

Special Populations

LD, ESL Students will need some assistance in this part. Post on the board a list of the parts of speech with simple definitions and examples. Encourage students to refer to this list frequently as they work the exercises. Always use examples so that students understand how a particular word can be used as more than one part of speech.

Reinforcement

1. Have the students follow the directions for the Exercise B on page 361 using these sentences:

1. a. My sister and I gave our dad a present on Father's Day. b. The principal will present the trophy to the winning team.
2. a. This bottle's label has a warning on it. b. Kim is warning the boys not to skate on the thin ice.
3. a. Daria rarely studies and is just getting by. b. Meet me by the water fountain.
4. a. Louis loaded the washing machine. b. Stella is washing her white sweater.
5. a. The boat plowed through the choppy waters. b. The workers were all through.
6. a. It is a short walk to the bus stop. b. You can walk there in five minutes.
7. a. We need help to move this piano. b. The Red Cross helps people during emergencies.
8. a. Ramona will train her dog to do tricks. b. The train stops in Vincennes, Indiana. at five o'clock.
9. a. Sam loaded the film into his camera. b. The photographer will film the parade.
10. a. Giorgio won the wrestling match. b. Can you match this sock with any of those in the drawer?

2. Have students use each word below in at least two different sentences, each time as a different part of speech.

1. picture   3. down   5. wish
2. cup   4. flower   6. fish

Exercises for Mastery

These **Exercises for Mastery** may be used for additional practice of the concepts presented in this section. Each exercise focuses on a single concept, and should be used after the page number indicated in parentheses.

Exercises for Mastery

Chapter 20

Using Prepositions and Conjunctions

▶ Recalling/Analyzing

A. Finding Prepositions Copy the following sentences. Underline the prepositions in each sentence. (Use after page 351.)

1. A stunt man perched on the tall flagpole.
2. The lamp beside the couch is broken.
3. Are those flowers along that fence geraniums?
4. Jeanette's baby sister toddled toward her mother.
5. An army helicopter landed among the tall pines.
6. The popcorn with butter costs more.
7. Penguins plunged into the icy water.
8. Did you paint your poster with watercolors?

B. Recognizing Prepositional Phrases Number your paper from 1 to 8. Write the prepositional phrases in the following sentences. Underline the object or objects in each phrase. (Use after page 353.)

1. A mole tunneled (under our back lawn.)
2. (Before breakfast,) the newspaper is delivered.
3. Richard paddled his canoe (around the lake.)
4. Christie searched (beneath her bed) (for her sneakers.)
5. The airplane disappeared (behind the clouds.)
6. Leave your boots (on the mat) (outside the door.)
7. We drove (to the drive-in window) (at the restaurant.)
8. (On New Year's Eve,) I stayed awake (past midnight.)

C. Using Pronouns as Objects of Prepositions Choose the correct pronoun from the parentheses. Write it on your paper. (Use after page 355.)

1. Dad adjusted the handlebars for (I, me).
2. That present is from Ella and (she, her).
3. Do you live near Tom and (he, him)?
4. Gino dedicated his poem to (we, us).
5. Sonia has been asking about (they, them).

362

Additional Resources

Skills Practice Book
Mixed Practice—page 140

D. Choosing the Right Prepositions Number your paper from 1 to 5. Choose the correct preposition from the parentheses. Write it on your paper. (Use after page 357.)

1. Spread the filling (<u>between</u>, among) the two layers.
2. (Between, <u>Among</u>) the stories in the collection, "Rip Van Winkle" is my favorite.
3. Keep this information (<u>between</u>, among) you and me.
4. Was Greta (between, <u>among</u>) the new members?
5. Decide (<u>between</u>, among) the wool or orlon yarn.

E. Using Conjunctions Rewrite the following sentences. Combine each pair with *and*, *but*, or *or*. Use commas where needed. (Use after page 359.) See answers in margin.

1. The letter on the chart may be an *E*. It may be an *F*.
2. I sprayed insect repellent on my arms. Mosquitoes bit me anyway.
3. Jarita has several assignments. They are all difficult.
4. You may have pudding for dessert. You may have an orange.
5. The car had engine trouble. We finally had to call a tow truck.
6. Rhea's arm is in a cast. She played baseball today.
7. The bread is delicious. The price is high.
8. You can wait in the car. You can come inside.

F. Using Words as Different Parts of Speech Write two sentences for each word below. Use the word as the part of speech shown in the parentheses. (Use after page 361.)

1. paper (Noun, Adjective)
2. phone (Noun, Adjective)
3. jam (Noun, Verb)
4. print (Noun, Verb)
5. water (Noun, Adjective)

363

Exercise E
1. The letter on the chart may be an E, or it may be an F.
2. I sprayed insect repellent on my arms, but mosquitoes bit me anyway.
3. Jarita has several assignments and they are all difficult.
4. You may have pudding for dessert or you may have an orange.
5. The car had engine trouble, and we finally had to call a tow truck.
6. Rhea's arm is in a cast, but she played baseball today.
7. The bread is delicious, but the price is high.
8. You can wait in the car, or you can come inside.

Using Grammar in Writing

These challenging and enjoyable activities allow the students to see how the concepts of grammar, usage, and mechanics may be applied in actual writing situations. Each exercise is designed to give students practice in several of the skills they have acquired in this section. The activities also provide opportunities for students to write creatively about a wide variety of interesting and unusual subjects.

As students complete these activities, remind them to follow the process of writing. Be sure to allow adequate time for prewriting activities. Individual conferences or peer-group sessions may be used for help with drafting and revision.

Students should be given time to do some research on the circulatory system before they begin writing their paragraphs for Exercise C.

Using Grammar in Writing

▶ Creative Application

A. Imagine you are a comet traveling through space. Write a paragraph telling what you see as you zip past, between, and among other heavenly bodies in the solar system.

B. You are on the committee to plan Field Day for the sixth grade. Your job is to design an obstacle course for the obstacle course relay. First, think of ten safe objects, such as tires, empty boxes, and hoops, to use as obstacles. Then write the directions for successfully completing the course.

C. Using Prepositions and Conjunctions in Science Your science class studied the systems of the human body. After a lecture on the circulatory system, you suddenly shrank into a red blood cell. Write about your adventures as you carried oxygen through veins to major organs of the body.

364

Additional Resources

Skills Practice Book
Using Prepositions
and Conjunctions
in Writing—page 141

Chapter 20 Review

▶ Recalling

A. Identifying Prepositional Phrases Write the prepositional phrases in the following sentences.

1. Who moved into the brick house across the street?
2. Uncle Tex sent me a cowboy hat from Dallas.
3. Hail pounded against the classroom windows.
4. Mom put my bowling trophy on a shelf in the living room.
5. He hid the secret message beneath a large pile of mystery books.
6. Is Justine's kitten under the raspberry bush?
7. Divide the cost of the food among the four boys.
8. Please don't leave without me.
9. I like all fruit except pineapple.
10. The girl behind Alexis is her sister.

▶ Structured Application

B. Using Conjunctions Rewrite each of the following pairs of sentences as one sentence. Choose a conjunction to join related ideas. Use commas where necessary. Leave out the words in italics. See answers in margin.

1. Zinc *is a* mineral. Copper *is a mineral.*
2. I play hockey. *I do* not *play* basketball.
3. Last July, we swam in the pond. It's too cold now.
4. The book was long. *The book was* interesting.
5. I drew a map of our town. Saul labeled the streets.
6. Amanda sings well. *Amanda* dances *well.*
7. The pilots got on the plane. The passengers didn't board until later.
8. My new wool sweater is bulky. *It is* warm.
9. I looked everywhere for my lost library book. I never found it.
10. Have you ever seen a sugar beet? *Have you ever seen* sugar cane?

365

Additional Resources

Skills Practice Book
Review—page 142

Test Booklet
Mastery Test—pages 119–120

Chapter 21

Chapter Objectives

1. To differentiate between fact and opinion

2. To demonstrate the relationships between ideas by putting them in order

3. To draw conclusions from a series of related facts

4. To recognize errors in thinking resulting from slanted language, overgeneralization, stereotyping, and the bandwagon fallacy

Motivating the Students

1. Read the following poem to students.

Thoughts

Thoughts are ideas,
And sometimes they're notions,
Springing from senses and emotions.
Deep in the darkness of the mind
Thought makes decisions, helps us find
Our way through all it means to live,
To learn, to love, create, forgive.
In this we humans are distinct:
The only creatures who can think.

—Mary O'Neill

Discuss the ideas in this poem, especially those in the first three lines. Point out that sometimes ideas are based on fact, and at other times they are opinions based on emotions, or the way a person feels. In this chapter, students will learn to identify the difference between fact and opinion.

Point out lines 5–7. Students will discover problem-solving techniques to help them find their way. They will also "learn" to draw conclusions.

2. Now have the students read the introduction to the chapter on page 367. Discuss the importance of clear thinking. Ask for suggestions on situations that occur during the school day when students need to think clearly.

Week 29

Chapter Management Guidelines   This chart may be used to help structure daily lesson plans.

Day 1	Day 2	Day 3	Day 4	Day 5
Chapter 21 Opener, p. 367; Part 1, "Recognizing Fact and Opinion," pp. 368–369	Part 2, "Seeing Relationships," pp. 370–371	Part 3, "Drawing Conclusions from Facts," pp. 372–373	Part 4, "Errors in Thinking," pp. 374–375	Chapter Review and selected end-of-chapter activities

Chapter 21

Clear Thinking

Imagine that you hear the following statements on the evening TV news.

> "Today, the legislature failed to pass the tax bill. School officials feel that this foolish action will cause local schools to suffer greatly."

Can you tell which statement is fact and which is opinion?

Now, suppose you read the following ad.

> "Everyone who jogs wears Speed Track jogging shoes. You should, too."

Should you go out and buy Speed Track jogging shoes?

You will often find yourself in situations that require you to think clearly and sensibly. To think clearly, you must be able to tell fact from opinion, recognize poor thinking, understand relationships, and draw conclusions.

In this chapter, you will learn to sharpen your thinking skills. You will learn to analyze what you read and hear. All of these skills will help you form sound opinions and make good decisions throughout your life.

367

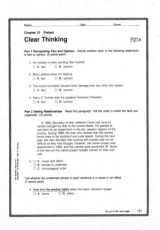

Part 1

Objective

To differentiate between fact and opinion

Presenting the Lesson

 All Students

1. Read and discuss pages 368–369.

2. Ask three students to give you a sentence that each feels expresses a fact. Write them on the board. Repeat the procedure with three opinions. Then, ask students to explain the difference between fact and opinion. Ask them to tell why they classified each item on the board as they did.

3. Make sure that students understand how to prove facts, and how to support opinions.

4. Assign and discuss Exercises A and B on page 369.

 Basic Students

Do Exercise A with the students as a group activity. As they suggest answers, ask them to provide the reasons for their answers. Then, assign Exercise B to be completed independently.

 Advanced Students

Ask the students to develop one of the opinions they wrote for Exercise B on page 369 into a paragraph. Remind students that an opinion must be supported with facts. Encourage students to use the process of writing as they complete this assignment.

Special Populations

ESL Recognizing the difference between fact and opinion relys on an ability to understand subtleties in language. Make sure that students understand these fine differences in the examples used in this part, as well as the terminology and vocabulary.

---

1 Recognizing Fact and Opinion

> **Focus**
>
> A **fact** can be proved true. An **opinion** is someone's personal feeling. It cannot be proved.

▶ Comprehension

You encounter facts and opinions daily. It is important to recognize the difference between them.

Recognizing Facts

A fact is an idea that can be proved true. These are facts.

Two stars in the Big Dipper point to the North Star.
The first astronaut walked on the moon July 20, 1969.

Proving Facts

There are several ways to prove facts. One way to prove a fact is by **personal observation**. For example, at night you can look at the Big Dipper in the sky. You can prove by observation that the first example is true.

The second way to prove a fact is to use a **reliable source**. The source may be a person or a reference work. For example, you could ask your history teacher when the first astronaut walked on the moon. You could also check the date in an encyclopedia, a written source.

Recognizing Opinions

An **opinion** is a statement that tells how a person feels about something. It cannot be proved true. These are opinions.

Owning a pet is a good idea.
Bird-watching is an interesting hobby.

Supporting Opinions

An opinion cannot be proved true. However, one opinion may be stronger than another. A sound opinion is supported with facts. For example, the statement about owning a pet is an unsupported opinion. However, you could support that statement with these facts: pets can be trained as guard animals; a pet can be a companion; pet care can teach a child to be responsible.

When you are supporting opinions, watch out for "empty sentences." For example, "I liked the movie because it was good" is an empty sentence. The statement just gives the same opinion twice. It presents no facts to support the opinion.

Exercises   Recognizing Facts and Opinions

▶ Classifying

A. Number your paper from 1 to 8. Then read the following statements. Next to each number, write whether the statement is a *Fact* or an *Opinion*.

1. Georgia O'Keeffe was an American painter.   Fact
2. Wallpapering is a tiresome job.   Opinion
3. Many bears hibernate in the winter.   Fact
4. Calcium helps build strong bones.   Fact
5. Greek food is delicious.   Opinion
6. Brasilia is the capital of Brazil.   Fact
7. The Celtics play in the Boston Garden.   Fact
8. That movie was terrific.   Opinion

▶ Critical Reasoning

B. Read each of the following topics. Write an opinion about each subject. Support each opinion with two facts.

Country and western music
Limited TV viewing time for teens
Ten-speed bicycles
Learning a foreign language

369

Reinforcement

1. Have the students follow the directions for Exercise A on page 369 using the following statements:

1. Louisa May Alcott was an American writer.   Fact
2. Lilacs bloom in the spring.   Fact
3. Riding a bicycle is fun exercise. Opinion
4. The Chicago Bears are a good football team.   Opinion
5. Maple syrup is made from sap.   Fact
6. Cockroaches are ugly bugs.   Opinion

2. Have the students follow the directions for Exercise B on page 369 using the following subjects: Answers will vary.

gardening
taking a baby-sitting class
swimming
twenty minutes of silent reading daily
Washington, D.C.

Enrichment

1. Have students look at several advertisements in magazines. For each advertisement, have students identify which statements are fact and which are opinion.

2. For additional enrichment activities, see the Unit Projects in the Teacher Notes on page 347. One or more of these projects have special activities for gifted and talented students.

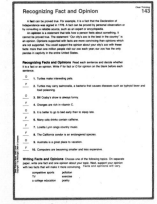

Additional Resources

Skills Practice Book—page 143

Teacher's Resource Binder
Reinforcement Activities—
page 103

Part 2

Objective

To demonstrate the relationships between ideas by putting them in order

Presenting the Lesson

All Students

1. Read and discuss pages 370–371.
2. Emphasize the different kinds of order to the students. Point out the examples given in each group. Ask the students to suggest some other examples that might fall in each category.

Other examples include:

Grouping If students were writing a report on elephants, they might group details into those about Asian elephants, and those about African elephants.

Logical Order In discussing gardening, one might talk about plants in the order of their difficulty to grow, from the most to the least difficult.

Cause and Effect One might discuss the Civil War in terms of its causes and the effect it had on the United States.

3. Assign and discuss Exercises A and B on page 371.

Basic Students

Ask the students to work in pairs for Exercises A and B. Review the different styles of organization. Have the students explain the reasons for their answers.

Advanced Students

Have students look at the following paragraph. Which facts are the causes? Which is the effect?

Kim and Steve wanted to build a campfire. The fire would not start. The firewood was wet. They had no kindling. The logs were green. The fire would not start is the effect. The other details are the causes.

Special Populations

LD Students with organizing or sequencing problems will have some difficulty with this part. Provide extra practice. Work through exercises with students. Make sure that students understand the organization and relationship between ideas.

---

2 Seeing Relationships

> **Focus**
>
> You can understand a group of facts better if you can put them in some kind of order.

▶ **Comprehension**

When you first open a jigsaw puzzle, the job of putting it together seems very difficult. However, when you sort the pieces into border pieces and like-colored pieces, the job begins to seem easier.

If you can put facts into some kind of order, they will be easier to understand. You will begin to see relationships among various facts.

Grouping
▶ **Classifying**

Look for similarities and differences in facts. Group facts together that are alike. Suppose that you were giving a talk on a new model car. Your facts might be grouped in two categories—advantages of this model and disadvantages.

Logical Orders
▶ **Inferring Sequence**

Another way to organize facts is to put them in some kind of sequence or order. Chronological order, or time order, is one type of sequence. It is the order in which things happen. For example, if you were writing about the space program, you might begin with the first program, Mercury. You would then continue with the Gemini and Apollo programs. Finally, you would end with the space-shuttle program. This is the order in which these programs took place.

Look for other kinds of order such as large to small, familiar to unfamiliar, easy to difficult, and many more.

370

Exercise A

1. City, county, state, region, country, continent. Grouped by smallest to largest.
2. *Games and entertainment*
   bean bags
   music
   prizes
   balls
   Refreshments
   lemonade
   hamburgers
   popcorn
   Decorations
   streamers
   posters
   Grouped by similarities

Exercise B

1. The severe freeze in Florida in 1983 led to entire orange crops being destroyed.
2. Because there were few oranges left unfrozen, there were few oranges for sale.
3. Because there were few oranges available for making juice, the price of orange juice went up.

Cause and Effect
▶ Making Inferences

Some events make other events happen. The first event is the cause. The second event is the effect. When you are studying a set of facts, look for cause and effect relationships.

Look at this set of facts. Which facts are the causes? Which is the effect?

Dave spent the day at the beach. Dave is sunburned. Dave has fair skin. Dave forgot his sunscreen.

Dave's sunburn is the effect. Each other detail is a cause.

Exercises   Seeing Relationships
▶ Generalizing

A. Look for relationships among the items in the following lists. Order or group the items. Explain your choice of order. See answers at bottom of page 370.

1. **Geography**

continent	state
city	country
region	county

2. **Items needed for a school carnival**

bean bags	hamburgers	posters
lemonade	music	popcorn
streamers	prizes	balls

▶ Making Inferences

B. Read the following facts. Write two possible cause and effect relationships. See answers at bottom of page 370.

In 1983, there was a severe freeze in Florida. Entire orange crops were destroyed. Few oranges were available in supermarkets. The price of orange juice rose.

371

Reinforcement

Have the students follow the directions for Exercise A on page 371 using the following lists:

Items needed for a ski trip

clothes	Clothes
skis	ski jacket
airplane ticket	waterproof pants
ski lodge reservations	hat
waterproof pants	mittens
hat	Equipment
ski poles	ski poles
bindings	skis
ski jacket	bindings
mittens	Travel Arrangements
	airplane ticket
	ski lodge reservations

Baking Muffins   chronological order

assemble the ingredients
eat
let the muffins cool
read the recipe
bake the muffins
pour the batter into the pan
mix the ingredients

1. read the recipe
2. assemble the ingredients
3. mix the ingredients
4. pour the batter into the pan
5. bake the muffins
6. let the muffins cool
7. eat

Additional Resources

Skills Practice Book—page 144

Teacher's Resource Binder
Reinforcement Activities—
page 104
Enrichment Activities—
pages 26–30

Part 3

Objective

To draw conclusions from a series of related facts

Presenting the Lesson

 All Students

1. Read and discuss pages 372–373. Point out each step for drawing a conclusion. Write the four steps on the board as you discuss them. Point out how one step leads logically to the next. Stress the idea that a conclusion should never be drawn until the first three steps have all been completed. Tell students that they are always exposed to details, facts, and other information. This information becomes valuable when they learn to order, analyze, and draw conclusions from it.

2. Assign and discuss the exercise on page 373.

 Basic Students

Do the exercise as a class activity. Before you begin, write the four steps for drawing a conclusion on the board. Walk students through each step. Have students refer to the steps listed on the board as you work.

 Advanced Students

Have the students write their own mini-mysteries and questions as in the exercise on page 373. Then, ask them to share their stories with the class. This might be done in small groups.

Special Populations

LD Some students will have difficulty drawing a conclusion from a series of facts. Provide additional practice.

With students, work through the four-step method for drawing a conclusion.

Then, have students complete the missing items in a series. You might use these series:

6, 10, 14, 18, <u>22</u>
left, right, top, <u>bottom</u>
breakfast, lunch, <u>dinner</u> (or supper)

---

3 Drawing Conclusions from Facts

> **Focus**
>
> After you think carefully about a set of related facts, you can draw a conclusion.

▶ Comprehension

A **conclusion** is an opinion or decision you reach after you study the available facts.

Drawing conclusions is a skill that people use often. If you ring a doorbell and get no answer, you may draw the conclusion that no one is home. Suppose that your mother tries to start her car. Nothing happens. She tries the lights and the horn, but neither works. She may draw the conclusion that the battery is dead. Follow these steps to draw a conclusion.

1. Study the facts. Begin by looking carefully at any information you have been given. Think about this situation.

> When astronauts returned from the first moon flight, they brought back rocks. Scientists found no evidence of water in the rocks. They also found only traces of carbon.

2. Compare the facts with what you already know. Scientists know that all plants and animals are made up of organic, or living, substances. They also know that carbon is present in all organic substances. Finally, scientists know that water is important to all living things.

3. See how the facts fit together. The scientists realized that if carbon is present in an organic substance, then carbon should remain after a plant or animal dies. Water should also remain. If there were life on the moon, then carbon and water should be evident in the moon rocks.

372

4. Draw a conclusion. The rocks contained only traces of carbon and no water. Therefore, the scientists concluded that it is not likely that living matter could exist on the moon.

Always state your conclusion carefully. Do not say more than you really know. Conclusions often contain qualifying words like these.

sometimes	perhaps	might	possibly
maybe	may	could	probably

Whenever you are given a set of facts, consider them carefully before you draw a conclusion.

Exercise   Drawing Conclusions
▶ Drawing Conclusions

Read this mini-mystery. Then answer the questions that follow.

Detective Briggs parked her car in the lot. She walked in the rain through the puddles toward the apartment building. She was going to question Dan Dubious, a well-known jewel thief. A robbery had been reported in Dan's apartment building.

"Detective Briggs, do come in and sit down," said Dan. "Let me take your wet coat."

"I don't mind if I do," said the detective. "Just let me take off my muddy shoes." She placed them on a mat next to Dan's shiny motorcycle boots.

"Well, Dan, where were you about a half an hour ago?" questioned Detective Briggs.

"Why, I was out riding my motorcycle," replied Dan. "I grabbed a bite to eat, and I just got home five minutes ago."

"Dan, you're going to have to come up with a better alibi than that," said Detective Briggs. "I don't think you ever left this building."

1. Do you believe Dan's alibi? No
2. Who probably committed the robbery? On what facts do you base your conclusion? Dan. His boots were shiny, so he obviously had not been out in the rain and mud.

373

Discuss with students how they had to see the relationship in each series before they could supply the missing item.

Reinforcement

Have the students follow the directions for the exercise on page 373 using the following mini-mystery.

Bessie, the maid, answered the door.

"You came so quickly, Ms. Flagpole. I'm so glad. My mistress is terribly upset. The cockatoo is very valuable and we can't imagine who could have taken him."

Jane Flagpole, well-known detective, entered the richly furnished library. She seated herself on the velvet couch and surveyed the others in the room. Bessie's husband, Thomas, the butler, sat in the plush chair next to the windows. The closed velvet curtains barred any sunlight from the room. Mrs. Ridgeworth, the owner of the missing cockatoo, paced nervously around the room.

"Mrs. Ridgeworth, what can you tell me about the theft?" inquired Jane.

"I wasn't here. I've just returned from a weekend trip. Bessie and Thomas were looking after things," replied Mrs. Ridgeworth.

"That's right, Ms. Flagpole. In fact, we sort of had the day off. I was upstairs blow-drying my hair and Thomas was down here, in that very chair, reading. I heard the bird squawking and the front door slam. I came running downstairs to see what was happening," Bessie explained.

"I think I may have seen the robber," offered Thomas. "I looked up from my reading and saw him through the window. Big fellow, he was. He dashed across the yard to a waiting car and sped away."

"Do you think you can find this awful thief?" pleaded Mrs. Ridgeworth.

"I think I have already found both thieves," replied Ms. Flagpole.

Bessie could not have heard the bird or the slamming door with the blow dryer going. Thomas could not have seen the thief through the curtained windows.

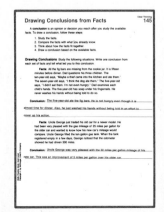

Additional Resources

Skills Practice Book—page 145

Teacher's Resource Binder
Reinforcement Activities—
   page 105
Enrichment Activities—
   page 31

Part 4

Objective

To recognize errors in thinking resulting from slanted language, overgeneralization, stereotyping, and the bandwagon fallacy

Presenting the Lesson

All Students

1. Read and discuss pages 374–375.
2. Make four columns on the board. Head each column with one of the errors in thinking presented in this part. Ask the students for examples of each error. Write the examples under the appropriate headings. Discuss why each item is an example of faulty reasoning.
3. Assign and discuss the exercise on page 375.

Basic Students

Work through the exercise together with the students. Refer them back to the list and description of errors in thinking as they work. Help them to see the errors in thinking. Guide students toward reaching the proper conclusion.

Advanced Students

Have the students write up four original situations that show poor thinking using each of the errors in reasoning listed in this lesson.

Special Populations

LD Students may have difficulty identifying the types of errors in the exercise on page 375. Start by identifying the errors for students. Then help them to understand how or why the wrong conclusion was reached.

ESL These students may have experience with stereotyping. If so, the lesson on stereotyping is a good opportunity to make classmates sensitive to this error.

---

4 Errors in Thinking

> **Focus**
>
> Errors in thinking can lead to poor conclusions.

▶ Comprehension

You have probably heard the expression, "Don't jump to conclusions." Sometimes people make errors in thinking and draw the wrong conclusion. Here are several problems that might lead to incorrect conclusions.

Slanted Language

Sometimes people choose words that they know will cause strong feelings in a reader or listener. Words such as these are called **slanted language**. For example, one person might describe a piece of art with positive words like *imaginative* and *creative*. Someone else might describe it with negative words such as *bizarre* and *disturbing*. When you notice slanted language, look for facts from which you can draw your own conclusion.

Overgeneralizations

A **generalization** is a fact that has been applied to a group of people, objects, or actions. For example, suppose that you live in a farming area. Five out of seven farmers grow corn. Two farmers grow soybeans. You could say, "Most of the farmers in my area grow corn." You have made a generalization.

An **overgeneralization** is a statement that is too broad to be true. For example, the statement, "All tall people are good basketball players," is an overgeneralization. Words such as *all*, *every*, *never*, and *nobody* often signal an overgeneralization. Correct an overgeneralization by using qualifying words such as *most*, *some*, *many*, or *usually* instead.

374

Stereotyping

One type of overgeneralization is called a **stereotype**. A stereotype wrongly states that an entire group shares certain characteristics. For example, perhaps you think of all wolves as killers. Old fairy tales may account for such ideas. The "big bad wolf" chased the three little pigs. A wolf ate Little Red Riding Hood's grandmother. The wolf has been stereotyped as mean and dangerous. To disprove a stereotype, you research the real facts. Research about the wolf shows that this creature is not the villain that many people think it is.

Bandwagon

Have you ever heard someone say, "They're just jumping on the bandwagon"? This statement refers to people who buy clothes or vote for a mayor simply because others are doing it. Try to avoid jumping on the bandwagon yourself. Never make decisions or act a certain way just because "everyone else is." Instead, look for facts to support the idea. If you can't find any, then the idea is probably not a good one.

Exercise   Correcting Errors in Thinking

▶ Critical Reasoning

Each of the following situations shows poor thinking. Tell what the error is. Then explain how or why the wrong conclusion was reached.

See answers in margin.

1. Rattlesnakes are deadly. Cobras are killers. Snakes are always dangerous. I should kill the snakes in my yard.
2. All of my friends are getting those sunglasses. I should get some, too.
3. Ginny mulishly stuck to her opinion. Ginny is stubborn.
4. Why don't you jog after school? Everyone else does.
5. All movie actors become fabulously wealthy. I want to be a movie actor.

375

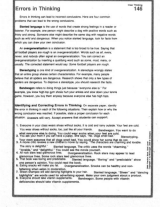

Using English in Math

This activity may be used to show how thinking skills can be used in math. Tell students that this type of question often appears on standardized tests. By learning how to see relationships in a series of numbers, they will better be able to answer this type of question.

Using English in Math

▶ Comprehension

You use the thinking skill of seeing relationships in math. Numbers and shapes may be grouped in many ways. For example, you know that some numbers are even and some numbers are odd. You also know that some numbers are whole numbers and some are fractions. You are also able to see sequences in numbers. For example, you know that in the sequence *5, 10, 15* . . . the next number is *20*. Finally, you can identify parts and wholes. All of these tasks require you to use thinking skills.

Exercises   Seeing Relationships in Math

▶ Inferring Sequence

A. The numbers in the following lists are arranged in special order. On your paper, write the number that will complete each sequence.

1. 3, 6, 9, 12, 15, __18__, 21, 24
2. 2, 4, 7, 11, 16, 22, __29__, 37
3. 896, 448, 224, 112, 56, 28, 14, __7__

▶ Analyzing/Drawing Conclusions

B. Look at each group of figures. Write the letter of the figure that is different from the others on your paper.   Correct answers are circled.

a.   b.   c.   d.   e.

a.   b.   c.   d.   e.

376

Chapter 21 Review

▶ Classifying

A. Recognizing Fact and Opinion Read each statement. Write whether the statement is a *Fact* or an *Opinion*.

1. Strawberry jam tastes better than grape jelly.   Opinion
2. Tofu, or bean curd, contains calcium.   Fact
3. A computer is a useful addition to every home.   Opinion
4. Stamp collecting is a dull hobby.   Opinion
5. Whales belong to the mammal family.   Fact

▶ Generalizing

B. Seeing Relationships What kind of relationship might exist among the facts in each of the following items?   See answers in margin.

1. historical dates
2. study habits and test scores
3. items on a menu
4. planets in the solar system

▶ Drawing Conclusions

C. Drawing Conclusions Read the following situation. Answer the question at the end.

When he heard the crash, Mr. Raymond rushed from the back room into the pet store.

"What happened?" he asked.

Eva, his assistant, replied, "I was busy working. Suddenly I heard a crash. I turned and saw the broken window. Look at the glass all over the sidewalk. Someone on the street must have thrown a rock."

"I don't think so. I suspect our monkey, Chi Chi, is the guilty party," suggested Mr. Raymond.

Why did Mr. Raymond think this?   The glass was on the sidewalk, not inside the pet store. Therefore, the rock was thrown from inside.

▶ Critical Reasoning

D. Recognizing Poor Thinking Read the following information. What is wrong with the conclusion? What is the error in thinking?

Accidents always happen when black cats cross your path. A black cat crossed my path today. I will have an accident.   The conclusion is based on superstition, not research. The error is overgeneralization.

377

Chapter Review

This review allows teachers to evaluate student understanding of the concepts presented in this chapter.

Exercise B Answers will vary.

1. arranged in time order or order by country
2. cause and effect
3. grouped into categories such as salads, soups, desserts
4. order of distance from the sun or order of size

Additional Resources

Skills Practice Book
Review—page 147

Test Booklet
Mastery Test—pages 123–126

Chapter 22

Chapter Objectives

1. To recognize paragraphs that state and support an opinion
2. To identify an opinion and find supporting reasons
3. To organize reasons in the order of their importance as part of a writing plan
4. To follow a writing plan when drafting an explanation of an opinion
5. To revise and proofread an explanation
6. To make and share a neat final copy of an explanation

Motivating the Students

1. Read the following passage from *To Kill a Mockingbird* to the students. Explain that it is part of a lawyer's closing statements to a jury. When you have finished reading the passage, ask students to state, in their own words, the opinion that is presented.

"But there is one way in this country in which all men are created equal—there is one human institution that makes a pauper the equal of a Rockefeller, the stupid man the equal of an Einstein, and the ignorant man the equal of any college president. That institution, gentlemen, is a court. It can be the Supreme Court of the United States or the humblest J.P. court in the land, or this honorable court which you serve. Our courts have their faults, as does any human institution, but in this country our courts are the great levelers, and in our courts, all men are created equal."

—Harper Lee

2. Read and discuss the chapter introduction on page 379. You may also wish to bring in an editorial page of a newspaper to continue the discussion of opinions. Tell students that in this chapter they will learn how to discover their own opinions and they will learn how to write about those opinions.

Special Populations

LD Some students will find it easier to use a tape recorder to catalog their ideas, opinions, and supporting details. Allow these students to use a tape recorder in the prewriting stages of this

Week 30

Chapter Management Guidelines
This chart may be used to help structure daily lesson plans.

Day 1	Day 2	Day 3	Day 4	Day 5
Chapter 22 Opener, p. 379; Part 1, "Thinking About Opinions," pp. 380–381	Part 2, "Prewriting: Discovering and Supporting Opinions," pp. 382–383	Part 3, "Prewriting: Developing and Organizing Reasons," pp. 384–385	Part 4, "Drafting Your Explanation," pp. 386–387	Part 5, "Revising Your Explanation," pp. 388–390

Chapter 22

The Process of Writing About Opinions

Look on the editorial page of a newspaper or near the front of many magazines. What do you find there? You find people's opinions. The editor of the paper writes his or her opinion in the form of editorials. Magazine readers express their opinions in letters to the editor.

You also express many opinions. For instance, you may tell your friend that a certain movie was the best you've ever seen. You may tell how you feel about your school, your neighborhood, or your favorite sports team. All of these are opinions.

In this chapter, you will learn how to write about an opinion you have. You will learn the importance of giving good reasons to support your opinions. Your skills will make it easier to understand the opinions of others.

379

chapter. After they have organized the material and made any necessary adjustments, they can then write their first drafts.

ESL Be sure that students understand the vocabulary used with the teaching of sequencing and order of importance. Encourage students to use familiar subjects for their paragraphs.

For general information on teaching composition to LD, ESL, and NSD students, see the "Guidelines for Teaching Special Populations" on pages T32–T35 in the front of this Teacher's Edition.

Related Chapters

You may wish to refer to related material in other chapters as you teach the following concepts:

1. Process of writing, Chapter 6, "Choosing a Process for Writing," page 101

2. Fact and opinion, and overgeneralization, Chapter 21, "Clear Thinking" page 367

Additional Resources

Skills Practice Book—pages 148–152
Test Booklet—pages 127–132
　　Pretest—pages 127–128
　　Mastery Test—pages 129–132
Teacher's Resource Binder
　　Reinforcement Activities—
　　　　pages 107–110
　　Enrichment Activities—
　　　　pages 34, 39–52
　　Process of Writing Transparencies
　　Ideas for Creative Teaching

Week 31

Chapter Management Guidelines

Day 1	Day 2
Chapter 22, Part 6, "Making and Sharing a Final Copy," p. 391	Chapter Review and selected end-of-chapter activities

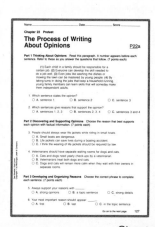

Part 1

Objective

To recognize paragraphs that state and support an opinion

Presenting the Lesson

● All Students

1. Read and discuss the introductory paragraph on page 380. Ask students what they would write in a letter to the principal of their school.

2. Read and discuss Example 1. Then, have students answer the questions on page 380. Make sure that students understand how the opinion is supported by reasons. Ask the students to put themselves in the principal's place. Would they be convinced to start a new club based on Ramona's letter?

3. Read and discuss Example 2 and the questions that accompany it on page 381. After the discussion, ask students to compare the paragraph with Example 1. Ask them if the writer of Example 2 used examples from her personal experience. Discuss why certain opinions can appropriately be supported by personal experience and others cannot.

This part sharpens the students' abilities to analyze and evaluate. It stresses individual styles of writing. By using both "student" and professional writing samples, it demonstrates both what students can do, and what more experienced writers can do. Since all writers and subjects are unique, writers working on the same type of paragraphs may produce very different products.

4. Read **Now It's Your Turn** on page 381. Encourage students to begin thinking about their opinions and to start recording these ideas in their journals.

▶ Basic Students

Make sure that students understand the difference between fact and opinion. Read the following statements to the students. Have them identify each as either a fact or an opinion. Emphasize that a fact can be proved, while an opinion cannot.

1. Many cats do not have tails. F

---

1 Thinking About Opinions

┌─ Focus ─────────────────────────────────┐
You can write about an opinion and give reasons to support it.
└───┘

You often share your opinions. For example, suppose you wanted to form a new club at school. You must explain to your principal why the club would be a good idea. You decide to write the principal a letter. What would you write?

Example 1

▶ Analyzing/Evaluating

Read and Think. Ramona wrote this explanation as part of her letter to her principal. As you read, look for her opinion and think about her reasons.

> I think we should have a club for left-handed people. We lefties could use the support, because being left-handed isn't easy. First of all, many school supplies like scissors are made for right handers. Even some school desks are designed only for people who write with their right hand. It's also harder for a lefty to learn how to do some things from a right-handed teacher. Once, during an arts and crafts unit, my teacher tried to teach me to knit. It was hopeless! Being left-handed even caused me a problem at the school picnic. My job was to serve punch. I quickly found I was in trouble! The spout was on the wrong side for me. The ladle was made for right-handed pouring.

Think and Discuss. Read the following questions. Discuss your answers to the questions with your classmates.

1. Which sentence tells Ramona's opinion?
2. What reasons does Ramona give to support her opinion?
3. Ramona uses examples and a story as supporting details. Find these details in Ramona's paragraph.

380

Example 2

▶ Analyzing/Evaluating

Read and Think. In this paragraph, the writer is telling why Dr. Martin Luther King, Jr., deserved to have a holiday created for him. Look for her reasons.

> Dr. Martin Luther King led a life worth celebrating. He believed that all people are equal, and have the right to equal opportunities no matter what color skin they have. Through his work, the country saw that black people were not being treated equally and were ready to work to change that. For example, blacks, especially in the South, used to be banned from many schools, restaurants, and stores. In some places, they were kept from voting. Dr. King showed people that they could protest this discrimination in a peaceful way. He led boycotts and marches, gave speeches, and inspired people across the nation.
>
> —MELISSA KIM

Think and Discuss. Think about these questions. Discuss them with your classmates.

1. What is the topic sentence of the paragraph?
2. What reasons are used to support the topic sentence?
3. What examples does the writer give to support her reasons?

▶ Generalizing

Now It's Your Turn

In both sample paragraphs, the opinion is stated clearly and directly. Both use reasons to support the opinions. Now you will learn how to write about your own opinions. Remember these two paragraphs. They will guide you when you express your spoken and written thoughts.

381

2. The Statue of Liberty was paid for by the contributions of private French and American citizens. F
3. Most Americans would enjoy a trip to Canada. O
4. The history of inventions is very interesting. O

◆ Advanced Students

Have the students draft a letter to the principal of their school asking for the formation of a new club or some other activity. Their letter should include at least three supporting reasons and an example or two from their own experience.

Special Populations

LD Students may have difficulty determining the difference between fact and opinion. Have students complete the exercise under **Basic Students** for additional drill. Refer to Chapter 21, "Clear Thinking," page 367 for additional information on fact and opinion.

ESL Because of cultural differences, some students may also have difficulty determining the difference between fact and opinion, especially when the information appears in the media. Discuss some television commercials and newspaper or magazine advertisements with students. Have them practice identifying the facts and opinions in each.

Reinforcement

Select several letters to the editor or other short opinion pieces from a local newspaper, magazine, or other publication. Read them to the students and discuss the following questions.

1. What is the writer's opinion?
2. Does he or she give reasons to support the opinion? What are they?
3. Does the writing persuade you to agree with the opinion?

Enrichment

Have students study news commentaries on local television. Many stations feature editorials at the end of the newscast. Then have the students select a news topic that they feel strongly about —something that affects them directly. Have them prepare a short oral report to present to the class, expressing their opinions on this topic.

Part 2

Objective

To identify an opinion and find supporting reasons

Presenting the Lesson

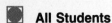 All Students

1. Read and discuss pages 382–383. Explain to students that opinions, unlike facts, cannot be proved. It is possible to persuade others to accept an opinion, but in order to do so, good reasons must be presented. Emphasize that the more one knows about a subject, the better one is able to express opinions about that subject. That is why it is important to be able to support opinions through reading and research.

2. Ask students to consider things they feel strongly about. Write some of these ideas on the board. Then ask students to think of some reasons that support these opinions. Stress the importance of using facts, not feelings, to support an opinion.

3. Assign and discuss Exercises A and B on page 383. Be sure that students begin keeping a record of their opinions in their journals or writing folders.

▶ Basic Students

Do Exercise A orally with the students. Make sure that students write several ideas in their writing folders or journals.

Help students select a topic for Exercise B. Have them think carefully about the opinions they have discovered while working on this part. Advise them to select the topic that they feel most strongly about or that they know the most about. Tell students that it is easier to write about a topic if they have strong opinions about it.

◆ Advanced Students

Encourage students to select a topic that requires an informed opinion. Have them research their topic carefully to gather supporting details. In addition to library research, they may wish to interview experts on their topic.

2 Prewriting: Discovering and Supporting Opinions

> ─ Focus ─
> Start the writing process by exploring your feelings. Develop an opinion and the reasons that support it.

Discover Your Opinions

▶ Comprehension

Opinions are what make people interesting. Opinions show what you value and how you feel. You have probably already formed strong feelings about certain things that happen in your life. You might have a favorite team, or a favorite music group. You may prefer a favorite ice cream flavor. You have your own ideas about the most interesting way to spend a Saturday afternoon. You can name the worst movie you've ever seen.

Brainstorm and talk with others to explore your own feelings. Search your journal for ideas that you think are important. Do some reading. Notice things that you would like to see changed. Decide what should remain the same. What ideas that you read or hear make you angry? Make a list of your opinions. Mark the ones you feel most strongly about.

Find Reasons for Support

When you have an opinion, you want to do more than just think about it. You also want others to understand or agree with your opinion. To make this happen, you must present good reasons for what you believe.

Try to go beyond feeling. The best reasons are factual. A reason that only gives another opinion is not really a reason at all. For example, your friend Burt says "I think the best

382

instrument to play is the trumpet. It sounds better than the other instruments." Burt's reason, that the trumpet "sounds better," is just another opinion. It is not good support.

You can find reasons to support opinions through reading and research. You may also find reasons in your experiences, or from talking with others. Try to find several strong reasons that will support your opinion.

Exercises   Finding and Supporting Opinions

▶ Creative Application

A. Discovering Opinions Complete the activities below. They will help you to discover your opinions. Keep these possible topics in your writing folder.

1. With some friends, look through a newspaper or magazine. Talk about what you read. What opinions do your friends have? Write down five of their opinions. Do you agree or disagree with them?
2. Ask questions about things that matter to you in your life. Who are your personal heroes or heroines? What are your pet peeves? What are your favorite pastimes? Why do you feel the way you do about these things?

▶ Creative Application

B. Starting To Explain Your Opinion Find a topic you feel strongly about. For ideas, look over the topics from Exercise A or those in the **Power Handbook** on pages 464-466. You might also check your journal. Next, begin your prewriting notes. Think of good reasons to support your opinion. Be sure your reasons are not just other opinions. Write down all your ideas.

383

Special Populations

LD Students will need some guidance as they work on the exercises. Refer to the notes under **Basic Students** for suggestions on assisting these students.

Reinforcement

1. Have the students follow the directions for Exercise A on page 383 using these activities:

A. Write "I believe" or "I think" ten times on a sheet of paper. Then complete each phrase with a different statement.

B. Look through your journal entries. Write five opinions that are recorded there. For each opinion, write several reasons that support it. Make sure the reasons are facts, not feelings.

2. Have the students read the following six ideas about keeping pets on leashes. Have them tell which ones are reasons and which are opinions.

1. Pets that run loose are pests. O
2. Pets that run loose can damage a home-owner's property. F
3. An unsupervised pet might bite a child. F
4. It is cruel to keep animals leashed all the time. O
5. An unleashed pet could be hit by an auto. F
6. Pets have a right to freedom just as people do. O

Additional Resources

Skills Practice Book—page 148

Teacher's Resource Binder
Reinforcement Activities—
page 107

Part 3

Objective

To organize reasons in the order of their importance as part of a writing plan

Presenting the Lesson

All Students

1. Read **Adding Supporting Details** on page 384. Emphasize that a good explanation of an opinion will contain several supporting reasons as well as details that help develop the reasons. Make students understand that details can include anything that develops an idea, or adds proof or support. Even a story or an anecdote can be a supporting detail.

2. Read and discuss **Organizing Your Reasons and Supporting Details** on page 384. Emphasize the importance of considering your audience when you are writing about an opinion. The audience may determine which ideas are most important and should, therefore, be saved for last.

3. Read **A Sample Writing Plan** on page 385. Emphasize that when beginning a writing plan, it is best to write down as many reasons as possible. Tell students that they can examine their reasons later and decide then which ones are most important, as Joanna did in the sample writing plan.

4. Assign and discuss Exercises A and B on page 385.

Basic Students

Choose one of the items in Exercise A. Do the exercise as a group activity. Have students find three supporting reasons for that opinion. Then, have the students select one of the remaining items to work on their own.

Help students organize their writing plans. Make sure that they have at least one detail to support each reason.

Advanced Students

Have students organize the notes for their writing plans twice, for two different audiences. Remind students that the order of importance will depend on the audience.

---

3 Prewriting: Developing and Organizing Reasons

> **Focus**
>
> As you gather your reasons, add supporting details. Organize your main points and supporting details.

Adding Supporting Details

▶ Classifying/Analyzing

You should have three or four good reasons to support your opinion. You should also have details that will help explain these reasons to your readers. These details may be examples, stories, facts, or statistics.

Look again at Ramona's letter in part 1. She gave several reasons why being left-handed is difficult. One was that it is harder for a lefty to learn how to do some things from a right-handed teacher. She developed this reason with an example—her teacher trying to teach her to knit. Ramona also used an anecdote, or brief story, to develop a reason. Add supporting details such as these to your prewriting notes.

Organizing Your Reasons and Supporting Details

Study your notes. Identify your main reasons and mark them with a check or star. Place each supporting detail with the reason that it helps to develop. Next, decide on the order you will use to present your reasons. Putting the strongest and most important reason last will leave it fresh in your reader's mind. To decide which reason is the most important, think about your audience. Who will read what you have written? Will it be the editor of the newspaper, your principal, or your classmates? One of your reasons will most strongly impress your audience. That reason should become your most important reason.

384

A Sample Writing Plan

Joanna brainstormed about some activities that were important to her. She decided to tell why gymnastics was so special to her. Her early prewriting notes are shown below.

Opinion: Gymnastics is fun.

Reasons: muscles more flexible   made new friends
in better physical condition   proud of myself
won medal in competition

After some thought, Joanna reworked her prewriting notes as shown below. She marked her main reasons with a star.

Opinion: Gymnastics is fun.

Reasons: ☆ in better physical condition
        muscles more flexible
   ☆ made new friends
   ☆ proud of myself
        won medal in competition

This example supports my statement about better physical condition.

I think this is most important reason. I'll mention it last.

This explains why I'm proud. It would make a good conclusion.

Exercises   Finding and Organizing Reasons

▸ Creative Application

A. Finding Reasons Below are three statements of opinion. Choose one and find three factual reasons to support it. Add two details to support each reason. You may need to use a reference source.

1. Thomas Jefferson was a talented man.
2. Everyone should learn to play an instrument.
3. Collecting _____ is a great hobby.

▸ Classifying/Analyzing

B. Making a Writing Plan First identify main reasons and supporting details. Then group supporting details with the reason each supports. Finally, put your main reasons in the order you want to present them. Remember to put your most important reason last.

385

Part 4

Objective

To follow a writing plan when drafting an explanation of an opinion

Presenting the Lesson

All Students

1. Read and discuss pages 386–387. Remind students that the purpose of a first draft is to get ideas down on paper. They should not be too concerned with form at this point. Later, they can perfect their writing through revision.

2. Review the words that signal overgeneralizations. Caution students against using these words in their paragraphs because overgeneralizations are difficult or impossible to support. Encourage students to use the following words instead: *most, few, usually, seldom,* and *some.* These can replace words such as *everyone, nobody, always,* and *never.*

3. Review signal words. Make sure that students understand how signal words are used to develop and build an explanation.

4. Discuss the revisions on the sample draft. Ask students to point out where Joanna has added signal words. Discuss how the signal words improve her paragraph. Point out Joanna's thoughts as she worked.

Discuss the ways that students might conclude their paragraphs. The final sentence should be interesting, but it should not introduce new information.

5. Assign and discuss the exercise on page 387. Remind students that their first draft need not be perfect. They should concentrate on getting their ideas down on paper. Later, during revision, they will have time to make changes and correct any errors.

▶ Basic Students

Before having students write their first draft, review the information presented in this part. Pay special attention to topic sentences and overgeneralizations. Remind students to follow their writing plans as they draft their explanations. Walk around the room and offer assistance as students work.

---

4 Drafting Your Explanation

> **Focus**
>
> Put your ideas into sentence and paragraph form. Use your prewriting notes as a guide for your rough draft.

▶ Comprehension

When you have finished your writing plan, you are ready to write your rough draft. Be sure to use your prewriting notes as a guide.

Follow your writing plan as you draft. Your writing plan gives you a good start toward your finished paper. As you draft, think about how your ideas are working together. As you know, you will continue to develop your ideas throughout the writing process. You will add some ideas and details and drop others that do not fit.

Write a strong topic sentence. Begin your explanation with a strong topic sentence. Avoid phrases such as "In my opinion . . ." or "I believe . . ." or "I think . . . ." State your opinion simply and clearly. For example, if you think that it is important to know how to cook, say so.

> Everyone over the age of ten should know how to prepare a simple meal.

Be sure your statement of opinion is accurate. Do not use words like *everyone, all, never,* and *no one* unless they say what you really mean. Otherwise your statement of opinion may be an overgeneralization. To learn more about overgeneralization, see Chapter 21, page 374.

Develop your paragraph. Follow the topic sentence with the reasons from your writing plan. Explain each reason simply and clearly. Finally, end your explanation with your most important reason.

Use signal words. Signal words can make your ideas work well together. They can "signal" a new idea. Signal words can also help your sentences flow together smoothly. They may show how one idea is tied to another. Here are some signal words that are often used in writing about opinions. Use these words or others like them as you draft and revise.

Signal Words for Explanations

For a main point or reason: first, next, in addition, another reason, most important, also, finally

For supporting details: for example, such as, for instance

Sample Draft

Joanna used her prewriting notes to develop the draft shown below. Notice her thoughts as she worked on her draft.

Gymnastics has changed my life.
~~Gymnastics is fun.~~ My whole body is in

better condition now than ever before. My

muscles are more flexible. I have made some
I have met girls from all over the state as I have
great new friends through gymnastics. I love *traveled*
                                                to meets.
to travel and eat out after meets. I am proud of

myself. I am proud of all the new things I can
Finally,
do. I am proud of the medal I won.

This is a better way to state my opinion. It covers all my reasons.

I should add a detail to explain this reason.

will
nal
last
ea.

Exercise   Drafting an Explanation
▶ Creative Application
Use your writing plan to make a first draft of your explanation. Begin your explanation with a good topic sentence that states your opinion. State your supporting reasons simply and clearly. Use signal words to show the organization of your ideas.

387

Additional Resources

Skills Practice Book—page 150
Teacher's Resource Binder
   Reinforcement Activities—
   page 109

◆ **Advanced Students**

Have students work as peer partners with basic students.

Special Populations

LD Students should refer to the steps in drafting an explanation as they work. Make a list or chart of these steps as presented on pages 386–387. Also, make a list of signal words. Post these in the classroom. Encourage students to refer to these charts often and to use them as a check-list in drafting their opinion paragraphs. You might also have advanced students work as peer partners with these students.

NSD Remind students of the importance of using Standard English in their paragraphs.

Reinforcement

Write the following five sentences on the board. Have the students copy them on their papers and mark every one that would be a good topic sentence for an opinion paragraph. Have them revise the poor sentences so that they will be good topic sentences.

1. I believe that pets should not be kept in an apartment.
2. Disneyland is a perfect spot for a family vacation.
3. Today's popular music may or may not be as good as the music from ten years ago.
4. Larry Bird is the best professional basketball player ever.
5. I like television comedies because they're good.

Part 5

Objective

To revise and proofread an explanation

Presenting the Lesson

 All Students

1. Read and discuss **Take a Second Look** on page 388. Discuss each point in the **Guidelines for Revising an Explanation.** Remind students that in an opinion paragraph they are trying to convince others to accept their opinion. It is important to revise with the audience in mind.

2. Read the sample revision on pages 389–390. Compare Joanna's revised draft to her first draft in part 4. Discuss how the revisions have made the explanation stronger. Point out that it is sometimes necessary to repeat the revision process. Students should continue to change and revise their work until they are satisfied with the results.

3. Read **Proofreading for Errors** on page 390. Stress the importance of saving proofreading for the final step. Proofreading should not be done until all content changes have been made. Encourage students to frequently refer to the **Power Handbook** for rules on capitalization, punctuation, and spelling.

4. Assign and discuss Exercises A and B on page 390.

 Basic Students

Remind students about the types of errors they should look for when proofreading. Help the students to identify problems that can be corrected in their final drafts.

 Advanced Students

Have students exchange their papers with a partner. Then, have them think of reasons why someone might disagree with their partner's opinion. Have them write down these reasons, along with other suggestions. Next, have the students revise their own papers, including reasons that would disprove the possible opposing arguments.

---

5 Revising Your Explanation

> **Focus**
>
> Review your draft. Make sure your reasons are presented clearly. Then carefully proofread what you have written.

Take a Second Look

▶ Comprehension/Analyzing

Has anyone ever said, "Take a second look," after you missed seeing something the first time? The revision stage is your second look in the writing process. It is a time to look over what you have written and to make changes. This is especially important when you write about your opinions. If you want others to agree with your opinion, weak writing will not convince anyone. See how you can improve what you say and how you say it. Ask yourself questions such as these when you revise.

> **Guidelines for Revising an Explanation**
>
> 1. Is my opinion clearly stated in my topic sentence?
> 2. Do I have good support for my topic? Do I have strong reasons?
> 3. Do I have enough supporting details to develop those reasons? Have I included examples, stories, facts, or statistics?
> 4. Is my most important reason mentioned last?
> 5. Could I add signal words to make my ideas clearer?

Try reading your draft aloud as you revise. Slow down and listen to your draft. Try reading your paper to someone else. Ask that person's opinion of your paper. This will help you review your ideas carefully.

388

Sample Revision

Joanna read her draft aloud several times. She continued to make changes. Notice her thoughts as she worked.

Gymnastics has changed my life. My whole body is in better condition now than ever before. My muscles are more flexible. *My parents even say that I am standing straighter.* Also, I have made some great new friends through gymnastics. I have met girls from all over the state as I have traveled to meets. ~~I love to travel and eat out after meets.~~ Finally, I am proud of myself. I am proud of all the new things I can do. *I am proud that I can stay calm in competition.* I am proud of the medal I won.

In addition, some of the older girls on my own team have helped me with my routines, and I've also been able to teach new exercises to the girls just starting out.

> *I can add this example here.*

> *I can replace that detail with two examples that are better.*

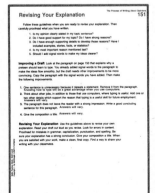

389

Special Populations

LD Students often have difficulty coping with details. Have students divide the proofreading process into these four separate steps.

1. Use the dictionary to check spelling.
2. Check names for capital letters.
3. Check for proper punctuation.
4. Read the paper out loud.

The final step will help students to catch errors they might otherwise miss.

LD, ESL For both groups stress content revision over the correction of grammar and usage errors. Provide assistance as needed while students work, or have advanced peer partners work with them.

NSD Pair students with Standard-English-speaking students to work on errors in usage.

Reinforcement

Copy the following paragraph on the board. Have the students revise it using the **Guidelines for Revising an Explanation** on page 388. Have them add signal words and correct overgeneralizations.

Photography is a terrific hobby. Everyone has a camera. Taking pictures can be quite simple with the new electronic cameras. You can take pictures that will help you remember many special times in your life. Best of all, photography can provide you with a way to express yourself creatively. There are many camera clubs that you can join. Also, you can enter your photographs in contests.

Joanna was happier with her explanation, but still not satisfied. She reviewed her writing and had these thoughts.

Problem: In my last reasons, I said "I am proud" four times.
Result: Joanna wrote, "Finally, now I feel good about myself. I am proud of my new skills and my ability to stay calm in competition."

Problem: My ending does not leave a strong impression.
Result: Joanna included the words printed on the medal. Her last sentence then read, "Most of all, I am proud of my new medal that says, 'second place, all-around competition'."

Proofreading for Errors

After you have completed your content changes, read through your writing again. This time, review it for errors in grammar, capitalization, punctuation, and spelling.

When you write to explain an opinion, you often use signal words and phrases at the beginning of sentences. These introductory words are usually followed by commas. Check carefully for the correct use of commas with signal words. Use the Guidelines for Proofreading on page 114 for further help. You may also wish to check the rules for capitalization and punctuation in the **Power Handbook**.

Exercises   Revising an Explanation
▶ Judging/Evaluating

A. Reading a Classmate's Draft As your teacher directs, help a classmate revise his or her writing. Read the draft. Refer to the "Guidelines for Revising an Explanation" on page 388. Write at least two ideas that the writer could use to improve his or her draft.

▶ Evaluating/Creative Application

B. Revising Your Explanation Read your draft aloud. Think about changes you want to make. Follow the suggestions of your classmate and the guidelines on page 388 to revise your writing. Carefully proofread your work for errors.

390

6 Making and Sharing a Final Copy

> **Focus**
>
> Choose a good title for your explanation. Then make a final copy.

▶ Comprehension

Decide on a good title for your explanation. Your title should briefly state the main idea of your explanation. Make your final copy as clean and neat as possible.

Here is Joanna's final copy.

A New Me

Gymnastics has changed my life. My whole body is in better condition now than ever before. My muscles are more flexible. My parents even say that I am standing straighter. Also, I have made some great new friends through gymnastics. I have met girls from all over the state as I have traveled to meets. In addition, some of the older girls on my team have helped me with my routines, and I've also been able to teach new exercises to the girls just starting out. Finally, now I feel good about myself. I am proud of my new skills and my ability to stay calm in competition. Most of all, I am proud of my new medal that says, "second place, all-around competition."

Exercise Making and Sharing a Final Copy

▶ Creative Application

Choose a good title. Then make a clean, final copy of your explanation. Proofread your final copy one last time for errors in copying. Choose a method from pages 116-117 and share your writing with your classmates.

391

Part 6

Objective

To make and share a neat final copy of an explanation

Presenting the Lesson

 All Students

Read and discuss page 391. Have students complete the exercise and turn in their final paragraphs. Use the following criteria to evaluate student work.

Guidelines for Evaluation

Strong The most successful writing will display the following characteristics: (5 points)

1. will state the opinion in a clear topic sentence that does not include "I think" or "I believe"
2. will support the opinion with two or three facts or reasons
3. will develop each reason with appropriate details
4. will demonstrate a clear sense of organization
5. will demonstrate coherence; will use transitional words and phrases as necessary
6. will contain no more than two or three minor errors in grammar, usage, and mechanics

Average A paragraph of average quality will meet most of the criteria of the successful response but may display one or two of these problems: (3 points)

1. may not state opinion concisely or clearly
2. may lack enough supporting detail
3. may display several errors in grammar, usage, and mechanics

Weak A weak paragraph will display only one or two of the characteristics of a successful response. It will also be characterized by several of the following problems: (1 point)

1. unclear statement of opinion
2. unsound or insufficiently developed supporting reasons
3. no clear sense of order
4. numerous errors in grammar, usage, and mechanics

Speaking and Listening

Objective

To use the process of explaining an opinion in a debate

Presenting the Activity

This page gives special emphasis to the speaking and listening skill of debating. This activity may be used to show students how the concepts presented in this chapter may be applied in an oral context. In addition to the instructions on this sheet, the students may wish to obtain a copy of the rules for debating. You might obtain these from an upper-level speech text.

Speaking and Listening

Taking Part in a Debate

▶ Comprehension

In a debate, two teams discuss one question or issue. For example, the statement "All students should study a foreign language," could be a debate topic. One team is "pro," or in agreement with the issue. The other team is "con," or not in agreement with the issue.

Each team has a set amount of time to present its opinion, reasons, and supporting details. The "pro" team goes first. Each team member presents a reason and some details. Then the "con" team presents its reasons. Finally, each team has a time for rebuttal, or a time to show weaknesses in what the other team has said. After the presentations and rebuttals, a judge decides which team has presented the stronger opinion.

If you are taking part in a debate, be well prepared. Have your reasons and evidence ready. Save your most important point until last. Speak slowly and clearly. Stress signal words like *first of all*, *secondly*, or *most importantly*.

If you are a judge, or part of the audience, listen with care to both teams. Take notes so you will remember what each person said. Then, decide which team should win the debate.

Exercise   Taking Part in a Debate

▶ Creative Application

Your teacher will give you a topic and tell you whether you are part of the "pro" or "con" team. Prepare at least two reasons along with their supporting details to support your opinion. When you are not debating, listen carefully. Take notes so that you can decide fairly who won.

392

Creative Writing

▶ Creative Application

A. Imagine that you are an important person in history. Next, select a current issue from your school, town, state, or nation. Decide how your important person would feel about this issue. Then, write an explanation. State an opinion and reasons as if you were this important person.

Here are some ideas for your explanation. How would Johnny Appleseed feel about a new highway that would run through the forest preserve? Would Babe Ruth think that today's baseball players are paid too much? What would Orville and Wilbur Wright think about space travel?

B. Write a skit for two people. It should involve an opinion that needs an explanation. For instance, have a driver explain to a police officer why he or she was speeding. Or, have a daughter explain to a parent why she should be allowed to have a slumber party. Your skit should present opinions, reasons, and supporting details. With a partner, perform your skit for the rest of the class.

393

Creative Writing

These activities provide opportunities for the students to use the skills they have learned in this chapter in an imaginative way. Remind students to use the writing process they have learned in this chapter when completing the activities. Provide a way for students to share their writing with the class.

Using English in Social Studies

▶ Comprehension/Drawing Conclusions

Did you know that you are a consumer? A consumer is anyone who buys or uses products or services. A wise consumer thinks carefully about the products that are available. Then he or she forms an opinion about which product is best. To do this, a consumer must have facts about a product.

An advertisement for a product is one place you must look for facts about a product. Ads often begin with a statement of opinion such as "Spotless Soap is best." The ad then tells why this is true. Look closely at the statements in an ad that tell why you should buy the product. Are factual reasons given or are these statements just more opinions? A wise consumer makes decisions based on facts.

Look at this ad. What opinion is stated? What are the reasons for this opinion?

The best way to start your day is with **Natural Crunch Cereal**. So great tasting you'll eat it for snacks, too. It's good for you. Has the nut-like taste of whole grain flakes. Enjoy the added flavor of dates, raisins, and nuts. Fortified with ten essential vitamins and minerals. All natural ingredients. Low in sugar.

Exercise Forming Opinions from Ads

▶ Drawing Conclusions/Creative Application

Cut out some ads from magazines and newspapers. Paste each ad on a sheet of paper. Examine the ad. Underline or write the opinion stated by the ad. List the reasons that tell why you should buy the product. Beside each reason, tell if the statement is fact or opinion. Tell what opinion you have formed about the product.

394

Chapter 22 Review

▶ Analyzing/Inferring Sequence

A. Organizing Ideas Below is a set of notes. The notes have not yet been organized into an effective prewriting plan. Copy the notes on your paper. Mark main reasons with a star. Find the supporting details that can be used with each main reason. Then, arrange the reasons and supporting details in the order you would present them. Rewrite the notes to show your organized writing plan. *Order of main reasons may vary. See suggested answers in n.*

Opinion: Molly is the best choice for class president.

Has experience*

Is well-liked*

Was the fifth-grade vice-president

Wants to raise money with a school car wash

Voted most popular girl in class

Has good plans*

▶ Interpretation/Critical Reasoning

B. Recognizing Opinions and Reasons Read the following paragraph. Then answer the questions. *See answers in margin.*

Every child should have a dog. In the first place, caring for a dog teaches a child about responsibility. A dog's owner must exercise, feed, and groom the pet. Secondly, a pet dog can be a watchdog. For example, the dog could protect its owner's family from strangers and burglars. Finally, a dog can be a child's best friend. A dog will always listen to problems and play any game.

1. What is the writer's opinion?
2. What reasons does the writer give to support his or her opinion?
3. What details support each reason?

395

Chapter Review

This review allows teachers to evaluate student understanding of the concepts presented in this chapter.

Exercise A
1. Is well-liked
   Voted most popular girl in class
2. Has good plans
   Wants to raise money with a school car wash
3. Has experience
   Was the fifth grade vice-president

Exercise B
1. Every child should have a dog.
2. teaches responsibility to children
   dog can become watchdog
   dog can be child's best friend
3. owner must exercise, feed, and groom pet
   protect family from strangers and burglars
   listens to and plays with child

Additional Resources

Skills Practice Book
Review—page 152

Test Booklet
Mastery Test—pages 129–132

Chapter 23

Chapter Objectives

1. To understand how books in the library are classified
2. To categorize books according to the Dewey Decimal System
3. To use the card catalog to locate books
4. To use an encyclopedia to locate and gather information
5. To recognize and use other reference books
6. To develop note-taking skills
7. To understand techniques for gathering information by interviewing
8. To understand graphic aids and use them when appropriate

Motivating the Students

1. If possible, arrange to have your class meet in the library for one or more class sessions.

If you do not have access to a school library, or yours cannot accommodate your entire class, assemble a collection of library materials for use in your classroom. Consider a field trip to the nearest public library.

2. Read the following passage to the students. Discuss the passage.

> Libraries have been important to people for over 6,000 years. Soon after the invention of writing, people realized the importance of assembling collections of their records into libraries.
>
> Very early libraries consisted of collections of clay tablets in Mesopotamia and papyrus scrolls in Egypt. Later, in the Middle Ages, when scholars couldn't get papyrus, they wrote on parchment made from thin layers of animal skin. Libraries then became collections of animal skins.
>
> Today, libraries contain an interesting variety of stored materials. These include audiovisual and computer equipment in addition to books. The modern library is a treasury of material waiting to be found.

Week 31

Chapter Management Guidelines   This chart may be used to help structure daily lesson plans

Day 3	Day 4	Day 5
Chapter 23 Opener, p. 397; Part 1, "The Classification of Books," pp. 398–399	Part 2, "The Dewey Decimal System," pp. 400–402; Part 3, "Using the Card Catalog," pp. 403–405	Part 4, "Using the Encyclopedia," pp. 406–408; Part 5, "Using Other Resources," pp. 409–411

Developing Library and Research Skills

Imagine that you have been given a safe filled with riches. However, you do not have the combination to open it. What a frustrating experience that would be! You have riches of another kind available to you in your library. Just as you need a combination to open a safe, you need certain skills to use a library.

This chapter will give you the "combination" you will need to unlock the riches in the library. It will teach you to find fiction books and nonfiction books, to use the card catalog, to use basic reference materials, and to conduct an interview.

397

3. Read and discuss page 397. Draw a safe on the board. Ask the students to suggest some topics they would like to learn more about. Write the student suggestions inside the safe.

Point out that a library is valuable only if a person knows what services it has to offer and how to locate and use the information the library holds. This chapter explains ways to locate and use library materials.

Special Populations

LD, ESL Provide "hands-on" experience whenever possible. Do exercises with the students. Give as much extra library practice as possible.

ESL Encourage students to find and borrow library books relating to their native cultures.

Related Chapters

You may wish to refer to related material in other chapters as you teach the following concepts:

1. Skimming and scanning, Chapter 7, "Study and Test-Taking Skills," page 126

2. Using the dictionary, Chapter 9, "Discovering the Dictionary and Thesaurus," page 161

3. Gathering report information, Chapter 24, "The Process of Writing a Report," page 420

Additional Resources

Skills Practice Book—pages 153–162

Test Booklet—pages 133–140
Pretest—pages 133–134
Mastery Test—pages 135–140

Teacher's Resource Binder
Reinforcement Activities—
pages 111–116
Enrichment Activities—
pages 35, 39–52, 77
Ideas for Creative Teaching

Chapter Management Guidelines

	Day 2
Chapter 23, Part 6, "Taking Notes," p. 413; Part 7 "The Interview," pp. 414–415	Part 8, "Getting Information from Graphic Aids," pp. 416–417; Chapter Review and selected end-of-chapter activities

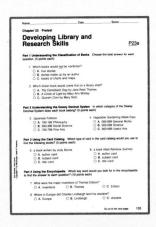

Part 1

Objective

To understand how books in the library are classified

Presenting the Lesson

 All Students

1. Read and discuss pages 398–399. Discuss the difference between fiction and nonfiction. Ask students to name some fiction and nonfiction books they have read.

2. Be sure students understand the arrangement of fiction books alphabetically by author's last name. Explain that nonfiction books are arranged by other classification systems. They will learn more about the Dewey Decimal System in part 2 of this chapter.

3. Assign and discuss Exercises A and B on page 399.

 Basic Students

To give reinforcement in alphabetizing, write these authors' names on the board and help students arrange them as they would appear in the fiction section of the library. Cleary, Blume, Bell, Clarke, D'Engle, White, Sobol, Whitney, Hamilton, Mitchell.

 Advanced Students

Have students draw a floor plan of the school or community library. Have them mark and color code the areas for fiction and nonfiction. Have them add features to their maps as they learn more about library resources later in this chapter.

Special Populations

LD Review alphabetizing with students before beginning the lesson. Provide a number of books from the classroom for students to separate into fiction and nonfiction and then have them alphabetize the fiction books.

---

1 The Classification of Books

> **Focus**
>
> There are two kinds of books, **fiction** and **nonfiction**.

▶ Comprehension/Classifying

Libraries can have thousands of books. Finding a particular book among so many may seem to be an impossible task. However, the job is not difficult when you learn how books are arranged in the library. Basically, books are divided into two groups: **fiction** and **nonfiction**.

Fiction

Fiction books are stories that were made up by a writer, or author. Since fiction comes from the author's imagination, it is not necessarily true. The writer of a fiction book may base a story on some real events or experiences, but then invent certain elements to make a good story. All fiction books are grouped together in the library.

Fiction books are arranged on shelves alphabetically according to the author's last name. For example, books by an author whose last name is Adams are placed before books by an author named Byars. Books by Byars are placed before those by Cleary.

If someone has written more than one book, all of those books are placed together on the shelf. They are then arranged alphabetically by the first word in the title. Words like *a, an,* or *the* are not considered in arranging titles alphabetically.

Nonfiction

Nonfiction books are about real people and events. They report facts or ideas. For example, a book about dinosaurs and a book about the history of fashion are nonfiction. These books

398

are classified and arranged according to their subjects. These subjects are grouped together in larger categories.

There are several classification systems for nonfiction. One is the **Library of Congress System**. Most university libraries use this system. The other classification system is the **Dewey Decimal System**. Most school and public libraries use this system. You will learn more about the Dewey Decimal System in part 2.

Exercises   Fiction and Nonfiction

▶ Inferring Sequence

A. On a separate sheet of paper, arrange these authors and fiction titles in the order in which they should appear on the shelves.

7   1. Snyder, Zilpha   *Eyes in the Fishbowl*
5   2. Sherburne, Zoa   *Jennifer*
10 3. Speare, Elizabeth   *The Witch of Blackbird Pond*
8   4. Snyder, Zilpha   *The Velvet Room*
4   5. Klein, Norma   *Mom, the Wolf Man, and Me*
3   6. Kjelgaard, Jim   *Outlaw Red*
1   7. Gault, William   *The Last Lap*
2   8. Kjelgaard, Jim   *Big Red*
6   9. Snyder, Zilpha   *Below the Root*
9   10. Speare, Elizabeth   *The Bronze Bow*

▶ Classifying

B. Number your paper from 1 to 6. Write *Fiction* or *Nonfiction* to identify each title.

1. *The History of China*   Nonfiction
2. *The Mystery of the Summer House*   Fiction
3. *The Autobiography of Kevin Ford*   Nonfiction
4. *Bicycle Repairs: A How-To Book*   Nonfiction
5. *Adventure in the Hidden Cave*   Fiction
6. *Short Story Masterpieces*   Fiction

Reinforcement

Have the students follow the directions for Exercise A on page 399 using these titles and authors:

5   1. Hamiliton, Virginia, *Justice and Her Brothers*
1   2. Babbitt, Natalie, *Goody Hall*
10 3. Verne, Jules, *Twenty Thousand Leagues Under the Sea*
6   4. Hobson, Sam B., and Hobson, George Carey, *The Lion of the Kalahari*
8   5. Lovelace, Maud Hart, *Betsy and Tacy Go Downtown*
7   6. Lewis, C.S., *Voyage of the Dawn Treader*
3   7. Bova, Benjamin, *The Winds of Altair*
9   8. Scholz, Jackson, *The Perfect Game*
2   9. Beyer, Audrey White, *Dark Venture*
4   10. Fisher, Leonard Everett, *A Russian Farewell*

Enrichment

1. Have one student give a brief plot summary of a book he or she has read. The rest of the class can then decide whether the book is fiction or nonfiction. For example, the student may say, "My book tells the story of George Washington Carver's life." The students would guess nonfiction.

2. For additional enrichment activities, see the Unit Projects in the Teacher Notes on page 347. One or more of these projects have special activities for gifted and talented students.

Additional Resources

Skills Practice Book—page 153
Teacher's Resource Binder
Reinforcement Activities—
    page 111
Enrichment Activities—
    page 35

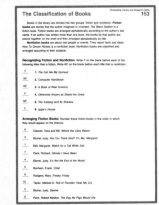

Part 2

Objective

To become familiar with the Dewey Decimal System of classifying nonfiction

Presenting the Lesson

 All Students

1. Read and discuss page 400 and the chart on page 401. Be sure students understand the relationship between the category of the book and its call number. Define, discuss, and give examples of any Dewey categories that might be unclear, such as philosophy or social science. If possible, provide examples from the library. Let the students examine the call numbers. Point out that some subjects may be grouped under more than one category. Plants, for example, could be found in 500 under science, or in 700 under gardening. Make the students aware that although most almanacs are found under 000, General Works, in some libraries they are classified under 300, Social Science. Check with your library to learn this arrangement.

2. Be sure students understand the terms *biography*, *autobiography*, and *collected biography*, and the assignment of the 920 and 921 numbers.

3. Assign and discuss Exercises A and B on page 402.

 Basic Students

Work with the students to complete Exercise A on page 402 and help them to use the titles to identify the general subject of each book. Then help them to relate that general subject to the Dewey System categories.

Review the biography, collective biography, autobiography, and short story collection categories before assigning Exercise B.

2 The Dewey Decimal System

> **Focus**
>
> The **Dewey Decimal System** classifies all nonfiction books into ten major categories. A specific identification number, a **call number**, is assigned to every nonfiction book.

▶ Comprehension

The **Dewey Decimal System** classifies all nonfiction books into ten categories. Most school and public libraries arrange their nonfiction books according to this identification system.

Each of the categories in the Dewey Decimal System is assigned a number, counting by hundreds. For example, the numbers 600–699 are assigned to Useful Arts. In this category, you will find cookbooks, garden books, and books about cars, among other subjects. Look at all ten categories in the chart on the next page.

In the Dewey Decimal System, a specific identification number is assigned to every nonfiction book. This number, known as the **call number**, is like the address of the book. It tells exactly where each book in the library can be found on the shelves. The call number of each nonfiction book is printed on its spine. Then the book is arranged in numerical order on a shelf in the library according to its call number.

The Dewey Decimal System

000–099	General Works	(encyclopedias, almanacs, handbooks)
100–199	Philosophy	(conduct, ethics, psychology)
200–299	Religion	(the Bible, mythology, theology)
300–399	Social Science	(economics, law, education, commerce, government, folklore, legend)
400–499	Language	(languages, grammar, dictionaries)
500–599	Science	(mathematics, chemistry, biology, physics)
600–699	Useful Arts	(farming, cooking, sewing, radio, nursing, engineering, television, business, gardening, cars)
700–799	Fine Arts	(music, painting, drawing, acting, photography, games, sports)
800–899	Literature	(poetry, plays, essays)
900–999	History	(biography, travel, geography)

A special section in the nonfiction area is the collection of biographies. A **biography** is the true story of a person's life written by another person. An **autobiography** is the true life story written by the person himself or herself. A **collective biography** contains the life stories of more than one person. The 920 call number is reserved for collective biographies. The 92 call number or the letter B may be used for individual biographies and autobiographies.

Most libraries keep fiction books that contain several short stories in a special section. These books are usually marked *SC,* for "Story Collection." Check your library for the location of this section.

401

◆ Advanced Students

If possible, provide some call slips from a public library for student examination. Demonstrate the completion of a call slip. Explain that large libraries use this method of locating a book.

You may wish to explain the second number under the Dewey Decimal number that appears on the spine of a book. In the number R 444f, for example, *R* is the first letter of the author's last name, *444* is the author's number, and *f* is the first letter of the book title.

Special Populations

LD Have students make a note card showing Dewey Decimal categories and numbers. They can use this card for reference in the library. See also notes for **Basic Students.**

Reinforcement

Follow the directions for Exercise A using books on these subjects:

the paintings of Claude Monet 700–799
recipes of New Orleans 600–699
Roman mythology 200–299
child psychology 300–399
the life of Albert Einstein 92
collection of Sherlock Holmes detective stories SC

Enrichment

Let the students know that a large number of libraries use a second system of classification, the Library of Congress system, which also uses a combination of letters and numerals. Give the students the following call numbers assigned to six nonfiction books according to the Library of Congress numbering. Each part of the classification number helps to identify certain information about the book. For example, in the number QA 765, the *Q* designates science, the *A,* computer science. Ask the students to put the call numbers in order according to the way in which the books would appear on the shelves. Tell them to begin with the first letter on the top line, and to use alphabetical order.

6 TG148 .M26	4 QA76.5 .C65	2 GF48 .A84
1 G860 .L35	3 GV885.1 .D52	5 QL506 .D34

Exercises   Using the Dewey Decimal System

▶Recalling

A. Number your paper from 1 to 10. Assign the correct category number to each of these books.

1. *The Rainbow Book of Nature* by Donald Peattie   500–599
2. *America in Legend* by Richard M. Dorson   300–399
3. *Ecology* by Peter Farb   500–599
4. *Illustrated Motor Cars of the World* by Piet Olyslager   600–699
5. *Making Mosaics* by Edmond Arvois   700–799
6. *Compton's Encyclopedia*   000–099
7. *The World of Ballet* by Anne Geraghty   700–799
8. *Ancient China* by John Hay   900–999
9. *Poetry Handbook* by Babette Deutsch   800–899
10. *The Story of Language* by Mario Pei   400–499

▶Classifying

B. Each book below belongs in one of the special categories of biography, autobiography, collective biography, or short story collections. Read the title of each book carefully. Decide on the right category. Copy each title and author. Then write the correct category for each book.

1. *Jules Verne: The Man Who Invented the Future* by Franz Born   biography
2. *O. Henry's Best Stories* edited by Lou P. Bunce   short story collection
3. *People in History* by R. J. Unstead   collective biography
4. *If You Could See What I Hear* by Tom Sullivan (with Derek Gill)   autobiography
5. *Martin Luther King: The Peaceful Warrior* by Ed Clayton   biography
6. *Stories Boys Like* compiled by Franklin M. Reck   short story collection
7. *My Animals and Me* by Nan Hayden Agle   autobiography
8. *Baseball's Greatest Pitchers* by Milton J. Shapiro   collective biography
9. *The Youngest General: A Story of Lafayette* by Fruma Gottschalk   biography
10. *Evel Knievel and Other Daredevils* by Joe Scalzo   collective biography

402

3 Using the Card Catalog

> ## Focus
> Use the **card catalog** to locate a book in the library.

▶ Comprehension

Most libraries have thousands of books. However, you can easily locate a specific book by using the card catalog.

The Card Catalog

The **card catalog** is a cabinet of small drawers filled with cards printed with information about every book in the library. The cards are arranged alphabetically according to the top line of each card. In the upper left-hand corner of each card in the catalog is the **call number** of the book listed on the card. This call number makes it easier to find the book.

On the outside of each drawer, there is a label that tells which letters of the alphabet are contained in that drawer. Inside each drawer there are **guide cards** that have tabs extending above the regular book cards. The tabs may have letters of the alphabet, complete words, or general subject headings printed on them. The guide cards separate the drawer of cards into small groups. Some libraries now have computerized card catalogs.

Types of Catalog Cards

▶ Classifying

There are usually three cards for the same book in the card catalog: the **author card**, the **title card**, and the **subject card**. All three cards give you the same information about the book, but in slightly different order. They provide the title of the book, the author, the publisher, the date of publication, the number of pages, a notation about illustrations, and the call number.

403

Part 3

Objective

To use the card catalog to locate books

Presenting the Lesson

All Students

1. Read and discuss pages 403–405. Point out that some libraries have two separate card files, one for author and title cards and another for subject cards. Check with the librarian to find out the arrangement for the card catalog. Also mention that many librarians are using computers to store card catalog information. The librarian can demonstrate how to find information on the computer.

2. If possible, obtain old card catalog cards of each type from the librarian. Duplicate or show these on an overhead projector for the class. Have students identify what type of card each is.

3. Assign and discuss Exercises A and B on page 405.

Basic Students

Have the students draw author, title, and subject cards for their mathematics or science book. Have the students use the general Dewey Decimal System category.

Pair students to work on Exercise A.

Advanced Students

Challenge the students to find the answers to each of the following questions, using only the card catalog:

Answers will vary.

1. Who is the author of the *Homer Price* series of books?
2. In what year was *Old Yeller* copyrighted?
3. Does your library have any books about the Loch Ness Monster?
4. How many books by Robb White are in your library?
5. Are there any other books by the author of *The Lion, the Witch, and the Wardrobe* in your library? If so, list one title. Who is the author?

6. Does your library have any books on careers in medicine?
7. How many books by Marilyn Sachs are in your library?
8. Are there any biographies about Eleanor Roosevelt? If so, who is the author of one of them?
9. Does your library have any books about arts and crafts of Native Americans?
10. Who is the author of the *Henry Reed* series?

Special Populations

ESL Pair students with native speakers of English for card catalog work in the library.

Reinforcement

Have the students follow directions for Exercise B on page 405 using these subjects. Answers will vary.

1. ballet
2. sea mammals
3. Grandma Moses
4. Martin Luther King
5. Niagara Falls
6. Chris Evert Lloyd
7. poems by Shel Silverstein
8. home computers
9. teradactyls
10. stamp collecting

Enrichment

Arrange for the class to visit a local library with a computerized catalog. Have the librarian demonstrate its use. Have students work in pairs to find a listing by author, title, and subject.

An author card has the name of the author on the top line. A title card has the title on the top line. A subject card has the general subject on the top line. All three cards for one book have the same call number in the upper left corner.

Look carefully at the following examples of card catalog cards for the book *Wildlife in Danger* by Alan C. Jenkins.

The Author Card

When you know the author of a book, use the card catalog to look up the author's name. All the cards for one author will be filed alphabetically by the first word in the title.

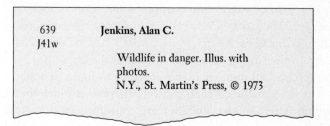

639
J41w

Jenkins, Alan C.

Wildlife in danger. Illus. with photos.
N.Y., St. Martin's Press, © 1973

The Title Card

When you know the title of a book, but not its author, look for the title card. Title cards are filed alphabetically by the first word. *A*, *an*, and *the* do not count as first words.

639
J41w

Wildlife in danger.

Jenkins, Alan C.

Wildlife in danger. Illus. with photos.
N.Y., St. Martin's Press, © 1973

404

Additional Resources

Skills Practice Book—page 156
Teacher's Resource Binder
Reinforcement Activities—
page 113

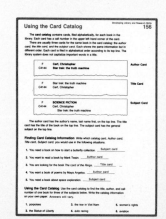

The Subject Card

If you have a general topic in mind but do not know any book titles or authors, use the subject cards. For example, if you were writing a report on wildlife, you would look in the card catalog under the subject heading WILDLIFE. The subject on every subject card is frequently in capital letters.

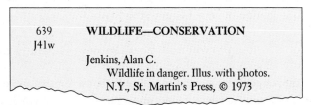

639
J41w

WILDLIFE—CONSERVATION

Jenkins, Alan C.
    Wildlife in danger. Illus. with photos.
N.Y., St. Martin's Press, © 1973

Some cards, called **cross-reference cards**, refer you to other subject headings related to the one on the card. Cross-references are listed after the words *See* or *See also*.

Exercises   Using the Card Catalog

▶ **Making Inferences**

A. What subject cards might give you information about the following topics? Try to think of several subjects for each topic.

1. How to study for a test   Study (Method of), Tests, Examinations
2. Famous women athletes   Athletes (Women), Sports
3. Rules of chess   Chess, Games (Rules)
4. History of the airplane   Airplane, Airplane History
5. How to grow a vegetable garden   Gardening, Vegetable Gardening

▶ **Structured Application**

B. Use the card catalog to find the title, author, and call number of a book on three of the following subjects.

1. skiing
2. detective stories
3. dinosaurs
4. poems by Robert Frost
5. Pablo Picasso
6. Harriet Tubman
7. The Alamo
8. U.S. Presidents
9. UFO's
10. math games

405

Part 4

Objective

To use an encyclopedia to locate and gather information

Presenting the Lesson

◐ All Students

1. Read and discuss the introduction to part 4 on page 406. Show some sample encyclopedia volumes to the class. Point out the letter and volume number on the spine. Also show the arrangement of articles and some article headings. Discuss how guide words in an encyclopedia are like the guide words in a dictionary.

2. If possible, have a set of encyclopedias for the class to use. Divide the class into the same number of groups as there are volumes of the encyclopedia. Assign one volume to each group. Ask each to prepare a short oral presentation about the contents of their volume, based on the following questions:

1. What is the first article in the volume? What is the last?
2. Name an article that is at least four pages long.
3. Name at least one famous person discussed in the volume. Is there a picture of the person?
4. Is there an article on any foreign country in the volume? Is there more than one? Name the countries you found.
5. In this fast survey of the volume, which article looked most interesting to you? Which article would you like to read completely?

3. Read and discuss **The Encyclopedia Index** on page 407. Stress that a single topic may be discussed in several different volumes. Test the students' understanding of the sample index on page 407. Give a topic, such as Lionel Rothschild, and ask the volume and page where information on the topic may be found. Vol. R p. 448

4. Read and discuss **The Encyclopedia Article.** Emphasize the use of boldfaced subheadings for skimming to get main ideas. As you discuss the use of charts and illustrations, you may wish to refer to part 8 in this chapter for information on graphic aids. Give special attention to the cross-reference feature.

4 Using the Encyclopedia

> **Focus**
>
> An **encyclopedia** is a valuable reference tool.

▶ Comprehension

When you need the answer to almost any question, go to the reference section of your library. The books in this section are usually marked with an *R* above the call number. In the reference section, you will find one of the most frequently used reference tools, the encyclopedia.

An **encyclopedia** is a reference book that contains general articles on many subjects. Most encyclopedias are made up of several volumes, covering a wide variety of subjects. Sometimes a whole set of encyclopedias is about one subject, such as art or biography. There are some special encyclopedias that consist of one volume on a single subject, such as baseball, mythology, ships, or careers.

Encyclopedias are easy to use. Information is arranged in the volumes alphabetically by subject. Articles about people are usually alphabetized by the last name. Other articles are organized by the key word in the subject.

Volumes are usually numbered to keep them in order. On the back, or spine, of each volume are letters or words to tell you which part of the alphabet is included in that volume. For example, in *The World Book Encyclopedia*, volumes are numbered in this way.

At the top of each page of the encyclopedia are guide words. They help you find the page that will have the article you need.

The Encyclopedia Index

Every set of encyclopedias has an index. The index may be a separate volume, or it may be part of the last volume. The index will direct you to every volume and page that contains information on your topic.

For example, if you were doing a report on the rotary engine, you might look in *The World Book* index. The sample index entry below directs you to three articles appearing in volumes *W*, *A*, and *G*. The index also tells you what page to look at in each of these volumes.

Rot [plant disease] **R:447**
  Alfalfa (Pests and Diseases) **A:330**
Rota [island, Pacific] **R:447**
Rotary bottom [tool]
  Plow *picture on* **P:511**
Rotary Club [organization]
  Rotary International **R:447**
Rotary-cut method [industrial process]
  Veneer **R:238**
Rotary drilling
  Petroleum (Methods of Drilling) **P:300**
  with picture

Rotary engine
  Wankel Engine **W:20** *with pictures*
  Automobile (The Gasoline Shortage)
    A:930–932
  Gasoline Engine *picture on* **G:64**

Rotary International [organization] **R:447**
  with picture
Rotary motion [physics]
  Machine *diagram on* **M:11**
Rotary pendulum
  Pendulum (Other Pendulums) **P:212**
Rotary plow
  Plow (Other Types of Bottoms) **P:512**

Rothschild, Guy de [German banker] **R:448**
Rothschild, House of [European history]
  Rothschild **R:448**
Rothschild, James Mayer [German banker]
  Rothschild, Mayer Amschel **R:448**
Rothschild, Karl Mayer [German banker]
  Rothschild, Mayer Amschel **R:448**
Rothschild, Lionel [British political leader]
    R:448
Rothschild, Mayer Amschel [German
  banker] **R:448**
Rothschild, Nathan Mayer [1777–1836.
    German banker] **R:448**
Rothschild, Nathan Mayer [1840–1915.
    British political leader]
  Rothschild, Lionel **R:448**
Rothschild, Salomon Mayer [German
  banker]
  Rothschild, Mayer Amschel **R:448**
Rotifer [microorganism] **R:448** *with pictures*
  Microscope *picture on* **M:425**
Rotogravure [printing]
  Intaglio **I:241**
  Printing (Printing by Gravure) **P:705**;
    (Gravure Presses) **P:705** *with picture*

407

Additional Resources

Skills Practice Book—page 157
Teacher's Resource Binder
  Reinforcement Activities—
    page 114

5. Exercises A–C require the use of an encyclopedia and might be assigned when the class visits the school library.

Basic Students

After the students have completed Exercise B on page 405, have them locate one of the articles in the encyclopedia. Ask them to supply the following information about the article:

1. List three subheadings in the article.
2. Briefly describe an illustration in the article.
3. Are there any "see also" cross-references at the end of the article? If so, what are they?

Advanced Students

Students may find it helpful to know the purpose of an encyclopedia yearbook. Have volunteers find out whether the encyclopedias in your school library have yearbooks. If so, the students should examine a recent yearbook, and report on their findings.

Special Populations

ESL Pair students with native speakers of English for reference work with encyclopedias.

Reinforcement

Have the students use an encyclopedia to locate an article for each of the following topics. They should give the letter and number of the volume in which the article can be found, as well as the guide words on the page where each is located.

Answers will vary according to encyclopedia used.

Argentina   calcium
electricity   Boston
Harry S. Truman   Nile River

Enrichment

Have students survey the different sets of encyclopedias in the school and/or public library. Ask them to answer the following questions:

How many volumes are there? Is there a yearbook? Is there an index? Are there illustrations? Are the articles easy to understand? Are additional resources listed after the articles?

Discuss the students' findings in class.

The Encyclopedia Article

Each encyclopedia entry includes a written article on the topic. If the topic is long, the article will be divided into parts. These parts are usually indicated by subheads in boldface type. By examining the subheads, you can tell at a glance what is covered in the article.

In addition to the written text, an article may contain photographs, charts, or other illustrations. An entry may also include cross-references, which refer the reader to related articles in the encyclopedia. Some encyclopedias also list additional references at the end of an article.

Exercises   Using an Encyclopedia

▶ Analyzing

A. Here are five topics. Choose an encyclopedia. Write its name on your paper. For each subject, write the key word that you would look up in the encyclopedia. Find the article on that topic. Write the letter or number of the volume and the page number of the article.

1. The talents of Benjamin Franklin Franklin
2. Beverly Sills's career in the opera Sills
3. Where active volcanoes can be found volcanoes
4. The description of a Neanderthal man Neanderthal
5. The economy of Thailand Thailand

▶ Structured Application

B. Choose one of the following topics and look it up in the index of an encyclopedia. List all articles on that topic. Give the titles of the articles, their volumes, and their pages.

1. Mummies   3. Soccer   5. Dentistry
2. Hercules   4. Fashion

C. Look up one of the following topics in an encyclopedia. List the cross-references that appear at the end of that article.

1. Computers   3. Reptiles
2. Extrasensory perception   4. Astronomy

408

5 Using Other Resources

Focus

The **reference section** has special books and materials that provide facts and information on countless topics.

▶ Comprehension

When you need specific information about a topic, go to the reference section of your library. There you will find valuable sources of current information. You have already learned about the encyclopedia. Here are some other common reference works found in a library.

Dictionaries

There are two types of dictionaries: **abridged** and **unabridged.** Abridged dictionaries contain fewer words and less detailed definitions than unabridged dictionaries. An unabridged dictionary, such as *Webster's Third New International Dictionary*, is the most complete collection of English words available. This edition has over 450,000 words.

A reference section may also contain dictionaries on specific topics. For example, there is a dictionary of Indian tribes of North America and another on American history.

409

Part 5

Objective

To recognize and use other reference books

Presenting the Lesson

All Students

1. Read and discuss the introduction on page 409. Explain that reference materials are often kept in a separate section of the library. Also point out that these materials are not usually allowed out on loan.

2. Read and discuss each type of reference source identified in the section. If possible, provide examples of each type of reference book. Be sure to point out the special features of each book.

3. Discuss and assign Exercises A and B on page 411. These exercises require the use of the library.

Basic Students

Review the kinds of reference materials discussed. Demonstrate how to use each one to find information.

Do Exercise A as a group activity. Have the group choose one country to research. Have them answer the questions in Exercise A as they apply to that country. Guide the use of each reference book listed in parentheses as students complete the questions.

Advanced Students

Ask students to locate each of the following books that are in the reference section of your library. Students should write a few sentences describing the contents of each reference book they located. Answers will vary.

1. *Current Biography*
2. *Who's Who in America*
3. *Guinness Book of World Records*
4. *Information Please, Almanac*
5. *Bartlett's Familiar Quotations*
6. *Roget's Thesaurus*
7. *Readers' Guide to Periodical Literature*
8. *American Heritage Dictionary*

Special Populations

ESL Encourage students to use special reference works to research information on their native country or culture.

Reinforcement

Have students make a list of three famous people they admire. They should find and list three sources of information in the library that they might use to learn more about each of the people on their lists. Encyclopedias may not be listed.

Enrichment

Have a reference work treasure hunt. Divide the class into groups. Have each group write four questions for each of the following topics. Groups should exchange lists and find answers in special reference works in the library. Sources should be listed with answers. See which group finishes first.

Topics:
An important sporting event
An international news event
The population of a country
A fact about a famous person

The Atlas

An **atlas** is a book of maps. To use an atlas, you refer to an index. The index gives you the page number of the map you want. It also gives the exact location of cities and towns on a map. In addition, the index of an atlas provides the populations of cities, states, and countries. Many atlases also include points of interest.

Magazines and Newspapers

Most libraries have current magazines and newspapers from all over the country. Libraries also save back issues of their magazines for future reference. These are often bound into book form. They are valuable sources of information. To find an article on a specific topic, refer to the *Readers' Guide to Periodical Literature*. Ask a librarian to help you use the *Readers' Guide*.

Almanacs and Yearbooks

Almanacs and **yearbooks** are collections of current facts and statistics. For example, you can find out who won last year's World Series or who are the current senators from the state of California. To find information in an almanac, use the index. Alamanacs are printed yearly. Use the most recent almanac for the most accurate information.

Vertical File

A vertical file is a file cabinet filled with newspaper and magazine clippings, and pamphlets. They are filed in folders alphabetically according to topic. A vertical file can often provide current information that is difficult to find elsewhere.

410

Exercise B
Answers will vary according to source.
1. careless smoking, overloaded outlets, playing with matches, storing flammable items improperly, faulty wiring, improper use of space heaters
2. 48,953
3. Sinhala
4. Black Sea, Sea of Mamara, Mediterranean Sea
5. Flag consists of three vertical panels of green, white, and red
6. Martha Layne Collins
7. Mackinac Bridge in Michigan
8. Rio Grande
9. Alamogordo, New Mexico
10. self-contained *underwater* breathing *apparatus*

Exercises Using Reference Materials

▶ Structured Application

A. Choose a foreign country that interests you. Then go to the reference section of the library to find the answers to the questions that are listed below. Write down the title of the source that you used for each answer.

1. Who is the current head or ruler of the country? What is the population? (Use an almanac or yearbook.)
2. Draw or trace a map of the country. (Use an atlas.)
3. Label the major bodies of water, mountain ranges, and large cities on the map you traced. (Use an atlas.)
4. What are the major exports of the country? (Use an encyclopedia.)
5. What are the major imports of the country? (Use an encyclopedia.)

B. Go to the reference section of your library. Number your paper from 1 to 10. Write the answers to the following questions. Also, write down the title of the reference work where you found the answer. You may use dictionaries, atlases, magazines, newspapers, almanacs, yearbooks, encyclopedias, and the vertical file.

See answers at bottom of page 410.

1. What are five fire hazards that can be found around the house?
2. What is the population of Santa Fe, New Mexico?
3. What is the official language of Sri Lanka?
4. What three seas touch the shores of Turkey?
5. Draw the flag of Italy.
6. Who is the current governor of Kentucky?
7. What is the longest suspension bridge in North America?
8. What river forms the southern border of Texas?
9. Where was the first large-scale nuclear test site in the United States?
10. What does *SCUBA* mean?

411

Additional Resources

Skills Practice Book—page 158

Teacher's Resource Binder
Enrichment Activities—
page 77

Part 6

Objective

To develop skills in note-taking

Presenting the Lesson

 All Students

1. Ask for student volunteers to recall what they read in their science texts last week. Praise them for what they have recalled. Point out that one way to remember even more information is to take notes.

2. Read and discuss page 412. Be sure students understand paraphrasing. If you wish, test their understanding by having them paraphrase a passage in their science or social studies text. Also stress the importance of using quotation marks when repeating exact words from a source. Be sure that students understand it is not acceptable to present someone else's words as their own.

Have students examine the sample note card on page 413. Emphasize the information each card should contain depending on the source. Make sure students understand this information is necessary when they credit sources for a report. Draw two more note cards on the board. Fill one out as a note card from a book, another from a magazine. Point out the different features of each.

3. Discuss and assign Exercises A and B on page 413 to be completed independently. Students will need access to an encyclopedia.

 Basic Students

Before assigning Exercise B, review the material discussed in this part. Give students additional practice in paraphrasing if necessary.

---

6 Taking Notes

> **Focus**
>
> When you do research, take notes. Taking notes as you read helps you to remember facts and ideas.

▶ Comprehension

You will often use the library to research a topic for a report. When you are gathering information for a report or composition, always take notes. Your notes will help you remember facts and ideas accurately.

Write notes on 3″ × 5″ note cards. On each card, write only one piece of information. That way you can organize your notes easily. Also be sure to include the source of the information on each card.

Note cards for books should include the title, the author, and the page number where you found the information. For magazines, include the name and date of the magazine, the title and page number of the article, and the author's name, if given. For encyclopedias, give the name of the encyclopedia, the volume number, and the title and page number of the article.

When you take notes, do not copy the author's words exactly. **Paraphrase** the material instead. To paraphrase, read the information carefully and write it in your own words. If you do copy an author's words exactly, you must enclose them in quotation marks.

At the top of the next page, you will see how a student paraphrased this excerpt from an encyclopedia.

> For centuries, musicians played *acoustical* guitars, which produce sound from the vibration of the strings. During the 1900's, *electric* guitars became popular. An electric guitar has an electromagnetic device that picks up the sound of the strings and sends it through an amplifier. An electric guitar can produce a greater range of sounds than an acoustical guitar.

412

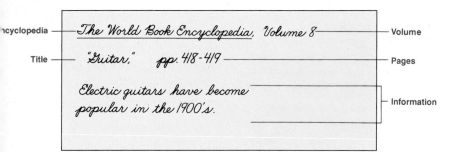

Encyclopedia — *The World Book Encyclopedia, Volume 8* — Volume

Title — "Guitar," *pp.* 418-419 — Pages

Electric guitars have become popular in the 1900's. — Information

Exercises Taking Notes on a Subject

▶ Structured Application

A. Read this article from *The World Book Encyclopedia*, Volume 14, page 478. Write three note cards based on the article. Put the notes in your own words.

OAKLEY, ANNIE (1860–1926), an American markswoman, starred in Buffalo Bill's Wild West Show for 17 years. She was popular throughout the United States and Europe. She was an expert shot with a pistol, rifle, or shotgun. Once, with a .22 rifle, she shot 4,772 glass balls out of 5,000 tossed in the air on a single day. At 90 feet (27 meters), she could hit a playing card with the thin edge toward her, and puncture a card five or six times while it fell to the ground. Since then, free tickets with holes punched in them have been called "Annie Oakleys."

Annie Oakley was born Phoebe Anne Oakley Mozee on Aug. 13, 1860, in a log cabin in Patterson Township, Ohio. She began shooting at the age of 9. After her father died, she supported the family by shooting small game. Only 5 feet (152 centimeters) tall, she was called "Little Sure Shot." Annie Oakley joined Buffalo Bill's Wild West Show in 1885 (see BUFFALO BILL).

—HOWARD R. LAMAR

▶ Creative Application

B. Choose any wild animal. Then look up the article on that animal in an encyclopedia. Read the article to find out how it survives in the wilderness. Make five note cards to help you remember the facts. Remember to paraphrase when you take notes.

413

Additional Resources

Skills Practice Book—page 159

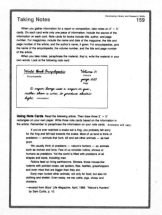

Part 7

Objective

To understand techniques for gathering information by interviewing

Presenting the Lesson

◼ All Students

1. Read and discuss the introduction on page 414. Talk about where students might locate expert sources. Point out that almost everyone is an expert on something. Your parents, for example, are experts on what you were like as an infant. A neighbor may be able to offer expert advice on a particular hobby. Also mention that universities, libraries, hospitals, and community service agencies are good places to find experts.

2. Read and discuss the four-step procedure for preparing for an interview. Emphasize the importance of being prepared. Talk about what happens at the interview. Explain that the success of the interview may be related to the questions written beforehand. Good questions make information gathering easier.

3. Discuss **At the Interview.** Discuss the difference between the questions prepared for the interview, and those that ask the expert to further explain a point.

4. Assign and discuss Exercises A and B on page 415.

▶ Basic Students

Work through Exercise A with the students. Then assign Exercise B to be done independently.

◆ Advanced Students

Have students role play interviewing. Each student should indicate an area that he or she is an expert on. List the students' names and specialties on the board. Each student should choose a subject and expert, prepare questions, and then conduct an interview.

---

7 The Interview

> **Focus**
>
> Sometimes an expert is the best source of information on a topic. **Interview** an expert to gather information.

▶ **Comprehension**

When you are writing a report, you may need first-hand information on your topic. In this case, your best source may be an expert. For example, if you were doing a report on a career as a paramedic, you could interview a paramedic to get first-hand information about the job.

There are two steps to completing an interview: preparation and the interview itself. Follow these guidelines to prepare for and conduct an interview.

Guidelines for Planning an Interview

1. **Contact the expert and politely request an interview.** Give your name and the reason you would like the interview. Arrange a convenient time and place to meet.

2. **Learn about the expert's background.** Then you will have some idea what information he or she will be able to provide.

3. **Know something about the topic.** It is important to have some basic knowledge about the subject. Then you will be able to ask good questions.

4. **Make a list of questions to ask the expert.** Make sure your questions require more than *yes* or *no* answers. Give the expert a chance to talk freely about the topic.

Guidelines for Conducting an Interview

1. **Be prompt.** Have ready your questions, your note paper, and your pen.
2. **Listen carefully.** Take notes.
3. **Ask questions.** If you do not understand what the expert is saying, ask him or her to clarify. Ask the person to repeat if you do not have time to write down all the information you need.
4. **Review your notes.** See if the expert answered your questions completely. If not, ask for a further explanation.
5. **Thank the expert for the interview.** Also send a thank-you letter. You will learn more about writing thank-you letters in Chapter 25.

Exercises   Conducting Interviews

▶ **Making Inferences**

A. Read the following list of topics. Then name an expert that you could interview to give you information on each one.

1. How to set up an aquarium
2. Kinds of fossils
3. How to write a children's book
4. How to open a bank account
5. The value of solar energy
6. Starting a vegetable garden
7. Eating nutritious foods
8. How to "tune-up" a bicycle
9. Blood types
10. How to train for a triathlon
11. Collecting stamps
12. Time zones in the United States
13. First aid
14. Identifying constellations

▶ **Structured Application**

B. Choose one of the topics from Exercise A. Make a list of questions that you would ask the expert in an interview.

415

Reinforcement

Have the students follow the directions given for Exercise A on page 415 using the following topics:

1. How to make banana bread
2. How to care for a rabbit
3. Kinds of rocks
4. When and how to plant tulips
5. How to become a lifeguard
6. Teaching children to read
7. How to start a coin collection
8. Taking good care of your teeth

Enrichment

Have students interview an expert. Suggested experts might include the gym teacher, music teacher, parents or neighbors, and community figures. Allow class time for students to share the information they gathered.

Additional Resources

Skills Practice Book—page 160

Teacher's Resource Binder
Reinforcement Activities—
page 115

Part 8

Objective

To understand graphic aids and use them when appropriate

Presenting the Lesson

All Students

1. Read page 416. Discuss each type of graphic aid and the information it offers.

2. If possible, have examples of the various graphic aids in the classroom. Point out the special features of each aid.

3. Assign and discuss the exercise on page 417.

Basic Students

Review the kinds of information learned from each graphic aid. Then, work through Exercise A with the students.

Advanced Students

Give the students a magazine article containing facts and figures. Have students prepare a graphic aid that helps to explain the information in the article.

Special Populations

LD Students might concentrate on one or two graphic aids at a time rather than five. Provide extra practice by studying additional examples of graphic aids in students' science or social studies texts.

---

8 Getting Information from Graphic Aids

> **Focus**
>
> **Graphic aids** include photographs and illustrations, diagrams, maps, charts and tables, and graphs.

▶ Comprehension

Some information is easier to understand if you can see it in pictures. Graphic aids allow you to see factual information.

Photographs and **illustrations** put ideas into picture form. Always read captions that appear with photographs and illustrations.

Diagrams identify the parts of an object. They tell how each part is related to other parts. Read all labels on diagrams.

Maps are drawings of areas of land and bodies of water. There are different kinds of maps. Some maps show the boundaries of countries and locations of cities. Others show geographical features like mountain ranges or deserts. Always read the legend on a map. The legend explains the symbols used on the map.

Charts and **tables** present groups of facts. Part of the information is usually in number form. Charts are often arranged in columns. Always read the title and the column headings.

Illustration

Queen Angelfish
Holocanthus ciliaris
12 to 18 inches long
(30 to 46 centimeters)

Diagram

Incandescent Lamp
(A, inert gas filling; B, coiled tungsten wire filament; C, glass envelope; D, glass support; E, metal base)

Map

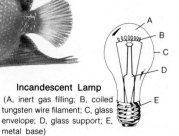

Dismal Swamp

416

A **graph** is a special kind of chart. It shows how one fact is related to another. When you study a graph, read the title. Also read the key to any symbols used in the graph. Next, read what is printed inside and next to the graph. Lastly, read the caption, if any.

Chart

Activity	Calories per hour
reading, writing, eating watching T.V.	80 to 100
walking moderately fast, making a bed	170 to 240
swimming, running, dancing, bicycling	350 and more

Graph

World Area Occupied by Continents

Asia 29.8%
Antarctica 8.9%
Africa 20.5%
Australia 5.2%
Europe 7.0%
N. America 16.4%
S. America 12.1%

Exercise   Using Graphic Aids

▶ Drawing Conclusions

Answer the following questions by referring to the graphic aids shown.

1. How long is a Queen Angelfish? 12 to 18 inches
2. What is the scientific name for a Queen Angelfish? Holocanthus ciliaris
3. What is inside an incandescent bulb? inert gas filling; coiled tungsten wire filament; glass envelope; glass support; metal base
4. What type of wire is used in the filament of an incandescent bulb? tungsten
5. In what two states is Dismal Swamp? Virginia, North Carolina
6. What body of water is south of Dismal Swamp? Albemarle Sound
7. How many calories per hour does a person burn while reading a book? 80 to 100
8. Which activity will burn more calories, walking fast or bicycling? bicycling
9. Which continent is the largest? Asia
10. What percentage of world area is occupied by Australia? 5.2%

417

Reinforcement

Have the students follow the directions for Exercise A using the following questions:

1. What kind of base is used in a lightbulb? metal
2. How many centimeters long is an angelfish? 30–46
3. How many calories per hour will you burn up watching TV? 80–100
4. What area of world is occupied by Africa? 20.5%
5. What continent occupies the smallest percentage of the world? Australia
6. In what state is the Albemarle Sound? North Carolina
7. What color is the Queen Angelfish? yellow, blue, and red
8. Which burns up more calories, reading or running? running

Enrichment

Have the students make a graph from information gathered in the class. Some possible topics might be:

1. Months birthdays fall in
2. Types of books liked
3. Favorite animals

Display the graphs in the room. Have the students make up questions from the graphs.

Additional Resources

Skills Practice Book—page 161
Teacher's Resource Binder
  Reinforcement Activities—
    page 116

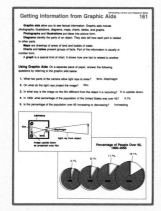

Using English in Art

This activity provides an opportunity for students to relate a research skill they have learned, interpreting graphic aids, to the subject of art. Provide for sharing of students' work. Perhaps graphic aids could be exhibited on a bulletin board.

Using English in Art

▶ Comprehension

There are many types of artists. You are probably familiar with painters, photographers, and sculptors. One special kind of artist is a graphic artist. Graphic artists prepare newspaper and magazine illustrations, posters, and pamphlets. Graphic artists also create illustrations, maps, and charts for encyclopedias and textbooks. They create advertising logos and design the packaging for the food you buy in the supermarket.

Exercise   Creating Graphic Aids
▶ Creative Application

Pretend that you are a graphic artist for a textbook company. Your assignment is to draw diagrams for a science book. Use the following information to draw a diagram of either a spider web or a tornado. Label the parts of your diagram.

A. A spider web is often spun between two branches. First, the web is anchored in several spots on each branch by short *foundation lines*. The foundation lines are then connected and a rough outer circle is made. Lines called *spokes* or *radials* extend from the outer circle to the *center*, or *hub*, of the web. The web is completed by *spiral* lines that circle around and around the web from the outer circle to the hub.

B. The funnel-shaped tornado is easy to recognize. The top of a tornado is a dark, heavy mass of swirling clouds, dirt, and debris. It is called the *cumulonimbus*. Extending down toward the ground is the *vertical updraft*. The air is swirling so rapidly here that large objects can be pulled high into the air. Finally, making contact with the earth, is the *tornado funnel*.

418

Chapter 23 Review

▶ Recalling

A. Using the Library Write the correct category for each of these nonfiction books. You may refer to the Dewey Decimal list on page 401.

1. *America's Journeys Into Space* by William Joffe Numeriff and Anthony J. Cipriano 500–599
2. *The Sierra Nevada* by Stephen Whitney 900–999
3. *Total Running* by Jim Lilliefors 700–799
4. *The New Roget's Thesaurus in Dictionary Form* 400–499
5. *Plants for Kids To Grow Indoors* by Adele Millard 600–699

▶ Structured Application

B. Using Reference Works Look at these sources of information. Then read each question or statement. Number your paper from 1 to 7. Next to each number, write down the reference source or sources you might use to find information. Answers may vary.

the card catalog   the vertical file   an atlas
an almanac or yearbook   an encyclopedia

1. What is the population of Austin, Texas? an atlas
2. Name a recent book about lasers. the card catalog
3. Who is the mayor of Denver, Colorado? an almanac or yearbook
4. What were some of the causes of the Civil War? an encyclopedia
5. Where would you find pamphlets on bicycle safety? the vertical file
6. How does a Wankel engine work? an encyclopedia
7. Where is the island of Madagascar? an atlas

▶ Structured Application/Drawing Conclusions

C. Using Graphic Aids Study the following illustration. Then write two note cards based on the information given.

Twig

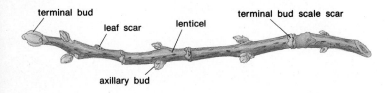

terminal bud   leaf scar   lenticel   terminal bud scale scar
axillary bud

419

Chapter Review

This review allows teachers to evaluate student understanding of the concepts presented in this chapter.

Additional Resources

Skills Practice Book
Review—page 162

Test Booklet
Mastery Test—pages 135–140

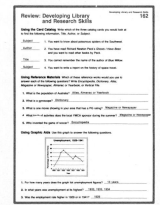

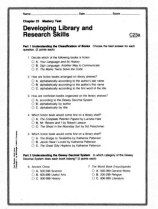

Chapter 24

Chapter Objectives

1. To choose and limit a topic for a report

2. To gather and record information for a report

3. To organize information for a report logically

4. To make an outline using correct form

5. To recognize and write an effective introduction

6. To develop the body of a report

7. To conclude a report and to credit sources

8. To revise and proofread a report

9. To make a clean, final copy and to share the report

Motivating the Students

1. Read and discuss the introduction on page 421. Point out that in all their compositions to date, the students have been writing about things that they know. Explain that in this chapter they will learn to write about things that they may not know a great deal about.

2. To develop the idea that report writing exists in many forms in the world outside of school, you might bring several *National Geographic* magazines to class. Select a few articles to show and read a brief passage from each. Explain that these writers are reporting on something that they have done or a place they have seen. Continue by pointing out that another form of report writing is the record a ship's captain keeps, which is called a log. Ships' logs serve to give important information to the ships' owners. Read the following log entry made by Christopher Columbus.

I left the city of Granada on the 12th day of May, in the same year of 1492, being Saturday, and came to the town of Palos, which is a seaport; where I equipped three vessels well suited for such service; and departed from that port, well supplied with provisions and with many sailors, on the 3d day of August of the same year, being Friday, half an hour before sunrise, taking the route to the islands of Canaria, belonging to your Highnesses, which are in the said Ocean Sea, that I might thence take my departure for navigating until I should

Week 32

Chapter Management Guidelines   This chart may be used to help structure daily lesson plans

Day 3	Day 4	Day 5
Chapter 24 Opener, p. 421; Part 1, "Prewriting: Finding a Topic," pp. 422–423	Part 2, "Prewriting: Gathering Information," pp. 424–425	Part 2, "Prewriting: Gathering Information," pp. 424–425

The Process of Writing a Report

Would you like to know what it's like to live and work inside a submarine? Are you interested in computers, or chimpanzees, or the Loch Ness monster? Would you like to share information about your favorite subjects with others?

You can learn about many subjects when you write a report. A report is a composition about a subject you have researched. It is based on facts.

In science class, you may be asked to write about optical illusions. In social studies, you might report on your state's natural resources. Organizing and writing a report is a skill that you can use in many different classes.

In this chapter, you will learn the process of writing a report. You will choose a subject. You will organize the information you gather on your subject. Then you will share your information in a written and oral report.

421

arrive at the Indies, and give the letters of your Highnesses to those princes, so as to comply with my orders. . . .

Mention that although the language may sound very formal and perhaps a little strange, this is a report to the King and Queen of Spain.

Have students suggest other types of report writing.

Explain that these are reports because each is built on facts and each requires research. Tell students that in this chapter they will learn more about report writing.

Special Populations

Refer to the suggestions on page T32–T35 in the front of this Teacher Edition for notes on adapting the teaching of composition for these students.

Related Chapters

You may wish to refer to related material in other chapters as you teach the following concepts:

1. Writing process, Chapter 6, "Choosing a Process for Writing," page 101

2. Scanning and skimming techniques, Chapter 7, "Study and Test-Taking Skills," page 127

3. Gathering facts, Chapter 23, "Developing Library and Research Skills," page 397

Additional Resources

Skills Practice Book—pages 163–171

Test Booklet—pages 141–148
  Pretest—pages 141–142
  Mastery Test—pages 143–148

Teacher's Resource Binder
  Reinforcement Activities—
    pages 117–122
  Enrichment Activities—
    pages 39–52, 78
  Process of Writing Transparencies
  Ideas for Creative Teaching

Week 33

Chapter Management Guidelines   This chart may be used to help structure daily lesson plans.

Day 1	Day 2	Day 3	Day 4	Day 5
Chapter 24, Part 3, "Prewriting: Organizing Notes," pp. 426–427	Part 3, "Prewriting: Organizing Notes," pp. 426–427	Part 4, "Prewriting: Making an Outline," pp. 428–429	Part 4, "Prewriting: Making an Outline," pp. 428–429	Part 5, "Drafting the Introduction," pp. 430–431

Part 1

Objective

To choose and limit a topic for a report

Presenting the Lesson

 All Students

1. Before introducing this chapter to the class, tell the school or local librarians that students will be using reference material extensively. If your school does not have a library, bring in a collection of materials to use in the classroom. Encourage students to use the public library as often as possible. If necessary, review with the students the skills needed for using the card catalog and finding information in reference books. You may wish to refer to Chapter 23, "Developing Library and Research Skills," page 397.

2. Read and discuss **How To Find a Topic** on page 422. Have the students suggest other places they might get ideas for a subject: newspapers, television, interviews, textbooks, or the card catalog.

3. Read and discuss **Limiting a Subject** on pages 422–423. Stress the fact that a subject must be narrowed until it is specific enough to be covered in a short report. Have the students narrow the topics in Exercise A by asking such questions as *Who?*, *What?*, *Where?*, *Which?*, and *How?* about the topic. Write the following example on the board. Guide the students in narrowing the topic.

Broad topic: Jungle Cats
Which one? Tiger
Where? Asia
What about them? Tigers are in danger of becoming extinct.
Narrowed topic: What is being done to save the tiger?

Suggest other prewriting techniques, if necessary, to help students in their choice of subject.

4. Assign Exercise B on page 423. Check each student's subject to make sure it is narrow enough to be covered in a five-paragraph report.

---

1 Prewriting: Finding a Topic

> ### Focus
> Think about a general subject that interests you. Then narrow it to a specific topic that can be covered completely in a short report.

How To Find a Topic

▶ **Comprehension**

Think about your interests. The best topic for a report is often the one subject that interests you the most. Think about your interests. Read through your journal. Have you mentioned any subjects that you might like to explore? You might also brainstorm with a friend to come up with a list of general subjects that would be fun to learn more about.

Visit the library. Look through magazines or books on subjects that interest you. Check such reference books as encyclopedias, almanacs, and special dictionaries for further suggestions. You may also discover ideas as you browse through an interesting exhibit at an art, science, or history museum.

Look again at Chapter 6, pages 102–103, for more ways to think of writing topics.

Limiting a Subject

Now you must choose one of the general subjects you have discovered, and narrow or limit it. That means that you must make the subject more specific. For example, imagine that you chose the general subject *soccer.* Will you write about the rules of the game, how soccer was invented, or a famous soccer player? Each of these is a specific topic.

These are several methods you can use to limit a subject. You can read about it in reference and nonfiction books. You

422

Week 34

Chapter Management Guidelines   This chart may be used to help structure daily lesson plan

Day 1	Day 2	Day 3	Day 4	Day 5
Chapter 24, Part 6, "Drafting the Body of the Report," pp. 432–433	Part 6, "Drafting the Body of the Report," pp. 432–433	Part 7, "Ending Your Report," pp. 434–435	Part 8, "Revising, Proofreading, and Sharing," pp. 436–437	Chapter Review and selected end-of-chapter activities

can ask *who, what, when, where, why,* and *how* questions about it. You can also use the table of contents and index in nonfiction and reference books. Both parts of a book could show you how other writers have broken down the subject.

Let's look at how one writer, Tony, limited his subject. Tony was interested in learning more about the American pioneers who settled in the West. He looked in the table of contents in a book about pioneers and jotted down these items.

Duties of a wagon master

Hardships on Oregon Trail

How pioneer children traveled west

Role of scouts

What happened to Native Americans

Why pioneers went west

Tony decided he wanted to learn more about the lives of the children on a wagon train.

Exercises   Finding a Topic

▶ Structured Application

A. Limiting a Topic Limit two of the topics below so that each could be covered in a short report of about five paragraphs.

Example: General topic—Medicine

Narrowed topic—How Penicillin Was Discovered

1. Marsupials   3. Jungle cats   5. Swamps
2. Mummies   4. Pyramids   6. Laser beams

▶ Creative Application

B. Finding Your Own Topic Make a list of five or more general topics for a report. Use the methods for finding topics suggested in this lesson. Choose one topic. Narrow it so that it can be covered thoroughly in a short report. You may wish to look over some of the report topics in the **Power Handbook**, pages 464–466.

423

Additional Resources

Skills Practice Book—page 163
Teacher's Resource Binder
 Reinforcement Activities—
  page 117

Basic Students

Work with the students in completing Exercise A, or have them work in groups or with partners.

If students choose topics that are too difficult or too broad, work with individuals or small groups to develop more reasonable subjects. Stress that even though students are working together during prewriting, each student will individually prepare a report.

Advanced Students

To help students see the many possibilities in one topic, have students narrow the same topic in three different ways. They may wish to develop one of these topics for their reports.

Special Populations

LD To help the students narrow their topics, provide a list of ten pairs of topics. Require that the smaller or narrower topic be identified. For example: hobbies—macramé, scientists—Marie Curie. For Exercise B, guide students in developing a list from which a topic can be chosen.

ESL Guide students in making lists and narrowing subjects that relate to American culture, such as holidays.

Reinforcement

Follow the directions for Exercise A on page 423.

1. Physical fitness   4. U.S. Civil War
2. Mining   5. Fashion
3. Flowers   6. Automobiles

Enrichment

1. Have the students select a topic and then find three books on that topic in the library. Have them compare the tables of contents from the books to see how each author chose to break down the general subject into narrower topics.

2. For additional enrichment activities, see the Unit Projects in the Teacher Notes on page 347. One or more of these projects have special activities for gifted and talented students.

Part 2

Objective

To gather and record information and take notes

Presenting the Lesson

 All Students

1. Read the introduction on page 424. Suggest that the students look in the library for special reference material, such as *The Encyclopedia of Wild Life*, a single volume, or sets of special encyclopedias. Mention that the reference section of the library usually includes general books about history, famous people, geography, and all areas of science. If your school has a library, talk about the location of reference materials in the library. Point out that many books may provide information about a broad subject, and therefore, students should locate specific topics in the tables of contents and indexes.

2. Read **Taking Notes** on page 424–425. Refer to Chapter 23, "Developing Library and Research Skills," page 397 for more information on note-taking skills. Emphasize that each card should contain only one item of information. Stress the importance of paraphrasing. Remind students that if they wish to use the wording from a book, it must be copied exactly and put in quotation marks. Then they can use the material as a direct quotation in the report. Point out that if they have difficulty putting information in their own words, it may be because they don't thoroughly understand this material. They should reread the information. Stress that students make sure their notes are accurate and are related to their topic. Show students where to locate the source information needed for the note cards by pointing out volume numbers, title pages, and dates of books, magazines, and reference books.

3. Have students study the sample note card on page 425. Point out the information that has been recorded. Have students suggest information for another note card from the encyclopedia

information given. Guide them in paraphrasing. Put the information on the board.

4. Assign Exercise A on page 425. Check the form and accuracy of their note cards. Then assign Exercise B.

 Basic Students

Before assigning the exercises, duplicate short articles from an encyclopedia

or other reference book. Work with the students in writing note cards based on the articles. Make sure the students include the appropriate information about the source in the correct form.

Do Exercise A on page 425 with the students.

Assign Exercise B.

---

2 Prewriting: Gathering Information

> **Focus**
>
> Gather information to develop your topic.

▶ Comprehension

There are several ways to find information for your report. Check the card catalog in the library and make a list of the books on your topic. To find magazine articles, look up your subject in the *Readers' Guide to Periodical Literature*. You can also read articles in encyclopedias and other reference books.

Taking Notes

As you read, take notes on 3″ × 5″ note cards. Use your own words. Do not copy information directly unless you are writing someone's exact words. Then put quotation marks around those words. Write only one piece of information on each card. Also, write down the source of the information. At the end of your report, you will list all of the sources you used.

When you write down the source, include the following:

Books—the title and author

Magazines—the name and date of the magazine, title of the article, author, and page numbers

Reference Books—the name of the reference book, volume number, title of the entry or volume, and page number

Here is an encyclopedia entry that Tony used. Notice how he reworded the material on his note card.

> As long as the pioneers of the 1840's kept moving westward, the Plains Indians allowed them to pass through their hunting grounds. Some tribes guided the early pioneers, or helped them at difficult river crossings. The Indians even traded vegetables and buffalo meat for tobacco or pieces of iron.

424

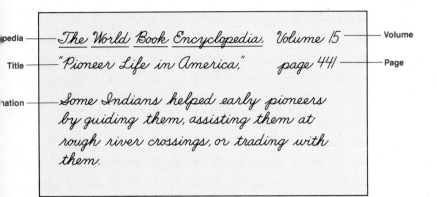

pedia — *The World Book Encyclopedia.* Volume 15 — **Volume**

Title — *"Pioneer Life in America,"* page 441 — **Page**

nation — *Some Indians helped early pioneers by guiding them, assisting them at rough river crossings, or trading with them.*

Exercises Taking Notes

▶ Generalizing/Structured Application

A. Writing Note Cards Read this article from *The World Book Encyclopedia*, Volume 14, pages 563–564. Write three note cards based on the article. Put the notes in your own words. Note cards will vary, but should follow the correct form.

MITCHELL, ARTHUR (1934-   ), was the first black American to dance with a major classical ballet company. He performed with the New York City Ballet from 1955 to 1970.

Mitchell was born in New York City and attended the School of American Ballet. In 1955, he joined the New York City Ballet.

While with the New York City Ballet, Mitchell began to teach ballet to underprivileged children. In 1969, he formed the Dance Theatre of Harlem, a professional ballet company and dance school in the city's chief black community. Mitchell directs the company, teaches in the school, and composes dances. As a *choreographer* (composer of dances), Mitchell created such works as *Holberg Suite* (1970), *Rhythmetron* (1972), and *Manifestations* (1976).

—DIANNE L. WOODRUFF

▶ Generalizing/Creative Application

B. Gathering Information Look through books, magazines, or encyclopedias that have information on your topic. As you read each source, write down any information that will help you develop your topic. Take notes on 3″ × 5″ note cards. Be sure notes are in your own words. Save these note cards.

425

Additional Resources

Skills Practice Book—page 164

Teacher's Resource Binder
  Enrichment Activities—
  page 78

Advanced Students

Before assigning Exercise B, discuss the newspaper as a source of information for current topics. Explain that the *New York Times* publishes an index that tells in what issue articles about a certain topic have appeared. Have students check the library for a copy of this index and find information on the topics of their reports. They should then find the listed articles, read them, and try to use that information in their reports. If the *Times* is not available, encourage students to look in other newspapers for articles on their topics.

Special Populations

LD, ESL Emphasize the use of tape recordings and video films as reference sources whenever possible. Allow students to work in groups to gather materials. See the notes under **Basic Students.**

Reinforcement

Provide each student with five 3″ × 5″ note cards. Direct them to look in books and magazines for the following:

1. One fact about pet care
2. One fact about weather
3. One fact about sports
4. One fact about animals
5. One fact about a country other than the United States

One fact must come from a magazine; the rest can come from books other than encyclopedias. Students should record each fact on an index card, along with the source of information. Remind them to follow the format presented in this lesson.

Enrichment

Show students a bibliography following a research article. Point out that this lists the sources the author used to write the article. Tell students that they, too, will list the sources they have used at the end of their reports.

Part 3

Objective

To organize information for a report logically

Presenting the Lesson

All Students

1. Read page 426. Review the concept of logical order. Explain the importance of organization. Tell students that unless they organize details in a logical way, they will confuse their readers. Examine the grouping of Tony's cards. Discuss how paragraphing will result from this organization. Explain that the details on the note cards in each group will be used as supporting details in paragraphs. Point out that Tony's groups are arranged in chronological order. Explain that this is one way of arranging details.

2. Assign and discuss Exercise A on page 427. Then, assign Exercise B on page 427. After students have completed Exercise B, have them explore other methods of organization. Have them read through their notes. They should look for any common thread that ties ideas together. Then have them think of one additional way that their report could be organized. Have them decide which is the better way.

Basic Students

Do Exercise A orally with the students. Have the students suggest topic sentences for each group of facts.

Work with each student individually on Exercise B. Remind all students to put aside notes that do not fit the narrowed topic. Also, remind students that they may have to gather more facts if they do not have enough information on a particular idea.

Advanced Students

Have students exchange note cards to check for logical order. Students should make suggestions for improvement.

---

3 Prewriting: Organizing Notes

> **Focus**
>
> The information that develops your report topic must be organized logically.

▶ Comprehension

You have done the reading for your report and taken notes. Now you are ready to organize your information.

Creating Idea Groups

Read through your notes. Most of your information is probably about two or three main ideas. List these main ideas. Then organize your notes by grouping each note card with the main idea it develops. For example, if you were writing a report about the start of the American Revolution, your notes might tell about three main ideas: the Continental Congress, the Boston Tea Party, and the Battle of Lexington. You would put all cards about the Continental Congress in one pile. Cards about the Boston Tea Party would go in another stack. Information about the Battle of Lexington would go in a third pile. Each idea group can become a paragraph in your report.

When you sort through your notes, leave out any that are not related to one of the main ideas. If you do not have enough notes on an idea, do more reading. Remember, you can add or take out information at any point in the writing process.

After Tony put his cards into idea groups, he read through them again. Then he wrote a topic sentence that summarized the information in each group of cards. These sentences will give Tony a good start when he begins drafting his report.

1. The children spent most of each day walking.
2. The children had many chores to do each day.
3. At the end of the day, the children could enjoy themselves.

426

Exercises   Organizing Notes

▶ Classifying/Generalizing

A. Organizing Notes into Main Idea Groups Look at the following notes. They are for a report on the neon tetra, a tropical fish. Imagine that each fact is on a note card. Organize the notes into two groups of related ideas. Then, write a summary topic sentence for each group. A.Tetras use gills to breathe. B.The tetras' shape allows them to swim at great speed.

A 1. Tetras breathe by pumping water past their gills.

B 2. The fish's shape has evolved over millions of years.

A 3. Water is pumped past the gills by the movement of the mouth.

A 4. The folds of the gills exchange oxygen for waste carbon dioxide.

B 5. Their shape allows for top speed and agility.

B 6. Long and narrow, tetras can cruise at speeds between three to six times their body lengths per second.

▶ Classifying/Generalizing/Creative Application

B. Organizing Your Notes Look at the note cards you wrote for Exercise B in part 2. Divide the cards into groups of related ideas. Then, write a sentence that summarizes the information in each group of cards.

427

Special Populations

LD, ESL Before assigning Exercise A, define any unfamiliar words. Have students restate each idea in their own words. See the notes under **Basic Students.**

Reinforcement

Follow the directions for Exercise A on page 427 using these notes on chipmunks. In addition, find the one note that does not fit well into either of the two groups. Cross out that note.

A 1. Chipmunks are approximately nine inches long from nose to tail tip.

B 2. Chipmunks store food in their burrows.

A 3. They weigh about three to four ounces.

   4. A chipmunk's sense of hearing is its most important sense.   unrelated

A 5. Chipmunks are much smaller than their cousins, the tree squirrels.

B 6. A chipmunk can carry as many as 900 acorns to its burrow per day.

B 7. Chipmunks carry food to their burrows in roomy cheek pouches.

   A. Chipmunks are quite small.

   B. Chipmunks have a unique food storage system.

Enrichment

To help students see the organization in professional writing samples, have each student select a short report from a magazine. Instruct each student to read a report and then describe how it is organized. Also, have them find the topic sentence of each paragraph. (Have the students use magazines geared to their age level such as *National Geographic World* and *Cobblestone.*)

Additional Resources

Skills Practice Book—page 165

Teacher's Resource Binder
  Reinforcement Activities—
    page 118

Part 4

Objective

To make an outline using correct form

Presenting the Lesson

All Students

1. Read and discuss page 428. Point out that the note card groups become a major part of the outline. The details become subtopics.

2. Have the students examine Tony's outline. Talk about the organization and the relation of subtopics to main topics. Mention that sometimes a main idea cannot be separated into subtopics. Then the outline will have a Roman numeral with no subtopics. Using the sample outline as a model, review the mechanics of outlining with the class. Refer students to the "Guide to Capitalization" and the "Guide to Punctuation" in the **Power Handbook.** Explain how to indent outlines properly.

3. Assign and discuss the exercise on page 429.

Basic Students

Give the students practice writing an outline. Use either the notes on neon tetra from Exercise A on page 427 or the notes on chipmunks from the **Reinforcement** exercise in the Teacher Notes. Have the students write the organized notes in outline form.

◆ Advanced Students

Have students examine a table of contents from a nonfiction book. Point out the similarity in organization of the table of contents to an outline. Discuss the relationship between main groups of information and supporting information.

---

4 Prewriting: Making an Outline

Focus

Use an **outline** to arrange your ideas in logical order.

▶ Comprehension

You are now ready to make a writing plan for your report. Usually, the plan is made in the form of an outline. An outline shows how each different part of a report works together to develop the topic.

Arranging Main Ideas

First, arrange the main idea groups in logical order. Each group of notes becomes a major division, or part, of the outline. The main idea of each group becomes the heading of the part. Number each heading with a Roman numeral followed by a period.

Arranging Facts

The important facts on your note cards become the subtopics of each main idea. List the subtopics under each main idea. Label each subtopic with a capital letter followed by a period. Indent the subtopics. Line up each subtopic so that it begins under the first letter of the main topic. Do not use just one subtopic under a main idea. If the main idea cannot be separated into at least two ideas, it should not be separated at all.

Write topics and subtopics in words, phrases, or sentences. However, use the same form for the topics and the subtopics throughout your outline.

An outline must have a title. It tells what the outline is about. You might want to use the title of your outline as the title of your report.

428

Here is Tony's outline for his report.

The Youngest Pioneers

I. Walked most of the day
   A. Walked 12–15 miles a day
   B. Rode in the wagons on the hottest afternoons

II. Did many chores each day
   A. Milked cows
   B. Fetched water
   C. Searched for prairie dog holes
   D. Gathered "buffalo chips" for fuel
   E. Studied school lessons
   F. Learned how to hook rugs, make quilts,
      preserve meat in salt

III. Free to enjoy themselves at the end of the day
   A. Played games like tag and hide-and-seek
   B. Sang around campfire

Exercise   Writing an Outline
▶ Creative Application

Write an outline for your report. Use your list of main ideas and your note cards. Use correct form, and remember to give your outline a good title.

429

Additional Resources

Skills Practice Book—page 166
Teacher's Resource Binder
Reinforcement Activities—
   page 119

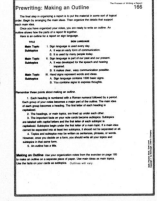

Part 5

Objective

To recognize and write an effective introduction

Presenting the Lesson

 All Students

1. Read page 430. Review the three parts of a report and the purpose for each. Stress that the introduction should do two things: State the topic of the report and catch the reader's attention. Ask the students to state what Tony's report is about in their own words. Compare Tony's first introduction and the improved version. Have the students find interesting phrases in the revised introduction and list them on the board. Have students explain how these phrases help make the paragraph interesting. Ask if Tony's revised introduction does both things an introduction should do.

2. Assign and discuss Exercises A and B on page 431.

 Basic Students

Do Exercise A orally. Write the students' suggested improvements for paragraph 2 on the board.

For Exercise B, work with individuals or small groups to help the students with their introductions.

 Advanced Students

Have the students write two introductory paragraphs for their reports, trying different approaches. Have students exchange papers and test their introductions on one another. Then have them choose the best introduction for their reports.

---

5 Drafting the Introduction

> **Focus**
>
> There are three parts to a written report: the **introduction**, **body**, and **conclusion**.

▶ Comprehension

A report has the same three main parts that any composition has. The **introduction** tells what the report is about. It is usually one paragraph. The **body** may have several paragraphs. These paragraphs explain the main idea of the report. The **conclusion** is a paragraph that summarizes the report.

Use your outline to guide you as you write your draft. It lists the ideas you want to include. It also shows the best order for presenting them. Refer to your note cards as well. They may contain some details not included in the outline.

Writing the Introduction

The introduction of a report should tell the reader what the report is about and catch the reader's interest.

There are several ways to begin an introductory paragraph. You may wish to begin by simply stating the main idea of your report. An example or an anecdote, a brief story that illustrates your topic, is another good way to begin. You might also discover a quotation during your research that would make an interesting beginning.

Look at Tony's first draft of his introduction.

> Many children traveled west during pioneer days. They made this journey in a covered wagon. They traveled a long way.

Although this short paragraph tells the main idea of the report, it does not catch the reader's interest. It also does not provide much information about the subject.

Now read Tony's revised introduction. Notice how he added strong details and specific words to create interest.

During the 1800's, thousands of children traveled west in long wagon trains. The trains moved slowly over the grassy plains. They crossed burning deserts and the cold, rugged mountains of the Oregon Trail. The children did their chores, studied their lessons, and played games. In many ways, their days were just like they would have been at home. This time, though, "home" was a wagon moving across 2,000 miles of unknown and often dangerous land.

Exercises   Writing an Introduction

▶ Analyzing/Drawing Conclusions

A. Discussing Introductions Read the introductions. Decide which one is good and which is poor. Explain the reasons for your choices. Rewrite the weak introduction to make it better.

1. Long ago, some people believed that gods lived among the stars. Others thought the stars held magical powers. Still others tried to predict the future by watching the changes in the sky. Today we know that stars are actually burning balls of gas. Good introduction. Interesting details support main idea. Variety in sentence structure and word choice.

2. Earthquakes under the ocean cause tidal waves. Tidal waves are gigantic and travel fast. They are interesting. Poor introduction. Tells main topic, but offers little information and few details. Word choice and sentence structure are dull.

▶ Creative Application

B. Writing an Introduction Write the introductory paragraph of your report. Make sure that it includes your main idea and offers information that will catch the reader's interest.

431

Additional Resources

Skills Practice Book—page 167

Teacher's Resource Binder
Reinforcement Activities—
page 120

Drafting the Introduction 167
The Process of Writing a Report

A report has the same three parts that any composition has. They are the introduction, the body, and the conclusion.

Special Populations

LD Discuss developing an introductory paragraph both by stating a broad idea and then giving specific details and in the reverse manner. Put the following visual model on the board.
Broad Area: Good eating habits
Specific: Breakfast is the most important meal of the day.
Specific: Breakfast is the most important meal of the day.
Broad: Good eating habits.
   Guide students in replacing the ideas from the model with material from their notes.
ESL Pair students with native speakers of English to help them draft their introductions.
NSD Remind students of the importance of using Standard English for report writing.

Reinforcement

Have students follow the instructions for Exercise A on page 431.
1. This report will be about the second war taking place in the colonies during the American Revolution. The second war was the frontier war. It's amazing that the colonies won the Revolution. They were fighting what was then a real superpower.
2. You can think of seeds as space capsules for infant plants. They contain an embryo plant, a food supply to feed the plant until it gets established, a tiny bit of water to keep it alive, and a tough outer coat or coats.

Enrichment

Make a collection of reports from magazines that are appropriate for sixth graders. *Scholastic Time, Scholastic Action,* or *Cobblestone Magazine* are good sources to try. Try to include some samples that begin with a quotation and some that begin with an anecdote. Study the introductory paragraphs with the students. Have the students analyze them. Do the paragraphs introduce the topic? Do they interest the reader? What details does the writer use? What specific words catch the reader's attention?

Part 6

Objective

To develop the body of a report

Presenting the Lesson

All Students

1. Read and discuss page 432 and the information preceding the sample body paragraphs on page 433. Remind the students that as they draft, they will probably make some changes. Encourage them to continually look for ways to make their reports better. This may mean adding information or changing its organization.

2. Discuss signal words as a way of showing organization and helping ideas to flow smoothly.

3. Demonstrate the relationship of the writer's outline to the body of the report. Do this by duplicating the body of Tony's report. Ask the students to underline the topic sentences in the paragraphs in red and compare them to the main topics in the outline. Then have the students find the supporting details from the outline and underline them in blue. Finally, have the students circle all of the signal words.

4. Assign the exercise on page 433. Have students exchange drafts. Classmates should check for good topic sentences. They should also evaluate whether the details in the paragraphs support the topic sentences. Students should write suggestions for improvement on a separate sheet of paper.

Basic Students

Work with individuals or small groups. Reinforce the idea that only one main idea should be presented in a paragraph.

Advanced Students

Remind these students that drafting is a time to get things down on paper and make changes that are needed. These students may be overly concerned with producing a perfect paper. Point out that the drafting stage does not produce a perfect paper.

---

6 Drafting the Body of a Report

> ┌─ *Focus* ─
> The **body** of a report presents information that develops the topic.

▶ Comprehension

The body of a report presents most of the information about the subject. Each main division in the outline becomes a paragraph in the body of the report. The subtopics are the supporting facts. Each paragraph might also include additional facts that are on your note cards but not on your outline.

Writing Body Paragraphs

As you write, remember that you can constantly rework your ideas. You might realize that the order you used in your outline could be improved. You might find new information or think of better ways to present the ideas you already have. Include these changes as you draft. Just be sure that the report still flows smoothly and develops one topic.

Using Signal Words

When writing paragraphs that give facts, you must let your reader know when an important idea is coming up. You must also show how your ideas fit together.

Use signal words to help make your ideas clear. Signal words such as *first*, *next*, or *finally* show that an important point follows. Phrases like *in addition* or *for example* can signal interesting details. Use signal words within a paragraph, or to link two paragraphs together.

For more information about using signal words, see Chapter 10, page 185 and Chapter 22, page 387.

432

Analyzing Body Paragraphs

▶Analyzing

Here are the body paragraphs of Tony's report. Tony followed his outline closely, but he also included some additional details.

The children spent most of the day walking alongside the wagons. Only on the hottest desert afternoons did many ride in the shelter of the jolting wagons. Every day except Sunday the wagons covered—and the children walked—twelve to fifteen miles. The only ones who did not walk were groups of older children. They herded the "cow column," the milk cows and spare horses and oxen that followed the wagon train. These children spent most of the long journey on horseback.

The children had work to do. They milked the cows, fetched buckets of water from the creeks, and gathered wild fruits and berries. They searched for prairie dog holes and alerted the hunters in the train to their locations. One of their most important jobs was gathering "buffalo chips." These were the disks of dried buffalo dung that were burned for cooking and warmth. The children also studied their school lessons. They used books that had been packed into the wagons. In addition, they learned skills such as how to hook rugs, make quilts, preserve meat in salt, start a fire from flint, and use an ax.

When the wagons finally pulled up at the end of a long day and the supper dishes were done, the children were free to have some fun. They could then get together with the children from other wagons to play games like tag and hide-and-seek. They could join the singing around the campfires and listen to the adults share their dreams of a new life in Oregon. Bedtime came early for those on a wagon train. Everyone had to be up before dawn to begin a new day.

Exercise   Drafting the Body of a Report

▶Creative Application

Write the body of your report. Follow your outline, making any improvements that occur to you. Be sure each paragraph has a strong topic sentence. Include details from your note cards. Use signal words to make ideas flow smoothly.

433

Special Populations

LD, ESL Through individual conferences, have students talk through their reports before beginning to draft the report.

ESL Continue to pair students with native speakers of English for this stage of the writing.

Reinforcement

Ask students to divide the following passage into paragraphs and underline the topic sentences.

Columbus and his men were not the first explorers to reach the Americas. Five hundred years or so before Columbus, Norsemen came to the shores of America. One of these Norsemen was named Leif Erickson. Leif was on his way from Greenland to Norway. His ship ran into a storm. Leif lost his course. The land he came to was America. Leif had reached the New World without meaning to go exploring. For that reason he is often called Lucky Leif. Leif found his way back to Greenland. His discovery led to other Norsemen coming to America. His story made his brother want to find these new lands. Leif's brother was not as lucky; he could not find them. Later, however, other Norsemen did.

Enrichment

Use the collection of reports from magazines that you gathered for the enrichment activity for part 5. Break the class into small groups. Give each group one report. This time, have the students analyze the body paragraphs. Have the students identify the topic sentence in each paragraph. Also have them identify the supporting details. Have them suggest an alternative method of organization for the information, if practical. Lastly, ask them to find any signal words used by the author.

Additional Resources

Skills Practice Book—page 168

Teacher's Resource Binder
Reinforcement Activities—
page 121

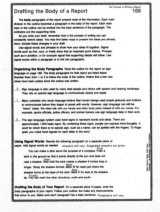

Part 7

Objective

To conclude a report and to credit sources

Presenting the Lesson

All Students

1. Read and discuss **Writing the Conclusion.** Reread the introduction and the body paragraphs of Tony's report with the class. Then read Tony's first and revised conclusions. Point out that no new information is presented in either ending. Tony either restates facts or draws conclusions from the information in the body of the report. Discuss the concluding sentences in both paragraphs. Point out which ones are restatements and which are conclusions drawn from the information in the report. Discuss the differences in the first and second versions. Have students suggest how the second one is better.

2. Read and discuss **Giving Credit.** Explain how the source information on these note cards will provide the information they need to list their sources. Have students look again at Tony's note card on page 425. Show students how that source now appears in his list of sources. Point out the pattern of indentation used in the list.

3. Assign the exercise on page 435.

Basic Students

Work with the students individually or in small groups as they draft the conclusions to their reports. Remind them that no new information should be presented in the conclusion.

Discuss in specific detail the format for listing sources. Explain that they are listed in alphabetical order by author's name. If there is no author, alphabetize by title. Make a copy of these guidelines for each student.

Magazine

Author's last name, First name
  "Title of article," *Title of magazine,*
  Month and year of magazine, pages
  000–000.

---

7 Ending Your Report

> **Focus**
>
> Write a clear conclusion for your report. Give credit to the sources you used for your information.

Writing the Conclusion
▶ Comprehension

The last paragraph of your report is very important. It ties together all of the ideas you have presented in the introduction and body paragraphs. The last paragraph also provides a clear, definite finish for the report.

The ending paragraph is often a summary of the main ideas. However, it should not just repeat an earlier part of the report. Such an ending would bore the reader. The final paragraph should be bright and fresh because it is your last chance to share your information with the reader. However, it should not introduce any new ideas.

Read Tony's first ending for his report.

> The children on a wagon train did ordinary things, like you and I. But they also did some out-of-the-ordinary things. Which was more fun—riding in a wagon train or on an airplane?

This is a weak concluding pargraph. It does not pull together or summarize the ideas of the report. Instead, it tries to compare a wagon train to a new topic—an airplane.

Tony's revised conclusion is much stronger.

> The children on a wagon train did the ordinary things that all children do. They worked, played, studied, ate, and slept. However, some of their experiences were difficult and far from ordinary. They suffered from hard wagon seats, tired feet, and fierce heat. They also faced long stretches of boredom as they traveled west. These children were true pioneers, just like their parents.

434

Book

Author's last name, First name.
  Book title.

Encyclopedia Article

"Article title," *Encyclopedia name.*
  Volume 00, pages 000–000.

Giving Credit

Your final step in drafting a report is showing where you got your information. You must credit your sources.

Look at your note cards. List the books and magazines that you used. Put the list in alphabetical order, using the author's last name. If no author is given, use the title of the book or article.

Here is Tony's list of sources. He included this list at the end of his report.

> My information was taken from these sources.
>
> Bartel, Pauline. "Wagons on the Oregon Trail," <u>Cobblestone</u>, December 1981, pp. 16–17.
>
> Havighurst, Walter. <u>The First Book of the Oregon Trail</u>.
>
> "Pioneer Life in America," <u>The World Book Encyclopedia</u>. Volume 15, pp. 440—443.
>
> <u>Westward on the Oregon Trail</u>. American Heritage Junior Library.

Notice that Tony underlined the titles of books and magazines. He put quotation marks around the titles of magazine and encyclopedia articles. Follow this example when you credit your sources. Look at the "Guide to Punctuation" and "Guide to Capitalization" in your **Power Handbook** for more information on titles.

Exercise   Writing Your Conclusion

▶ Creative Application

Write the last paragraph of your report. Make sure that it ties your ideas together and shows the reader that the report is over. Finally, list the sources you used for your report. Use the examples in this lesson as a guide.

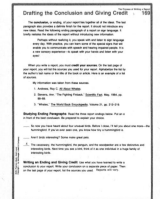

435

Have the students work in small groups. Each student should read his or her conclusion to the group. The group should comment on the strong points and weak points of the conclusion. They should ask these questions: Does the ending hold the reader's attention? Does it provide a strong ending to the report? Is any new information introduced in the conclusion?

Special Populations

LD, ESL Pair students with stronger writers as they draft their conclusions. See the notes under **Basic Students.**

Reinforcement

Have the students put these sources for a report in the proper format.

Under the Apple Trees by John Burroughs.

"Chipmunks: Lively Lords and Ladies of Our Woodlands" by Lawrence Wishner, *Smithsonian,* October 1982, page 76.

"Chipmunks," Volume 3 of *The World Book Encyclopedia*, pages 300–307.

Burroughs, John. *Under the Apple Trees*.
"Chipmunks," *The World Book Encyclopedia*. Volume 3, pp. 300–307.
Wishner, Lawrence. "Chipmunks: Lively Lords and Ladies of Our Woodlands," *Smithsonian,* October 1982, page 76.

Enrichment

Continue the analysis of the report collection from magazines. In this discussion, concentrate on the conclusions. Ask the students to decide whether or not they are good conclusions. They should support their opinions with sound reasons based on the material presented in the lesson.

Additional Resources

Skills Practice Book—page 169
Teacher's Resource Binder
   Reinforcement Activities—
     page 122

Part 8

Objectives

1. To revise and proofread a report
2. To make a clean, final copy and to share the report

Presenting the Lesson

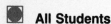 **All Students**

1. Read and discuss page 436. Discuss the **Guidelines for Revising** on page 436. Emphasize that a report should not include the opinions of the writer or statements that are not based on fact. Remind students that these facts should be written in their own words. Have students examine the sample revision. Discuss the changes and the reasons for those changes.

2. Talk about the importance of a neat final copy.

3. Assign Exercise A. Have the students use the **Guidelines for Revising** on page 436. Review how to use proofreading symbols, if necessary.

4. Assign Exercise B. You may wish to use the following guidelines as you evaluate the reports.

Guidelines for Evaluation

Strong The most successful writing will display the following characteristics: (5 points)

1. will state the topic of the report in an interesting introductory paragraph
2. will contain information that is accurate and appropriate to the topic
3. will present each main topic in a separate paragraph
4. will present facts and ideas in a logical order
5. will demonstrate coherence; will use signal words and phrases necessary to maintain coherence
6. will contain a conclusion that introduces no new ideas and summarizes the topic
7. will have used and credited at least two sources
8. will contain no more than five or six minor errors in grammar, usage, and mechanics

---

8 Revising, Proofreading, and Sharing

Focus

Carefully revise and proofread your report. It should be clear and error-free. Share your work with your classmates.

▶ Comprehension

When writing a report, you are sharing many facts. These facts must be presented clearly and accurately. To do so, you must revise your report carefully. Use the guidelines below to help you.

> **Guidelines for Revising a Report**
>
> 1. Does my introduction state the topic of the report? Is the introduction interesting?
> 2. Is the body of my report informative?
> 3. Are the ideas presented in logical order?
> 4. Did I begin a new paragraph for each main idea? Did I develop each idea thoroughly?
> 5. Does my conclusion summarize the main ideas of my report? Does it show that my report is finished?
> 6. Is my writing lively and clear?

Look at this revised paragraph from one writer's report.

Midas was ^a character^ in Greek mythology. ^The god^ Dionysus gave [*I should tell who Dionysus was.*]

Midas the power to turn everything he touched [*Who?*]

into gold. ^At first, Midas^ ~~He~~ thought this was the perfect power.

Soon it caused trouble. Midas could not even eat. *because his food turned to gold.* [*This is part of my story.*]

~~I wish I could have Midas's power just for a day!~~ [*I'd better say how the story ends.*]

Finally, Dionysus told Midas to bathe in the river Pactolus. Midas lost his touch, but the river sand turned to gold.

436

Proofreading

After you revise your report, you must proofread it carefully. Pay special attention to proper names and unusual or technical words. Check the accuracy of dates, figures, and other facts. Finally, check your spelling, punctuation, capitalization, and grammar.

Making a Final Copy

When you have revised your report, give it a good title. Then make a clean, final copy. Include any revisions you have made. Check to make sure that your handwriting is easy to read. Also, make sure you left margins and indented each paragraph. If you planned to use pictures or graphs as part of your report, add them to your final copy. Proofread your work one last time. Neatly make any necessary changes.

Exercises   Revising a Report

▶ Analyzing/Creative Application

A. Revising Your Report Revise your report, using the guidelines given on page 436. Carefully proofread your report. Then make a clean, final copy. Include a good title, and any charts or pictures you have made. Put the list of sources you used at the end of your report.

▶ Creative Application

B. Sharing Your Report Brainstorm with your classmates to think of ways you might share your report. Here is one idea to get you started.

You might group together all reports on similar subjects. For example, you might have groups of science, history, and sports reports. Then ask your librarian if you might have a week to display each group of reports in the library. Add pictures or other items to make the display more interesting. For example, the "Sports Week" display might include a soccer ball, hockey stick, swim goggles, books about sports, and your reports.

437

Additional Resources

Skills Practice Book—170

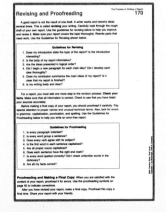

Average A paragraph of average quality will meet most of the criteria of the successful response but may display one or two of these problems: (3 points)
1. introduction may not be interesting
2. may contain one or two errors in paragraphing or organization
3. may contain a weak conclusion that lacks finality
4. may not use or credit correctly the required number of sources
5. may display several errors in grammar, usage, and mechanics

Weak A weak paragraph will display only one or two characteristics of a successful response. It will also be characterized by several of the following problems: (1 point)
1. unclear topic
2. no sense of order or coherence
3. no identifiable conclusion
4. improper crediting of sources
5. numerous errors in grammar, usage, and mechanics

 Basic Students

Before they make their final copies, have the students read their rough drafts to someone else—a writing partner, a tutor, or a writing group—and discuss any problems in sentence structure. Ask students to correct run-on sentences and to combine short, choppy sentences.

 Advanced Students

Have students explore the possibility of using graphic aids to illustrate some of the information in their report. Refer to Chapter 23, "Developing Library and Research Skills" for a review of the kinds of graphic aids and the suitability of each to a particular kind of information. Have students prepare one or more suitable graphic aids to accompany their report.

Special Populations

LD Do not overemphasize neatness for students with small motor dysfunction.

LD, ESL Consider the possibility of these students preparing the final copy of their reports on tape recordings.

Speaking and Listening

Objectives

1. To recognize the similarities in report writing and news broadcasting
2. To prepare a simulation of a news broadcast

Presenting the Activity

This page gives special emphasis to the speaking and listening skills of presenting a news broadcast. This activity may be used to show students how the concepts of report writing presented in this chapter may be applied in an oral context.

Before making this assignment, review the concepts presented in Chapter 14, "Sharpening Speaking and Listening Skills" on page 251.

Speaking and Listening

Preparing and Presenting a News Report

▶ **Comprehension**

The news reports you see on television are much like the reports you have learned to write. Each news story begins with a *lead*. Like the topic sentence in a report, the lead states the topic of the news story and catches the listeners' attention.

The lead is followed by facts. These facts tell the *who, what, when, where, why,* and *how* of the story. The report usually ends with a summary statement.

Carefully watch a television news program. Notice that the reporters look directly into the camera. In this way, they have eye contact with their television audience. They know their copy, or report, well. They seldom glance at their copy.

Exercise   Presenting a News Program

▶ **Creative Application**

With your class, prepare a news show. First, form several groups. Each group will be responsible for preparing a story about something interesting that has happened in your school in the past month.

Once your group has decided on a story, gather information. You may wish to interview people who are part of your story. Then write the story. Make sure to write a lead that will catch the audience's attention. Then add facts that develop your lead. These facts should tell the *who, what, when, where, why,* and *how* of your story. End with a summary statement. Now, choose one person in your group to be the on-camera reporter.

Practice the entire program with the on-camera reporters. Other reporters can be the audience. If you are on camera, remember to look directly at the audience, speak clearly, sit straight, and keep your hands still. Look at your written story only when necessary. After you have practiced, "broadcast" your news reports to another class.

438

Creative Writing

▶ Creative Application

A. Imagine that you are an inventor. You have invented a fantastic new product. Write a report about your product.

First, make a list of details about your product. Include facts about what it looks like, what it does, and what it is made of. Then, organize your notes into an outline. Finally, draft your report. Remember to revise and proofread your report.

B. Imagine that you are a British redcoat spy in the American Revolution. Your assignment is to penetrate General Washington's lines. You are to bring back information about the number of Revolutionary soldiers and how well trained they are. You are to report on supplies, ammunition, and troop morale.

Write a short report on your findings. Be sure to include all of the requested information.

Creative Writing

These activities provide opportunities for imaginative applications of the skills presented in this chapter.

When you assign part B, discuss the definition of *morale* with the students ("moral or mental condition in relation to courage, discipline, confidence, enthusiasm, etc."). Explain that the morale of the troops could determine how hard they would fight.

439

Using English in Reading

This activity allows the students to see how the skills used in writing a report may be applied to sharing information about a book. You may want to point out that in this case the gathering of information is done when the book to be reported on is read.

Using English in Reading

▶ Comprehension

You often read both fiction and nonfiction books just for the enjoyment they give you. When you find a good book, you can share your discovery with your friends. You can tell them about it, or you can write a book report.

Once in a while, you will read a book you do not enjoy. In that case, you should tell what you did not like about the book. Then people who read your book report can decide for themselves whether they might like it anyway.

Book reports can be long or short. They may include many details or few. All book reports, however, must include the information listed below.

1. The title of the book
2. The author of the book
3. What the book is about and whether it is fiction or nonfiction
4. Reasons why you like or dislike the book

When you report on a fiction book, tell when and where the story takes place. Then tell a little about the people or animals in the story and at least one problem they face. Don't tell the whole story.

When you report on a nonfiction book, tell about the subject covered in the book. You might tell a few especially interesting or unusual facts that you learned.

Give good reasons why you like or dislike the book. Whoever reads this report will be interested in your opinion.

Exercise   Writing Your Own Book Report

▶ Creative Application

Write a book report about a book you have read recently. Be sure to include the information every book report needs. Correct your mistakes and make a clean copy. Share your report with your class.

440

Chapter 24 Review

▶ Classifying

A. Organizing Notes into Main Idea Groups Look at these notes for a report on the ostrich. Imagine that each note is on a separate note card. Organize the notes into four groups of related ideas. Divide your paper into four columns. Label the columns *Looks*, *Behavior*, *Diet*, and *Offspring*. Write each fact in the correct column.

Has large feathers, or plumes, once popular for decorating hats   Looks

Does not bury its head in the sand   Behavior

Eats plant food—leaves, seeds, fruit   Diet

Can run very fast—40 to 60 miles per hour   Behavior

Eggs weigh about three pounds each   Offspring

Does not fly—uses wings only for turning or braking   Behavior

Protects itself by running away or kicking   Behavior

Adult bird weighs up to 200 pounds   Looks

Babies are the size of full-grown chickens   Offspring

▶ Analyzing/Generalizing

B. Revising and Proofreading a Paragraph The following paragraph has several errors. Make it a better paragraph by making these changes.   See corrected paragraph in margin. Topic sentence will vary.

1. Write a good topic sentence.
2. Correct four misspelled words.
3. Correct two errors in capitalization.
4. Take out a sentence that does not belong.

Walt Disney's first hit was a carton called "steemboat Willie." It was the first cartoon to have sound. The star of this animated show was a tiney mouse named mickey. Walt Disney was born in Chicago. Mickey went on to star in hunderds of cartoons.

441

Chapter Review

This review allows teachers to evaluate student understanding of the concepts presented in this chapter.

Exercise B

Walt Disney, one of history's most famous movie producers, was once an unknown cartoonist. Walt Disney's first hit was a cartoon called "Steamboat Willie." It was the first cartoon to have sound. The star of this animated show was a tiny mouse named Mickey. Mickey went on to star in hundreds of cartoons.

Additional Resources

Skills Practice Book
Review—page 171

Test Booklet
Mastery Test—pages 143–148

Chapter 25

Chapter Objectives

1. To use the correct form for writing a friendly letter

2. To identify the purpose of social notes and to write them correctly

3. To identify and use the correct form for a business letter

4. To use the correct form for addressing envelopes

5. To fill out forms neatly and accurately

Motivating the Students

Read the following fictional ad to the students.

WANTED: Letter Writer

Famous athlete is looking for a person to answer correspondence. Should be a good speller and have good knowledge of English and grammar. Neat handwriting a must. Send a letter explaining why you would be perfect for the job to Johnson Employment Agency, 25¼ Mercer Street, New York, New York, 10013.

Discuss the skills asked for in the ad. Point out that these skills are important in any letter—whether it is to a friend, or to apply for a job.

Read and discuss the chapter introduction on page 443. Stress the fact that letter writing is an important skill. In this chapter students will learn how to write many types of letters for a variety of purposes.

Special Populations

LD Some students will have difficulty with the details of capitalization and punctuation. Provide sample letters on charts or posters so that students can refer to models of correct letter form.

ESL Students may be acquainted with different letter writing conventions. Encourage students to discuss these differences. Make sure they understand the forms presented in this chapter.

NSD Stress the importance of using Standard English when writing letters and filling out forms.

Week 35

Chapter Management Guidelines This chart may be used to help structure daily lesson plans

Day 1	Day 2	Day 3	Day 4	Day 5
Chapter 25 Opener, p. 443; Part 1, "Writing a Friendly Letter," pp. 444–446	Part 2, "Writing Social Notes," pp. 447–448	Part 3, "Writing Business Letters," pp. 449–451	Part 4, "Addressing an Envelope," pp. 452–453; Part 5, "Filling Out Forms," pp. 454–455	Chapter Review and selected end-of-chapter activities

Chapter 25

Writing Letters and Filling Out Forms

Sending a letter has always been a special occasion. In past centuries, a letter was so important it was often sealed with wax. The sender left a mark by pressing his or her ring into the wax. The letter was then given to someone who might have to travel a great distance to deliver it.

Letters are still a part of important occasions. You use your letter-writing skills when you receive a gift, share news with a friend, or send invitations to a party. You have probably been writing letters since you were very young. Knowing how to write letters will continue to be an important skill in your life.

This chapter will help you to write clear, interesting letters. You will write social notes. You will also write a business letter to order materials or request information. Finally, you will learn how to address envelopes correctly, so that your letters reach the people they are meant for.

443

Related Chapters

You may wish to refer to related material in other chapters as you teach the following concepts:

1. Capitalization rules, the "Guide to Capitalization," in the **Power Handbook**

2. Punctuation rules, the "Guide to Punctuation," in the **Power Handbook**

Additional Resources

Skills Practice Book—pages 172–180

Test Booklet—pages 149–154
Pretest—pages 149–150
Mastery Test—pages 151–154

Teacher's Resource Binder
Reinforcement Activities—
pages 123–126
Enrichment Activities—
pages 8, 39–52, 79
Ideas for Creative Teaching

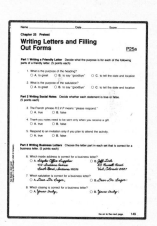

Part 1

Objective

To use the correct form for writing a friendly letter

Presenting the Lesson

All Students

1. Read and discuss pages 444–445. Emphasize the importance of using a conversational tone in friendly letters. Point out that each topic in a friendly letter should be covered in a separate paragraph.

2. After reading **Parts of a Friendly Letter** on page 445, have the students locate each part in the sample letter on page 444. Be sure that students understand the purpose of each part.

3. Review the rules for capitalization and punctuation in letters on page 446. Again, refer to the sample letter as an illustration of correct usage.

4. Assign and discuss Exercises A and B on page 446. Provide these addresses of pen pal organizations.

Student Letter Exchange
910 Fourth Street S.E.
Austin, MN 55912

International Friendship League
Beacon Hill
55 Mt. Vernon Ave.
Boston, MA 02108

Basic Students

After students complete Exercise A, have them exchange papers with a proofreading partner. They should make corrections on their papers according to the proofreader's suggestions.

---

1 Writing a Friendly Letter

> **Focus**
>
> A friendly letter is a way to share news with a friend.

▶ **Comprehension**

When you have something to say to a friend, you can write a friendly letter. Your letter should sound natural, as if you were speaking to the person. Write about things that interest you and your friend. Share stories and experiences. Ask questions. Talk about your feelings. Use vivid details and strong verbs to make your descriptions come alive.

Read the following friendly letter. Notice the form and purpose of each part of the letter.

Heading 1201 West Leonard Street
Pensacola, Florida 32501
October 5, 1987

Salutation

Dear Miguel,   Body

Today our class went to a wooded area for a science lesson. We had to find specimens of different leaves. When I found some poison ivy, I thought of you right away! Remember when we went on that hike at camp and the poison ivy found you? Boy, did you itch!

Have you been doing a lot of skateboarding? We formed a neighborhood skateboarding team. You have much better hills in Georgia, so I bet you're really good.

Closing   Your friend,

Signature   Jerry

444

The Parts of a Friendly Letter

A friendly letter has five parts. Each part has its own purpose and form.

Part	Form	Purpose
Heading	The **heading** is written in the upper right-hand corner.	The **heading** tells where you are and when you are writing. It consists of three lines: house number and street name city, state, ZIP code month, day, year
Salutation or Greeting	The **salutation**, or **greeting**, is written on the line below the heading and begins at the left margin.	The **salutation**, or **greeting**, is the way you say "hello" to your friend. It can be casual, such as *Dear Mary, Hi,* or *Greetings.*
Body	The **body** begins on the line below the salutation. Each paragraph is indented.	The **body** of a letter is for talking to your friend. Arrange the body in paragraphs for each subject you discuss.
Closing	The **closing** should line up with the first line of the heading.	The **closing** is a simple way of saying "goodbye." Some common closings are *Love, Sincerely,* or *Your friend.*
Signature	After the closing, skip a line. Your **signature** should line up with the first word in the closing.	In a friendly letter, only your first name is needed unless you don't know the person well.

445

 Advanced Students

After the students have completed the exercises for this part, ask each of them to choose a favorite character from a story or from history. Students should put themselves in the character's place and write a letter. Suggest that the letter be about an incident in the story in which the character appears, or about an historical event with which the person is connected. For example, George Washington might write a letter to his wife Martha about the morale of his troops at Valley Forge.

Special Populations

LD Students often have poor handwriting, spelling, and punctuation skills. This might make them insecure about writing letters. Reassure students that the letters they write need not be mailed. This is an opportunity for them to practice and improve their skills.

ESL Students may not be accustomed to the informal tone and style in the friendly letter. They may also write dates differently, putting the day before the month. Encourage discussion about these differences.

NSD Encourage the use of Standard English, even though the language in friendly letters is informal.

Reinforcement

1. Have the students follow the directions for Exercise A on page 446 using these letter parts: See answers on page 446.

1. 451 sixth avenue inglewood california 90305 october 15 1987
2. sincerely gregory
3. 1001 cecil road jacksonville florida 33054 november 30 1987
4. always marcia
5. 379 julian avenue st louis missouri 63122 may 3 1987
6. dear kerry
7. 95 abott road concord new hampshire 03301 july 9 1987
8. dear grandmother
9. 200 allwood drive austin texas 78704 february 21 1987
10. your friend eric

Chapter 25   **445**

2. Have students write a letter to a real or imaginary friend about a parade. They can write about a parade they have seen or been a part of, or they can write about an imaginary parade.

Enrichment

For enrichment activities, see the Unit Projects in the Teacher Notes on page 347. One or more of these projects have special activities for gifted and talented students.

Exercise A
1. 336 Old Mill Road
   Phoenix, Arizona 85040
   August 7, 1987
   Heading
2. Dear Lorna Jill,
   Salutation
3. 852 Main Street
   Mount Prospect, Illinois 60056
   June 3, 1987
   Heading
4. Missing you,
   Tiffany
   Closing and Signature
5. Dear Aunt Lynn and Uncle Tom,
   Salutation
6. Sincerely yours,
   Jeff Rodriguez
   Closing and Signature

Reinforcement
1. 451 Sixth Avenue
   Inglewood, California 90305
   October 15, 1987
   Heading
2. Sincerely,
   Gregory
   Closing
3. 1001 Cecil Road
   Jacksonville, Florida 33054
   November 30,1987
   Heading
4. Always,
   Marcia
   Closing
5. 379 Julian Avenue
   St. Louis, Missouri 63122
   May 3, 1987
   Heading
6. Dear Kerry,
   Greeting
7. 95 Abott Road
   Concord, New Hampshire 03301
   July 9, 1987
   Heading
8. Dear Grandmother,
   Greeting
9. 200 Allwood Drive
   Austin, Texas 78704
   February 21, 1987
   Heading
10. Your friend,
    Eric
    Closing

Using Correct Capitalization and Punctuation

Using correct capitalization and punctuation will make your letter much easier for your friend to read. Review the following rules for letter writing.

Heading
1. Capitalize all proper names.
2. Place a comma between the name of the city and state.
3. Put the ZIP code after the state. No comma is needed between the state and the ZIP code.
4. Place a comma between the day and the year.

Salutation
5. Capitalize the first word and any proper nouns in the salutation.
6. Use a comma after the salutation.

Closing
7. Capitalize only the first word of the closing.
8. Use a comma after the closing.

Exercises   Writing Friendly Letters

▶ Structured Application
A. In your best handwriting, copy the following parts of a letter. Use correct capitalization and punctuation. Write the information on separate lines where necessary. Then label each part correctly.

See answers in margin.

1. 336 old mill road phoenix arizona 85040 august 7 1987
2. dear lorna jill
3. 852 main street mount prospect illinois 60056 june 3 1987
4. missing you tiffany
5. dear aunt lynn and uncle tom
6. sincerely yours jeff rodriguez

▶ Creative Application
B. Practice your letter-writing skills by writing to a pen pal. Request a pen pal from a pen pal organization. Your teacher can give you the names and addresses of pen pal organizations. In your letter, tell your age and a little about yourself. You may even be assigned a pen pal in a foreign country. When you send your first letter, write neatly. English may be a foreign language to your pen pal.

446

Additional Resources

Skills Practice Book—page 172
Teacher's Resource Binder
   Reinforcement Activities—
      page 123

2 Writing Social Notes

> **Focus**
>
> A social note can be a thank-you note, an invitation, or a note of acceptance or regret.

▶ Comprehension

Social notes are a form of courtesy that people appreciate. These notes have the same form as a friendly letter except that they are much shorter. Generally, social notes use only the date in the heading.

Writing a Thank-You Note

Here are some occasions that call for thank-you notes.

1. When you have received a gift
2. When someone has done you a special favor
3. When you have spent the night at someone's house

A Sample Thank-You Note

> *July 18, 1987*
>
> Dear Mr. and Mrs. Johnson,
>
> Thank you for inviting me to your summer cottage last weekend. It was great to visit with Jack again.
>
> Riding in your boat was exciting, and now I can say I know how to water-ski.
>
> I really enjoyed myself and hope that Jack can visit me soon.
>
> Sincerely,
> Todd Monroe

447

Part 2

Objective

To identify the purpose of social notes and to write them correctly

Presenting the Lesson

 All Students

1. Read the introduction on page 447. Stress the two main differences between friendly letters and social notes: the length, and the use of only the date in the heading. Courtesy should also be emphasized as the purpose of social notes.

2. Read **Writing a Thank-You Note** on page 447. Most students will be familiar with the thank-you note. Stress the importance of punctuality when writing a thank-you note.

3. Read and discuss **Writing an Invitation** on page 448. Students will already be familiar with invitations, but mainly with the preprinted variety sold in stores. Tell students that a handwritten invitation is much more personal and friendly.

4. Read and discuss **Notes of Acceptance or Regret** on page 448. Students may think that a note of acceptance is not really necessary when they can just tell the person they are coming to the event. Point out that with a note, the person planning the event will have a record of who is coming and can better make plans. In addition, it is a courtesy to write a response to the person who took the time to invite you.

5. Assign and discuss the exercise on page 448.

 Basic Students

Before assigning the exercise, have the students discuss the purpose of each social note described in this part.

 Advanced Students

Have the students design an invitation for a social event. The invitation should feature original art and text.

Special Populations

ESL Encourage students to discuss the social customs of their cultures regarding invitations, thank-you notes, and notes of acceptance or regret. This is a good opportunity for students to demonstrate their knowledge.

Reinforcement

Have the students follow the directions for the exercise on page 448 using these situations:

A. 1. A note to a friend, after he has given you a book
   2. A note to your cousins who have just sent you pictures of their new house
B. 1. A note to an aunt inviting her to a performance of a play that you are performing in
   2. A note to a friend who lives out of state inviting him or her to visit you next summer
C. 1. A note to a friend explaining that you can not attend a Valentine's Day party
   2. A note to your grandmother telling her that you can spend part of your summer vacation at her house

Enrichment

The students may want to write a note or letter inviting someone to speak to the class on a topic they have been studying in one of their classes.

Writing an Invitation

Everyone enjoys receiving an invitation. You write an invitation to ask someone to a party or special event. An invitation should contain a complete heading and this information:

1. Type of activity
2. Purpose of activity
3. Where the activity will take place
4. The day, date, and time of the activity
5. How the person should reply

Notes of Acceptance or Regret

Many invitations contain the letters *R.S.V.P.* near the end. This is an abbreviation for a French phrase that means "please respond." Respond to an invitation as soon as possible. Use the same form you use for a thank-you note. For both notes of acceptance or regret, thank the person for the invitation.

Exercise   Writing Social Notes

▶ Creative Application

Choose one situation from group *A*, one from *B*, and one from *C*. Write the appropriate form of social note for each situation.

A. 1. A note to your aunt and uncle after they have taken you on a tour of their city.
   2. A note to your grandmother for letting you spend the weekend with her.

B. 1. A note asking a friend to go on a camping trip with you and your family.
   2. A note inviting a new classmate to a party.

C. 1. A note telling your cousin you will not be able to spend the weekend at her house.
   2. A note telling a friend you will not be able to attend a skating party.

448

Additional Resources

Skills Practice Book—
    pages 173–175
Teacher's Resource Binder
    Reinforcement Activities—
       page 124
    Enrichment Activities—
       page 8

3 Writing Business Letters

┌─ *Focus* ─────────────────────────────────┐
│   You can get information or order a product by writing a │
│ business letter. │
└──┘

▶ Comprehension

A business letter is written for a specific purpose. It is used to request information or order materials. A business letter is more formal than a friendly letter.

Parts of a Business Letter

1. Heading The heading of a business letter is the same as the heading for a friendly letter.

2. Inside Address The inside address contains the name and address of the person or company to which you are writing. The inside address comes below the heading, but begins at the left margin.

3. Salutation The salutation of a business letter is more formal than that of a friendly letter. If you are writing to a specific person, use *Dear* followed by a person's name.

Dear Mr. Anderson: *Dear Ms. Garcia:*

If you do not know the name of the person to whom you are writing, use a general greeting such as the following.

Dear Sir or Madam:

The salutation begins two lines below the inside address at the left margin. The salutation of a business letter ends with a colon (:).

449

Part 3

Objective

To identify and use the correct form for a business letter

Presenting the Lesson

 All Students

1. Survey the students to discover if any have ever written a business letter. Ask those who have written a business letter to explain their reasons for writing.

2. Read and discuss pages 449–451. Have students find each part in the sample letter on page 450. Particular emphasis should be given to punctuation, especially the use of the colon. Point out that the body of a business letter should include a discussion of specific details as opposed to the descriptive details of a friendly letter. Tell students that not all of the information listed in the guidelines may be applicable to every letter. Emphasize that neatness and organization are necessary in a business letter if the writer expects to receive a response.

3. Assign and discuss the exercise on page 451. Encourage students to mail the letters they write.

 Basic Students

Before assigning the exercises, have the students work as a group to organize the following information into a business letter. Have them correct errors in punctuation and capitalization.

The heading is:
      3419 center road
      detroit,michigan 40007
      july 10,1987
The inside address is:
      sports illustrated
      4301 hampton avenue
      st.louis,missouri 63109

The body should include the following information:

You would like to order three *sports illustrated* posters that you saw advertised in the magazine. The catalog numbers are 4543, 7203, and 4601. The posters are three for $10 plus $1 for postage and handling. You are sending a check for the full amount.

◆ Advanced Students

Have the students write a letter of application for a specific job. The letter should include all the information they would want an employer to have, such as their age, previous experience, and qualifications for the job. They might write a letter of application for a job such as baby-sitting, yard work, dog walking, or house-watching for someone who is vacationing.

Special Populations

ESL Explain formal language. It is the language and tone used in business situations. It should be used in letters to all but those people one knows well. Neither contractions nor slang is used in formal language. Vocabulary is often more difficult, and sentences are longer than is typical of informal language.

Reinforcement

Have the students choose one of the following items and write the letter described. Instruct them to supply any names and facts needed to complete the letter, using their own name and address as the letterwriter.

1. You need information about basketball for a report you are writing. Write to the Basketball Hall of Fame, P.O. Box 175, Highland Station, 460 Alden Street, Springfield, Massachusetts, 01109, for the free booklet "Basketball Was Born Here." Include a self-addressed stamped envelope.
2. You finally received your address labels, but the ZIP code is wrong. The 1,000 labels cost $1.00 plus 25¢ for handling from Imperial Products, 482 Sunrise Highway, Rockville Centre, New York 11570.
3. Your string art kit arrived in the mail, but the instruction booklet was missing. Write to Kelly's String Art Division, Dept. BH-88, Box 36195, Cincinnati, Ohio 45236.

Study the following business letter. Notice how all the parts of the letter work together in a clear, well-organized manner.

A Business Letter

Heading
51 Bank Street
Stamford, Connecticut 06901
September 22, 1987

Inside Address
Tropical Shell Institute
Dept. BH-8
Box 21490
Fort Lauderdale, Florida 33335

Salutation
Dear Sir or Madam:

Body
In the August issue of <u>Better Homes and Gardens</u>, I read your advertisement for your shell collection offer and catalog. I would like to order both of these items. Please send me the following order as soon as possible.

1 shell collection (150 shells)	$12.95
1 catalog	1.00
postage	3.00
total	$16.95

I am enclosing a money order for the amount of $16.95.

Closing
Sincerely,

Signature
Laurie Douvris
Laurie Douvris

450

450 Chapter 25

4. Body The body of a business letter should be short and courteous. It should clearly state your subject.

The **letter of request** should tell what specific information you need as well as why and when you need that information.

An **order letter** should include the name of the product and the number you want. You should also tell where you saw the advertisement. Include the catalog number, size, color, and price. List postage and handling separately. Add up the total price of the order. Finally, tell what you are enclosing with the letter, such as a check, subscription form, or money order.

A **letter of complaint** should politely state the nature of the problem and ask about how the problem might be corrected.

5. Closing The closing appears on the second line below the body. The closing should line up with the heading. The most common closings for a business letter are these.

Sincerely,   Respectfully yours,
Very truly yours,   Yours truly,

6. Signature Write your signature below the closing. Then print or type your name below the signature.

Exercise   Writing Business Letters

▶ Creative Application
Write a business letter to order or request one of these items.

1. You plan to visit California. Write to ABC Guest Relations, 41–51 Prospect Avenue, Hollywood, California 90027. Ask for tickets to your favorite TV show on ABC. Include all necessary information.
2. Write for information on the programs and ways you or your classmates may help people in countries suffering from famine. Write to Group Programs 3-2-1, The U.N. Committee for UNICEF, 331 E. 38th St., New York, NY 10016.

451

Part 4

Objective

To use the correct form for addressing an envelope

Presenting the Lesson

 All Students

1. Read and discuss pages 452–453. You may wish to bring in examples of correctly addressed envelopes to show the class.

2. Stress the importance of accuracy when addressing an envelope. A letter can be delayed as the result of a wrong address or ZIP code.

3. Assign and discuss the exercise on page 453.

 Basic Students

Draw an envelope on the board. As a group activity, have the students write in the addresses for the following examples. Tell them to use their own address as the return address.

1. Hobbit House/ P.O. Box 12684/ Dallas, Texas 75225
2. Ms. Jan Bleeker/Lincoln Junior High School/ 700 West Lincoln Street/ Mount Prospect, Illinois 60056

 Advanced Students

Have the students research the various classes of mail and postal rates. Have them share the information with the rest of the class in the form of an oral or written report. You might bring to class preprinted information on this topic. The materials are available at post offices.

Special Populations

LD Students with difficulties in visual or spatial perception will need assistance in working the exercises in this part. Students may not be able to visualize or determine "half-way down the envelope," or "indent from one-fourth to one-third of the way from the left edge." Provide a marked sample envelope for students to use as a guide.

---

4 Addressing an Envelope

Focus

Your letter will reach its destination quickly if the envelope is addressed and stamped correctly.

▶ Comprehension

Use the following checklist when addressing envelopes.

> ### Guidelines for Addressing Envelopes
>
> 1. Make sure the envelope is the right size for the paper. Do not fold the paper more than three times.
> 2. Put your return address on the envelope in the upper left-hand corner.
> 3. Write the address almost half-way down the envelope. Indent the address about one-fourth to one-third of the way from the left edge.
> 4. Check the correctness of street numbers and ZIP codes.
> 5. Use standard postal abbreviations for states.

Here is an example of a correctly addressed envelope.

Miss Faith Copeland
510 South Fulton Avenue
Mt. Vernon, NY 10550

Miles Kimball
2244 Bond Street
Oshkosh, WI 54091

452

Envelopes for social notes are usually smaller in size. In this case, the return address may be put on the back of the envelope.

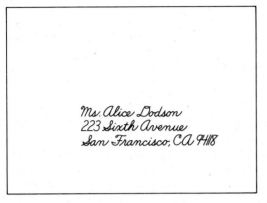

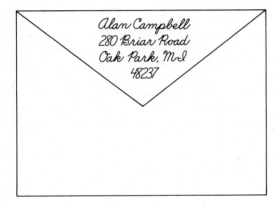

Exercise   Addressing Envelopes

▶ Structured Application

Draw three envelopes on your paper. Use the addresses from the organizations in the exercise on page 451. Address three envelopes correctly to these organizations. Use your home address as the return address.

453

Reinforcement

Have the students draw four envelopes on their papers. Have them address the envelopes to the following organizations, using their own address as the return address, and correcting all capitalization and punctuation errors.

1. Friends of the earth
   529 commercial street
   san francisco, california 94111
2. helmut's hobby specialties
   2728 esplanade avenue
   davenport, iowa 52803
3. h-way products
   1650 mayfield lane
   madison, wisconsin 53704
4. garden camera
   135 west 29th street
   new york, new york 10001

Additional Resources

Skills Practice Book—page 178

Teacher's Resource Binder
Reinforcement Activities—
   page 126
Enrichment Activities—
   page 79

Part 5

Objective

To fill out forms neatly and accurately

Presenting the Lesson

All Students

1. Read and discuss page 454. Stress the importance of reading the instructions on any form carefully before beginning to write down the information.

2. Assign and discuss the exercises on page 455. For Exercise B, you may wish to provide the forms for the students.

Basic Students

When assigning Exercise B, help the students determine which form they would like to fill out. Have them select one that will help them obtain something that they do not have already. First, ask if students have a public library card. If not, this is the form they should fill out and submit.

Advanced Students

Have the students design a form to collect information about the students in the class. The form should ask for an address, telephone number, birthday, and other information that students may want to collect and compile for a class directory. Have the students make copies of the form and pass it out to all the students in the class.

Reinforcement

Obtain copies of catalog or mail order forms. Have the students fill these out. Because they will not actually mail these forms, students can enjoy ordering any products that they want. Check to see that all of the required information is included on the forms.

Enrichment

Have students ask older brothers and sisters, parents, and neighbors about forms they fill out for work, school, or other activities. You might help students to make a bulletin board display.

---

5 Filling Out Forms

┌─ *Focus* ──────────────────────────────────┐
│ Fill out forms neatly and accurately.   │
└──┘

▶ Comprehension

During your lifetime, you will probably fill out thousands of forms. When you register for school, you fill out information forms and medical forms. To get a library card, you must fill out a form. Every time you apply for a job, you will fill out an application form. Here are some guidelines to help you fill out forms correctly.

Guidelines for Filling Out Forms

1. Read all of the instructions carefully before you begin to write. Then you will avoid needless errors.

2. Print the information requested. Printing is easier to read than handwriting. Read instructions to see whether you should use pencil or pen.

3. Correct any errors neatly. If you are using pencil, erase the mistake carefully and write in the correction. If you are using ink, draw a single line through the error. Then write the correction neatly above it.

4. Proofread the form to make sure you have filled in all of the necessary information.

Sometimes when you are filling out forms, you will need special information. For example, when you fill out a school health form, you may need to write the name, address, and telephone number of your family doctor. Some forms require the name, address, and telephone number of a close relative that does not live with you. You may also need to know your mother's or father's business address and phone number. Try to have all the necessary information with you whenever you fill out a form.

454

Additional Resources

Skills Practice Book—page 179

Exercises Filling Out Forms

A. Copy this form on your paper. Then complete it correctly. Use your imagination to supply the information asked for.

VILLAGE OF DARIEN DOG LICENSE APPLICATION EXPIRING DEC. 31st Please Print in black ink. 1987	VILLAGE USE ONLY TAG NO _____ FEE _____ _____

DATE _____ 19____

NAME _____

ADDRESS _____

PHONE _____

☐ DOG ☐ CAT	BREED		AGE		MALE ☐ FEMALE ☐

NAME	COLOR

RABIES TAG NO.	DATE VACCINATED	VACCINATED BY

A RABIES CERTIFICATE OR A COPY THEREOF WHICH HAS BEEN ISSUED WITHIN ONE YEAR PRIOR TO DATE OF ISSUANCE OF LICENSE MUST ACCOMPANY APPLICATION.

FEE $3.00 OR $5.00— SEPARATE APPLICATION FOR EACH DOG

WRITTEN SIGNATURE OF OWNER **X** _____

B. Look at the activities listed below. Choose one. Get the proper form and complete it correctly.

1. Complete an application for a social security card.
2. Fill out the forms for opening a savings account.
3. Apply for and obtain a library card at your local community library.
4. Complete the forms for bicycle registration.
5. Complete the forms for participation in a local park district or community center activity.

455

Using English in Social Studies

This activity may be used to emphasize the importance of letter-writing skills in social studies, and as a means for obtaining information.

Students may find additional addresses by consulting "The Directory of the Chamber of Commerce of the United States" or "The Washington D.C. Directory" in the library. Below are more addresses that students may write to.

Hungarian Embassy
3910 Shoemaker St., N.W.
Washington, D.C. 20008

Iceland Embassy
20022 Connecticut Avenue, NW
Washington, DC 20008

Italian Embassy
1601 Fuller St., N.W.
Washington, D.C. 20009

Using English in ➤ Social Studies

▶ Comprehension

You can learn about foreign countries by writing to embassies or consular offices. The material you receive will help you gather information for reports, learn about a country in which a pen pal or relative lives, or learn about countries you might like to visit someday. Your letter-writing skills can help you learn about faraway countries.

Exercise Writing to Foreign Countries
▶ Creative Application

Here are the addresses of embassies and consular offices for five countries. Choose one, or get the address of the consular office of another country that interests you. Then write a letter of request asking for information about the country you have chosen.

Review what should be included in a letter of request on page 451. After you have written the letter, address an envelope for it. Use the materials you receive to make a display about the country.

1. Canadian Consulate
   General
   Suite 1200
   310 S. Michigan
   Chicago, IL 60604

2. Korean Consulate General
   Suite 600
   500 N. Michigan Avenue
   Chicago, IL 60611

3. Indian Embassy
   2107 Massachusetts
   Avenue NW
   Washington, DC 20008

4. Australian Embassy
   1601 Massachusetts
   Avenue NW
   Washington, DC 20036

5. Irish Embassy
   2234 Massachusetts
   Avenue NW
   Washington, DC 20008

456

Chapter 25 Review

▶ Recalling/Analyzing

A. Mastering Forms of Letters and Envelopes Number your paper from 1 to 10. Tell whether each statement is True or False. Rewrite the false statements so that they are correct. See answers in margin.

1. A friendly letter should sound like a conversation.
2. A friendly letter must include an inside address.
3. The closing contains only your name.
4. Only respond to invitations that you cannot accept.
5. ZIP codes must always appear in addresses.
6. A letter of request is another name for an invitation.
7. The salutation often begins with "Dear."
8. A business letter is informal.

▶ Creative Application

B. Writing Letters and Addressing Envelopes Read the following invitation from Bruce Weinstein. Then write a note of acceptance or regret. Draw an envelope and address it properly, using your own home address for the return address.

> 4402 Nancy Lane
> Phoenix, Arizona 85040
> October 17, 1987
>
> Dear Ellen,
>
> You are invited to attend a Halloween party at my house on Saturday, October 31, at 7:30 P.M. This is going to be a costume party, so start thinking of something original.
>
> Sincerely,
> Bruce
>
> R.S.V.P.

457

Cumulative Review

These exercises provide a cumulative review of the concepts presented in this unit. Each exercise challenges the students to apply several of the skills they have acquired while studying this unit.

To evaluate writing that presents an opinion in Exercise A, see the Guidelines for Evaluation in the Teacher Notes on page 391.

To evaluate report writing in Exercise B, see the Guidelines for Evaluation in the Teacher Notes on page 436.

(These Unit Projects are continued from T. E. page 347.)

For Gifted and Talented Students These students can organize the information that is collected and write summaries. The material could be bound to form an album of local history and displayed in the school or local library.

For an alternative activity, have students prepare a documentary videotape on the history of the neighborhood. Direct students to film scenes in the neighborhood, talk to and film local merchants, and accompany class members to film their interviews. Have the students develop the research material gathered by the class into a narration to accompany the videotape.

Computer Activity: Annotated Bibliography

The class can create an annotated bibliography of reference books by using a simple word processing program. The bibliography may be used by the class for future reports or writing assignments. First briefly review the form used for listing sources in a bibliography. Have students use the word processor to type the author and title of a book or reference source that they used to gather information for a report. Finally, they will type two or three notations about the source. A notation might indicate if all or only certain parts of the book proved useful. Students might give helpful tips for use, such as mentioning tables or graphs the source contains.

Cumulative Review

Composition

▶ Creative Application

A. Writing Opinions Briefly explain why everyone should know how to give first aid.

▶ Recalling

B. Writing Reports Complete each sentence below with the word or words necessary to make each a correct statement.

1. As you read, write what you need to remember on note cards in your own words .
2. To arrange main ideas and details in logical order, you write an outline .
3. A report has the same three main parts as any composition: the introduction , the body , and the conculsion .
4. The introduction of a report should catch the reader's attention and tell what the report is about.
5. When you show where you got your information, you are giving credit to your sources .

▶ Creative Application

C. Letter Writing Write a business letter requesting a list of programs available for the type of computer you own or would like to own. Write to Public Domain Exchange, 673 Hermitage Lane, San Jose, California 95134. The list will cost $2.00. Draw an envelope on your paper and address it correctly.

Grammar

▶ Classifying/Structured Application

Prepositions and Conjunctions Write whether each word in italics is a preposition or conjunction. If it is a preposition, write the prepositional phrase. Then rewrite the sentence. Replace the word in italics with a different preposition or conjunction.

1. A skunk scampered *along* the fence in our yard.　P
2. The birthday card is *for* Lucy.　P

458

3. The kite was ripped, *and* it still flew. C
4. Two squirrels darted *up* the oak tree. P
5. Michael likes crossword puzzles *or* word search puzzles. C
6. Some landowners freed slaves *before* the Civil War. P
7. Were you scared when we drove *in* the tunnel? P
8. A hummingbird hovered *near* the bushes. P

Related Skills

▶ Drawing Conclusions

A. Clear Thinking Read the following sets of facts. Write a reasonable conclusion for each.

1. There is a bad thunderstorm outside. Lightning flashes frequently. The lights in your house are flickering. The electricity in your house may go off.
2. You want a part-time job. A neighborhood store advertises for an "experienced clerk." You have never worked as a clerk. You apply, explaining that you learn quickly and work hard.

▶ Recalling

B. Library and Research Skills On your paper, fill in the blanks with the word or words necessary to make complete statements.

1. Fiction books are arranged on shelves in alphabetical order by the author's last name .
2. The Dewey Decimal System classifies nonfiction books and assigns each book a call number.
3. Reference books, such as dictionaries and encyclopedias, are in a special section.
4. Always consult the index of an encyclopedia to find every volume and page that contains information on a topic.
5. A picture of something with its parts labeled is a graphic aid .

459

They should also note any difficulties they encountered or negative qualities the book had. The student should repeat the entire process for one additional source. If a printer is available, have students print this information. If not, make the material available for viewing on the terminal screen before students make information gathering trips to the library.

For Gifted and Talented Students

These students should collect all the printed annotated entries. Then they should alphabetize, organize, and collate them according to the report topic. If it is not possible to print material, suggest that some of these students write an alphabetizing program, or use software that is commercially available, and alphabetize the entries on the screen according to report topic. This will make the material more accessible for all students.

Additional Resources

Test Booklet
End-of-Year Test—pages 167–176

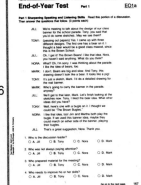

460

POWER HANDBOOK

461

Guidelines for the Process of Writing

These guidelines remind students of the steps they should follow as they write. Encourage students to use the guidelines as a reference during each stage of their writing. The revising and proofreading sections of these guidelines combine items from all of the writing chapters into a complete checklist for students.

Guidelines for the Process of Writing

Prewriting

1. Select a topic and narrow it. Write your topic as a main idea. Decide whether you are writing a **narrative**, a **description**, or an **explanation**.
2. Identify your purpose and your audience.
3. Make a list of details that you could use to develop your main idea.
4. Put your details into a logical order. Choose an order that suits the type of writing you are doing. Some common orders are **time order**, **order of importance**, and **natural order**.
5. As you organize your details, see if you can cover your main idea in one paragraph. If not, organize your details into several paragraphs.
6. Use your organized details to make a **writing plan**.

Drafting

1. Choose a method of drafting that works best for you. (See page 110.)
2. With your topic in mind at all times, begin to write. Follow your writing plan. However, do not hesitate to change your writing plan if necessary.

Revising

1. Read your draft. Keep questions such as these in mind:
   a. Do you like what you have written? Will others want to read it?
   b. Does your writing make sense? Have you achieved your purpose?
   c. Is your writing organized well? Is each paragraph well written? Does each have a strong topic sentence?
   d. Do all of the sentences in each paragraph tell about the main idea? Are they arranged correctly? Should any sentence be moved?
   e. Should any details be left out? Should any be added?
   f. Does every sentence express a complete thought?
   g. Is there variety in the sentence patterns? Do the sentences flow smoothly from one idea to the next?
   h. Is every word the best possible word? Have you chosen language that suits your audience?
2. Mark changes on your paper as you think of them. Keep making changes until you are satisfied with what you have written.

462

Proofreading

Proofread your revised draft. Consider questions such as those that follow. Refer to the pages indicated for specific help.

Grammar and Usage

a. Is every word group a complete sentence? (18–19)
b. When you use a pronoun, is it clear about whom you are writing? (210–211, 213–214, 216)
c. Is the form of each adjective correct? (283–299)
d. Is the form of each adverb correct? (301–308)

Capitalization

a. Did you capitalize the first word in each sentence? (474)
b. Did you capitalize all proper nouns and adjectives? (468)
c. Did you capitalize titles correctly? (476)

Punctuation

a. Does each sentence have the correct end mark? (480–484)
b. Did you use these punctuation marks correctly: commas, apostrophes, quotation marks, hyphens, colons, question marks, underlining? (480–499)

Spelling

a. Did you check unfamiliar words in a dictionary? (162–166)
b. Did you spell plural and possessive forms correctly? (50–55)

Sharing the Final Copy

1. Make a clean copy of your writing. Make all changes and correct all mistakes. Then check your work, asking the following questions:
   a. Is your handwriting easy to read?
   b. Is your paper neat?
   c. Did you leave wide margins?
   d. Is every paragraph indented?
2. Proofread your final copy, reading aloud. Correct any mistakes by erasing neatly and writing in the changes.
3. Choose a method of sharing your writing. Use the suggestions on pages 116–117.

463

Topics for Writing

These writing topics are provided for those students who have difficulty choosing topics on their own or who need some idea starters. The topics are organized into groups and can be used in conjunction with the writing chapters in this book.

Caution students not to rely too heavily on these topics. Rather, encourage students to think of these topics as springboards to their own creativity.

Topics for Writing

Journal Starters

You may also use Creative Writing Ideas as journal starters.

I wish I could trade places with:
    my mom/my dad
    someone in prehistoric times
    a friend
    a famous movie star/sports hero
When I come in last . . .
When I hear my favorite music . . .
By the time I'm 30 years old I will have . . .
The best place to live would be . . .
The kindest person I've ever known is . . .
I feel very lonely when . . .
Today I read in a magazine/newspaper . . .
For me, the greatest honor would be . . .
Sometimes I worry about . . .
A best friend should . . .
A dream I have over and over is . . .
When I'm in high school . . .
A movie that really made me think was . . .
The hardest thing for me to do is . . .
I would like people to think that I'm . . .

Narratives

Tell a story about:
the mystery solved by Sally Sleuth
a trip to _____
the time _____ came to America
something that made you very proud
a lesson learned the hard way
how _____ became rich and famous
a time when you couldn't believe your eyes
an elephant so tiny that it fits in a tea cup
a second chance
a frightening experience
an embarrassing moment
a day that started like any other day, but ended in a very unusual way
someone who won't give up—no matter what
a race with time
a day that wouldn't end
the best Saturday ever
a place where fish fly, birds swim, and the ant is king
waking up to find that your hair has turned purple
someone who lives to the age of 127
a dog that not only brings his owner the newspaper, but reads it to him
a time when the laugh was on you

Descriptions

Describe each of the following:
a gnome

the view from the 67th floor of a skyscraper

how your favorite movie character walks

a frog that can leap fifteen yards

the taste, smell, appearance, and texture of any food

the sound of your favorite music

the sights and sounds of a shopping center

night sounds

a gremlin

the perfect brother or sister

your favorite place indoors

your favorite article of clothing

a sports event

a typical family celebration

a sunset

how an insect bite feels

the smell of tar and gasoline on a hot day

Paul Bunyan's Blue Ox, Babe

Explaining *How*

Explain how to:
make paper-mâché

do origami

make a combination pizza

live with braces on your teeth

use dental floss

study for a test

fix a flat bicycle tire

be a true friend

arrange flowers

tune a guitar

play checkers

pack a backpack

pitch a tent

snorkel

play darts

Explain how each of these items works:
a bagpipe

a fire alarm

a lightbulb

a steam engine

a hang glider

a tape recorder

medieval armor

Explaining *Why*

Give reasons for or against the following:
believing in superstitions

TV time should be limited

a new fashion

winning is not important

movie ratings

intramural sports program at school

conservation is everyone's responsibility

Topics for Writing

465

Give reasons why:

_____ is the best book you've ever read.

_____ is the best kind of pet.

_____ is your favorite music.

everyone needs friends.

you like to participate in a particular sport.

_____ should be added to the lunch program.

everyone should take fire drills seriously.

Reports

Write a report about:

the knights of the Round Table

a famous inventor

a famous sports figure

a famous explorer

a lunar eclipse

meteor showers

what happens in an earthquake

tidal waves

geysers

a famous pirate

the history of baseball

the story of photography

mummies

carrier pigeons

submarines

koala bears

the origin of Santa Claus

how snowflakes are formed

Jessie James

stained glass windows

how tornados develop

black holes in space

how pearls are formed

Creative Writing

an announcement that will change the way you live

an advertisement for a campaign poster—to elect you as President of the United States

a tall tale in which a sports star is the hero

a newspaper story about a strange event

your acceptance speech for an academy award

what if . . .

the wheel had never been invented

all clocks had stopped

your pet could talk

you could see into the future

there were no tears

dragons ruled the earth

what happens to . . .

last year's calendar

an old tennis ball

your first toy

write about . . .

yellow

sour

fuzzy

tired

confidence

466

Guides to Capitalization, Punctuation, and Spelling

Capitalization

Punctuation

Spelling

467

Capitalization

Additional Resources

Skills Practice Book—pages 181–189

Test Booklet—pages 155–160
  Pretest—pages 155–156
  Mastery Test—pages 157–160

Teacher's Resource Binder
  Reinforcement Activities—
    pages 127–132
  Enrichment Activities—
    page 80
  Ideas for Creative Teaching

Punctuation

Additional Resources

Skills Practice Book—pages 190–203

Test Booklet—pages 161–166
  Pretest—pages 161–162
  Mastery Test—pages 163–166

Teacher's Resource Binder
  Reinforcement Activities—
    pages 133–145
  Ideas for Creative Teaching

Spelling

Additional Resources

Teacher's Resource Binder
  Reinforcement Activities—
    pages 146–152

Guide to Capitalization

Part 1

Objective

To apply the general rules for capitalizing proper nouns and proper adjectives

Teaching Suggestions

1. Read and discuss pages 468–469. Stress the difference between common and proper nouns. Discuss the examples of proper adjectives and how they are formed from proper nouns. Encourage students to give examples for each item discussed.

2. Make sure that students understand that in a proper noun of several words, only the important words are capitalized. Articles and prepositions of four or fewer letters are not capitalized unless they occur first or last in the proper noun.

3. Read and discuss Exercises A, B, and C on page 469. Before students begin Exercise C, make sure they know what a movie review is. You might bring to class an example of a review from a newspaper or magazine and share it with students.

Practice

1. Have the students follow the directions for Exercise A on page 469 using these sentences:

1. howard carter discovered the egyptian tomb of tutankhamen.
2. mustapha has studied the koran for many years.
3. i went to the movie with mary and mrs. hunter yesterday.
4. the story of adam and eve is in the book of genesis.
5. paul especially likes mexican food.
6. who was narcissa whitman?
7. dr. hernandez examined audrey's broken leg.
8. that chair is built in the victorian style.
9. mr. and mrs. schultz live in the apartment next to ours.
10. the painting was done by john singleton copley.

Guide to Capitalization

Guide to Capitalization

Proper Nouns and Proper Adjectives

> A **common noun** is a general name of a person, place, thing, or idea.

princess   city   ship   honesty

> Capitalize proper nouns. A **proper noun** names a particular person, place, or thing.

Princess Diana   Tulsa   *Titanic*

A proper noun can be made up of one or more words. Capitalize a important words in a proper noun.

New Year's Day   Kalamazoo River   Johnny Appleseed

> Capitalize proper adjectives. A **proper adjective** is made from a proper noun.

Danish — Denmark   Portuguese — Portugal

Proper adjectives are often used with common nouns. Do no capitalize the common noun.

French dressing   Greek alphabet   Siamese cat

> Capitalize the names of people and pets.

Begin every word in a name with a capital letter. An initial stands for a name. Write initials as capital letters. Put a period after an initial.

Susan B. Anthony   A. J. Foyt   Muggins

Often, a word for a family relation is used as the name of a particular person, or as part of the name. *Mom* and *Grandpa Lewis* are two examples. Capitalize a word used in this way.

Capitalize a title used with a person's name.

A **title** is a term of respect used in front of a name. Many titles have short forms called **abbreviations**. Capitalize abbreviations of titles. Follow an abbreviation with a period.

Mister — Mr.   Mistress — Mrs.   Doctor — Dr.

The title *Miss* has no abbreviated form. Do not use a period after this title. *Ms.* has no long form.

Did Mr. Lee interview Dr. Smith or Mayor Gentry?

Capitalize the word *I*.

Margaret and I walked to the library.

Key to Writing

Take special care when capitalizing unusual names such as MacDonald or Rip Van Winkle.

Practice

A Number your paper from 1 to 10. Copy the following sentences. Change small letters to capital letters wherever necessary.

1. A television series was based on books by laura ingalls wilder.
2. The names linda ann rigby and spencer a. marks were engraved on the plaque.
3. Some people think that thomas edison was a genius.
4. *Dachshund* is a german word meaning "badger dog."

469

2. Have the students follow the directions for Exercise B on page 470 using these sentences:

1. the cowboys drove the cattle along the chisholm trail.
2. anthony and mike are going swimming at holiday sands beach.
3. confucius was a chinese philosopher.
4. my mother and sister work at the john hancock building.
5. we took the train from chicago, illinois, to salt lake city, utah.
6. emily lives in minneapolis, minnesota.
7. we held the picnic at greenway park.
8. thanksgiving day is always the last thursday in november.
9. during fall, the birds fly south to florida.
10. the bus stopped at the corner of euclid avenue and east ninth street.

Additional Resources

Skills Practice Book—page 181
Teacher's Resource Binder
  Reinforcement Activities—
    page 127
  Enrichment Activities—
    page 80

5. The famous scientist, dr. george washington carver, was born a slave.
6. We watched coach burns give an award to t. j. kelly.
7. Stacy and i played tennis against kenny and maria.
8. Mr. and mrs. torres have a cat named trigger.
9. The best teacher i ever had was professor eileen black.
10. Czar nicholas was a russian emperor.

B Number your paper from 1 to 10. Copy the following sentences. Change small letters to capital letters wherever necessary.

1. Chief william brant and chief red jacket signed a treaty with moses cleaveland.
2. Tomorrow, grandpa and i will cut miss quinlan's lawn.
3. President lincoln met harriet beecher stowe.
4. Daffodils, hyacinths, and dutch tulips bloom in early spring.
5. The leader of althea's Bluebird group is mrs. hartley.
6. My uncle mike once met governor charles s. robb.
7. For years, researcher jane goodall lived with a band of apes.
8. One of the speakers was the american artist, andrew wyeth.
9. Either lottie or i can take you to ms. franklin's office.
10. When did marian anderson begin her career?

C Writing

Write a movie review. Include the names of the main characters and the names of the actors or actresses who played these characters. Briefly tell what happened. Then tell why you think the movie was good or bad. Capitalize all proper nouns and adjectives.

470

2 More Proper Nouns

Capitalize the names of particular places and things.

1. Capitalize cities, states, and countries.

   Laredo, Texas, is near Mexico.

2. Capitalize streets, bridges, parks, and buildings.

   The tour guide showed us the Empire State Building, the Brooklyn Bridge, Wall Street, and Central Park.

3. Capitalize geographical names. Do not capitalize *north*, *south*, *east*, or *west* when they refer to directions. Capitalize these words only when they refer to a particular section of the country or world.

   The Millers turned south and drove to Death Valley.
   In the United States, the Mississippi River is the dividing line between the East and West.
   The Adirondack Mountains are located in the North; the Blue Ridge Mountains extend from the North to the South.

Capitalize the names of months, days, and holidays.

Do not capitalize the names of the four seasons: spring, summer, winter, and fall.

   We celebrate Father's Day and the first day of summer in June.

Capitalize the names of races, religions, nationalities, and languages.

   Modern American Indian artists often use traditional designs in their work.
   Judaism, Christianity, and the Muslim religion share a belief in one God.
   The Russians and the Chinese have frequent arguments about their common border.
   Does this junior high school offer French?

471

Part 2

Objectives

To apply specific rules for capitalizing the names of particular places and things; the names of months, days, and holidays; and the names of special groups

Teaching Suggestions

1. Read and discuss pages 471–472. Have students give additional examples for each of the rules presented in this section. Have the students write their examples on the board, making sure to capitalize correctly.

2. Discuss the **Key to Writing** on page 472. Make sure that students understand how meanings can be confused as the result of incorrect capitalization.

3. Assign and discuss Exercises A, B, and C on page 472. Allow students some time to discuss this topic before they begin writing their paragraphs for Exercise C.

Practice

Have the students follow the directions for Exercise A on page 472 using these groups of words:

1. anchorage, alaska
2. the eastern european holidays
3. three miles north of flathead lake
4. winter on nantucket island
5. the salt river indian reservation
6. summer in the big horn mountains
7. california's imperial valley
8. friday, the first day of spring
9. danish cheese
10. the united nations
11. irish linen
12. sandy's chicken shack
13. the eiffel tower in paris, france
14. italian language
15. lutheran church
16. bradfield sports club
17. the largest city in the south
18. the first tuesday in april
19. the fourth of july
20. the new york yankees

Guide to Capitalization

> **Capitalize words referring to God and to religious scriptures.**
>
> | | | |
> |---|---|---|
> | the Deity | the Bible | the Gospel |
> | the Lord | the Talmud | the Book of Genesis |
> | Allah | the Koran | the New Testament |

> **Capitalize the names of clubs, organizations, and business firms.**
>
> Carolyn's dog is registered with the American Kennel Club.
> Have you heard of the International Kitefliers Association?
> Don's father works for American Plastics, Incorporated.

 Key to Writing

Carefully follow capitalization rules. Incorrect capitalization can confuse meaning in your writing.

Little Rock (Arkansas)
little rock (pebble)
I am going west. (direction)
I am going out West. (area of country)

Practice

A Number your paper from 1 to 10. Copy the following sentences. Change small letters to capital letters wherever necessary.

1. Some of the Romance languages are french, italian, and spanish.
2. Pope john paul II is the leader of the roman catholic church.
3. The first monday in september is labor day.
4. Gabriel joined the united states marine corps.
5. The richardsons will drive north to the great lakes.
6. On december 2, 1980, glacier bay became a national park.

472

7. Wendy walked across jefferson bridge and turned west on maple street.
8. The transamerica pyramid is the tallest building in san francisco.
9. Dolores tests computers for the digital equipment company.
10. The elmwood photography club meets every monday in the carnegie library.

B Number your paper from 1 to 20. Copy each of the following groups of words. Change small letters to capitals wherever necessary.

1. denver, colorado
2. african art
3. ten miles east of pikes peak
4. the cub scouts
5. an east wind
6. buckingham palace
7. filipino traditions
8. thanksgiving celebration
9. cathedral square in moscow
10. the arab oil fields
11. a dutch windmill
12. the tribes of the west
13. a jewish temple
14. in houston on tuesday
15. baptist minister
16. national football league
17. a spring hurricane
18. the campfire girls
19. telecom telephone company
20. thursday, july 12

C **Writing**

Imagine that you dreamed you were a crew member on a Viking ship. In your dream, you discovered an island tribe. Briefly describe the island, the tribe, its language, religion, and any other interesting details. Capitalize correctly.

Part 3

Objective

To apply the rules for capitalizing the first words in sentences and the first words in most lines of poetry

Teaching Suggestions

1. Read and discuss page 474. Make sure that students understand that not all poems follow the capitalization rule given, but that many do.

2. Assign and discuss Exercises A and B on pages 474–475.

Practice

Have the students follow the directions for Exercise A using these sentences and poems:

1. susan lives in somerset, a small town near the pennsylvania turnpike.
2. jim was born on april 20, 1972.
3. does the bike path run south of the arkansas river?
4. lake superior is the largest of the great lakes.
5. inez is going to the canadian rockies this summer.
6. dr. hammond is the representative from the seventh congressional district.
7. the blue forest tennis club plays at jackson park in the spring.
8. i wandered lonely as a cloud
   that floats on high o'er vales and hills,
   when all at once i saw a crowd
   a host, of golden daffodils
   beside the lake, beneath the trees,
   fluttering and dancing in the breeze.
   —William Wordsworth, "Daffodils"
9. the sun is a smoldering fire,
   that creeps through the high
   gray plain,
   and leaves not a bush of cloud
   to blossom with flowers of rain.
   —Vachel Lindsay, "An Indian Summer Day on the Prairie"
10. there was a road ran past our house
    too lovely to explore
    i asked my mother once—she said
    that if you followed where it led
    it brought you to the milkman's door.
    (that's why I have not traveled more.)
    —Edna St. Vincent Millay, "The Unexplorer"

---

3 First Words

> **Capitalize the first word of every sentence.**

Workers digging the foundation found a mastodon bone.
When will the eclipse begin?
Look out!

> **Capitalize the first word in most lines of poetry.**

I'll tell you how the sun rose
A ribbon at a time.
The steeple swam in amethyst,
The news like squirrels ran.
—EMILY DICKINSON, "I'll Tell You How the Sun Rose"

Sometimes, especially in modern poetry, the lines of a poem do not always begin with a capital letter.

so much depends
upon

a red wheel
barrow

glazed with rain
water

beside the white
chickens
—WILLIAM CARLOS WILLIAMS, "The Red Wheelbarrow"

Practice

A Number your paper from 1 to 10. Copy the following sentences. Capitalize wherever necessary.

1. the second sunday in may is mother's day.
2. is cotton still an important crop in the south?
3. last year, we had a dry summer and a rainy fall.

Additional Resources

Skills Practice Book—page 184
Teacher's Resource Binder
  Reinforcement Activities—
    page 131

4. do you like italian food? we can get pizza at tina's restaurant.

5. there is a program on television tonight about japan.

6. dr. adams teaches english at alma college.

7. this month has five saturdays.

8. have you seen any movies by d. w. griffith?

9. carol and her family go out east in july.

10. a bird came down the walk:
    he did not know i saw;
    he bit an angleworm in halves
    and ate the fellow, raw.

    —EMILY DICKINSON, "A Bird Came Down the Walk"

B Rewrite each of these sentences. Use proper capitalization.

1. the school orchestra will play two works by wolfgang amadeus mozart.

2. dad went to a lions' club dinner on saturday night.

3. on wednesday, i'll be late for dinner. my girl scout troop is meeting after school.

4. what is the spanish word for *table*?

5. our plane flew east over the atlantic ocean.

6. we celebrate flag day on june 14.

7. are you visiting montreal, in quebec? there, canadians speak french.

8. have you ever seen the sears tower in chicago?

9. governor smith's mansion is on ninth avenue.

10. the Rhino is a homely beast,
    for human eyes he's not a feast,
    but you and i will never know
    why Nature chose to make him so.
    farewell, farewell, you old rhinoceros,
    i'll stare at something less prepoceros.

    —OGDEN NASH, "The Rhinoceros"

475

Guide to Capitalization

Power Handbook   **475**

Part 4

Objective

To apply the rules for capitalizing outlines and titles

Teaching Suggestions

1. Read and discuss pages 476–477. Give attention to capitalization, underlining, and quotation marks in titles. Ask students to give examples of each type of title discussed. Have them write the titles on the board, making sure to capitalize correctly.

2. Assign and discuss Exercises A, B, and C on page 477. Before students complete Exercise C, have them spend some time browsing in either a school or public library. Have them begin the exercise by making a list of the publications they might enjoy reading. This exercise could also spark interest in outside or unassigned reading.

Practice

1. Have the students follow the directions for Exercise A on page 477, using these phrases:

1. *mister mom* (motion picture)
2. *where the red fern grows* (book)
3. *it's not the end of the world* (book)
4. "the pit and the pendulum" (short story)
5. *mona lisa* (painting)
6. *popular mechanics* (magazine)
7. "our solar system" (student report)
8. "junkyard dogs or dandies?" (magazine article)
9. "how To make a radio" (student report)
10. jingle bells (song)

2. Have the students follow the directions for Exercise B using this outline:

rocks
I. types
   A. igneous
      1. basalt
      2. granite
   B. sedimentary
      1. limestone
      2. shale
   C. metamorphic
      1. marble
      2. quartz
II. uses
   A. in building
   B. as jewelry

Additional Resources

Skills Practice Book—page 185

Teacher's Resource Binder
  Reinforcement Activities—
    page 132

Guide to Capitalization

4 Outlines and Titles

Capitalize the first word of each line of an outline.

Notice that the major divisions of an outline are marked with Roman numerals (I., II.). The next most important divisions are identified with capital letters (A., B.). After that, numerals mark the divisions.

Capitalization and Punctuation
I. Use of capital letters
   A. Proper nouns and adjectives
   B. First words
      1. Sentences
      2. Poetry
      3. Outlines
      4. Titles
II. Use of periods

Capitalize the first word, last word, and all important words in a title.

Do not capitalize an article (*the*, *a*, *an*), or a short preposition (*in*, *for*, *from*, *by*), unless it comes first or last.

  Raiders of the Lost Ark (movie title)
  Anne Morrow Lindbergh, *Gift from the Sea* (book)
  Lewis Carroll, "The Walrus and the Carpenter" (poem)

Titles are also underlined or enclosed in quotation marks. Look on page 497 for rules on using these marks. Follow this general rule for punctuating titles. Place quotation marks around titles of short works such as stories, poems, newspaper articles, and reports. Underline the titles of longer works such as books, movies, magazines, newspapers, and television series. In printed works, these titles are in italics instead of underlined.

476

Practice

A Number your paper from 1 to 10. Copy the following titles. Capitalize them correctly.

1. "highwire trapeze artist breaks record" (newspaper article)
2. *the peaceable kingdom* (painting)
3. "the brain is wider than the sky" (poem)
4. "mine strike in fifth week" (magazine article)
5. *pets of the world* (magazine)
6. *the return of the king* (book)
7. "what makes the aurora borealis?" (student's report)
8. "the world's deepest caves" (article)
9. "the kiteflying tournament" (pupil's report)
10. *where the red fern grows* (book)

B Rewrite the following outline using correct capital letters.

indians of the northeast
I. groups
  A. lake indians
  B. woodland indians
II. important foods
  A. lake indians
    1. wild rice
    2. fish and shellfish
  B. woodland indians
    1. corn, squash, and beans
    2. deer and other game

C **Writing**

A severe windstorm has knocked down power lines. You will be without electricity for three days. You do have oil lamps so that you can read. Write a short paragraph telling what books, magazines, and newspapers you would read while waiting for the return of television. Capitalize correctly.

477

Additional Practice

Use Exercises A–D after completion of the chapter.

A Capitalizing Correctly

Copy the following sentences. Change small letters to capital letters wherever necessary.

1. the "grasshopper and the ant" is a famous fable by aesop.
   <small>T ... G ... A</small>
2. cathy and i walked rex across the seventeenth street bridge.
   <small>C ... I ... R ... S ... S ... B</small>
3. the future photographers' club meets every wednesday at the hillside community center.
   <small>T ... F ... P ... C ... W ... H ... C ... C</small>
4. central middle school offers spanish and french classes.
   <small>C ... M ... S ... S ... F</small>
5. last sunday, reverend h. s. russel preached to the methodist congregation.
   <small>L ... S ... R ... H ... S ... R ... M</small>
6. mike's shoe repair is a new shop in centerville mall.
   <small>M ... S ... R ... C ... M</small>
7. *journey to the soviet union* is a book by samantha smith.
   <small>J ... S ... U ... S ... S</small>
8. what are the three colors of the mexican flag?
   <small>W ... M</small>
9. mr. and mrs. richards went to a hawaiian luau in honolulu, hawaii.
   <small>M ... M ... R ... H ... H ... H</small>
10. michele ordered chinese fortune cookies at the oolong restaurant.
    <small>M ... C ... O ... R</small>

B Mastering Capitalization

Copy the following sentences. Change small letters to capital letters wherever necessary. If a sentence is correctly capitalized, write *Correct* on your paper.

1. "Vasilisa the beautiful" is a russian folktale.
   <small>B ... R</small>
2. We met rabbi cohen at the beth hillel synagogue.
   <small>R ... C ... B ... H ... S</small>
3. Bev turned south to get to the library. Correct
4. Dr. cortez studies south american art.
   <small>C ... S ... A</small>

478

Additional Resources

Skills Practice Book
Mixed Practice—pages 186–187
Using Capitalization in Writing— page 188

Mixed Practice (I): Guide to Capitalization — 186

Using Capitalization in Writing — 188

5. Grandpa read us an interesting article, "the origin of popcorn."

6. In november, i will help cook our thanksgiving dinner.

7. Fred's football team practices in the lot on kent street.

8. The boy scouts toured the united nations building last summer.

9. French, flemish, and german are spoken in belgium.

10. San juan is the capital of puerto rico.

C Capitalizing Outlines

Copy the following outline. Capitalize it correctly.

reptiles

I. extinct
  A. dinosaurs
  B. giant flying reptiles
  C. giant swimming reptiles
II. living today
  A. turtles
  B. snakes
  C. alligators and crocodiles
  D. lizards
  E. tuatara

D Capitalizing Poems

Copy the following poem. Capitalize it correctly.

brown and furry
caterpillar in a hurry;
take your walk
to the shady leaf or stalk.

—CHRISTINA GEORGINA ROSSETTI, "The Caterpillar"

479

Additional Resources

Skills Practice Book
Review—page 189

Test Booklet
Mastery Test—pages 157–160

Guide to Punctuation

Part 1

Objective

To use the period after sentences, abbreviations, and initials, and in outlines

Teaching Suggestions

1. Read and discuss pages 480–481. Review the definitions of declarative and imperative sentences. Explain that a period is used at the end of every imperative sentence that does not show strong emotion.

2. Ask students to suggest additional examples of abbreviations they know. Have them write their own names with initials. Point out that some abbreviations, such as the postal abbreviations for states, do not require periods.

3. You might review outlining with students. Emphasize the importance of outlining as an organizational tool for both writing and studying.

For additional information on outlining, refer students to Chapter 24, "The Process of Writing a Report," pages 428–429.

4. Assign and discuss Exercises A and B on pages 481–482. Abbreviations in Exercise A not presented in the text include the following:

ft.	feet
Ave.	Avenue
Aug.	August
Co.	Company
Inc.	Incorporated
Dr.	Doctor
mi.	miles
Ln.	Lane

5. Assign Exercise C on page 482. Remind students to use the process of writing when completing this exercise.

Guide to Punctuation

1 The Period

> Use a period at the end of a declarative sentence and most imperative sentences.

Declarative: The next clue is hidden under that rock.

Imperative: Look under that rock for the next clue.

> Use a period after an abbreviation. To save time and space we often use words in a shortened form. These forms are called **abbreviations**.

The names of states, days, and months are often abbreviated. Except for such abbreviations as *Mr.*, *Mrs.*, *Ms.*, A.M., and P.M., avoid using abbreviations when you write sentences. Look at these abbreviations.

P.O.	Post Office	in.	inch
U.S.A.	United States of America	doz.	dozen
St.	Street	ht.	height
Mt.	Mountain	wt.	weight
R.R.	Railroad	lb.	pound
D.C.	District of Columbia	oz.	ounce

Some special abbreviations are written without periods.

FM	frequency modulation	PBS	Public Broadcasting System
CB	citizens' band	USAF	United States Air Force
M	meter	ml	milliliter

480

The two-letter state abbreviations such as IL, OH, and CA are written with capital letters and no periods. If you are not sure whether an abbreviation is written with periods, look in a dictionary.

Use a period after an initial. We often shorten a name to its first letter, which is called an initial. Always use a period after an initial.

P. Travers—Pamela Travers
J. C. Penny—James Cash Penny

Use a period after each number or letter that shows a division of an outline or that precedes an item in a list.

Punctuation (an outline)
I. End marks
  A. The period
    1. Sentences
    2. Abbreviations and initials
    3. Outlines and lists
  B. The question mark
  C. The exclamation point

Talent Show Act (a list)
1. tumblers
2. tap dancer
3. singer
4. band

Practice

A Number your paper from 1 to 10. Copy the following phrases, putting periods where necessary.

1. 4 ft. 10 in.
2. Washington, D.C.
3. P.O. Box 12
4. Bedford Ave.
5. Aug. 30
6. Butterford Chocolate Co., Inc.
7. Dr. H. M. Ritchie
8. 500 mi.

481

Practice

1. Have the students follow the directions for Exercise A on page 481 using these phrases:
  1. 3 doz.
  2. Ravensbane Rd.
  3. Mt. St. Helens
  4. 7 ft. 5 in.
  5. Dr. Eric A. Cook
  6. Bill's Bicycle Co., Inc.
  7. 50 mi.
  8. Monticello Blvd.
  9. (list) cities in Michigan
    1. Detroit
    2. Lansing
    3. Flint
    4. Holland
    5. Kalamazoo
  10. (outline) Isaac Newton
    I. His life
      A. As a child
      B. As a scientist
        1. Student
        2. Teacher
        3. Author
      C. As a government worker
    II. His work
      A. In physics and astronomy
      B. In mathematics

2. Have the students follow the directions for Exercise B on page 482, using these phrases:
  1. West 25th Street   W. 25th St.
  2. Bismarck, North Dakota   Bismark, N.D.
  3. 3 quarts   3 qts.
  4. October 19   Oct. 19
  5. National Aeronautics and Space Administration   NASA
  6. Amazon River   Amazon R.
  7. Lucasfilm, Limited   Lucasfilm, Ltd.
  8. Mindscape, Incorporated   Mindscape, Inc.
  9. 45 square yards   45 sq. yds.
  10. Berkley High School, Berkley, Michigan   Berkley H.S., Berkley, MI

Additional Resources

Skills Practice Book—page 190
Teacher's Resource Binder
  Reinforcement Activities—
    pages 133–134

9. Pine Tree Ln.
10. (outline) Super-8 Movie-Making
    I. Major equipment needed
      A. Camera
        1. For silent movies
        2. For sound movies
      B. Projector
    II. Other materials needed
      A. Film
      B. Splicer

B Rewrite each of the following phrases, using abbreviations where possible.

1. East 126th Street   E. 126th St.
2. New York   NY
3. Reverend Marsh   Rev. Marsh
4. 4 gallons   4 gals.
5. Platte River   Platte R.
6. Raleigh, North Carolina   Raleigh, NC
7. December 9   Dec. 9
8. Benander Game Company   Benander Game Co.
9. 10 square feet   10 sq. ft.
10. Durapools, Incorporated   Durapools, Inc.

C **Writing**

Write a short note to a friend. Give directions from his or her house to a park or shopping center where you plan to meet on Saturday. Correctly punctuate abbreviations in your note.

The Question Mark and the Exclamation Point

Use a question mark at the end of an interrogative sentence. An **interrogative sentence** is a sentence that asks a question.

Where are we?   When do the geese migrate?

Use an exclamation point at the end of an exclamatory sentence and some imperative sentences. An **exclamatory sentence** is a sentence that expresses strong feelings.

Jackie struck out!   It's a home run!

Use an exclamation point at the end of an imperative sentence that shows surprise or other strong emotion.

Look out!   Hurry!

Use an exclamation point after an interjection. An **interjection** is a word or group of words used to express strong feeling.

Oh! How beautiful!   Wow! What an ending!

Key to Writing and Speaking

When you write conversation, use question marks and exclamation points to show how items are being said.

Practice

A Number your paper from 1 to 10. Copy each sentence. Add periods, question marks, and exclamation points wherever necessary.

1. Ouch! This pan is hot!
2. How many more play rehearsals do we have?
3. W. E. B. DuBois was a writer and a professor.

483

Additional Resources

Skills Practice Book—page 191

Teacher's Resource Binder
Reinforcement Activities—
pages 135–136

Part 2

Objectives

1. To use the question mark after interrogative sentences
2. To use the exclamation point after exclamatory sentences

Teaching Suggestions

1. Read page 483. Be sure students understand *interrogative, exclamatory*, and *interjection* sentences.
2. Ask student volunteers to write examples of sentences using each end mark on the board.
3. Assign and discuss Exercises A and B on pages 483–484. Then assign Exercise C. Students should brainstorm on the scientist and his discovery before they begin to write their interviews. You might have students write their interviews in simple dialogue form, rather than expecting them to use quotation marks at this time. Have students identify each speaker this way:

Reporter:

Scientist:

No quotation marks are necessary.

Practice

Have the students follow the directions for Exercise A on page 483 using these sentences:

1. Wait! You forgot your umbrella!
2. Which boat belongs to Dr. Greene?
3. E. B. White illustrated that book.
4. Do Mr. and Mrs. Petrovic live here?
5. Hey! That's a terrific game!
6. Dan moved to 125 N. Ridge Ave.
7. Watch out for that huge dog!
8. Mr. A. J. Nash traveled to St. Louis.
9. Did you hear the thunder last night?
10. Sir Hillary climbed Mt. Everest.
11. Is that mine or yours?
12. They eat dinner at 5:30 every night.
13. That's not fair!
14. What should I do about it?
15. I guess I'll leave now.
16. Help! Police!
17. How does that machine work?
18. There's a spider crawling on your leg!
19. When was the party?
20. That's terrific news!

4. Mail this letter to Ms. Deborah K. Sobol.
5. Fire! Move fast!
6. Did Vanessa try out for the soccer team?
7. The poet Hilda Doolittle signed her poems H.D.
8. Oh, no! You didn't forget the picnic, did you?
9. Take your watch to Melbourne, Inc, Jeweler for repair.
10. Have you seen the Lincoln Memorial in Washington, D.C.?

B Number your paper from 1 to 10. Copy the following sentences. Add the missing punctuation.

1. Mr. and Mrs. Gregory go to St. Augustine every winter.
2. Great! We got the last four tickets!
3. Dr. Evans will be in his office until 4:30.
4. What circus did P.T. Barnum manage?
5. Ms. Carol F. Lunt will speak at the N.H.S. banquet.
6. My new address is 600 W. 24th St.
7. Don't touch that broken glass!
8. We stopped at an L.C. Carran gas station.
9. How much does that album cost?
10. Wow! We got sixteen inches of snow last night.

C **Writing**

A scientist has discovered a cure for a disease. The discovery has made this person famous. Write a brief account of the interview the scientist gives to some reporters. Remember, the reporters have many questions. The scientist has many facts to share. Everyone is excited. Correctly punctuate the interview.

484

The Comma

Commas signal the reader to pause. This pause keeps the reader from running together words or ideas that should be separate.

Use commas to separate the items in the series. There are always three or more words in a series.

The Jungle Pet Store sells mynah birds, lizards, turtles, and tropical fish.

In a series, place commas after each word except the last. It is important to insert commas carefully when you write a series. Notice how the meaning of this sentence changes when the commas are removed.

The grocery clerk packed Anna's bag with soda, crackers, broccoli, soup, cream, cheese, and peanut butter.

The grocery clerk packed Anna's bag with soda crackers, broccoli soup, cream cheese, and peanut butter.

If *yes*, *no*, or *well* begin a sentence, use a comma after them.

Yes, we're walking.   Well, we'll meet you there.

When you use *and*, *but*, or *or* to combine two sentences, put a comma before these words.

We ran fast. We nearly missed the bus.
We ran fast, but we nearly missed the bus.

Use commas to set off the name of a person spoken to.

One comma is needed when the name starts or ends the sentence. A comma is needed before and after a name in the middle of the sentence. Look at the way commas are used in these sentences.

Peter, what is your favorite color?
Mail this letter please, Joseph.
I think, Abigail, that you are taller than Sara.

485

Part 3

Objective

To use the comma to separate items in a series, after introductory words, before a conjunction in a compound sentence, after an appositive, in dates, and in addresses

Teaching Suggestions

1. Read and discuss pages 485–486. Be sure students understand the word *pause*. Stress that a series always consists of three or more words. Refer students to Chapter 15, "Revising and Combining Sentences," page 269, for more information on using commas in compound sentences.

2. Assign Exercises A, B, and C on page 486. For Exercise C, encourage students to make full-size posters, and to display their finished products in the classroom.

Practice

Have the students follow the directions for Exercise A on page 486 using these sentences:

1. No, I didn't see a flying saucer.
2. Well, we'd better start the game.
3. Jane ran quickly and won the race.
4. Houston, Cleveland, Pittsburgh, and Cincinnati are in the Central Division of the National Football League.
5. Sybil cut the lawn three days ago, but now the grass is high again.
6. Either mother went to the grocery store, or she hasn't come home from work yet.
7. Yes, the T.V. set has been repaired.
8. Well, summer has finally arrived.
9. Barry used eggs, milk, salt, and bread to make French toast.
10. Rick, Becky, Antonio, and Heather are waiting at the corner for the bus.
11. Angela, would you like more salad?
12. My sister's dog, Scruffy, is friendly.
13. Perhaps, Dorothy, we will find the buried treasure here.
14. Our team's best hitter, Joe, sent the ball over the outfield fence.
15. The next meeting will be held on Wednesday, March 19.

16. On May 12, 1987, our class will visit the planetarium.
17. Caracas, Venezuela, is in the mountains.
18. Stevie Wonder, the singer, has entertained many people.
19. The Willamette River flows through Portland, Oregon.
20. I think, Dennis, that your story was very interesting.

Use commas to set off an appositive. An **appositive** follows a noun and renames the noun. It is used to give more information. Notice how commas set off the appositive in this sentence.

Mr. Lopez our swim coach, retired last week.

Use commas to separate the parts of a date. If a date is in the middle of a sentence, use a comma after the last part.

Our field trip to the Brookfield Zoo is on Friday, May 13.
On November 7, 1962, Eleanor Roosevelt died.

Use a comma to separate the name of a city from the name of a state or country.

We once lived near Trenton, New Jersey.
My parents traveled to Zurich, Switzerland, last year.

 Key to Writing

Do not overuse commas. Too many commas make a sentence harder to read instead of easier.

Practice

A Number your paper from 1 to 10. Copy these sentences. Place commas where they are needed.

1. Albany, New York, is on the Hudson River.
2. Friday, May 5, was our opening night.
3. Denmark, Sweden, and Norway are Scandinavian countries.

486

Additional Resources

Skills Practice Book—page 192
Teacher's Resource Binder
Reinforcement Activities—
pages 137–138

4. Will you drive us, or should we take the bus?
5. Catherine added garlic, oregano, parsley, salt, and pepper
   to the spaghetti sauce.
6. Well, what do you think?
7. The candidate, Ms. Wingreen, made a speech in San
   Diego, California.
8. You know, Adele, I'll be away tomorrow.
9. On October 7, 1943, my father was born in Charleston,
   South Carolina.
10. Dad, this is Al Cresco, a friend of mine.

The following paragraphs are missing several commas. Copy these paragraphs, adding commas wherever they are needed.

The first bicycle, the *draisienne*, was built by Baron Karl de Drais. The German inventor first exhibited his *draisienne*, or "dandy horse", on April 6, 1818, in Paris, France. It was made of wood, and the rider made it go by paddling his or her feet along the ground. It was clumsy, heavy, and inefficient.

A Frenchman, Pierre Lallement, was given the first patent for a bicycle in 1866. This bicycle, also called the "bone shaker", had pedals attached to the front wheel. Later models included the high-wheeled bicycle, the tandem bicycle, the quadricycle, and the racer. Bicycles have come a long way since the *draisienne!*

Writing

Imagine that a sheriff in the old "Wild West" has received word that a dangerous bank robber may be in his area. He decides to make a "wanted" poster. Write the information he puts on the poster. Include the city, state, and date the criminal was last seen. Also list a series of physical characteristics of the bandit. Give the robber's real name, using his nickname as an appositive.

487

Part 4

Objective

To use commas in quotations, letters, and to avoid confusion in sentences

Teaching Suggestions

1. Read about and discuss the use of commas in direct quotations on page 488. Point out that the comma at the end of a direct quotation is always placed inside the quotation marks.

2. Read about and discuss the use of commas in letters.

3. Read about and discuss the use of a comma whenever the reader might otherwise be confused. Tell students that it is a good idea to always read their work out loud. In this way they will notice sentences that need commas to avoid confusion. These sentences are not always obvious if the work is read silently.

4. Assign Exercises A and B on page 489. Ask students to exchange papers for proofreading. Have them point out errors.

5. Assign Exercise C on page 489.

Before students begin Exercise C, you might refer them to Chapter 25, "Writing Letters and Filling Out Forms," page 443, for information on proper letter format.

Practice

Have the students follow the directions for Exercise A on page 489 using these sentences:

1. "The statue is three thousand years old," Annette told me.
2. I, too, eagerly wait for your decision.
3. As I sang loudly, the song ended.
4. "In this song," said the singer, "I want you to join me in the chorus."
5. "I will mow the grass on Friday," I promised my father.
6. At the end of the hay ride, cider and doughnuts were served.
7. "I told Jenny," Eric remarked, "that this plane is a jumbo jet."
8. "I hope," murmured Selma as she strung her bow, "that I can hit the bull's-eye."
9. After you move the T.V., set the rocker over there.
10. "The film lasts nearly ninety minutes," the theater manager advised us.

Guide to Punctuation

4 Other Uses for Commas

Use a comma to set off the explanatory words of a direct quotation.

Notice where the comma is placed in this direct quotation.

> Courtney announced, "The movie will begin in ten minutes."

The explanatory words *Courtney announced* come before the quotation. A comma is placed after the last explanatory word. Now read this quotation.

> "I want to go home," moaned Lisa.

The explanatory words come after the quotation. A comma is placed inside the quotation marks and after the last word of the quotation. Sometimes the quotation is separated into two parts.

> "One of the people in this room," the detective said, "is the murderer."

A comma is used after the last word of the first part. Another comma is used after the last explanatory word. You will learn more about punctuating quotations in part 7 of this guide.

Use a comma after the greeting of a friendly letter and after the closing of any letter.

> Dear Agnes,   Sincerely yours,

Use a comma whenever the reader might be confused.

Some sentences can be very confusing if commas are not used.

> Going up the elevator lost power.
> In the grocery bags were in demand.

Notice how much clearer a sentence is when a comma is used.

> Going up, the elevator lost power.
> In the grocery, bags were in demand.

488

Practice

A Copy these sentences. Add commas where they are needed.

1. Benjamin said, "I'd like to visit Boston some day."
2. "This chili is delicious," said my father.
3. As Sheila wrote, the teacher talked.
4. "It seems to me," Carol said, "that this puzzle is too hard."
5. In the story, books were forbidden.
6. When I called, my friend invited me to the show.
7. "Who," the caterpillar asked Alice, "are you?"
8. According to the paper, apples may soon cost fifty cents.
9. In the forest, trails for bikers have been made.
10. "Come here, Midnight," Ned called.

B Rewrite these sentences using punctuation correctly. If the sentence has no errors, write *Correct*. See answers in margin.

1. While Vickie painted Eric sanded the table.
2. "Tomorrow's weather" the forecaster said ",will be sunny."
3. Tony had macaroni salad and dessert. (three items)
4. Ms. Gajda said, "The concert is at seven o'clock."
5. "The radio is too loud", my mother complained.
6. When our team lost the players felt depressed.
7. After jumping the horse trotted, to the next hurdle.
8. Yvette asked, "What's on TV tonight?"
9. After, Mr. Knowlea left his puppy whined.
10. "Three weeks ago today" Meg said "I got my new bike."

C Writing

While visiting an aunt, Samantha discovers a packet of letters in the attic. One is from Lydia Darragh to a colonel in the American Revolutionary Army. Lydia reports overhearing British General Howe planning an attack on Washington's troops at Valley Forge. Write the letter. Include the letter opening, closing, and Howe's words quoted by Lydia.

489

Exercise B
1. While Vickie painted, Eric sanded the table.
2. "Tomorrow's weather," the forecaster said, "will be sunny."
3. Tony had macaroni, salad, and dessert.
4. Correct
5. "The radio is too loud," my mother complained.
6. When our team lost, the players felt depressed.
7. After jumping, the horse trotted to the next hurdle.
8. Correct
9. After Mr. Knowlea left, his puppy whined.
10. "Three weeks ago today," Meg said, "I got my new bike."

Guide to Punctuation

Additional Resources

Skills Practice Book—
pages 193–194

Teacher's Resource Binder
Reinforcement Activities—
page 139

Part 5

Objectives

1. To use the apostrophe to show possession and in contractions

2. To use the hyphen to separate a word at the end of a line and in compound numbers

Teaching Suggestions

1. Read about apostrophes on page 490. If necessary, review possessive nouns in Chapter 3, "Nouns for Precise Meaning," on page 45. Remind students that an apostrophe replaces the missing letter in a contraction. Therefore, the apostrophe should always be placed where the letter or letters are dropped. The correct spelling of the contraction for *do not* is *don't*, not *do'nt*. The correct spelling of the contraction for *are not* is *aren't*, not *are'nt*.

2. Read about hyphens on page 490. It may also be helpful to note this guideline: If a word ends in double consonants, usually divide the word between the consonants. Stress that proper nouns should never be divided at the end of a line.

3. Assign and discuss Exercises A, B, and C on page 491. Encourage students to write Exercise C in the form of a journal entry.

Practice

1. Have the students make these words show possession:

1. men's	7. Judge Schwartz's
2. sheep's	8. dancers'
3. ghost's	9. Rebecca's
4. nose's	10. fans'
5. Curtis's	11. Sam Jones's
6. pigeon's	12. deer's

2. Have the students write the contractions of these words:

they'll	1. they will	6. you are	you're
couldn't	2. could not	7. he will	he'll
she'll	3. she will	8. what is	what's
shouldn't	4. should not	9. that is	that's
could've	5. could have	10. have not	haven't

---

5 The Apostrophe and the Hyphen

Use an apostrophe to show possession. To form the possessive singular noun, add an apostrophe and *s* after the apostrophe.

city + 's = city's   Carlos + 's = Carlos's

To form the possessive of a plural noun that does not end in *s*, add an apostrophe and an *s* after the apostrophe.

gentlemen + 's = gentlemen's   geese + 's = geese's

To form the possessive of a plural noun that ends in *s*, add only an apostrophe.

birds + ' = birds'   cities + ' = cities'

Use an apostrophe in a contraction. A **contraction** is a word made joining two words and omitting one or more letters. An apostro replaces the missing letters.

can + not = can't	we + are = we're	they + are = they'
will + not = won't	does + not = doesn't	she + would = she
you + will = you'll	he + had = he'd	are + not = aren't

Use a hyphen after the first part of a word at the end of a line. W you write, you sometimes run out of room at the end of a line. T you may have to split the word. Put a hyphen at the end of a sylla Then write the second part of the word on the next line.

Before you choose a career, inves-
tigate many fields.

Never divide words of one syllable, such as *slight* or *bounce*. If you are in doubt about dividing a word, look it up in a dictionary.

Do not write a single letter at the end or beginning of a line. For example, these divisions would be wrong: *a- mong, inventor- y*.

490

1. twenty two gallons
2. eighty eight children
3. her fifteenth recital
4. thirty five arguments
5. ninety nine nightmares

e a hyphen in compound numbers from twenty-one through ety-nine.

eventy-six trombones   Twenty-third Psalm

ctice

Number your paper from 1 to 10. Make contractions from the words in 1 to 4. Make the words in 5 to 8 show possession. Hyphenate the words in 9 and 10.

1. it is   it's
2. she is   she's
3. we would   we'd
4. had not   hadn't
5. children   children's

6. mechanics   mechanics'
7. Chris   Chris's
8. cyclist   cyclist's
9. seventy nine   seventy-nine
10. seventh   sev-enth

Copy the following phrases. Decide whether you can divide the word in italics into two parts, each part having more than one letter. If you can, divide the word as you would at the end of a line. Add the necessary hyphens.

Example: the thirty eight *cannons*
the thirty-eight can-nons

1. forty-five *minutes*   min-utes
2. the fifty-ninth *correction*   cor-rec-tion
3. Twenty-second *Amendment*   Amend-ment
4. thirty-four *years*
5. eighty-one *trailers*   trail-ers

6. seventy-nine years *ago*
7. ninety-three *skateboards*   skate-boards
8. twenty-nine *cents*
9. my sixty-fourth *experiment*   ex-per-i-ment
10. forty *clarinets*   clar-i-nets

Writing

Write a daily entry in a ship's log. Include events of the day, the number in your crew, and the cargo your ship is carrying. Write out all numbers. Use some possessive forms and contractions.

491

Guide to Punctuation

Additional Resources

Skills Practice Book—
pages 195–196

Teacher's Resource Binder
Reinforcement Activities—
pages 140–141

Part 6

Objectives

1. To use a colon in business letters and to state time

2. To use a semicolon between two related sentences

Teaching Suggestions

1. Read and discuss the top of page 492. Point out that the colon has limited uses. It should not be overused.

2. Read about the semicolon on page 492. Point out that a semicolon marks a degree of separation greater than a comma but less than a period. Stress that a semicolon separates two sentences (independent clauses), not two phrases. The semicolon, like the colon, should not be overused.

3. Assign and discuss Exercise A on page 493.

4. Assign Exercise B. Have students write their paragraphs in the form of a diary or journal entry.

Practice

Have students correctly punctuate the following sentences, putting in the needed commas, colons, and semicolons.

1. We have a fire drill at 8: 30 P.M.
2. Dear Mrs. Peabody,
   Thank you for the fruit. It was my favorite. I really enjoyed your visit with us last month and hope we can see you again soon.
          Fondly,
          Jane
3. The sisters came home from school; it was time for a snack.
4. Please send me a copy of the letter, my umbrella, and tennis balls.
5. Dear Sir or Madam;
6. Let's go to the lunchroom now, before it's too late.
7. Emma wasn't tired; she had a hard time falling asleep.
8. She looked at her clock; it was only 7:30 A.M.
9. That new girl seems so confused, and I'm starting to get upset.
10. Alexa read two books, a newspaper, and a magazine before 10:00.

---

6   The Colon and the Semicolon

Use a colon after the greeting in a business letter.

Dear Mrs. Winter: Dear Sir:

Use a colon between the numerals that tell hours and minute

8:30 A.M.   3:30 P.M.

Remember to capitalize the letters and to use periods after each lett in the abbreviations *A.M.* and *P.M.*

Use a semicolon to combine two related sentences.

There are two ways to combine two related sentences into one. Th first way is to use a conjunction such as *and*, *but*, or *or* to connect th sentences. When you write this kind of sentence, use a comma befo the conjunction.

> Judge Marino announced her decision, and the courtroom emptied quickly.

The second way to combine two related sentences is to use semicolon (;). The semicolon takes the place of both the comma ar the conjunction.

> Judge Marino announced her decision; the courtroom emptie quickly.

 ### Key to Writing

Correct use of the semicolon will help you avoid writing run-on sentences.

Incorrect: The conductor raised her baton the concert began.
Correct: The conductor raised her baton; the concert began.

492

Guide to Punctuation

Practice

A Copy the following business letter. Use colons, semicolons, and commas where they are needed.

June 14, 1987

Dear Mr. Grant:

   Our puppet theater in Tyler, Texas, will present the story "Cinderella" this weekend. Please print the schedule in the Tuesday paper. The play will be shown on Saturday, July 9, at 11:00 A.M. and 3:00 P.M. It will also be shown on Sunday, July 10, at 10:30 A.M., 2:30 P.M., and 7:00 P.M.

Sincerely yours,
Toy Chest Puppet Theater

B Writing

Up, Up, and Away Day was a special day for your class. Each student wrote a message to be tied to a helium balloon. While holding onto the balloons, you were suddenly lifted into the air. You waved to shouting classmates as you began a five-day journey.

Write a diary. Start each entry with the date and time. Describe where you went that day and what you saw below you. What did people on the ground say as they saw you drift above them? Your last entry should describe how you landed safely and how you returned to school.

493

Additional Resources

Skills Practice Book—page 197
Teacher's Resource Binder
Reinforcement Activities—
page 142

Part 7

Objective

To use quotation marks correctly in direct quotations

Teaching Suggestions

1. Read and discuss pages 494-495. Emphasize that only the words actually spoken should be enclosed in quotation marks. Words identifying the speaker or describing the situation are not enclosed in quotation marks. The words of a direct quotation must be set apart from the rest of a sentence by a comma or end mark in addition to the quotation marks. Indirect quotations are never punctuated with quotation marks.

2. Read **Divided Quotations** on page 495. Some students may have difficulty with this lesson, but they should be introduced to the process. Refer students back to this explanation as they work on the exercises. You might point out that if the quotation is a single sentence, it should be punctuated in that way even if it is interrupted by phrases such as *he said,* or *she commented.* The word after the interrupting phrase should not be capitalized. If there are two sentences, they should be treated as such, both beginning with capital letters and ending with proper end punctuation.

3. Read the **Key to Writing** on page 495. Ask students for examples of other explanatory words that might be used in writing conversations. Other explanatory words include: *wondered, pondered, questioned, wished,* and *dreamed.*

4. Assign Exercises A and B on page 496. Allow students experiencing difficulties to work in pairs on these exercises.

5. Assign Exercise C. Remind students to use the process of writing as they complete this exercise.

Practice

1. Have the students follow the directions for Exercise A on page 496 using these sentences:

1. "Are you hungry?" asked my father.
2. "This typewriter is easy to use," remarked Elise.
3. Frank murmured, "Is it already three o'clock?"

Guide to Punctuation

7 Quotation Marks

When you write what a person has said, you are writing a **quotation**. When you write the person's exact words, you write a **direct quotation**. If you do not write the exact words, you are writing an **indirect quotation**. Study these sentences.

Direct quotation: Steven whispered, "I'm hiding."
Indirect quotation: Steven said that he was hiding.

> Put quotation marks before and after the words of a direct quotation.

Notice that Steven's exact words are set apart by quotation marks in the first sentence.

Quotation marks (" ") are two pairs of small marks that look like apostrophes. They tell the reader that the exact words of the speaker or writer are being quoted.

> Separate the words of a direct quotation from the rest of the sentence with a comma or end mark in addition to quotation marks.

Julie exclaimed, "The band is marching!"
"The band is marching!" Julie exclaimed.

Notice that, in the first sentence above, the comma comes *before* the quotation marks. The second sentence starts with the quoted words. Here the end mark is placed *inside* the quotation marks.

> Place question marks and exclamation points inside quotation marks if they belong to the quotation itself.

Michael asked, "Did the bird's wing heal?"
"It's perfect!" answered Marianne.

In the first sentence, the question is quoted. Therefore, the question mark is placed inside the quotation marks. In the second sentence, the speaker is showing strong emotion. The exclamation point is also placed inside the quotation marks.

Place question marks and exclamation points outside quotation marks if they do not belong to the quotation. Remember to capitalize the first word of a direct quotation.

Did Dad say, "Come home at seven o'clock"?
I was shocked to hear her say, "I'll go"!

Divided Quotations

Sometimes a quotation is divided. Explanatory words, like *she said* or *he asked*, are in the middle of the quotation.

"My favorite movie," Lewis said, "is the original *King Kong*."

Notice that two sets of quotation marks are used in this quotation. The explanatory words are followed by a comma. This sentence has a comma after the explanatory words because the second part of the quotation does not begin a new sentence. Use a period after the explanatory words if the second part of the quotation is a sentence.

"We wrote that," said the students. "It is a group poem."

In this sentence, the second part of the quotation begins with a capital letter because it is the start of a new sentence.

Key to Writing

Said is a common explanatory word used in writing. Try to use a variety of explanatory words when you write. Try some of these.

explained	announced	exclaimed	requested
commented	expressed	asked	noted

495

4. Mamie explained, "The bike path goes past these gardens."
5. "All aboard," the conductor called.
6. Cornelius whispered, "This movie is very good!"
7. "What's on the television tonight?" Gloria asked.
8. Andy wondered, "Will the bus come?"
9. Tom thought he was almost finished. correct
10. "I've solved the mystery," the super detective declared.
11. "Be careful," Adam warned. "There's broken glass in the street."
12. "Beyond the next bend," cried the riverboat pilot, "is a sand bar."
13. "Turn off the water," Cora shouted. "I'm finished washing the car."
14. "This book is interesting," explained Monique. "It is about the Sioux Indian tribe."
15. "I suppose," observed Hattie, "that you are tired."

2. Have the students follow the directions for Exercise B on page 496 using these sentences: Answers will vary.
1. Alex wanted to know where the quarterback was.
2. Danny insisted that we stop for lunch.
3. Dina was wondering why that building is painted blue.
4. Kendra ordered toast with her eggs.
5. Nancy invited Karen over for dinner.

Exercise B
1. Mom said, "Be careful walking home."
2. "I'm getting cold," Robin complained.
3. "Where has the kitten hidden?" Wendy asked.
4. Sheila thought, "The sunrise over the lake is the most beautiful I have ever seen."
5. "Where can I find a good place to eat?" the stranger asked.
6. "The other way was shorter," Hector insisted.
7. Dad reminded us, "Take your keys before locking the door."
8. "I'd like two eggs with bacon and toast," Kevin said.
9. Martin asked, "When will the test begin?"
10. "How can I help Mrs. Sundelius?" Mary wondered.

Guide to Punctuation

Practice

A Number your paper from 1 to 10. Add all the necessary quotation marks. Some sentences are correct.

1. "Drop anchor," bellowed the captain.
2. The cashier asked, "Will there be anything else?"
3. "Take the game home," Sally said. "You can keep it."
4. "What was that noise?" asked my sister.
5. Dora said she'd come at about 8:30 on Saturday. Correct
6. "You can pat Prince," said Linda. "He won't bite."
7. "Last call for dinner," announced the train porter.
8. "What would you do," Mr. Rocher asked, "if the rope broke?"
9. Mike suggested that we knot the tug-of-war rope. Correct
10. "No," answered Ethan. "My jacket is maroon."

B Number your paper from 1 to 10. Change the following indirect quotations to direct quotations. See suggested answers in margin.

1. Mom told us to be careful walking home.
2. Robin complained that she was getting cold.
3. Wendy asked where the kitten had hidden.
4. Sheila thought that the sunrise over the lake was the most beautiful she had ever seen.
5. The stranger asked where he could find a place to eat.
6. Hector insisted that the other way was shorter.
7. Dad told us to take our keys before locking the door.
8. Kevin said he'd like two eggs with bacon and toast.
9. Martin asked when the test would begin.
10. Mary wondered how she could help Mrs. Sundelius.

C Writing

Imagine that you are a musical instrument in a band or orchestra. The musicians are taking a brief break. You have a short conversation with the instrument next to you. Write the brief conversation you have. Use direct quotations.

496

Additional Resources

Skills Practice Book—page 198
Teacher's Resource Binder
Reinforcement Activities—
pages 143—144

8 Punctuating Titles

Put quotation marks around the titles of stories, poems, reports, articles, and chapters of a book.

"Spring Song" (poem)   "The Ransom of Red Chief" (story)

Underline the title of a book, magazine, play, motion picture, or TV series. When these titles are printed, they are in italics.

Mary Jane by Dorothy Sterling   *Mary Jane* by Dorothy Sterling

Underline the title of a painting or the name of a ship.

Washington Crossing the Delaware (painting)
Queen Elizabeth II (ship)

Practice

A Copy the following titles. Add quotation marks and underlining as needed.

1. "Rapunzel" (story)
2. "Fog" (poem)
3. Webster (TV series)
4. "The Muscles" (chapter)
5. Cricket (magazine)
6. Back to the Future (movie)
7. Summer of the Swans (book)
8. "New Bridge Opens" (article)
9. Freaky Friday (book and movie)
10. "Salute to a Tree" (poem)

B Writing

The year is 2020. Aliens have landed on Earth. It looks as if the town they have landed near has been deserted for about 35 years. In a brief paragraph, describe what the aliens find in the town. Include the titles of books, magazines, and videocassettes.

497

Part 8

Objective

To punctuate titles correctly

Teaching Suggestions

1. Read and discuss page 497. Tell students that the names of newspapers are treated like the names of magazines. Both are underlined or set in italics. Make sure that students can recognize italic print.

2. Assign Exercise A on page 497. Then assign Exercise B. Students might enjoy working on Exercise B in pairs or small groups.

Practice

Have students follow the directions for Exercise A on page 497 using the following titles:

1. "Twelve Dancing Princesses" (story)
2. The Outsider (book and movie)
3. "The Autumn Traveler" (poem)
4. Good Morning America (TV show)
5. "Rocks and Minerals" (chapter)
6. Edmund Fitzgerald (ship)
7. American Gothic (painting)

Additional Resources

Skills Practice Book—page 199

Teacher's Resource Binder
Reinforcement Activities—
page 145

Additional Practice

These exercises may be used for additional practice of the concepts presented in this section. Each exercise focuses on a single concept, and should be used after the page number indicated in parentheses.

Guide to Punctuation

Additional Practice

Use Exercises A–E after completion of the guide.

A Using Commas and End Marks Correctly

Number your paper from 1 to 10. Copy the following sentences. Supply the missing commas, periods, question marks, and exclamation points.

1. It was wild.The soccer game was still going on at 8:30 P.M.
2. Ashton, are you going to the movie with us?
3. "Satellites," Ms. Lee said, "are used for communications, weather reporting, and navigation."
4. Do you mean Paris, France, or Paris, Ontario?
5. Well, Tracy has money, and she wants to buy the ring.
6. Get help fast!
7. Wow! I never saw such a huge cave before.
8. On July 20, 1969, the United States landed two astronauts on the moon.
9. Let's move to a seat with a better view of the screen.
10. "Shouldn't you take an umbrella?" Ned asked.

B Using Apostrophes and Hyphens Correctly

Rewrite the following sentences. In each sentence, make a contraction of the words in italics. Change any underlined word to show possession. Add hyphens where necessary.

1. *He will* mail Mother thirty-six invitations.   He'll, Mother's
2. *They have* always bought cider at the apple orchard.   They've
3. Bret dog *did not* wake up when lightning hit.   Bret's, didn't
4. The twenty-two members of the band performed well.
5. Isabelle temperature was ninety-nine degrees.   Isabelle's
6. *We had* finished the game when it began to rain.   We'd
7. Alice *could not* see the acrobats performance.   couldn't, acrobats'
8. I collected seventy-five dollars for the Heart Association.
9. You *should not* phone Cara house again tonight.   shouldn't, Cara's
10. Our seats are in section thirty-one.

498

Additional Resources

Skills Practice Book
Mixed Practice—pages 200–201
Using Punctuation in Writing—
    page 202

C Using Colons, Semicolons, and Commas Correctly

Copy the following business letter using colons, semicolons, and commas where they are needed.

April 12, 1987

Dear Ms. Walker:

We are glad you and your class have decided to visit the science museum in San Diego, California. The museum opens at 9:30 A.M.. There is an electricity demonstration at 10:00 A.M., 1:30 P.M., and 4:00; there is also a program in the auditorium at 11:15 A.M. and 3:30 P.M.

We're looking forward to seeing you on Thursday, May 3, and hope you'll enjoy your visit.

Very truly yours,
Sarah Carson

D Punctuating Quotations Correctly

Number your paper from 1 to 5. Add all the punctuation marks and capital letters that are needed.

1. "Beat the eggs," Julia said, "and pour them in a skillet."
2. "I have some money, but I'm saving it," I told Alonzo.
3. Heather asked, "Where is my basketball, Terence?"
4. "Which do you like?" asked Henry. "Is this photo better?"
5. "Paul, have you ever read about old castles?" asked Ed.

E Punctuating Titles Correctly

Number your paper from 1 to 5. Copy the following titles. Use quotation marks or underlining as needed.

1. Family Ties (TV show)
2. "Paul Revere's Ride" (poem)
3. It's Like This, Cat (book)
4. "Rip Van Winkle" (story)
5. What's Up, Doc? (movie)

499

Additional Resources

Skills Practice Book
  Review—page 203

Test Booklet
  Mastery Test—pages 163–166

Guide to Spelling

Objectives

1. To develop habits for good spelling
2. To understand and apply common spelling rules
3. To become familiar with the use and spelling of words often confused

Teaching Suggestions

1. This "Guide to Spelling" can help your students to become better spellers. Although the Guide is designed to be used primarily as a reference tool, you might find it helpful to read and discuss the Guide with your students early in the school year. Encourage students to refer to the Guide whenever they encounter spelling difficulties, especially as they revise and proofread their writing.

2. The Guide begins with "How To Become a Better Speller." This section contains general suggestions for improving spelling habits. Encourage NSD and ESL students to be especially careful about how they pronounce words. Explain to them that incorrect or lazy pronunciation can lead to spelling errors. Work with these students to overcome pronunciation difficulties.

Your students should enjoy creating memory devices to help overcome spelling problems. First, introduce your students to the memory devices in the Guide. Then, encourage them to make up their own memory devices for words they have trouble spelling. To aid retention, assist students in creating posters or a bulletin board display of memory devices.

3. The second part of the "Guide to Spelling" is a five-step method for mastering the spelling of particular words. Ask students to apply this method to any frequently misspelled words. You may want to display the five steps on a poster in your classroom.

4. The third part of the Guide is "Rules for Spelling." Discuss each of these rules thoroughly with your students. Supply additional examples for each rule. To help your students master the rules, practice exercises have been provided in these Teacher Notes.

Guide to Spelling

Guide to Spelling

How To Become a Better Speller

Make a habit of looking at words carefully.

When you come to a new word, be [sure] you know its meaning. If you are [not] certain, look up the word in a diction[ary].

Practice seeing every letter. Many [peo]ple see a word again and again but [never] really look at it. When you see a new [word] or a tricky word, like *government*, lo[ok at] all the letters. To help you reme[mber] them, write the word several times.

When you speak, pronounce words carefully.

Sometimes people misspell words [be]cause they say them wrong. Be sure [that] you are not blending syllables toge[ther]. For example, you may write *prob[ly for]* *probably* if you are mispronouncing [it].

Find out your own spelling enemies and attack them.

Look over your papers and make a [list of] the misspelled words. Also keep a l[ist of] new words that are difficult for you. S[tudy] these words until you can spell them [cor]rectly and easily.

500

memory devices to help
problem spellings.

Some words are difficult to remember. In these cases, a memory device may help you. A memory device is a trick, or a catchy sentence, that you can remember easily. The device tells you how to spell the word. Here are three examples:

principal   The princi*pal* is my *pal*.
tragedy   Every *age* has its tra*ge*dy.
embarrass   I turned *really red* and felt *so* silly.

ofread what you write.

To make sure that you have spelled all words correctly, reread your work. Examine it carefully, word for word. Don't let your eyes race over the page and miss incorrectly spelled words.

a dictionary.

You don't have to know how to spell every word. No one spells everything correctly all the time. A good dictionary can help you to be a better speller. Use a dictionary whenever you need help with spelling.

5. The "Guide to Spelling" ends with "Homophones: Words Often Confused." This list of words, definitions, and example sentences will be helpful to all students, but especially to ESL students. Encourage your students to check this list whenever they have trouble remembering the spelling of a particular homophone.

6. This "Guide to Spelling" is a valuable reference tool. However, its effectiveness will be enhanced when students use it in conjunction with their dictionaries. After you have introduced your students to the Guide, review with them important dictionary skills. These skills are taught in Chapter 9, "Discovering the Dictionary and Thesaurus," on pages 161–175.

Guide to Spelling

501

Mastering Specific Words

When you notice that you are having trouble with a certain word, take a few minutes to study it carefully. Give it all your attention. If you spend the time and energy to learn it correctly once, you will save yourself all the trouble of correcting it many times.

Follow these steps to master a specific word.

Steps for Mastering Specific Words

1. **Look at the word and say it to yourself.**

Pronounce it carefully. If it has two or more syllables, say it again, one syllable at a time. Look at each syllable as you say it.

2. **Look at the letters. Spell the word aloud.**

If the word has two or more syllables, pause between syllables as you say the letters.

3. **Without looking at the word, write it.**

Be sure to form each letter properly. Take your time.

4. **Now look at your book or list to see if you have spelled the word correctly.**

If you have, write it once more. Compare it with the correct spelling again. For best results, repeat the process once more.

5. **If you have misspelled the word, notice where the error was.**

Then repeat steps 3 and 4 until you have spelled the word correctly three times in a row.

Rules for Spelling

Adding Prefixes and Suffixes

Prefixes

A prefix is a word part added to the beginning of a word to change its meaning. When a prefix is added to a word, the spelling of the word stays the same.

Prefix	Base Word	New Word
un- (not)	+ named	= unnamed (not named)
re- (again)	+ enter	= reenter (enter again)
dis- (not)	+ appear	= disappear (not appear)
il- (not)	+ legible	= illegible (not legible)
pre- (before)	+ set	= preset (set before)
im- (not)	+ mature	= immature (not mature)
mis- (incorrectly)	+ state	= misstate (state incorrectly)
in- (not)	+ formal	= informal (not formal)

The Suffixes -ly and -ness

A suffix is a word part added to the end of a word to change its meaning. When the suffix -ly is added to a word ending with l, both l's are kept. When -ness is added to a word ending in n, both n's are kept.

Base Word	Suffix	New Word
mean	+ **-ness**	= meanness
practical	+ **-ly**	= practically

The Final Silent e

When a suffix beginning with a vowel is added to a word ending with a silent e, the e is usually dropped.

make + ing = making
confuse + ion = confusion
expensive + ive = expensive

advise + or = advisor
believe + able = believable
fame + ous = famous

503

Additional Resources

Teacher's Resource Binder
Reinforcement Activities—
page 146

Practice

Prefixes

Add the prefixes as shown and write the new word.

1. re + appear   reappear
2. in + considerate   inconsiderate
3. dis + obey   disobey
4. over + exert   overexert
5. sub + marine   submarine
6. bi + weekly   biweekly
7. pro + noun   pronoun
8. sub + way   subway
9. inter + state   interstate
10. a + foot   afoot

The Suffixes -ly and -ness

Add the suffixes as shown and write the new word.

1. entire + ly   entirely
2. peaceful + ly   peacefully
3. friend + ly   friendly
4. come + ly   comely
5. usual + ly   usually
6. kind + ness   kindness
7. full + ness   fullness
8. barren + ness   barrenness
9. dry + ness   dryness
10. shy + ness   shyness

The Final Silent e

Find the misspelled words. Spell them correctly.

1. Latly, I have been feeling lonsome.   lately, lonesome
2. That dyeed egg is blueish.   dyed, bluish
3. Refrigerateing bananas is inadviseable.   Refrigerating, inadvisable
4. This homly dog is pricless to me.   homely, priceless
5. Aerobic danceing can be tireing.   dancing, tiring
6. Mom is hopful that this old grill will work.   hopeful
7. The skateers raced in the freezeing weather.   skaters, raced, freezing
8. I watched a truely enjoyable movie.   truly
9. The game is in the nineth inning, and the score is tieed.   ninth, tied
10. The bear wadeed across the rushing stream.   waded

Words Ending in *y*

Add the suffixes as shown and write the new word.

1. bury + ed   buried
2. dry + ing   drying
3. copy + ing   copying
4. crafty + ly   craftily
5. rainy + er   rainier
6. thirty + eth   thirtieth
7. enjoy + ment   enjoyment
8. merry + ment   merriment
9. silly + est   silliest
10. dirty + ed   dirtied

Words with *ie* or *ei*

Find the misspelled words. Spell them correctly.

1. Karen recieved an unusual package in the mail.   received
2. The cheif is the leader of the tribe.   chief
3. I left my reciept on the counter.   receipt
4. Do you beleive everything you see on television?   believe
5. My neice is two years old.   niece
6. We learned about the British system of wieghts and measures.   weights
7. Drivers must yeild the right of way to pedestrians.   yield
8. Detective Raney caught the theives.   thieves
9. The horse nieghed loudly when it saw the snake.   neighed
10. Terry's dog will retreive a frisbee.   retrieve

When a suffix beginning with a consonant is added to a word ending with a silent *e*, the *e* is usually kept.

hate + ful = hateful   hope + less = hopeless
bore + dom = boredom   sure + ly = surely
safe + ty = safety   move + ment = movement

The following words are exceptions:

truly   argument   ninth   wholly   judgment

Words Ending in *y*

When a suffix is added to a word that ends with *y* following a consonant, the *y* is usually changed to *i*.

noisy + ly = noisily   carry + age = carriage
happy + est = happiest   fifty + eth = fiftieth
try + ed = tried   heavy + ness = heaviness

Note this exception: When *-ing* is added, the *y* remains.

bury + ing = burying   cry + ing = crying
deny + ing = denying   apply + ing = applying

When a suffix is added to a word that ends with *y* following a vowel, the *y* usually is not changed.

joy + ful = joyful   pay + ment = payment
stay + ing = staying   annoy + ed = annoyed

The following words are exceptions: paid, said.

Words with *ie* or *ei*

When the sound is long e (ē), the word is spelled *ie* except after *c*.

The following rhyme provides some rules which will help you.

I before *e*
Except after *c*,
Or when sounded like *a*
As in n*ei*ghbor or w*ei*gh.

504

Additional Resources

Teacher's Resource Binder
Reinforcement Activities—
pages 147–148

I before E

belief	relieve	yield	fierce	achieve
niece	brief	field	chief	shield

Except after C

receive	ceiling	perceive	deceit
conceive	conceited	receipt	

Or when sounded like A

weight   eight
neigh

These words are exceptions:

either	weird	species
neither	seize	leisure

Doubling the Final Consonant

Words of one syllable, ending with one consonant following one vowel, double the final consonant before adding -*ing*, -*ed*, or -*er*.

sit + ing = sitting	sad + er = sadder
hop + ed = hopped	stop + ing = stopping
shop + er = shopper	let + ing = letting

The final consonant is **not** doubled when it follows two vowels.

meet + ing = meeting	loan + ed = loaned
break + ing = breaking	train + er = trainer

Words with the "Seed" Sound

Only one English word ends in *sede: supersede.*
Three words end in *ceed: exceed, proceed, succeed.*
All other words ending in the sound of "seed" are spelled *cede.*

concede   precede   recede   secede

505

Doubling the Final Consonant

Find the misspelled words. Spell them correctly.

1. The swimer dove into the pool. swimmer
2. The parachutist jumped from the plane. jumped
3. Two men were caught stealling the race horse. stealing
4. That fish is a keepper! keeper
5. Pete stired the sauce until it was smooth. stirred
6. The bathroom faucet has been leakking for a week. leaking
7. Twelve cousins were seatted around the picnic table. seated
8. Shopers lined up at the door, waiting for the store to open. shoppers
9. The rabbits hoped around in their pen. hopped
10. Phil loanned me his extra jacket. loaned

Words with the "Seed" Sound

Find the misspelled words. Spell them correctly.

1. The tide receeds twice a day. recedes
2. The Southern states seceeded from the Union. seceded
3. The parade proceded to the pier at the edge of town. proceeded
4. The fire chief succeded in controlling the blaze. succeeded
5. An overture preceeds either an opera or a musical. precedes
6. This new list of students superseeds the old one. supersedes
7. The drivers were warned not to excede the speed limit. exceed
8. The tennis champion conceeded to his opponent. conceded

Additional Resources

Teacher's Resource Binder
  Reinforcement Activities—
    pages 149–151

Homophones: Words Often Confused

Choose the right word from the words in parentheses.

1. Kim and Art were (quite, quiet) thirsty after the race. _quite_
2. Alchemists tried to change (led, lead) into gold. _lead_
3. We'd better stop (hear, here) for the night. _here_
4. (Their, They're, There) perhaps the smartest students in the class. _They're_
5. (You're, Your) picture was in this morning's newspaper! _Your_
6. Woody is going (too, to, two) Miami next week. _to_
7. I don't know (weather, whether) it will snow. _whether_
8. Jenny accidentally knocked a puzzle (piece, peace) off the table. _piece_
9. A screw on the frame of my glasses is (lose, loose). _loose_
10. The butterfly broke out of (its, it's) cocoon. _its_
11. Do you know (whose, who's) glove this is? _whose_
12. I will do anything (except, accept) sing. _except_
13. The (capital, capitol) building has a gold dome. _capitol_
14. You seem to (loose, lose) everything. _lose_
15. (Their, There) bowling scores were high. _Their_

Complete each of the following sentences with a pair of homonyms.

1. _____ time for the puppy to have _____ dinner. _It's, its_
2. They signed a _____ of paper promising _____ in the land. _piece, peace_
3. Our school _____ taught a lesson about the _____ of gravity. _principal, principle_
4. _____ is the place to _____ good music. _Here, hear_
5. I don't care _____ the _____ is rainy or sunny. _whether, weather_

Words Often Confused

Sometimes your problems in spelling are caused by the language itself. In English there are many words that are easily confused. These words sound the same, or nearly the same, but are spelled differently and have different meanings. Words of this type are called **homophones**. Here are some examples of homophones.

horse—hoarse pare—pear—pair tail—tale do—dew—due

When you have problems with homophones, general spelling rules won't help you. The only solution is to memorize which spelling goes with which meaning.

Here is a list of homophones and other words frequently used and frequently confused in writing. Study the sets of words, and try to connect each word with its correct meaning.

accept means to agree to something or to receive something willingly.
except means to keep out or leave out. As a preposition, _except_ means "but" or "leaving out."

▶ My brother will _accept_ the job the grocer offered him.
▶ Michelle likes every flavor of ice cream _except_ pistachio.

capital means chief, important, or excellent. It also means the city or town that is the official seat of government of a state or nation.
capitol is the building where a state legislature meets.
the Capitol is the building in Washington, D.C., in which the United States Congress meets.

▶ The _capital_ of Illinois is the city of Springfield.
▶ The _capitol_ of Illinois is a stately building in Springfield.
▶ The senators arrived at the _Capitol_ in time to vote.

hear means to listen to.
here means in this place.

▶ Every time I _hear_ this song, I feel happy.
▶ Reference books are found _here_ in the library.

506

Additional Resources

Teacher's Resource Binder
Reinforcement Activities—
page 152

it's is the contraction for *it is* or *it has*.
its shows ownership or possession.

▶*It's* nearly midnight.
▶The boat lost *its* sail during the storm.

lead (lēd) is a heavy, gray metal.
lead (lēd) means to go first, to guide.
led (lĕd) is the past tense of *lead* (lēd).

▶Water pipes are often made of *lead*.
▶These signs will *lead* us to the hiking trail.
▶Bloodhounds *led* the detectives to the scene of the crime.

loose means free or not tight.
lose means to mislay or suffer the loss of something.

▶The rider kept the horse's reins *loose*.
▶If you *lose* your book, report the loss to the library as soon as possible.

peace is calm or stillness or the absence of disagreement.
piece means a portion or part.

▶After two years of war, *peace* was finally achieved.
▶This statue was carved from a *piece* of jade.

principal means first or most important. It also refers to the head of a school.
principle is a rule, truth, or belief.

▶A *principal* export of Brazil is coffee.
▶Our school *principal* organized a safety council.
▶One *principle* of science is that all matter occupies space.

quiet means free from noise or disturbance.
quite means truly or almost completely.

▶The only time our classroom is *quiet* is when it's empty.
▶The aquarium tank is *quite* full.

507

their means belonging to them.
there means at that place.
they're is the contraction for *they are*.

▶ Our neighbors sold *their* house and moved to a farm.
▶ Please take the squirt guns over *there*.
▶ My sisters have never skied, but *they're* willing to try.

to means in the direction of.
too means also or very.
two is the whole number between one and three.

▶ The surgeon rushed *to* the operating room.
▶ The lights went off, and then the heat went off, *too*.
▶ Only *two* of the four mountaineers reached the peak.

weather is the state of the atmosphere referring to wind, moisture, temperature, etc.
whether indicates a choice or alternative.

▶ Australia has summer *weather* when the United States has winter.
▶ *Whether* we drive or take the train, we will arrive in three hours.

who's is the contraction for *who is* or *who has*.
whose is the possessive form of *who*.

▶ *Who's* been chosen to be a crossing guard?
▶ *Whose* skateboard was left on the sidewalk?

you're is the contraction for *you are*.
your is the possessive form of *you*.
▶ *You're* going to the costume party, aren't you?
▶ Please bring *your* sheet music to choir practice.

Thesaurus

509

Thesaurus

This "Thesaurus" is included as an aid to student vocabulary selection in speaking and writing. Encourage students to use this "Thesaurus" whenever they draft and revise any type of writing.

Introduce the thesaurus carefully and thoroughly to your students. Lead them slowly through the introduction, being sure that they understand how to use the index and that they know the meaning of *entry word*, *synonym*, and *antonym*.

The thesaurus is introduced in Chapter 9, "Discovering the Dictionary and Thesaurus," pages 161–175.

How To Use This Thesaurus

What Is a Thesaurus?

A strong vocabulary adds power to your speaking and writing. It allows you to express your ideas clearly. This thesaurus can help you to develop a strong vocabulary.

A thesaurus is a tool writers use to improve their writing. In a thesaurus, words with similar meanings—synonyms—are listed in groups. These groups of synonyms can help you find the best word to express an idea. They can also help you add variety to your speaking and writing.

Using This Thesaurus

To find synonyms for a word, first find the word in the index on page 522. The index lists, in alphabetical order, every synonym that appears in the thesaurus. Look at the following portion of the index.

fabulous *see* TERRIFIC	520
fantastic *see* STRANGE	520
fearful *see* AFRAID	512
fearless *see* BRAVE	514
finish *see* END	514
fit *see* RIGHT	518
frightened *see* AFRAID	512
FUNNY	
furious *see* ANGRY	512

Some of the words in the index are printed in capital letters. These words are called **entry words.** *Funny* and *Brave* are entry words. An entry word has a general meaning. It is the word under which one group of synonyms is organized.

The words in small letters in the index are synonyms for entry words. *Fabulous* is a synonym for *terrific. Furious* is a synonym for *angry.*

Suppose you wanted to find a synonym for the word *amusing.* First you would look up *amusing* in the index. The index would tell you to look at the entry for *funny* on page 515. Here is what you would find.

510

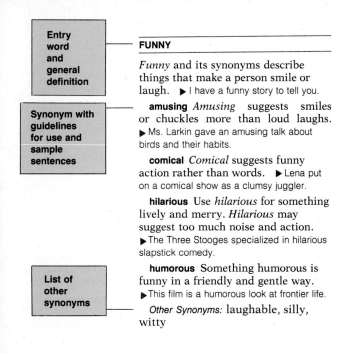

Entry word and general definition

Synonym with guidelines for use and sample sentences

List of other synonyms

FUNNY

Funny and its synonyms describe things that make a person smile or laugh. ▶ I have a funny story to tell you.

amusing *Amusing* suggests smiles or chuckles more than loud laughs. ▶ Ms. Larkin gave an amusing talk about birds and their habits.

comical *Comical* suggests funny action rather than words. ▶ Lena put on a comical show as a clumsy juggler.

hilarious Use *hilarious* for something lively and merry. *Hilarious* may suggest too much noise and action. ▶ The Three Stooges specialized in hilarious slapstick comedy.

humorous Something humorous is funny in a friendly and gentle way. ▶ This film is a humorous look at frontier life.

Other Synonyms: laughable, silly, witty

Understanding the Entries

The entry begins with the entry word, *funny*. This general word is then defined and used in an example sentence. Following the definition and example sentence are synonyms for *funny*. These synonyms include *amusing*, the word you looked up in the first place. The group also includes *comical* and *hilarious*. Each synonym is followed by a sentence or two that tells how the word should be used. Then the word is used in an example sentence. Be sure to read all the synonyms before you decide which one best expresses your idea.

At the end of some entries, there is a list of other synonyms. These words are not defined and not used in example sentences. Be careful about using these words. Before you choose one, look it up in a dictionary. Study its meaning. Then decide whether it is really the right word for you to use.

Thesaurus

511

AFRAID

The words in this group mean "feeling fear."

Afraid shows that the fear has lasted for a while and will probably last longer. ▶ Tony is afraid of cats.

alarmed Use *alarmed* to show that fear came on suddenly and was caused by danger. ▶ Everyone was alarmed by the tornado warnings.

fearful Use *fearful* to show fear of something that may happen. ▶ I'm fearful that the river will flood.

frightened A frightened person feels fear because something has happened. ▶ The earthquake frightened the people in the city.

scared *Scared* is like *frightened*. However, *scared* is less formal than *frightened*. A scared person is not as afraid as a frightened one. ▶ A loud noise scared us.

wary A *wary* person is being careful because something dangerous may happen. ▶ Parents teach children to be wary of strangers.

Ant: unafraid, calm
see also **BRAVE**

ANGRY

Angry means "upset by something that hurts or is against one." ▶ The rumors about me made me angry.

annoyed An annoyed person isn't very angry. The annoying thing usually has lasted for a while. ▶ A barking dog annoyed Carla all night.

enraged An enraged person is extremely upset and may be shouting. ▶ We were enraged by the vandalism.

furious A furious person is so enraged that he or she is out of control. ▶ Senator Wilson was so furiou that he couldn't speak.

upset Use *upset* to show that a pe son feels nervous and troubled. Thi a mild word. ▶ I was so upset that I couldn't eat.

Ant: glad, happy, pleased

ANSWER

To *answer* is to say or do something a way of reacting to a question or request. ▶ Will you answer my questio

reply *Reply* is more formal. ▶ Mr. Summers will reply to your letter.

respond *Respond* suggests cooperation. ▶ When we asked for volunteers, dozens responded.

retort To retort is to answer in an angry or clever way. ▶ "That's none your business," Anderson retorted.

Ant: see **ASK**

ASK

To *ask* is to request something that person wants. A person may ask for information or for help. ▶ We asked directions to the aquarium.

demand To demand is to ask for what a person thinks he or she deserves. ▶ The reporter demanded a answer from the mayor.

inquire *Inquire* suggests that the person has a serious reason for aski It is more formal than *ask*. ▶ Call th hospital to inquire about Dan's condition.

request To request is to ask in a formal, courteous way. ▶ "We reque recess, your honor," said the lawyer.

Ant: see **ANSWER**

512

word *bad* has two main mean-
: "not satisfactory," and "evil."
n did a bad job of fixing the leak. Steal-
s bad. **Caution:** many people use
carelessly. Before you use *bad* or a
nym, think. Decide what is wrong
what you are describing. You
not need any of these words.

reless *Careless* describes a thing
without caring about doing a
job. ▶ Careless drivers should not
our roads.

l *Evil* suggests deliberately doing
ng. Badness shows in nearly
ything an evil person does. ▶ Evil
imprisoned people without a trial.

or A poor thing makes us wonder
could ever be any better. ▶ The
closed because of poor attendance.

cious A vicious thing is cruel. It
be done to hurt someone. ▶ He
d vicious rumors about her.

cked A wicked thing is wrong in
ght and deed. ▶ They had a wicked
to cheat elderly people.

e also **MEAN**
t: see **GOOD**

UTIFUL

tiful and its synonyms mean
asing and nice to look at." *Beauti-*
uggests that a thing is perfect in
important way. ▶ A beautiful vase
a single rose.

ractive Use *attractive* to show that
ng's beauty draws attention.
wore an attractive sweater.

gant Use *elegant* to show good
, grace, and excellence. ▶ The Taj
al is an elegant palace.

gorgeous A gorgeous thing is
brilliant or dazzling. It may almost be
gaudy. ▶ Darlene has a gorgeous red
convertible.

lovely *Lovely* suggests beauty that is
cozy or comforting. ▶ We pitched our
camp beside a lovely lake.

stunning A stunning thing has
striking beauty. Its beauty can
astonish a person. ▶ From the mountain
peak, we saw a stunning sunrise.

Other Synonyms: fair, handsome,
pretty
Ant: homely, hideous, ugly

BIG

Big and the other words in this group
mean "great in size or amount." ▶ A
big shopping mall will be built here.

colossal A colossal thing is "bigger
than life." It seems much bigger than
things like it usually are. ▶ At our
family reunions, we have colossal meals.

enormous An enormous thing is
bigger than the norm for things like it.
The meaning is nearly the same as the
meaning of *colossal*. ▶ Alissa grew some
enormous tomatoes in her vegetable garden.

immense Long ago, *immense* meant
"not measurable." An immense thing
seems too great to measure. The
amount of sand in the world is
immense. A large car is not. ▶ It's hard
to imagine the immense size of the universe.

mammoth *Mammoth* is the name of a
prehistoric animal similar to an
elephant. It suggests something big
and heavy. ▶ The ship struck a mammoth
iceberg.

Other Synonyms: gigantic, huge,
large, monumental
Ant: see **SMALL**

513

Thesaurus

BRAVE

All the words in this group have the meaning of *brave:* "facing up to dangers or troubles." ▶ Brave drivers delivered the medicine in the storm.

bold *Bold* may suggest cockiness. A bold person is quick to meet a challenge. ▶ Perry was a bold explorer.

courageous A courageous person not only faces up to trouble but welcomes the challenge. ▶ Courageous men and women volunteered to rescue flood victims.

daring *Daring* suggests taking risks. A daring person may look for dangerous situations. ▶ The astronauts made a daring attempt to fix the satellite.

fearless *Fearless* means "without fear." A fearless person doesn't think about personal safety. ▶ One fearless doctor dashed into the burning building.

Other Synonyms: plucky, valiant
Ant: see **AFRAID**

BREAK

Break and its synonyms all mean "to divide into pieces." ▶ Tree branches broke in the storm.

shatter To shatter is to break so that pieces scatter. ▶ The glass shattered on the floor.

smash To smash is to break something into small pieces, making noise by doing it. *Smash* is a blend of *smack* and *crash.* ▶ The car smashed through the window of a shop.

wreck *Wreck* means "destroy." Use *wreck* for large things, especially vehicles. Do not use it for the breaking of small things, such as a glass. ▶ Pounding waves wrecked the dock.

Other Synonyms: crack, crumble, crush, snap

BRIGHT

A *bright* thing reflects light well o shines with its own light. ▶ The n is bright tonight.

brilliant *Brilliant* suggests light strong enough to draw a person's attention. ▶ A brilliant flash lit the sk

gleaming *Gleam* comes from an Germanic word meaning " worm." *Gleaming* suggests light li the light from a firefly. ▶ On each were gleaming drops of dew.

glistening *Glistening* suggests sm gleams of light reflected from s thing smooth. ▶ Ripples disturbed glistening pond.

glowing *Glowing* suggests warm even light coming from the thing itself. *Glowing* is used for somethi heated until it gives off light. ▶ W told stories over the glowing embers of fire.

Other Synonyms: blazing, radiant shiny
see also: **SHINE**
Ant: dark, dim

END

To *end* something is to stop it. ▶ movie ended sooner than I thought it we

bring to a close Use the phrase *bring to a close* to suggest ending something in a planned way. A person may bring a meeting to a close, for example. ▶ We brought t meeting to a close by introducing the n officers and singing the club song.

finish To show that a person has completed something, especially a use *finish.* ▶ We finished decorating school lobby.

Thesaurus

514

lt Use *halt* for a sudden stop. *Halt*
gests that the end was not planned
xpected. ▶ Work on the bridge was
d by a blizzard.

her Synonyms: close, conclude,
,

t: continue, keep up, persist

LAIN

xplain means "to make under-
dable." ▶ Can you explain this math
lem?

arify *Clarify* means "to make
r." Use it to emphasize that
ething was "foggy" or murky
re it was explained. ▶ Jack clarified
easons for his disappearance.

monstrate When explaining
udes showing how something
ks or why something is so, use
onstrate. ▶ Phyllis demonstrated how
s in a canal work.

escribe *Describe* emphasizes giving
cture in words. ▶ Please describe
countryside in Scotland.

terpret Use *interpret* to stress
ing something in other words to
ain it. ▶ Jack interpreted Professor
's theories for us.

NY

ny and its synonyms describe
gs that make a person smile or
h. ▶ I have a funny story to tell you.

nusing *Amusing* suggests smiles
chuckles more than loud laughs.
s. Larkin gave an amusing talk about
s and their habits.

mical *Comical* suggests funny
on rather than words. ▶ Lena put
comical show as a clumsy juggler.

---

hilarious Use *hilarious* for something
lively and merry. *Hilarious* may
suggest too much noise and action.
▶ The Three Stooges specialized in hilarious
slapstick comedy.

humorous Something humorous is
funny in a friendly and gentle way.
▶ This film is a humorous look at frontier life.

Other Synonyms: laughable, silly,
witty

GET

The words in this group have the general meaning of *get:* "to come to
have." ▶ Ann got tickets for the play.

acquire Use *acquire* to show that
getting a thing took a long time.
Acquire also suggests collecting or
accumulating things. ▶ Nancy has
acquired a large coin collection.

gain *Gain* shows that a person
worked to get something valuable.
▶ From helping in the hospital kitchen, Rico
gained skill as a cook.

obtain *Obtain* suggests work and
desire. ▶ At last we obtained the funds.

receive *Receive* does not suggest that
a person worked for a thing or even
wanted it. ▶ I received a catalog in the
mail.

Other Synonyms: amass, buy, collect,
earn, procure, purchase, realize,
reap, secure, win

Ant: see **GIVE**

GOOD

The word *good* has two general meanings, "okay; meeting standards," and
"morally right." ▶ You did a good job. It
is good to help needy people. **Caution:** Do
not use *good* carelessly. If you use *good*
or a synonym, think. Decide what you
like about what you are describing.

515

honorable An honorable person knows what is right and behaves in the right way. ▶ Ms. Gordon had an honorable career in the Senate.

pure A pure person or thing is free from guilt or badness. A person may have pure reasons for doing something, even if it turns out wrong. ▶ His motives were pure.

satisfactory A satisfactory thing meets a person's needs or wishes. It is no more or less than what was expected. ▶ Your work is satisfactory.

Ant: see **BAD**

GROUP

A *group* is a number of people, animals, or things that are together. ▶ Every afternoon, we run in a group.

band A band is a group joined for a purpose. One purpose may be to make music, and that is a common use of *band*. ▶ A band of rebels controls the mountains.

crew A crew is a group brought together by their work. *Crew* doesn't suggest that they chose to get together, as *band* does. ▶ A crew of electricians arrived today.

crowd A crowd is a large group. *Crowd* suggests people squeezed together. It may suggest disorder. ▶ A crowd waited outside the theater.

gang *Gang* can mean workers who do a job as a group. ▶ The construction gang worked on the foundation. It can mean a group of lawbreakers. ▶ A gang of hoodlums committed the crime.

mob A mob is disorderly and may be lawless. Do not use *mob* just to mean "a large crowd." ▶ "Sheriff," he warned, "there's an angry mob outside."

ANIMAL GROUPS Specific words a used for groups of animals; for example: bevy of swans, brood of chicks, colony of ants, drove of catt (or oxen), flight of birds, flock of sh (or camels), gaggle of geese, herd o elephants, hoard of gnats, pack of dogs (or wolves), pride of lions, sch of fish, swarm of bees (or eels), tro of kangaroos.

HELP

To *help* is to do something to make things easier or better for others. ▶ Jack helped with the chores.

aid *Aid* is more formal than *help* Use *aid* when the help is serious. ▶ Hundreds aided the flood-relief effort.

assist *Assist* is also more formal than *help*. Use *assist* to show that what the helper does is much less important than what the other does. ▶ Ted assisted a scientist in her experiments.

rescue To rescue is to save from danger. ▶ Dan rescued Carl from the

support *Support* may mean to giv approval or understanding. Howev it may mean meeting a person's ne either by giving money or what is needed. ▶ We support Senator Giles's stand on taxes.

Ant: interfere, hinder

IMPORTANT

Something *important* has great me ing or great influence. ▶ I have imp tant news.

grave Something *grave* is import. and serious. It may be threatening. ▶ Every volunteer knows that there are g risks in this mission.

516

rious *Serious* suggests something
important. ▶ I have to make a
us decision.

rgent Use *urgent* for something that
portant and should get
ediate attention. ▶ The show was
upted by an urgent bulletin.

al Do not use *vital* just to mean
portant." Something vital is
lutely necessary. ▶ A compass is
dy on a hike, but vital on a boat.

nt: unimportant

GH

augh is to make sounds that show
piness or ridicule. ▶ Everyone
hed when Tina told her story.

nuckle To chuckle is to laugh softly
ow tones. A person may chuckle
n something is mildly amusing.
sa chuckled when she saw that she
ld finish in time.

iggle A giggle is a high-pitched
gh. An embarrassing or silly thing
y make a person giggle. ▶ I giggled
ndy's ridiculous hat.

ar To roar is to laugh loudly or
sterously. ▶ The crowd roared when I
ated a chicken.

nicker To snicker is to make a sly
gh, often at someone else's
fusion. ▶ When I forgot my lines, a
of my "friends" snickered.

ther Synonyms: cackle, chortle,
w

E

e and its synonyms all have the
eral meanings "to be pleased with,
njoy." ▶ Is there anyone who doesn't
summer?

admire To admire is to like
something because it impresses. A
person looks up to what he or she
admires. ▶ I admire the shuttle astronauts'
skill and courage.

adore To adore is to like something
so much that you honor it. Don't
waste *adore* by using it just to mean
"like very much." ▶ Hiking and
camping taught me to adore nature.

enjoy To enjoy means "to get
pleasure from." ▶ People enjoy comedy
movies.

love To love is to feel a strong, deep,
and tender affection. People
sometimes use *love* to exaggerate their
likes. ▶ I love hamburgers with onions! In
writing, avoid using *love* that way. ▶ I
love my parents.

MAKE

To *make* is to bring into being.
▶ We'll make omelets for lunch.

construct *Construct* suggests putting
together according to a plan. ▶ With
this kit, you can construct a model plane.

create To create is to bring into
being something that did not exist.
▶ Computer companies created new jobs.

manufacture *Manufacture* once
meant "make by hand." Now,
manufacture means made by machine.
▶ The factory will manufacture farm
equipment.

Ant: demolish, destroy, dismantle

MANY

Many means "a great number of."
Caution: whenever you can, tell how
many, instead of using *many* or one of
its synonyms. ▶ Many people returned
the dangerous toy. Over forty people returned the dangerous toy.

517

Thesaurus

a lot The phrase *a lot* is used in casual speech to mean "very many" or "very much." Avoid it in most writing and speaking.

a number of Many people use *a number of* to mean "many." This phrase is more formal than *a lot,* but it is just as vague. Try to use a more precise synonym or use a figure.

countless *Countless* means "too many to count." It may give emphasis by exaggerating. ► I've been to Jean's house countless times.

numerous *Numerous* is more formal than *many.* It suggests many more than expected. ► We received numerous requests for tickets.

several *Several* means "more than two but not many." ► Many people called, and several sent letters.

MEAN

One meaning of *mean* is "bad-tempered or unkind." ► It was mean of you not to answer my letter.

bad-tempered A bad-tempered person is irritable or cranky. ► You're bad-tempered this morning!

nasty A nasty person is very unpleasant or harmful. The word suggests that people are disgusted by the person's meanness. ► He was so nasty that I walked away.

selfish A selfish person cares too much for his or her own interests. He or she gives little thought to others. ► Carol is too selfish to lend me her ruler.

unkind *Unkind* means "not kind." It is stronger than *bad-tempered.* An unkind person treats others harshly or cruelly. ► You were unkind not to invite Janet.

518

QUIET

All the words in this group mean "without sound." *Quiet* suggests dom from excitement or confusio ► We stayed at a quiet country inn.

hushed *Hushed* suggests that s a person might expect is missing softened. ► The crowd was hushed the curtains opened.

noiseless *Noiseless,* of course, n "without noise." *Noiseless* stresse that there is no noise and often suggests movement without soun ► A noiseless spider spun a web in the morning sun.

silent *Silent* means "without an sound of any kind." ► Space is utt silent.

still *Still* usually means "withou sound or movement." ► In the tim before dawn, the forest was still.

RIGHT

Right has two general meanings: rect" and "proper." ► Your answe right.

correct *Correct* means "fitting t facts," or "matching a standard." may suggest that there are no err ► You have the correct answer. It ma suggest that a thing is proper: ► I want to see correct behavior.

fit *Fit* is used for something tha just what is needed in some situa or for some purpose. ► We bough equipment fit for an Arctic expedition.

proper *Proper* is used for a thing good judgment says is right. ► S always shows proper respect for her pa

Other Synonyms: accurate, exact fitting

Ant: see **WRONG**

e words in this group share the
ing of *run:* "to go by moving the
aster than in walking." ▶ We ran
ver when rain began to fall.

h Use *dash* for a sudden quick
ver a short distance. ▶ Janet
d from the room.

lop *Gallop* is used for a horse's
t running. It suggests running
ut thinking. ▶ A horde of shoppers
ed into the market.

e Use *race* to suggest moving
mely fast or too hastily. ▶ We
through the house, dusting and
ming.

mper *Scamper* suggests small,
movements, like those that a
rel would make. ▶ Dozens of tots
pered in the field.

er Synonyms: jog, trot

words in this group share the gen-
meaning of *say:* "to utter words;
eak." ▶ "We'll begin work tomorrow,"
id.

nounce *Announce* is a more
al word than *say.* ▶ Henderson
unced that he will not run for mayor.

To cry is to speak loudly or
ly. ▶ "I found the treasure!" he cried.

claim To exclaim is to speak with
ement, as in surprise or anger.
u're Ted Atwood!" she exclaimed.

r To roar is to speak in a
tering or boisterous way.
e're number one!" roared Rita.

her Synonyms: assert, blurt, boast,
ment, declare, growl, grumble,
ark, shout, state, whisper

SEE

To *see* is to get information through
the eyes. ▶ We saw a boat on the horizon.

glimpse To glimpse is to see briefly.
▶ Through the fence, I glimpsed a garden.

inspect To inspect is to look at
carefully, to examine. ▶ We inspect
each part of the engine for tiny cracks.

observe To observe is to pay special
attention to something. ▶ Satellites
observe weather on the earth.

sight To sight is to see something for
which one has been looking. ▶ Astronomers have sighted the comet.

spot To spot is to pick out something that is hard to find. ▶ We
spotted Hank in the crowd.

watch To watch is to observe
something closely to find out
something. ▶ If you watch Martina serve,
you'll learn something. However, it is also
used to mean looking at something
without close attention. ▶ They spent
the evening watching television.

SMALL

Something *small* is little in size or
value. It is less than things like it usually are. ▶ Mr. Carson drives a small car.

little Use *little* to show that something is small without comparing it to
other things. ▶ We have a little time left.

miniature Use *miniature* for a copy or
model that is much smaller than the
original. ▶ In the box was a set of
miniature tools.

tiny Use *tiny* for something so small
that it can only be noticed by looking
carefully. ▶ There is a tiny scratch on this
table.

Ant: see **BIG**

519

SMART

Smart and the other words in this group mean "intelligent, alert, clever." *Smart* is an informal word.
▶ She is a smart girl.

bright *Bright* is also an informal word. It emphasizes alertness. It suggests a lively mind. ▶ Andy is so bright that he is already learning to read.

clever *Clever* suggests a mind that comes up with new or unusual ideas. ▶ Clare's idea is clever.

gifted *Gifted* emphasizes an inner intelligence or talent rather than learning or experience. ▶ Carl is a gifted musician.

intelligent *Intelligent* emphasizes the ability to learn or to deal with new situations. ▶ We need intelligent leaders for the hard times ahead.

STRANGE

Something *strange* is out of the ordinary, peculiar, or odd. ▶ I have a strange story to tell you.

fantastic Use *fantastic* for a thing so wildly different from experience that it seems to have come from a dream. ▶ The ship was attacked by fantastic furry creatures.

mysterious Use *mysterious* for a thing that is unknown, unexplained, or secret. ▶ Duane is behaving in a mysterious way.

peculiar Use *peculiar* for a thing that is puzzling or difficult to explain. ▶ Dr. Christie had a peculiar machine with her.

weird Use *weird* for a thing so strange that it doesn't seem to be real. ▶ A weird green light filled the sky.

Other Synonyms: extraordinary, unfamiliar, unusual
Ant: familiar, ordinary, usual

TEACH

To *teach* is to show someone how something or help someone learn something. ▶ Teach me to play the

coach *Coach* combines the mea of *instruct* and *train*. Coaching in volves step-by-step guidance. ▶ the dance, Carl coached me in the lat steps.

instruct To instruct is to teach according to some system, usual particular subject. ▶ Lois will inst you in the use of the computer.

train To train is to develop a particular skill, or to teach a per do a particular job or follow a particular career. ▶ Renata has b trained in first-aid.

Other Synonyms: drill, educate, school

TERRIFIC

The words in this group are ofte in casual speech to mean "unusu fine or enjoyable." This is not the use for these words. Each has a s ic meaning of its own. *Terrific* act means "terrifying, dreadful." ▶ rific fire raged through the village.

fabulous *Fabulous* means "incre ible, astounding." It refers to thi that might be in a fable rather th real life. ▶ They described a fabulo of glass on the moon.

remarkable A remarkable thing one that people notice because it exceptional for its type. ▶ She ha remarkable strength.

...nsational A sensational thing
...es strong feeling or great
...ement. ▸The end of the game was
...ational.

...nderful Something wonderful
...es wonder or amazement. ▸Toni
...n a wonderful display of magic.

...VEL

...words in this group share the gen-
... meaning of *travel:* "to go from one
...e to another." ▸Someday I'm
... to travel to China.

...rney *Journey* once meant "a day's
...el." Now, it suggests a long and
...cult trip. ▸They journeyed through
...ungles of the Amazon.

...am *Roam* suggests freedom and
...sure. ▸I could spend hours roaming
...gh a hardware store.

...nder *Wander* emphasizes aimless-
... or lack of purpose. ▸We
...dered through the mall until the rain
...ped.

...K

...*alk* is to go on foot at a normal
...e, not running. ▸We can walk to the
... from here.

...ce Use *pace* for walking back and
...h. Often, pacing suggests
...ousness or boredom. ▸I paced the
...ay, waiting to see Dr. Hirsch.

stride Use *stride* for walking with
long steps, in a vigorous or bold
way. ▸Dan strode to the counter and
demanded a refund.

strut Use *strut* for walking in a
proud or showy way. ▸The winners
strutted off the field.

trudge Use *trudge* for the way a tired
or unhappy person would walk. ▸The
losers trudged off the field.

Other Synonyms: hike, march,
parade, saunter, step, stroll, tramp,
tread

WRONG

Wrong has several meanings. The one
shared by the words in this group is
"not what is true, correct, or
wanted." ▸We made a wrong turn.

inaccurate Something inaccurate is
wrong because it is not exact or
precise. ▸Your count of tickets was
inaccurate.

incorrect *Incorrect* simply means
"not correct." It is more formal than
wrong. Many people consider it more
polite. ▸Your information is incorrect.

mistaken *Mistaken* suggests being
wrong by accident. ▸I was mistaken
about the bus schedule.

521

Index

522

Thesaurus

Thesaurus

523

Thesaurus

Index

528

Reference books
  taking notes from, 424
  using to find and develop topics,
    107, 422
  see also Resources
Religions, capitalization of names of,
  471
Reports, 421–41
  body of, 432–33
  conclusion of, 434–35
  crediting sources, 435
  finding and limiting topic for,
    422–23
  gathering information for, 424–25
  introductions for, 430–31
  organizing notes for, 426–27
  outlining, 428–29
  parts of, 430
  revising, 436–37
  titles of, 476
Request, letter of, 451
Research
  for explanatory writing, 180
  to find ideas for writing, 103
  see also Reference books; Resources
Resources, 403–11
  almanacs and yearbooks, 410
  atlases, 410
  card catalogs, 403–405
  dictionaries, 409
  encyclopedias, 406–408
  graphic aids, 416–17
  magazines and newspapers, 410
  interviews, 414–15
  vertical files, 410
Restatement
  as context clue, 148
  key words signaling, 149
Return address, 452, 453
Reviewing, in the SQ3R method, 133
Revising, 112–15
  description, 338–39
  explanatory writing, 186–88
  guidelines for, 238, 462
  narrative, 238–39

opinions, 388–89
  reports, 436–37
Rhyme, 320
Rhythm, 320–21
rise, raise, 82
R.S.V.P., 448
Run-on sentences, 270

-s
  to form plurals, 50
  to form present tense, 73
Sacred words, capitalization of, 472
Salutations
  in business letters, 449, 450
  in friendly letters, 445, 446
Scanning, 131–32
"seed" sound, spelling words with,
  505
Semicolons, 492
Sensory details, in description, 332,
  334
Sensory images, 323
Sensory order, 337
Sentences, 17–43, 270–81
  beginning with *here, there,* and
    where, 28, 198
  capitalization in, 474
  colons in, 492
  combining, 272–73
  commas in, 485–86
  compound predicates in, 36–37
  compound subjects in, 34–35
  declarative, 30, 480
  defined, 18
  end punctuation of, 30, 480, 483
  exclamatory, 30, 483
  fragments, 18–19
  groups of words added to, 277–78
  imperative, 30, 480, 483
  interrogative, 30, 483
  predicates of, 20–21, 22–23, 36–37
  punctuation in, 480, 483
  run-on, 270
  subjects in different positions,
    28–29

Editorial Credits

Executive Editor: Kathleen Laya
Managing Editor: Geraldine Macsai

Executive Editor for Language Arts: Bonnie L. Dobkin
Senior Editor: James M. LiSacchi
Editor: Julie A. Schumacher
Associate Editors: Christine Iversen, Susan Nisson, Virginia Swanton
Assistant Editor: Marcia Mann
Rights and Permissions: Irma Rosenberg, Betty Godvik
Editorial Assistant: Nanci Connors

Senior Designer: Mary MacDonald
Design and Art Supervision: Dale Běda, Donna Cook, Laima T. Gecas, Luis Ramirez, Chestnut House
TE: Diane R. Johnson
Cover Design: Mary MacDonald, Laima T. Gecas

538

Acknowledgments

Associated Book Publishers Ltd.: For "The Paint Box" by E.V. Rieu, from *The Flattered Flying Fish* copyright by Methuen & Company. Atheneum Publishers, Inc.: For an excerpt from "Your Thing," from *Today Is Saturday* by Zilpha Keatley Snyder; copyright © 1969 by Zilpha Keatley Snyder. Alan Bold: For "Lullaby" by Alan Bold, from *A Very First Book of Poetry*, compiled by John Foster. Tricia Connor: For "How To Blow Your Nose" by Tricia Connor, from *Enter* Syndicated strip, Children's Television Workshop, New York. Crown Publishers Inc.: For "Rain Song," from *The Complete Cheerful Cherub* by Rebecca McCann; copyright 1932 by Covici-Friede, Inc., copyright renewed © 1960 by Crown Publishers, Inc. The Dial Press: For a brief excerpt from *The Unicorn and the Lake* by Marianna Mayer; copyright © 1982 by Marianna Mayer. Harper & Row Publishers, Inc.: For "Cynthia in the Snow," from *Bronzeville Boys and Girls* by Gwendolyn Brooks; copyright 1956 by Gwendolyn Brooks Blakely. For "A Dragonfly," from *Eleanor Farjeon's Poems for Children* (J.B. Lippincott); copyright 1933, © 1961 by Eleanor Farjeon. For "So Will I" by Charlotte Zolotow from *River Winding*: Poems by Charlotte Zolotow (Thomas Y. Crowell), copyright 1970 by Charlotte Zolotow. For a brief excerpt from *Sounder* by William Armstrong; copyright 1969. Holt, Rinehart and Winston: For "The Dark Gray Clouds," from *The Sun Is a Golden Earring* by Natalia M. Belting; copyright © 1962 by Natalia Belting. Beatrice Janosco: For "The Garden Hose" by Beatrice Janosco; reprinted by permission of the author. Alfred A. Knopf, Inc.: For "Windshield Wipers Wipe the Windshield," from *Nuts to You and Nuts to Me: An Alphabet of Poems* by Mary Ann Hoberman; copyright © 1974 by Mary Ann Hoberman. Little, Brown and Company: For "The Rhinoceros" by Ogden Nash; Copyright 1933 by Ogden Nash, first appeared in *The New Yorker*. Alonzo Lopez: For "I Go Forth to Move about the Earth," by Alonzo Lopez, from *The Whispering Wind*; copyright © 1972 by Doubleday and Company, Inc. Lothrop, Lee & Shepard Books (A Division of William Morrow and Company): For "The Sidewalk Racer," from *The Sidewalk Racer And Other Poems of Sports and Motion* by Lillian Morrison; copyright © 1977 by Lillian Morrison. Macmillan Publishing Company: For "Some People," from *Poems* by Rachel Field; copyright 1957 by Macmillan Publishing Company. The New York Times: For "Moonlight" by Maud E. Uschold; copyright © 1951 by The New York Times Company. Peter Pauper Press: For a haiku poem by the poet Shosen from *Japanese Haiku* translated by Peter Beilenson; copyright 1955 by Peter Pauper Press. The Putnam Publishing Group: For an entry "cook" from *The New Roget's Thesaurus in Dictionary Form* edited by Norman Lewis; copyright © 1961 by G.P. Putnam's Sons. Random House, Inc.: For a brief excerpt from "A Christmas Memory" by Truman Capote, from *Selected Writings of Truman Capote*; copyright 1956 by Truman Capote. For "The Night Is a Big Black Cat" by G. Orr Clark, from *The Random House Book of Poetry for Children*, edited by Jack Prelutsky. Marian Reiner: For "Foghorns," from *I Thought I Heard the City* by Lilian Moore; copyright ©1969 by Lilian Moore. Scholastic Inc.: For a brief excerpt from "The Science of Fighting Fires" by James Baggett, from *Science World* (November 1, 1985). Charles Scribner's Sons: For "Coyote and the Money Tree" by Tina Naiche, adapted from *And It Is Still That Way*, Legends told by Arizona Indian Children, with notes by Byrd Baylor; copyright © 1976 by Byrd Baylor. For a brief excerpt from "Bull Fighting a Tragedy," reprinted from *By-Line: Ernest Hemingway* edited by William White; copyright © 1967 By-Line Ernest Hemingway, Inc. Simon & Schuster, Inc.: For p. 737 of *Webster's New World Dictionary*, Student Edition; copyright © 1981 by Simon & Schuster, Inc. World Book, Inc.: For an entry from the Index, and articles on "Arthur Mitchell" by Dianne L. Woodruff and "Annie Oakley" by Howard R. Lamar, and an excerpt from the article "Guitar" by Winston Irving Tan, from *The World Book Encyclopedia*; copyright © 1986 by World Book, Inc. Every effort has been made to trace the ownership of all copyrighted material found in this book and to make full acknowledgment for its use. Portions of the material in this book were previously published under the title *Building English Skills*, © McDougal, Littell & Co.

Additional Acknowledgments for Teacher's Edition

Atheneum: For "Flashlight" and "Balloons," from *Flashlight and Other Poems* by Judith Thurman; copyright © 1976 by Judith Thurman. Boy Scouts of America: For a brief excerpt from *Revised Handbook for Boys*, Thirty-Eighth Printing; copyright 1945 by Boy Scouts of America. Doubleday and Co.: For a brief excerpt from *Go Tell It On the Mountain* by James Baldwin; copyright 1953. For "Adjectives" and "Thoughts," from *Words Words Words* by Mary O'Neill; copyright © 1966 by Mary O'Neill. Norma Millay Ellis: For "The Unexplorer," from *Collected Poems*, Harper and Row; by Edna St. Vincent Millay; copyright 1922, 1950 by Edna St. Vincent Millay. Encyclopaedia Britannica, Inc.: An excerpt reprinted from "Turtle" in *Compton's Encyclopedia* © 1986 by Encyclopaedia Britannica, Inc. Golden Press: For an excerpt on "Marco Polo," from *The Golden Book Encyclopedia*, Volume IX, by Bertha Morris Parker; copyright © 1959 by Golden Press, Inc. Harcourt Brace Jovanovich, Inc.: For a brief excerpt from *The Story of the Dictionary* by Robert Kraske; copyright © 1975 by Robert Kraske. For "Snow Toward Evening" by Melville Cane, from *So That It Flower*; copyright 1926 by Harcourt Brace Jovanovich, Inc.; renewed copyright 1954 by Melville Cane. Harper and Row, Publishers Inc.: For a brief excerpt from *Charlotte's Web* by E.B. White; copyright 1952 by Harper and Row. For "What Did?" and "How to Make a Swing with No Rope or Board or Nails," from *A Light in the Attic* by Shel Silverstein; copyright © 1981 by Snake Eye Music, Inc. For "Recipe for a Hippopotamus Sandwich" and "Spaghetti," from *Where the Sidewalk Ends* by Shel Silverstein; copyright © 1974 by Snake Eye Music, Inc. Holiday House, Inc.: For an excerpt from "Iskwas," from *The Great White* by Jane and Paul Annexter; copyright © 1966 by Holiday House, Inc. Holt, Rinehart and Winston: For a brief excerpt from *Lassie Come Home* by Eric Knight; copyright © 1981 by Holt Rinehart & Winston. J.B. Lippincott Company: For a brief excerpt from *Where the Lilies Bloom* by Vera and Bill Cleaver; copyright © 1969 by Vera and William J. Cleaver. For a brief excerpt from *To Kill a Mockingbird* by Harper Lee; copyright 1960 by Harper Lee. Little, Brown and Company: For "The Eel" and "The Octopus," from *Verses from 1929 On* by Ogden Nash; copyright 1942 by Ogden Nash, first appeared in *The New Yorker*. Rand McNally & Company: For a brief excerpt from *The American Reader* by

Paul M. Angle. Harold Ober Associates: For an excerpt from "The Big Wave" by Pearl S. Buck, from *Jack and Jill*, October 1947; copyright 1947 by the Curtis Publishing Co., copyright 1948 by Pearl S. Buck, renewed 1975 by Pearl S. Buck. G.P. Putnam's Sons: For a brief excerpt from *The Man Who Was Thursday* by G. K. Chesterton. The authors and editors have made every effort to trace the ownership of all copyrighted selections found in this book and to make full acknowledgment for their use. Portions of the material in this book were previously published under the title *Building English Skills*, © McDougal, Littell & Company.

Continued from Student Letter page.

Cleaver, Vera and Bill, from *Where the Lilies Bloom*. ▶*The Kissimmee Kid*
English, Ann, "Dark Windy Night."
Farjeon, Eleanor, "A Dragonfly," *Eleanor Farjeon's Poems for Children*. ▶*Then There Were Three*
Field, Rachel, "Some People," *Poems*. ▶*The Rachel Field Story Book*
Fletcher, John G., "The Skaters."
Hemingway, Ernest, from *Bull Fighting: A Tragedy*.
Hoberman, Mary Ann, "Windshield Wipers Wipe the Windshield," *Nuts to You and Nuts to Me: An Alphabet of Poems*.
Janosco, Beatrice, "The Garden Hose."
Knight, Eric, from *Lassie Come Home*.
Lamar, Howard R., "Annie Oakley," *The World Book Encyclopedia*.
Lee, Harper, from *To Kill a Mockingbird*.
Lopez, Alonzo, "I Go Forth to Move About the Earth," *The Whispering Wind*.
Mayer, Marianna, from *The Unicorn and the Lake*. ▶*The Black Horse*
McCann, Rebecca, "Rain Song," *The Complete Cheerful Cherub*.
Moore, Lilian, "Foghorns," *I Thought I Heard the City*. ▶*Go With the Poem*
Morrison, Lillian, "The Sidewalk Racer," *The Sidewalk Racer and Other Poems of Sports and Motion*. ▶*Overheard in a Bubble Chamber and Other Science Poems*
Naiche, Tina, "Coyote and the Money Tree," *And It Is Still That Way*.
Nash, Odgen, "The Eel," "The Octopus," *Verses from 1929 On*. ▶*Custard and Company; Poems by Ogden Nash*
O'Neill, Mary, "Adjectives," "Thoughts," *Words, Words Words*. ▶*Hailstones and Halibut Bones*
Parker, Bertha Morris, "Marco Polo," *The Golden Book Encyclopedia*.
Rieu, E. V., "The Paint Box," *The Flattered Flying Fish*. ▶*Voyage of Argo*
Shosen, untitled haiku, *Japanese Haiku*.
Silverstein, Shel, "What Did?" "How to Make a Swing with No Rope or Board or Nails," *A Light in the Attic*; "Recipe for a Hippopotamus Sandwich," "Spaghetti," *Where the Sidewalk Ends*. ▶*The Missing Piece*
Snyder, Zilpha Keatley, "Cast a Spell," *Today Is Saturday*. ▶*The Egypt Game*
Thurman, Judith, "Balloons!" "Flashlight," *Flashlight and Other Poems*. ▶*The Magic Lantern: How Movies Got to Move*
Uschold, Maud E., "Moonlight."
White, E. B., from *Charlotte's Web*. ▶*The Trumpet of the Swan*
Woodruff, Dianne L., "Arthur Mitchell," *The World Book Encyclopedia*.
Zolotow, Charlotte, "So Will I," *River Winding*. ▶*The Summer Night*

▶An additional work by the author

Photographs

Cleo Freelance Photo: 90. Click/Chicago, Ltd.: Gary Irving 243; William Means 16; Ron Seymour 126; Howard L. Beckstrom 300; Norman Mosallem 366. Four By Five: 4; 268; 316. H. Armstrong Roberts, Inc.: 442. The Image Bank: Elyse Lewin 282. International Stock Photo: George Ancona 224, 348; Ray Solowinski 396. Magnum Photos, Inc.: Paul Fusco 194. Tom Stack & Associates: Tom Stack 208. West Light Photographic: Tony Duffy 60, 378. Woodfin Camp and Associates: 243. James Ballard, 250. Jim Cronk: 330. Joseph A. DiChello, Jr.: 420. Kathryn Muus: 160. Paul Robert Perry: 100, 176. Jim Whitmer 44, 146.

Illustrations

Bradley Clark: 276; Floyd Cooper: 13, 49, 212, 260, 292, 333, 352, 354, 364, 399, 439; David Cunningham: 125, 372, 373; Ben Denison: 130, 139, 150-151, 191, 244; Jacqueline Denison: 24, 222, 240, 340, 381; Len Ebert: 6; Larry Frederick: 12, 48, 54, 164, 183, 210, 228-229, 238, 258-259, 308, 319, 334, 339, 360, 383, 389, 391, 393, 394, 425; Jeremy Guitar: 18, 20, 27, 143; Lydia Halverson: 254, 286, 400, 448; JAK Graphics: 104, 109, 117, 158, 342, 416, 417, 419, 427; Tani Johnson: 8, 93, 155, 163, 206, 285, 294, 304, 314, 318, 327; Dorothy Kavka: 3, 249; Christa Kieffer: 144, 270, 290, 409, 446; Diana Magnuson: 174, 181, 187, 188, 189, 214, 324, 325; Bob Masheris: 7, 51, 53, 83, 88, 94, 153, 170, 199, 219, 413, 414, 429, 431, 435; Diane McKnight: 347; Ed Parker: 66, 306, 341; Jim Pearson: 113, 119; Todd Reifers: 46, 62, 63, 97, 169, 196, 262, 265, 303, 322, 323; Judy Sakaguchi: 34, 42, 72, 134-135; Robert Steele: 321, 368, 371; Arvis Stewart: 275, 406-407; Pat Traub: 79.

We wish to express our appreciation to Dr. Barry Moore, curator of the International Collection of Children's Art, University Museums, Illinois State University, and to his staff for their consultation and research.

540

Additional Classroom Management Materials Copy Masters

- Individual Record Sheet

- Class Record Sheet

- Conversion Table for Computing Percentage Grade

- Letters to Parents

- Scope and Sequence

McDougal, Littell English
Gold Level, Grade 6

May be duplicated for teachers use

Student _____

Teacher _____

School _____

Chapter		Pretest	Assignments	Speaking & Listening	Mastery Test	Chapter Grade
1	How Language Grows					
2	Writing and Understanding Sentences					
3	Nouns for Precise Meaning					
4	Verbs for Writing Power					
5	Learning About Paragraphs					
6	Choosing a Process for Writing					
7	Study and Test-Taking Skills					
8	Building Your Vocabulary					
9	Discovering the Dictionary and Thesaurus					
10	The Process of Explaining *How*					
11	Mastering Subject-Verb Agreement					
12	Understanding Pronouns					
13	The Process of Narrative Writing					
	Midyear Test	✕	✕	✕	✕	✕
14	Sharpening Speaking and Listening Skills					
15	Revising and Combining Sentences					
16	Adjectives for Creative Expression					
17	Adverbs for Clear Description					
18	Appreciating the Language of Poetry					
19	Description and the Process of Writing					
20	Using Prepositions and Conjunctions					
21	Clear Thinking					
22	The Process of Writing About Opinions					
23	Developing Library and Research Skills					
24	The Process of Writing a Report					
25	Writing Letters and Filling Out Forms					
	Guide to Capitalization					
	Guide to Punctuation					
	End-of-Year Test	✕	✕	✕	✕	✕

Guideline for Record-Keeping

Pretest/Mastery Test: Record scores from separate test booklet.
Assignments: Record cumulative grade from all written or oral assignments.
Speaking and Listening (Optional): Record evaluation from charts on page T30 or record a class participation grade.
Chapter Grade: Record final grade based on all scores except for the pretest. Weight each section to suit particular classroom requirements.

Class Record Sheet

Student Names

Unit ____
Chapter (insert chapter number in box below)
▼

Grade for Assignments															
Speaking and Listening															
Mastery Test Score															
Overall Grade															
Grade for Assignments															
Speaking and Listening															
Mastery Test Score															
Overall Grade															
Grade for Assignments															
Speaking and Listening															
Mastery Test Score															
Overall Grade															
Grade for Assignments															
Speaking and Listening															
Mastery Test Score															
Overall Grade															
Grade for Assignments															
Speaking and Listening															
Mastery Test Score															
Overall Grade															
Grade for Assignments															
Speaking and Listening															
Mastery Test Score															
Overall Grade															
Grade for Assignments															
Speaking and Listening															
Mastery Test Score															
Overall Grade															

Guidelines for Record Keeping

Assignments: Record cumulative grade from all written or oral assignments.
Speaking and Listening (optional): Record evaluation from charts on page T30 or record a class participation grade.
Mastery Test: Record score from separate test booklet.
Overall Grade: Record final grade based on preceding scores. Weight items to suit particular classroom requirements.

This chart may be reproduced and used for each Unit in the text.

Conversion Table for Computing Percentage Grade

McDougal, Littell English provides teachers with a wealth of activities, not only in the student text, but also in the Skills Practice Book, Teacher's Resource Binder, and Teacher's Edition. The table below may be used to help teachers compute grades for any activities that they wish to make part of the student's permanent records.

Total number of items

Incorrect	6	7	8	9	10	11	12	13	14	15	16	17	18	19	20	21	22	23	24	25	26	27	28	29	30	31	32	33	34	35	
1	83	86	88	89	90	91	92	92	93	93	94	94	94	95	95	95	95	96	96	96	96	96	96	97	97	97	97	97	97	97	1
2	67	71	75	78	80	82	83	85	86	87	88	88	89	89	90	90	91	91	92	92	92	93	93	93	93	94	94	94	94	94	2
3	50	57	63	67	70	73	75	77	79	80	81	82	83	84	85	86	86	87	88	88	88	89	89	90	90	90	91	91	91	91	3
4	33	43	50	56	60	64	67	69	71	73	75	76	78	79	80	81	82	83	83	84	85	85	86	86	87	87	88	88	88	89	4
5	17	29	38	44	50	55	58	62	64	67	69	71	72	74	75	76	77	78	79	80	81	81	82	83	83	84	84	85	85	86	5
6		14	25	33	40	45	50	54	57	60	63	65	67	68	70	71	73	74	75	76	77	78	79	79	80	81	81	82	82	83	6
7			13	22	30	36	42	46	50	53	56	59	61	63	65	67	68	70	71	72	73	74	75	76	77	77	78	79	79	80	7
8				11	20	27	33	38	43	47	50	53	56	58	60	62	64	65	67	68	69	70	71	72	73	74	75	76	76	77	8
9					10	18	25	31	36	40	44	47	50	53	55	57	59	61	63	64	65	67	68	69	70	71	72	73	74	74	9
10						9	17	23	29	33	38	41	44	47	50	52	55	57	58	60	62	63	64	66	67	68	69	70	71	71	10
11							8	15	21	27	31	35	39	42	45	48	50	52	54	56	58	59	61	62	63	65	66	67	68	69	11
12								8	14	20	25	29	33	37	40	43	45	48	50	52	54	56	57	59	60	61	63	64	65	66	12
13									7	13	19	24	28	32	35	38	41	43	46	48	50	52	54	55	57	58	59	61	62	63	13
14										7	13	18	22	26	30	33	36	39	42	44	46	48	50	52	53	55	56	58	59	60	14
15											6	12	17	21	25	29	32	35	38	40	42	44	46	48	50	52	54	55	56	57	15
16												6	11	16	20	24	27	30	33	36	38	41	43	45	47	48	50	52	53	54	16
17													6	11	15	19	23	26	29	32	35	37	39	41	43	45	47	48	50	51	17
18														5	10	14	18	22	25	28	31	33	36	38	40	42	44	45	47	49	18
19															5	10	14	17	21	24	27	30	32	34	37	39	41	42	44	46	19
20																5	9	13	17	20	23	26	29	31	33	35	38	39	41	43	20
21																	5	9	13	16	19	22	25	28	30	32	34	36	38	40	21
22																		4	8	12	15	19	21	24	27	29	31	33	35	37	22
23																			4	8	12	15	18	21	23	26	28	30	32	34	23
24																				4	8	11	14	17	20	23	25	27	29	31	24
25																					4	7	11	14	17	19	22	24	26	29	25
26																						4	7	10	13	16	19	21	24	26	26
27																							4	7	10	13	16	18	21	23	27
28																								3	7	10	13	15	18	20	28
29																									3	6	9	12	15	17	29
30																										3	6	9	12	14	30
31																											3	6	9	11	31
32																												3	6	9	32
33																													3	6	33
34																														3	34

Number of Incorrect Items

Date _____

Dear Parent,

In this year's study of language arts, your child will be using *McDougal, Littell English, Gold Level.* This text is designed to lead students toward mastery of essential skills in writing, grammar, clear thinking, speaking and listening, vocabulary development, and other related language areas. These concepts are presented in four units that emphasize the relationships among the different skills. Extensive exercises are provided for development and drill.

Your assistance and reinforcement will add to the effectiveness of the text and your child's classroom experience. It would be helpful for you to become familiar with the subjects covered in the lessons and to encourage your child to share with you what he or she is studying.

No language arts program is complete if it is limited to study alone. Lessons in a text or classroom can develop the structure for a student's language experience, but cannot replace the language experience itself. Here are some ways you can contribute to your child's language development.

Guide your child's television viewing to include some of the better young people's specials and series. Talk about the programs with your child.

Encourage your child to read by letting him or her see you read. Make sure that reading materials—books, newspapers, magazines—are present in your home.

Provide a quiet place and time for reading, letter writing, and school assignments.

I am confident that, with your assistance, your child's understanding and effective use of language will increase throughout this year. If you have any questions or suggestions, please feel free to contact me.

Sincerely,

Fecha _____

Estimados Padres,

Durante este año escolar, sus hijos van a estudiar el *nivel dorado* de la serie de inglés *McDougal, Littell English*. Este texto esta diseñado con el fin de desarrolar en sus hijos las habilidades esenciales de escribir, pensar claramente, escuchar, ampliar su vocabulario, comprender la gramática, y desarollar otras destrezas relacionadas. Los temas del libro están presentados en cuatro unidades que dan énfasis a la relación entre las varias destrezas. Hay amplia oportunidad para la práctica y el estudio.

Les sugiero que se familiaricen con el programa y con la clase de sus hijos. Así Uds. comprenderán el sentido de las lecciónes y podrán animar a sus hijos a compartirlo con Uds.

Ningún programa de idioma es completo si nos limitamos únicamente al estudio. Los ejercicios del texto y las presentaciones de la clase aumentan el entendimiento de cada lección. Aún así, falta la experiencia misma donde los estudiantes pueden poner en práctica lo que aprenden en la escuela. Es aquí donde Uds. pueden hacer una gran contribución. Pienso que las siguientes actividades tienen el mismo valor tanto en inglés como en espãnol:

> Guíen a sus hijos para que vean los programas de televisión que son propios para niños de su edad. Discutan con sus niños estos programas.

> Despierten en sus hijos el deseo y hábito de la lectura. Cuando Uds. estén leyendo, asegúren que sus hijos los vean. Mantengan libros y revistas en casa.

> Seleccionen un sitio apropriado para leer y escribir.

Sé que con su ayuda y interés en el transcurso del año escolar, sus hijos tendrán un gran éxito en este programa. Les pido que se comuniquen conmigo si tienen preguntas o sugerencias.

Atentamente,

Date _____

Dear Parent,

During the past few months, using the textbook *McDougal, Littell English, Gold Level,* your child has been increasing his or her language skills in the following ways:

Developing vocabulary by studying the origins and meanings of words

Developing ways to write smooth, clear sentences

Learning to use the process of writing

Improving skills in studying and test taking

Identifying and using nouns, verbs, and pronouns correctly in sentences

Learning to write effective narratives

In the coming months, your child will write descriptions, explanations, reports, and letters; develop ways to improve speaking and listening skills; learn about the language of poetry; develop important skills in clear thinking; and study correct grammar and usage. He or she will constantly use the process of writing to develop such skills as choosing a topic for a piece of writing, finding and organizing information, revising ideas and organization, and proofreading for correctness.

Your continued help and encouragement are most important as your child takes on these challenges. Here some ways you can reinforce and further expand your child's language development.

Help your child improve speaking and listening skills by having regular discussions about school activities, events in the news, and family experiences. Listen carefully to what your child is saying. Develop the habit of asking questions about what interests him or her.

Make sure your child sees you take time for reading and writing. If possible, provide all kinds of reading materials, especially in those areas that interest your child. Ask questions about what he or she reads. Encourage writing as a means of communication by asking your child to leave notes, make lists, or write out directions.

I am sure that, with your continued help, your child will make further progress in developing language skills throughout this school year. If you have any questions or suggestions, please feel free to contact me.

Sincerely,

Fecha _____

Estimados Padres,

Durante los meses pasados, sus hijos han desarrollado las siguientes habilidades del idioma inglés con nuestro texto *McDougal, Littell English,* del *nivel dorado*:

Ampliando el vocabulario, con el estudio del origen y significado de palabras.

Desarrollando la manera de escribir oraciones claras y fluentes.

Aprendiendo como usar el proceso de escribir.

Mejorando su habilidad para estudiar y tomar exámenes.

Identificando y usando los sustantivos, verbos, y pronombres.

Aprendiendo como escribir narraciones efectivas.

Mejorando las destrezas de hablar y escuchar.

En los próximos meses, sus hijos escribirán descripciones, explicaciones, y reportes; estudiarán el uso correcto de la gramática; aprenderán el lenguaje de la poesía; desarrollarán destrezas importantes en pensar claramente. Sus hijos usarán constantemente el proceso de escribir para escojer un tema para una composición, encontrar y organizar información, revisar ideas y organización, y corregir lo que han escrito.

Les pido que continuen dando a sus hijos el apoyo y aliento que hasta hoy les han brindado. Así podrán alcanzar estas metas con éxito. Les sugiero las siguientes actividades para repasar el desarrollo del idioma en sus hijos:

Hablen con sus hijos sobre actividades de la escuela, incidentes en las noticias, y experiencias familiares. Así Uds. ayudarán a que sus hijos desarrollen las habilidades de hablar y escuchar. Pongan atención a lo que sus hijos les dicen. Tengan el hábito de hacer preguntas sobre lo que les interesa a sus hijos.

Estén seguro que sus hijos los vean a Uds. cuando estén leyendo y escribiendo. Si es posible, hagan provisión para que sus hijos tengan materiales de lectura sobre sus areas de interés. Animen a sus hijos a comunicarse en forma escrita. Pidan que les dejen notas, que hagan listas, o que escriban instrucciones.

Creo que con su ayuda y apoyo, sus hijos continuarán su progreso en el estudio del idioma durante el año. Les pido que se comuniquen conmigo si tienen preguntas o sugerencias.

Atentamente,

Date _____

Dear Parent,

Throughout this past school year, through the classroom use of *McDougal, Littell English, Gold Level,* your child has developed a variety of skills in writing, clear thinking, speaking and listening, vocabulary development, grammar, and other areas of language study. It is important to maintain these skills at a high level throughout the coming vacation.

Here are some ways you can assist your child in maintaining these skills:

> Encourage reading for pleasure. Help your child to visit a library regularly. Accompany your child, if possible. It would also be helpful to have a dictionary for young people available at home, so that your child can continue to develop vocabulary and comprehension skills. Discuss with your child what she or he has learned or enjoyed in this independent reading.

> Encourage your child in writing letters, keeping a diary, or writing original stories or poems for fun. Offer to read your child's writing, not to criticize, but to provide an audience. This will give your child a stronger feeling for communication through writing, and will provide more incentive for clear and correct writing.

> Sharpen your child's thinking skills by giving him or her opportunities to solve problems and evaluate results independently. Encourage your child to share what he or she has learned. Also encourage your child to analyze and ask questions about various events and situations.

Encouraging your child to participate in more purposeful activities such as these will help to lessen an addiction to watching television throughout the summer.

I hope these suggestions will help to make the coming vacation stimulating as well as enjoyable for both you and your child.

Sincerely,

Fecha _____

Estimados Padres,

En el transcurso de este año escolar, sus hijos han aprendido una variedad de habilidades del idioma, tales como hablar, escribir, escuchar correctamente, y pensar claramente. También han desarrollado su vocabulario, el conocimiento de la lengua, y otras destrezas relacionadas estudiando el texto *McDougal, Littell English*, del *nivel dorado*. Es sumamente importante que sus hijos conserven estos conocimientos ya adquiridos durante las vacaciones de verano que se aproximan. Su ayuda, en inglés o español, tiene mucho valor. Les sugiero las siguientes actividades para ayudar a sus hijos a mantener las habilidades que han aprendido:

> Despierten en sus hijos el interés y hábito de la lectura, animándolos a visitar la biblioteca con frecuencia. Acompáñenlos cada vez que les sea posible. Tengan un diccionario juvenil en casa para el desarrollo y comprensión del vocabulario. Discutan con ellos lo que han aprendido o disfrutado en su lectura.

> Animen a sus niños para que escriban sus propias cartas, un diario, o cuentos y poesías originales. Lean en voz alta lo que han escrito, no para criticar, sino para que tengan oyentes. Esta experiencia fomentará en sus hijos el deseo de expresarse por escrito correctamente.

> Desarrollen en sus hijos la habilidad de pensar claramente, dándoles la oportunidad de resolver problemas y evaluar los resultados por sí solos.

> Animen a sus hijos a compartir lo que han aprendido. Denles la oportunidad de analizar y hacer preguntas sobre varios eventos y situaciones.

Cuando sus hijos participan en actividades educativas y creativas, como éstas, perderán interés en ver tantos programas de televisión.

Espero que estas sugerencias sean productivas y les ayuden a Uds. y a sus hijos a disfrutar un verano grato e interesante.

Atentamente,

Contents

Vocabulary Development

Word Origins	Cherry K	Pink 1	Plum 2	Brown 3	Aqua 4	Silver 5	Gold 6
History of Language, Borrowed Words, Compound Words, Clipped Words, Words from Names or Initials, Echoic Words, Technical Words			●	●			●

Language Acquisition

	Cherry K	Pink 1	Plum 2	Brown 3	Aqua 4	Silver 5	Gold 6
Using Word Parts To Unlock New Words Base Words, Prefixes, Suffixes			●	●	●	●	●
Using Context Clues To Discover Meanings Definition and Restatement, Examples, Comparison and Contrast				●	●	●	●
Using the Dictionary To Learn About Words Using Alphabetical Order and Guide Words To Find the Word, Understanding the Pronunciation, Finding the Best Definition		●	●	●	●	●	●
Using the Thesaurus To Choose Specific Words				●	●	●	●

Language Enrichment

	Cherry K	Pink 1	Plum 2	Brown 3	Aqua 4	Silver 5	Gold 6
Developing Specific Vocabulary Rhymes, Homophones and Homographs, Synonyms and Antonyms, Words Referring to the Senses	●	●	●	●	●	●	●
Using the Thesaurus To Choose Specific Words				●	●	●	●
Vocabulary To Match the Situation (Levels of language)					●	●	●

Writing

Sentences

	Cherry K	Pink 1	Plum 2	Brown 3	Aqua 4	Silver 5	Gold 6
Using Words for Specific Purposes Clarity and Precision, Persuasion (judgment words, connotations, slanting), Creative Expression (simile, metaphor)			●	●	●	●	●
Writing Good Sentences Writing Complete Thoughts	(ORAL)	●	●	●	●	●	●
Avoiding Fragments, Avoiding Run-on and Stringy Sentences	(ORAL)	●	●	●	●	●	●
Combining Sentences					●	●	●
Writing Interesting Sentences Using Specific Words and Details, Using Strong Verbs, Using Figurative Language		●	●	●	●	●	●

Process of Writing

	Cherry K	Pink 1	Plum 2	Brown 3	Aqua 4	Silver 5	Gold 6
Prewriting Selecting a Mode of Expression			●	●	●	●	●
Using Appropriate Prewriting Techniques		●	●	●	●	●	●
Choosing and Narrowing a Topic	(ORAL)	●	●	●	●	●	●
Determining Purpose and Audience				●	●	●	●
Gathering Information		●	●	●	●	●	●
Organizing Information Using Chronological Order, Natural or Spatial Order, Order of Importance	(ORAL)	●	●	●	●	●	●
See also: Narrative, Descriptive, and Explanatory Writing							
Drafting Choosing a Method for Drafting, Drafting Narratives, Drafting Descriptions, Drafting Explanations, Drafting Reports	(ORAL)	●	●	●	●	●	●
Drafting Introductions, Drafting Bodies, Drafting Conclusions of Compositions						●	●
Revising Refining Ideas, Organization, Word Choice		●	●	●	●	●	●
Proofreading Correcting Errors in Form: Grammar, Usage, Capitalization, Punctuation, Spelling		●	●	●	●	●	●
Proofreading Symbols		●	●	●	●	●	●
Publishing and Sharing Making a Final Copy		●	●	●	●	●	●
Sharing the Final Copy		●	●	●	●	●	●

Paragraphs and Compositions

	Cherry K	Pink 1	Plum 2	Brown 3	Aqua 4	Silver 5	Gold 6
The Concept of Paragraphs and Compositions Definition, Identifying the Main Idea, Finding and Writing Topic Sentences		●	●	●	●	●	●
Developing a Paragraph Specific Details, Examples, Facts and Figures, Definitions		●	●	●	●	●	●
See also: Process of Writing, Prewriting, Narrative Paragraph, Descriptive Paragraph, Explanatory Paragraph							
Narrative Writing Developing Character, Setting, and Plot; Identifying Main Events; Use of Chronological Order	(ORAL)	(ORAL)	●	●	●	●	●
Using Dialogue						●	●
Using Description				●	●	●	●
See also: Process of Writing							
Descriptive Writing Choosing Words and Details	(ORAL)	●	●	●	●	●	●
Use of Natural or Spatial Order			●	●	●	●	●
Use of Sensory Details	(ORAL)	(ORAL)	●	●	●	●	●
Use of Similes and Metaphors				●	●	●	●
See also: Process of Writing							
Explanatory Writing Writing That Explains How				●	●	●	●
Writing That Explains Why					●	●	●
Writing That Persuades							●
See also: Process of Writing							
Creative Writing					●	●	

Scope and Sequence

Reports

Reports	Cherry K	Pink 1	Plum 2	Brown 3	Aqua 4	Silver 5	Gold 6
The Concept of a Report Definition				●	●	●	●
Basis in Study and Research				●	●	●	●
Planning the Report Using Prewriting Techniques for Choosing a Subject, Narrowing the Topic, Gathering Ideas, Finding Sources, Taking Notes, Organizing Ideas, Making an Outline				●	●	●	●
Drafting the Report Introductory Paragraph, Body, Conclusion, Giving Credit to Sources						●	●
Revising the Report Revising for Content, Proofreading, Sharing the Report				●	●	●	●

Related Writing Skills

Related Writing Skills	Cherry K	Pink 1	Plum 2	Brown 3	Aqua 4	Silver 5	Gold 6
Writing a Book Report Title, Author, Main Characters, Setting, Plot, Evaluation		●	●	●	●	●	●
Writing Friendly Letters Form of Friendly Letters, Addressing Envelopes		●	●	●	●	●	●
Social Notes, Invitations and Replies to Invitations, Thank-You Notes		●	●	●	●	●	●
Writing Business Letters Form of Business Letters, Order Letters, Letters of Request, Letters of Complaint, Addressing Envelopes					●	●	●
Filling Out Forms							●
Using Grammar in Writing		●	●	●	●	●	●
Writing in Other Subject Areas		●	●	●	●	●	●

Speaking and Listening

Speaking

Speaking	Cherry K	Pink 1	Plum 2	Brown 3	Aqua 4	Silver 5	Gold 6
Nonverbal Aspects Using Body Movement To Express Emotion or Ideas		●	●	●	●	●	●
Adjusting Volume, Pitch, Tone, and Rate of Delivery to the Situation			●	●	●	●	●
Informal Speaking Situations Using the Telephone, Taking a Message, Giving Directions, Making Introductions, Social Discussion	●	●	●	●	●	●	●
Formal Speaking Situations Sharing Writing Aloud		●	●	●	●	●	●
Oral Reports and Demonstration Talk	●	●	●	●	●	●	●
Reading Aloud		●	●	●	●	●	●
Telling a Story	●	●	●	●	●	●	●
Giving and Following Directions				●	●	●	●
Making Announcements, Making Introductions to Groups			●		●	●	●
Discussions					●	●	●
Debate							●
Interviewing					●	●	●
Giving a Speech						●	●
Drama	●			●	●		●

Listening

	Cherry K	Pink 1	Plum 2	Brown 3	Aqua 4	Silver 5	Gold 6
Listening for Specific Purposes Following Directions, Listening for Information, Listening for Motive and Bias, Listening to Literature	●	●	●	●	●	●	●
Manners in Listening	●	●	●	●	●	●	●
Evaluation Evaluating Others' Speaking Skills			●	●	●	●	●
Evaluating Personal Listening Skills	●	●	●	●	●	●	●

Clear Thinking

	Cherry K	Pink 1	Plum 2	Brown 3	Aqua 4	Silver 5	Gold 6
Analyzing Writing Models and Literature Excerpts	●	●	●	●	●	●	●
Using Facts Differentiating Between Fact and Opinion			●	●	●	●	●
Clarifying Facts				●	●	●	●
Using Facts To Make Judgments and Draw Conclusions					●	●	●
Logical Reasoning Recognizing Generalizations, Stereotypes, and Slanted Language					●	●	●
Identifying Sequence, Cause and Effect, and Other Relationships; Identifying Fallacies	●	●	●	●	●	●	●
Organizing Ideas Classifying	●	●	●	●	●	●	●
Sequencing	●	●	●	●	●	●	●
Outlining	●	●	●	●	●	●	●
Problem-solving				●	●	●	●
Judging and Evaluating	●	●	●	●	●	●	●
Making Choices	●	●	●	●	●	●	●
Also check Revising							

Study and Research Skills

Study Skills	Cherry K	Pink 1	Plum 2	Brown 3	Aqua 4	Silver 5	Gold 6
Types of Reading Skimming and Scanning, In-depth (Study-type) Reading					●	●	●
Using a Study Method SQ3R (Study, Question, Read, Record, Review)						●	●
Note-Taking Restating in Your Own Words					●	●	●
Separating Fact from Opinion				●	●	●	●
Evaluating Sources						●	●
Using Modified Outline Form				●	●	●	●
Taking Notes from Oral Material				●	●	●	●
Using Memory Aids				●	●	●	●
Using Graphic Aids Pictures, Diagrams, Charts, Maps, Graphs, Tables						●	●
Test-Taking How To Prepare for a Test					●	●	●
Taking the Test				●	●	●	●
Types of Directions and Questions				●	●	●	●

Research Skills	Cherry K	Pink 1	Plum 2	Brown 3	Aqua 4	Silver 5	Gold 6
Using the Dictionary Using Alphabetical Order and Guide Words To Find the Word			●	●	●	●	●
Recognizing the Information in an Entry			●	●	●	●	●
Finding the Right Meaning and Pronunciation			●	●	●	●	●
Using the Thesaurus					●	●	●
Using the Library Kinds of Books (Fiction/Nonfiction)	●	●	●	●	●	●	●
Book Arrangement and Classification					●	●	●
Dewey Decimal System					●	●	●
Card Catalog					●	●	●
Using Nonfiction and Reference Books Table of Contents and Index			●	●	●	●	●
Encyclopedia, Almanacs, Atlases					●	●	●
Readers' Guide to Periodical Literature and Other Reference Works							●
Using People as Resources Finding a Good Source, Interviewing				●		●	●

Literature

Types of Literature

	Cherry K	Pink 1	Plum 2	Brown 3	Aqua 4	Silver 5	Gold 6
Nonfiction Biography, Autobiography, Journals, Diaries, Anecdote, Feature Articles, Essays, Satire			●	●		●	●
Fiction Oral Tradition, Legend, Myth, Fable, Folk Tale, Tall Tale, Ballad, Short Story (Fantasy, Realistic Fiction)	●	●	●	●	●	●	●
Poetry Listening to or Reading Poetry, Reading Poetry Aloud, Analyzing Poetry (Structure, Images, Rhythm, Rhyme, Alliteration, Assonance, Consonance, Onomatopoeia, Personification, Simile, Metaphor, Mood)	●	●	●	●	●	●	●
Drama Definition, Plot, Character, Setting, Stage Directions, Terms of Production, Oral Interpretation				●			●

Analyzing Literature

	Cherry K	Pink 1	Plum 2	Brown 3	Aqua 4	Silver 5	Gold 6
Elements of Literature Character, Setting, Plot, Mood, Narrator, Point of View, Theme	●	●	●	●	●	●	●
Analyzing Meaning	●	●	●	●	●	●	●
Appreciating Literature Meaning		●	●	●	●	●	●
Techniques for Reading Enjoyment			●	●	●	●	●
Sharing Literature with Others	●	●	●	●	●	●	●

Cross-Curricular Application

	Cherry K	Pink 1	Plum 2	Brown 3	Aqua 4	Silver 5	Gold 6
Art	●		●	●	●		●
Computer Studies						●	●
Drama				●	●	●	●
Health/Safety	●	●	●	●	●	●	●
Mathematics	●	●	●	●	●	●	●
Music	●		●	●	●	●	●
Reading		●	●	●	●	●	●
Science	●	●	●	●	●	●	●
Social Studies	●	●	●	●	●	●	●
Spelling			●	●	●	●	●

Grammar

Sentences	Cherry K	Pink 1	Plum 2	Brown 3	Aqua 4	Silver 5	Gold 6
Identifying Sentences Definition	●	●	●	●	●	●	●
Distinguishing Between Sentences and Fragments	●	●	●	●	●	●	●
Run-on Sentences			●	●	●	●	●
Kinds of Sentences Declarative	●	●	●	●	●	●	●
Interrogative	●	●	●	●	●	●	●
Imperative			●	●	●	●	●
Exclamatory			●	●	●	●	●
Sentence Parts: The Subject Complete Subject		●	●		●	●	●
Simple Subject—Definition					●	●	●
Understood Simple Subject			●	●	●	●	●
Finding the Simple Subject The Subject in Unusual Positions						●	●
The Subject in Declarative Sentences						●	●
The Subject in Interrogative and Exclamatory Sentences						●	●
Compound Subject							●
Sentence Parts: The Predicate Complete Predicate		●	●	●	●	●	●
Finding the Simple Predicate or Verb		●	●	●	●	●	●
Identifying Main Verbs and Helping Verbs				●	●	●	●
Finding Separated Parts of the Verbs							●
Finding Verbs in Unusual Order: Questions, Commands, Sentences Beginning with *There*, *Here*, and *Where*						●	●
Linking Verbs (Definition)						●	●
Identifying the Direct Object						●	●
Sentence Structure Study of the Simple Sentence	●	●	●	●	●	●	●

Parts of Speech	Cherry K	Pink 1	Plum 2	Brown 3	Aqua 4	Silver 5	Gold 6
Nouns Definition	●	●	●	●	●	●	●
Singular and Plural Nouns	●	●	●	●	●	●	●
Common and Proper Nouns		●	●	●	●	●	●
Possessive Nouns			●	●	●	●	●
Use of Nouns as Subjects		●	●	●	●	●	●
Use of Nouns as Direct or Indirect Objects of Verb						●	●
Use of Nouns as Objects of Prepositions						●	●
Verbs Definition: Action and State-of-Being (or Linking) Verbs	●	●	●	●	●	●	●
Main Verbs and Helping Verbs				●	●	●	●
Forming the Present Tense of Regular Verbs	●	●	●	●	●	●	●
Forming Past Tenses of Regular Verbs	●	●	●	●	●	●	●
Using Principal Parts of Verbs To Form Other Tenses						●	●
Forming Tenses of Irregular Verbs	●	●	●	●	●	●	●
***See also* Usage: Verbs**							
Adjectives Definition	●	●	●	●	●	●	●
Kinds (what kind, how many, which ones)				●	●	●	●
Articles				●	●	●	●
Proper Adjectives						●	●
Predicate Adjectives							●
Comparative and Superlative Forms	●	●	●	●	●	●	●
Pronouns Classed as Adjectives							●
***See also* Usage: Adjectives and Avoiding Confusion of Adjectives and Adverbs**							
Adverbs Definition. Kinds (how, when, where, to what extent)		●	●	●	●	●	●
Comparative and Superlative Forms					●	●	●
***See also* Usage: Adverbs and Avoiding Confusion of Adjectives and Adverbs**							
Pronouns Definition	●	●	●	●	●	●	●
Personal Pronouns, Compound, Forms of Pronouns	●	●	●	●	●	●	●
Possessive Pronouns				●	●	●	●
Use of Pronouns as Subject of Sentences	●	●	●	●	●	●	●
Use of Pronouns as Predicate Pronouns						●	●
Use of Pronouns as Direct or Indirect Objects of Verbs, Use of Pronouns as Objects of Prepositions	●	●	●	●	●	●	●

***See also* Usage: Pronouns**

	Cherry K	Pink 1	Plum 2	Brown 3	Aqua 4	Silver 5	Gold 6
Conjunctions Definition, Coordinating, Combining Parts of Sentences, Sentences, or Clauses					●	●	●
Prepositions Definition						●	●
Object of Preposition,						●	●
Prepositional Phrase						●	●
Special Problems with Prepositions						●	●

Usage

Verbs

	Cherry K	Pink 1	Plum 2	Brown 3	Aqua 4	Silver 5	Gold 6
Problems with Making the Subject and Verb Agree General Rules for Agreement of Subject and Verb		●	●	●	●	●	●
Irregular Verbs *To Be*	●	●	●	●	●	●	●
Other Commonly Used Irregular Verbs	●	●	●	●	●	●	●

Pronouns

	Cherry K	Pink 1	Plum 2	Brown 3	Aqua 4	Silver 5	Gold 6
Using the Correct Form of Personal Pronouns Using Pronouns as Subject of Sentences	●	●	●	●	●	●	●
Using Pronouns as Predicate Pronouns						●	●
Using Pronouns as Direct or Indirect Objects of Verbs, or as Objects of Prepositions	●	●	●	●	●	●	●
Other Problems Including Using *I* or *Me* Last		●	●	●	●	●	●
Coordinating Pronouns and Antecedents						●	●
***See also* Grammar: Parts of Speech, Pronouns**							

Adjectives

	Cherry K	Pink 1	Plum 2	Brown 3	Aqua 4	Silver 5	Gold 6
Forming Comparisons and Using Them Correctly Correct Use of Comparative and Superlative Forms	●	●	●	●	●	●	●
Special Cases (including *good/better/best*)					●	●	●

Adverbs

	Cherry K	Pink 1	Plum 2	Brown 3	Aqua 4	Silver 5	Gold 6
Forming Comparisons and Using Them Correctly Correct Use of Comparative and Superlative Forms					●	●	●
Special Cases (including *well, better, best*)					●	●	●
Avoiding Double Negatives					●	●	●

Avoiding Confusion of Adjectives and Adverbs

	Cherry K	Pink 1	Plum 2	Brown 3	Aqua 4	Silver 5	Gold 6
Choosing Between Adjective and Adverb Forms of a Modifier						●	●
Using *Good* and *Well* Correctly						●	●

Words Often Confused

Words Often Confused	Cherry K	Pink 1	Plum 2	Brown 3	Aqua 4	Silver 5	Gold 6
Using Troublesome Pairs of Verbs Correctly						●	●
Recognizing and Using Correctly Homonyms and Other Words Often Confused			●		●		
Possessive Pronouns and Contractions				●	●	●	●

Mechanics

Capitalization

Capitalization	Cherry K	Pink 1	Plum 2	Brown 3	Aqua 4	Silver 5	Gold 6
The Word _I_		●	●	●	●	●	●
Proper Nouns Personal Names and Titles and Their Abbreviations		●	●	●	●	●	●
Names of Buildings, Streets, Cities, States, Countries		●	●	●	●	●	●
Months, Days, and Holidays		●	●	●	●	●	●
Nationalities, Races, Religions, Names for the Deity and Scriptures				●	●	●	●
Geographical Names and Directions, Organizations, Events and Documents, Other Nouns				●	●	●	●
Proper Adjectives						●	●
First Words Sentences		●	●	●	●	●	●
Lines of Poetry					●	●	●
Quotations				●	●	●	●
Letters		●	●	●	●	●	●
Outlines				●	●	●	●
Titles of Books, Plays, Poems, Articles, Essays, Movies, TV Series		●	●	●	●	●	●

Scope and Sequence

Punctuation

	Cherry K	Pink 1	Plum 2	Brown 3	Aqua 4	Silver 5	Gold 6
The Period Sentences	●	●	●	●	●	●	●
Initials, Abbreviations			●	●	●	●	●
Outlines					●	●	●
The Question Mark Sentences		●	●	●	●	●	●
Exclamation Point Sentences			●	●	●	●	●
The Comma Uses in Letters: Dates, Addresses and Locations, Letter Parts			●	●	●	●	●
Uses in Sentences: Series, Introductory Words, Nouns of Direct Address, Quotations, Compound Sentences, Appositives, for Clarity				●	●	●	●
The Semicolon							●
The Colon					●	●	●
The Apostrophe Possessives			●	●	●	●	●
Contractions and Other Omissions			●	●	●	●	●
The Hyphen						●	●
Quotation Marks				●	●	●	●
Underlining			●	●	●	●	●

Spelling

	Cherry K	Pink 1	Plum 2	Brown 3	Aqua 4	Silver 5	Gold 6
Study Plan for Spelling				●	●	●	●
Rules for Common Problems Problems with Adding Suffixes: Final *e*, Final *y*, Doubling the Final Consonant			●	●	●	●	●
Adding Prefixes; Adding the Suffixes -*ly* and -*ness*; Spelling words with the *seed* sound; Spelling Words with *ie* and *ei*			●	●	●	●	●
Homonyms and Other Words Often Confused		●	●	●	●	●	●

Proofreading

	Cherry K	Pink 1	Plum 2	Brown 3	Aqua 4	Silver 5	Gold 6
Checking Sentences for Grammatical Correctness; Checking Paragraphs for Form; Checking Punctuation, Capitalization, and Spelling; Rewriting for Appearance		●	●	●	●	●	●
***See also:* Process of Writing: Revising**							

Outlining

	Cherry K	Pink 1	Plum 2	Brown 3	Aqua 4	Silver 5	Gold 6
Form. Use in Note-Taking. Use in Planning a Report ***See also:* Composition, Reports, Study and Research Skills, Clear Thinking**				●	●	●	●